FORMAL ORGANIZATION

A Systems Approach

FORMAL

ORGANIZATION

A SYSTEMS APPROACH

ROCCO CARZO, Jr.

and

JOHN N. YANOUZAS

The Pennsylvania State University

1967

RICHARD D. IRWIN, INC. and

THE DORSEY PRESS. Homewood, Illinois

© RICHARD D. IRWIN, INC., 1967

First Printing, April, 1967
Second Printing, March, 1968

Library of Congress Catalog Card No. 67–14357

Printed in the United States of America

THIS BOOK is dedicated to

those ladies who helped us to endure the

pains of birth, *DOLORES* and *ELENI*

PREFACE

Like any new and developing discipline, the study of formal organization is characterized by opposing theories and conflicting research findings. We do not propose a new theory but recommend an approach to the subject—the systems approach. In this approach, the formal organization is treated as an open system, that is, as a set of interdependent elements which act to achieve certain goals and to maintain an orderly state of affairs in exchanges with the environment. Through the systems approach, it is hoped that the reader will develop an understanding of human behavior in formal organization and develop skills in making decisions about practical problems of organizational design.

The early contributions to the study of formal organization, called traditional theory in the literature, have generated much controversy. Since these early contributions and the subsequent controversy reveal so much about the nature of formal organization, we devote most of Part I to a discussion of concepts and shortcomings of the theory. In Part II, behavior patterns of formal organization are classified into subsystems of behavior. Part III is devoted to a discussion of analytical techniques for making decisions about organizational design and Part IV is concerned with changing individual and organizational behavior.

The material of this book is introductory. It is designed for a one- or two-semester beginning course. The mathematics used does not require preparation beyond the level of algebra and elementary statistics. The mathematical material has been arranged so that the instructor may bypass it without loss of continuity. In our own classes, we have found the mathematical models and their application to problems at the end of the chapters to be useful and stimulating. They have helped our students to appreciate the importance of formulating organizational relationships in a precise manner. In addition, they have stimulated lively class discussion and have helped clarify some of the issues raised in the text.

Many people helped in the formulation and writing of this book. We are grateful to Dean Ossian R. MacKenzie and Professor Max D. Richards for providing the academic freedom and time to write. Professors Jeremiah J. O'Connell, John G. Hutchinson, John F. Mee, Robert B. Fetter, Keith Davis, R. Stansbury Stockton, Vernon E. Buck, Barry M. Richman, Edgar H. Schein, Larry L. Cummings, D. W. Conrath, and Warren B. Brown read major portions of the book and gave many helpful suggestions. We are especially indebted to Professors Warren G. Bennis, R. William Millman, and Paul S. Greenlaw who read the entire manuscript and spent many hours trying to improve our efforts. Several graduate students who helped were Messrs. Joseph Hagen, William Foulds, Gregg Weiss, and Carlyle Griffin. Mr. Michael Sibol checked our mathematics and helped to develop problems at the end of the chapters.

PINE COTTAGE   ROCCO CARZO, JR.
UNIVERSITY PARK, PENNSYLVANIA   JOHN N. YANOUZAS
                        April, 1967

TABLE OF CONTENTS

CHAPTER   PAGE

PART I. FUNDAMENTAL CONCEPTS

1. INTRODUCTION   3
   Social Order. FORMAL ORGANIZATION: Why Organize? Why Study
   Formal Organization? FORMAL ORGANIZATION AS A SYSTEM: The
   Problem of Interdependence. Steady-State Behavior. Relations with
   the Environment. Spontaneous Behavior. Elaboration of Behavior.
   Generality of Concepts. Plan of the Book.

2. TRADITIONAL ORGANIZATIONAL THEORY 23
   TRADITIONAL THEORY. THE THEORY, IN BRIEF. DEPARTMENTATION:
   Purpose Departmentation. Functional Departmentation. Place De-
   partmentation. Clientele Departmentation. APPLICATIONS OF DE-
   PARTMENTATION: Application of Purpose Departmentation. Application of Functional Departmentation. Application of Place Depart-
   mentation.

3. ADMINISTRATION IN TRADITIONAL THEORY 43
   UNITY OF COMMAND. SPAN OF SUPERVISION: Narrow Span of
   Supervision. ORGANIZATIONAL AUTHORITY: Line and Staff Author-
   ity. Development of Staff Concept by the Army. The Staff Concept
   in Religious Organization. Staff Concept in Business Organization.
   AMOUNT OF ORGANIZATIONAL AUTHORITY: Centralization and De-
   centralization. The Practice of Decentralization. Departmentation,
   Authority, and Size of Administrative Unit. Authority and Service
   Activities. Authority and Span of Supervision.

4. PROBLEMS OF TRADITIONAL THEORY 71
   SPECIALIZATION. SPECIALIZATION AND ADMINISTRATION. SPAN OF
   SUPERVISION. THE PROBLEM: Flat versus Tall Organization. The
   Dilemma. IMPORTANT CONSIDERATIONS: The Fordham Model. Notes
   on the Model. The Lockheed Model. DIVISION OF AUTHORITY: Hard-
   wood Experiments. Participative Management. Appeal Channels.

PART II. BEHAVIOR PATTERNS

5. NONFORMAL BEHAVIOR 107
   That "Mysterious Something." LIGHTING EXPERIMENT. RELAY AS-
   SEMBLY TEST ROOM: Interview Program. Bank Wiring Room. CLAS-
   SIFICATION OF BEHAVIOR: Formal Behavior. Nonformal Task—

CHAPTER   PAGE

Oriented Behavior. Nonformal Social Behavior. DYSFUNCTIONS OF FORMAL ORGANIZATION: Problems of Structure. Rules and Work Processes. Informal Pressures. Line and Staff Conflicts. POWER STRUGGLES: The Milo Study. Analysis.

6. SOCIAL ORGANIZATION AND BEHAVIOR 139

CHARACTERISTICS OF INFORMAL ORGANIZATION: Status and Role. Social Processes. Illustration of Processes and Structure. Shared Values and Their Function in Organization. Controlling Behavior. THE SLADE COMPANY: Structure. Informal Processes. Group Norms. Group Performance. SOCIOMETRIC ANALYSIS: Sociometric Choice and Data. Sociogram. Sociometric Matrix. Multiplication Rules. FRIENDSHIP PATTERNS: Simple Patterns. Squared Matrix of Friendships. Cubed Matrix of Friendships. Matrix of Symmetrical Relationships. APPLICATIONS OF MATRIX ANALYSIS: The Slade Illustration. Practical Applications.

7. POWER AND POWER STRUCTURE 182

An Illustration of Power. DEFINITION OF POWER: Use or Presentation of Force. Ability to Influence through Force. Mutual Dependence. Scope of Power. PERSPECTIVE ON POWER. POWER STRUCTURE. SOURCES OF POWER: Power Process. Organizational Sources. Individual Sources. Group Sources. MEASURE OF POWER: Individual Power. Notes on the Measure of Individual Power. Power in Coalitions. Notes on the Measure of Power in Coalitions.

8. EMERGENT SYSTEM 235

SUBSYSTEMS: Technical Subsystems. Social Subsystem. Power Subsystem. Summary of Characteristics. System Overlays. EMERGENT BEHAVIOR: Compromise. Behavior Is Orderly and Purposeful. Structure and Processes. CLASSIFICATION OF BEHAVIOR AND SET THEORY: Set Operations.

PART III. ORGANIZATIONAL DESIGN

9. MARKOV CHAIN ANALYSIS 261

MARKOV CHAINS: Application of Matrix Algebra to Markov Chains. The Steady State. Design of Organization and Markov Chains. Design No. 1. Design No. 2. Design No. 3. General Procedure. Analysis. Notes on the Model.

10. LEARNING 291

LEARNING CURVES: Tabular and Graphical Presentation. Analytic Model. Logarithmic Function. Notes on the Model. A MODEL FOR INDIVIDUAL LEARNING: Definitions. The Estes-Burke Learning Model. GROUP LEARNING: Leavitt Experiment. Guetzkow and Simon Experiment. Carzo and Yanouzas Experiments. A GROUP LEARNING MODEL: Individual Learning. Group Learning. Test of Group Learning Model.

11. BASIC FRAMEWORK FOR ORGANIZATIONAL DESIGN 324

PURPOSE OF DESIGN: Limits of Rationality. The Method of Design. Design and Efficiency. THE PARABLE OF THE SPINDLE: Technical and Behavioral Implications. DESIGN FRAMEWORK: Basis for Design. Desired Performance. Actual Performance. Processes. Structure. Flows and Processes. Flows and Decision Process. Flows and

CHAPTER   PAGE
Action Process. Subsystems on Each Flow. The Total System. A
SIMULATION MODEL: Level Equations. Decision Functions or Flow
Rate Equations. Simulation of Behavior. Notes on the Model.

12. CONTROL 362
DESIGN FOR CONTROL: Effect of Feedback. POSITIVE AND NEGATIVE
FEEDBACK: Delays. Coupled Feedback Loops. Rationality. Delays
and Rationality. DISTORTION OF MESSAGES. DISCONTINUITIES IN
THE SYSTEM.

13. WAITING LINE THEORY AND ORGANIZATIONAL DESIGN . . . 389
DISCONTINUITIES IN THE SYSTEM. THE WAITING LINE MODEL: Distribution of Arrival and Service. Times. Queue Discipline. Inputs
to the System. INFINITE POPULATION: Average Number of Units
in the System. Average Number of Units in Waiting Line. Average
Waiting Time in the Line. Average Time in the System. Summary
of Pertinent Equations. FINITE POPULATION: The Service Factor.
Efficiency Factor. Average Number of Units Being Serviced. Aver-
age Number of Units Waiting for Service. MULTIPLE-STATION
SYSTEM, FINITE POPULATION. DECISION CRITERIA: Implications for
Organizational Design. Effects of Crew Size. Notes on the Model.
WAITING LINE THEORY AND SPAN OF SUPERVISION: The Waiting
Line Model. Note on the Model Applied to Span of Supervision.

14. SYSTEM RELIABILITY IN ORGANIZATIONAL DESIGN 431
Pearl Harbor. A COMPARISON OF SYSTEMS. MEASURES OF SYSTEM
RELIABILITY: Single-Channel System. Two-Channel System. Three-
Channel System. A More Comprehensive Model. General Form of
Reliability Model. Decision Criteria. DESIGN IMPLICATIONS. The
Problem. Some Guidelines.

PART IV. ELEMENTS OF CHANGE

15. MOTIVATION IN ORGANIZATION 469
EXPLANATION BY HISTORIANS. SOCIOECONOMIC EXPLANATIONS: Humoral Models. Instinct and Drive Models. Economic Man Model.
Need-Satiation Model. MOTIVATION AND EXCHANGE: Preferences
and Selection. Exchange of Values. ANALYTICAL TECHNIQUES FOR
CHOOSING BEHAVIOR PATTERNS: Marginal Utility Analysis. Indifference Analysis. Activity-Satisfaction Analysis. Shift of Desired Goal.

16. ORGANIZATIONAL CHANGE 500
DEFINITION OF CHANGE: Change to a New Steady State. Some
Conditions of Change. SYSTEMS APPROACH AND CHANGE: Effects
of Change. Major Organizational Variables and Change. Linking
the Technical and Social Subsystems.

EPILOGUE

EPILOGUE 527
TODAY: Leadership. Exchange. Structure. Adaptation. THE FU-
TURE: Revolutionary Predictions. Moderate Predictions.

CHAPTER   PAGE

APPENDIX

APPENDIX. FINITE QUEUING TABLES 539

INDEXES

AUTHOR INDEX 577
GENERAL INDEX 581

PART I

Fundamental Concepts

1

INTRODUCTION

Whenever men come into contact with one another for any extended period of time they tend to order their relationships and display orderly behavior. The contacts may occur by chance or casually, as in a meeting between strangers that eventually develops into a friendship relation. The contacts may have a purpose, as in meetings between buyers and sellers in a marketplace. Nevertheless, the tendency toward order and orderliness goes on without any design or predetermination.

There is abundant evidence to show this tendency of man to order his relationships without any conscious design. It is clearly evident, for example, in the operation of a capitalistic economic system. The self-sufficient households of ancient society, where man had to perform virtually all the tasks necessary to satisfy the food, clothing, and shelter needs of his family, have given way to economic systems with a high degree of specialization where man makes little or no direct contribution to family needs. He works in a factory or office, receives a money wage for performing some specialized task, and eventually exchanges this wage in the open marketplace for the goods and services needed by his family. The economy of the United States is an example of such a system. Although the government controls much of the economic activity, hundreds of thousands of products are produced and exchanged in

3

the marketplace without government intervention. A private enterprise economy, where there is relative freedom from government controls and where there are millions of producers and consumers of many products and services, would appear chaotic. On the contrary, the markets for goods and services and the relations between consumers and producers in the United States are quite orderly. Samuelson offers the fact of unregulated exchange as proof of order and orderliness in competitive markets. He states:

Hundreds of thousands of commodities are produced by millions of people more or less of their own volition and without central direction or master plan.

This functioning alone is convincing proof that a competitive system of markets and prices—whatever else it may be, however imperfectly it may function—is not a system of chaos and anarchy. There is in it a certain order and orderliness. It works.

A competitive system is an elaborate mechanism for unconscious coordination through a system of prices and markets, a communication device for pooling the knowledge and actions of millions of diverse individuals. Without a central intelligence it solves one of the most complex problems imaginable, involving thousands of unknown variables and relations. Nobody designed it. It just evolved, and like human nature, it is changing; but at least it meets the first test of any social organization—it is able to survive.[1]

The operation of a competitive system may be understood, according to Samuelson, by making the simplifying assumption that everything has a price. The prices of commodities and services are determined by supply and demand. If the demand for a particular commodity is greater than its supply, the price will rise and producers will offer more of the commodity for sale. Similarly, if producers offer more items than consumers are willing to buy at the price offered, competition will force the price down. At the lower price, consumers will buy more and producers will supply less of the commodity. This process will continue until an equilibrium price is established. At this price ". . . the amount willingly supplied and amount willingly demanded are equal"[2] or supply equals demand. Other things being equal, the equilibrium price will be maintained over the long run. Similar reasoning applies to the markets for the factors of production such as labor and capital. This trial and error

---

[1] Paul A. Samuelson, *Economics* (6th ed.; New York: Mc-Graw Hill Book Co., 1964), p. 37. Used by permission.
[2] *Ibid.*, p. 63.

process, then, solves the problems of what and how much shall be produced, and for whom things are to be produced. The problem of how things are produced is solved through competition among producers, with the more efficient producers displacing producers with costlier methods of production. In other words, an order in the economic system evolves by a trial and error process of interaction between and among the buyers and sellers of goods and services and the factors of production.

Social Order

Another example of this tendency is the way that men order their social relations. Men living in the same community or working close to each other in a factory have a tendency to interact, that is, talk to each other, exchange favors, play games, have meals together, or simply exchange glances. From these contacts, they develop sentiments toward each other such as liking, disliking, attraction, or respect. Eventually, the frequency and duration of interactions and the sentiments of group members toward each other become patterned, and a social structure develops. "Each member's status in the group depends on his relations with the others—their sentiments toward and interaction with him. As a result, integrated members become differentiated from isolates, those who are widely respected from those who are not highly regarded, and leaders from followers."[3]

Furthermore, the group will develop a value structure, that is, their shared beliefs or ideas about what is important in life, play, or work. Group members might share beliefs on the importance of such items as home ownership, athletic ability, travel, education, and financial independence. The group will also develop standards of conduct which dictate how its members ought to behave. For example, workers in a factory may agree not to exceed a certain rate of production. Anyone who exceeds this rate is labeled a "rate buster." There are certain sanctions that the group employs against those who violate its norms of conduct. The "rate buster," for example, may get the "silent treatment" from the other members of the group. "Finally, aside from the norms to which everybody is expected to conform, differential role expectations also emerge,

---

[3] Peter M. Blau and W. Richard Scott, *Formal Organizations* (San Francisco: Chandler Publishing Co., 1962), p. 3. Copyright © 1962 by Chandler Publishing Company.

expectations that become associated with various social positions. Only women in our society are expected to wear skirts, for example."[4]

FORMAL ORGANIZATION

This book is about formal organization. In contrast to systems that arise through unconscious ordering, such as those described above, formal organizations are systems in which men and capital are *deliberately* related for the accomplishment of some *explicit* purpose. Social organization, for example, does not arise as a result of design or deliberation, but it evolves naturally whenever men interact with each other over extended periods of time. While the formal organization exists for the accomplishment of specific objectives (it is a means to an end), the social organization is important to members for its own sake (it is an end in itself), that is, it fulfills a basic need that men have to associate with others. In fulfilling this need for human association, men eventually order their relationships and form a social organization.

Why Organize?

If people tend to organize naturally, why is it necessary to design a formal organization? The most obvious answer to this question seems to lie in the premise that formal organization is necessary to achieve objectives. However, this answer is not completely acceptable, because certain goals are attained when people order their relationships without formal design. In our description of a competitive economic system, for example, we noted that the problem of output determination or how much of a particular commodity will be produced is solved by the interaction of producers and consumers in the marketplace. Related problems such as what shall be produced, how they shall be produced, and for whom they are produced, are solved in a similar manner.

Perhaps a better answer to the question: "Why organize?" is that natural systems are unable to evaluate alternatives or to institute the decision-making processes of formal organizations. This

---

[4] *Ibid.*, p. 4.

premise is also untenable because living systems go through a selection process to achieve their goals. We have said, for example, that living systems such as economic and social systems try to achieve a state of order, an equilibrium or what we later call a steady state. When there is a change in its environment and the change throws the system into a state of imbalance, the system seeks ways to eliminate the effect of the disturbance and return to a steady state. From the various possible alternatives, the system selects that behavior pattern which seems most likely to maintain a steady state. In effect, then, natural systems approximate the decision processes of formal organizations.

As an example of this type of behavior, let us use the social organization of a factory. Specifically, we draw from the well known study of Coch and French at the Harwood Manufacturing Corporation.[5] The researchers were concerned with the problem of employee resistance to change. The company tried to institute changes in the jobs and work methods of its production workers. Employee attitudes toward these changes were markedly negative. Despite the fact that the company gave a monetary allowance or a bonus to employees who experienced job changes, they resisted. "This resistance expressed itself in several ways, such as grievances about the piece rates that went with the new methods, high turnover, very low efficiency, restriction of output, and worker aggression against management."[6] Part of the resistance could be attributed to a feeling by employees that the job changes would disturb the social order. For example, the researchers indicated that employees would resist change because of the possibility of failure on the new job and a loss of status in the eyes of fellow employees. Furthermore, employees may resist because they are reluctant to leave friends or break social ties, and they may be uncertain about being accepted in a new and different social system. They could have accepted the job changes, but they chose the alternative of resistance because to them, this was the best way to maintain the social order.

Why Then? Although human beings display organizing ten-

---

[5] Lester Coch and John R. P. French, Jr., "Overcoming Resistance to Change," *Human Relations*, Vol. I (August, 1948), pp. 512–32. We return to this study in later chapters.

[6] *Ibid.*, p. 512.

dencies, they order their relationships slowly. Social organization evolves by successive approximation, that is, it emerges from a trial and error process. Social organization would be adequate for the accomplishment of objectives if resources were unlimited and there were no wars, illness, ignorance, or natural disorders such as floods, storms, and earthquakes. If there were enough goods and services to fully satisfy every human desire, it would not matter if the system produced excessive amounts of any commodity or service, and it would not matter if the factors of production such as labor and capital were used inefficiently. Resources are scarce, however, and it does matter how they are employed. While the free interplay of forces in the marketplace may eventually solve the problems of how resources shall be employed and what goods and services shall be produced, a nation may be unable (because of scarce resources) or unwilling to withstand the wastes of a trial and error process. The effects of an economic depression, for example, may be so severe as to cripple a nation and prevent its normal progress toward recovery and eventual stability. Similarly, a nation threatened by invasion or insurgence can ill afford to wait until an army or police force develops naturally. A businessman cannot wait until his employees become organized. While they are going through the trial and error process of developing an optimum organization, the businessman must bear the losses coincident with the unwise use of resources, and in the meantime, he might be clobbered in the marketplace by his competitors. Thus, a nation finds it necessary to institute government controls in economic affairs and to organize armies formally for national defense, and the businessman usually has a formal organization before he begins operations.

Efficiency. The primary reason for formal organization, then, is the attainment of objectives through the efficient use of resources. Every organization is constrained by limited resources. With a fixed amount of resources, an organization cannot take advantage of all the possible opportunities available to it. When available resources are applied to one purpose, the attainment of other possible goals is prevented. Thus, the problem of formal organization is to determine the best possible allocation of resources. The formal organization has attained *efficiency* when it employs resources to that alternative which produces the greatest result.[7]

---

[7] Herbert A. Simon, *Administrative Behavior* (New York: Macmillan Co., 1957), p. 179.

Let us illustrate this point with a simplified problem of business organization. Consider a business with only so many workers, only so much material, and so much machine capacity. Specifically, let us suppose a company that produces swim trunks and walking shorts wants to determine the best allocation of its limited resources between these two products. Suppose that the capacities of its resources are defined as shown in Table 1–1.

TABLE 1–1

Capacities of Productive Resources

Resources	Walking Shorts		Swim Trunks
Workers..........................	2,000	or	1,000
Cutting and sewing machines..........	1,000	or	2,000
Cloth material......................	1,333	or	1,200

As implied by the information of Table 1–1, the resources are interchangeable, that is, they may be used to produce either swim trunks or walking shorts or some combination of the two products. The capacities of these resources are shown graphically in Figure 1–1.

FIGURE 1–1

Graph of Resource Capacities

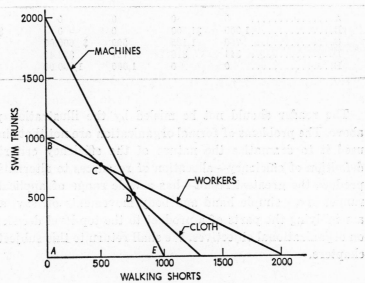

Although the company's machines are capable of producing 2,000 swim trunks when no walking shorts are produced, labor capacity limits the production of this product to 1,000 units. Similarly, machine capacity limits the production of walking shorts to 1,000 units when no swim trunks are produced. In the language of linear programming, the area bounded by *A, B, C, D,* and *E* is called a technical feasibility polygon. In other words, it is technically feasible for the firm to produce any combination of swim trunks and walking shorts that falls within the area of the polygon. Let us consider the five possibilities represented by the points *A, B, C, D,* and *E.* Recall that the efficiency criterion requires an assignment of resources to the alternative that produces the greatest result. In a business situation, results may be measured by profits. Assume that profit per unit is $1.50 for swim trunks and $1.20 for walking shorts. Total profit for each alternative is shown in Table 1–2. According to the results of the table, alternative *C* (750 swim trunks and 500 walking shorts) is the optimum output combination and represents the best allocation of resources.

TABLE 1–2

Evaluation of Alternative Uses of Resources

Alternatives	Swim Trunks		Walking Shorts		Total Profits
	Units	*Profits*	*Units*	*Profits*	
A.................	0	0	0	0	0
B.................	1,000	$1,500	0	0	$1,500.00
C.................	750	1,125	500	$ 600.00	1,725.00
D.................	544	816	727	872.40	1,688.40
E.................	0	0	1,000	1,200.00	1,200.00

The reader should not be misled by the illustration provided above. The problems of formal organization are not that simple. We used it to dramatize the nature of the efficiency criterion. The definition of efficiency—allocation of resources to alternatives that produce the greatest result—has a wide range of applicability. It ranges from simple hand and body movements of, say, a worker assemblying the parts of a product to the top-level decisions made on organizational objectives. We shall return to this subject in later chapters.

Why Study Formal Organization?

Despite its growing importance, formal organization has received, until very recently, inadequate attention in modern thought and study; Boulding, in his treatise on "the organizational revolution," states the problem quite succinctly:

Yet this revolution has received little study and is not something of which we are particularly conscious. It has crept upon us silently. It is something which we accept as "natural" almost without thinking. And yet, the whole movement raises problems with which we are ill equipped to deal. In our political and economic thinking, and in our ethical thinking as well, we are still often a hundred years behind the times—still thinking in terms of a society in which organizations are rather small and weak, and in which the family is the dominant institution.[8]

The growth in number and size of formal organizations has made them the dominant form of institution in modern society. They are the manifestation of a highly specialized and interdependent society and a relatively high and continually rising standard of living. Accompanying these rising standards are demands for more and more goods and services and for the organizations to supply these wants. Formal organizations pervade in all aspects of modern life, and they command the attention, time, and energy of most people. This fact alone is justification for the study of formal organizations. However, the design for explicit purpose and the efficiency criterion provide more compelling reasons. For emphasis, let us restate some of our previous discussion on these points.

Design for Explicit Purpose. Formal organizations are different from other social institutions in that they are designed to accomplish an explicit purpose. In other words, organization is a means to an end. The businessman, for example, does not organize for the sake of organization, but to produce a product or service and to reward those who contribute to that end. The head of a state government agency, a health department, for example, desires an organization not for aesthetic reasons but rather as a means for achieving the statutory objectives with which his agency is charged.

Efficiency Criterion. Every organization is constrained by limited

---

[8] Kenneth E. Boulding, *Organizational Revolution* (New York: Harper & Row, 1953), p. 4.

resources. With a fixed amount of resources, an organization cannot take advantage of all opportunities available to it. Thus, the problem of formal organization is one of determining the best possible allocation of resources. The formal organization has attained *efficiency* when it applies resources to the alternative which produces the greatest result. It is not enough, for example, to produce an automobile that is desirable to consumers; the automobile must be produced efficiently. At most, the automobile manufacturer will want an output which requires the least expenditure of capital and human resources or, in broader terms, he seeks an arrangement of resources that results in the largest difference of revenues over costs. The organizer, therefore, arranges men and capital in a manner that promises the greatest possible advantage.

The formal organization is characterized by rules, regulations, and a status structure that orders the relations among its members. Through organization, the administrator attempts to remove some of the uncertainties of a human situation, to take advantage of the benefits of specialization, to facilitate the decision process, and to ensure that decisions are implemented properly. *This formal design, which attempts to regulate human behavior for the efficient accomplishment of explicit goals, makes the formal organization unique among the social institutions of modern society and worthy of special study.*

FORMAL ORGANIZATION AS A SYSTEM

One way that the formal organization achieves efficiency is through specialization. A man working alone on a project could hardly achieve the productivity of men working on specialized parts of the project. Adam Smith, in his *Wealth of Nations*, illustrated this point in his description of a pin factory. By dividing the work of pin making into specialized tasks and assigning each worker to a single task, the factory could produce thousands of pins per man per day. Whereas, if each worker had to make the entire pin himself, he could produce only a few pins per day.

Another way that a formal organization achieves efficiency is through concerted action. Men who are united in a common cause, for example, can exert more physical force than men standing separate from and independent of each other. The power of labor unions is another example of a property of organization that is not available to individuals acting alone. A single worker with common skills and nothing more than his own services to offer or withhold from employment would have little or no bargaining power against a large employer. However, an organized work force represented by a labor union with the ability to call a stop to all operations is in a very strong bargaining position.

Even in activities requiring mental skills, there is reason to believe that organized effort is more productive that unorganized effort. In decision making, for example, which is largely a mental task, evidence seems to indicate that group decisions (where the members interact before arriving at a decision) are significantly better than decisions made by individuals.[9]

Each of these ways is possible because there are connections among the parts. The benefits of specialization could not be realized, for example, without an organizational structure that relates those who perform specialized tasks or some agency to coordinate their efforts toward the overall task. In essence, the formal organization is a system. A *system* is defined as anything that consists of interdependent elements. The behavior or state of each element is dependent upon the behavior or state of the other elements.

The Problem of Interdependence

How does one study a situation where everything is dependent on everything else—especially something as complex as an organization? Stafford Beer describes this problem as one of astronomical proportions. He uses a system of n elements. If this were not a system, a study of the set of n elements would only involve n investigations. "Once we declare the set of things to be a system, however, there are not only the n elements themselves to examine, but $n(n-1)$ relations between the elements to be examined."[10] For example, a system of seven elements would involve 42 relations. "If we define a state of this system as the pattern produced in the network when each of these relations is either in being or not in

---

[9] Earnest J. Hall, Jane S. Mouton and Robert R. Blake, "Group Problem Solving Effectiveness under Conditions of Pooling versus Interaction," *Journal of Social Psychology*, Vol. 59 (1963), pp. 147–57. Besides presenting the results of an experiment concerned with quality of group and individual decision making, the authors also provide a brief annotation of literature on the subject.

[10] Stafford Beer, *Cybernetics and Management* (New York: John Wiley & Sons, Inc., 1964), p. 10.

being (which is not a very detailed account of the relationships), then there will be 2^{42} different states of the system. This is a fantastically large number : more than four million of millions."[11]

The extreme complexity and variety of relationships in an organization does not prevent analysis. It is not necessary to examine all possible relationships. We can learn a great deal about an organization by examining its parts and a limited number of relationships. What we say about the relationships among a few parts is not necessarily incorrect just because we say nothing about all the relationships in an organization.[12]

Moreover, complexity and variety are reduced by a natural tendency of human beings to order their relationships. This factor is crucial to the study of organizations. In essence, we are able to study and draw conclusions about the ways that people behave in organizations because their behavior is orderly and generally predictable. It is called *steady-state behavior*. Let us examine some well-known facts and scientific explanation about this behavior.

Steady-State Behavior

Steady-state behavior is not only characteristic of human beings but it is true for all living things. In fact, this tendency to order relationships is one of the characteristics that distinguishes the living from the nonliving or physical world. According to the second law of thermodynamics, the general trend of events in the physical world is ". . . directed toward a chaotic state, characterized by maximum disorder, or, in other terms, toward thermodynamic equilibrium, where all processes come to a stop. In living organisms, however, we find a preservation of order and an avoidance of equilibrium."[13] The second law of thermodynamics is only applicable to *closed systems*, that is, systems which are isolated from their environment. Several chemicals reacting in an insulated vessel is an example of a closed system. Eventually the chemicals will move from an ordered state to one of maximum disorder. According to the language of thermodynamics, the probability that

---

[11] *Ibid.*, pp. 10–11.

[12] George C. Homans, *The Human Group* (New York: Harcourt, Brace & World, Inc., 1950), p. 10.

[13] Ludwig von Bertalanffy, *Problems of Life* (London: C. A. Watts & Co. Ltd., 1952), p. 145.

the elements in a system are randomly distributed is called its *entropy*. The trend of events in a closed system is toward a random distribution. In closed systems, then, entropy change is always positive. It never decreases. Entropy increases to a maximum, at which point there is complete disorder and all processes come to a stop. At this point, the system is in its most probable state. In other words, it is almost certain that the elements of the system are randomly distributed or completely disordered.

In contrast to closed systems, *open systems* continuously exchange materials, energy, or information with their environments. They take in something (an input) and give off something (an output) to the environment. All living systems, from the simple cell to complex formal organizations, nations, and societies, are open systems. Open systems also experience the tendency toward disorder, breakdown, and loss of energy, but they are able to counter this tendency by taking in inputs of higher energy and order than their outputs. Thus, open systems are able to rebuild energy, repair breakdowns, and restore order. Living systems ". . . maintaining themselves in a steady state can avoid the increase of entropy and may even develop towards states of increased order and organization."[14]

The tendency towards steady-state behavior goes on despite changes in the environment. When an open system ". . . is thrown into a state of imbalance by a change in its environment . . . the system behaves in such a way as to eliminate the effect of this change and to return to a steady state which is as nearly like the former state as is possible."[15] It is also possible, of course, for the system to fail in its efforts to maintain a steady state. When the magnitude of the environmental change is so great that the internal processes of the system are unable to compensate, the system will not return to a steady state but will experience death. Thus, the human being dies and the business organization suffers bankruptcy. In passing, it is interesting to cite two vivid examples of organizations that survived after extreme shocks: the Ford Motor Company and the General Dynamics Corporation. Reportedly, Ford lost $200 million on its introduction of the Edsel automobile, and General

---

[14] Ludwig von Bertalanffy, "General Systems Theory," *General Systems*, Vol. 1 (1956), p. 4.

[15] D. F. Bradley and M. Calvin, "Behavior: Imbalance in a Network of Chemical Transformations," *General Systems*, Vol. 1 (1956), p. 65.

Dynamics experienced a $425 million loss on its jet airliners, the Convair 880 and 990;[16] but yet, each company survived and returned to profitable operations.

Relations with the Environment

Formal organizations are a part of a larger order, which may be a community, a nation, or society in general. The formal organization must exchange values, material, or energy, with this larger order or what might be considered as its environment. The business firm, for example, draws its work force from the community, sells its products or services to consumers in the society, purchases its supplies from other firms, competes with still other firms in the sale of its products or services and in the purchase of capital and human resources, bargains with labor unions over the working conditions, and must exist in a community as an institution that utilizes community services such as light, power, and water. As an employer, the business firm is a source of wealth to the community. Its employee benefits may cover every aspect of human welfare from providing educational funds for the children of employees to employee retirement benefits. As a member of society, the business firm must abide by laws which restrict its buying and selling activities and its relations with employees, and it must contribute to the support of the community by paying taxes. As part of the community and society, the business firm is influenced, and even governed, by the culture and order in the environment. An American firm, for example, is strongly influenced by the precepts of political freedom, democracy, and the general independence of individual action considered so sacred in the American way of life. Likewise, the business exercises a strong influence in the American society. Capitalism, the profit motive, and free enterprise, for example, are also sacred precepts in the American way of life.

The motives of men are, in part, influenced by this environment. Men work for an organization to make money. They may want this money to support a family, buy a home or car, or pay for a vacation. Formal organizations appeal to these externally determined motives by paying their men to work. Men, of course, have many

---

[16] Richard Austin Smith, "How a Great Corporation Got Out of Control," *Fortune*, Vol. 65, No. 1 (January, 1962), pp. 69–184.

other externally determined reasons for working, such a prestige, or the respect that goes with just having a job.

Cultural influences also play an important part in determining organizational behavior. Japanese industrial enterprise provides a striking example of the effects of cultural influences.[17] Family life and regard for elders are strong determinants of behavior in Japanese organizations.

Since the ethic of the society is for young men to be diligent yet self-effacing before their superiors, they are supposed to rejoice in the fact that their elders take the credit for their efforts. Only in rare circumstances would it be ethical for a junior executive to be promoted over his senior. In Japan, executives patiently wait their turn for promotion, and their ultimate reward is based much more upon loyalty, devotion, and contribution to the group than upon individual initiative or outstanding individual achievement. The young man who attempts to push himself ahead of others is subject to severe criticism, if not outright rejection by the group, for such tactics would destroy the entire web of authority and security within the enterprise.[18]

While the Japanese factory provides an example that is unique in terms of Western culture, it dramatizes the fact that an organization exists in relation to its environment.

Spontaneous Behavior

An organization also displays characteristics which require no stimulus from its environment, and this fact reveals another difference between living and inanimate things such as machines. Although an organization has some machinelike characteristics, such as feedback and control, much of the behavior in organizations is spontaneous or is generated internally. In contrast, machines are set in motion only by external forces such as an electrical impulse. Biologically, there is no question about the difference between living organisms and machines. Some of the "spontaneous" movements of living things are given by von Bertalanffy:

---

[17] James C. Abegglen, *The Japanese Factory* (New York: The Free Press, 1958).

[18] F. Harbison and C. A. Myers, *Management in the Industrial World; An International Analysis* (New York: McGraw-Hill Book Co., 1959), p. 255. Used by permission.

Organisms go through progressive transformations, which we call growth, development, senescence, and death. They are produced only by their kin by the process known as reproduction. Organic structures and functions are admirably fitted for the "purpose" they serve. An astounding multiplicity of processes goes on in the simplest cell, so arranged that its identity is maintained in this ceaseless and tremendously complicated play. Equally, every living being displays in its organs and functions a purposeful construction, adapted to the environment in which it normally exists.[19]

On a social level in organizations, spontaneous activities evolve which have no necessary relation to the environment. We have mentioned the formation of social groups which arise when men associate. As men form friendships and develop sentiments toward one another, they express their sentiments in activities. These activities may take the form of helping each other at work. Homans describes this situation as it occurred in the Bank Wiring Observation Room of the Western Electric Company's Hawthorne Works.

There were few occasions when helping another man was required by the necessity of the work—indeed it was forbidden by the company; yet it took place just the same, and many of the men testified that helping and being helped made them feel better. Everyone took part in helping; it was not confined, as were some other activities, to soldering units. In fact it was one of the activities that united the whole group instead of dividing it into cliques. . . .[20]

Elaboration of Behavior

Despite the fact that men are placed in an ordered situation when employed in a formal organization, they tend to elaborate their behavior beyond the demands of a job. This tendency not only complicates relationships but affects the organization as a whole. Homans describes the phenomenon as follows:

When a number of persons have come together to form a group, their behavior never holds to its first pattern. Social life is never utilitarian: it elaborates itself, complicates itself, beyond the demands of the original situation. The elaboration brings changes in the motives of individuals . . . change in the attitudes of persons, brought about by their membership in groups, . . . the elaboration also means changes in their activities

---

[19] Bertalanffy, *Problems of Life, op. cit.*, p. 2.

[20] Homans, *op. cit.*, p. 118. For a full description of the research at Hawthorne, see F. J. Roethlisberger and W. J. Dickson, *Management and the Worker* (Cambridge, Mass.: Harvard University Press, 1939).

and interactions—changes, in fact, in the organization of the group as a whole.[21]

In the first few paragraphs of this chapter, we described this tendency as an unconscious ordering of relationships. Thus, in addition to job relations, we find, for example, that men order their relations even further into social organizations. Later in the book, we characterize social organization as a subsystem of formal organization. This subsystem along with others is a fact in organization life. Subsystems are important for our consideration not only because of their existence but also because they play a major part in determining the course of events in the formal organization.

Generality of Concepts

In this chapter and in other parts of the book, we use concepts that have been developed in the social, biological, and physical sciences. The illustrations taken from the physical and biological sciences are perhaps not analogous to situations in formal organizations. But, there is growing evidence that the concepts, models, and laws of other fields are applicable to the study of formal organizations. Concepts such as wholeness, interdependence, open system, order, and steady state seem especially applicable to formal organizations. The recognition that there are isomorphies among several different fields of study is not new, of course. In fact, it has led von Bertalanffy to call for a "General System Theory." He states:

. . . there exist models, principles, and laws that apply to generalized systems or their subclasses, irrespective of their particular kind, the nature of their component elements, and the relations of "forces" between them. It seems legitimate to ask for a theory, not of systems of a more or less special kind, but of universal principles applying to systems in general.

In this way we come to postulate a new discipline, called General System Theory. Its subject matter is the formulation and derivation of those principles which are valid for "systems" in general.[22]

Mary Parker Follett, who was impressed by advancements in the biological and social sciences, such as the trend in physiology to

---

[21] Homans, *op cit.*, p. 109.

[22] Ludwig von Bertalanffy, "General Systems Theory," *Main Currents in Modern Thought*, Vol. II, No. 4 (March, 1955) pp. 75–76.

view the organism as consisting of integrated parts and in psychology to take the "whole man" approach or what is known as "gestalt psychology," proposed a similar approach to the study of organizations.[23] As early as 1927, Follett emphasized the necessity for understanding "the total situation." She cautioned against organizational analysis whereby all factors were considered in isolation from one another, but rather she emphasized that they must be considered in relation to one another:

What I am emphasizing is not merely the totalness of the situation, but the nature of the totalness. . . . what you have to consider in a situation is not all the factors one by one, but also their relation to one another. This means, among other things, that when a factor is added to or subtracted from a situation, you have not that situation minus or plus that factor, for all the rest will be changed. . . . the whole is determined not only by its constituents, but by their relation to one another. . . . the whole is determined also by the relation of whole and parts.[24]

Plan of the Book

The preceding sections have established the framework to be undertaken in the following chapters of this book. Formal organization is characterized as a system not only because its component parts interact with each other but also because the entire system interacts with its environment. In this regard, formal organization is viewed as an open system.

One purpose of this book is to provide an introduction to concepts about formal organization. Another purpose is to familiarize the reader with some models for evaluating alternative organizational designs.

The point of departure is made from the contributions of those organizational theorists who are referred to as "traditionalists." In Chapters 2 and 3, our intent is to describe traditional theory and to provide some illustrations of its application. Then, in Chapters 4 and 5, we point out some of the shortcomings of traditional theory both in terms of its narrow assumptions about the ways that people behave in organizations and in terms of arriving at decisions about organizational design. Although traditional theory is concerned

---

[23] Mary Parker Follett, "The Psychology of Control" reprinted in Henry C. Metcalf and Lyndall F. Urwick (eds.), *Dynamic Administration* (New York: Harper & Row, 1940), pp. 183–209.

[24] *Ibid.*, pp. 192–95.

with organization, it fails to recognize the importance of (1) the fact that people in organization elaborate their behavior, (2) environmental influences, and (3) the interdependence of the parts of an organization. Viewing organization as a system not only takes into account the formally prescribed behavior but it also encompasses social and power behavior.

In Chapters 6, 7, and 8, we conceptualize behavior in terms of systems behavior and discuss how the subsystems interact to form what we call an emergent system.

A major premise of this book is that behavior in organizations generally displays order and orderliness; that is, it tends toward a stable condition. We elaborate on this thesis in Chapter 9, the first chapter on organizational design. We recognize that organizational relationships change over time and that organizations go through periods of shock and disturbance, but after each disturbance, the organization will again tend toward stability even though it may be at a different level of performance.

We maintain that the first step in evaluating alternative organizational designs is to determine the level at which behavior will settle down under each design or, indeed, whether it will settle down at all. In Chapter 10, we examine models of the so-called "learning curve" and discuss individual and group learning models that have been used for understanding and predicting behavior.

In Chapter 11, a framework for organizational design is explored by identifying organizational patterns in terms of inputs, outputs, feedback, delays, and flows. These serve as a foundation for certain aspects of design which are presented in Chapters 12, 13, and 14.

The subject of control or feedback control systems is taken up in Chapter 12. The problem of delays is covered in Chapter 13, where we apply waiting line theory to organizational design. The communication system in existence prior to the Pearl Harbor attack and the more recent defense setup called "Fail Safe," along with a model for determining system reliability are discussed in Chapter 14.

In the final section of the book, there are two chapters concerned with organizational change. In these chapters, it is assumed that a given level of performance is undesirable. In order to change behavior to the desired level, we maintain that it is first necessary to understand what motivates man in organization (Chapter 15). In the final chapter we examine the systems approach and its usefulness in analyzing and implementing change.

DISCUSSION QUESTIONS AND PROBLEMS

1-1. When people become members of a formal organization, does their natural tendency to organize diminish, disappear, or intensify? Explain.

1-2. Can a social organization be characterized as a system? Explain.

1-3. Does the fact that people tend to order their relationships and stabilize behavior have any significance in the design of formal organization? Explain.

1-4. If people did not have a tendency to order their relationships and display orderly behavior, do you think it would be possible to devise a formal organization? Why?

1-5. Is it possible to allocate resources in an optimum manner for the total organization, yet use them inefficiently in one part of the organization? Explain.

1-6. How can the inefficient use of resources at some subordinate level in an organization be justified?

1-7. Is it possible for a formal organization to derive energy from its own output? Explain.

1-8. Give illustrations of formal organizations that are less open to the environment than others.

1-9. Should the designer of a formal organization seek ways to suppress the tendency of its members to elaborate their behavior? Explain.

1-10. What is the "system approach" to the study of formal organization? What are the implications of this approach in the design of formal organization?

$\mathcal{2}$

TRADITIONAL
ORGANIZATIONAL
THEORY

Although one may find some references in ancient literature on the importance of formal organization, it was not until the early part of the 20th century that widespread interest developed in the subject. This lack of interest in earlier periods may have been a cause and/or an effect of the lack of understanding about human behavior in formal organizations. Nevertheless, the extent of understanding left much to be desired. Doubts about the knowledge of formal organizations were, perhaps, best expressed by Leo Tolstoy through his hero, Prince Andrew, in *War and Peace*. Prince Andrew made the following observation about man's state of knowledge:

What theory and science is possible about a matter the conditions and circumstances of which are unknown and cannot be defined, especially when the strength of the acting forces cannot be ascertained? . . . a detachment of five thousand is worth thirty thousand, as at Schön Grabern, while at times fifty thousand run from eight thousand, as at Austerlitz. What science can there be in a matter in which, as in all practical matters, nothing can be defined and everything depends on innumerable conditions, the significance of which is determined at a particular moment which arrives no one knows when?[1]

---

[1] Leo Tolstoy, *War and Peace*, trans. Louise and Aylmer Maude (New York: Oxford University Press, Inc., 1942), p. 713.

Tolstoy's view was pessimistic but not inappropriate to the condition of the literature over one hundred years ago when this classic novel was written. In this modern era, our ability to analyze the "innumerable conditions" and to make prescriptions for organizational design have improved considerably, but the theory is still at an embryonic stage of development.

Perhaps the strongest indication that the discipline is still new and developing is the controversy that prevails in present-day literature over what is considered traditional organizational theory. Much of this controversy is examined in Chapters 4 and 5. In this and the following chapter, the traditional theory about formal organizations is examined. The approach in this chapter and Chapter 3 is strictly descriptive, that is, no attempt is made to evaluate or present criticisms of the theory. Our reasons for following this approach are both academic and practical. First, we want to present the theory simply, uncluttered with long discussions about its validity. This approach also allows us to get familiar with terminology and to form a basis for communication about the discipline. Second, we wish to give proper credit to the traditionalists. Their efforts represent a significant contribution to knowledge. Their principal contribution was in simplifying and classifying what is indeed a complicated subject (most of the criticism of the traditionalist's theory is based on the premise that they made it too simple). Third, we find it necessary to present the traditional theory because its concepts form the basis for much of modern theory. Later in the book, some of the more modern thoughts are presented and some criteria for the design of formal organization are offered.

TRADITIONAL THEORY

It may be misleading and, according to some, unfair to label a theory "traditional," but we do it only in the sense that the ideas classified as traditional are the ones that prevailed in the early development of organizational theory and practice. Traditional organizational theory can be traced historically, for instance, to 19th-century prototype industrial, military, and ecclesiastic organizations.[2] In this section we lump the ideas of several contributors.

---

[2] For a philosophical speculation concerning the origin of the term "traditional organizational theory," see John M. Pfiffner and Frank P. Sherwood, *Administrative Organization* (Englewood Cliffs, N.J.: Prentice-Hall, Inc., 1960), pp. 53–54.

In this effort we do not mean to undermine the work of the traditional theorists but merely to describe it as briefly as possible.

Frederick W. Taylor,[3] Henri Fayol,[4] Luther Gulick,[5] J. D. Mooney and A. C. Reiley,[6] and Max Weber[7] were perhaps the most prominent of the men associated with the early development of the traditional theory.[8] All of these men were dissatisfied, in one way or another, with the organizational practices of their time. Taylor, for example, was concerned with the problem of "soldiering," that is, the practice of workmen producing less than their capabilities permitted. "Underworking, that is, deliberately working slowly so as to avoid doing a full day's work, 'soldiering,' . . ." according to Taylor, ". . . constitutes the greatest evil with which the working people of both England and America are now afflicted."[9] Taylor saw three causes for this condition of low production:

First. The fallacy, which has from time immemorial been almost universal among workmen, that a material increase in the output of each man or each machine in the trade would result in the end in throwing a large number of men out of work.

Second. The defective systems of management which are in common use, and which make it necessary for each workman to soldier, or work slowly, in order that he may protect his own best interest.

Third. The inefficient rule-of-thumb methods, which are still almost universal in all trades, and in practicing which our workmen waste a large part of their effort.[10]

Taylor and his colleagues were concerned principally with the operational level of organization or shop management, but their emphasis on planning, standard practices, proper work tools, and proper work methods based on time and motion study gained wide-

---

[3] Frederick W. Taylor, *Scientific Management* (New York: Harper & Row, 1947).

[4] Henri Fayol, *General and Industrial Management*, trans. Constance Storrs (London: Sir Isaac Pitman & Sons, Ltd., 1949).

[5] Luther Gulick, "Notes on the Theory of Organization," in Luther Gulick and Lyndall F. Urwick (eds.), *Papers on the Science of Administration* (New York: Institute of Public Administration, 1937).

[6] James D. Mooney and Alan C. Reiley, *Onward Industry* (New York: Harper & Row, 1931), or the later edition: James D. Mooney, *Principles of Organization* (rev. ed.; New York: Harper & Row, 1947).

[7] H. H. Gerth and C. Wright Mills, *From Max Weber* (New York: Oxford University Press, Inc., 1946), chap. viii.

[8] In our coverage of traditional theorists we may have done an injustice both to those not included because they were ignored and to those included since the coverage is brief.

[9] Taylor, *op. cit.*, pp. 13–14.

[10] *Ibid.*, pp. 15–16.

spread acceptance and developed into what became known as the "scientific management movement." Taylor said that by substituting scientific for rule-of-thumb methods, enormous gains in efficiency could be achieved. According to Taylor, the worker would benefit by receiving higher wages, and the employer would benefit by realizing lower labor costs.

Taylor also made an attempt to extend the principle of specialization into the organization of managerial levels. "Functional management," Taylor explained, "consists in so dividing the work of management that each man from the assistant superintendent down shall have as few functions as possible to perform. If practicable the work of each man in management should be confined to the performance of a single leading function."[11] Taylor felt that by breaking down the task of the foreman, the benefits of specialization would accrue. Furthermore, it would be easier to find and train a man to perform one specialized function. His organizational scheme, labeled the "functional foreman," subdivided the task into eight parts: route clerk, instruction card clerk, cost and time clerk, shop disciplinarian, inspector, gang boss, speed boss, and repair boss.

According to Taylor, equally as important as his recommendations concerning the routinization of work and "functional management" is the approach he used to solve organizational problems. He attempted to replace rule-of-thumb and traditional methods, and personal opinions and judgments, by what he called "scientific investigation and knowledge." While the use of the term "science" has not received the approbation of some people, Taylor's attempt to apply it to the solution of organizational problems is a noteworthy development.

Other contributors to the traditional theory, such as Fayol, Gulick, Mooney, and Weber, were more concerned with the administrative level of organization. While Taylor sought to solve organizational problems by the objective rationality of measurement, Max Weber, the German social historian, stressed the importance of a hierarchical structure, positions, authority, and rules in solving the recurring problems of organization. Bureaucracy, according to Weber, was management by rules without regard for human emotion. Weber believed that bureaucracy was an absolute necessity for government and the modern corporation. According to Weber:

---

[11] Taylor, *op. cit.*, p. 99.

"The decisive reason for the advance of bureaucratic organization has been its purely technical superiority over any other form of organization."[12] "Precision, speed, unambiguity, knowledge of the files, continuity, discretion, unity, strict subordination, reduction of friction and of material and personal costs—these are raised to the optimum point in the strictly bureaucratic administration, and especially in its monocratic form."[13] Bureaucracy develops toward perfection, the more it is ". . . 'dehumanized,' the more completely it succeeds in eliminating from official business love, hatred, and all purely personal, irrational, and emotional elements which escape calculation."[14]

Weber's bureaucratic organization is a model of perfection. It could be likened to a model of a machine without friction. In Weber's bureaucracy, everyone's job and authority are clearly defined. Appointments to office are made strictly on a candidate's technical proficiency and not on family or political connections. All behavior in the organization is closely regulated by rules and by superior officers in the hierarchy of authority. Technical proficiency, a disregard for personal feelings, and governance by rules and regulations, in Weber's view, are supposed to promote efficiency.

Henri Fayol, the French industrialist, took a different approach to organizational theory. Based on his industrial experience as an executive, he induced a set of "general principles of administration." Principles such as "division of work," "authority," "unity of command," and "subordination of individual interests," according to Fayol, have a universal applicability.[15] As opposed to Weber's approach, which is descriptive, Fayol sought to prescribe organizational principles.

Based on an historical study of military, industrial, government, and ecclesiastic organizations, Mooney and Reiley identified and correlated four organizational principles which "underlie all associated effort."[16] The principles that Mooney and Reiley found in their study of organizations are:

1. *The coordinative principle*—the orderly arrangement of group effort is necessary in order to provide a unity of action in the pursuit of a common objective.

---

[12] Gerth and Mills, *op. cit.*, p . 214.

[13] *Ibid.*

[14] *Ibid.*, p. 216.

[15] Fayol, *op. cit.*, pp. 19–42.

[16] Mooney, *op. cit.*, p. 1.

2. *Scalar principle*—the formation of a hierarchical process through which the coordinating authority operates in the entire organization.
3. *Functional principle*—functional differentiation between various types of duties is necessary to attain a given purpose.
4. *Staff principle*—the differentiation of authority into two categories, command (supervisory) authority and staff (advisory and informational) authority, emphasizes the service of knowledge in the sphere of execution.[17]

Since the ideas of the traditionalists were so similar in content, we briefly summarize them below.

THE THEORY, IN BRIEF

As expected from the emphasis on efficiency, traditional theory prescribes an organizing process that begins with objectives. The objectives are the values that the organization seeks to achieve. Once the objectives have been determined, the next step is to determine the work necessary to achieve those objectives. For maximum efficiency, the theory specifies that the work be divided into simple tasks. Tasks are then allocated to jobs or positions, each of which requires routine and repetitive movements of a single worker. These jobs are grouped into administrative units to meet the need for coordination. There is only one boss at the head of each unit. Furthermore, each supervisor has a span of supervision, that is, each supervisor has limitations and therefore should have only a few subordinates reporting directly to him. Administrative units are then grouped into higher level administrative units. This grouping continues until the organization takes the shape of a pyramid with one supreme official at its apex. Authority to discharge the duties of each job is distributed to each jobholder. The means employed to discharge duties and the jurisdictional area of each official is delimited by laws or administrative regulations. Personnel assignments are made on the basis of the requirements of the job and each individual's ability to perform the tasks. Finally, the rewards given to organization members are based on job performance.

It is apparent from the above that the *work* required to achieve objectives and *efficiency* are the basis for the organizing process. The central problem, according to traditional theory, is to make

---

[17] *Ibid.*, pp. 5–46.

sure that work gets done efficiently through a careful definition of tasks into specialized jobs and then by coordination of the jobs through a hierarchy of administrative units. Gulick emphasizes this breakdown of work as the basis for organization in the following statement:

.... Wherever many men are . . . working together the best results are secured when there is a division of work among these men. The theory of organization, therefore, has to do with the structure of co-ordination imposed upon the work-division units of enterprise. Hence, it is not possible to determine how an activity is to be organized without, at the same time, considering how the work in question is to be divided. Work division is the foundation of organization; indeed, the reason for organizing.[18]

The concepts of traditional theory that we examine in detail in this chapter and the next are: (1) departmentation; (2) unity of command; (3) size of the supervisory unit; and (4) type and amount of authority assigned and delegated to subunits of the organization.

DEPARTMENTATION

In traditional theory, especially in the writings of Luther Gulick, four bases for grouping specialized jobs into larger specialized units or departments are provided. They are: (1) *purpose*, that is, according to an output, such as a product or service; (2) *function*, that is, according to the kind of work that must be performed; (3) *place*, that is, according to the geographical location served by the organization and/or where the work is to be done; and (4) *clientele*, that is, according to the type of persons for whom the work is done.[19] Before illustrating each of these bases for grouping specialized jobs, let us first portray specialization as the division of a large rectangle into smaller units, shown in Figure 2-1. This breakdown is important for the following illustrations.

FIGURE 2-1

Breakdown of a Whole Task

A_1	B_1	C_1	D_1
A_2	B_2	C_2	D_2
A_3	B_3	C_3	D_3
A_4	B_4	C_4	D_4

[18] Gulick, "Notes on the Theory of Organization," *op. cit.*, p. 3.
[19] Gulick, *op. cit.*, pp. 15–30. These four bases of departmentation may be used simultaneously in one organization. Multiple departmentation is illustrated in subsequent sections.

Purpose Departmentation

Organization on the basis of purpose involves differentiating and grouping activities according to an output of the organization, such as a service or product. This means that all of the functions required to supply a service or product, even if the activities are dissimilar, are placed in the same group or department. For instance, if the purpose of an organization is to create four products, the functions, A, B, C, and D, required for each product would be grouped in each product department. Figure 2–2 depicts a case in which each of four purposes (products) require four functions. Figure 2–3 illustrates a grouping in terms of a traditional organizational structure.

FIGURE 2–2

Departmentation on the Bases of Purpose or Function

| | PURPOSES (PRODUCTS) | | | |
	NO 1	NO 2	NO 3	NO 4
FUNCTIONS (ACTIVITIES)	A_1	A_2	A_3	A_4
	B_1	B_2	B_3	B_4
	C_1	C_2	C_3	C_4
	D_1	D_2	D_3	D_4

Functional Departmentation

Organization on the basis of functions requires the differentiation and grouping of similar work activities. All of the similar activities are grouped together and identified by some functional classification, such as manufacturing, engineering, marketing, teaching, financing, building, and transporting. In creating some values, an organization may be required, for instance, to perform 16 activities: 4 similar activities under function A, 4 under function B, 4 under

FIGURE 2–3

Purpose Organization

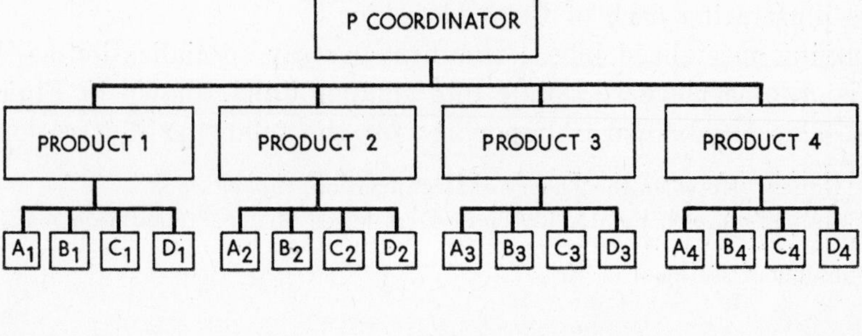

FIGURE 2–4

Functional Organization

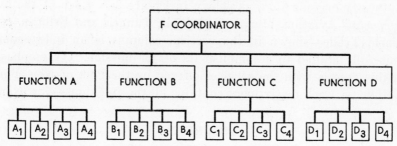

function C, and 4 under function D. This type of breakdown is shown in Figure 2–2 by reading it horizontally. In this case, the dominant type of departmentation is based on the functions that need to be performed. Figure 2–4 illustrates how activities would be grouped in traditional organizational structure based on functions.

FIGURE 2–5

Purpose and Functional Departmentation of the Port of New York Authority

	AVIATION DEPARTMENT	MARINE TERMINALS DEPARTMENT	TERMINALS DEPARTMENT	TUNNELS AND BRIDGES DEPARTMENT	WORLD TRADE DEPARTMENT
PLANNING FUNCTION	PLANNING DIVISION ECONOMICS DIVISION	PLANNING DIVISION	PLANNING & ANALYSIS DIVISION	PROJECT ENGINEERING DIVISION RESEARCH DIVISION	TRADE DEVELOPMENT DIVISION OPERATIONS PLANNING DIVISION
OPERATIONS FUNCTION	AERONAUTICAL SERVICE DIVISIONS PUBLIC SERVICE DIVISIONS	OPERATIONS DIVISION	OPERATIONS DIVISION	OPERATIONS DIVISION	TRAFFIC MANAGEMENT DIVISION
PROPERTIES FUNCTION	PROPERTIES DIVISION	PIERS RENTALS DIVISION COMMERCIAL RENTALS DIVISION	PROPERTIES DIVISION		RENTALS DIVISION
CONSTRUCTION FUNCTION	CONSTRUCTION DIVISION	CONSTRUCTION DIVISION			
					PROMOTION DIVISION

The tabular method of separating purposes and functions, illustrated in Figure 2–1, may be applied to the Port of New York Authority organization, as shown in Figure 2–5. Each of the five purposes—Aviation, Marine Terminals, Tunnels and Bridges, and World Trade—shown in the vertical columns is an independent unit fully staffed to accomplish its major mission. The emphasis in this case is with the services offered by the Port of New York Authority. Each department contains all the functions—for exam-

FIGURE 2–6

Place Departmentation in the Organization of the Port of New York Authority

	AVIATION DEPARTMENT	MARINE TERMINALS DEPARTMENT	TERMINALS DEPARTMENT	TUNNELS AND BRIDGES DEPARTMENT	WORLD TRADE DEPARTMENT
OPERATIONS PROCESS	LA GUARDIA AIRPORT JOHN KENNEDY INTERNATIONAL AIRPORT NEWARK AIRPORT TETERBORO AIRPORT W. 30TH ST. HELIPORT P. A. DOWNTOWN HELIPORT	BROOKLYN P. A. MAR. TERM. ELIZABETH P. A. MAR. TERM. ERIE BASIN P. A. MAR. TERM. HOBOKEN P. A. MAR. TERM. P. A. GRAIN TERMINAL PORT NEWARK	BUS TERMINAL PORT AUTHORITY BUILDING TRUCK TERMINAL NEW YORK TRUCK TERMINAL NEW JERSEY GEORGE WASHINGTON BRIDGE BUS STATION	GEORGE WASHINGTON BRIDGE HOLLAND TUNNEL LINCOLN TUNNEL BAYONNE BRIDGE GOETHALS BRIDGE OUTERBRIDGE CROSSING	PORT COMMERCE WORLD TRADE CENTER

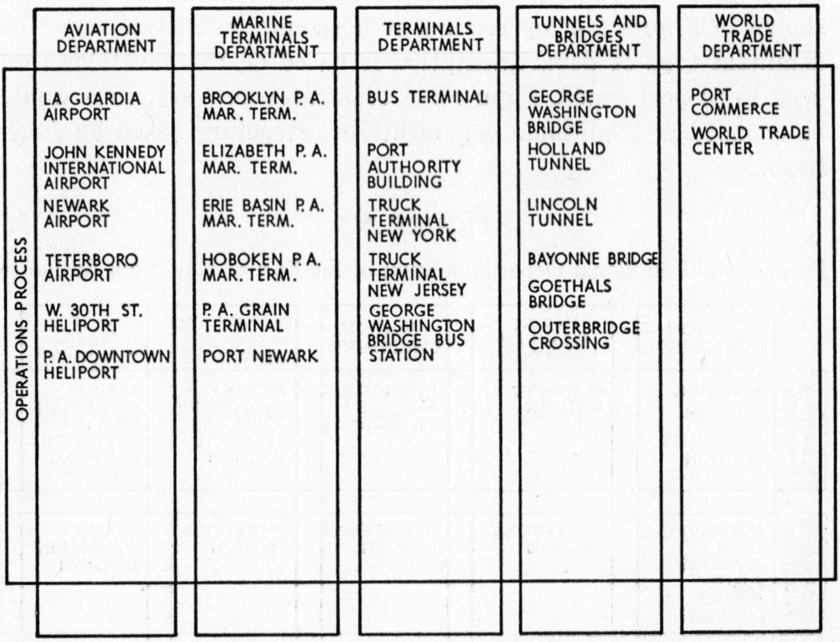

ple, planning, operations, properties, and construction—necessary to carry out its purpose. An abridged version of the Port of New York Authority's organization chart is shown in Figure 2–10. Each of the departments mentioned above is shown as a line department, as opposed to a staff department, designated by heavy-line connections. The functions of each department mentioned above are not shown on the abridged chart, but they did appear on the original chart.

FIGURE 2–7

Purpose Departmentation within Place

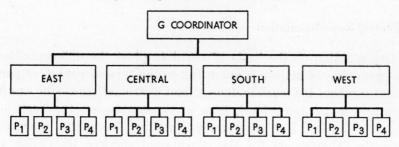

Place Departmentation

Organization on the basis of place requires differentiation and grouping of activities according to the location where work is to be performed or an area to be served by the organization. Thus, regardless of the similarity or dissimilarity of functions and purposes, grouping is based on geographical considerations.

Place departmentation may occur in the same organization where there is purpose and functional departmentation. Figure 2–6 presents a case in which place is used to departmentalize activities within the operations (functional) division of each of the departments (purposes) of the Port of New York Authority.

In the organization of the Port of New York Authority, there is place departmentation within the purposes and functions, but it is possible also for the opposite to occur, that is, specialization based on purposes and functions within place departmentation.

Figures 2–7 and 2–8 show purpose (P_1, P_2, P_3, P_4) and functional (A, B, C, D) departmentation within place organization. These

FIGURE 2–8

Functional Departmentation within Place

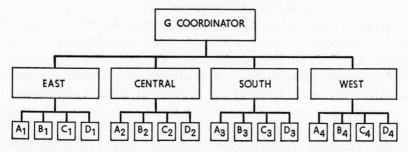

illustrations do not, of course, exhaust all of the possible combinations of purpose, functional, and place departmentation.

Clientele Departmentation

Organization on the basis of client involves the differentiation and grouping of activities according to the type of person or persons for whom the work is done. Client characteristics—for example, age, sex, income level, type of consumer—are the basis of departmentation. For instance, universities frequently maintain separate departments for the educational services they offer to adults and resident students. Loan departments in large banks may organize on the basis of consumer or commercial services offered to its clients. Department stores often group work on the basis of the client's sex, for instance, men's apparel versus women's apparel; or on the basis of income level, for example, bargain basements for lower income customers; or on the basis of age, for example, children's, women's, and men's clothing.

APPLICATIONS OF DEPARTMENTATION

Many institutions publish their organization charts and give the reasons for the groupings shown in the diagrams. In order to give the reader a feel for actual organization, we present some of these charts below and discuss them in terms of traditional theory.

Application of Purpose Departmentation

According to traditional theorists, purpose departmentation is especially useful to organizations which supply many different services or products because it facilitates the coordination of all of the activities required by each purpose.

Moreover, purpose departmentation permits the establishment of semiautonomous subunits within a large organization. For instance, the E. I. du Pont de Nemours Company, the organization of which is shown in Figure 2–9, is divided into product (purpose) operating divisions. Each of the product divisions operates much like an independent company. Other large business organizations, for example, General Motors, General Electric Company, Ford Motor Company, Westinghouse Electric, Lockheed Aircraft, Inter-

FIGURE 2–9

Organization of E. I. du Pont de Nemours & Company*

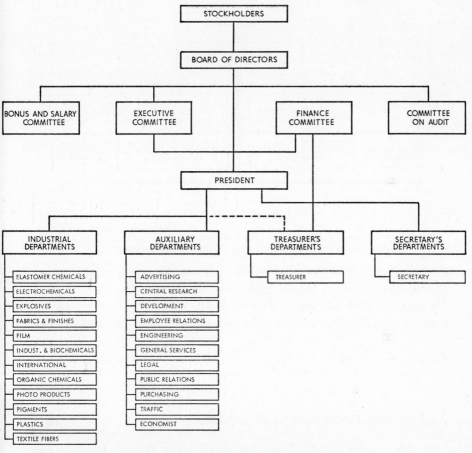

* Reproduced by permission of E. I. du Pont de Nemours & Company.

national Business Machines, Monsanto Chemical Company, and Radio Corporation of America, are organized in a similar manner. Each of Du Pont's product departments, for example, explosives, electrochemicals, film, and so on, operates with almost complete autonomy with its own manufacturing, sales, research, and control departments. Each of the product departments (called industrial departments) is headed by a general manager who is accountable to the Executive Committee for a prescribed rate of return on investment.

Nonbusiness organizations, for example, hospitals, schools, and

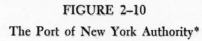

FIGURE 2–10

The Port of New York Authority*

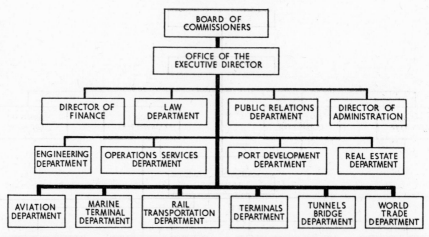

* The organization chart and other material included in this chapter about the Port of New York Authority was obtained directly from the Authority and is published with permission.

governmental agencies, also utilize product or service departmentation. For instance, the abridged organization of the Port of New York Authority, shown in Figure 2–10, demonstrates the use of service organization along with functional departmentation. The major activities of the Authority, shown by the heavy line, are departmentalized on the basis of the service (product) offered, while the auxiliary activities are organized on the basis of functions.

Application of Functional Departmentation

Traditional theorists claim that this type of departmentation not only emphasizes the basic activities (functions) of an organization by placing them in a dominant and prestigious position but it also allows occupational specialization and the benefits that are to be derived from using specialized skills of human beings.

In a business organization these groupings or departments based on functional departmentation carry labels such as production, marketing, finance, and personnel. While this terminology is used extensively in manufacturing enterprises, it is not universally accepted as standard organizational nomenclature in business organization, much less in nonbusiness organizations. Figures 2–11 and 2–12 depict organizational structures based on functional departmentation, yet the terms used to express the major functions are

FIGURE 2–11

Diamond Crystal Salt Company Organization Structure*

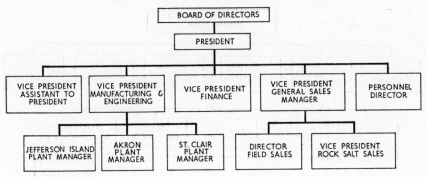

*Produced from a description in K. K. White, *Understanding the Company Organization Chart* (New York: American Management Association, 1963), pp. 158–59.

different. Functional departmentation in both of these cases exists also at lower levels in the hierarchy. For instance, in the case of the Farm Bureau Insurance Company, the organization within the operations department includes functions such as plans and organization, standards and procedures, operations reports and controls, and others. However, lower level subdivisions within the manufacturing and engineering department of the Diamond Crystal Salt Company are based on place departmentation. The other bases of departmentation may be used at lower levels within the functional departments. It is evident from the cases illustrated in Figures 2–11 and 2–12 that more than one basis of departmentation is used in actual practice.

FIGURE 2–12

Farm Bureau Insurance Company Organization Structure*

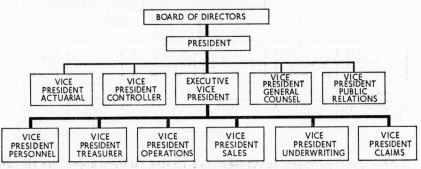

* Reproduced from *Studies in Personnel Policy*, No. 139, with the permission of The National Industrial Conference Board and the Farm Bureau Insurance Companies of Michigan.

FIGURE 2-13

U.S. Army Infantry Division Abridged Organization Structure*

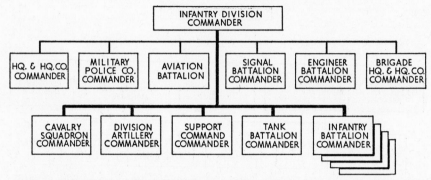

* This abridged version of the organization of an infantry division was obtained from the following manual: U. S. Army Infantry School, *Infantry Reference Data, ROAD* (Fort Benning, Ga.: Command and Staff Department, September, 1962), p. 45.

The organization of a U.S. Army Infantry Division and a sanitarium, indicated in Figures 2–13 and 2–14, illustrates the use of functional departmentation in nonbusiness organizations. The infantry division is a relatively large public organization, with a regular complement of over 12,000 men, and the sanitarium is a

FIGURE 2-14

Chestnut Lodge Sanitarium Organization Structure*

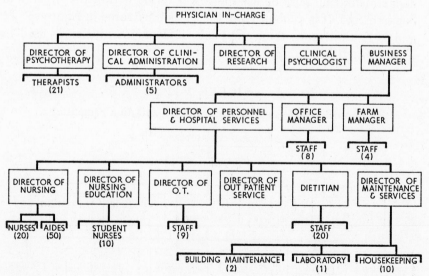

* Reproduced from Alfred H. Stanton and Morris S. Schwartz, *The Mental Hospital* (New York: Basic Books, Inc., 1954), p. 101.

relatively small psychiatric organization composed of 165 personnel. Even though size, ownership, and mission of these organizations are quite different, the basis upon which they are organized is similar. The dominant scheme in both of them is based on the functions which create the values or goals of the organization.

Application of Place Departmentation

Advocates of traditional theory claim that place departmentation is not only useful in cases which involve a wide physical dispersion of activities but it can also be applied to the organization of activities in one location. An illustration of the former is the division of a manufacturing department into several places. The chart of the manufacturing and engineering departments of the Diamond Crystal Salt Company, shown in Figure 2–11, illustrates organization based on location.

Marketing departments are frequently divided into subdivisions covering wide geographic areas. Large city police departments use this basis of departmentation in dividing police work into several precincts or districts. This type of departmentation is used even when the areas covered are small. For instance, the security work done by an internal protection department in a large retail department store can be organized on the basis of floor area.

While the principal reason for place departmentation may be to solve the problem of supervising physically dispersed activities, differences in environmental conditions also make this type of departmentation useful. If environmental factors are relevant to the functioning of an organization, then geographic considerations cannot be ignored. Cultural and legal factors are especially relevant to an organization which operates in several different countries.

SUMMARY

This chapter is devoted to presenting a brief statement of traditional organizational concepts. The views of several prominent traditional theorists reveal that they were dissatisfied with the organizational practices of their time. Traditional theory evolved for the purpose of introducing into organization some rationality. Taylor used the objective rationality of measurement; Weber described the technically superior rational bureaucracy; Fayol induced from his experiences some "general principles"; and Mooney and Reiley identified and correlated in various organizations four basic elements of organization.

The common elements of traditional organization theory are specialization and departmentation, unity of command, span of supervision, and allocation of authority. For maximum efficiency, traditional theory specifies that work be broken down into specialized tasks. This chapter includes an elaboration of the basic patterns of departmentation—purpose, function, client, and place— and illustrations of their applicability. The four types of departmentation are not exclusive of each other. Many organizations use a multiple basis of departmentation.

Dividing work into subunits according to some basis of departmentation is the initial step in the traditional approach to organizing. Once the work has been grouped into subunits, there still remains the problem of relating subordinates to superiors and each subunit to the others. This involves coordination. The traditional concepts basic to coordination are unity of command, span of supervision, and allocation of authority. These concepts are included in the next chapter.

DISCUSSION QUESTIONS AND PROBLEMS

2-1. Try to name some of the "innumerable conditions" (Tolstoy quote) that are necessary for the success of an organization. Frame your answer in terms of cause and effect relationships; for example, a change in X causes a change in Y.

2-2. Starting with a general statement of objectives for a business firm, outline the steps in the organizing process as indicated by traditional theory.

2-3. Is it appropriate for all organizations to use the same basis for departmentation? Why?

2-4. Do all organizations have to give some consideration to purpose, function, clientele, and place specialization, regardless of the basis of departmentation selected for their organization plan? Explain your answer.

2-5. Mr. Michaels is responsible for operating three summer camps in Pennsylvania. Two of these residence camps are located in the northwestern corner of the state, and the third one, Camp Highpoint, is near the center of the state. Each of the camps operate for two sessions each summer. They accommodate boys and girls between the ages of 5 and 15. Each camp is adjacent to a lake and has a swimming area as well as a dock for rowboats, canoes, and sailboats. Large flat pastures at two of the camps have been cleared and developed into baseball fields, croquet areas, and volleyball, badminton, and basketball areas. Camp Highpoint is still developing its fields for use as athletic areas. The director at Camp Highpoint is concerned with the seemingly poor operation of the mess facilities and is looking to the directors of other camps for help in improving the operation. Currently, each of the camps can handle 200 children per session. Mr. Michaels is anxious to keep the program growing and looks forward to the day, three years from now, when each camp will be able to handle 500 children each session. Using the traditional basis for departmentation, develop alternative organization structures that would facilitate effective management of these facilities.

2–6. The Cadet Wing at the Air Force Academy is divided into 24 squadrons. Each squadron is made up of approximately 280 cadets. Every year, at the end of the summer program, the wing commander is responsible for staging a field day. All cadets compete athletically in an effort to accumulate enough team points to win the general's streamer for their squadron. Activities involve the obstacle course run (wooded area); fieldball, rugby, soccer, lacrosse (upper athletic area); tug-of-war, 100-yard dash, shot put, and broad jump (lower athletic area). Individual performances are recorded so that individual champions can be determined. The event takes place on a Saturday. A crowd of 2,000 to 3,000 usually concentrates in the lower athletic area to observe the competition. This area is closest to the parking lots. Medical personnel should be in the areas to treat routine injuries as well as emergencies. Since many high ranking officers and their wives will attend, some provisions must be made for special parking and seating accommodations. Facilities must be prepared prior to the event. Reports of the 70 field judges involved must be collected and processed quickly for winners to be determined. Arrangements must also be made to put away scorers' tables, chairs, and so on, and return the fields to their original state.

If you were the wing commander, how would you organize to handle the field day?

2–7. The Shears Company is made up of two large local department stores. Their total sales volume is approaching $30 million annually. One store is located in the heart of Percieville, the other is in the Suburban Shopping Center. The shopping center store also operates a service station for customer convenience. In each of the two stores, several areas are rented to independently owned businesses; these include a flower shop, a beauty salon, and a shoe repair shop. Departments include furniture, clothing, specialty foods, dining rooms, hardware, housewares, sporting goods, jewelry and cosmetics. The total number of employees ranges from 200 to 300 (peak seasons and holidays). The Shears board of directors had decided to expand the operation by adding two more stores in the next three years. Plans to cater to a greater number of people include the setting up of a bargain basement in the downtown store.

How would you organize?

3

ADMINISTRATION IN TRADITIONAL THEORY

In this chapter, we continue the review of traditional theory, especially as it pertains to administration. Traditional theory is very specific about the administrative structure of formal organization. Its prescriptions about the chain of command, size of supervisory unit, and the dispersion of authority, seemingly leave little doubt about administration in formal organization (in Chapter 4, we indicate that there are some doubts). The underlying premise of the traditional structure is that specialized jobs can be coordinated best by one head, or one boss, that is, there shall be unity of command. This requirement that everybody in the organization reports to only one boss gives traditional structure the appearance of a pyramid with one supreme coordinating boss at the top. We will see this structure develop as the administrative concepts of traditional theory are examined in this chapter.

UNITY OF COMMAND

According to traditional theory, unity of command facilitates order because it charges one official with an area of responsibility and establishes a chain of command whereby every organization member knows to whom he reports and who reports to him. There is no confusion over who is responsible for organizational activities and over who gives orders and who carries them out. Unity of command forms the basis, therefore, for the hierarchy of authority because it defines the path of authority which extends from the top to the bottom of the formal organization. Fayol explained the importance of the unity of command in the following manner: "Should it be violated, authority is undermined, discipline is in jeopardy, order disturbed and stability threatened. . . . A body with two heads is in the social as in the animal sphere a monster, and has difficulty surviving."[1]

SPAN OF SUPERVISION

Size of Supervisory Unit. A supervisory unit is composed of a supervisor and his immediate subordinates. The size of a supervisory unit is determined by the number of subordinates reporting to the supervisor. In traditional literature, the terms "span of control," "span of management," and "span of supervision" have been used to denote size of the supervisory unit. There are some interesting complications involved in trying to determine the size of the supervisory unit. Let us illustrate.

Suppose that we want to organize a relatively small group composed of 64 workers. With respect to span of supervision, this group can have a uniform ratio of subordinates to superior ranging from 64:1 to 2:1. For convenience, let us examine four ratios, 64:1, 8:1, 4:1, and 2:1. These alternatives (*A* through *D*) are illustrated in Figure 3–1.

The most obvious fact about this ratio is that as the span of supervision decreases from 64:1 to 2:1, there is an increase in the number of supervisors and levels of organization. In each of the four alternatives, *A, B, C,* and *D,* the number of workers supervised is constant, that is, 64, and the ratio in the span of supervision is also constant for each alternative. For example, in alternative *D,* the span of supervision for each superior throughout the entire organization hierarchy is two.

Table 3–1 summarizes the number of supervisors and levels for each of the alternatives, *A, B, C,* and *D.* Reducing the span of supervision from 64:1 to 2:1 increases the number of supervisors from 1 to 63 and the number of organization levels from two to six.

---

[1] Henri Fayol, *General and Industrial Management,* trans. Constance Storrs (London: Sir Isaac Pitman & Sons, Ltd., 1949), pp. 24–25.

FIGURE 3-1

Alternative Ratios of Span of Supervision

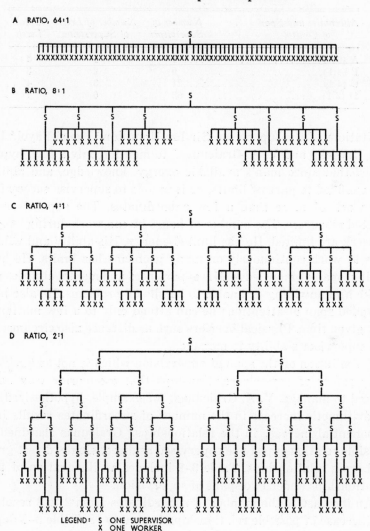

LEGEND: S ONE SUPERVISOR
         X ONE WORKER

Narrow Span of Supervision

Determining the appropriate span of supervision is not a simple problem. Early attempts to solve this problem were based on the

TABLE 3–1

Supervisors and Levels with Alternative Spans of Supervision

Alternative and Span of Control	Number of Supervisors	Number of Levels of Supervision	Total Levels
A (64:1)	1	1	2
B (8:1)	9	2	3
C (4:1)	21	3	4
D (2:1)	63	6	7

limitations of the supervisor. Sir Ian Hamilton,[2] Henri Fayol,[3] Lyndall Urwick,[4] and V. A. Graicunas,[5] to mention only a few, hypothesized that since man's available energy, knowledge, and abilities are confined to narrow limits, he is unable to supervise successfully the work of more than a few subordinates. The supervisor has limited resources. The number of hours he can work during one day or week are limited. He has limited energy. His ability and willingness to work continuously on many problems has limits. He has a limited span of knowledge. His experiences and mental abilities may make him unwilling or unable to handle all problems. He also has a bounded span of attention; he can attend only to a few matters at any given time. Physical barriers such as distance also circumscribe the supervisor's ability to manage.

A limitation on the span of supervision which is not as obvious is the number of possible relationships that a superior may be required to manage. V. A. Graicunas, for example, hypothesized that an arithmetic increase in the number of subordinates results in an exponential increase in the relationships.[6] Graicunas classified the possible relationships to be supervised as direct single, direct group, and cross relationships. Table 3–2 includes an illustration of these relationships under two spans of supervision.

An increase in the number of subordinates from 2 to 3 results in an increase of possible relationships from 6 to 18. Table 3–3 depicts

---

[2] Sir Ian Hamilton, *The Soul and Body of an Army* (New York: George H. Doran Co., 1921).

[3] Fayol, *op. cit.*

[4] Lyndall F. Urwick, "Organization as a Technical Problem," in Luther Gulick and Lyndall F. Urwick (eds.), *Papers on the Science of Administration* (New York: Institute of Public Administration, 1937), pp. 52–57.

[5] V. A. Graicunas, "Relationship in Organization," *Ibid.*, pp. 181–87.

[6] *Ibid.*, p. 185.

TABLE 3–2

Types of Superior-Subordinate Relationships

Example 1—Two Subordinates	Example 2—Three Subordinates
A | B C	A | B C D
Direct Single Relationships	Direct Single Relationships
A to B A to C	A to B A to C A to D
Direct Group Relationships	Direct Group Relationships
A to B with C A to C with B	A to B with C A to B with C and D A to B with D A to C with B and D A to C with B A to D with C and B A to C with D A to D with C A to D with B
Cross Relationships	Cross Relationships
B to C C to B	B to C B to D C to B C to D D to B D to C

the connection between possible relationships and various numbers of subordinates under one supervisor.

The total number of relationships under each span of supervision can be computed using equation (3–1) :[7]

$$r = n(2^{n-1} + n - 1) \tag{3-1}$$

where

n = number of persons supervised.
r = number of relationships.

---

[7] Ibid., p. 186.

TABLE 3-3

Number of Relationships with Various Numbers of Subordinates

Number of Subordinates	Number of Relationships
1	1
2	6
3	18
4	44
5	100
6	222
7	490
8	1,080
9	2,376
10	5,210
11	11,374
12	24,708

Each supervisor according to traditional theory must manage not only individual subordinates but also the interactions among individuals and groups. Therefore, according to the theory, the number of subordinates reporting to any one supervisor should be limited to a very few. Traditional organization literature suggests that there exists an ideal number of subordinates that can be managed effectively by one superior.[8] This ideal ratio of subordinates to superior has been called the principle of "span of control" or "span of supervision" and is stated as follows:

Principle of Span of Supervision. The number of subordinates supervised directly by a single executive should be limited to a small number. No executive should supervise directly the work of more than four or, at the most, six subordinates—especially when their work is interrelated.

ORGANIZATIONAL AUTHORITY

When anyone, say a worker, is assigned to a work activity, he has an obligation to perform successfully—he has responsibility. Coincident with this responsibility, implicitly or explicitly, each worker has the authority to act or the authority to perform the activities required by the assigned work. Although we assume that authority and responsibility occur coincidently, it should be emphasized that the literature of organization theory usually treats them as if they are assigned separately. Writers on the subject stipulate that the

---

[8] Hamilton, *op. cit.;* Graicunas, *op. cit.;* and Fayol, *op. cit.*

assignment of authority should be equal to responsibility.[9] Urwick states, for example, the need for this balance as follows: "To hold a group or individual accountable for activities of any kind without assigning to him the necessary authority to discharge that responsibility is manifestly both unsatisfactory and inequitable."[10]

This same coincidence of authority and responsibility extends to the administrative levels of organization. In a superior-subordinate relationship, for example, the supervisor's authority is derived from his responsibility to coordinate the work of subordinates.

In this context, *authority* constitutes official permission to use the resources of the organization. Thus, an individual worker needs authority to use equipment or to withdraw materials from storage, the industrial foreman needs authority to command his men to do a given job, a hospital nurse needs authority to issue medicine to a patient, the surgeon needs authority to command the actions of an entire operating team, a baseball coach must have authority to call for the execution of a particular play, and a general manager of a baseball team needs authority to consummate a player deal.

There is another aspect to authority at the administrative level. In order to coordinate the efforts of subordinates, a superior needs to obtain their compliance to orders and commands. For this reason, administrative authority also includes official permission to use some of the possessions of the organization as inducements. Thus, a supervisor is permitted to offer rewards or to impose penalties for the purpose of gaining compliance. Included in the definition of authority, then, is the understanding that in superior-subordinate relationships, the superior has permission to invoke sanctions in order to obtain compliance from subordinates.

In the traditional literature, this authority is called "legal" or "official authority."[11] The source of this authority is not to be found in the individual, but rather it is derived from the organization.[12] It is an attribute of office or formal position. An organization member has authority because he occupies a certain position and not because

---

[9] For instance, see James D. Mooney, *The Principles of Organization* (rev. ed.; New York: Harper & Row, 1939), pp. 17–23; Lyndall Urwick, *The Elements of Administration* (New York: Harper & Row, 1939), pp. 45–46; Fayol, *op. cit.*, pp. 21–22; and Taylor, *op. cit.*

[10] Urwick, *op. cit.*, p. 46.

[11] Fayol, *op. cit.*, p. 21.

[12] For a discussion summarizing the issues concerning official versus personal authority, see Harold Koontz and Cyril O'Donnell, *Principles of Management* (New York: McGraw-Hill Book Co., 1955), pp. 48–54.

of personal characteristics. In this regard, Weber states: "In the case of legal authority, obedience is owed to the legally established impersonal order. It extends to the persons exercising authority of office under it only by virtue of the formal legality of their commands and only within the scope of authority of the office."[13]

James D. Mooney identified authority as the foundation of the first principle of organization—the coordinative principle. He labeled authority as the "supreme coordinative power" and stated that "in every form of organization, this authority must rest somewhere, else there would be no directive for any coordinated effort."[14] Locating its "resting" place in the formal organization involves defining authority according to type and amounts. Two types of authority distinguished in traditional theory are line and staff authority.

Line and Staff Authority

A relationship in which the occupant of one position can exercise direct command over the occupant of another position is called *line authority*. A superior who exercises direct command over a subordinate has line authority.

A relationship in which the occupant of one position can advise or counsel but not command the occupant of another position is called *staff authority*. A person occupying a position with staff authority does not command others, but rather his responsibility is discharged by providing information, advice, and recommendations. The principal value of staff authority is that specialized knowledge and technology can be injected into the organization to aid the incumbents of positions which have line authority.

Development of Staff Concept by the Army

Though the staff patterns used by current military organizations are fashioned according to the staff organization of Gustavus Adolphus, the Swedish king who ruled during the 17th century, there exist traces of staff specialists in the armies of Egypt (circa 1500 B.C.), Assyria (circa 722 B.C.), Persia (circa 500 B.C.), Athens and

---

[13] A. M. Henderson and Talcott Parsons, *Max Weber: The Theory of Social and Economic Organization* (New York: Oxford University Press, Inc., 1947), p. 328.

[14] Mooney, *op. cit.*, p. 6.

Sparta (circa 480 B.C.), Philip of Macedonia and Alexander the Great (circa 300 B.C.), and Caesar (circa 100 B.C.).[15]

The military staff appeared in ancient armies primarily as new military tactics and arms were developed. For instance, the development of siege tactics by the Assyrians meant that specialized engineering personnel were needed in the army. The river-crossing tactics used by Alexander the Great required specialists in portable missile-throwing artillery to cover the crossing troops.

During the 17th century the military forces under Gustavus Adolphus included staff differentiation of the regimental headquarters unit for the following staff positions: (1) a chief quartermaster; (2) two judge advocates; (3) two chaplins; (4) four surgeons; (5) four provost marshals; (6) one assistant provost marshal; and (7) clerks. Moreover, the organization of the top headquarters unit was essentially the same as in the regimental headquarters. In addition to the staff positions differentiated at the regimental level, the command level staff included various chiefs of arms such as chief of artillery, chief of engineering, chief of scouts, and chief of staff. Each of these chiefs advised Gustavus on matters related to his specialty. Military staffs gained more importance as military tactics and weaponry became more complex.

During the 17th century, the Gustavian system with some modifications appeared in the organization of the armies of Prussia, France, and Spain. The Prussians, after they were defeated by Napoleon at Jena in 1806, introduced several staff reforms which were instrumental in the Prussian victory over France in 1870. According to Karl von Clausewitz, who along with Generals Scharnhorst, Gneisenau, and Von Moltke are the principal innovators of staff efficiency, the purpose of the general staff is "to convert the ideas of the commanding general into orders, not only by conveying the former to the troops, but far more by working out all the necessary matters of detail, thus relieving the mind of the general from a great amount of trouble."[16]

The relative importance of the general staff in the Prussian Army appears to be unique, because its official role is not merely to

---

[15] J. D. Hittle, *The Military Staff* (3rd ed.; Harrisburg, Pa.: Stackpole Co., 1961). Hittle provides some traces of the development of military staffs between the time of Caesar and 17th century staffs.

[16] Bronsart von Schellendorf, "The Duties of the General Staff," reprinted in *Staffs of Various Armies* (Washington, D.C.: U.S. Government Printing Office, 1899), p. 9.

take a passive position, but rather the general staff was expected to act as a "junior partner" to the line commanders. The general staff not only was more active in assisting the top commanders but it was also duplicated at lower echelons. Field staffs were added in the organization of the Prussian military forces as early as 1828.[17]

The staff organization of the German Army during World War II (see Figure 3-2) was essentially the same as the staff organization

FIGURE 3-2

Staff Organization, German Army Corps (World War II)*

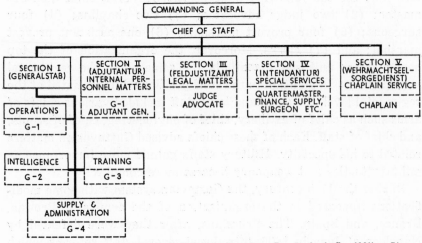

* SOURCE: J. D. Hittle, *The Military Staff* (3rd ed.; Harrisburg, Pa.; Stackpole Co., 1961), p. 74.

of the early 19th-century Prussian Army. The U.S. Army staff organization, as indicated by the broken boxes in Figure 3-2, resembles the staff organization employed by the German Army during World War II.

The Gustavian system has undergone some modifications, but the concept of providing line commanders with a set of "auxilliary brains" is still the fundamental basis for modern military staff organizations. Gustavus did not invent something new; he merely revived some basic organizational concepts which had not been used previously in the organization of various armies. Gustavus Adolphus modified them and applied them to several levels of organization. Even today his modifications are reflected in the staff organization of the armies of the United States, France, Great Britain, West Germany, and other nations.

---
[17] Hittle, *op. cit.*, pp. 67–76.

The Staff Concept in Religious Organization

While the line-staff type organization is primarily a military concept, business and religious organizations and government and other public institutions utilize this means of organization. In fact, traces of this concept have been detected in ecclesiastic organization dating back to earliest era of the history of the Catholic Church. The installation of the staff concept in the Catholic Church, however, cannot be ascertained, because, as James Mooney states: "The staff principle is woven into the fabric of church rules and discipline, affecting every individual in every relation."[18]

Mooney's study of the Catholic Church reveals that the staff principle operates in a formal and informal way. The application of the formal principle is represented by the Sacred College, which elects the Pope in conclave, and the Curia Romana through its several divisions, which acts as a collective advisory council to the Pope. In addition to these two collective staff bodies, vital decisions are also made by the Councils of the church. These Councils are called into session at the diocesan, provincial, national, patriarchal, or ecumenical level. These Councils are composed of various holders of high ecclesiastic office and special advisors.

Staff authority is also used within the line authority relations existing between superiors and subordinates in the Catholic Church. Mooney refers to this informal application of the staff principle as "compulsory staff service."[19] It was used as early as the sixth century by the St. Benedict monastic order. Essentially, this concept requires that on vital matters each superior must consult all of his subordinates before rendering a decision. For instance, the abbot of a Benedictine monastery must consult both elder and young monks before making a final decision.

In addition to the "compulsory staff" concept, the organization of staff in the Catholic Church includes a staff concept which is unique, namely "staff independence."[20] The staff man, according to this concept, is not dependent upon the person whom he advises. This separation removes the staff from line pressures that might prevail otherwise.

---

[18] Mooney, op. cit., p. 116.
[19] Ibid., pp. 119–21.
[20] Ibid., pp. 121–24.

Staff Concept in Business Organization

While the application of the staff concepts has a long history in military and religious organizations, not until recently has it appeared in business organizations. One of the first applications of this concept to a business organization was reported by Harrington Emerson, who applied it to the organization of the Santa Fe Railroad during the first decade of the 20th century.[21] Du Pont used the concept of general staff as early as 1908.[22]

The functional differentiation of advisory and service activities found in the military staff organization, for instance, the general staff and special staff, also exists in the organization of business staffs. On the basis of a survey study of 31 business organizations, Paul Holden, Lounsbury Fish, and Hubert Smith categorized the functions of staffs as : control, service, coordinating, and advisory.[23] The business version of staff organization appears to elaborate the task of staff units, because the control, service, and coordinative activities imply that staff units exercise some degree of authority over the line organization. Frederick Taylor's "functional management" played an important part in the development of staff specialization. Even though Taylor did not use the line-staff classification, he suggested that staff work or as he called it, "brain work" should be differentiated : "All possible brain work should be removed from the shop and centered in the planning or laying out department, leaving for the foreman and gang bosses work strictly executive in its nature."[24] Taylor's classification roughly resembles the line-staff classification. In fact, many of the activities that he removed from the "shop" and placed in the "planning department" are staff activities in modern business organizations.

The modification of the line-staff concept to serve as a basis not

---

[21] Harrington Emerson, *The Twelve Principles of Efficiency* (New York: Engineering Magazine Co., 1924), especially chap. ii.

[22] Ernest Dale, *Staff In Organization* (New York: McGraw-Hill Book Co., 1960), pp. 186–87. A survey of 300 business firms reported that approximately 70 percent employ staff assistance for the president. See: "Handy Men with Growing Power," *Business Week*, October 19, 1957, pp. 193–97.

[23] Paul E. Holden, Lounsbury S. Fish, and Hubert L. Smith, *Top-Management Organization and Control* (New York: McGraw-Hill Book Co., 1951), pp. 36–58.

[24] Frederick W. Taylor, "Shop Management," in *Scientific Management* (New York: Harper & Row, 1947), pp. 98–99.

only for the differentiation of authority but also for the differentiation of activities, for example, control activities, service activities, and so on, complicates this seemingly simple concept.[25] The inclusion of control and service activities in the staff organization frequently requires line authority. For instance, control activities such as accounting, product inspection, and fire protection are meaningless unless some command authority is vested in them. Service activities such as purchasing and maintenance frequently are given authority that overrides the line organization. This hybrid type of authority, which has been labeled *functional authority*,[26] is really line authority limited to a specified function that can be assigned to a specialized department. This command authority is limited to the specialized function. For instance, an inspection department of a manufacturing firm may have the authority to command the production department concerning the quality characteristics of a product.

The introduction of functional authority in organization, and the tendency to perceive line and staff as types of departments, creates certain dysfunctions in organization. A discussion of these conflicts is included in Chapter 5.

AMOUNT OF ORGANIZATIONAL AUTHORITY

Another aspect of traditional theory which has received considerable attention is the delegation of authority, or as Mooney defined it "the conferring of a specified authority by a higher authority."[27] Essentially this means, even in the simplest organization, that authority must be delegated in order to get work done.

The principal issue in the delegation of authority involves the

---

[25] Not only does the line-staff classification result in specialization with respect to type of authority, but it also provides a rough guide for the separation of activities into those which are directly (line) and indirectly (staff) related to the attainment of organizational goals. Ralph C. Davis argues that the department concerned with activities which are "organic" to the accomplishment are line departments, while those departments which contribute to the "secondary" and "collateral" organization goals are staff departments. See his *The Fundamentals of Top Management* (New York: Harper & Row, 1951), pp. 205–11, 337–38.

[26] See Koontz and O'Donnell, *op. cit.*, chap. viii; William H. Newman, *Administrative Action* (Englewood Cliffs, N.J.: Prentice-Hall, Inc., 1950), chap. ix; and Holden, Fish, and Smith, *op. cit.*, sec. 3.

[27] Mooney, *op. cit.*, p. 17.

amount of authority to delegate, that is, the centralization of authority in one or a few organization positions as opposed to the
dispersion of authority throughout most or all of the levels of the
organizational hierarchy.

The early contributors to organizational theory, such as Max
Weber and Frederick W. Taylor, were not unique in their concern
over the issue of the dispersion of authority. The designers of the
Constitution of the United States, for example, were also concerned
with the problem of centralization versus decentralization. In the
tableau of history this issue has acquired many different labels, for
instance, autocracy versus democracy, monism versus pluralism, to-
talitarianism versus freedom, sectarianism versus ecumenism, fed-
eralism versus confederation, social mold versus social contract,
organizationalism versus anarchy. Once the political and emotional
overtones, shibboleths and labels are removed, the basic issue involves the question of how much authority to delegate, regardless of
whether the institution is business, education, military, church, or
government.

Centralization and Decentralization

Traditional theory prescribes that authority be equal to responsibility, that is, if a person is assigned certain duties, he *should* also
have the permission to commit the resources of the organization
necessary to perform the job. The authority to commit resources
may range from permission to perform a simple act like drawing
necessary tools from a toolroom to permission to perform a major
act like an expenditure of $500,000. Thus, if authority is directly
related to responsibility, the dispersion of authority throughout the
organization depends upon the definition of the jobs and positions.

The dispersion of authority occurs only in terms of degree. Henri
Fayol referred to the relativity of the dispersion of authority in
terms of centralization and decentralization,[28] or as he suggested,
"centralization . . . is always present to a greater or less

---

[28] The terms "centralization" and "decentralization" have been used to
describe the geographic dispersion of organizational units, for instance, the
decentralization of warehouses in Chicago, New York, and Atlanta as opposed
to one central warehouse in Chicago, or the location of sales offices in London,
Tokyo, and San Francisco. The use of these terms in this section of the book is
limited to the dispersion of authority in the organization, for example, the
decentralization of authority to several levels of an organization as opposed to
the centralization of authority to one level.

extent . . . it is a matter of finding the optimum degree for the particular concern."[29] Especially in large organizations, some amount of authority must be delegated, because it may be impossible for one person to coordinate all of the organizational activities. Yet, this does not mean that authority must be delegated completely to the managers of the lower subunits. To the extent that some authority is retained by central management, there exists a degree of centralization in every organization. At a minimum, according to traditional theory, central management always retains *residual authority,* which is the authority to recall from subordinates that authority which had been previously delegated to them. Thus, the dispersion of authority among the levels of an organization cannot be dichotomized into a pattern which is entirely centralized or completely decentralized. In effect, some degree of each pattern of authority dispersion is likely to be found in every organization.

Practitioners have found convenient ways to withhold some authority and yet permit decentralization. This is done usually by delegating operating authority and retaining policymaking authority. A rough definition of *operating authority* is the authority needed to make detailed, specific and repetitive decisions. *Policymaking authority* is confined roughly to formulating basic long-term objectives and adopting courses of action that provide general guides to operating decisions and practices. Let us turn to several examples of this practice.

The Practice of Decentralization

The annals of history include numerous records of organizations that have implemented the idea of decentralization. Commonly known examples include the General Motors Corporation, E. I. du Pont de Nemours & Company, General Electric Company, and Sears, Roebuck & Company.

Decentralization at General Motors. The most widely known and possibly most successful application of decentralization is the General Motors Corporation, referred to by Donaldson Brown as "centralized control with decentralized responsibility."[30] The organiza-

---

[29] Fayol, *op. cit.,* p. 33. For a critical appraisal of decentralization of authority, see: John Dearden, "Mirage of Profit Decentralization," *Harvard Business Review,* Vol. 40, No. 6 (November–December, 1961), pp. 140–48.

[30] Donaldson Brown, *Centralized Control with Decentralized Responsibility,* Annual Convention Series No. 57 (New York: American Management Association, 1927).

tion of General Motors is composed of two seemingly conflicting concepts—centralization and decentralization. These seemingly conflicting ideas are put into practice at General Motors essentially by an organization of semiautonomous operating divisions. Corporate strategy, formulated by top-management committees, provide unifying guidelines for the decisions that are made by the executives in each of the operating divisions.

Top management, operating through groups called the Executive Committee and the Financial Committee, formulates overall company goals and policies. The operating division managers and executives from the Operations, Legal, and Financial staffs participate in top-management policy formulation through membership on 10 policy groups which work with an overall coordinating group called the Administrative Committee.[31] But, the "central management," according to Peter Drucker's analysis of the General Motors organization, does not function only as a formulator of policy, but it is also "at the same time the servant of the divisional managers, helping them to be more efficient and more successful in their autonomy, and the boss of the corporation."[32]

The "divisional manager," according to Drucker, is limited in his decision making only by the broad goals and policies established by "central management." But, within these limits the divisional manager "operates on his own as the boss of his outfit" and:

He is in complete charge of production and sales. He hires, fires and promotes. . . . decides the factory layout, the technical methods and equipment used. He works out the capital requirements of his division and plans for expansion and for new plants—though central management must approve of major investments. The divisional manager is in charge of advertising and public relations for his division. He buys his supplies independently from suppliers of his own choice. He determines the distribution of production within the several plants under his jurisdiction, decides which lines to push and decides on the methods of sales and distribution.[33]

Each operating division has the authority to plan and execute a program which is measured and evaluated by the following objec-

---

[31] Earnest Dale, *Planning and Developing the Company Organization Structure*, Research Report No. 20 (New York: American Management Association, 1956), pp. 100–106.

[32] Peter F. Drucker, *Concept of the Corporation* (New York: John Day Co., Inc., 1946), p. 49.

[33] *Ibid.*, p. 56.

tive yardsticks: (1) base pricing measures the productive efficiency and rate of return of capital invested in each of the divisions; and (2) competitive market standing indicates the efficiency of each division as a seller. These two sets of measurements show the overall efficiency of the performance of each operating division.[34]

With this type of organization, General Motors is benefiting from both centralization through centralized planning, financing, and staff services, and decentralization through the fast, "on-the-spot" decision making that characterizes small organization. Decentralization also helps to develop managers by giving them experience in making decisions.

Decentralization at General Electric. The General Electric Company, which is organized into more than 100 operating product departments and realizes sales in billions of dollars annually, has a high degree of decentralization. Until 1940, General Electric was managed "by a central cluster of autocrats, with one superb autocrat placed grandly at the top."[35] During the last few years of the reign of Gerald Swope, the last of the "superb autocrats," it became apparent that important operating problems were not being solved and fundamentally sound ideas often failed because of the highly centralized management. *Fortune* characterized General Electric's problem as follows:

Why couldn't management make good the president's ideas? The reasons are now evident. Appliances were designed by engineers, unaided by stylists or marketing specialists; quantities to be produced were specified by men too remote from selling. In other words, management down under was centralized as to function (manufacturing, engineering, selling, etc.) with no one manager having full responsibility for the profit position of a particular product.[36]

Ralph Cordiner, who was appointed to the presidency in December, 1950, felt that General Electric's basic problem was not its gigantic size but rather its product diversity; therefore, he introduced some drastic changes in the General Electric organization. Cordiner's reorganization plan required the fragmentation of the firm into product departments (Operating Departments), each with relative independence from central authority. Each manager,

---

[34] *Ibid.*, pp. 65–66.

[35] William B. Harris, "The Overhaul of General Electric," *Fortune*, Vol. 52, No. 6 (December, 1955), p. 112.

[36] *Ibid.*, p. 112.

FIGURE 3-3

Abridged Organization of the General Electric Company*

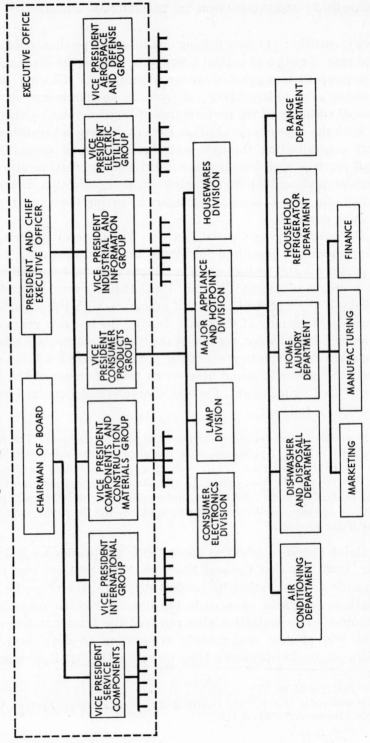

* Source: The General Electric Company.

under the Cordiner plan, was given a great deal of freedom to make decisions on matters affecting the products of his department. Accordingly, each manager was held accountable for results, which in financial terms meant profit and loss responsibility for his department. Although he operated like an independent businessman, he could still call on the vast corporate resources of General Electric. For instance, the manager of the Home Laundry Department, indicated in Figure 3-3 as one of the five product departments in the Major Appliance Division, has the authority to make decisions concerning the product design, manufacturing, pricing, and marketing of the home laundry products. In the words of Ralph Cordiner:

Today, General Electric's products are engineered, manufactured, and marketed by nearly a hundred decentralized Operating Departments, each of them bearing full operating responsibility and authority for the Company's success and profitability in a particular product or service field. The special skills and knowledge required for each operating business are thus brought to bear by a local business managerial team which can concentrate on the opportunities of a specific product or marketing area. Through these integrated managerial teams, each with a specific profit-and-loss responsibility for the operation of a defined business, we achieve the flexibility, drive and "human touch" that comes from direct participation in the daily problems of a business.

To demonstrate that the responsibility, authority and accountability of these Operating Departments is real, not window dressing, consider their pricing authority. The price of a product can be raised or lowered by the managers of the Department producing it, with only voluntary responsibility on their part to give sensible consideration to the impact of such price changes on other Company products.

As further evidence of the freedom provided by decentralization to the Operating Departments, consider the fact that the operating budget of the General Electric Company is not a document prepared by the Executive Offices in New York. It is an addition of the budgets prepared by the Operating Department General Managers, with the concurrence of the Division General Managers and Group Executives. These budgets include planned sales volume, product development plans, expenditures for plant and equipment, market targets, turnover of investment, net earnings, projected organization structure and other related items.[37]

The Operating Department manager can make expenditures up to $500,000 without top-management approval. Larger expendi-

---

[37] Ralph J. Cordiner, *The New Frontiers for Professional Managers* (New York: McGraw-Hill Book Co., 1956), pp. 58–60. Used by permission.

tures, when justified and approved by top officials, may be drawn from the corporate treasury.

The decentralization of authority into Operating (product) Departments solved the day-to-day operating problems, but the fragmentation created a need for some coordination and long-range planning. This function is assigned to the Office of the President, comprised of the president, the chairman of the board, and six group vice presidents, and the Service Components, composed of 10 vice presidents. The Office of the President and the Service Components combined is called the Executive Office (enclosed in the broken-line box in Figure 3–3).

The vice presidents of the Service Components, for instance, research, engineering, marketing, public relations, accounting, and manufacturing have authority only to review and appraise the performance of the Operating Departments. The Service Components are required to spend at least 50 percent of their time on long-range planning and forecasting. For this reason, the Service Components are considered as "Futures Divisions."[38]

At General Electric some policy decisions, that is, the formulation of broad goals and "directive policies" emanate from the Executive Office.[39] These goals deal with the fundamental nature of the firm. The following is a statement of goals of the General Electric Company:

GENERAL ELECTRIC COMPANY OBJECTIVES

1. To carry on a diversified, growing, and profitable world-wide manufacturing business in electrical apparatus, appliances, and supplies, and in related materials, products, systems, and services for industry, commerce, agriculture, government, the community, and the home.
2. To lead in research in all fields of science and all areas of work relating to the business in order to assure a constant flow of new knowledge that will make real the Company theme, "Progress Is Our Most Important Product."
3. To operate each business venture to achieve its own favorable customer acceptance and profitable results; especially by plan-

---

[38] Harris, op. cit., p. 237.

[39] In a speech given at the International Management Congress, Ralph J. Cordiner, chairman of the board, General Electric Company, indicated that as the chief executive of General Electric in the last 13 years he issued only six "directive policies," or "company-wide rules" which transcend the authority of any other individual in the firm. See *The Nature of the Work of the Chief Executive*, given at the International Management Congress, the *Comité international de l'organisation scientifique*, New York, September 16, 1963.

ning the product line or services through decentralized operating management, on the basis of continuing research as to markets, customers, distribution channels, and competition, and as to product or service features, styling, price range, and performance for the end user, taking appropriate business risks to meet changing customer needs and to offer customers timely choice in product and service availability and desirability.

4. To design, make, and market all Company products and services with good quality and with inherent customer value, at fair, competitive prices.

5. To build public confidence and friendly feeling for products and services bearing the Company's name and brands.

6. To provide good jobs, wages, working conditions, work satisfactions, stability of employment, and opportunities for advancement for employees, in return for their loyalty, initiative, skill, care, effort, attendance and teamwork.

7. To manage the human and material resources of the enterprise for continuity and flow of progress, growth, profit, and public service in accordance with the principles of decentralization, sound organization structure, and professional management.

8. To attract and retain investor capital through attractive returns as a continuing incentive for wide investor participation and support.

9. To cooperate with suppliers, distributors, retailers, contractors, and others who facilitate the production, distribution, installation, and servicing of Company products and systems.

10. To meet the Company's social, civic, and economic responsibilities with imagination and with voluntary action which will merit the understanding and support of all concerned among the public.[40]

The principal premise of the theory of decentralization is that each purpose (product) can be achieved best if it is treated as an independent unit. Thus, decentralization of authority is not limited to business organizations, but it can be applied to any organization with multiple purposes. For example, the Port of New York Authority, a semi-government agency, utilizes a decentralized form of organization.

Decentralization at the Port of New York Authority. The authority and responsibility of the autonomous subunits within the Port of New York Authority (discussed in Chapter 2 and shown in Figure 2–10) is described as follows:

---

[40] Ralph J. Cordiner, *The New Frontiers for Professional Managers, op. cit.,* pp. 55–57.

The directors of the six line departments are held accountable by the Executive director on a net revenue basis for operations and maintenance of the facilities under their supervision in accord with public service policies of The Port Authority. Each line department director has authority over all expenditures within the units under his supervision, and he has the right of prior review or approval of expenses charged to his department's facilities. He initiates or approves plans to enlarge or modify facilities under his supervision.

By illustrating these successful cases of decentralization we do not mean to imply that this is the best way to organize. Decentralization or its opposite alternative are approaches to organization, but they are not "good" or "bad" *per se*. The degree to which an organization can be decentralized depends, according to traditional theory, upon the nature and diversity of organizational goals, the amount of duplication in activities and resources that is economically feasible, the capability of divisional personnel to make decisions, the ability of central personnel to manage remotely and to refrain from restricting divisional personnel in exercising their authority, and the prevailing environmental conditions of, and the demands placed upon, the formal organization.

Departmentation, Authority, and Size of Administrative Unit

Departmentation refers to the grouping of specialized activities into departments or subunits of an organization. The dispersion of authority and the size of the administrative unit are related to departmentation to the extent that some patterns for grouping activities facilitate decentralization and small administrative units, while others lend themselves to centralization and large administrative units. However, before we pursue these relationships, the term "administrative unit" must be defined. An *administrative unit* is an organizational unit which contains the sufficient component parts to operate autonomously. An administrative unit characteristically resembles a total organization. In other words, it is a unit which can make virtually all of the decisions and take virtually all of the actions necessary to achieve a general purpose. In a business organization, for example, this means that an administrative unit is capable of making the necessary decisions and performing the activities needed to finance, manufacture, and distribute a given product. In a military organization an administrative unit is a task force capable of making the decisions and performing all of the duties necessary in achieving a given military mission. In a hospital organization this means that an administrative unit can perform the full line of medical services needed to accomplish its goals.

Departmentation and Size of Administrative Unit. Grouping organizational components according to purpose permits smaller administrative units than departmentation on the basis of function. This result can be illustrated with a hypothetical example. Suppose that four functions, *A, B, C,* and *D* must be performed on each of four products of a business organization. Departmentation on the basis of function is shown in Figure 3–4. In the diagram, *S* represents

FIGURE 3–4

Functional Departmentation and Administrative Unit

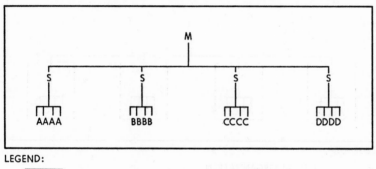

LEGEND:

TOTAL ORGANIZATION AND ADMINISTRATIVE UNIT

supervision, *M* indicates general management, and the solid-line box encloses the administrative unit or the total organization in this case. Since the functions *A, B, C,* and *D* require coordination for each product, the coordinating authority for each product must be placed at the level of general management, *M*.

If the organizational components are grouped according to purpose (or product), the organization would be designed according to Figure 3–5. The administrative units indicated by broken-line boxes include all of the functions necessary to produce one product. In comparison to the functional departmentation of Figure 3–4, the purpose departmentation of Figure 3–5, requires more administrative units but each of the four units is smaller. In addition, the coordinating authority for each product is placed at a lower level of the organization, that is, at level *S* and there are fewer hierarchical levels involved in the administrative unit.

Departmentation and Dispersion of Authority. As we indicated above, departmentation by purpose or product permits the establishment of administrative units at lower levels in the organization than does departmentation by function. It was also possible to place the coordinating authority for each product at lower levels. In terms of the dispersion of authority, then, organization by product allows a greater degree of decentralization than the functional-type organization. This result may be illustrated further with more specific examples of business firms, shown in Figures 3–6 and 3–7.

In these illustrations, it is assumed that manufacturing, market-

FIGURE 3–5

Purpose Departmentation and Administrative Unit

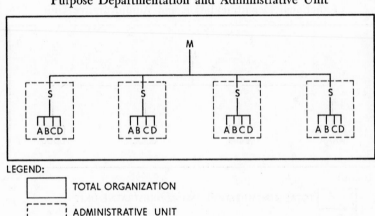

ing, and finance are all the functions necessary (of course, there are others, such as personnel, engineering, and purchasing functions) to complete a product. In the purpose-type organization (Figure 3–7), each of the products divisions can be managed as an autonomous unit. The coordinating authority for each product can be assigned to vice presidents at level 2. The delegation of coordinating authority for each product in the functional-type organization, Figure 3–6, cannot be delegated below the president, level 3.

Authority and Service Activities

The delegation of authority and the arrangement of service activities are related since the assignment of work creates a responsibility which in turn, according to traditional theory, must be accompanied by authority. Service activities which may be demanded by

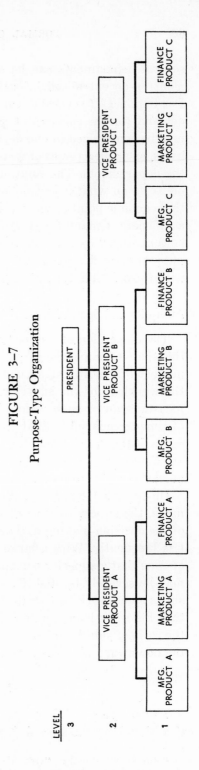

FIGURE 3-6
Functional-Type Organization

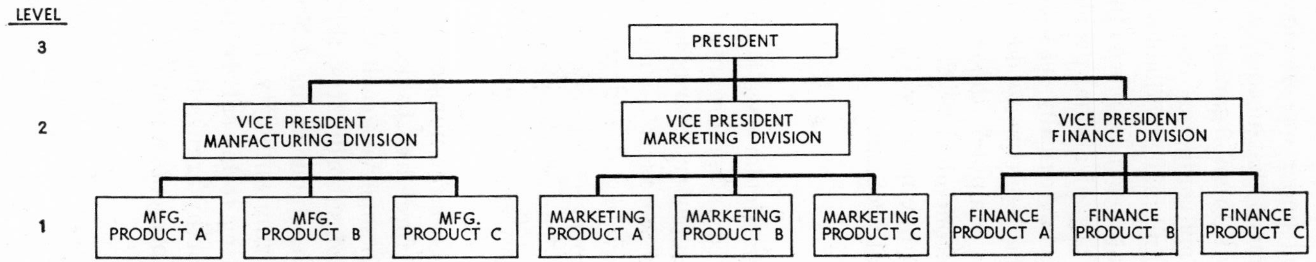

FIGURE 3-7
Purpose-Type Organization

several departments can be centralized under one service department or decentralized in each department that needs the service.
For instance, if several departments within an organization have a
demand for the services of an electronic computer, these services
may be centralized in one department and made available to all the
users, or an electronic computer installation can be placed in each of
the departments. The solution to this organizational problem may
be based on what is economically or technologically feasible. From
the economic point of view, if each of the departments does not have
a sufficient demand for the full use of a computer, this service may
be centralized, because it would be uneconomical to employ a computer in each department. The waiting line model of Chapter 13 is
used to solve this type of organizational problem.

Authority and Span of Supervision

The dispersion of authority in any particular case is affected by
the span of supervision policy adopted in an organization. The
number of subordinates assigned to a superior determines, in part,
the workload of the superior. In other words, if a superior has a
narrow span of supervision, he can devote a considerable amount
of time to each subordinate. He can supervise "closely," and retain
much of the decision-making authority. Though close supervision is
not a necessary consequence of a narrow span of supervision, it is
at least possible to occur.

On the other hand, if a superior has a large number of subordinates, the supervisory work load may force him to delegate much
of the decision-making authority and to supervise each subordinate
less frequently. With a large number of subordinates, the amount
of time that a superior can spend with each one of his subordinates
may be severely limited. By decentralizing authority, the superior
shifts some work and/or decision making to his subordinates, and
thus his work load can be reduced. Worthy argues that increasing
the ratio of subordinates to superior represents a method of forcing
the downward delegation of authority.[41]

SUMMARY

This chapter and the previous one describe the major concepts of
traditional organizational theory, including the bases of specializa-

---

[41] James C. Worthy, "Organizational Structure and Employee Morale,"
American Sociological Review, Vol. 15 (April, 1950), pp. 169–79.

tion and grouping of work, unity of command, span of supervision, delegation of authority, and types of authority.

In traditional theory, organizing is based on the method of departmentation—functional, purpose, place, and/or client. Each of these types of specialization serve a particular purpose, and it is not unusual to find organizations using more than one basis of departmentation. Administration in traditional theory is confined almost entirely to the coordination of specialized jobs.

Coordination in traditional theory is prescribed in terms of unity of command, span of supervision, and division of authority. Traditional theory prescribes that specialized jobs can be coordinated best through a unity in command, that is, each subordinate should have only one boss. With minor exceptions, each individual in the organization is subjected to one chain of command or one channel of authority.

To determine the number of subordinates that should report to a supervisor, traditional theory suggests an ideal number. The recognition that a supervisor's physical and mental capabilities are limited has led to the conclusion that the most effective span of supervision is six or less.

According to traditional theory, authority is delegated as a concomitant to responsibility, and it is derived from the position that one occupies not from personal characteristics. The delegation of authority means essentially that an organization member has permission to commit organizational resources. Included in this definition is the permission for supervisors to use organizational resources as sanctions for the purpose of gaining cooperation from subordinates.

Traditional theory prescribes an ideal type of organization with major emphasis on a formalized structure within which members of organizations operate. Some of the problems of traditional theory are presented in the following chapter.

DISCUSSION QUESTIONS AND PROBLEMS

3–1. Compare supervisors under different environmental conditions and speculate about their spans of supervision. For example, compare the span of supervision of a noncommissioned officer under battle conditions to that of a foreman in a public utility plant which has been generating electrical power for a city for 25 years. Give a full explanation of your conclusions.

3–2. Compare supervisors with different backgrounds in the following areas and speculate about their spans of supervision:
   a) Education.
   b) Experience.
   c) Charisma.
   d) Intelligence.
   e) Physical characteristics, such as size, age, beauty, and strength.

3–3. Speculate about spans of supervision of supervisors who have subordinates with different backgrounds in the following areas:
   a) Education.
   b) Profession, such as engineers, lawyers, and scientists.
   c) Average number of years with the organization.
   d) Average age.

3–4. Using equation (3–1), how many relationships are possible with $n = 14$?

3–5. Draw an organizational chart for a factory to show line and staff relationships. Assume that the line positions are titled as follows:
   a) Factory manager.
   b) Foreman (assume that there are five foremen).
   c) Workers (assume that each foreman has six subordinates).
   Assume that the staff positions are titled as follows:
   a) Production controller.
   b) Cost controller.
   c) Quality controller.

3–6. Expand the chart of problem 3–5 to show that each of the staff officers has functional authority over each of the foremen. What implications do these relationships have with respect to requirements of the concept of "unity of command"?

3–7. Is it reasonable to hold someone accountable for performance in an organization when he does not have the authority to control all the factors that influence performance? Explain your answer.

3–8. Why is a decentralized organizational arrangement more costly than a centralized one? Why, then, do companies like General Motors and General Electric use such organizational designs?

3–9. Is departmentation by purpose or product the only arrangement that facilitates the decentralization of authority? Why?

4

PROBLEMS OF TRADITIONAL THEORY

A serious criticism of the traditional theory is that it lacks precision, or a comprehensive framework for analysis[1] (this criticism is also applicable to more modern theory). Although traditional theorists talk of the advantages of various organizational arrangements, their arguments are usually one-sided, and they offer almost no objective criteria for selecting one method of organizing over other methods. For example, traditional arguments about the principle of span of supervision are usually restricted to the benefits gained by holding the number of subordinates reporting to a supervisor to very narrow limits. A more comprehensive analysis would emphasize overall efficiency criteria. An organization that follows a policy of a very narrow span of supervision must grow by increasing its levels of supervision. Accordingly, a comprehensive analysis requires that the benefits of a narrow span of supervision be weighed against the benefits that must be given up when the levels of supervision are increased. Of course, an even more com-

---

[1] Simon has argued that although traditional analysis has been at a theoretical level, it has lacked a theory and: "Since no comprehensive framework has been constructed within which the discussion could take place, the analysis has tended either to . . . logical one-sidedness . . . or to inconclusiveness." See Herbert A. Simon, *Administrative Behavior* (2nd ed.; New York: Macmillan Co., 1957), p. 35.

prehensive approach requires that all elements affected by the arrangement be considered in the analysis.

In the design chapters of this book, we offer broader and more objective decision criteria than does traditional theory. In the last part of this chapter, we present decision models which are a reasonable approximation of the techniques needed for organizational analysis. The purpose of this chapter is to examine the shortcomings of traditional theory. In the first part of this chapter, we concentrate on three specific concepts, namely, specialization, the span of supervision, and division of authority, and we evaluate their validity as prescriptions for increasing organizational efficiency. Chapters 5, 6, 7, and 8 are devoted to an examination of the ways in which people behave in organizations—especially that behavior not covered in the traditional theory. We begin with the idea of specialization.

SPECIALIZATION

The shortcomings of the traditional theory are especially apparent in the narrow approach taken toward specialization. While specialization is inherent in any organized activity, the traditional approach tends to define jobs so narrowly that only the barest minimum of skills and abilities are required to perform the tasks. James Worthy has criticized this approach as follows:

> The gravest weakness [of specialization] was the failure to recognize and utilize properly management's most valuable resource: the complex and multiple capacities of people. On the contrary, the scientific managers deliberately sought to utilize as narrow a band of personality and as narrow a range of ability as ingenuity could devise. The process has been fantastically wasteful for industry and society.[2]

Studies of operating organizations indicate that the narrow approach to specialization has been practiced widely. The trend since World War I, according to some writers ". . . has been to reduce the content of worker's jobs to their simplest components and to abstract from them all skill and responsibility."[3] What evidence is there to substantiate the claim made by James Worthy that the narrow approach to specialization is a "waste of resources"? Per-

---

[2] James C. Worthy, *Big Business and Free Man* (New York: Harper & Row, 1959), pp. 69–70.

[3] Charles R. Walker, *Modern Technology and Civilization* (New York: McGraw-Hill Book Co., 1962), p. 76.

haps the best way to answer this question is to cite the results of cases where jobs were broadened or enlarged beyond the limits dictated by a traditional approach. Here is Charles Walker's summation of several attempts at job enlargement:

> It is probably inevitable that the trend of a half a century or more during which the jobs of workers had been shrinking in content and skills should cause a reaction, a swing of the pendulum to some degree in the other direction. Significantly that swing began, not because of the preaching of humanitarians or the cries of radicals about turning men into robots, but because practical production men found that it often paid to enlarge the job and so release more responsibility, skill, and judgment to the mass production worker.
>
> . . . the enlarged job gives the worker greater variety and hence is presumably more interesting, but . . . it also demands greater skill and judgment. Some of the advantages reported were reduced spoilage and number of rejects (due to a greater sense of product responsibility by the individual worker), improved quality, higher morale, reduced absenteeism and turnover, and decreased number of accidents.[4]

The traditional approach to specialization also suffers from a narrow definition of the efficiency criterion. The values to be achieved with specialization in the traditional view are primarily economic. Dividing work into very simple, repetitive-type jobs is supposed to be more efficient because it makes workers more productive in a material sense. This view is almost completely devoid of other human values, such as a worker's satisfaction with his job. What has been the effect of the traditional approach on worker attitudes? Let us examine two studies on the subject.

Walker, Guest, and Turner produced some studies about men involved in assembly-line operations.[5] In one article, Guest stated that ". . . the extreme subdivision of labor (the man who puts a nut on a bolt is the symbol) conjoined with the 'endlessly moving belt' has made the assembly line the classic symbol of the subjection of man to the machine in our industrial age."[6] From interviews with over 400 assembly-line workers in automobile manufacturing, Guest reproduced one interview which he felt was typical. The

---

[4] *Ibid.*, pp. 76–77. Used by permission.

[5] Charles R. Walker and Robert H. Guest, *The Man on the Assembly Line* (Cambridge, Mass.: Harvard University Press, 1952); and Charles R. Walker, Robert H. Guest, and Arthur N. Turner, *The Foreman on the Assembly Line* (Cambridge, Mass.: Harvard University Press, 1956).

[6] Robert H. Guest, "Men and Machines: An Assembly-Line Worker Looks at His Job," *Personnel* (a publication of the American Management Association), Vol. 31, No. 6 (May, 1955), pp. 496–503, reprinted in: Walker, *Modern Technology and Civilization, op. cit.*, p. 98.

interview revealed strong worker dissatisfaction. The following quote, though it is lengthy, portrays vividly the nature of assembly-line jobs and employee attitudes toward these jobs.

. . . this worker's dissatisfaction was not due primarily to the things that are usually considered important to a job. People often say, "Pay a man enough and he'll be satisfied." But this man's pay was good. His job was secure. He worked for a sound company. He had substantial seniority. He had a pension, hospitalization and disability benefits when he became sick, and a good boss. . . . Working conditions, heating, lighting, cafeteria facilities, and safety conditions were, I would say, as good as if not better than average.

Yet Joe despised his job.

The simple fact is that the impact of "sound" engineering principles had had a marked effect on his total outlook on the job.

What "Sound" Engineering Has Taken Away

For this man, and for hundreds of others with whom we have had experience, the engineer, in applying the principles of mass production to the extreme, had factored out virtually everything that might be of real, personal value to the worker. The sense of anonymity implicit in much of what this particular worker said can be traced back to some of the basic characteristics of his immediate job.

The conveyor belt determined the *pace* at which he worked. He had no control over his pace.

Because it was broken down into the simplest motions possible, the job was highly *repetitive*.

Simple motions meant that there was little or no need for *skill*.

The tools and the work procedure were predetermined. And when techniques changed, it was the engineer—not the worker—who controlled the change.

He worked on a *fraction of the product* and never got a sense of the whole. (He admitted that in 12 years of work he had almost never seen a finished car roll off the final line.)

Some attention was required. Too much to allow him to daydream or carry on any sustained conversation with others; but not enough to allow him to become really absorbed in his work.

Men on the line work as an aggregate of individuals with each man performing his operation more or less independently of the others. The lack of an intimate group awareness appeared to reinforce the same sense of anonymity fostered by the conveyor-paced, repetitive character of the job itself.[7]

A study by Chris Argyris resulted in similar findings.[8] His research was concerned with a seemingly healthy organization. The

---

[7] *Ibid.*, pp. 501–2.

[8] Chris Argyris, "The Organization: What Makes It Healthy?" *Harvard Business Review*, Vol. 36, No. 6 (November–December, 1958), pp. 107–16.

company's traditional indicators of employee morale were impressive. The company had very low indexes of employee turnover, absenteeism, and grievances. However, when Argyris questioned the employees about their attitudes, he found them to be apathetic and indifferent toward their jobs and surroundings. They desired to be directed rather than give directions to others. They did not want to become involved in company affairs other than the responsibilities of their immediate jobs. Argyris concluded these are *not* the needs of healthy, mature individuals. "Mature individuals, in our culture," according to Argyris, "tend to need to be relatively independent, to be responsible about and involved in their activities, to seek challenging creative work, to aspire to higher positions, and to be active, and to utilize many of their abilities."[9] If these are the needs of mature adults, what happened to the workers studied by the researcher? Argyris hypothesizes that these employees once had the needs that are characteristic of healthy individuals. "But, in an attempt to adapt to a work world that ideally prefers that they behave like infants, they have finally capitulated and have adapted by becoming apathetic, indifferent, noninvolved, and so forth. They have created their present immature needs in order to remain relatively free from inner tension and psychological illness."[10]

What difference does it make that employees are dissatisfied with their jobs, apathetic, indifferent, and noninvolved? The administrator may argue that he is forced to use the traditional approach to specialization because it promises the greatest material benefits, such as profit maximization in the case of business enterprise. However, if we accept the findings of research efforts on job enlargement (discussed at the beginning of this section), the administrator's argument may not be valid. Greater utilization of the physical and mental capabilities of the human resource may increase the scope of organizational accomplishment, that is, the organization may become more efficient. Furthermore, apathy and indifference may have long-run implications for the efficient attainment of goals. For example, Argyris predicts that the dissatisfaction of employees manifested by apathy and indifference may result in demands for increased wages; these increases may be viewed "not as rewards for production but as management's moral obligation for placing the employees in the kind of working world where frustration, failure and conflict are continuously being

---

[9] *Ibid.*, p. 111.
[10] *Ibid.*

experienced." According to this thesis, wage costs will tend to rise regardless of productivity changes.

Moreover, it is possible that employee dissatisfactions may develop into general unrest and eventually into a work stoppage. Roethlisberger makes this point in talking about "logical plans to promote efficiency."

> The application of the most economical way of performing certain operations to concrete work situations involves individuals in their relations to one another. It involves attitudes, feelings, and sentiments. At times these factors cannot be conveniently disregarded, ... From a technical standpoint, many things in business can be done more efficiently; but if in the process of introducing changes toward this end a strike is produced, what do we mean by "efficiency"?[11]

There is even a broader consideration implicit in the problem of employee attitudes. It involves values or purposes which the organization attempts to achieve. The narrower view of organizational purpose is restricted to material achievements, such as profits as the prime goal (and some say the only goal) of business institutions. The broader view would include a recognition of the fact that organizations have multiple objectives. Included in these objectives would be a regard for personal values, such as the working conditions necessary to provide some degree of satisfaction to employees. There has been much discussion in the literature about expanding the traditional approach to setting organizational goals. James Worthy, for example, has criticized prevailing theories about business organization and has called for a new theory that more adequately reflects the multiple goals of business:

> Such a theory will recognize that business is a social organ with functions far beyond the mere promotion of material prosperity, and with motivations far broader than simple self-interest. It will give consideration to the pervasive influence of religious forces in American life, the profound consequences of the rise of the large, publicly owned corporation, and certain unique features of American historical development. It will, in other words, shake off outmoded economic doctrine and take a fresh look at the truth about today's business.[12]

This broader view of organizational goals implies that the administrator has responsibilities far beyond those dictated by mate-

---

[11] F. J. Roethlisberger, *Management and Morale* (Cambridge, Mass.: Harvard University Press, 1956), p. 146.

[12] Worthy, *op. cit.*, pp. 31–32.

rial achievements. The fragmentation and routinization of work to the point where it loses significance has implications not only for organizations that live by this action but also for society in general. The organization may suffer because the rewards for submissive compliance produce apathy, indifference, noninvolvement, and alienation on the part of group members. They become highly dependent and incapable of solving problems and making decisions. The organization may become rigid and its members unwilling to accept and adapt to changes necessary for growth and changing socioeconomic conditions. Furthermore, a democracy built on a foundation of free choice will suffer because the dependency rewarded and fostered in organizations may carry over into everyday life.

SPECIALIZATION AND ADMINISTRATION

In the traditional theory, administration is confined almost entirely to the coordination of specialized jobs. Little attention is given to the administrative problems of decision making and communication flow. Although the traditionalists seem to recognize the importance of decision making when they discuss concepts like "planning," they seem to ignore its importance in discussions of administration in an organizational context.

The underlying premise of the traditional structure is that specialized jobs can be coordinated best by one head or one boss, that is, there shall be unity of command. Everybody in the organization, according to this "principle," is subject to one chain of command or one channel of authority. One obvious defect of this method of organizing is that while it takes advantage of specialization at the worker level (horizontal specialization), it may not realize the benefits of specialization as it applies to decision making (vertical specialization). The benefits of specialization are derived from dividing work in such a way that the skills required to perform the tasks can be mastered easily. Likewise, the benefits of expertise in decision making are derived from ". . . subdivision of the decisions governing the organization into numerous component decisions, and a restriction of the activities of each member of the organization to a very few of these components."[13]

Furthermore, much of the traditional literature prescribes that

---

[13] Herbert A. Simon, *Administrative Behavior* (New York: Macmillan Co., 1957), p. 137.

the flow of information be limited to the chain of command or the channels of authority. The reason given for this requirement is that communications by organization members with other members outside of the channels of authority tends to undermine the superior-subordinate relationship. However, this requirement may place undue restraints on the decision process. Decision makers may need access to sources of information that lie outside of the chain of command. If the sources of information are limited to those that are provided by the single channel of authority, then it is evident that decisions will be only as good as the quality and extensiveness of the information carried in the one channel.

There are some exceptions in traditional literature to this rule that communication flow adhere to the chain of command, notably in the works of Henri Fayol and Frederick W. Taylor. Henri Fayol recognized that it is sometimes necessary to bypass the chain of command. Thus, he proposed an arrangement that is referred to as "Fayol's Bridge." It is illustrated in Figure 4–1. Suppose that F

FIGURE 4–1

Fayol's Bridge

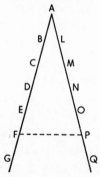

SOURCE: Reproduced from Henri Fayol, *General and Industrial Management*, trans. Constance Storrs (London: Sir Isaac Pitman & Sons, Ltd., 1963), p. 34.

needs to contact P. Strict adherence to the principle of unity of command requires F to follow the chain of command to A and then to P. It is quicker and simpler, according to Fayol, for F to go directly to P through the connection FP. However, Fayol was careful to maintain the hierarchical relationship by insisting that the connection between F and P be approved or authorized by their respective superiors E and O and that F and P keep their superiors fully informed of their deliberations.[14] Taylor's "functional fore-

---

[14] Henri Fayol, *General and Industrial Management*, trans. Constance Storrs (London: Sir Isaac Pitman & Sons, Ltd., 1963), pp. 34–35.

manship" was another example in the traditional literature that proposed multiple channels of communication and, in this case, multiple channels of authority. However, Gulick, another traditionalist, rejected this idea, when he stated:

Even as great a philosopher of management as Taylor fell into this error in setting up separate foremen to deal with machinery, with materials, with speed, etc., each with the power of giving orders directly to the individual workman. The rigid adherence to the principle of unity of command may have its absurdities; these are, however, important in comparison with the certainty of confusion, inefficiency and irresponsibility which arises from the violation of the principle.[15]

Gulick's proposal for strict adherence to unity of command requires that whenever there is a disagreement between organization members, the dispute is resolved not on its merits but on the relative rank of the disputants. Strict compliance to unity of command creates a further problem with respect to specialization of the decision process. In the discussion above, we emphasize that decision makers may need access to several sources of information besides the chain of command. When disagreements arise and organization members are forced to revert to the formal lines of authority, the resolution of the conflict will reflect the type of specialization represented by the chain of command rather than the decision process. Simon gives the following example to illustrate the point: "If the training officer of a city exercises only functional supervision over the police training officer, then in case of disagreement with the police chief specialized knowledge of police problems will determine the outcome while specialized knowledge of training problems will be subordinated or ignored."[16]

SPAN OF SUPERVISION

After work has been divided into specialized jobs, traditional theory prescribes that these jobs be grouped according to (a) purpose, (b) function, (c) clientele, or (d) place.[17] The traditional theory specifies further that jobs should be grouped so that no employee

---

[15] Luther Gulick, "Notes on the Theory of Organization," in Luther Gulick and Lyndall Urwick (eds.), *Papers on the Science of Administration* (New York: Institute of Public Administration, 1937), p. 9.

[16] Simon, *op. cit.*, pp. 25–26.

[17] For a discussion on the ambiguity among these terms see Simon, *op. cit.*, pp. 30–32.

reports to more than one boss; that is, there should be *unity of command*.[18] Furthermore, the theory prescribes that subordinates reporting directly to any one supervisor should be limited to a very small number, that is, the assignment of subordinates to a supervisor should adhere to the principle of *span of supervision*. We discussed each of these ideas in the preceding chapter. Since we want to examine the controversy about the span of supervision in detail, let us review some of the discussion of the preceding chapter.

THE PROBLEM

The reasons why the magnitude of the number of subordinates reporting to a single executive is considered a problem are rather obvious. The supervisor has limited resources. The number of hours that he can work during a day or week are limited. He has limited energy. His ability and willingness to work on many problems at once has limits. He has a limited span of knowledge. His experiences and mental abilities may make him unwilling or unable to handle all problems. He also has a limited span of attention—he can attend only to a few things at a time. Physical barriers such as distance also circumscribe the executive's ability to supervise. Employees and operations spread over a wide geographic area make supervision by one man difficult—especially when problems are peculiar to one area, require personal attention, and demand close supervision. A not so obvious problem, emphasized by the theory, is that relationships between and among supervisors and subordinates are much more complex and involved than that which is represented by direct lines of command. The theory emphasizes, for example, that in addition to direct single relationships of the chain of command, there are direct group and cross relationships among the members of the group.

The recognition that the supervisor as a human being has limitations which are accentuated by such physical barriers as time and distance, and amplified still further by the complex relationships that characterize organizations, has led to the conclusion that every supervisor should have a narrow span of supervision. Some writers are very specific about this prescription. For example: "No superior can supervise directly the work of more than five or, at the most,

---

[18] The problems with respect to unity of command are taken up in the next chapter.

six subordinates *whose work interlocks.*"[19] No explanation, other than experience, is given as the basis for limiting the span to a specific number.

The critics of the span-of-supervision principle emphasize that other, and perhaps more difficult, problems are created when the number of subordinates assigned to an executive is limited to a very few. In Figure 3–1, we saw that a movement from a wide span of 64 to 1, to narrower spans of 8 to 1, 4 to 1, and 2 to 1, requires an increase in the number of supervisors and supervisory levels. An increase in number of supervisors causes corresponding increases in administrative expenses for executive salaries, office space, and secretarial assistance. Communication in an organization with many levels becomes subject to different interpretation at each level and has a tendency to become distorted. The more levels there are in an organization, the greater is the likelihood that the final recipient of a communication will get the wrong message or emphasis in a message. Communication through many levels takes time and creates the well-known problem of red tape. Many levels of supervision in an organization also dilute the influence of the most senior executive, and the resulting "administrative distance" that develops between top and lower line officials may have a demoralizing effect on the latter. The obvious answer to the problems raised by the critics is to have wide spans of supervision.

Flat versus Tall Organization

The traditional organization with its narrow span of supervision and many supervisory levels is shaped like an elongated pyramid and is referred to in the literature as a "tall" organization. With wider spans of supervision, the traditional pyramid-shaped organization becomes wide at the base and shorter in height. An organization with relatively wide spans of supervision and relatively few levels of supervision is referred to as "flat" organization.

Empirical evidence and published charts about existing organizations reveal conflicting practices. Organization charts of the U.S. Army and German Army units in 1944 show strict adherence to narrow spans of supervision. Abbreviated charts of units from each army are shown in Figures 4–2 and 4–3.

---

[19] Lyndall F. Urwick, "The Manager's Span of Control," *Harvard Business Review*, Vol. 34 (May–June, 1956), p. 41. Emphasis is Urwick's.

FIGURE 4–2

The Campaign in Northern France (1 August 1944)

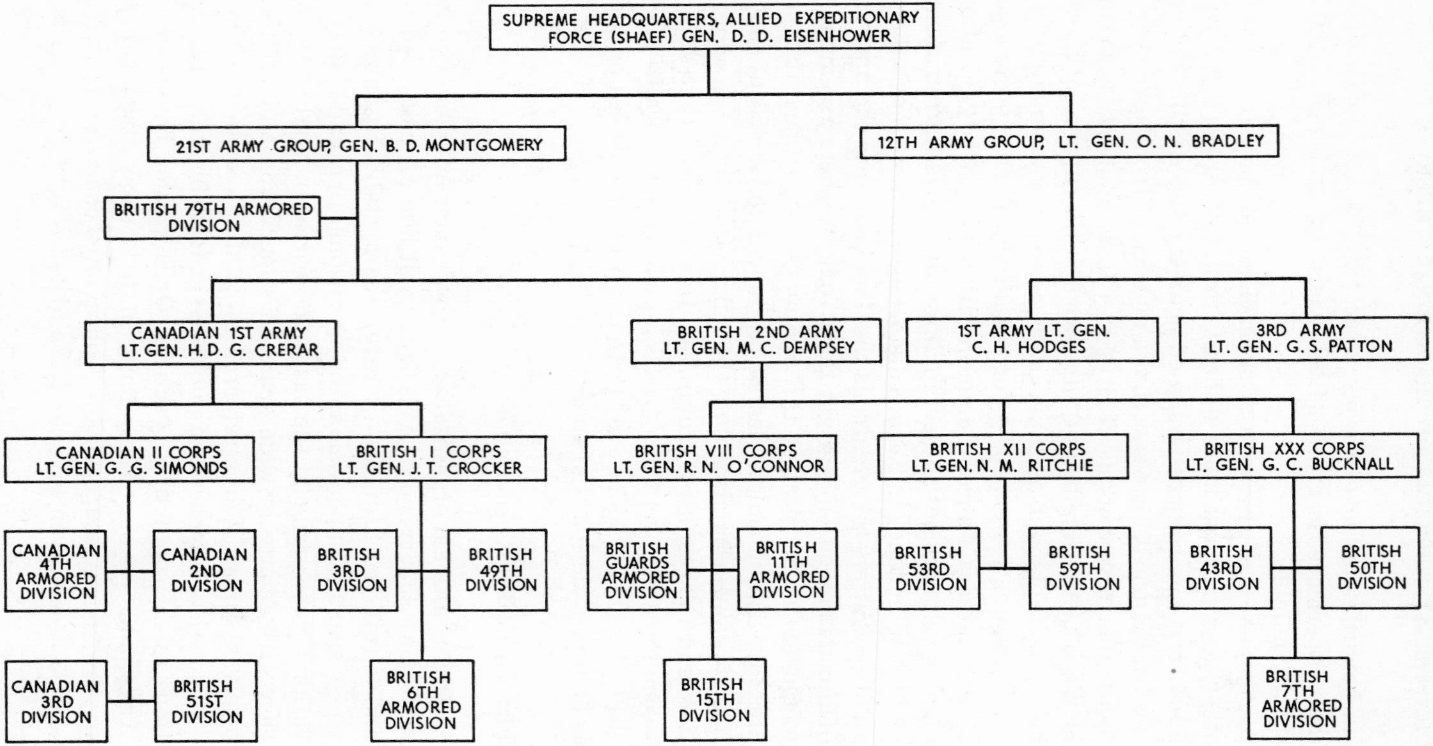

FIGURE 4–5

Gerdan Army—Western Front (15 December 1944)

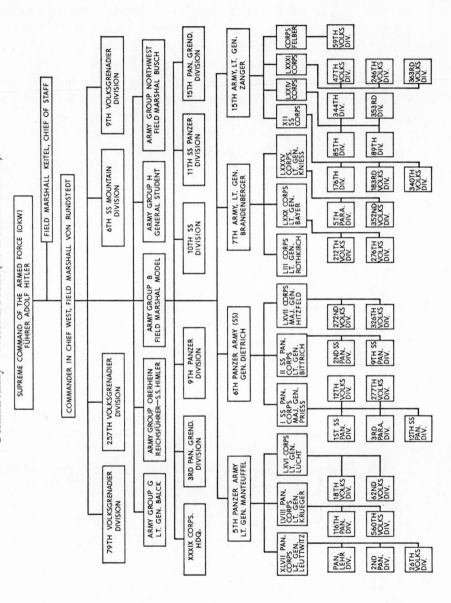

A survey conducted by James H. Healey of 1,915 manufacturing firms in Ohio revealed that the chief executives of 70 percent of the main plants and 60.6 percent of the branch plants used a span of three to seven subordinates. Healey concluded that in practice the span of supervision "tends to agree with the span advocated in theory,"[20] and in cases where executives have spans greater than eight, they are "inclined to advocate a span lower than that which is actually utilized by the respondents."[21]

There is also evidence to show that many organizations use wide spans of supervision. The U.S. Army, which for a large part of its history adhered to a span of three to six, recently was reorganized in a manner which violates the narrow-span idea. The organization of an infantry division in 1965 (see Figure 2–13) reveals that up to 13 tactical battalions can be included in the span of supervision of the division commander. Essentially, this was accomplished by eliminating the regimental command echelon.

The organization of the Executive Department of the U.S. government also utilizes a wide span of supervision. A commission studying the organization of the executive branch of the government found that the President supervises 74 subordinates.[22] If special advisory commissions and interdepartmental committees are included, the President's span has on some occasions increased to approximately 300.[23] The Commission found that:

> The executive branch is not organized into a workable number of major departments and agencies which the President can effectively direct, but is cut up into a large number of agencies, which divide responsibility and which are too great in number for effective direction from the top.[24]

The Commission recommended a reorganization which required a consolidation of departments, thereby reducing the President's span to about one third of what it was prior to the study. However, even with this recommendation, the number of subordinates reporting to the President is much greater than that prescribed by traditional theory.

---

[20] James H. Healey, *Executive Coordination and Control* (Columbus, Ohio: Bureau of Business Research, The Ohio State University, 1956), p. 242.

[21] *Ibid.*, p. 245.

[22] "General Management of the Executive Branch," *A Report to Congress by the Commission on Organization on the Executive Branch of the Government* (Washington, D.C.: U.S. Government Printing Office, 1949), Vol. I, pp. 47–50.

[23] "The Presidency: Can Any One Man Do the Job?" *U.S. News & World Report*, November 22, 1957, pp. 52–53.

[24] "General Management of the Executive Branch," *op. cit.*, p. 3.

A survey study by the American Management Association discloses additional evidence on industry practices.[25] The data gathered concerning the spans of the presidents of 100 large and 41 medium-sized firms reveals that the median span for the large firms is between eight and nine, and for the medium-sized firms it is between six and seven. A span of greater than six was reported by 74 percent of the large firms and 46 percent of the medium-sized firms.

An example of an organization that successfully employs wide spans of supervision is Sears, Roebuck. As reported by James Worthy, the merchandising vice president has 44 senior executives reporting directly to him. Furthermore, the typical retail store at Sears has ". . . forty-odd department managers reporting to a single store manager."[26] According to Worthy, Sears found that this flat type of structure with maximum decentralization develops self-reliance, initiative, and decision-making skills. Under this organization, the department store manager, with over 40 department managers reporting directly to him, does not have time to solve all the problems and therefore is forced to delegate decision-making authority to subordinates. When managers of departments were asked to manage, they learned to manage. "They cannot be running constantly to superiors for approval of their actions; they have to make their own decisions and stand or fall by the results. In the process, they make mistakes—but that, too, contributes to their growth and maturity."[27] Having to rely heavily on department managers, store managers took greater care in the selection, placement, and development of subordinates. The broad, flat type of organizational structure, according to Worthy, gets the job done better and permits individuals to develop and grow in ways that are not possible in the traditional organizational structure.[28]

---

[25] Ernest Dale, *Planning and Developing the Company Organization Structure*, Research Report No. 20 (New York: American Management Association, 1950), pp. 57–59.

[26] Worthy, *op. cit.*, p. 109. For a brief report on the Sears study, see James C. Worthy, "Organizational Structure and Employee Morale," *American Sociological Review*, Vol. 15 (April, 1950), pp. 169–79.

[27] *Ibid.*, p. 110.

[28] Worthy does not provide any validating evidence with his study. Some doubts have been expressed about the Worthy findings. For further examination of the problem of organizational structure and effects upon performance and morale, see, for example, L. Meltzer and J. Salter, "Organizational Structure and Performance and Job Satisfaction of Physiologists," *American Sociological Review*, Vol. 27, No. 3 (1960), pp. 351–61; L. W. Porter and E. E.

The Dilemma

This review of existing practice suggests that some organizations succeed using a narrow span of supervision while others succeed with a wide span of supervision. We conclude, therefore, that the principle of traditional theory which prescribes a narrow span of supervision, and the remedy of wide spans recommended by the critics, *are not* generally applicable to organizations. In effect, we are saying that generalizations cannot be made about this problem.

This conclusion does not mean that the ideas of traditional theorists and their critics are insignificant. Indeed, their contributions to theory are legitimate and warrant the time and attention of anyone concerned with organizational problems. Our point is that they were too quick to generalize. In each case, the generalizations stemmed from a one-sided argument. In the case of traditional theory, narrow spans (resulting in a tall organization) were prescribed because of human limitations of the supervisor. In the case of more modern writers, wide spans (resulting in a flat organization) are recommended because of the communication and decision problems created by an organization with many levels.[29] Furthermore, neither the traditional theory nor its critics offer any objective criteria for deciding which type of design is best—the flat organization, the tall organization, or some variation of the two types. Evidence of actual organizational practices seem to indicate that generalized prescriptions such as narrow or wide spans are invalid. Each supervisory situation is peculiar enough to warrant an independent decision based on local conditions. We can illustrate how this need can be met with a mathematical model of the problem.

We can develop a mathematical model which expresses the relationships among pertinent variables in the problem and provides

---

Lawler, III, "The Effects of 'Tall' Versus 'Flat' Organization Structures on Managerial Satisfaction," *Personnel Psychology*, Vol. 17, No. 2 (1964), pp. 135–48; L. W. Porter and E. E. Lawler, III, "Properties of Organization Structure in Relation to Job Attitudes and Behavior," *Psychological Bulletin*, Vol. 64, No. 1 (1965) ; H. Jules, "Types of Institutional Structures," *Psychiatry*, Vol. 20 (1957) ; B. P. Indik, "Some Effects of Organization Size on Member Attitudes and Behavior," *Human Relations*, Vol. 16, No. 4 (1963), pp. 369–84; A. R. Anderson and S. Warkov, "Organizational Size and Functional Complexity: A Study of Administration in Hospitals," *American Sociological Review*, Vol. 26, No. 1 (1961), pp. 23–28.

[29] In order to dramatize the problems involved in span of supervision, we have overstated each position.

specific criteria upon which an objective decision can be made. Once this model has been developed, we can apply it to a particular situation by supplying the numerical values to the model which reflect local conditions. A model is developed in the next section.

IMPORTANT CONSIDERATIONS

Much of traditional theory about the span of supervision stems from the Graicunas theorem which says that the *possible relationships* increase exponentially as additional subordinates are assigned to a supervisor. The prescriptions to restrict the span of supervision to very narrow limits are based on the implicit assumption that *possible relationships* have some effect on the *frequency* of contacts between supervisor and subordinates, and among subordinates themselves. Even if the number of relationships among subordinates resulted in an equal amount of contacts, this does not mean that a supervisor has to become involved or must mediate all the interactions among his subordinates. The more important relationships are those between supervisor and subordinates. While there may be many possible relationships between a supervisor and his subordinates, the frequency of contacts between the parties is dependent on many more factors than their organizational relationship. Another element which was not given proper attention in the theory was the *duration of time* of each contact. Here again, the time of each contact is not solely dependent on the organizational relationship between supervisor and subordinate. Clearly, the *frequency* and *time* of contacts between supervisor and subordinates are the important aspects of the problem,[30] but what are the factors that effect the magnitude of these two elements?

One factor that affects the frequency and time of contacts is the managerial ability of the supervisor. It is likely, for example, that supervisors with exceptional managerial talent are more successful in regulating the frequency and time of interactions with subordinates and, therefore, may use wider spans of supervision than executives with lesser talents. Another factor that affects interac-

---

[30] Luther Gulick, a writer whom we have classified as a member of the traditional school, did recognize the importance of frequency and time of contacts and the futility of trying to generalize about the span of supervision. See Luther Gulick and Lyndall F. Urwick (eds.), *Papers on the Science of Administration* (New York: Institute of Public Administration, 1937), pp. 8–9.

tions between supervisor and subordinates is the nature of the work. Some types of work require more contacts between supervisor and subordinates than other types of work. For example, we would expect frequent contacts between a soldier in battle and his noncommissioned officer. We would expect relatively few contacts between supervisor and subordinates in cases of professors, priests, and scientists. The amount of change that takes place in an organization will influence contacts between supervisors and subordinates. "In a stable organization the chief executive can deal with more immediate subordinates than in a new or changing organization."[31] The degree to which authority is delegated to subordinates will also affect superior-subordinate contacts. We would expect, for example, that a management which employs the technique of decentralization would require fewer contacts between supervisor and subordinates than one which uses centralization.

Furthermore, the extent to which men understand organizational objectives and policies and the extent to which they are experienced and trained in organizational processes will have an important effect on their need to interact. "Knowing what the boss wants" and being able to predict the behavior of other members of the organization requires fewer and less time-consuming contacts. Clearly, these abilities stem from close and continuing associations with the boss and other members of the organization. For example, Waino Suojanen has argued that the principle of a narrow span is invalid because it does not take into consideration the "institutionalization" of organization and the development of primary groups.[32] According to this premise, men who associate for extended periods of time, develop patterns of behavior—set ways of doing things. They learn each other's customs and habits. They learn to work together on an informal basis. These factors facilitate communication and understanding and actually reduce the frequency of contacts and the demands made upon the supervisor.

The Fordham Model

Now that it has been established that time and frequency of contacts are the important factors in the span-of-supervision prob-

---

[31] *Ibid.*

[32] Waino Suojanen, "The Span of Control—Fact or Fable?" *Advanced Management*, Vol. 20 (November, 1955), pp. 5–13.

lem, let us proceed with a model for making a decision.[33] The objective of the Fordham model may be stated as follows:

Objective: Select that span of supervision which maximizes the efficiency of the organization.

Simplifying Assumptions. The first assumption of the model is a constant span of supervision throughout the organization, that is, each supervisor has the same number of subordinates. The illustration of Figure 4–4 shows each supervisor with two subordinates. The problem, then, is to find the optimum span for all supervisors in the organization.

For notation, let:

n = number of organization levels (In Figure 4–4, $n = 3$).
r = span of supervision or number of subordinates reporting directly to one supervisor (In Figure 4–4, $r = 2$).

Efficiency of Organization is the dependent variable of the model (r is the independent variable) and is defined as the total efficiency of all individuals divided by the total number of individuals, or:

$$\text{Efficiency of organization} = \frac{\text{Total efficiency of all individuals}}{\text{Total number of individuals}} \quad (4\text{--}1)$$

Since time and frequency of contacts are so important to the model, let us examine the contacts of an individual in an organization. A supervisor, for example, has contacts with his superior, his equals, and his subordinates. Some of the time spent in these contacts is "productive," and some of the time is "nonproductive." *Productive time* is the time spent on activities directly related to the primary responsibility of the supervisor. *Nonproductive time* is the time spent on activities that are indirectly related to the primary responsibility of the supervisor. Productive time of the supervisor is the time spent on directing the work of subordinates and solving problems directly related to the output of his manufacturing facility. Anything else is nonproductive time. The use of these two terms is unfortunate because "nonproductive" connotes wasted time, which may or may not be true. We use them because they are standard terms.

Let c denote the fraction of an individual's contact time with

---

[33] Adapted from S. Fordham, "Organization Efficiency," *Journal of Industrial Economics*, Vol. 6, No. 3 (1958), pp. 209–15, and Daniel Teichroew, *An Introduction to Management Science* (New York: John Wiley & Sons, Inc., 1956), pp. 48–51.

others that is nonproductive. Returning to the illustration of Figure 4–4, we see that a supervisor at level 2 has one superior, r subordinates, and $r - 1$ equals, and his nonproductive time is:

$$c + (r - 1)c + rc = 2rc$$

The remaining fraction of his contact time, therefore, is productive time or:

Productive time of a supervisor at level 2 = $1 - 2rc$ (4–2)

There is another important element in this model. Much has been said in this and previous chapters about the benefits of specializa-

FIGURE 4–4

Three-Level Organization with Uniform Span of Supervision

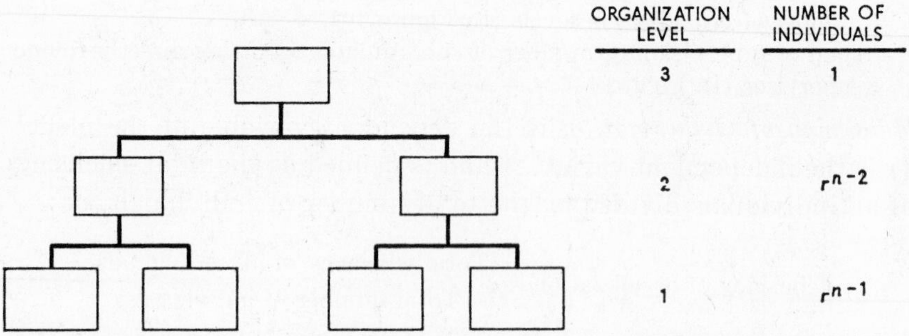

	ORGANIZATION LEVEL	NUMBER OF INDIVIDUALS
	3	1
	2	r^{n-2}
	1	r^{n-1}

tion. Generally, we stated that men who are specialized and organized are more productive than men standing separate and independent from each other. Let us incorporate this condition into the model. Assume that the productivity of a man working alone is unity and that the increase in productivity due to specialization is denoted by the parameter s. If we show the benefits of specialization through an individual's contacts with his equals and call it effectiveness, then:

Effectiveness of a supervisor at level 2 = $1 + (r - 1)s$ (4–3)

Combining equations (4–2) and (4–3), we define the efficiency of an individual in the organization as:

Efficiency of an individual = (Productive time) (Effectiveness)   (4–4)

Applying (4–4) to a supervisor at level 2, we obtain:

Efficiency of a supervisor at level 2 = $(1 - 2rc)[1 + (r - 1)s]$ (4–5)

Since there are r^{n-2} or r supervisors at level 2, the total efficiency for that level is

Total efficiency for level 2 = $r(1 - 2rc)[1 + (r - 1)s]$ (4–6)

Expanding equation (4–1), for the simple organization of Figure 4–4, we obtain:

$$\text{Efficiency of a three-level organization} =$$
$$\frac{\begin{array}{c}\text{Total efficiency}\\ \text{of level 3}\end{array} + \begin{array}{c}\text{total efficiency}\\ \text{of level 2}\end{array} + \begin{array}{c}\text{total efficiency}\\ \text{of level 1}\end{array}}{\text{Total number of individuals}} \quad (4\text{–}7)$$

Let us now derive the total efficiency for levels 1 and 3. At level 3, the supervisor has 0 superiors, r subordinates, and 0 equals. His nonproductive time, therefore, is rc and his productive time is $(1 - rc)$. Since the supervisor at level 3 has 0 equals, his effectiveness is unity. Applying (4–4) to the supervisor at level 3, we obtain:

$$\text{Efficiency of the supervisor at level 3} = 1 - rc \quad (4\text{–}8)$$

Since there is 1 supervisor at level 3, the total efficiency for that level is the same as (4–8).

An individual at level 1 has 1 superior, 0 subordinates, and $r - 1$ equals. His nonproductive time is $c + (r - 1)c$ or rc. His productive time is $(1 - rc)$. Since an individual at level 1 has $r - 1$ equals, his effectiveness is $[1 + (r - 1)s]$. Therefore:

$$\text{Efficiency of an individual of level 1} = (1 - rc)[1 + (r - 1)s] \quad (4\text{–}9)$$

Since there are r^{n-1} or r^2 *individuals at level* 1:

$$\text{Total efficiency at level 1} = r^2(1 - rc)\,[1 + (r - 1)s] \quad (4\text{–}10)$$

Substituting (4–6), (4–8), and (4–10) for the numerator, and $(1 + r + r^2)$ for the denominator in equation (4–7), we obtain:

$$\text{Efficiency of a three-level organization} =$$
$$\frac{(1 - rc) + r(1 - 2rc)\,[1 + (r - 1)s] + r^2(1 - rc)[1 + (r - 1)s]}{1 + r + r^2} \quad (4\text{–}11)$$

Solving the Model. We may assume that equation (4–11) is a general model for any three-level organization that adheres to the "principle" of unity of command and has a uniform span of supervision for all supervisors. Since c and s are the parameters or fixed constants of the problem, the efficiency of an organization, equation (4–11), is dependent on r, the span of supervision. The solution to the model then, may be obtained by enumerating alternative spans of supervision and selecting that span which maximizes organizational efficiency. Assume that 5 percent of total available time is spent on each contract, that is, $c = 0.05$. This means that 24 minutes out of an eight-hour day (0.05×480 minutes) is spent on each contact. Also, assume that there is a 10 percent improvement in effectiveness due to specialization, that is, $s = 0.10$. Now, let us enumerate several alternative spans of supervision in Table 4–1.

TABLE 4–1

Organizational Efficiency as a Function of the
Span of Supervision in a Three-Level
Organization
$c=0.05, s=0.10$

Span of Supervision r	Organizational Efficiency
(1)	(2)
2	0.94571
3	.96538
4	.97905
5	.98387
6	.97907
7	.96439
8	.93973
9	.90505
10	.86036

From column (2) of Table 4–1, it can be seen that a span of supervision of $r = 5$ maximizes organizational efficiency. Thus, we have obtained the objective or solved the model by designing the three-level organization so that each supervisor has five subordinates.

Contact time is an important parameter in this model. An organization with a slightly different value for c than 0.05 is radically different with respect to the span of supervision required for optimum efficiency. For example, a three-level organization with $c = 0.059$ and, as in the previous case, $s = 0.10$, has maximum organization efficiency with a span of supervision at $r = 3$. This result can be seen from Table 4–2.

TABLE 4–2

Alternative Spans of Supervision
in a Three-Level Organization
$c=0.059, s=0.10$

Span of Supervision r	Organizational Efficiency
2	0.92051
3	.92592
4	.92385
5	.91129

Notes on the Model

Again, we emphasize that the Fordham model is simple—too simple perhaps to be of practical advantage. The simplifying assumption of a constant span of supervision, for example, both in the development and solution of the Fordham model is still too abstract. The fact that there are usually significant differences in managerial talent among supervisors, and differences in other conditions such as the social climate of each supervisory situation, make the assumption of a uniform span of supervision quite untenable. Another problem with the Fordham model is that it is deterministic, or it assumes certainty. In Chapter 13, we overcome the problems of a uniform span and certainty by examining a model that determines an optimum span for *each* supervisor under *probabilistic* conditions.

Despite these deficiencies, the Fordham model illustrates the use of objective criteria for making a decision on span of supervision—a missing ingredient of both traditional theory and more contemporary thought. Furthermore, the model demonstrates the importance of contact time in the span-of-supervision problem. Also, the Fordham model gives a more comprehensive approach than usual formulations by providing a parameter to show the effect of specialization on efficiency.

The Lockheed Model

A span-of-supervision model developed at the Lockheed Missiles & Space Company employs those variables considered to be "most significant" for Lockheed along with judgments concerning the relative importance of each.[34]

Based on an analysis of the situation at Lockheed, the designers of this model concluded that there are seven key variables in setting the span of supervision: (1) similarity of functions; (2) geographic contiguity of subordinates; (3) complexity of functions; (4) direction and control required by subordinates; (5) coordination of subordinates required; (6) planning importance, complexity, and

---

[34] This model was reported by Harold Stieglitz in "Optimizing Span of Control," *Management Record*, Vol. 24 (September, 1962), pp. 25–29.

TABLE 4-3

Criteria for Assigning Weights to Span of Supervision Variables

Degree of Supervisory Burden

Span Variables					
Similarity of functions	Identical — 1	Essentially alike — 2	Similar — 3	Inherently different — 4	Fundamentally distinct — 5
Geographic contiguity	All together — 1	All in one building — 2	Separate buildings, one plant location — 3	Separate locations, one geographic area — 4	Dispersed geographic areas — 5
Complexity of functions	Simple repetitive — 2	Routine — 2	Some complexity — 4	Complexity varied — 6	Highly complex and varied — 8 / 10
Direction and control	Minimum supervision and training	Limited supervision — 3	Moderate periodic supervision — 6	Frequent continuing supervision — 9	Constant close supervision — 12 / 15
Coordination	Minimum relationships with others	Relationships limited to defined courses — 2	Moderate relationships easily controlled — 4	Considerable close supervision — 6	Extensive mutual nonrecurring relationships — 8 / 10
Planning	Minimum scope and complexity	Limited scope and complexity — 2	Moderate scope and complexity — 4	Considerable effort required guided only by broad policies — 6	Extensive effort required areas and policies not charted — 8 / 10

SOURCE: Reproduced from Harold Stieglitz, "Optimizing Span of Control," *Management Record*, Vol. 24 (September, 1962), p. 27. The seventh variable, organizational assistance, was treated separately; therefore, it is not included in the supervisory index.

time required; and (7) organizational assistance received by supervisor.

Once the key variables are identified, each one is assigned a weight. The more critical a variable is, the more heavily it is weighted. For instance, direction and control is assigned a maximum weight of 15 points while similarity of functions has a maximum of 5 points. The maximum weights and scale of numerical values for each variable are shown in Table 4–3. These weights were derived at Lockheed by "Common sense, experience and experimentation."[35]

Each managment position is rated, that is, point values are determined, for each of the span variables. The point values are summed for each position to form a supervisory index. The higher the supervisory index, the greater is the supervisory burden and the narrower is the suggested span. For middle-management positions, the supervisory index was aligned to a suggested standard span as shown in Table 4–4.

TABLE 4–4
Middle-Management Index and Suggested Span

Supervisory Index	Suggested Standard Span
40–42	4–5
37–39	4–6
34–36	4–7
31–33	5–8
28–30	6–9
25–27	7–10
22–24	8–11

SOURCE: Reproduced from Harold Stieglitz, "Optimizing Span of Control," *Management Record*, Vol. 24 (September, 1962), p. 29.

The results obtained at Lockheed reveal that in one situation, the average span was increased from 3.8 to 4.2 subordinates and the supervisory levels reduced from 5 to 4. At the middle-management level, the mean span was increased from 3.0 to 4.8 subordinates and the levels reduced from 6 to 5. In another case, the average span was broadened from 4.2 to 4.8 subordinates and the levels cut from 7 to 5.

According to the analysts who designed this model, it is not

[35] *Ibid.*, p. 26.

intended to provide a completely objective method to replace judgments. It is offered as a guide to setting the span of supervision. Judgments are still needed, for instance, in selecting the key variables and assigning weights to each one. As Harold Stieglitz concluded, this model "represents an attempt to bring a little more objectivity, a little bit more organized thinking, to the determination of span and levels of management."[36]

DIVISION OF AUTHORITY

According to traditional theory, the direction for the course of events in formal organization flows downward only through the hierarchy of authority. Coordinative or administrative authority ends at the supervisory level. There is a clean break between supervisors and workers. Supervisors manage and workers work.

Critics of this approach contend that it does not achieve the quality of coordination that is necessary for the endurance of cooperation. Chester I. Barnard points out that a "cooperative system" requires balance among the elements of organization. Barnard's imperatives of technical effectiveness and human efficiency are both important elements in sustaining cooperation.[37] While traditional theory is concerned with technical effectiveness, it ignores human values such as individual growth and employee needs to participate in the decisions which determine their destiny while at work.

A serious charge is made by Douglas McGregor against the implicit assumptions of traditional theory with regard to limiting administrative authority to a few select people in the organization. The implicit assumptions of traditional theory, called by McGregor "Theory X," are that:

1. The individual human being has an inherent dislike for work and avoids it if he can.
2. Because of this dislike for work, most people must be coerced, controlled, directed, and threatened by punishment to get them to put forth adequate effort toward the achievement of the organizational goals.
3. The average human being prefers to be directed, wishes to avoid

---

[36] *Ibid.*, p. 29.

[37] Chester I. Barnard, *The Functions of the Executive* (Cambridge, Mass.: Harvard University Press, 1956), pp. 19–20, 56–57, and p. 256.

authority and responsibility, has relatively little ambition, and wants security above all.[38]

The results of several research projects cast additional doubt about these implicit assumptions and the adequacy of the traditional approach to the delegation of authority. There is some research evidence to indicate that lower level participation is a feasible alternative in the organizational division of administrative authority. Let us examine some of these studies.

Harwood Experiments

Research reported by Lester Coch and John R. P. French, Jr., about a change implemented at the Harwood Manufacturing Company indicates that resistance to change can be reduced by permitting employees to participate in the planning of the change.[39] An experiment was designed to give four groups different treatment with respect to implementing a change in job methods. One group did not participate in planning the change; they were merely told about the planned change. A second group was permitted to participate in designing the planned change through elected representatives, and two other groups were allowed total participation in formulating the change. The first group was designated the "control" group, whereas the participation groups were referred to as "experimental" groups.

Prior to this experiment, the general attitude of workers toward change was negative. Learning curves of several hundred experienced operators, computed after some job changes had been introduced, revealed that 38 percent of the operators recovered to the standard unit rating, while 62 percent either became chronically substandard operators or quit during the relearning period.

The results of this experiment reveal that the performance of the participation groups was superior to that of the no-participation group. The no-participation group "improved little beyond their early efficiency rating . . . resistance developed . . . aggression against management occurred,"[40] and 17 percent of the members quit during the 40 days following the introduction of change.

---

[38] Douglas McGregor, *The Human Side of Enterprise* (New York: McGraw-Hill Book Co., 1960), pp. 33–34.

[39] Lester Coch and John R. P. French, Jr., "Overcoming Resistance to Change," *Human Relations*, Vol. 1 (1948), pp. 512–32.

[40] *Ibid.*, p. 522.

The two full-participation groups improved their performance after the change. Their output increased to a level about 14 percent higher than the prechange level, they required no additional training after the second day, they cooperated with their superiors, and no one quit during the 40 days after the change.

The members of the control group were returned to their original jobs, and after two and one-half months, 13 of them were reassembled for a second experiment. The reassembled group was given the total participation treatment in introducing a change. Their performance in the second experiment showed a marked difference. Their efficiency rating improved rapidly like that of the other experimental groups. There were no indications of aggression and no turnover after 19 days. The few anxieties that did arise were resolved in a meeting of elected representatives. The conclusion drawn from this experiment by Coch and French is that permitting participation makes it possible to remove group resistance to change.[41] Several other studies have suggested similar results about the effect of participation.[42]

There have been other methods developed to modify the traditional methods of delegating authority. They can be identified either as practical efforts to expand the decision-making base in organization through group management or attempts to develop appeal channels. A brief description of some of these methods is presented in the following sections.

Participative Management

Several attempts to modify the traditional delegation of authority have emerged, primarily from practice. These organizational plans vary in the degree to which authority is redistributed among the lower levels of the organization. Most of these plans attempt to

---

[41] For an interesting debate concerning the merits of participative management and in particular the validity of the results obtained from the Harwood experiments, see the following articles: William Gomberg, "The Trouble with Democratic Management," and Warren G. Bennis, "A Reply: When Democracy Works," both appearing in *Trans-action*, Vol. 3, No. 5 (July–August, 1966), pp. 30–35 and pp. 35–36. A continuation of this debate is found in *Trans-action*, Vol. 3, No. 6 (September–October, 1966), pp. 35–37.

[42] For instance, see J. R. P. French, Jr., J. Israel, and D. As, "An Experiment on Participation in a Norwegian Factory," *Human Relations*, Vol. 13 (1960), pp. 3–19; N. R. F. Maier and L. R. Hoffman, "Group Decision in England and the United States," *Personnel Psychology*, Vol. 15 (1962), pp. 75–87; and J. Misumi, "Experimental Studies on 'Group Dynamics' in Japan," *Psychologia*, Vol. 2 (1959), pp. 229–35.

involve the lower level participants in some phase of decision making. Some of these arrangements permit the employees or their representatives to participate in the making of major decisions, while others allow employees to get involved in relatively minor decisions or in the methods of implementing decisions. The rationale, according to the proponents of this plan, is that organizational design, particularly the distribution of authority, represents a value which is desired by the participants of the organization.

One example of employee participation in major organizational decisions is the "consultative hierarchy" developed at the Glacier Metal Company of Great Britain.[43] "Consultative hierarchy" was designed for the purposes of (1) providing worker representation in making decisions on day-to-day operating problems as well as general policy; (2) improving communications between workers and management; and (3) giving "all operatives a feeling of direct communication with the consultative hierarchy."[44]

We do not attempt to describe in detail the consultative hierarchy, because it involves a series of continuous developments which began in 1948 and are still occurring. Briefly, the consultative hierarchy is composed of a network of committees, representing all of the interest groups in the organization, which either make decisions or sponsor discussions in the decision-making process. This committee network includes the Works Council, the Representative Committees, and the committees of the executive organization.

The Representative Committees include shop committees representing workers and a Works Committee composed of representatives from the shop committees, shop stewards, local trade union officials, and a secretary. Through the years these committees have sought to provide a direct channel of communication between employees and management, machinery for the joint consideration of matters affecting the employees and the factory, and the means for developing cooperation in obtaining efficiency. The Works Committee has dealt with management–trade-union relations, procedures for avoiding disputes, policies on such matters as payments, grading, and retirement.

---

[43] See Elliott Jaques, *The Changing Culture of a Factory* (London: Tavistock Publications, Ltd., 1951); Wilfred Brown, *Explorations in Management* (New York: John Wiley & Sons, Inc., 1960); and Elliott Jaques, "Social Analysis and the Glacier Project," *Human Relations*, Vol. 17, No. 4 (1964), pp. 361–75.

[44] Jaques, *The Changing Culture of a Factory, op. cit.*, p. 64.

The Works Council, composed of nine members elected from and by the Works Committee and nine specified management representatives, makes decisions on all policy matters. In 1964, it produced a policy document covering most of the firm's policies.

Executive committees representing all strata of management have been formed to deal with a wide variety of problems including projects, such as the organization of the sales and production work, appeals procedures, analysis of project organization of research and development, and analysis of pricing methods.

The results of this experience do not lend themselves to rigorous scientific validation. We offer it here, not as a validated method of organizing, but merely as an arrangement which has been effective for a considerable number of years.

Other participative schemes have been developed with more limited purposes. For instance, the introduction of "multiple management" at McCormick and Company is essentially an attempt to develop a training medium for executive personnel.[45] This plan involves four junior boards under the senior board of directors. The junior boards, composed of assistant department managers and others, make decisions to supplement the judgments of top management.

Another participative plan, called "bottom-up" management, was developed by William B. Given, Jr. at the American Brake Shoe Company.[46] This organizational plan attempts to circumvent the rigidities of the formal chain of command by assigning men to positions without an exact and narrow definition of responsibilities. Bottom-up management encourages and rewards those participants who take the initiative to suggest new and creative ideas involving work and functions other than their own. Also managers are appraised, compensated, and promoted according to the extent that each creates an organizational climate conducive to bottom-up management.

Appeal Channels

Another approach to modify the rigidities of the chain of command is the development of channels of appeal which bypass the

---

[45] Charles P. McCormick, *Multiple Management* (New York: Harper & Row, 1938).

[46] William B. Given, Jr., *Bottom-Up Management* (New York: Harper & Row, 1949).

formal hierarchy. The reasons given for the appeal channels is that the chain of command of traditional theory impairs individual freedom, by virtue of the chain of superior-subordinate relationships, and weakens the organization as well as the position of the people who serve it. Under the traditional approach, according to advocates of appeal systems, each subordinate becomes highly dependent upon his superior. W. G. Scott, for example, explains that the ability of each subordinate to appeal his superior's decisions and commands to higher management is restricted because he is so dependent upon his superior.[47]

To rectify this condition, several practical methods have been introduced. Union-management negotiations, grievance procedures, suggestion systems, and the Inspector General in the Armed Forces are some of the formal methods open to an individual to bypass his immediate superior. There are less formalized methods; for example, there is the "open door" policy which means that executives are accessible to anyone in the organization.

SUMMARY

The object of this chapter is to examine a few of the problems that are created in the application of the basic concepts of traditional theory—specialization, unity of command, span of supervision, and delegation of authority. While traditional theory may solve some of the problems of organization, it creates some also.

Specialization, for instance, is supposed to bring about efficiency because it makes each job simple and repetitive. However, if jobs are defined so narrowly that only the barest and minimum human skills are required, not only are human resources wasted but the dysfunctions of specialization may have long-run implications for the efficient attainment of organizational goals. Attempts to despecialize, that is, to enlarge jobs, suggest that this solution yields values that are beneficial to both the organization and the individual.

The prescribed limits to the span of supervision in traditional theory creates the dilemma between "tall" and "flat" organization.

---

[47] The rationale for organizational justice, and some appeal systems existing in labor unions, the Roman Catholic Church, the federal government, the U.S. Army, and in business firms, are presented by William G. Scott in *The Management of Conflict: Appeal Systems in Organizations* (Homewood, Ill.: Richard D. Irwin, Inc., and Dorsey Press, 1965).

Neither the traditional theorists nor their critics offer any objective criteria for resolving the dilemma. The conclusion reached in this chapter is that each situation is peculiar and warrants a decision based on local conditions. To this end, illustrative models are offered. The Fordham model is offered as a means of solving this problem, assuming the existence of certain parametric values. A model that is not as abstract, the Lockheed model, is presented also.

The division of authority according to the traditional theory is supposed to bring about an orderly accomplishment of work and the coordination of effort. Dysfunctions arise, however, because it is based primarily upon the division of work and it ignores decision making and the needs of the people involved. Several alternatives have been suggested—participative management and appeal channels. These alternatives take into account some of the behavioral patterns of organizational participants. In Chapter 5 we illustrate further that the assumptions of traditional theory about the way people behave in formal organization are far too simple.

DISCUSSION QUESTIONS AND PROBLEMS

4-1. What are the weaknesses in the traditional approach to the establishment of narrow limits to the span of supervision? How does the span of supervision affect the shape of the organization?

4-2. If job specialization promotes efficiency, how can job enlargement be justified? Does the success achieved through job enlargement invalidate the idea of specialization?

4-3. Discuss some of the decisions that would have to be made in order to use the Lockheed model in setting the span of supervision. In what ways is the Lockheed model better than the traditional method of establishing the span of supervision?

4-4. What are the implications of "participative management" to the objectives of a formal organization and the efficiency criterion?

4-5.
  a) Find the total efficiency of an organization where $n = 4$ levels.
  b) Use the model derived in (a) to find the efficiency of an organization if:

1) $c = 0.04$	$s = 0.1$	$r = 1$
2) $c = 0.04$	$s = 0.1$	$r = 2$
3) $c = 0.04$	$s = 0.1$	$r = 3$
4) $c = 0.04$	$s = 0.1$	$r = 4$
5) $c = 0.04$	$s = 0.1$	$r = 5$
6) $c = 0.04$	$s = 0.1$	$r = 6$
7) $c = 0.04$	$s = 0.1$	$r = 8$

      8) $c = 0.04$ $s = 0.1$ $r = 9$
      9) $c = 0.01$ $s = 0.1$ $r = 4$
    10) $c = 0.15$ $s = 0.1$ $r = 4$
    11) $c = 0.20$ $s = 0.1$ $r = 4$

  c) Plot the values of efficiency of an organization you found in (*b*) as a function of r. Discuss the significance of your results.

4–6.

  a) Find the total efficiency of an organization where $n = 5$ levels.
  b) Use the model derived in (*a*) to find the efficiency of an organization if:

     1) $c = 0.1$ $s = 0.1$ $r = 1$
     2) $c = 0.1$ $s = 0.1$ $r = 2$
     3) $c = 0.1$ $s = 0.1$ $r = 3$
     4) $c = 0.1$ $s = 0.1$ $r = 4$
     5) $c = 0.1$ $s = 0.1$ $r = 5$
     6) $c = 0.1$ $s = 0.1$ $r = 6$
     7) $c = 0.1$ $s = 0.1$ $r = 8$
     8) $c = 0.1$ $s = 0.1$ $r = 9$
     9) $c = 0.01$ $s = 0.1$ $r = 4$
    10) $c = 0.15$ $s = 0.1$ $r = 4$
    11) $c = 0.20$ $s = 0.1$ $r = 4$

  c) Plot the values for efficiency of an organization you found in (*b*) as a function of r. Discuss the significance of your results.

4–7. Develop a general model for the efficiency of an organization comprised of n levels. Assume $r \geq 2$.

4–8. What are the shortcomings of traditional theory as applied to the span of supervision? What factors does the Graicunas model fail to take into account?

4–9. What are the advantages of the Fordham model over the traditional theory of span of supervision?

4–10. What are the limitations of the Fordham model?

4–11. What would be the effect of participative management of the time required to make a decision?

PART II

Behavior Patterns

5

NONFORMAL
BEHAVIOR

The design of formal organization is intended to order relationships and channel human behavior toward the efficient attainment
of objectives. In traditional theory, this requirement produced a
rather extreme form of organization. One of the essential characteristics of the traditional or bureaucratic model is its formality. It
has definite purpose, clearly defined jobs, written rules, and an
established chain of command. Theoretically, the traditional model
leaves nothing undefined, imprecise, or ambiguous. It is organization based primarily on work, and allowance is made only for
work-oriented behavior. Formal organization, in traditional theory,
is supposed to infuse its members with a strong sense of duty and
a willingness to adapt their behavior to the needs of the organization.

The means for obtaining adaptive behavior is through rewards
and punishments. Appropriate behavior, sentiments, and attitudes
are rewarded, while inappropriate responses are punished. In traditional theory this view of rewards and punishments is based on the
assumption that man is motivated by a drive for personal enrichment—he is an economic man. When offered higher earnings for
more output through a wage incentive plan, for example, he will
exert maximum effort in order to maximize his earnings. The doctrine of self-interest has long prevailed in traditional theory as well

as in practice. The self-interest doctrine is illustrated in one of Adam Smith's basic assumptions: "Every individual is continually exerting himself to discover the most advantageous employment for whatever capital he can command." It does not take much study to realize that this same doctrine still prevails. As an example, note the view of the president of one of the world's largest corporations: "Of all the motivations to which the human mechanism responds, none has proved so powerful as that of financial gain . . . self-enrichment is a dream which must rank with the most compelling forces in shaping the destinies of the human race."[1]

While the concept of self-interest based on financial reward is important in explaining human behavior, it presents an incomplete and inadequate picture of human needs. It says nothing, for example, about the desire to feel important, to be respected, or to have prestige. Of equal importance to the study of formal organization is the human desire to associate, to belong, or to be accepted as a member of a group on an informal basis. Elton Mayo has stated, "The desire to stand well with one's fellows, the so-called human instinct of association, easily outweighs the merely individual interest and the logical reasoning upon which so many spurious principles of management are based."[2] He concluded that "If one observes either industrial workers or university students with sufficient care and continuity, one finds that the proportionate number actuated by motives of *self-interest logically elaborated* is exceedingly small. They have relapsed upon self-interest when social association has failed them."[3]

Thus, there is reason to question the assumption that man is motivated simply by self enrichment. Also, as we shall see below, man does not hold to the pattern of behavior prescribed by the formal organization. He elaborates his behavior and relationships beyond the formal requirements of a job. One of the first studies to reveal nonformal organizational behavior was directed by Elton Mayo at the Hawthorne plant of the Western Electric Company. Since it is such a classic in the field of organizational research, we feel that the

[1] Crawford H. Greenewalt, *The Uncommon Man* (New York: McGraw-Hill Book Co., 1959), pp. 37–38.

[2] Elton Mayo, *The Social Problems of an Industrial Civilization* (Boston: Division of Research, Graduate School of Business Administration, Harvard University, 1945), p. 43.

[3] *Ibid.*

reader should become fully acquainted with the project. Thus, much attention is given to the study below.

Early industrial research was concerned with the effects of physical factors such as illumination and ventilation on productivity. The results of these experiments were inconclusive. Elton Mayo, who had conducted this type of experiment at a Philadelphia textile mill, concluded in 1933 that, "Where human beings are concerned, one cannot change one condition without inadvertently changing others. . . ."[4]

Mayo, who had been appointed in 1926 as the first head of the department of industrial research at Harvard University, became involved in a study then in progress at the Hawthorne plant of the Western Electric Company. Mayo, along with Fritz J. Roethlisberger, T. N. Whitehead, William J. Dickson, and others, introduced some experimental controls into the Hawthorne plant research project. The Hawthorne experiments, under his direction, lasted about five years and involved about 20,000 individual employees. The results, labeled by *Fortune* magazine as the "fruitful errors of Elton Mayo,"[5] did not immediately produce a new interpretation of the relationship between man and work. This point is evident from the following descriptions of that research.

That "Mysterious Something"

In an attempt to explain the relationship of man to work, Stuart Chase once said that we are "forgetting that under the factory roof is a human society, as authentic as that of a South Sea Island fishing village . . . the worker is driven by an inner urge to find an environment where he can take root, where he belongs and has a function. . . ."[6] Stuart Chase refers to this urge to belong, to associate, and to participate as that "mysterious something [which] is hidden deep in human nature. Fatigue experts did not find it. Stop

---

[4] Elton Mayo, *The Human Problems of an Industrial Civilization* (2nd ed.; Boston: Division of Research, Graduate School of Business Administration, Harvard University, 1946), p. 56.

[5] *Fortune*, Vol. 34, No. 5 (November, 1946). Some critics of the Hawthorne experiments question their credibility as sound empirical research. These experiments are included in this book because we consider them as a classic study in revealing the importance of social factors in formal organization.

[6] Stuart Chase, *Men at Work* (New York: Harcourt, Brace & World, Inc., 1941), pp. 26–27. Copyright 1941, 1943, 1944, 1945, by Stuart Chase. Reprinted by permission of Harcourt, Brace & World, Inc.

watch boys overlooked it. All decent managers of factories have
known intuitively that it was there, but they have not known what
it was."[7] This "mysterious something," and nonformal behavior in
formal organization, is the subject of this chapter.

LIGHTING EXPERIMENT

The most widely known attempt to study the "mysterious something" occurred as a by-product of a search for physical factors
which were thought to affect productivity. The initial results, however, appeared to be so contradictory that the research group ended
up searching for the answer to the question concerning the "distribution of human satisfaction."[8] Stuart Chase described the study
as follows:

The Western Electric Company had the courage to attack this question
head on. It is a progressive company with the latest schemes for pensions,
sickness, and accident benefits, safety councils, recreation clubs, thrift
plans. . . . Yet this benevolent and progressive company was ripe with
tension and frustration in the prosperous 1920's.
In 1924 Western Electric, in co-operation with the National Academy
of Sciences, undertook a study. . . . The investigation began with lighting. It was generally assumed that the better the light the greater would
be the output. . . . The "control group" worked under a constant amount
of light. The "test group" received variable amounts. . . . The test group
is given increased light. Its output goes up. . . . But the output of the
control group—without a candle power of extra light—goes up
too. . . . But screwier results are to follow. Light for the test group is
now decreased below that of the control group. Its output goes up again!
So does that of the control group! What in heaven's name is going on?
The research staff was forced to conclude that intensity of light was a
minor factor in producing induction coils, where the motions of the
workers are largely automatic. To verify this they put two workers in a
locker room with no light at all except what came through a crack under
the door. The workers maintained output, even in the dark.
. . . Groping for an answer, they planned a new and more ambitious
experiment. In this test a group of employees were subjected to changes
in hours of work, in rest pauses, rates of pay, types of supervision; and
their output was measured before and after the changes. Besides the
fundamental question of what makes workers work, the investigators
hoped to find answers to six other questions: Do employees on a forty-
eight-hour week really get tired out physically? Are rest pauses desirable? Is a shorter work day desirable? What is the effect of changing the

---

[7] *Ibid.*, p. 10.
[8] *Ibid.*, p. 12.

type of working equipment? Why does production fall off in the after-noon? What is the attitude of the workers toward their work and toward the company?[9]

RELAY ASSEMBLY TEST ROOM

The more ambitious Relay Assembly Test Room experiment pro-vided some answers concerning the fundamental question of what human factors affect productivity. The following is a brief descrip-tion of the experiment, along with some conclusions, written by Stuart Chase.

THE TEST ROOM

It was decided to use a group of girls assembling telephone relays. A telephone relay is a small gadget, looking something like a pocket whistle, made up of thirty-five separate parts. The task of the girls was to take these parts out of trays and put them together. It was a typical machine-age repetitive job.

Two girls were selected who were skilled at assembling relays, and they picked four companions. Five of the group were about twenty years old, three of Polish families, one of Italian, one of Czech. The sixth had been born in Norway, and was about thirty years old. They were all moved into a special room separated by a thin partition from the big relay depart-ment where 100 employees worked.

Here the six girls sit, at one long bench, trays of tiny metal parts in front of them. Their nimble fingers fly. Every minute or so a relay is finished, dropped into a chute, and carried out into a box on the floor, where it is collected. On each girl's chute is placed a little machine operating a kind of ticker tape which counts every relay coming through. For five years these tickers will click—from 1927 to 1932—giving an accurate record of hourly, daily, weekly output.

Five of the girls were assemblers, while the sixth was the "layout operator," who prepared the trays of parts so the girls could assemble them more easily. A seventh person was also in the room—the observer. He represented the research staff. His job was to record everything of significance that happened. He was to be the counselor and friend of the girls, telling them about the experiment, talking over proposed changes, inviting their comments, listening to their complaints.

The idea was to let the girls work along as they had been doing in the regular department, and count the relays coming down the chute. This would give a base rate of output. Then, following the plan, shift the pay-ment for a few weeks, and count the relays. Then introduce rest pauses of various kinds, and count the relays. Then vary the hours in the working day, give Saturday off and what not, and count the relays. If more relays per week went through the tickers, the change of course would be proved

---

[9] *Ibid.*, pp. 11–14.

a good one and could be extended over the plant. If fewer relays went through the ticker, the change was obviously bad, and should not be adopted. It was all as clear as A B C.

If the investigators had been disturbed by what happened in the lighting experiments, they were knocked galley west by what happened to these six girls with flying fingers in the relay room. Things didn't happen the way they were expected to happen. Assumptions as to cause and effect were found to be completely false. As the weeks grew into months and years, the mystery became deeper and deeper. What was the matter with these girls? Why didn't they do what the efficiency books said they ought to do?

Being true scientists, however, the investigators kept doggedly on, recording faithfully what happened, even if they did not know what caused it or what it meant.

Here in brief outline is the mystery story, divided into chapters:

Periods 1 and 2, lasting seven weeks. These periods were devoted to getting the base output figures. The girls were found to average about 2,400 relays a week each. They worked the regular forty-eight hours, including Saturdays.

Period 3, lasting eight weeks. A variation in wages was introduced, putting the girls on a group piecework basis. Output went up.

Period 4, lasting five weeks. Two rest pauses of five minutes each were introduced, at ten in the morning and at two in the afternoon. Output went up.

Period 5, lasting four weeks. The rest pauses were increased to ten minutes each. Output went up sharply.

Period 6, lasting four weeks. Six five-minute rest pauses were tried. The girls complained that the rhythm of their work was broken. Output fell off slightly.

Period 7, lasting eleven weeks. Rest pauses were reduced to two, one of fifteen minutes in the morning, with a hot snack provided by the company, and one of ten minutes in the afternoon. Output went up.

Period 8, lasting seven weeks. The same conditions as Period 7, except that the girls were dismissed at four-thirty instead of five o'clock. Output went up sharply.

Period 9, lasting four weeks. The same as Period 7, except that closing time was moved to four o'clock. Output remained on a level.

Period 10, lasting twelve weeks. Back to the exact conditions of Period 7, with closing time at five o'clock. Were the girls discouraged by losing an hour a day of liberty? They were not; output went up with a rush!

The research staff began to tear their hair. Their assumptions were disintegrating. Some unmeasured force was constantly pulling output up no matter how they juggled hours, wages, and rest pauses.

So after trying Saturdays off for twelve weeks, in Period 11, with output on a level, they prepared for the greatest test of all. They would throw the whole experiment back to where it started and take away everything they had given the girls over a year and a half. Surely this would crush their spirits and reduce the number of relays going through the counters. Surely every rule of common sense and factory management indicated that.

Period 12, lasting twelve weeks. The girls went back to the exact physical conditions of Period 3—no rest pauses, no company hot lunch, a full forty-eight hour week. Output jumped to an all-time high—3,000 relays a week, a cool 25 per cent above the original Period 3!

THE UNKNOWN FACTOR

The staff swooned at their desks. They thought they were returning the girls to the original conditions of the experiment, but they found that the original conditions had gone forever. The experiment had changed under them, and the group they now had was not the group they had started with. Because of some mysterious X which had thrust itself into the experiment, this group of six girls was pouring 25 per cent more relays into the chutes, though working arrangements were precisely like those at the beginning of the test.

What was this X? The research staff pulled themselves together and began looking for it. They conferred, argued, studied, and presently they found it. It wasn't in the physical production end of the factory at all. It was in the girls themselves. It was an attitude, the way the girls now felt about their work and their group. By segregating them into a little world of their own, by asking their help and co-operation, the investigators had given the young women a new sense of their own value. Their whole attitude changed from that of separate cogs in a machine to that of a congenial team helping the company solve a significant problem.

They had found stability, a place where they belonged, and work whose purpose they could clearly see. And so they worked faster and better than they ever had in their lives. The two functions of a factory had joined into one harmonious whole.

With this discovery, the results of the lighting experiments became clear. Both groups in the lighting test had come to feel important. So their output went up regardless of the candle power sprayed upon them.

The relay room showed other significant results. Cumulative fatigue was not present at any time, as proved by regular medical examination of the girls. They always worked well within their physical capacity. If monotony was present, it was blotted out in group interest, as the output curves bore witness.

It was found that each girl had a definite style in her work. She placed the parts so and assembled them so. Sometimes she put little frills on the job; the higher the IQ, the more frills. This helped to give her a real interest in the task. Beware, you stop-watch men, of destroying little habits like this. You may run into the paradox of decreasing output by saving motions.

There was a visible increase in contentment, and an 80 per cent decrease in absenteeism. The girls were eager to come to work in the morning—a phenomenon as startling as a small boy eager to go to school. Early suspicions gave way to complete trust in the observer and in the integrity of the experiment. The girls came to feel that they had no boss.

They moved about as they pleased, talked as they pleased. Nobody silenced them.

With this sense of freedom came a sense of responsibility, and they began to discipline themselves. They evolved into a compact social unit, working as a team, helping each other, making up each other's work when one of the group was not feeling well, giving parties for one another outside the factory. They squabbled a bit, but underneath they were members of the same gang. They had found here some of the clan unity which the machine age has stripped away from so many industrial workers. They stayed in the factory, but they came out of the cage.

Human societies since Adam have depended on nonlogical social rules expressed in folkways and ceremonials. In handicraft days each member of the community was assigned his place and function, and he took pride in that place and in his work. The factory system has broken down these ancient folkways and substituted an economic logic. It doesn't work out. It does not connect with human nature. It spreads a sense of defeat and frustration. The relay test room substituted a new set of rules for the set which had been lost. In that place, and with those girls, they worked. The girls were integrated, better balanced, and happier.

Underneath the stop watches and bonus plans of the efficiency experts, the worker is driven by a desperate inner urge to find an environment where he can take root, where he belongs and has a function; where he sees the purpose of his work and takes pride in achieving it. Failing this, he will accumulate frustrations and obsessions, and every so often break out in violent conflict. "Fatigue" and "monotony" are more effects of this frustration than causes of it.[10]

Interview Program

The results of the Relay Assembly experiments produced a considerable amount of speculation, because the behavior that was observed did not conform to the assumptions of economic rationality. The cause of this "mysterious" behavior was not completely uncovered by the Relay Assembly experiments. The second research phase in the Hawthorne experiments involved an interview program covering about 21,000 employees. This program uncovered some of the psychological and sociological variables that affect work and productivity in the factory. The depth interviews revealed that the cause of employee discontent is not confined solely to the physical environment. The following conclusions were drawn from the interview program:

1. Some complaints are subjective and cannot be treated as objective facts. They may be themselves symptoms of other problems, such as personal and social disorders.

---

[10] *Ibid.*, pp. 15–27.

2. Material goods, physical events, wages, and hours of work must be interpreted as conveyers of social value.
3. An understanding of employee grievances requires that the position or status of the employee in the social system be taken into account.
4. The meaning an employee assigns to his position depends upon the degree to which that position permits him to fulfill the social demands needed in his work.
5. The social organization represents a system of values from which the individual participant derives satisfaction or dissatisfaction on the basis of his social status and expectations.
6. The ultimate significance of work is defined by social experiences both within and outside the factory.[11]

Bank Wiring Room

The investigators concluded, however, that the interview program could not uncover the more detailed and spontaneous subtleties of the employees' social organization. In order to do this, the investigators planned an experiment which would allow them to observe and record the overt behavior of a small group of employees working in the Bank Wiring Room of the Hawthorne plant. The observer, who was instructed to act as a detached but friendly spectator, kept a daily record of individual output, quality rating, conversations, and significant events. An interview was held with each worker before the study began and twice during the course of the study for the purpose of securing information about employee attitudes, thoughts, feelings, and personal history and background. Each worker was given a physical and mental examination before the study began. The following is a summary account of the findings of this phase of the research at Hawthorne:

1. In the performance of their work the employees subscribed to a "logic" which did not always agree with the "logic" of the management or the job technology. For instance, individuals restricted output even though it meant that they could increase their earnings by producing at the standards set by management.
2. Norms or standards of behavior and attitudes with respect to output, treatment of supervisor, and interpersonal relations, were established tacitly by the group, and effective controls operated to ensure individual conformity to the norms of the social organization.
3. The social organization of the Bank Wiring Room was not cotermi-

---

[11] These conclusions are drawn from F. J. Roethlisberger and William J. Dickson, *Management and the Worker* (Cambridge, Mass.: Harvard University Press, 1939), pp. 269, 373–76.

nous with the technical organization based on occupational lines. For instance, each of the two social configurations detected in the Bank Wiring Room contained both wiremen and soldermen.

4. The social organization was based on sentiments, status, social customs, codes of behavior, and interactions. This system of relationships was not necessarily the same as the formal relationships nor did it recognize the same values. Each job had some social values ranked in a social scale that may not have coincided with the technical order of the formal organization.

5. The scores of the dexterity and intelligence tests of each worker were not related to their output.[12]

These discoveries about the behavior of men at work provided important new knowledge about the necessary preconditions for cooperation. For instance, the social behavior which develops around work routines is not necessarily an obstacle to efficiency, because it provides a setting which makes workers willing to cooperate. This does not mean necessarily that the formal and nonformal behavior coincide in terms of goals, values, structures, and processes. The existence of an informal organization within a formal organization does not *per se* have a debilitating or strengthening influence. It exists and persists, it can be identified and measured, it may overlap and conflict with the expectations of the formal organization, but above all, it cannot be ignored or treated like an extinct disease. F. J. Roethlisberger summarizes it in the following way:

. . . man at work is a social creature as well as an "economic man." He has personal and social as well as economic needs. Work provides him with a way of life as well as a means of livelihood. To understand his satisfactions and dissatisfactions at work, one must understand the social as well as the physical and economic setting in which his work takes place.[13]

CLASSIFICATION OF BEHAVIOR

Before we examine the behavior that does not conform to what is expected from the traditional prescriptions, a clarification of the meaning of formal and nonformal behavior would be helpful.

---

[12] *Ibid.*, pp. 445–46, 456, 458, and 508–10.

[13] F. J. Roethlisberger, "A 'New Look' for Management," *Worker Morale and Productivity*, General Management Series No. 141 (New York: American Management Association, 1948), p. 12.

Formal Behavior

By formal behavior we mean that behavior which is prescribed by the formal organization. Formal prescriptions about behavior include standards with respect to activities required to perform a job or task, as well as social behavior related to task performance. For instance, the task-oriented activities may involve a prescribed method of operating a machine, selling a product to a customer, performing an appendectomy on a patient, teaching typing skills to a student, and requisitioning military supplies. Some aspects of social conduct may also be required for effective job performance. For example, salesclerks may be required to engage in social pleasantries with their customers, executives and salesmen may be expected to dress in suit and tie, clergymen may be expected to engage in social contacts with the parishioners, and teachers may be required to confer with parents. The social demands of some occupations may be more important than the technical skills required for performance.

Nonformal Task—Oriented Behavior

The prescriptions concerning formal behavior may be stated explicitly in terms of policies, standards, rules, and procedures, or they may be understood and accepted tacitly.

As far as the formal organization is concerned, nonformal behavior is unintended. By this we do not want to imply that it is necessarily undesirable behavior. Like formal behavior, nonformal behavior may be task-oriented or social. An illustration of nonformal task-oriented behavior, presented previously in Chapter 1, involved one employee in the Bank Wiring Room helping another perform the required work. It was a common practice in the Bank Wiring Room. Even though "helping" was not prescribed and in fact not permitted by the company, it occurred nonetheless.

Nonformal Social Behavior

Nonformal social behavior involves any socializing on the job which is not related to work performance. For instance, employees playing games, joking, or gambling are examples of nonformal social behavior in formal organization. Informal group norms or standards, union practices, external reference group values, ethnic expectations or other cultural factors may be the bases for nonformal social behavior in formal organization.

Treating nonformal behavior as an unintended result permits us in the next section to examine behavior in terms of the dysfunctions of formal organization. By "dysfunctions" we refer to those aspects of formal organization that cause behavior which is neither intended nor anticipated.[14]

DYSFUNCTIONS OF FORMAL ORGANIZATION

Nonformal behavior may be a result of contradictions that appear in the design of traditional organization. Design features such as structure, rules and procedures, which are supposed to produce behavior that is fully oriented toward the objectives of the organization, may actually produce nonformal behavior. The very characteristics that seem to make formal organization more advantageous than unorganized activity tend to prevent human processes from following a formally prescribed pattern. In other words, there are many aspects of traditional organization which are dysfunctional. Let us be more specific with references to structural and procedural problems.

Problems of Structure

It is axiomatic that communication is an absolute necessity in organization. Decisions, for example, must be communicated to those who are to implement the decision or take the action required by the decision. Also, the decision maker, if he is to make a wise choice from available alternatives, must have enough information to know what alternatives are available and to evaluate the alternatives for selection of one or several which best accomplish objectives. Thus, there must be communication to the decision maker on which he will base his decisions, and there must be communication from the decision maker in order to implement the decisions.

---

[14] According to Robert K. Merton, unintended consequences may be functional, dysfunctional, or irrelevant to a system. See Merton's *Social Theory and Social Structure* (Glencoe, Ill.: Free Press, 1957), p. 51; and "The Unanticipated Consequences of Purposive Social Action," *American Sociological Review*, Vol. 1 (1936), pp. 894–904.

Separating the work of an organization into several specialized jobs requires a coordinating function to ensure their continued contribution to the overall task. The coordinating function creates a status relationship, with the coordinator as the superior and the specialized jobholders as subordinates. This status is in certain respects dysfunctional, because it inhibits the free flow of communication. The superior in the status relationship has two responsibilities which work at cross-purposes. On the one hand, his decision-making responsibility requires that he be adequately and correctly informed by subordinates. On the other hand, his responsibility for evaluating the performance of subordinates creates the condition whereby he will most likely get less than adequate and correct information from subordinates. The tendency under this state of affairs is to "let the boss hear only the good news." According to Hoslett, "the subordinate tends to tell his superior what the latter is interested in, not to disclose what he doesn't want to hear, and to cover up problems and mistakes which may reflect adversely on the subordinate. He tends to tell the boss those things which will enhance his position and indicate his success in meeting the problems of the day."[15] This tendency, of course, produces distortions in the upward flow of communication. Hoslett also points out that this status relationship also creates a distortion in the downward flow of communication. In his efforts to maintain the status differences, the superior is less than candid in his relationships with subordinates. He does not wish to admit mistakes or reveal conditions which would reflect adversely on his ability and judgment. "To do so would undermine his position as a superior being in the formal organization."[16]

Leon Festinger has pointed out that placing individuals into hierarchically arranged positions automatically introduces certain impediments to the free flow of communications.[17] H. H. Kelley,[18] and J. Thibaut,[19] have found through experimental research that

[15] Schuyler Dean Hoslett, "Barriers to Communication," *Personnel* (a publication of the American Management Association), Vol. 28 (September, 1951), p. 109.

[16] *Ibid.*

[17] L. Festinger, "Informal Social Communication," *Psychological Review*, Vol. 57 (1950), pp. 217–82.

[18] H. H. Kelley, "Communication in Experimentally Created Hierarchies," *Human Relations*, Vol. 4 (1951), pp. 39–56.

[19] J. Thibaut, "An Experimental Study of the Cohesiveness of Underprivileged Groups," *Human Relations*, Vol. 3 (1950), pp. 251–78.

lower level participants tend to screen upward communications selectively, especially when there is a need for a "psychological substitute" for upward advancement. Industrial research reported by W. H. Read[20] reveals that there is a relationship between the accuracy of upward communications and mobility aspirations among subordinate managers. He found support for the hypothesis that the accuracy of upward communications is related negatively to mobility aspirations. Those executives with aspirations for advancement tend to refrain from reporting anything that might hinder their advancement.

To illustrate how status differences are dysfunctional to formal organizational processes, we refer to a study of a government law enforcement agency made by Peter Blau.[21] The agency consisted of 16 agents, a supervisor, and a clerk. The principal duties of the agents were to investigate businesses to see if they violated the laws administered by the agency. The cases were assigned by the supervisor, and each agent usually worked alone on a case. In processing a case, an agent would audit the company's books, interview the employer and some employees, and if violations were found, negotiate with the employer and submit a written report to the supervisor.

Often, the agent had to make difficult legal decisions. When the agent could not solve the problems that arose in conjunction with these decisions, he was supposed to consult his supervisor. However, the supervisor evaluated the performance of agents on each case, and he also rated each agent on an annual basis. These ratings influenced an agent's chances for promotion. "Agents were therefore reluctant to expose their ignorance to the supervisor by asking him often for advice. The comment of one of them was typical: 'I try to stay away from the supervisor as much as possible. The reason is that the more often you go to the supervisor, the more you show your stupidity.' "[22] Although the agents were not permitted to consult with each other, their need for advice from someone other

---

[20] W. H. Read, "Upward Communication in Industrial Hierarchies," *Human Relations*, Vol. 15, No. 1 (1962), pp. 3–15.

[21] Peter M. Blau, "Patterns of Interaction Among a Group of Officials in a Government Agency," *Human Relations*, Vol. 7, No. 3 (1954), pp. 337–48. For similar cases involving dysfunctions, see Peter M. Blau, *The Dynamics of Bureaucracy* (Chicago: University of Chicago Press, 1955), pp. 33–48; and V. F. Ridgeway, "Dysfunctional Consequences of Performance Measurements," *Administrative Science Quarterly*, Vol. 1, No. 2 (1956), pp. 240–47.

[22] *Ibid.*, p. 338.

than the supervisor induced them to ignore this rule. "All agents, including the most competent ones, often discussed their problems with colleagues."[23] In other words, they used unofficial channels of communications to fulfill the needs of the decision process. This is nonformal task-oriented behavior that was forbidden by the formal organization.

Zaleznik reports similar results in his study of a machine shop.[24] He reports that machine operators would go to machinists for help more often than to foremen, especially if the workers felt that they were being evaluated by the foremen on ability to do the job. "An operator therefore will tend to feel that too many requests for help addressed to the foreman may imply that he, the operator, does not know his work."[25]

Status differences are necessary for coordination, but they inhibit the free flow of communication. Less than adequate and correct information means that formal organizational processes are inadequate and must be supplemented by unofficial processes for the accomplishment of organizational objectives. It is interesting to note that in the government agency study, Blau states that the unofficial processes followed by agents reduced their anxieties about making correct decisions and, therefore, improved their performance. Also, the fact that group members frequently consulted with each other made the group more cohesive. Moreover, and most important for the decision process, the use of unofficial channels made more information and advice available to the decision maker and generally improved decision making. In this case, nonformal task-oriented behavior appeared to be beneficial to the formal organization.

Rules and Work Processes

The formal organization has an action orientation, i.e., certain work must be performed to accomplish its objectives. After the work has been broken up into individual tasks or jobs, work processes are usually specified in some sort of operating procedure. At the operating levels of an organization, there may be a high degree

[23] *Ibid.*

[24] Abraham Zaleznik, *Worker Satisfaction and Development* (Boston: Graduate School of Business Administration, Harvard University, 1956), p. 37.

[25] *Ibid.*, p. 37.

of specificity in operating procedures, depending on the nature of the job and its relation to equipment used in the work process. Jobs that are highly specialized or involve a great deal of machine processing will be closely defined in content and process. The activities of a machine operator involved in an assembly-line operation, for example, will be circumscribed by the movements required to operate the machine and to "keep up" with the assembly line. Furthermore, time and motion studies may result in even greater circumscription of movements. In order to avoid wasted time and motions, a job may be defined and the worker trained so that efforts are reduced to a minimum. Thus, the worker may get instructions on proper body movements in walking, carrying, lifting, grasping, and turning.

At the administrative level of an organization, procedures may be less confining, but nonetheless they exist and are necessary to ensure effective completion of the overall task. Thus, instructions will specify the manner in which customers' orders, production schedules, shipping schedules, invoices, budgets, blueprints, payrolls, and collective bargaining agreements are prepared and processed. The obvious purpose of organizational procedures is to standardize work processes and to ensure that all necessary work is done correctly. The reduction of work processes to standard practice allows the organization to enjoy the benefits of specialization and facilitates the coordination of specialized activities. Standard practice means, of course, that a job can be done in the same manner over and over again, and the routine nature of the job allows the worker to be very productive. Standard practice also facilitates coodination, because standardization of individual jobs allows other jobs to be complementary and eventually build toward the overall task.

Formal rules and procedures, however, are dysfunctional with respect to work processes for a number of reasons. They may fail to cover the complete task; they may not be applicable to all situations of the job; they may conflict with other procedures or orders from administrators; and they may not specify the best way of performing a task. In some cases, the individual has to exercise his own inventiveness and work out a way to complete the task or to cope with situations not covered by instructions. In other cases, organization members may even develop better ways of meeting job requirements than those specified by instructions. In all these cases,

the people involved may still meet the requirements of formal organization or even produce better results than the formal requirements, but they may perform their tasks in unofficial ways.[26] It is,
of course, possible that nonformal activity may have results which
are not directed to the goals of the organization.

In order to illustrate nonformal task-oriented behavior, we draw
from a study by Ralph Turner, which deals with the job of a Navy
disbursing officer.[27]

Most of the clients of the disbursing officer are enlisted men and
are, therefore, of lesser rank. However, many of his clients are
officers of senior rank, and the disbursing officer finds that orders
from superiors often conflict with military regulations governing
the disbursement of funds. While the regulations give the disbursing officer enough authority to defy superiors who make illegal or
questionable demands, it is not in his best personal interest to
follow such a practice. A commanding officer is not accustomed to
having his orders questioned, and when he issues an order for the
disbursement of funds he expects compliance. Ordinarily, in business, government, and even military institutions, an order from a
superior officer supersedes existing regulations, and a subordinate
is relieved from personal responsibility if the order causes him to
violate regulations. However, the disbursing officer does not have
this way out; he is personally accountable and financially liable for
his actions regardless of orders. If the disbursing officer cannot
resolve a conflict between an order and a regulation, the Navy
allows two alternatives. The matter may be forwarded to the Bureau of Supplies and Accounts or referred to the commanding officer,
who may order the disbursing officer to make the expenditure "under protest," whereby the commanding officer assumes full responsibility. The first method takes several months of processing, and
senior officers are often unwilling to wait that long. The second
method can be even more disastrous because of the apparent affront-
ery to the commanding officer. Turner reports that a disbursing
officer is very reluctant to use either method, because it leaves him
in poor standing with senior officers and his career could be ruined
by the commanding officer who makes out "fitness reports" and can

---

[26] Robert Dubin, *The World of Work* (Englewood Cliffs, N.J.: Prentice Hall,
Inc., 1959), pp. 67–70.

[27] Ralph H. Turner, "The Navy Disbursing Officer as a Bureaucrat," *American Sociological Review*, Vol. 12 (June, 1947), pp. 342–48.

assign the disbursing officer to all kinds of undesirable military duties. This case illustrates a situation in which an official of an organization must behave in a nonformal manner in order to perform his job.

Informal Pressures

The person occupying a particular position may also be subject to informal pressures which conflict with formal procedures. The disbursing officer, for example, is subject to pressures of informal organization. The disbursing officer belongs to the same informal organization as some of his clients. This is especially true aboard ship, where within the confines of a vessel, a small group of officers live, work, and play poker together. "Say, 'Pay,' I sure could use about twenty dollars before payday," or, "Isn't there some way I can get flight pay this month?" is the sort of appeals which come constantly from friends. As a human being the disbursing officer wants to help his friends, and the penalty for brusque disposal of such requests may be social ostracism.[28] Another type of informal pressure is simulated friendship, whereby a superior officer will treat the lower ranking disbursing officer as an equal by taking him into confidence on personal and organizational matters. The purpose, of course, is to gain favors from the disbursing officer.

Still another type of informal pressure is the exchange system. The officer who assigns staterooms, for example, finds it easy to get extra food from the galley. In exchange for hard-to-get supplies, the supply officer can expect special favors from officers. "Such exchanges are not usually verbalized as such among officers, but the officer who does another a favor has no doubt that it will be returned. The exchange structures extend so far that it is often difficult for a man to secure those services and equipment which are essential to his job unless he can promise some return."[29] In effect, the exchange system means preferential treatment for those who are able to reciprocate with favors. The disbursing officer is able to grant favors by rendering unusually prompt and careful attention to the business of clients.

Under these kinds of pressures, the realistic and most common type of disbursing officer gives regulations secondary importance.

---

[28] *Ibid.*, p. 345.
[29] *Ibid.*, p. 346.

He thrives on the ambiguity of regulations, applying a constraining interpretation to those who do not rate in the informal structure, and for those of importance he is an expert on "loopholes."

Many conscientious disbursing officers turn to unofficial practices because of obvious injustices in regulations. They find that many claims are payable within the intent of regulations, but payment is not possible because one or several of the many specifications in the regulation raises some technicality that cannot be met. "Differential treatment of clients on this basis is hard to maintain, so the officer soon finds himself giving such aid without reference to justification, or more frequently, under varying pressures and moods, wavering between a regulation attitude and an opportunistic attitude."[30]

Line and Staff Conflicts

Line authority usually describes a relationship whereby one person directly commands the activities of another or others in an organization. Thus, an official who makes work assignments, delegates authority, and supervises the work of others has line authority. Staff authority usually describes a relationship whereby one person indirectly influences the work of another or others in an organization. Thus, an official who advises, recommends, and makes suggestions to others has staff authority. The receiver of these influences is obliged to carry out the directions received in a line relationship, but he may accept or reject the advice or suggestions received in a staff relationship. In our discussions we shall often make reference to line and staff departments and line and staff officials. However, these distinctions are for convenience, and it should be recognized that executives of an organization usually have both line and staff authority. For example, in addition to their command authority, line officials may render advisory services when they are members of committees which make recommendations to superior executives or when they give advice to other line officials. Also, staff department heads, in addition to their advisory functions, exercise line authority over subordinates in their own departments. In summary, then, any references to line and staff indicates an authority relationship. Line authority describes a command relationship, and staff authority describes an advisory rela-

---

[30] *Ibid.*, p. 348.

tionship. References to line officials and departments mean that the officials or departments *predominantly* exercise command authority. References to staff officials and departments mean that the officials or departments *predominantly* exercise advisory authority.

According to traditional theory and practice, staff departments are supposed to assist line executives in work that requires technical knowledge and detailed attention. The staff department is supposed to remain advisory, but it usually develops into a line capacity with both the higher and lower elements of the organizational hierarchy. Staff specialists become "experts" in their specialty, and

FIGURE 5-1

Development of Line and Staff Authority

CONDITION I—SIMPLE LINE ORGANIZATION

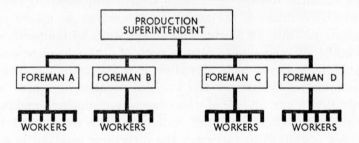

CONDITION II—LINE AND STAFF ORGANIZATION

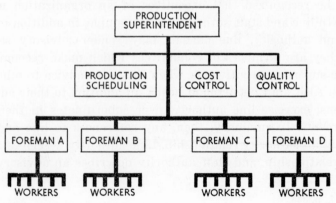

FIGURE 5–1 (Continued)

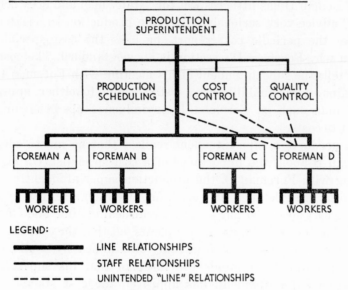

CONDITION III– LINE, STAFF, AND UNINTENDED RELATIONSHIPS

top-management officials rely on them for "authoritative" advice. As lower management officials realize that staff recommendations are backed by top management, a line of command is established that covers a particular aspect of the work. Let us illustrate this condition by diagramming a hypothetical production department, shown in Figure 5–1.

Under Condition I, we see a simple line arrangement with all foremen reporting directly to the production superintendent on all matters. The superintendent finds that there are some problem areas that need detailed attention and constant study. He separates the problem areas into production scheduling, cost control, and quality control. He then proceeds to establish staff positions in each area and hires specialists for the new positions. The new line and staff structure is shown as Condition II of Figure 5–1. He instructs the specialists to study their respective problem areas intensively and to submit recommendations to him. After careful study and discussion, the production superintendent accepts the recommendations and issues the appropriate orders for implementation.

After some time under the new methods and standards, the cost control specialist notices that Foreman D's section has been incurring costs that are substantially above standard. In his discussion with Foreman D about the discrepancy, the cost specialist realizes that Foreman D has little respect for "staff" men and does not take "staff" advice very seriously. After the production superintendent receives the periodic cost report, he asks the cost specialist to explain why Foreman D's section is above standard. The cost specialist tells the superintendent of his meeting with Foreman D and complains of his inability as a "staff" man to either impress a "line" man such as Foreman D or influence his behavior with respect to costs.

The production superintendent realizes that he must "educate" Foreman D about the importance of a cost specialist. On his next meeting with Foreman D, the production superintendent explains why costs need detailed and constant attention. He also explains that the cost specialist has spent a great deal of time and effort on developing the cost standards. He points out that the cost specialist is an expert on costs and that he relies on him heavily in all matters involving costs. He reminds the foreman that his superior, the production superintendent, has approved the cost standards for implementation and ends the conversation by telling the foreman "to get his costs in line with standard." With this backing, the cost specialist finds on his next meeting with Foreman D that he is given preferential treatment and his suggestions are given very careful attention. As soon as he learned that the superintendent relied on the cost specialist as an authority and gave full support to the new cost standards, the foreman no longer treated the specialist as a "staff" man but as a man in authority on matters of cost. After similar experiences with the other staff men, Foreman D would find himself in a relationship with each specialist, as shown in Condition III of Figure 5–1. The broken lines are unintended "line" relationships.[31] Although they may not be shown on the official organization chart, these unintended "line" relationships may also exist between the other foremen and staff specialists.

A formal structure with a line and staff arrangement has certain dysfunctional aspects because it suffers from two false assumptions: (1) that staff specialists are able and willing to operate without formal authority, and (2) that their advice and suggestions will readily be accepted and applied by lower line officials.

---

[31] When this line relationship is intended, it is labeled as "functional authority" in traditional theory.

Under the true line and staff arrangement, the staff officer finds he has little power. His advice may go unheeded and unheralded because he has no authority to implement his decisions in the organization. The lower line officers may resent and reject staff advice because it threatens the sacred position of the line. Melville Dalton, after a study of three industrial plants, concluded that line officers fear staff innovation for a number of reasons:

> In view of their longer experience, presumably intimate knowledge of the work, and their greater remuneration, they fear being "shown up" before their line superiors for not having thought of the processual refinements themselves. They fear that changes in methods may bring personnel changes . . . and quite possibly reduce their area of authority. Finally, changes in techniques may expose forbidden practices and departmental inefficiency.[32]

These frustrations may lead to a power struggle. The staff officer may seek more authority by reporting his frustrations and criticisms of line operations to higher line officials. Evidence indicates that staff officers, by virtue of their specialized knowledge, their continual contact with top management, and better education, are able frequently to gain from top management the necessary authority over line operations. Eventually, the acceptance of staff recommendations and suggestions by lower management officials as authoritative and representative of the views of higher management tends to create an order that is quite different from the prescribed formal relations between line and staff and is often more representative of the real working relationships of the group. The consequences are unintended but real.

POWER STRUGGLES

To have meaning, a decision must be followed by action. A decision that cannot be put into action has little value to an organization.[33] The most obvious consideration in this regard is the question of *feasibility*. If the organization does not have, or cannot acquire,

---

[32] Melville Dalton, "Conflicts Between Staff and Line Management Officers," *American Sociological Review*, Vol. 15 (June, 1959), p. 349.

[33] Of course, there is the decision that calls for no action, such as a decision to do nothing. However, we treat this kind of a decision as a special case and deal only with action-oriented decisions. Decisions that do not involve action, therefore, are ruled out of our discussion. A judgment that a work of art is beautiful, for example, does not fall within our definition of a decision.

the resources required by a decision, the decision cannot be put into action and, therefore, is of no value to the organization other than to reveal the impracticality of the course of action selected.

Another important consideration is the *formal authority* to implement decisions. Formal authority means that the person who possesses it has permission to commit some of the resources of the organization. Strictly speaking, if a decision maker does not have the formal authority to bring about the action required by his decision, the decision is of no value. For example, one of the authors could decide that the Empire State Building be destroyed. Without the formal authority that would come from unrestricted ownership, the action required by the decision could not be legally realized.

The existence of formal authority does not necessarily mean that the decision maker is able to initiate action. Through his formal authority, he may be able to commit an organization's resources, make commands, and delegate authority, but still be unable to gain the cooperation of other members of the organization. His proposed actions may be opposed by leaders of the union or of the informal organization, who might instruct members to refuse to carry out the decision. In this case, the decision maker has the necessary authority but not the *power* to implement the decision.

Chapter 7 is devoted to the concept of power. At this point, power is defined simply as an ability to get things done or to bring about the action required in a decision. It is evident from our previous illustrations that much of the work of organizations is done unofficially or without formal authority. In other words, some people in organizations have more power than authority. In any event, power is necessary to implement decisions. Important for our discussion at this juncture is the fact that people in organizations compete for power. To illustrate power struggles in an organization, we have selected a study by Melville Dalton which was concerned with a company of 8,000 employees called the Milo Fractionating Center.[34]

The Milo Study

Milo, a manufacturing plant, was under the direct control of a central headquarters called the Office. In the formal organization,

---

[34] Melville Dalton, *Men Who Manage* (New York: John Wiley & Sons, Inc., 1961). The names of the company and personnel are fictitious.

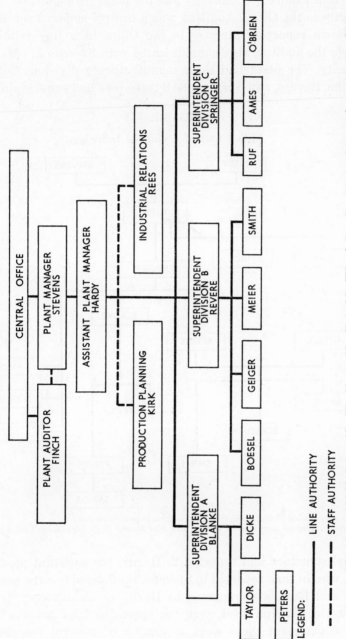

FIGURE 5–2

Milo Formal Chart Simplified

LEGEND: ——————— LINE AUTHORITY
        – – – – – – STAFF AUTHORITY

SOURCE: Adapted from Melville Dalton, *Men Who Manage* (New York: John Wiley & Sons, Inc., 1961), pullout page between pp. 10 and 11.

shown in Figure 5–2, Stevens was the plant manager and reported directly to the Office. Auditing was a control agency over Milo and is shown reporting directly to the Office in a line relationship. Finch, the auditor, also communicated with Stevens in an advisory capacity. The plant had three manufacturing divisions headed by Blanke, Revere, and Springer. All three men had equal status in the

FIGURE 5–3

Milo Chart of Unofficial Influence*

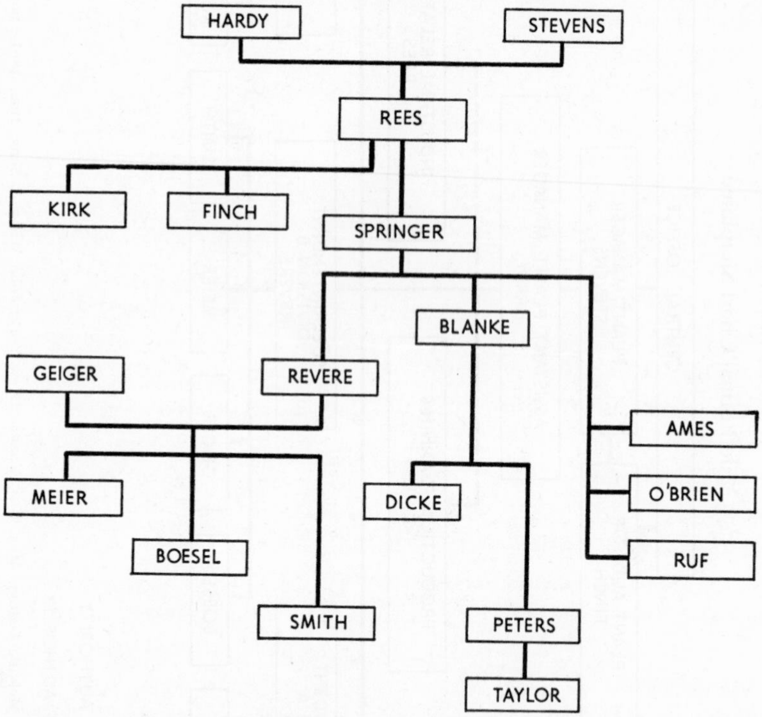

* Relative vertical position on chart indicates status in power structure.
Source: Adapted from Melville Dalton, *Men Who Manage* (New York: John Wiley & Sons, Inc., 1961), p. 22.

formal structure and reported to Hardy, the assistant plant manager, who in turn reported to Stevens. Staff departments, headed by Kirk and Rees, also reported to Hardy in an advisory capacity. Below the division level were the operating departments, and in each department there were a number of general foremen. For example, Taylor and Dicke were department heads in Division A, and Peters was a general foreman. There were many more general foremen, staff offices, and departments than the number shown in

Figure 5–2. However, the number shown is enough to illustrate power struggles.

Dalton found that the people at Milo did not operate according to the formal structure shown in Figure 5–2. Actual working relationships at Milo displayed the order shown in Figure 5–3. Power struggles played an important part in determining the unofficial organization at Milo.

Hardy and Stevens. In the unofficial pattern of relations, Hardy, the assistant plant manager, was placed on an equal level with Stevens, the plant manager. An examination of organizational processes clearly showed Hardy as the dominant executive. This relationship was especially evident during executive meetings. "Appearing nervous and worried, Stevens usually opened meetings with a few remarks and then silently gave way to Hardy who dominated thereafter. During the meeting most questions were directed to Hardy. While courteous, Hardy's statements usually were made without request for confirmation from Stevens."[35] At executive luncheons, Hardy usually dominated the conversations and was the target of questions. Hardy's approval, not Stevens', was considered indispensable to the more important promotions. During breakdowns and emergency stops, supervisors expressed concern over the ire of Hardy rather than Stevens. Even production employees referred to Hardy as the "master" and Stevens as his "dog."

Socially, Stevens was called a "lone wolf," and was considered "unsocial and distant." While Stevens was inactive in community affairs, Hardy was very active and was considered to be a "social lion." Hardy was under 40 and, like most Milo managers, was a member of the Masonic Order. Stevens, on the other hand, was past 60 and a rejected non-Mason. In contrast to Stevens, Hardy came up through the ranks, having served as division and department head. These qualities gave Hardy intimate knowledge of, and enabled him to have close relations with, his associates; all of which placed him in the dominant power position in the plant.

Rees. As the staff head of industrial relations, Rees was supposedly in an advisory capacity. However, he occupied a very prominent position in the unofficial order primarily because he was sent from the Office to strengthen the department. Rees's power position may be illustrated with reference to a meeting which was

---

[35] *Ibid.,* p. 23.

called to discuss the problem of whether or not to install an incentive system on maintenance work. At the meeting, Hardy stated his opposition to the use of incentives and concluded that Milo should stop using incentives because they caused too much trouble and cost too much. Rees arose and said:

> I agree that maintenance incentives caused a lot of trouble. But I don't think it's because they're not useful. It's because there are too many people not willing to toe the mark and give them a try. The [Office] put that system in here and by God we're going to make it work, not just tolerate it.[36]

This and other incidents led Milo executives to view Rees as the unofficial spokesman of the Office. Several executives stated their belief that Rees had powerful ties with the Office and to oppose him would be "suicide."

Although Rees overpowered Hardy on the matter of incentives, Hardy still placed above Rees in the unofficial organization because he exercised more influence in the overall affairs of Milo. In actual practice, then, Hardy exercised more than his formal authority in all organizational processes, except in the area of industrial relations. Rees dominated in matters of industrial relations, and in this sphere, Hardy exercised less than his formal authority. As unofficial spokesman for the Office, Rees served as the connecting link between Finch (the auditor), and the Office. Milo executives noticed that Finch and Kirk worked very closely with Rees, and these three were the only staff executives to sit with Hardy and Stevens during lunch in the cafeteria. In the unofficial chart, therefore, Finch and Kirk are shown reporting to Rees.

Division Heads. Officially, Blanke, Revere, and Springer were the division heads and supposedly had equal status in the Milo organization. However, Springer, head of Division C, placed above the other division heads, just below Rees in the unofficial power structure. Before his appointment as division head, Springer spent four years in the Office, after which he was assigned to Division B as a processing superintendent. Hardy was the head of Division B at the time, and he and Springer worked very closely together in gaining favors from the former plant chief. From this close working relationship, Hardy and Springer developed a strong social relationship. This social relationship persisted even after Hardy was

---

[36] *Ibid.*, p. 25.

promoted to assistant plant manager and Springer was promoted to the head of Division C. Blanke and Revere knew of the relationship between Hardy and Springer, and before approaching Hardy for important favors, they first conferred with Springer. In the unofficial structure, therefore, Springer placed first below Rees and above Blanke and Revere.

Revere, who was 59 years old, was the least influential of the division heads. Revere was a widower with married children and no longer wished to become deeply involved in plant affairs. In fact, he had been reluctant to accept the promotion from department to division head. He did not want the additional responsibility, but Hardy had decided that Revere was the best candidate for the job and forced him to choose between the promotion and early retirement. Forty-two-year-old Geiger, who officially was subordinate to Revere, appeared in the unofficial structure on an equal level with the division head. Part of Geiger's power was attributed to the fact that he headed the major production unit in the division. Also, Geiger, who was born in Germany, received the full support of Boesel and Meir, both of whom were of German descent. Moreover, Geiger had given Blanke full support from below in the latter's bid for division head, which undoubtedly proved important in Geiger's bid for power. Blanke and Dicke were also of German extraction, and all five men were referred to by some as "Nazis" during World War II. Although the charges were unfounded, it revealed the ethnic consciousness in the organization. The German ethnics were partly responsible for the power structure of both Divisions A and B.

Analysis

Dalton explains the power relations at Milo in terms of the personalities of the executive personnel. He states that the existence of unofficial power positions "creates a pressure on the formal framework to accelerate new positions and reassignments beyond the 'normal' rate of promotion and retirement."[37] The men with power, promote, reorganize, and make the necessary adjustments in organizational processes to meet changing conditions, and it was these men who made the organization a dynamic, going concern.

[37] *Ibid.*, p. 30.

"To them rules and procedures are not sacred guides but working tools to be revised, ignored, or dropped, as required in striking balances between company goals on one side, and their personal ends and the claims of their supporters on the other."[38] The power of men like Hardy, Blanke, Geiger, and Ames is attributable to their individual drive, initiative, and executive abilities beyond just meeting official directives. These attributes were not characteristic of men with little power.

Although Rees's power stemmed principally from his role as unofficial spokesman of the Office, he, along with Hardy, Blanke, Geiger, Ames, Springer, Peters, Meir, Dicke, and Boesel, was skillful in forming informal power alliances, not for intrigue, but for the purpose of "dealing with situations too urgent and dynamic for formal handling."[39] At one time or another, all of these men used more authority than was formally assigned to them, and they displayed organizational behavior that was above and beyond the scope of their formally assigned jobs. There were other men, namely, Taylor, Revere, and Smith, who were not able to fill the requirements of their formal tasks. They were also unable or unwilling to form informal alliances and, therefore, were ineffective in bringing about official action of any importance.

The personality characteristics attributable to age differences were also factors in the power struggles at Milo. The older executives were less prone to take chances and accept changes. The younger executives, who were more willing to take chances and who were more flexible, were most successful in the power struggle and eventually exercised the greatest influence at Milo. The most influencial executives—Hardy, Dicke, Meir, Ruf, Geiger, Ames, Springer, Blanke, and Peters averaged 42.2 years, while the least influencial executives—Revere, Stevens, Taylor, and Smith averaged 55.5 years of age.

SUMMARY

In this chapter, nonformal behavior in organization is explored with the view of further illustrating the inadequacy of traditional model. The examples of organizational dysfunctions presented in this chapter reveal that some organizational elements, for example,

---

[38] *Ibid.*

[39] *Ibid.*

hierarchical structure, rules and work processes, and differentiation of line and staff authority themselves are causes of nonformal behavior. We point out that nonformal behavior may be task-oriented or social, and it need not necessarily be considered undesirable.

Some examples reveal that nonformal behavior is necessary in order to perform a task successfully. However, in many cases, organizational dysfunctions create frustrations which lead to power struggles. It is evident from the examples presented that a considerable amount of the work of organization is done unofficially or without formal authority. Power relations develop in such an environment. Some people in organizations have more power than, while others have less power than, and still others have power equal to their delegated authority.

It is evident from the discussions in this chapter that nonformal behavior is a fact of life in formal organization. It is evident, also, that these types of behavior cannot and should not be ignored. Social and power behavior, as well as formal behavior, are essential elements to the accomplishment of organizational goals. The next three chapters present more intensive treatment of these behavior elements. They are classified and placed in perspective to the total system of formal organization. Chapter 6 deals with social behavior.

DISCUSSION QUESTIONS AND PROBLEMS

5-1. Try to outline or detail a description of that "mysterious something."

5-2. What made the Hawthorne experiments so important for the study of formal organization?

5-3. Since many of the traditional features of formal organization are dysfunctional, does this mean that they should be abolished or disregarded? Explain.

5-4. Is it legitimate for an organization to expect its members to perform successfully in situations not anticipated by rules and procedures? Explain.

5-5. How do the dysfunctions of organization affect the delegation of authority? Do you think it is possible to avoid these problems? Explain.

5-6. What pressures encourage individuals to violate the chain of command? Do you think these reasons are valid, or are they merely a reflection of human desire for disobedience? Explain.

5–7. Discuss the problems associated with dichotomizing between line and staff authority.

5–8. A performance appraisal program designed to evaluate and, hence, reward employees according to their contribution is generally considered desirable. What are some of the organizational problems that might arise in implementing an employee appraisal plan?

5–9. Illustrate with some examples from personal experience what is meant by nonformal task-oriented behavior and nonformal social behavior.

5–10. Is unintended nonformal behavior undesirable? Illustrate some cases in which it is beneficial to the organization, to the individual, and to both.

5–11. One of the Nittany Company rules is that all personnel who drive their cars to work must park them in an assigned area. Any violations to this rule are subject to a fine. Mr. Gregg, a foreman on one of the assembly lines occasionally would drive his car to the company's personnel office and park it illegally. He did this usually when he wanted to obtain personnel records quickly. On one such occasion, the violation was detected and Mr. Gregg was fined $5. Mr. Gregg protested to his superior, who replied that "those are the rules of the game and no one is excluded." Mr. Gregg paid the fine and he ceased his practice of parking illegally. Thereafter, when he needed personnel records he relied on the company's interdepartmental mail, even though the mail did not serve his needs for obtaining information quickly.

What do you think of the result of this incident? What would you have done if you were Mr. Gregg? What would you have done if you were Mr. Gregg's superior? What organizational arrangements might be made to solve this type of problem?

5–12. Based on time study standards established by the engineering department, each member of the floor maintenance crew of the Midtown Hospital is expected to keep a specified area of floor space clean. This involved sweeping the floor every day and mopping the floor once every three days.

The nurses on the second floor have complained to the head nurse that the floor is not clean, and on some occasions the nurses have swept the floor in their area. The head nurse has complained repeatedly to the supervisor of the maintenance department, but no corrective action has been taken.

If you were in charge of the nursing department, what would you do? What would you do if you were in charge of the maintenance department? Should the maintenance department be classified orzationally as a division of the nursing department? Why?

SOCIAL ORGANIZATION
AND BEHAVIOR

There are two well-accepted beliefs about social organization and behavior in formal organization. First, there is the belief that social behavior and social organization always exist in formal organization. This belief has been well supported by empirical evidence. It seems that whenever men associate on a continuous basis, they interact, develop and express sentiments toward each other, and engage in activities that are different from, or in addition to, activities required by job specifications. Second, it is believed that social organization provides the basis for cooperative behavior. It stimulates men to cooperate because it fulfills a basic human need to associate on a social basis. It is as Roethlisberger has said ". . . a product of man's inherent desire for continuous intimate association."[1] Informal groups, according to this same author, ". . . give people a place, a feeling of 'belonging,' and a sense of importance. They make people feel that they command respect, have the power of independent choice, and are not just cogs in a machine." Similarly, Chester Barnard has said that social interactions ". . . are consequences of cooperation, and constitute one set of social factors

---

[1] F. J. Roethlisberger, "A 'New Look' for Management," *Worker Morale and Productivity*, General Management Series No. 141 (New York: American Management Association, 1948), p. 13.

involved in cooperation."[2] The social organization, then, plays a most important role in any cooperative enterprise. It is the purpose of this chapter to examine this phenomenon in depth and to present some techniques for analyzing social behavior in formal organization.

In Chapter 5, we included some extensive descriptions of the research at the Hawthorne plant of the Western Electric Company. The conclusions of the researchers may be summarized as follows: (1) Workers do not act as isolated individuals, but rather *there is a natural camaraderie with fellow workers.* (2) *Workers do not behave on the basis of logical or systematic thinking.* This became increasingly evident to the researchers as the research approach at Hawthorne changed from the experimentally controlled conditions of the Relay Assembly Test Room to the investigation of group behavior in the actual operations of the Bank Wiring Observation Room. The latter study revealed that the work group under observation developed some uniform behavior patterns that did not coincide with the behavior prescribed by the job requirements. The social relations observed in this study followed a pattern of conduct which revealed an organization within the formal structure of relations. This was labeled by the researchers as an informal organization.

In this text, the terms "social organization" and "informal organization" are used interchangeably. The use of the term "informal" in place of "social" does not imply that social organization has no form. Social organization does in fact have form, even if it is relatively fluid and subject to change. While "social organization" is more descriptive, the term "informal organization" is used more frequently in the literature.

CHARACTERISTICS OF INFORMAL ORGANIZATION

In order to dramatize the nature of informal organization, we make a somewhat artificial comparison between it and the technical part of formal organization. We say artificial because it is virtually impossible to distinguish between formal and social behavior in formal organization. While most of the relationships in the two systems are overlapping and difficult to separate, it is important to

---

[2] Chester I. Barnard, *The Functions of the Executive* (Cambridge, Mass.: Harvard University Press, 1956), p. 41.

understand the factors that enter into the social inclinations of people in formal organization. Thus, the arbitrary distinction is made in order to advance toward our goals of understanding and analysis.

As described previously, formal organization has technical requirements which arise from its explicit goals. The goals require the performance of a certain amount of work. Men are assigned to specific jobs to perform this work. There is usually a design which relates men and jobs in a formal hierarchy of authority. Social organization does not arise as a result of design or deliberation, but it evolves naturally whenever men interact with each other over extended periods of time. While the formal organization is a means to an end, the social organization is important to members for its own sake, that is, it fulfills a basic need for human association.

The social organization is like the formal organization in that it attempts to regulate behavior. The codes of behavior and customs of the social organization are based on mores and shared beliefs, while the rules and regulations of the formal organization are based on the need for efficiency. Members of the social organization, for example, may share the belief that job security is important. To protect their jobs they might resist a change (even though it offers greater rewards) to more efficient laborsaving methods by restricting output. Both types of organization have standards or norms of conduct, and enforcement methods called sanctions. The norms of both may range from a definitive specification of output to what is acceptable moral behavior. Drunkenness, stealing, and fighting may be unacceptable to both systems. Of course, there is some behavior which is acceptable to one and not the other, and there are different degrees of acceptability in acts considered offensive. The organizations differ in the sanctions levied against offenders. Members of the social group might ostracize an offender, give him the "silent treatment," or refuse to help him in his work assignments. Formal sanctions might take the form of a transfer, demotion, reprimand, or complete dismissal. Sanctions of the social group are usually social in nature, while the formal group tends to exercise economic sanctions. Both can be very effective.

The status structure of the social organization is determined by the feelings or sentiments that members of a group have for each other. Thus, one member may become the leader because he is the most popular, the most respected, or the most liked by the other members of a group. The sentimental structure of the social organization is not characteristic of the formal structure. Generally, men hold status in the formal structure because of their skills, abilities, and experience. Status in the formal organization is determined by the position or responsibilities of a job rather than by sentiments. Likewise, authority in the formal organization stems from a position held or a work assignment and is delegated from some higher authority. Informal authority, on the other hand, is given by those who are its subjects. It is based on sentiments and attaches to a person rather than a position or job assignment.

Status and Role

In the technical part of formal organization, we define *status* as the relative position of a job, and it is independent of the person who holds a job. The job defines the rights and duties and is ranked or has a given status in the hierarchy of formal organization by some scale of values such as job importance. The status of an individual in an organization is dependent upon his position. His importance to the organization is dependent upon the relative importance of his job. The rights and duties of a job and its status are static as prescribed by the technical system, while role represents the dynamic aspects of a status, or as Ralph Linton explained: "When he puts the rights and duties which constitute status into effect, he is performing a role."[3] More specifically, a *role* can be defined as the actual deeds performed by a person in a position.[4] When a person carries out the duties or performs the tasks of his assigned job, he is playing a *technical role*. These deeds may involve physical actions such as manual labor or mental activities such as decision making. Some sociologists include in the definition of role the pattern of attitudes which a person exhibits in a social situa-

---

[3] See Ralph Linton, *The Study of Man* (New York: D. Appleton-Century Co., 1936), p. 113. Copyright, 1936, by D. Appleton-Century Co., Inc. Reprinted by permission of Appleton-Century-Crafts.

[4] Although this definition may appear to be specific, we recognize that the role concept is relatively vague. For a survey of the various meanings of this concept, see L. J. Nieman and J. W. Hughes, "The Problem of the Concept of Role—A Re-Survey of the Literature," *Social Forces*, Vol. 30 (1951), pp. 141–49.

tion.[5] In the real world the fact that status and role cannot be defined clearly serves to emphasize their inseparability. Linton concluded that: "Role and status are quite inseparable. . . . There are no roles without statuses or statuses without roles."[6]

When a person engages in social activities in addition to, or unintended by, the formal requirements of a job, he is playing a *social role*. As indicated earlier, social organization has a status structure based on differential sentiments and feelings of its members toward each other. In contrast to formal status, then, social status is dependent upon the attributes of a person. Thus, in addition to playing more than one role a person may hold a status position in the social system as well as in the technical system of formal organization.[7]

The informal organization, much like formal organization, can be characterized by structure and processes. The processes which characterize the informal organization are social activities, interactions, and sentiments.[8]

Social Processes

The element *activity* involves the physical movements and actions of man, or according to George Homans it "refers to things that people do: work on the physical environment, with implements and with other persons."[9] The following, for example, describe actions of people: walk, lecture, drill a hole, write a report, punch out, and decides. This concept can be used to describe a wide range of human actions and it also lends itself to measurement. For instance, the number of holes that a worker drills can be measured, or it is also possible to measure drilling activities in relative terms of input to output units.

---

[5] The following represent some of the developments of role along these lines: George H. Mead, *Mind, Self and Society* (Chicago: University of Chicago Press, 1934); and R. E. Park and E. W. Burgess, *Introduction to the Science of Society* (2nd ed.; Chicago: University of Chicago Press, 1924).

[6] Ralph Linton, *op. cit.*, p. 114. The coincidence of statuses and roles is also stressed by E. Wight Bakke in *The Fusion Process* (New Haven, Conn.: Labor and Management Center, Yale University, 1953).

[7] In the next chapter, we extend this statement to include power systems.

[8] We are indebted to George C. Homans for these fundamental concepts of behavior. See his *The Human Group* (New York: Harcourt, Brace & World, Inc., 1950), chap. ii.

[9] *Ibid.*, p. 34.

Interaction is an element which refers to a contact between two or more people. While action may be occuring during an interaction between two or more people, the concept of interaction is confined to the contacts between people. For instance, if Bill is talking to John, who is listening, the actions occurring are talking and listening, but there is also a contact between Bill and John which we can call an interaction. Interactions lend themselves to measurement in terms of the *direction* of interactions, the *frequency* of interactions, the *length* of an interaction, the *type* of interaction, the *content* of interaction. Interactions need not be confined to oral or written messages. Interactions can occur by any means that involves the passing of a message between people, for instance, a look, a frown, hand and body motions. Note that this concept does not mean that an interaction requires understanding between two or more people.

Formal communications usually follow a path which is defined clearly by the chain of command, but social communications flow through an informal channel. This informal network is known commonly as the "grapevine" or the "rumor mill."

These terms carry the connotation that the social communications network is not well defined, that it is circuitous like the stems of a grapevine, and that the information conveyed is false, distorted, and not selective. Some of these connotations stem partly from the results of laboratory and classroom experiments. However, evidence uncovered in field research studies[10] reveals that the grapevine operates quickly, selectively, and along well-defined paths. The information conveyed has a high degree of veracity which does not decline noticeably in the transmission process. According to Caplow, distortion of information is minimized as the channels are solidified and persons known to distort messages are excluded from the network.[11]

Sentiments, according to Homans, refer to "internal states of the human body,"[12] which are usually identified as beliefs, ideas, or

---

[10] Theodore Caplow, "Rumors in War," *Social Forces,* Vol. 25 (October, 1946–May, 1947), pp. 298–302; and Keith Davis, "Management Communications and the Grapevine," *Harvard Business Review,* Vol. 31 (September–October, 1953), pp. 43–49.

[11] Caplow, *op. cit.*

[12] Homans, *op. cit.,* pp. 37–38. In a subsequent treatment of social behavior, George Homans drops the distinction between activities and sentiments. He suggests that sentiments are not "internal states" inferred from overt behavior, but rather sentiments are activities because they are directly observable. See his *Social Behavior: Its Elementary Forms* (New York: Harcourt, Brace &

feelings such as likes, dislikes, hunger, fears, and anger. In terms of organization, friendliness between group members is an important and a complex sentiment concerning the like or dislike that one person feels toward another. It represents a decision made consciously or unconsciously which leads a person to seek association with another or to avoid association with another. Though the decision to seek friendship may be complex, difficult to explain and measure because of its subjective nature, it is relevant to social behavior. Our inability to discern various sentiments of friendship is no reason to ignore them.

Illustration of Processes and Structure

To illustrate the formal and informal processes and how they may overlap, let us examine a part of a hypothetical formal organization composed of five machine jobs—cutting, boring, grinding, polishing, and painting.[13] A certain type and amount of action is required to perform the work. The relationships among jobs are defined by the formal structure. The spatial layout and the job relationships required by the formal part of the organization are illustrated in Figure 6–1.

This set of jobs represents a formal group which is managed by a group supervisor. Each box in Figure 6–1 represents a required activity, and the lines and arrows indicate the prescribed relations between jobs. According to formal prescription, interactions should be confined to those contacts required by the flow of work. The decisions on: routing and scheduling work; supplying materials, tools, and equipment; maintaining machines; and others are made by the group supervisor. The formal structure of this group may be described in terms of the formally designated positions and the relationships among these positions. In addition to the relationships implied by the flow of work and the decision process, there are, of course, the superior-subordinate relationships of the supervisor and the five workers.

The formal actions, spatial layout, and relationships, however,

World, Inc., 1961), p. 34. In this book we maintain the distinction between activities and sentiments because sentiments help to explain the unique character of social organization, that is, its base in the sentiments or feelings of the people involved.

[13] Other organizational processes such as manufacturing, marketing, and financing could have been used just as well.

FIGURE 6–1

Formal Layout and Relationships of Five Factory Jobs

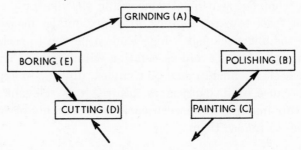

do not represent all that occurs in this group. The required activities, interactions, and decisions may be "elaborated" by the social behavior of the machine operators. For instance, if the activities of each machine operator were observed, we would probably find that each man performs more, or perhaps less, activities than those prescribed, or that the job is being done in a manner that is different from the way it is supposed to be done.

Another type of deviation from the prescribed requirements of work may be in the interactions that actually occur. Figure 6–2

FIGURE 6–2

Social Interactions in the Formal Group

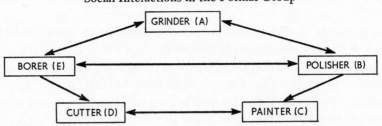

indicates with the lines and arrows how the direction of actual interactions may occur. A sociometric analysis of the interactions may also reveal deviations from the prescribed interactions in terms of frequency, length, type, and content.[14] In a subsequent section of this chapter, a sociometric analysis of this hypothetical group reveals that though there is a formal design for teamwork, a

---

[14] Sociometric analysis is taken up in a subsequent section of this chapter. Briefly, it refers to an analysis of social behavior and relationships based on certain techniques of measurement.

division of subgroups exists. The operators of the boring, grinding, and polishing machines function as a clique, and the cutter and painter form another small group. Also, the activities of each of the subgroups may be noticeably different from those of the others.

Shared Values and Their Function in Organization

The informal processes and structure are based on the values and beliefs shared by participants in the informal organization.[15] These are the motive forces which unite the members of the informal group and guide their conduct. *Values* are the criteria or standards that guide individuals in their selections of the appropriate behavioral alternatives in a given situation.

Defining Goals. At all levels in the organization, people mold values, beliefs, opinions, and myths into an ideology which influences the behavior of the individual. Sentiments concerning conflict, cooperation, superiority, inferiority, authoritarianism, democracy, equality, and others form the basis for defining the goals of an informal organization. The values which are shared by informal group members may not be necessarily in accord with the logic of the formal part of the organization. In such a case, individuals may seek these values only because the informal collectivity provides some protection. For instance, in a formal organization which is autocratically structured, an informal group may formulate and operate for the purpose of bringing about some degree of equality between the autocrats and those who are governed. Equality is a cultural value which may be transmitted into the formal organization through the informal group. This value, if shared by a sufficient number of individuals, helps the group to define its goal and to identify its character.

Prescribing Conduct. Shared values may serve as a basis for the development of group norms and role expectations. The social norms which develop in an informal group define the human behavior expected of each group member. These norms may consist of explicitly or tacitly understood rules. They may prescribe social behavior on how to dress, terminology to use, relations with the

---

[15] The results of an industrial study of work groups, reported by Leonard R. Sayles, reveals that though in most types of work groups the members share common values, there is an exception. Sayles points out that a class of work groups labeled "apathetic" is characterized by "internal disunity and frictions." See his *Behavior of Industrial Work Groups* (New York: John Wiley & Sons, Inc., 1958), pp. 8–40.

boss, and who to associate with, as well as work behavior, that is, how to do the work, when to do it, and how much work to do. For example, an informal group which shares working-class values may establish a dress norm for manual labors which would not tolerate the conduct of a group member who comes to work wearing a suit, necktie, and dress hat. Norms involving activities such as gambling, stealing, escaping, and playing exist in formal organizations even though they appear to be alien to the performance of the organization. For instance, hospital patients, prison inmates, and war prisoners in forced labor camps may not be motivated to accept the hospital, prison, or labor camp standards. Their conduct may be guided by the norms of the informal organization.[16]

With respect to prescribing work behavior, one of the common informal group norms involves the determination of an equitable standard of output or what is known as "a fair day's work." To restrict the output of each worker at a level which is considered "fair," the informal group may establish an output norm which does not coincide with the output standards set by the formal organization.[17] Each group member is expected to produce no more than the norm. Under an incentive system, workers who respect the norm, but who at the same time are capable of producing in excess of it, may receive less money than they could have received if they violated the norm. From the organizational point of view, governing behavior in this manner often appears to be irrational, but as the Hawthorne studies and others have revealed, "man at work is a social creature as well as an 'economic man.' "[18]

Controlling Behavior

The perpetuation of an informal group requires the development of controls aimed at making the group members conform to the

---

[16] See H. Rowland, "Friendship Patterns in the State Mental Hospital," *Psychiatry*, Vol. 2 (1939), pp. 363–73; G. M. Sykes, "The Corruption of Authority and Rehabilitation," *Social Forces*, Vol. 34 (1956), pp. 257–62; and G. M. Sykes, *Society and Captives* (Princeton, N.J.: Princeton University Press, 1958).

[17] This statement should not be taken to imply that the restriction of output is due entirely to group norms. For other explanations of output restriction, see D. Roy, "Quota Restriction and Gold Bricking in a Machine Shop," *American Journal of Sociology*, Vol. 57 (1952), pp. 427–42; W. F. Whyte, *Money and Motivation* (New York: Harper & Bros., 1955); D. J. Hickson, "Motives of Workpeople Who Restrict Their Output," *Occupational Psychology*, Vol. 35 (1961), pp. 110–21.

[18] Roethlisberger, *op. cit.*, p. 13.

group culture. If individual conduct is in violation of the informal group's norms, the deviation is not likely to go unnoticed. If the violator does not alter his behavior after some "lighthearted razzing," the group members may take more serious remedial action; the ridicule may be followed by social ostracism or physical violence.

Informal group control may perform some beneficial functions for its members. First, group norms may be established to protect its members against arbitrary policies and orders of the formal organization and to protect its members against overambitious individuals. For instance, group output norms may be established to protect an individual against excessively high standards of the formal organization, and also to protect group members against overambitious individuals commonly referred to as "rate busters." Second, while the protective function may serve to attract members to the group and strengthen group ties, it may also enhance the group's ability to perform other functions which otherwise could not be undertaken. For example, while the informal organization may restrict output, it may also police and enforce formal safety regulations, or it may encourage high-quality workmanship. Group norms may not only be established with respect to maximum output but they may also set a minimum output standard. In such a case, a group may be as intolerant of workers who produce below the norm as of those who produce above it.

The following material illustrates the social processes operating within a formal organization. It is a case study of an actual organization.

THE SLADE COMPANY[19]

This study describes the behavior of 38 skilled workers employed in the plating room of the Slade Company. They performed tasks such as plating, oxidizing, and preparing metal parts for painting. The plating room production schedule was made up on a daily basis and fluctuated widely to reflect changes in demand.

The work conditions in the plating room varied. In some parts of the department, workers had to contend with acid odors, hot and

---

[19] The original Slade Company case is copyrighted by the President and Fellows of Harvard College; it is listed in the *Intercollegiate Bibliography* (Boston: Intercollegiate Case Clearinghouse, Harvard Graduate School of Business Administration, 1960), Vol. VI, and it appears in Paul R. Lawrence and John A. Seiler, *Organizational Behavior and Administration* (rev. ed.; Homewood, Ill.: Richard D. Irwin, Inc., and Dorsey Press, 1965), pp. 76–88.

cold temperatures, cold water, steaming acid, and caustic soda; other parts of the room were relatively dry, stable in temperature, and free of steam and odor. The hourly wage rate, $1.25 per hour, was slightly below the average starting wage rate for the community. Plating room workers, however, had the opportunity to work up to 76 hours per week. The first 60 hours were paid on a straight-time basis, and overtime on Saturday was paid at time and one half. Double time was given for work on Sunday. This gave the plating room workers gross wages equal to, or in excess of, the community average.

Though the plating room workers were organized on the basis of formal activities and work groups, there also existed several informally organized groups. The informal associations which existed were based on common social activities, interactions, and sentiments. Group norms defined what was and what was not legitimate behavior.

Structure

Two informal groups were prominent in the plating room—the Sarto group and the Clark group. Three workers were considered peripheral members of these two groups. Except for three workers who belonged to no group, all other workers belonged to smaller groups, called dyads and triads. Figure 6–3 shows the workers' station assignments and the flow of work in the plating room. Figure 6–4 shows how the workers were organized on an informal basis.

In terms of formal hierarchy, the 38 plating room workers were supervised by one foreman, Otto Schell, who reported to the production manager. The physical facilities included six aisles, five tanks, one rack assembly, one polishing station, one degreasing station, one rack maintenance station, and one rack drying station. The plating room layout and the flow of work are depicted in Figure 6–5.

The informal groups designated in Figure 6–4 by the encircling lines are not coterminous with the formally designated work groups. Each of the two large informal groups had an informal leader, indicated in Figure 6–4 by boxes. Tony Sarto and Harry Clark were informal leaders who personified the values shared by their respective groups. According to the formal structure, Sarto and Clark

FIGURE 6-3

Work Station Assignments and Flow of Work in the Plating Room

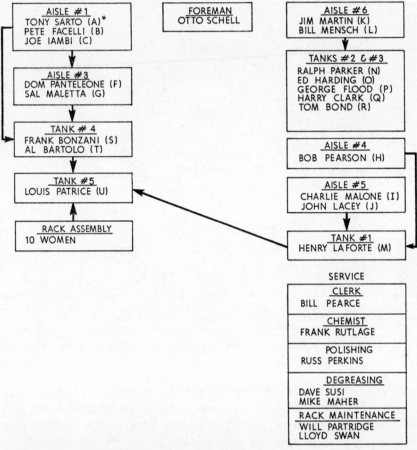

* The letter in brackets after each name is used in Tables 6-5, 6-6, 6-7, and 6-8 instead of the name of each worker.

were on the same level as the other workers, but in the informal organization of the plating room they were considered as leaders. The workers in each of the two large groups sought advice and help from the informal leaders and accepted their instructions.

Informal Processes

The activities actually performed by the workers in the plating room reveal that in some instances activities were elaborated beyond those required by the work, and in other instances fewer

FIGURE 6–4

Informal Groups in the Plating Department

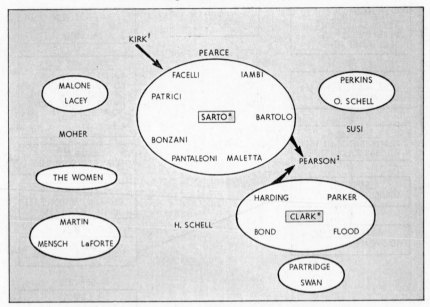

SOURCE; From Paul R. Lawrence and John A. Seiler, *Organizational Behavior and Administration* (rev. ed.; Homewood, Ill.: Richard D. Irwin, Inc., and Dorsey Press, 1965), p. 83.
* Indicates informal group leader.
† Attempted to associate with the Sarto group.
‡ Though Pearson was not an active member of any group, the two large groups regarded him with affection.

activities were performed than required. For instance, though Tony Sarto was not required to train new workers, he undertook the task of training men to perform work according to the high quality standards practiced by the entire Sarto group. On other occasions, Tony Sarto's advice was sought by the foreman and the chemist with respect to solving unique "finishing" problems. Other workers, such as Herman Schell, sought to perform the least amount of work possible. Schell never helped others in any way. He even refused to break in his assigned helper. He was the only worker in the room who executed a deliberate slowdown during the period when jobs were being time studied.

Besides work-related activities, the plating room workers engaged in numerous social activities. The individuals of the Sarto group ate lunch together, operated an organized "punch-in and punch-out" system, and worked as a team when weekend work was required. Sarto group members also associated together in off-

FIGURE 6–5

Plating Room Layout

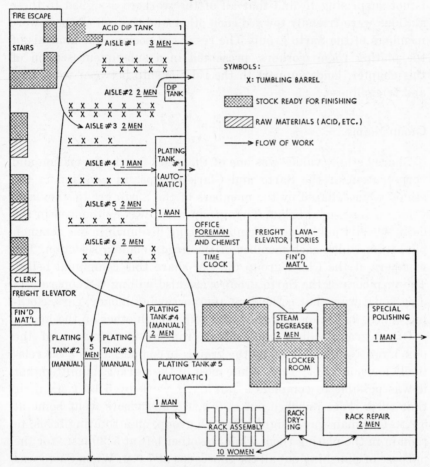

SOURCE; From Paul R. Lawrence and John A. Seiler, *Organizational Behavior and Administration* (rev. ed.; Homewood, Ill.: Richard D. Irwin, Inc., and Dorsey Press, 1965), p. 78.

the-job activities; for example, they often organized trips and parties. Occasionally, the Sarto and Clark groups joined in extraplant social activities.

Probably the most interesting pattern detected in the plating room is the relationship between activities, interactions, and friendliness. The designated work flow from specified aisles to tanks (see Figure 6–5) established a set of interactions which bolstered the friendship bonds within each of the two large informal groups. For instance, the work flow from Aisle No. 1 to Aisle

No. 3 to Plating Tank No. 4 and then to Plating Tank No. 5 required interactions among the men who manned these stations. It is not surprising to find that all of the workers assigned to these stations were friendly toward each other and that all of them were members of the Sarto group. The results of sociometric analysis of the plating room workers, presented in a subsequent section of this chapter, lends support to the relationship between work flow and friendliness.

Group Norms

Shared ethnic values was one of the bases for the formation and perpetuation of the Sarto and Clark groups. In addition to the ethnic values shared by the members of the Sarto group, they also valued a communal belief. This group norm was epitomized in the daily lunch ritual by each member placing his lunch in one common pile, from which each member of the group made a selection. The members of the Clark group did not share this communal belief. The members of the Sarto group were also willing to cooperate in a personal way, that is, lending and borrowing money, cars, clothing, lunch, and so on, and they also helped each other on the job.

Other group values are evident from an examination of the punch-out system devised by the groups to compensate for the relatively low hourly pay rate. While most of the workers admitted that it was possible to complete a fair day's work by 5:30 P.M., their time cards were punched out at 7 P.M. Supervisors went home at 5 P.M. One man was assigned by each group, on a rotating basis, to remain in the plating room while the other left at 5:30 P.M., for the purpose of punching out all the timecards at 7 P.M. When Sarto was asked if he would rather work shorter hours at a higher pay rate, he responded: "It wouldn't come close to an even trade." The others, that is, the isolates, the dyads, and the triads, either arranged within their small groups for "punch-outs" or they remained until 7 P.M., or they paid someone to remain behind to "punch out" their time-cards. The latter practice was considered improper by the members of the Sarto group. The Sarto group also operated a "punch-in" system for group members who were unavoidably delayed in the morning between 7 A.M. and 8 A.M. This practice never occurred without prior arrangements by the man who expected to be late, and it was not employed to "cover up" tardiness beyond 8 A.M., which was the starting time for the plating room foreman. The Sarto group established an exception to this punch-out norm for "extra orders." Whenever it was necessary to produce a rush order, the Sarto group actually worked until 7 P.M. The goal of the output norm was explained by Sarto in the following manner:

You know our hourly pay rate is quite low, compared to other companies. What makes this the best place to work is the feeling of security you get. No one ever gets laid off in this department. With all the hours in the week, all the company ever has to do is shorten the work week when orders fall off. . . . When things are going well, as they are now, the company is only interested in getting out the work. It doesn't help to get it out faster than it's really needed—so we go home a little early whenever we can. . . .

The punch-out norm gave the workers some control over the work environment and, according to their perceptions, it lessened their dependence upon management.

Group Performance

An examination of performance and rewards for the Sarto and Clark groups reveals that, on the average, these groups had a higher productivity rating and a higher wage rate than the smaller groups and isolates. Table 6–1 shows the average productiv-

TABLE 6–1

Productivity Ratings and Rewards on the Basis of Group Affiliation

	Average Productivity Rating for the Group*	Quality of Jobs Assigned	Average Hourly Wage Rate for the Group†
Sarto group	2.0	High	$1.30
Clark group	4.0	High	$1.20
Others	5.5	Regular	$1.11½

* This rating is an arithmetic average of the individual ratings provided by the workers of the plating department. Grading was done on a scale of 1 (high producer) to 10 (low producer).
† The group average wage rate is the arithmetic means of individual hourly wage rates, and it represents management's evaluation of the men.

ity ratings and wage rates for the Sarto group, the Clark group, and the others.

Another value which was implicit in the Sarto group productivity norm was related to the quality of work. First, of all the Sarto group members were engaged in jobs which involved highly specialized or high-quality work. For instance, Tony Sarto's assignment was in Aisle No. 1 where all the high-quality plating and highly specialized acid-etching was done. The output from Aisle No. 1 normally went to Tanks No. 4 and No. 5, Sarto-manned stations, which completed the work on high-quality items. In order to maintain the quality norm, the Sarto group performed a training function. The company did not provide any special training for new workers, but the Sarto group, especially Tony Sarto, taught the new men how to produce high-quality work. This activity was not required by the formal part of the organization. The training of new men performed several functions simultaneously. In addition to providing instructions concerning the work, it also served as a method of indoctrinating new workers to the Sarto group norms, and it perpetuated the manning of high-quality work stations by Sarto men. Second, the Sarto group expected its members to exhibit a certain amount of inventiveness in improving the work process. Tony Sarto himself was instrumental in solving many problems which arose from changes in customer specifications.

Given the situation at the Slade Company, that is, low wage rates, poor working conditions, no training, and fluctuating product demand, it appears that the group norms of the Sarto group served both to protect the interest of the workers and in some ways to help management. The Sarto group values concerning the quality of workmanship emphasized inventiveness and training. Both of these results were beneficial to management. The cost of these norms, with respect to the goals of the formal organization, was the "spreading out" of 10 hours of work to 12 hours and the loss of some formal control over the workers. In this case, the informal processes did not alter the formally designated work process, but it elaborated the formal organization by establishing more specific controls and a training process. In fact, the flow of work, for instance, the flow of high-quality assignments from Aisle No. 1 to Tanks No. 4 and No. 5, was used by the informal group as a way of identifying its values and perpetuating itself.

The punch-out system, which was necessary to effectuate the group output norms, not only gave the Sarto group an extra reason to exist, but it also provided a daily control function which tended to strengthen group cohesiveness.[20]

While group cohesiveness was not correlated to efficiency or worker satisfaction in the Slade Company case, other studies disclose that group cohesion is correlated to high production,[21] stable control,[22] high-quality production,[23] low turnover and absenteeism,[24] and worker satisfaction.[25] However, the research evidence is not conclusive. Research studies conducted by Stanley Schachter *et al.*,[26] Stanley E. Seashore,[27] and L. Berkowitz[28] reveal that group cohesion is not correlated directly with high productivity. Leon Festinger argues that cohesiveness may be related to the amount of control that a group has over its individual members, but the productivity norm is determined by other factors.[29]

SOCIOMETRIC ANALYSIS

The network of interpersonal relations that exists within the informal organization is of interest if we seek to understand group behavior. Since the processes of social behavior—activities, interactions, and sentiments—are important components of the social

---

[20] For an interesting discussion concerning a positive relationship between cohesiveness and the accomplishment of a satisfying endeavor by a group. See Josephine Klein, *The Study of Groups* (London: Routledge & Kegan Paul, Ltd., 1956), pp. 134–35 and pp. 148–49.

[21] Daniel Katz and Robert L. Kahn, "Some Recent Findings in Human-Relations Research in Industry," in Guy E. Swanson *et al.* (eds.), *Readings in Social Psychology* (New York: Henry Holt & Co., 1952), pp. 621–22.

[22] Stanley E. Seashore, *Group Cohesiveness in the Industrial Work Group* (Ann Arbor: Institute for Social Research, University of Michigan, 1954), chap. v.

[23] Elton Mayo and George F. Lombard, *Teamwork and Labor Turnover in the Aircraft Industry of Southern California* (Boston: Graduate School of Business Administration, Harvard University, 1944), p. 27.

[24] *Ibid.*

[25] *Ibid.*

[26] Stanley Schachter *et al.*, "An Experimental Study of Cohesiveness and Productivity," *Human Relations*, Vol. 4 (1951), pp. 229–38.

[27] Seashore, *op. cit.*, pp. 98–99.

[28] L. Berkowitz, "Group Standards, Cohesiveness, and Productivity," *Human Relations*, Vol. 7 (1954), pp. 509–19.

[29] Leon Festinger *et al.*, *Social Pressures in Informal Groups* (New York: Harper & Bros., 1950), especially chap. v.

structure of a group, we can learn something about group behavior by subjecting these elements to analysis.[30]

Sociometric analysis involves the measurement of social elements and relationships. While many techniques of social measurement have emerged in recent years, we are concerned primarily with sociometric choice, sociograms, sociometric matrices, and matrix algebra. These sociometric tools are helpful in our attempt to understand informal group structure and channels of communication. Specifically, our goal in using sociometry is to identify informal groups, the members of an informal group, and the patterns of interactions and relationships.

Likewise, the same type of analysis can be used to understand influence patterns, especially if the activities that people emit are treated as exchanges in a motivational relationship. Treating activities as motivators is important to organizational analysis, because in this way we can relate a basic aspect of group dynamics— friendship patterns—to a system of rewards and punishments. George Homans, for example, looks upon activities, from the motivational point of view, as exchanges of "help for approval, in which each activity emitted by one man is rewarded by an activity of the other man. . . ."[31]

Sociometric Choice and Data

The key factor in applying sociometry to the analysis of social relations is sociometric choice. Sociometric choice is an individual's expression of preference to associate with other persons. Choice of friends, for example, can be used as a means for differentiating interpersonal relations. This differentiation is based upon the assumption that individuals usually prefer to associate with others who enhance their feelings of personal worth, belongingness, and satisfaction.

In terms of behavior in formal organization, the choice preference of association may not be equivalent to the job relationships prescribed by the formal organization. For example, the formal job relationships of the hypothetical group, depicted in Figure 6–1, are

---

[30] For a more complete description and use of sociometric analysis, see Gardner Lindzey and Edgar F. Borgatta, "Sociometric Measurement," in Gardner Lindzey (ed.), *Handbook of Social Psychology* (Reading, Mass.: Addison-Wesley Publishing Co., Inc., 1954), pp. 405–48.

[31] Homans, *Social Behavior, op. cit.*, p. 54.

not the same as the pattern of social interactions, as shown in Figure 6–2, and possibly other sociometric choices of the members of the group.

The gathering of such sociometric data can be accomplished by direct observations of social behavior or through the interrogation method. Techniques like the Bales interaction process analysis have been used to obtain data by direct observation.[32] The interrogation method includes such techniques as sociometric tests and questionnaires. The questionnaire technique involves questions such as: With whom would you like to work? With whom would you like to eat lunch? Who would you prefer as your leader?[33]

Many variations of these techniques have been developed.[34] Their prime purpose is to gain knowledge about social relations. After gathering these data through observation and/or interrogation, the investigator may display his findings through a sociogram.

Sociogram

The sociogram, first described by J. L. Moreno, is a diagrammatic method of showing interpersonal sentiments of attraction (choice) and repulsion (rejection) among members of a group.[35] This technique has been used to identify and describe a variety of attraction-repulsion patterns. For instance, Moreno found recurring patterns which have been referred to as "overchosen," "isolates," "mutual pairs," and "triads."[36]

To illustrate some of these patterns, let us refer to the social interactions of the hypothetical group composed of a grinder (A), polisher (B), painter (C), cutter (D), and borer (E) presented originally in Figure 6–2. Assuming that the social interactions

---

[32] Robert F. Bales, *Interaction Process Analysis* (Reading, Mass.: Addison-Wesley Publishing Co., Inc., 1950).

[33] See, for instance, J. L. Moreno, *Who Shall Survive?* (New York: Beacon House, Inc., 1934); J. L. Moreno and H. H. Jennings, *Sociometric Control Studies*, Sociometric Monographs No. 7 (New York: Beacon House, Inc., 1947); and H. H. Jennings, "Leadership and Sociometric Choice," *Sociometry*, Vol. 10 (1947), pp. 32–49.

[34] See: J. H. Jacobs, "The Application of Sociometry to Industry," *Sociometry*, Vol. 8 (1954), pp. 181–98; R. M. Stogdill, "The Sociometry of Working Relationships in Formal Organizations," *Sociometry*, Vol. 12 (1949), pp. 276–86; M. Patchen, "Alternative Questionnaire Approaches to the Measurement of Influence in Organizations," *American Journal of Sociology*, Vol. 69, No. 1 (1963), pp. 41–52.

[35] Moreno, *Who Shall Survive?*, *op. cit.*

[36] Lindzey and Borgatta, *op. cit.*, pp. 410–13.

represent sentiments of choice among the group members, a socio-gram of choices is shown in Figure 6–6.

FIGURE 6–6

Sociogram of Interpersonal Feelings of Attraction

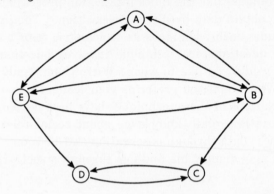

The lines and arrows represent feelings of attraction or choice. The line and arrow, for example, from A to B means that A likes B; the line and arrow from B to A indicates that B likes A. This particular relationship is a mutual choice pair as opposed to the relationship between B and C, which is a one-way choice relationship. The same method can be used to depict rejections also.

The pattern revealed in the sociogram of Figure 6–6 is relatively simple. No single member of this group is overchosen, that is, no individual received a number of choices that exceeds the number received by any other member. Also, there are no isolates—no member received zero choices and made zero choices.

This group includes four mutual choice pairs, also referred to as symmetrical relationships :

A likes B and B likes A
A likes E and E likes A
B likes E and E likes B
C likes D and D likes C

This group also includes a triad, that is, there are three members, A, B, and E, who are connected by mutual choices.

The same type of analysis could have been undertaken with the other elements of social behavior or even the formal activity relationships among the group members depicted in Figure 6–1.

Sociometric Matrix

Interpersonal feelings such as those depicted in a sociogram can be shown just as easily in a table or matrix. The presentation of social relationships in matrix form can be accomplished simply by listing the members of a given group along the rows and columns of a matrix in the same order. The number 1 can be used, for instance, to show a choice of one member by another, and a zero can be used to represent no choice. The matrix presentation simplifies the otherwise tedious task of diagramming or listing relationships among various individuals of a group.

Table 6–2 includes the sociometric responses shown previously in the sociogram of Figure 6–6.

TABLE 6–2

Matrix of Interpersonal Feelings of Attraction

TO

	A (Grinder)	B (Polisher)	C (Painter)	D (Cutter)	E (Borer)
A (Grinder)	0	1	0	0	1
B (Polisher)	1	0	1	0	1
C (Painter)	0	0	0	1	0
D (Cutter)	0	0	1	0	0
E (Borer)	1	1	0	1	0

FROM

The number 1 in the rows represents a choice from one individual to another and the number 1 in the columns indicates the individual receiving a choice. Reading across row A, we can say that A has chosen B and E, row B indicates the friendship choices of B are A, C, and E, row C reveals that C likes D, the choice of D is C as shown in row D, and row E indicates that E likes A, B, and D. A zero is placed in the cells of the principal diagonal because there is no interpersonal relationship of each individual to himself. A zero in the other cells represents no choice. Rejections can also be shown in the same manner. One of the limitations of this method is that only one response, either choices or rejections, can be treated at once. Another limitation is that there can be no weighting of the responses. The responses must be made in the form of yes or no.

Without an adequate technique for manipulating these data, the analysis would be limited to identifying who likes whom and summarizing the choices received by each of the group members.[37] Identification of the structure of relationships and channels of communication by inspecting the matrix would be possible only when dealing with simple patterns of small groups. Identifying complex patterns and large groups in this manner would be difficult and unwieldy. The application of matrix algebra permits us to analyze both small and large groups, and complex and simple patterns. Before proceeding with the application of matrix algebra to social analysis, let us explain briefly some fundamental rules of matrix manipulation.

Multiplication Rules

The procedure for multiplying a row vector times a matrix, a matrix times a column vector, and a matrix times a matrix can be accomplished as follows: The rule for multiplying a row vector times a matrix states that the number of rows in the matrix must be equal to the number of elements in the row vector. The result of this multiplication is another row vector. Suppose we have a row vector p consisting of three elements and a matrix T consisting of three rows and we wish to find their product. Using general notation, their product would be :

$$pT = (a_1 a_2 a_3) \begin{pmatrix} t_{11} t_{12} t_{13} \\ t_{21} t_{22} t_{23} \\ t_{31} t_{32} t_{33} \end{pmatrix}$$

$$= (a_1 t_{11} + a_2 t_{21} + a_3 t_{31}, a_1 t_{12} + a_2 t_{22} + a_3 t_{32}, a_1 t_{13} + a_2 t_{23} + a_3 t_{33})$$

The rule for multiplying a matrix times a column vector states that the number of columns in the matrix must equal the number of

---

[37] Statistical methods can be applied to these data summaries to determine whether or not differences are statistically significant. For a brief description of statistical methods, along with further references, see Lindzey and Borgatta *op. cit.*, pp. 415–16.

elements in the column vector. The result of the multiplication is another column vector. Suppose we have a matrix T consisting of three columns and a column vector x consisting of three elements, and we wish to find their product. Their product would be:

$$Tx = \begin{pmatrix} t_{11}t_{12}t_{13} \\ t_{21}t_{22}t_{23} \\ t_{31}t_{32}t_{33} \end{pmatrix} \begin{pmatrix} x_1 \\ x_2 \\ x_3 \end{pmatrix}$$

$$= \begin{pmatrix} t_{11}x_1 + t_{12}x_2 + t_{13}x_3 \\ t_{21}x_1 + t_{22}x_2 + t_{23}x_3 \\ t_{31}x_1 + t_{32}x_2 + t_{33}x_3 \end{pmatrix}$$

The rules for matrix multiplication, for instance, matrix A multiplied times matrix B, state that the number of columns in matrix A must be equal to the number of rows in matrix B and that the result, which is also a matrix, must have the same number of rows as the matrix A and the same number of columns as the matrix B. Suppose we have a matrix A consisting of three columns and a matrix B consisting of three rows, and we want to find their product. The result would be:

$$AB = \begin{pmatrix} a_{11}a_{12}a_{13} \\ a_{21}a_{22}a_{23} \\ a_{31}a_{32}a_{33} \end{pmatrix} \begin{pmatrix} b_{11}b_{12} \\ b_{21}b_{22} \\ b_{31}b_{32} \end{pmatrix}$$

$$= \begin{pmatrix} a_{11}b_{11} + a_{12}b_{21} + a_{13}b_{31}, \ a_{11}b_{12} + a_{12}b_{22} + a_{13}b_{32} \\ a_{21}b_{11} + a_{22}b_{21} + a_{23}b_{31}, \ a_{21}b_{12} + a_{22}b_{22} + a_{23}b_{32} \\ a_{31}b_{11} + a_{32}b_{21} + a_{33}b_{31}, \ a_{31}b_{12} + a_{32}b_{22} + a_{33}b_{32} \end{pmatrix}$$

These rules also apply when a matrix is raised to a power. Squaring of a matrix, for example matrix A, requires that we multiply matrix A times matrix A or we can state it as A^2. Squaring matrix A would give us the following results:

$$A^2 = A \cdot A = \begin{pmatrix} a_{11}a_{12}a_{13} \\ a_{21}a_{22}a_{23} \\ a_{31}a_{32}a_{33} \end{pmatrix} \begin{pmatrix} a_{11}a_{12}a_{13} \\ a_{21}a_{22}a_{23} \\ a_{31}a_{32}a_{33} \end{pmatrix}$$

$$= \begin{pmatrix} a_{11}a_{11} + a_{12}a_{21} + a_{13}a_{31}, \ a_{11}a_{12} + a_{12}a_{22} + a_{13}a_{32}, \ a_{11}a_{13} + a_{12}a_{23} + a_{13}a_{33} \\ a_{21}a_{11} + a_{22}a_{21} + a_{23}a_{31}, \ a_{21}a_{12} + a_{22}a_{22} + a_{23}a_{32}, \ a_{21}a_{13} + a_{22}a_{23} + a_{23}a_{33} \\ a_{31}a_{11} + a_{32}a_{21} + a_{33}a_{31}, \ a_{31}a_{12} + a_{32}a_{22} + a_{33}a_{32}, \ a_{31}a_{13} + a_{32}a_{23} + a_{33}a_{33} \end{pmatrix}$$

In order to obtain the cube of matrix A, we must multiply A times A^2.

Generally, matrix multiplication is not *commutative*, that is,

$$AB \neq BA$$

However, matrix multiplication is *associative*, hence,

$$ABC = A(BC) = (AB)C$$

Also, matrix multiplication is *distributive*, thus,

$$A(B + C) = AB + AC$$
$$(B + C)D = BD + CD$$

FRIENDSHIP PATTERNS

In this section relatively simple and complex patterns of behavior are subjected to sociometric analysis. For simple patterns we rely upon sociograms for analysis. But, for more complex patterns, matrix algebra is applied.

Simple Patterns

By entering each sociometric friendship choice in a matrix we have a display of all the choices made and received in a group. In this analysis, we are interested in the connecting links between members of a group. In the simple patterns of this section, we illustrate one-link, two-link, and three-link paths. One-link paths in a group of three members—A, B, and C—may be shown as follows:

$$Ⓐ \longrightarrow Ⓑ \longleftarrow Ⓒ$$

In the diagram above, there are one-link paths from A to B and C to B. A two-link path from A to B to C can be shown as follows:

$$Ⓐ \longrightarrow Ⓑ \longrightarrow Ⓒ$$

A three-link path from A to B to C to B may be shown as follows:

$$Ⓐ \longrightarrow Ⓑ \rightleftarrows Ⓒ$$

Analysis of larger groups and more complex relationships requires use of matrix analysis. We illustrate this technique below.

Squared Matrix of Friendships

By squaring the original matrix of friendship choices we can detect the patterns that show all of the connecting paths of two links. Cubing the original matrix reveals all of the connections involving three-link paths. By raising the power of the original matrix to n we can find all of the n-link paths in a group. Let us see how this is done using the data from Table 6–2, which is labeled as the A matrix.

To determine the pattern of relationships that exists among the members of this group, the original matrix, that is, the R matrix must be manipulated algebraically. By squaring the original matrix R, each number in the R^2 matrix represents the number of two-link paths that exist between any pair of members of the group. The results of squaring the R matrix are shown as follows:

$$
R^2 = R \cdot R =
\begin{pmatrix}
0 & 1 & 0 & 0 & 1 \\
1 & 0 & 1 & 0 & 1 \\
0 & 0 & 0 & 1 & 0 \\
0 & 0 & 1 & 0 & 0 \\
1 & 1 & 0 & 1 & 0
\end{pmatrix}
\begin{pmatrix}
0 & 1 & 0 & 0 & 1 \\
1 & 0 & 1 & 0 & 1 \\
0 & 0 & 0 & 1 & 0 \\
0 & 0 & 1 & 0 & 0 \\
1 & 1 & 0 & 1 & 0
\end{pmatrix}
=
\begin{array}{c}
A \\
B \\
C \\
D \\
E
\end{array}
\begin{pmatrix}
A & B & C & D & E \\
2 & 1 & 1 & 1 & 1 \\
1 & 2 & 0 & 2 & 1 \\
0 & 0 & 1 & 0 & 0 \\
0 & 0 & 0 & 1 & 0 \\
1 & 1 & 2 & 0 & 2
\end{pmatrix}
$$

Excluding the numbers in the principal diagonal, the numbers in the other cells reveal that, for instance, there exists one path of two links from A to C, that is, A to B to C, or there exists two paths composed of two links from B to D, that is, B to E to D and B to C to D. The connections, however, are not necessarily symmetrical, that is, the connection from A to C, shown above, is a one-way connection. The reverse is not true, because no connection exists from C to B. The symmetrical relations between group members require a different treatment, which is discussed below.

The squared matrix reveals one more aspect of relationships within a group. The numbers appearing in the principal diagonal of the matrix indicate the number of two-link connections that exist from each person to himself, that is, the number of mutual choices in which each person is involved. The principal diagonal of the R^2 matrix reveals that A, B, and E are each involved in two paths of two-link (mutual choice) connections, and C and D are each involved in one path of a two-link relationship. These results can be checked with the original sociogram shown in Figure 6–6. In fact, by visual inspection of the sociogram, we could have detected the results obtained through the more tedious task of squaring the original matrix. This is possible, however, only because the group is relatively small and the pattern of relationships is relatively simple.

Cubed Matrix of Friendships

By cubing the original R matrix, it is possible to obtain the number of three-link paths from each member of the group to any other member of the group. For instance, there exists two paths of three links going from A to D, that is, A to B to C to D, and A to B to E to D. The resulting matrix is:

$$R^3 = R \cdot R^2 = \begin{pmatrix} 0 & 1 & 0 & 0 & 1 \\ 1 & 0 & 1 & 0 & 1 \\ 0 & 0 & 0 & 1 & 0 \\ 0 & 0 & 1 & 0 & 0 \\ 1 & 1 & 0 & 1 & 0 \end{pmatrix} \begin{pmatrix} 2 & 1 & 1 & 1 & 1 \\ 1 & 2 & 0 & 2 & 1 \\ 0 & 0 & 1 & 0 & 0 \\ 0 & 0 & 0 & 1 & 0 \\ 1 & 1 & 2 & 0 & 2 \end{pmatrix} = \begin{matrix} & \begin{matrix} A & B & C & D & E \end{matrix} \\ \begin{matrix} A \\ B \\ C \\ D \\ E \end{matrix} & \begin{pmatrix} 2 & 3 & 2 & 2 & 3 \\ 3 & 2 & 4 & 1 & 3 \\ 0 & 0 & 0 & 1 & 0 \\ 1 & 1 & 3 & 0 & 2 \\ 3 & 3 & 1 & 4 & 2 \end{pmatrix} \end{matrix}$$

The cubed matrix indicates, for example, that there exists two paths of three links going from A to D, that is, A to B to C to D and A to B to E to D. The figures in the principal diagonal reveal the number of paths of three-link connections from a given person back to himself. For example, the two paths of three links that exist from A back to A are as follows: A to B to E to A and A to E to B to A.

Raising the power of the original matrix to higher powers reveals more circuitous relationships among group members, that is, the R^4 matrix discloses the number of paths comprised of four-link connections, the R^5 matrix provides the number five-link connections, and so on.

Matrix of Symmetrical Relationships

It is possible to identify cliques within a group.[38] A clique consists of three or more individuals who choose each other as friends. For

---

[38] Clique and subgroup are used synonymously in this chapter.

example, three individuals, A, B, and E of Figure 6–6 are members of a clique because there is a mutual choice between A and B, A and E, and B and E. A clique may be identified also by cubing a matrix of mutual choices or symmetrical relationships of a group. The principal diagonal of the cubed matrix indicates whether or not a clique exists. For a clique to exist there must be at least three people in the group with two three-link relationships indicated in the principal diagonal. Again referring to Figure 6–6, it can be seen that A, B, and E each have two three-link relationships that lead back to themselves. The two three-link relationships of A, for example, are (1) A to B to E to A, and (2) A to E to B to A. Let us illustrate how a clique may be determined by matrix algebra.[39] First, we form a matrix of the symmetrical relationships of Figure 6–6 and call it the S matrix. The mutual choices are indicated in matrix by the number one. All of the other cells contain zeros.

$$
S = \begin{array}{c} \\ A \\ B \\ C \\ D \\ E \end{array}
\begin{array}{c}
\begin{array}{ccccc} A & B & C & D & E \end{array} \\
\left(\begin{array}{ccccc}
0 & 1 & 0 & 0 & 1 \\
1 & 0 & 0 & 0 & 1 \\
0 & 0 & 0 & 1 & 0 \\
0 & 0 & 1 & 0 & 0 \\
1 & 1 & 0 & 0 & 0
\end{array}\right)
\end{array}
$$

$$
S^2 = S \cdot S =
\begin{pmatrix}
0 & 1 & 0 & 0 & 1 \\
1 & 0 & 0 & 0 & 1 \\
0 & 0 & 0 & 1 & 0 \\
0 & 0 & 1 & 0 & 0 \\
1 & 1 & 0 & 0 & 0
\end{pmatrix}
\begin{pmatrix}
0 & 1 & 0 & 0 & 1 \\
1 & 0 & 0 & 0 & 1 \\
0 & 0 & 0 & 1 & 0 \\
0 & 0 & 1 & 0 & 0 \\
1 & 1 & 0 & 0 & 0
\end{pmatrix}
=
\begin{array}{c} A \\ B \\ C \\ D \\ E \end{array}
\begin{pmatrix}
2 & 1 & 0 & 0 & 1 \\
1 & 2 & 0 & 0 & 1 \\
0 & 0 & 1 & 0 & 0 \\
0 & 0 & 0 & 1 & 0 \\
1 & 1 & 0 & 0 & 2
\end{pmatrix}
$$

$$
S^3 = S \cdot S^2 =
\begin{pmatrix}
0 & 1 & 0 & 0 & 1 \\
1 & 0 & 0 & 0 & 1 \\
0 & 0 & 0 & 1 & 0 \\
0 & 0 & 1 & 0 & 0 \\
1 & 1 & 0 & 0 & 0
\end{pmatrix}
\begin{pmatrix}
2 & 1 & 0 & 0 & 1 \\
1 & 2 & 0 & 0 & 1 \\
0 & 0 & 1 & 0 & 0 \\
0 & 0 & 0 & 1 & 0 \\
1 & 1 & 0 & 0 & 2
\end{pmatrix}
=
\begin{array}{c} A \\ B \\ C \\ D \\ E \end{array}
\begin{pmatrix}
2 & 3 & 0 & 0 & 3 \\
3 & 2 & 0 & 0 & 3 \\
0 & 0 & 0 & 1 & 0 \\
0 & 0 & 1 & 0 & 0 \\
3 & 3 & 0 & 0 & 2
\end{pmatrix}
$$

The results of this manipulation indicate that a three-member subgroup or clique exists within the five-man group. The numbers

---

[39] It is not necessary to use matrix algebra when analyzing a small group such as the one illustrated in Figure 6–6. It is appropriate, however, for large groups such as the work group of the Slade Company.

in the principal diagonal identify those individuals who are members of the subgroup, and who are involved in three-link symmetrical connection starting from each member and coming back to him. The number in the diagonal cell of each individual is equal to $(n-1)(n-2)$, where n is the number of members in the subgroup. The zeros that appear in the diagonal cells of C and D mean that these individuals are not elements of the three-member, three-link subgroup.[40]

In a friendship pattern such as the one depicted in Figure 6–7 and Table 6–3, it is evident that there are no cliques according to our definition that a clique is composed of a subgroup of three or more individuals with symmetrical sentiments of friendship. In other words, a clique is composed of three or more individuals with a direct one-step mutual connection between every possible pair of

FIGURE 6–7

Sociogram of Interpersonal
Feelings of Friendship

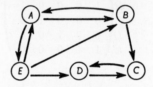

TABLE 6–3

S Matrix of Friendships

TO

		A	B	C	D	E
	A	0	1	0	0	1
FROM	B	1	0	0	0	0
	C	0	0	0	1	0
	D	0	0	1	0	0
	E	1	0	0	0	0

[40] For a more elaborate treatment of matrix analysis of social structure, see Duncan R. Luce and Albert R. Perry, "A Method of Matrix Analysis of Group Structure," *Psychometrika*, Vol. 14 (1949), pp. 94–116.

$$S^3 = S \cdot S^2 = \begin{pmatrix} 0 & 1 & 0 & 0 & 1 \\ 1 & 0 & 0 & 0 & 0 \\ 0 & 0 & 0 & 1 & 0 \\ 0 & 0 & 1 & 0 & 0 \\ 1 & 0 & 0 & 0 & 0 \end{pmatrix} \begin{pmatrix} 2 & 0 & 0 & 0 & 0 \\ 0 & 1 & 0 & 0 & 1 \\ 0 & 0 & 1 & 0 & 0 \\ 0 & 0 & 0 & 1 & 0 \\ 0 & 1 & 0 & 0 & 1 \end{pmatrix} = \begin{array}{c} \\ A \\ B \\ C \\ D \\ E \end{array}\begin{pmatrix} A & B & C & D & E \\ 0 & 2 & 0 & 0 & 2 \\ 2 & 0 & 0 & 0 & 0 \\ 0 & 0 & 0 & 1 & 0 \\ 0 & 0 & 1 & 0 & 0 \\ 2 & 0 & 0 & 0 & 0 \end{pmatrix}$$

members in the subgroup. The cube of the symmetrical matrix in Table 6–3 yields zeros in every cell of the principal diagonal.

This sociometric analysis permits us to determine whether or not a subgroup exists, the size of an existing subgroup, and the identity of individual subgroup members. The analysis is based on sentiments which are expressed in terms of an absolute value, for instance, one or zero. This method of analysis cannot be used on values which are relative; for instance, sentiments expressed in terms of degrees of friendship.

APPLICATIONS OF MATRIX ANALYSIS

Matrix analysis of social behavior has several practical uses in understanding and designing organizations. In this section we illustrate its usefulness, first, by applying matrix analysis to the Slade case, and, second, by examining some applications that have been attempted in practice.

The Slade Illustration

As indicated previously, matrix analysis need not be limited to sociometric choices of friendships. Activities and interactions, the other elements of social behavior, are amenable to the same type of treatment. In the case of the plating room workers of the Slade Company, the connections based on activities can be scrutinized using matrix algebra. The activities of the plating room employees are connected in a prescribed manner to form a flow of work. Each job, composed of given activities, serves as a step in a chain of events. For instance, the job activities of the workers assigned to Plating Tank No. 4 are dependent on the activities of those men assigned to Aisles No. 1 and No. 3, and the job activities of Aisle No. 3 are dependent on the output of Aisle No. 1. To show all of the activity connections and paths of the plating room, a 38 by 38 matrix is needed. For simplicity, the matrix of activities indicated in Table 6–4 excludes the following workers: 10 rack assembly wo-

TABLE 6–4*

R Matrix of Related Activities of Plating Room Workers

	A	B	C	D	E	F	G	H	I	J	K	L	M	N	O	P	Q	R	S	T	U
A	0	1	1	0	0	1	1	0	0	0	0	0	0	0	0	0	0	0	1	1	1
B	1	0	1	0	0	1	1	0	0	0	0	0	0	0	0	0	0	0	1	1	1
C	1	1	0	0	0	1	1	0	0	0	0	0	0	0	0	0	0	0	1	1	1
D	0	0	0	0	1	0	0	0	0	0	0	0	0	0	0	0	0	0	0	0	0
E	0	0	0	1	0	0	0	0	0	0	0	0	0	0	0	0	0	0	0	0	0
F	1	1	1	0	0	0	1	0	0	0	0	0	0	0	0	0	0	0	1	1	0
G	1	1	1	0	0	1	0	0	0	0	0	0	0	0	0	0	0	0	1	1	0
H	0	0	0	0	0	0	0	0	0	0	0	1	0	0	0	0	0	0	0	0	0
I	0	0	0	0	0	0	0	0	0	1	0	0	1	0	0	0	0	0	0	0	0
J	0	0	0	0	0	0	0	0	1	0	0	0	1	0	0	0	0	0	0	0	0
K	0	0	0	0	0	0	0	0	0	0	0	1	0	1	1	1	1	1	0	0	0
L	0	0	0	0	0	0	0	0	0	0	1	0	0	1	1	1	1	1	0	0	0
M	0	0	0	0	0	0	0	1	1	1	0	0	0	0	0	0	0	0	0	0	1
N	0	0	0	0	0	0	0	0	0	0	1	1	0	0	1	1	1	1	0	0	0
O	0	0	0	0	0	0	0	0	0	0	1	1	0	1	0	1	1	1	0	0	0
P	0	0	0	0	0	0	0	0	0	0	1	1	0	1	1	0	1	1	0	0	0
Q	0	0	0	0	0	0	0	0	0	0	1	1	0	1	1	1	0	1	0	0	0
R	0	0	0	0	0	0	0	0	0	0	1	1	0	1	1	1	1	0	0	0	0
S	1	1	1	0	0	1	1	0	0	0	0	0	0	0	0	0	0	0	0	1	1
T	1	1	1	0	0	1	1	0	0	0	0	0	0	0	0	0	0	0	1	0	1
U	1	1	1	0	0	0	0	0	0	0	0	0	1	0	0	0	0	0	1	1	0

* Each letter represents a worker. To identify each worker, see Figure 6–3, in which each name is followed by a letter corresponding to the ones used in this table.

men; 2 repairmen; 1 special polisher; 1 clerk; 2 steam degreasers; and 1 foreman.

By raising the power of the matrix, indicated in Table 6–4, we can determine the number of two- and then three-step paths relating various workers.

A visual inspection of the principal diagonal of the R matrix raised to the third power, indicated in Table 6–5, reveals that the prescribed activities of 15 of the 21 individual workers provide a large number of paths of three-link connections for $A, B, C, F, G, K, L, N, O, P, Q, R, S, T$, and U.

TABLE 6–5

Cubed R Matrix of Activities
of Plating Room Workers

	A	B	C	D	E	F	G	H	I	J	K	L	M	N	O	P	Q	R	S	T	U
A	38	39	39	0	0	36	36	1	1	1	0	0	4	0	0	0	0	0	39	39	39
B	39	38	39	0	0	36	36	1	1	1	0	0	4	0	0	0	0	0	39	39	32
C	39	39	38	0	0	36	36	1	1	1	0	0	4	0	0	0	0	0	39	39	32
D	0	0	0	0	1	0	0	0	0	0	0	0	0	0	0	0	0	0	0	0	0
E	0	0	0	1	0	0	0	0	0	0	0	0	0	0	0	0	0	0	0	0	0
F	36	36	36	0	0	30	31	0	0	0	0	0	5	0	0	0	0	0	36	36	25
G	36	36	36	0	0	31	30	0	0	0	0	0	5	0	0	0	0	0	36	36	25
H	1	1	1	0	0	0	0	0	1	1	0	0	4	0	0	0	0	0	1	1	0
I	1	1	1	0	0	0	0	1	2	3	0	0	5	0	0	0	0	0	1	1	1
J	1	1	1	0	0	0	0	1	3	2	0	0	5	0	0	0	0	0	1	1	1
K	0	0	0	0	0	0	0	0	0	0	30	31	0	31	31	31	31	31	0	0	0
L	0	0	0	0	0	0	0	0	0	0	31	30	0	31	31	31	31	31	0	0	0
M	4	4	4	0	0	5	5	4	5	5	0	0	2	0	0	0	0	0	4	4	9
N	0	0	0	0	0	0	0	0	0	0	31	31	0	30	31	31	31	31	0	0	0
O	0	0	0	0	0	0	0	0	0	0	31	31	0	31	30	31	31	31	0	0	0
P	0	0	0	0	0	0	0	0	0	0	31	31	0	31	31	30	31	31	0	0	0
Q	0	0	0	0	0	0	0	0	0	0	31	31	0	31	31	31	30	31	0	0	0
R	0	0	0	0	0	0	0	0	0	0	31	31	0	31	31	31	31	30	0	0	0
S	39	39	39	0	0	36	36	1	1	1	0	0	4	0	0	0	0	0	38	39	32
T	39	39	39	0	0	36	36	1	1	1	0	0	4	0	0	0	0	0	39	38	32
U	32	32	32	0	0	25	25	0	1	1	0	0	9	0	0	0	0	0	32	32	20

In fact, this group of 15 individuals, enclosed in boxes in Table 6–5, represents a subset of the 21-man plating room group. This 15-man subgroup can be distinguished from the others because each one of these workers has 20 or more three-link paths leading to some other member of the subgroup. The activities prescribed by the formal organization require these workers to interact with others within the subgroup.

A survey of the friendship preferences of the plating room workers, as indicated in Figure 6–4, reveals the existence of several subgroups which coincide to a considerable degree with the pattern of relationships based on activities.

TABLE 6–6

S Matrix of Friendship Sentiments
of Plating Room Workers

	A	B	C	D	E	F	G	H	I	J	K	L	M	N	O	P	Q	R	S	T	U
A	0	1	1	0	0	1	1	0	0	0	0	0	0	0	0	0	0	0	1	1	1
B	1	0	1	0	0	1	1	0	0	0	0	0	0	0	0	0	0	0	1	1	1
C	1	1	0	0	0	1	1	0	0	0	0	0	0	0	0	0	0	0	1	1	1
D	0	0	0	0	1	0	0	0	0	0	0	0	0	0	0	0	0	0	0	0	0
E	0	0	0	1	0	0	0	0	0	0	0	0	0	0	0	0	0	0	0	0	0
F	1	1	1	0	0	0	1	0	0	0	0	0	0	0	0	0	0	0	1	1	1
G	1	1	1	0	0	1	0	0	0	0	0	0	0	0	0	0	0	0	1	1	1
H	0	0	0	0	0	0	0	0	0	0	0	0	0	0	0	0	0	0	0	0	0
I	0	0	0	0	0	0	0	0	0	1	0	0	0	0	0	0	0	0	0	0	0
J	0	0	0	0	0	0	0	0	1	0	0	0	0	0	0	0	0	0	0	0	0
K	0	0	0	0	0	0	0	0	0	0	0	1	1	0	0	0	0	0	0	0	0
L	0	0	0	0	0	0	0	0	0	0	1	0	1	0	0	0	0	0	0	0	0
M	0	0	0	0	0	0	0	0	0	0	1	1	0	0	0	0	0	0	0	0	0
N	0	0	0	0	0	0	0	0	0	0	0	0	0	0	1	1	1	1	0	0	0
O	0	0	0	0	0	0	0	0	0	0	0	0	0	1	0	1	1	1	0	0	0
P	0	0	0	0	0	0	0	0	0	0	0	0	0	1	1	0	1	1	0	0	0
Q	0	0	0	0	0	0	0	0	0	0	0	0	0	1	1	1	0	1	0	0	0
R	0	0	0	0	0	0	0	0	0	0	0	0	0	1	1	1	1	0	0	0	0
S	1	1	1	0	0	1	1	0	0	0	0	0	0	0	0	0	0	0	0	1	1
T	1	1	1	0	0	1	1	0	0	0	0	0	0	0	0	0	0	0	1	0	1
U	1	1	1	0	0	1	1	0	0	0	0	0	0	0	0	0	0	0	1	1	0

Table 6–6 discloses the friendship choices made by the plating room workers, and Table 6–7 contains the cubed matrix of expressed mutual sentiments of friendships. The fact that the principal diagonal of the S^3 matrix of sentiments has at least three entries that are greater than or equal to two, shows the existence of subgroups. In fact, there are three subgroups within the plating room.

This fact can be determined by observing the numbers which appear in the principal diagonal, 42, 2, and 12. These numbers appear in those positions on the principal diagonal which correspond to those individuals who are members of a subgroup. For instance, all the individuals with the number 42 in the principal

TABLE 6-7

Cubed S Matrix of Friendship
Sentiments of Plating Room Workers

	A	B	C	D	E	F	G	H	I	J	K	L	M	N	O	P	Q	R	S	T	U
A	42	43	43	0	0	43	43	0	0	0	0	0	0	0	0	0	0	0	43	43	43
B	43	42	43	0	0	43	43	0	0	0	0	0	0	0	0	0	0	0	43	43	43
C	43	43	42	0	0	43	43	0	0	0	0	0	0	0	0	0	0	0	43	43	43
D	0	0	0	0	1	0	0	0	0	0	0	0	0	0	0	0	0	0	0	0	0
E	0	0	0	1	0	0	0	0	0	0	0	0	0	0	0	0	0	0	0	0	0
F	43	43	43	0	0	42	43	0	0	0	0	0	0	0	0	0	0	0	43	43	43
G	43	43	43	0	0	43	42	0	0	0	0	0	0	0	0	0	0	0	43	43	43
H	0	0	0	0	0	0	0	0	0	0	0	0	0	0	0	0	0	0	0	0	0
I	0	0	0	0	0	0	0	0	0	1	0	0	0	0	0	0	0	0	0	0	0
J	0	0	0	0	0	0	0	0	1	0	0	0	0	0	0	0	0	0	0	0	0
K	0	0	0	0	0	0	0	0	0	0	2	3	3	0	0	0	0	0	0	0	0
L	0	0	0	0	0	0	0	0	0	0	3	2	3	0	0	0	0	0	0	0	0
M	0	0	0	0	0	0	0	0	0	0	3	3	2	0	0	0	0	0	0	0	0
N	0	0	0	0	0	0	0	0	0	0	0	0	0	12	13	13	13	13	0	0	0
O	0	0	0	0	0	0	0	0	0	0	0	0	0	13	12	13	13	13	0	0	0
P	0	0	0	0	0	0	0	0	0	0	0	0	0	13	13	12	13	13	0	0	0
Q	0	0	0	0	0	0	0	0	0	0	0	0	0	13	13	13	12	13	0	0	0
R	0	0	0	0	0	0	0	0	0	0	0	0	0	13	13	13	13	12	0	0	0
S	43	43	43	0	0	43	43	0	0	0	0	0	0	0	0	0	0	0	42	43	43
T	43	43	43	0	0	43	43	0	0	0	0	0	0	0	0	0	0	0	43	42	43
U	43	43	43	0	0	43	43	0	0	0	0	0	0	0	0	0	0	0	43	43	42

diagonal, that is, A, B, C, F, G, S, T, and U are members of one clique composed of eight members. The number 42 does not occur by accident, because the number appearing in the principal diagonal must equal to $(n-1)(n-2)$ or $(8-1)(8-2)$ which is equal to 42. The same is true of the other two subgroups, that is $(3-2)(3-1)$ equals 2 and $(5-2)(5-1)$ equals 12. Thus, with the cubed matrix we are able to determine the existence of three cliques in the plating room, determine the number of members in each clique, and identify the individuals in each clique.

The cubed supermatrices of activities and sentiments each contain several submatrices. A comparison of the two supermatrices reveals the existence of similar patterns of submatrices, the subgroups defined by the formally prescribed activities are also friendship groups. It appears that in the interdependence of certain prescribed activities there exists a basis for the development of friendship subgroups. These sociometrically arranged subgroups, as indicated in Table 6–1, produce superior quantity and quality output.

Practical Applications

Not only is sociometric analysis useful in determining and locating informal groups, informal leaders, and informal communications, but it can be used in facilitating change and improving performance.

Education. The earliest sociometric applications occurred in the field of education. Moreno and others used sociometric analysis to understand students and to help them to improve their interpersonal relations by counseling and regrouping them on the basis of sociometric choices.[41] School administrators and teachers were also studied. Attempts were made to sensitize teacher observations and judgments about their students.[42]

Industry. One of the first industrial applications of sociometry

---

[41] For example, see: Moreno, *Who Shall Survive?, op. cit.;* J. L. Moreno, "Sociometry in the Classroom," *Sociometry,* Vol. 6 (1943), pp. 425–28; J. L. Moreno and H. H. Jennings, "Sociometric Methods of Grouping and Regrouping," *Sociometry,* Vol. 7 (1944), pp. 397–414; L. Kerstetter and J. Sargent, "Reassignment Therapy in the Classroom," *Sociometry,* Vol. 3 (1940), pp. 292–306; A. D. Johnson, "An Attempt at Change in Interpersonal Relationships," *Sociometry,* Vol. 2 (1939), pp. 43–48; L. D. Zeleny, "Sociometry in the College Classroom," *Sociometry,* Vol. 3 (1940), pp. 102–4; D. Faunce and J. A. Beegle, "Cleavages in Relatively Homogeneous Group of Rural Youth: An Experiment in the Use of Sociometry in Attaining and Measuring Integration," *Sociometry,* Vol. 11 (1948), pp. 207–16.

[42] For example, see: M. L. Northway, "Outsiders: A Study of the Personality Patterns of Children Least Acceptable to their Age Mates," *Sociometry,* Vol. 7 (1944), pp. 10–25; M. E. Bonney, "Sociometric Study of Agreement Between Teacher Judgments and Student Choices: In Regard to the Number of Friends Possessed by High School Students," *Sociometry,* Vol. 10 (1947), pp. 133–46; N. E. Gronlund, "The Accuracy of Teachers' Judgments Concerning the Sociometric Status of Sixth-Grade Pupils, Part I and Part II," *Sociometry,* Vol. 13 (1950), pp. 197–225 and 329–57.

was reported by J. H. Jacobs in 1945.[43] While Jacobs does not report specific results of this study, he concludes that industrial uses for sociometric analysis include: a method of testing morale; a means of determining the intangible factors of cooperation and productivity; a method of recording social adjustment to work; an aid to management in selecting and rating personnel; and a method of identifying informal groups.

A sociometric analysis of a group of executives was reported by C. G. Browne.[44] This study suggests that there is a positive correlation between the frequency of interactions and a questionnaire measure of delegation of authority and leadership. Browne indicates that sociometric data are useful in studying and modifying communication channels, leadership style, and personnel relations.

Another sociometric study conducted by B. Speroff and W. Kerr relates industrial safety and sociometric choice.[45] This investigation suggests that accident proneness appears to be related in a negative manner to sociometric choice. Speroff and Kerr suggest that industrial accidents could be reduced by assigning workers on the basis of sociometric choice.

A research study, reported by H. Van Zelst, reveals that sociometrically arranged work teams among bricklayers are superior over casually arranged work teams in terms of job performance and degree of job satisfaction.[46] The sociometrically selected work teams produced more, maintained a higher level of quality, reduced labor turnover, and expressed a more "comfortable feeling" at work. The major limitation to this approach, according to Van Zelst, is in "the shifting of workers to different jobs while avoiding any change in job duties which would affect job performance, necessitate retraining of workers, etc."[47] Another similar study, conducted by Speroff, found no significant correlation between sociometric choice and job satis-

---

[43] Jacobs, op. cit., pp. 181–98.

[44] C. G. Browne, "A Study of Executive Leadership in Business: Part IV, Sociometric Pattern," Journal of Applied Psychology, Vol. 35 (1951), pp. 34–37.

[45] B. Speroff and W. Kerr, "Steel Mill 'Hot Strip' Accidents and Interpersonal Desirability Values," Journal of Clinical Psychology, Vol. 8 (1952), pp. 89–91.

[46] R. H. Van Zelst, "Validation of a Sociometric Regrouping," Journal of Abnormal and Social Psychology, Vol. 47 (1952), pp. 299–301; and R. H. Van Zelst, "Sociometrically Selected Work Teams," Personnel Psychology, Vol. 5 (1952), pp. 175–85.

[47] R. H. Van Zelst, "Sociometrically Selected Work Teams," op. cit., p. 184.

faction.[48] Outside of these studies little has been reported on the application of sociometry in industry.

Military. Interest in the military services concerning morale, social adjustment, leadership, and informal groups has resulted in several sociometric studies. A study reported by J. G. Jenkins reveals a relationship between the morale of Navy pilots and sociometric choices and rejections.[49] The air squadron with high morale was characterized by friendship choices among commanding and executive officers. There was also a high incidence of pilot in-group friendship choices. In the air squadron with low morale, there were considerable pilot in-group rejections as well as a lack of friendship choices among the commanding and executive officers. There were no cliques within the high-morale squadron, while the low-morale squadron included distinct cliques. D. M. Goodacre, III, used sociometric choices to predict combat effectiveness for 12 Army squads performing under field conditions.[50]

The value of friendship choices to the U.S. Army is reflected in the introduction of an Army regulation which permits an infantryman who has been assigned to foreign duty to select three other soldiers to form an overseas replacement team.

The few studies presented in this section suggest that sociometric analysis can serve a valuable function in understanding social behavior in a variety of organizations. Although this technique is potentially a useful tool in organizational analysis, it involves some unresolved problems. Its excessive dependence upon sociometric choices and rejections, the scarcity of theoretically based research, inadequate attention to the selection of sociometric criteria, and inadequate quantitative treatment of data are some of the limitations that have been pointed out.[51]

SUMMARY

This chapter attempts to distinguish social organization from formal organization, especially as the former may exist within the

---

[48] B. J. Speroff, "Job Satisfaction and Interpersonal Desirability Values," *Sociometry*, Vol. 18 (1955), pp. 69–72.

[49] J. G. Jenkins, "The Nominating Technique as a Method of Evaluating Air Group Morale," *Journal of Aviation Medicine*, Vol. 19, No. 1 (1948), pp. 12–19.

[50] D. M. Goodacre, III, "The Use of a Sociometric Test as a Predictor of Combat Unit Effectiveness," *Sociometry*, Vol. 14 (1951), pp. 148–52.

[51] See Lindzey and Borgatta, *op. cit.*, pp. 441–44, for an elaboration on the limitations of sociometric analysis.

latter. It is necessary to study social organization because it exists within formal organization and because it has an effect on the way that people behave in formal organization. Social organization arises spontaneously, and its structure is usually determined by shared beliefs and social processes. Its principal function is to organize and control the social interactions, friendships, and conduct of its members. It serves as an instrument for the accomplishment in an informal way of that which is not realized through the formal organization.

The structure of the social group is a function of the social processes which take place within an informal group. The social processes are based on three elements of behavior—activities, interactions, and friendship sentiments. The structure of any social group can be defined by obtaining sociometric data about individuals of an organization and subjecting these data to analysis. Analysis of these data can be accomplished with the aid of matrix algebra. By manipulating sociometric data, it is possible to identify a social group, its size and its members.

The social organization is only one of the subsytems of the formal organization. Power and power relations, another component of formal organization, is the next subject of discussion.

DISCUSSION QUESTIONS AND PROBLEMS

6–1. Since informal organization arises spontaneously and is relatively fluid, how can it be characterized as an organization?

6–2. What is the relationship of informal organization to formal organization? Why do informal organizations exist?

6–3. Define what is meant by status and role in both the formal and informal organizations. Illustrate each with an example.

6–4. Discuss the sanctions that are used in informal organizations. How do they differ from the sanctions of the formal organization.

6–5. Compare and contrast the communication media of the informal and formal organizations with respect to speed, accuracy, and direction.

6–6. Shared values function as a means of effecting internal control over group members. This control may be to the benefit or to the detriment of the formal organization. Explain.

6–7. Give several examples of values that may or may not guide the conduct of an informal group to achieve the goals of the formal organization.

6–8. How can sociometric analysis be used in designing organizations. What are its limitations?

6–9. The Dolphin Corporation is a small scientific company engaged in the production of underwater breathing apparatus. The company has a staff of eight engineers. Four of the engineers (A, B, C, D) are supposedly professionally oriented (those people who identify themselves with the values of science and knowledge) and work under Mr. Harkness in the research laboratory. The other four engineers (E, F, G, H) are supposedly organizationally oriented (those who identify with the company itself and would value administrative positions, promotion to supervisory positions, etc.) and comprise the technical service group under Mr. Leland. A study was made to see with whom each man would like to work. The matrix in Table A shows each man's choices. The number 1 indicates that the man in that row has chosen the man in that column.

TABLE A

	Harkness	Leland	A	B	C	D	E	F	G	H
Harkness	0	1	0	0	0	0	0	0	0	0
Leland	1	0	0	0	0	0	0	0	0	0
A	1	0	0	0	1	1	0	0	0	0
B	0	1	0	0	0	0	1	1	0	1
C	1	0	1	0	0	1	0	0	0	0
D	1	0	1	0	1	0	0	0	0	0
E	0	1	0	0	0	0	0	1	0	1
F	0	1	0	0	0	0	1	0	0	1
G	1	0	1	0	1	1	0	0	0	0
H	0	1	0	0	0	0	1	1	0	0

Use the preceding information to answer the following questions:

a) Does the informal organization follow the lines of the formal organization?

b) What seems to be the positions of engineers B & G?

c) Identify the cliques through the use of matrix algebra.

d) To what would you ascribe the cliques.

6–10. Archer Engineering, Inc., is a small machine shop manufacturing motor parts. In addition to the owner, who supervises the men in the shop, there is an office staff composed of three secretaries. In the factory there are three older man and four young men. Several of the people in the company are relatives of the owner. An investigation of who each person liked in the company uncovered the choices shown in Table B. Notation here is the same as in Problem 1.

TABLE B

	Owner	Sec. A	Sec. B	Sec. C	YMA	YMB	YMC	YMD	OMA	OMB	OMC
Owner	0	1	1	1	0	0	0	1	1	1	1
Sec. A	1	0	1	1	0	0	0	1	0	0	0
Sec. B	1	1	0	1	0	0	0	1	0	0	0
Sec. C	1	1	1	0	0	0	0	1	0	0	0
YMA	0	0	0	0	0	1	1	0	0	0	0
YMB	0	0	0	0	1	0	1	0	0	0	0
YMC	0	0	0	0	1	1	0	0	0	0	0
YMD	1	1	1	1	0	0	1	0	0	0	0
OMA	0	0	0	0	0	0	0	0	0	1	1
OMB	0	0	0	0	0	0	0	0	1	0	1
OMC	0	0	0	0	0	0	0	0	1	1	0

a) Identify the cliques and indicate how many people are in each clique.

b) Indicate if age plays any part in the informal organization.

6-11. The Pierson Storm Door Company is a small company that manufactures and sells storm doors. The organization is made up of a president, two salesmen, a production manager and six workers. Each man in the company was asked to choose who he would like to work with. Table C includes all of the choices made.

TABLE C

	President	Sales. A	Sales. B	Prod. Mgr.	Worker A	Worker B	Worker C	Worker D	Worker E	Worker F
President	0	1	1	1	0	1	0	0	0	0
Sales. A	1	0	1	0	0	0	0	0	0	0
Sales. B	1	1	0	0	0	0	0	0	0	0
Prod. Mgr.	1	0	0	0	0	0	0	1	1	1
Worker A	0	0	0	0	0	1	1	0	0	0
Worker B	0	0	0	0	1	0	1	0	0	0
Worker C	0	0	0	0	1	1	0	0	0	0
Worker D	0	0	0	1	0	0	0	0	1	1
Worker E	0	0	0	1	0	0	0	1	0	1
Worker F	0	0	0	1	0	0	0	1	1	0

a) Identify the cliques and how many people are in each.

b) How many mutual choices is the production manager involved in? How many cliques?

c) How many three-step chains is the president involved in? (They do not have to be symmetrical.)

6-12. The starting players on a professional football team were requested to indicate which players they liked. The pattern shown in Table D evolved.

a) Identify the cliques and the number of people in each.

b) How many cliques is the fullback in?

c) How many three-step chains (they do not have to be symmetrical) is the fullback (FB) involved in?

d) How many mutual choices is the quarterback (QB) involved in?

TABLE D

	QB	LHB	RHB	FB	LE	LT	LG	C	RG	RT	RE
QB	0	1	0	1	0	0	0	0	0	0	1
LHB	1	0	0	1	0	1	1	0	0	0	0
RHB	0	0	0	1	1	0	0	0	1	1	1
FB	1	1	1	0	0	0	1	1	0	0	0
LE	1	0	1	0	0	1	0	0	0	1	1
LT	0	0	0	0	1	0	1	0	1	0	0
LG	0	1	0	1	0	1	0	1	0	1	1
C	1	0	0	1	1	0	1	0	1	0	0
RG	0	0	0	0	0	1	0	1	0	1	0
RT	0	0	0	0	1	0	0	0	1	0	1
RE	1	0	1	1	1	0	0	0	1	0	0

6–13. An office supervisor wants to raise the efficiency of his group of five secretaries. The supervisor reasons that efficiency can be increased by moving those secretaries who like each other adjacent to each other. The existing arrangement shows:

| Sec. A | Sec. B | Sec. C | Sec. D | Sec. E |

The results of a questionnaire asking who likes who are shown in Table E.

TABLE E

	Sec. A	Sec. B	Sec. C	Sec. D	Sec. E
Sec. A	0	1	1	1	1
Sec. B	1	0	1	1	0
Sec. C	1	1	0	0	1
Sec. D	1	1	0	0	0
Sec. E	1	0	1	1	0

a) What is the best office arrangement, assuming that the work is homogeneous and that the supervisor's reasoning is valid?

b) How many cliques is secretary A involved in? Secretary B?

6–14. Suppose that the supervisor in problem 6–13 obtained the results shown in Table F.

TABLE F

	Sec. A	Sec. B	Sec. C	Sec. D	Sec. E
Sec. A	0	0	1	0	1
Sec. B	1	0	0	0	1
Sec. C	1	0	0	1	0
Sec. D	1	0	1	0	0
Sec. E	0	1	0	1	0

a) On the basis of mutual choices, what would be the best seating arrangement?

b) Who are the members of each clique?

6-15. The coach of a major college basketball team feels that in order to get the best performance from his starting five, all members of the starting five must like each other. The coach feels that all eight of his players have equal ability. The coach conducted a survey of who liked who on the team. The results are shown in Table G.

TABLE G

	A	B	C	D	E	F	G	H
A	0	0	1	1	0	1	0	1
B	0	0	0	0	0	0	0	0
C	1	0	0	1	0	1	0	1
D	1	0	1	0	0	1	0	1
E	0	0	0	0	0	0	1	0
F	1	0	1	1	0	0	0	1
G	0	0	0	0	1	0	0	0
H	1	0	1	1	0	1	0	0

Which members of the team should be on the starting five?

6-16. A floor in the Memorial Hospital is staffed by six people—three nurses (F, G, H), two aides (A and B), and one porter (P). The supervisor of this staff has been aware of "increasing friendliness" accompanied by decreasing efficiency within the staff. The supervisor wishes to identify the source of this increasing friendliness so that she might be able to remedy the situation. The supervisor asked each staff member which staff member he or she liked. The results are shown in Table H.

TABLE H

	F	G	H	P	A	B
F	0	1	1	0	1	1
G	1	0	1	1	1	1
H	1	1	0	0	1	1
P	1	1	0	0	1	1
A	1	1	1	1	0	1
B	1	1	1	0	1	0

a) How many cliques exist within the staff and who are the members of each clique?

b) Who might be the reason for the increasing friendliness? (Hint: Before taking her survey, the supervisor was sure that a clique of five people—F, G, H, A, and B existed.)

7

POWER AND POWER STRUCTURE

In this chapter, we are concerned with still another pattern of behavior in formal organization—the behavior that is associated with power relationships. Formalized task-oriented behavior, social behavior, and power behavior are the behavior patterns of formal organization discussed in this book. Although it is conceptually convenient and necessary to discuss these patterns in separate parts of the book, it should be recognized that they are not independent systems. They are subsystems of the formal organization and, as we shall see in the next chapter, make up the emergent system.

Each subsystem has influence mechanisms. The formal or technical subsystem assigns each organization member to a specialized job and attempts to govern his behavior through job specifications and a statement of expected performance. In addition, the organization provides managerial positions with responsibilities for decision making and coordinating the work of subordinate positions. Thus, a person occupying a managerial position must be able to influence subordinates to implement his decisions and, in general, direct their behavior toward the goals of the formal organization. In order to fulfill this responsibility, managerial positions are supplied with formal authority. Through this authority, the manager may invoke official sanctions to gain the compliance of subordinates. According to traditional theory, the direction for the course of events in a formal organization flows downward only through the hierarchy of authority. However, research conducted in actual organizations and in laboratory situations indicates that authority which is based on the official position provides only one potential source of influence. It is often unsuccessful. There are many more bases for influence in an organization.[1] When influence is successful and it involves the presentation of force, it is called power.

An Illustration of Power

The following newspaper account involving the Philadelphia Eagles professional football team provides an interesting example of how the course of events in a formal organization was influenced by men who did not occupy administrative positions in the hierarchy of formal authority.

Thursday, September 5, 1963.[2] Eagles quarterbacks Sonny Jurgensen and King Hill were AWOL Wednesday and efforts of embarrassed officials to locate them were unsuccessful. They walked out of the Philadelphia club's Hershey training camp without notice in a "no-contract, no-work" maneuver without precedent among National Football League players.

Their sudden departure left the team without a quarterback three days before the final exhibition game with the New York Giants . . . and only 11 days before the Eagles open the league season against the Pittsburgh Steelers . . .

Jurgensen and Hill told teammates they were taking the drastic step in order to get Vince McNally, Eagles' general manager, to sit down and negotiate a contract with them.

The two quarterbacks are among six Eagles who haven't signed for the 1963 season. Unlike major league baseball, unsigned NFL players are allowed to train with a team because of an option clause that binds a player to the club for a year in addition to the one for which he signs.

Jurgensen is anxious to sign a contract calling for a salary increase while Hill is fighting a salary cut. Reports had Jurgensen receiving in excess of $25,000 and Hill approximately $20,000 last season.

McNally said he had no idea what the quarterbacks planned to do. "We're trying to get in touch with them to see if we can work out something," he said. This was proving difficult since no one knew where the players might be reached.

Safetyman Don Burroughs, the only player on the squad with quarterback experience and assistant coach Sonny Grandelius filled in for the missing quarterbacks as the Eagles drilled against Giants' plays and

---

[1] W. G. Bennis, N. Berkowitz, M. Affinito, and M. Malone, "Authority, Power, and the Ability to Influence," *Human Relations*, Vol. 11 (1958), p. 144.

[2] *The Philadelphia Inquirer*. Reprinted with the permission of Triangle Publications.

sharpened some of their own offensive maneuvers. Burroughs hasn't played quarterback since leaving Colorado State nine years ago.

Friday, September 6, 1963.[3] Quarterbacks Sonny Jurgensen and King Hill won their one-day strike against the Eagles Thursday. They signed new contracts making Jurgensen the highest paid player in the club's history and giving Hill an increase instead of a salary cut.

It was learned reliably that Jurgensen received a $4,000 boost that upped his salary to $30,000, one of the highest in the National Football League. Hill reportedly settled for a boost in the neighborhood of $1700 that placed him in the $20,000 bracket.

"We got what we wanted," said a serious Jurgensen after the meeting and an equally serious Hill added: "I'm satisfied."

Jurgensen and Hill did not have administrative authority but they had power. It was not the owners or managers who determined the outcome in this situation but two football players on the team. Although the owners and managers contributed to the outcome by agreeing to terms, they were not the influencers but the object of influence. The power of Jurgensen and Hill was evident from their ability to employ sanctions and to obtain a desired result from the Eagles' management. The walkout was an application of sanctions, and the salary increase was the intended result.

In this case, there were several sources of power. One source of power was job importance. The quarterback is undoubtedly the most important position on the team. Offensive maneuvers are built around the quarterback. He handles the ball on virtually every play and must either hand the ball off lateral or forward pass it to an eligible receiver, or run with it himself. The quarterback position requires extraordinary skills, both physical and mental. He must be a superb ball handler and passer. Since he, along with the coaches determines team strategy, he must display above-average intelligence. Since he calls virtually every play during the game, his tactical decision-making skills must be superior. The demands on a quarterback in professional football leave little room for error or anything less than perfection. In short, he must be very proficient in all aspects of his job. Anyone who qualifies for the quarterback position on a professional football team has power in his dealings with a team's managers. This factor gained even greater than ordinary importance in the Jurgensen-Hill situation because when

---

[3] *The Philadelphia Inquirer.* Reprinted with the permission of Triangle Publications.

both players agreed to walk out together, it left the team with no quarterback.

Another source of power to the players was their quarterbacking skills and especially their passing ability. According to the *Inquirer;* "Sonny Jurgensen and King Hill are the keys to the Eagles' offense. Between them they account for all of the passing except an occasional toss by halfback Timmy Brown." Furthermore, both players were very familiar with the complicated Eagles' offense.

Another source of power to the players was the coalition formed in their agreement to walk out together. Prior to the walkout, each man, acting individually, failed to negotiate a favorable contract. Apparently, neither Jurgensen nor Hill had the individual power to induce management to act as desired. However, their concerted action was overwhelming, and the Eagles' management was forced to capitulate.

By all accounts, management was completely surprised by the action. If they considered the possibility of such action, the management had good reason to question its occurrence. First of all, as mentioned in the newspaper article, such behavior was unprecedented among National Football League players. Second, there was the peculiar contract clause which bound players to a team for one year after a contract had expired. Third, it was unlikely that the two men would act in concert on a highly personal matter such as salary. Last, but not least, there is the "glory of the game" which seemingly is more important than material benefits. Nonetheless, they did walk out, and the fact that they caught management completely by surprise contributed to the power of the players.

The combination of these factors plus the fact that the timing of the maneuver was opportune (they walked out 3 days before an exhibition game with the New York Giants and 11 days before the League opener with the Pittsburgh Steelers), made any other alternative such as the use of a substitute player or the hiring of a new quarterback unthinkable to the Eagles' management. In short, the team was in dire need of their services. Frank McNamee, the Eagles' president, summed it up well when he was quoted in the *Inquirer* as saying: "They had us over a barrel and there was nothing else we could do but eat crow."[4]

---

[4] A similar incident occurred in professional baseball when Sandy Koufax and Don Drysdale, pitchers for the Los Angeles Dodgers, agreed to "hold out"

DEFINITION OF POWER

Power is a mode of influence. It is an interpersonal concept.[5] It always refers to a relation or relations between or among people.[6] *Influence* is defined as an ability of an individual or group to induce others to produce an intended result. There are, of course, many ways to induce others to produce an intended result. We are interested in two ways: persuasion and coercion. *Persuasion* involves an effort to influence by argument, reasoning, or a presentation of ideas. The person who is the object of persuasive efforts may refuse to produce without fear of reprisal. *Coercion,* on the other hand, involves an effort to influence through the use or presentation of force, and the person who refuses to obey a command may expect reprisal. People who can produce an intended result through the use or presentation of force have power. *Power* may be defined, then, as an ability to influence through coercion. The power of an executive, for example, is his ability to gain the obedience of subordinates through the application (or possible application) of sanctions. When subordinates refuse to obey his commands, he may apply negative sanctions such as demotion, layoff, reduction in pay, reprimand, or expulsion from the system. The executive may also apply positive sanctions for obedience such as promotion, commendation, or an increase in salary. His ability to use sanctions is derived from his formal position in the administrative hierarchy of authority. In this case, power and administrative authority are equivalent. The expert employee who seeks higher wages may apply sanctions by resigning or threatening to resign. His ability to apply sanctions is derived from the fact that he possesses skills that are scarce and extremely valuable to the organization. In this case, power is not equivalent to administrative authority. Indeed, the expert employee may have no administrative authority.

---

prior to the 1966 season until both had received contracts that were satisfactory to each member of the coalition. They were successful in their collective bargaining for higher salaries. The power of this coalition was based upon their successful performances during the previous season when, as starting pitchers, they were credited with 49, or over one half, of the Dodger victories. For a more complete account of this event, see Sandy Koufax, *Koufax* (New York: Viking Press, Inc., 1966).

[5] Harold D. Lasswell and Abraham Kaplan, *Power and Society* (New Haven, Conn.: Yale University Press, 1950), p. 75.

[6] This relation may refer to one person and another person, a group and another group, or a group and a person.

Use or Presentation of Force

It is important to emphasize that the power relation does not always involve the use or threat of force. It is probably more correct to say that the use or threat of force is seldom employed in the power relation. The executive does not threaten his subordinates everytime he issues an order, and the expert employee does not threaten to resign everytime that he seeks concessions from his superior. It must, however, be apparent to the person who is the object of power that the power holder will use sanctions when necessary.

Power does not attach to those who are unable or unwilling to use force. An executive who has the right to use sanctions but is unwilling to employ them when necessary has authority but not power. The "presentation of force" in our definition means, therefore, that the power holder has a predisposition or capacity to use available sanctions and this is recognized by "others" in the relationship.

Power may be described as a latent force. Power is not applied. It becomes manifest through force which is applied. Force is visible and apparent. When an executive applies sanctions to a subordinate, he is using force and showing his power. The application of sanctions also identifies him as a power holder and gives evidence of his willingness to use force.

When a power holder uses force, he gives direction to the course of events. An executive, for instance, does not apply negative sanctions for the sheer joy of seeing someone punished nor does he apply positive sanctions because he wants to do good things for others, but rather he is trying to ensure satisfactory results on organizational objectives.[7] By applying sanctions, he is serving notice that satisfactory performance is expected. The subordinates who perform unsatisfactorily are punished or go unrewarded, while those who produce satisfactory results or perform in an exemplary manner are rewarded. The point is that sanctions are the *means* used to produce an intended result in the power relation. Even when sanctions are not used, the threat or possibility of their use still represents the means for producing intended results.

---

[7] Here, we are assuming rationality, that is, behavior oriented toward the goals of the organization rather than emotional behavior.

Ability to Influence Through Force

The application of sanctions involves the deprivation or rendering of something that is valuable to those who are the object of power. The "ability to influence through force," then, means that the power holder possesses, or is in a position to give or withhold, something that is valued by those from whom he seeks compliance.

In terms of formal action, a power relation exists when an executive has formal authority and is able to promote, demote, or fire subordinates, and subordinates value their jobs or a promotion enough to be willing to carry out his orders. A subordinate or a person in a position which does not carry formal administrative authority may also have power. The services of an employee may be considered so valuable to an organization that management would readily consent to his demands for higher wages or better working conditions. If management refused to grant his demands for higher wages or better working conditions, the employee could employ the sanctions at his disposal, that is, quit or refuse to render his services. A salesman who has developed and extracted personal loyalty from large customer accounts, a football player with unusual skills, a medical doctor who has brought great prestige to a university through his research and publications, an employee with expert knowledge about a machine or process, and an inventor of profit-making products are all examples of people who are valuable to an organization. They are valuable because the rendering of their services is beneficial, and the cessation of these services would be harmful, to an organization. Given the predisposition to use these valued services as sanctions, that is, to refuse to render them unless certain demands are satisfied, these people have power. The salesman, for example, may demand and be successful in gaining participation in decisions that affect his customers. The expert employee may be able to participate in decisions affecting his working conditions.

There is the possibility, of course, that the one making demands or threatening the use of force has overvalued his services. Management may reject the demands of an employee for higher wages, for example, because it feels that the wages demanded exceed the value of his services. The management of a company experiencing labor difficulties may be willing to incur heavy losses rather than meet the "excessive" demands of a labor union. The salesman may not be able to gain a participating voice in all decisions affecting his customers. The management may refuse to allow him a "voice" in the prices charged his customers. It may be willing to risk the loss of his services and the business of his customers rather than relinquish its prerogative to set prices.

One person is unsuccessful in influencing others through the use of force because "others" do not place sufficient values on his possessions. When the possessions of the person desiring certain results are not valued sufficiently by the others, the power relationship has either failed or never existed in the first place. The definition of power, therefore, assumes that "others" in the relationship consider the things possessed by those seeking compliance, giving orders, or making demands have sufficient value to warrant the response desired. In other words, in the definition of power, it must be assumed that efforts to influence through force are always successful. When the efforts are unsuccessful, there is, by definition, no power relationship.

Mutual Dependence

Actually, both parties to the power relation possess something of value. One party to the relationship is trying to achieve an intended result and, therefore, he *values* the responses of the other party. To obtain the desired responses, he must possess, or be in a position to provide or withhold, something of *value* to the other party. In effect, power involves *mutually dependent relations,* with each party to the relation dependent upon the other for gratification. Richard Emerson has stated the power-dependent relation in the following manner:

Social relations commonly entail *ties* of *mutual dependence* between the parties. A *depends* upon B if he aspires to goals or gratifications whose achievement is facilitated by appropriate actions on B's part. By virtue of mutual dependency, it is more or less imperative to each party that he be able to control or influence the other's conduct. At the same time, these ties of mutual dependence imply that each party is in a position, to some degree, to grant or deny, facilitate or hinder, the other's gratification. Thus, it would appear that the power to control or influence the other resides in control over the things he values, which may range all the way from oil resources to ego-support, depending upon the relation in question. In short *power resides implicitly in the other's dependency.*[8]

---

[8] Richard M. Emerson, "Power-Dependence Relations," *American Sociological Review,* Vol. 27 (February, 1962), p. 32.

Scope of Power

Power does not necessarily mean that one man or group has complete control over the behavior of another man or group. The power relation is generally limited to a behavior area. Thus, a supervisor may have power over a subordinate's work behavior but not over his personal life away from the job. An inspector may have power over a group of workers only in matters that deal with the quality of their performance. A union may have power over the management of a firm in matters that deal with the working conditions of employees but not over how the company distributes its profits.

Power also has limitations with respect to time periods. A military pilot, for example, may have power over his copilot on all matters concerning the flight of their aircraft. This relation may hold even though the copilot is of higher military rank than the pilot. However, the power relation may not exist after both men return to the ground and resume normal military decorum. Thus, the power of the pilot over the copilot existed only during the time of flight and covered all matters of flight. The supervisor mentioned above has power over subordinates only during working hours.

Power may extend to one person, several persons, a group, or several groups, but the number of people covered in any power relation is definitely limited.[9] Furthermore, power does not cover all relations of the power holder. A personnel director, for example, may come into contact with many employees from many departments of a company, but his power is limited to members of the personnel department. A union official may have power over the members of his own union but not over members of another union or over nonunion members. It is obvious that a complete statement of a power relation would have to include references to behavior area, time period, and the people involved.

PERSPECTIVE ON POWER

Again, we emphasize that there are several influences on behavior in formal organization. The reason for stressing power relationships, as we do in this chapter, is to underscore its importance as a

---

[9] Laswell and Kaplan, *op. cit.*, p. 77, call the number of people covered in a power relation "the domain of power."

major element in determining the course of events in an organization. It is a necessary mode of influence in any organization. While it is not always necessary to initiate action, power is necessary to sustain action in a given direction, that is, toward organizational goals. Furthermore, power provides order to the organization and sustains it through periods of change. In this regard, Bierstedt has stated:

. . . power is required to inaugurate an association in the first place, to guarantee its continuance, and to enforce its norms. Power stands behind every association and sustains its structure. Without power there is no organization and without power there is no order. The intrusion of the time dimension and the exigencies of circumstance require continual readjustments of the structure of every association, not excepting the most inelastically organized, and it is power which sustains it through these transitions.[10]

We may dramatize the importance of power by making further comparisons between persuasive and coercive influence. As we noted, a person attempting to influence behavior through persuasion, appeals to reason and understanding. He seeks agreement on issues and tries to convince others through argument. He tries to win over a person as to the proper course of action. Power, on the other hand, is coercive.[11] It does not involve appeals or arguments but relies on force. "We submit voluntarily to [persuasion], while power requires submission."[12] An executive with an engineering background has power over his subordinates not from his superior knowledge about engineering (this is competence rather than power) and not from a presentation of his ideas (this is persuasion rather than power) but from his ability to apply the sanctions of reward or punishment to those who are subject to his commands. "The competence may be unappreciated and the [persuasion] may be ineffective, but the power may not be gainsaid."[13]

---

[10] Robert Bierstedt, "An Analysis of Social Power," *American Sociological Review*, Vol. 15 (December, 1950), pp. 730–36, reprinted in Robert Dubin, *Human Relations in Administration* (Englewood Cliffs, N.J.: Prentice-Hall, Inc., 1961), pp. 245–46.

[11] For a different classification, see John R. P. French, Jr., and Bertram Raven, who make a distinction between coercive power and reward power: "The Bases of Social Power," in Dorwin Cartwright and Alvin Zander (eds.), *Group Dynamics* (2nd. ed.; Evanston, Ill.: Row, Peterson & Co., 1962), p. 615.

[12] Bierstedt, *op. cit.*, p. 240.

[13] *Ibid.* The example of the executive is adapted from Bierstedt's illustration of the power of a teacher over his pupils. The teacher's power stems from his

While persuasion will produce results, it does not have the sustenance of power. It will not sustain a goal oriented relationship or an organization which oftentimes requires performance that is disagreeable to the one asked to perform but very beneficial to the one making the request or to the organization. An organization requires coordinated action and, therefore, requires behavior which may seem unreasonable to individuals but necessary for overall effectiveness. Furthermore, an organization is likely to pass through periods of tribulation, and its demands for extraordinary effort may seem unreasonable to those upon whom the demands are made, but necessary for the survival of the organization. Obviously, performance that is based on an appeal to reason and understanding will not be forthcoming when demands seem unreasonable. Dahl's definition of power provides a good summary of the sustaining characteristics of power. He states, "A has power over B to the extent that he can get B to do something that B would not otherwise do."[14]

When organizational processes are entirely in compliance with the formal organizational structure, power is the same as formal authority and belongs to those who occupy administrative positions. Men who occupy administrative positions in the formal organization have a mandate to manage an area of responsibility. This mandate gives them the right to use sanctions which presumably enables them to obtain satisfactory performance from subordinates on organization objectives.

The definition of power as synonymous with formal authority and the identification of force solely with formal sanctions such as demotion, layoff, promotion, or commendation is a narrow approach to the subject of power. It is narrow because, as we learned in earlier chapters, organizational processes are seldom in complete compliance with the formal organizational structure. Furthermore, it is easy to understand that not all people in positions of authority have the predisposition to use force. Also, we shall learn that there are more and stronger sources of power than formal authority. Moreover, it will soon become apparent that sanctions can take many more forms than formal action. It is important, therefore, to

---

ability to withhold academic credit from students who do not meet his requirements.

[14] Robert A. Dahl, "The Concept of Power," *Behavioral Science*, Vol. 2 (1957), pp. 202–3.

broaden our approach by examining the other major sources of power. This broader approach reveals that people other than formally designated administrators possess power and that organizational processes follow patterns that conform to a power structure rather than to the formally designated structure.

POWER STRUCTURE

Structure in the technical part of the organization is based on the relationships among jobs or positions. Structure in the social organization is based on friendship choices. Structure in the power organization is based on values controlled by various members of the organization, that is, a person controls things considered valuable by others and he is able to influence their behavior in exchange for these things.[15]

The dependence relationship between two people is the basis for the formation of a power structure. A power structure exists if there are two or more unequal power-dependence relations.[16] A power relationship is the situation whereby M is dependent upon S and S is dependent upon M for gratification of certain values; that is, M has something that S considers valuable, and, therefore, S is willing to do what M asks or provide to M those things that M values or wants. In a case where this dependence is equal, we have $Dms = Dsm$ or the dependence of M upon S is equal to the dependence of S upon M. Since this dependency can be defined with respect to its potential influence of M upon S and S upon M, we can state the relationship in terms of the power of M over S and S over M.

$Pms = Psm$ means that the power of M over S equals the amount that S has over M. A completely balanced situation is shown by Emerson in the following manner:

$$
\begin{array}{ccc}
Pms & = & Dsm \\
\| & & \| \\
Psm & = & Dms
\end{array}
$$

---

[15] Again it is emphasized that the distinction made between these systems is for convenience. We show the overlap in Chapter 8.

[16] Emerson, *op. cit.*, pp. 33–34, argues that equal opposing power does not neutralize power. He suggests that even in "a balanced condition, power is in no way removed from the relationship." While we agree with Emerson's statement that power exists even in "balanced" power dependence situations, this discussion about structure is not concerned with the mere existence of power but rather with power relations which create a dominance structure.

An unbalanced (or unequal) power relationship is represented as follows:

$$Pms = Dsm$$
$$\vee \qquad \vee$$
$$Psm = Dms$$

An unequal power relationship between M and S means that M has a power advantage over S because the dependence of S upon M is greater than the dependence of M upon S. A power structure which is a static picture of difrential dominance relations among all members of a group may be shown graphically. By adding F and P we can illustrate a power structure. Let us suppose that M has a power advantage over S, F, and P, and that S dominates F and P, and F dominates P. These power-dependence relations can be shown graphically as depicted in Figure 7–1.[17]

FIGURE 7–1

Power Relations of M, S, F, and P

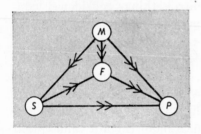

Using the notation $M \gg S$, we indicate that M has power over S. This is a one-link power relationship. The one-link power relationships in Figure 7–1 are:

$$M \gg S \qquad S \gg F$$
$$M \gg F \qquad S \gg P$$
$$M \gg P \qquad F \gg P$$

In this analysis of power relations, we assume that: (1) no individual can have power over himself; (2) each power-dependence relation is unequal, that is, in every power connection there is one individual who has power over the other; and (3) power need not be transitive, that is, if $M \gg S$ and $S \gg F$, it does not mean necessarily that $M \gg F$. If M has power over F we can show it by $M \gg F$, but we cannot automatically assume transitivity.

Another way of depicting power relations is by means of matrices similar to the ones used in Chapter 6. The relationships in Figure 7–1 are depicted in a power matrix (Table 7–1) by using the

---

[17] The application of this sociometric analysis to power relations is adapted from John G. Kemeny, J. Laurie Snell, and Gerald L. Thompson, *Introduction to Finite Mathematics* (Englewood Cliffs, N.J.: Prentice-Hall, Inc., 1956), pp. 307–12.

TABLE 7–1

Power Matrix

OBJECT OF POWER

		M	S	F	P
	M	0	1	1	1
POWER HOLDER	S	0	0	1	1
	F	0	0	0	1
	P	0	0	0	0

number 1 in the row cells of the power holder to represent power over the person in a given column and zero to represent no power advantage. Summing the values in the row of each individual reveals that M has three one-link power advantages, S has two, F has one, and P has zero. Let us refer to this one-link matrix as a D matrix

$$D = \begin{pmatrix} 0 & 1 & 1 & 1 \\ 0 & 0 & 1 & 1 \\ 0 & 0 & 0 & 1 \\ 0 & 0 & 0 & 0 \end{pmatrix}$$

A two-link power relationship involves three people and it may be indicated as $M \gg S \gg F$. The two-link power relationships of each individual can be obtained by squaring the original D matrix:

$$D^2 = \begin{pmatrix} 0 & 0 & 1 & 2 \\ 0 & 0 & 0 & 1 \\ 0 & 0 & 0 & 0 \\ 0 & 0 & 0 & 0 \end{pmatrix}$$

In matrix D^2 the sum of the values in the rows discloses that M has three two-link power advantages, S has 1, F has none, and P has none. The two-link relationships can be written as

$$M \gg S \gg F$$
$$M \gg F \gg P$$
$$M \gg S \gg P$$
$$S \gg F \gg P$$

If we measure power as the total number of one- and two-link power advantages, the power of each individual may be expressed as the sum of the row entries in the matrix $T = D + D^2$.

$$T = D + D^2 = \begin{pmatrix} 0 & 1 & 1 & 1 \\ 0 & 0 & 1 & 1 \\ 0 & 0 & 0 & 1 \\ 0 & 0 & 0 & 0 \end{pmatrix} + \begin{pmatrix} 0 & 0 & 1 & 2 \\ 0 & 0 & 0 & 1 \\ 0 & 0 & 0 & 0 \\ 0 & 0 & 0 & 0 \end{pmatrix} = \begin{pmatrix} 0 & 1 & 2 & 3 \\ 0 & 0 & 1 & 2 \\ 0 & 0 & 0 & 1 \\ 0 & 0 & 0 & 0 \end{pmatrix}$$

The T matrix reveals a power structure in which:

The power advantages of M = 6
The power advantages of S = 3
The power advantages of F = 1
The power advantages of P = 0

FIGURE 7–2

Formal Positions of M, S, F, and P

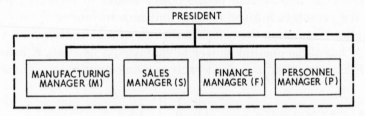

The analysis just completed must be conditioned, because the power advantages held may be limited by time and subject matter.[18]

FIGURE 7–3

Power Relations of M, S, F, and P for Personnel Selection Decisions

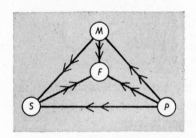

In a continuing relationship between people in an organization, it is possible for power roles to be different from problem to problem. For instance, if the four individuals, M, S, F, and P, depicted in Figure 7–1, occupy formal positions, as indicated in Figure 7–2, we would have to determine the scope of the power relations with respect to solving various types of problems. Let us suppose that for inventory decisions, the manufacturing manager has a power advantage as indicated in Figure 7–1, but for personnel selection decisions, the power relations may be as represented in Figure 7–3 and Table 7–2.

[18] In a subsequent section of this chapter, we introduce the idea that power relations may be stated in terms of a probability of success.

TABLE 7–2
Power Matrix for Personnel Selection Decisions
OBJECT OF POWER

		M	S	F	P
	M	0	1	1	0
POWER	S	0	0	1	0
HOLDER	F	0	0	0	0
	P	1	1	1	0

The power matrix T for the personnel selection problem, composed of one-link D and two-link relations D^2, is as follows:

$$T = D + D^2 = \begin{pmatrix} 0 & 1 & 1 & 0 \\ 0 & 0 & 1 & 0 \\ 0 & 0 & 0 & 0 \\ 1 & 1 & 1 & 0 \end{pmatrix} + \begin{pmatrix} 0 & 0 & 1 & 0 \\ 0 & 0 & 0 & 0 \\ 0 & 0 & 0 & 0 \\ 0 & 1 & 2 & 0 \end{pmatrix} = \begin{pmatrix} 0 & 1 & 2 & 0 \\ 0 & 0 & 1 & 0 \\ 0 & 0 & 0 & 0 \\ 1 & 2 & 3 & 0 \end{pmatrix}$$

The T matrix for personnel selection problems reveals a power structure in which:

The power advantages of P = 6
The power advantages of M = 3
The power advantages of S = 1
The power advantages of F = 0

Although it is limited to static analysis, this model may be used to analyze power relationships which are of a recurring and repetitive nature. More importantly, perhaps, is its use as a method of counting for the purpose of estimating probabilities for power relationships (taken up under the section, "Measures of Power").

SOURCES OF POWER

The power relation has been described as a mutually dependent relation in which each party is dependent upon the other for gratification. The decision maker, for example, relies on others to implement his decisions. He is dependent upon them for certain responses or for the accomplishment of intended results. The respondent or the one who implements decisions relies on the decision maker for the satisfaction of his needs. In effect, each party to the relation dispenses with something that is valuable to the other, and one is able to control the behavior of the other to the degree that he controls the things valued by the other. Herein lies the sources of power.

Power Process

The acquisition of things considered necessary to establish power relations and their subsequent transformation into influence mechanisms is called the power process. The formation of coalitions, the development of expert skills, or the efforts to attain status in the administrative hierarchy, are examples of power processes. Oftentimes power processes are called: "politics" or "political maneuvering." Miller and Form, for example, have observed that ". . . political processes run through the social structure of industry." In order to perform these processes, men ". . . must learn to play the appropriate role. Such roles require adaptability to the techniques of conflict, accommodation, and cooperation. If they are successful, they may gain power status. If they fail, others rise to take their place."[19] As power seekers learn to play the "role," that is, as they gain control over things valued by others and make it known that they are willing and able to employ these possessions as sanctions, they attain status in the power structure. Since values are so important to power processes, let us examine the sources from which these values may be acquired.

Although there are many, we are concerned only with the major sources of power. We classify the sources of power according to their attributes. Power stems from attributes of organization, individuals, and/or groups. None of these attributes is mutually exclusive of the others, nor are the attributes necessarily independent. All three, two, or any one of the attributes may serve as a source of power. An individual, for instance, may have valuable personal characteristics and/or occupy a position of formal authority and/or be a member of an informal organization or group. Either one or any combination of the three attributes could provide him with the ability to render or withhold things that are valuable to others.

Among the more important organizational attributes related to power are formal position in the administrative hierarchy or authority, job importance, and location. Since we have already examined formal position as a source of power, the discussion below

---

[19] Delbert C. Miller and William H. Form, *Industrial Sociology* (New York: Harper & Bros., 1951), p. 339.

is limited to the other two attributes. Among those individual attributes related to power are expertise, interest and tenure, and personal characteristics. Group attributes related to power include informal organization and coalitions.

Organizational Sources

Location. One of the reasons why people are able to gain power that is greater than the administrative authority allocated to their position is that they are located strategically in the flows of information and/or in the relationships between or among organizational components. Consider, for example, the information that flows to and from decision centers in an organization. Communication channels to decision centers carry information about objectives, environmental conditions, past performances, and the availability of resources. The decision center or decision maker needs this information to formulate alternative courses of action and to select the alternative which permits optimum results. After the decision has been made, communication channels carry the decision to others for implementation. Before the information is transmitted to and from decision centers, it usually requires some transformation. For example, it has to be gathered and consolidated into some summary form. It may require analysis. The information may need to be interpreted or judgments made about its meaning. It may also require judgments regarding the timing of transmittals.

The people who are placed in information processing positions are valuable not only because they occupy integral positions with respect to other parts of the system but also because the other parts (especially decision centers) are dependent upon them for an accurate and timely appraisal of facts. Some examples of duties that involve information processing to decision centers are sales forecasting, cost control (or virtually any accounting activity that prepares reports on financial performance), quality control, and personnel performance appraisal. Some examples of duties that involve information processing from decision centers are planning, (such as the preparation of budgets, schedules, blueprints, designs, strategies, projects), and line supervision where decisions must be interpreted and orders given to those who must do the work required by decisions. The dependency that arises between the people who process information and the people who need the information provides the basis for the power relationship. March and Simon call these activities "uncertainty absorption."

Uncertainty absorption takes place when inferences are drawn from a body of evidence and the inferences, instead of the evidence itself, are then communicated.

By virtue of specialization, most information enters an organization at highly specific points. Direct perception of production processes is limited largely to employees in a particular operation on the production floor. Direct perception of customer attitudes is limited largely to salesmen. Direct evidence of the performance of personnel is restricted largely to immediate supervisors, colleagues and subordinates.

In all of these cases, the person who summarizes and assesses his own direct perceptions and transmits them to the rest of the organization becomes an important source of informational premises for organizational action. The "facts" he communicates can be disbelieved but they can only rarely be checked. Hence, by the very nature and limits of the communication system, a great deal of discretion and influence is exercised by those persons who are in direct contact with some part of the "reality" that is of concern to the organization. Both the amount and the *locus of uncertainty absorption* affect the *influence structure of the organization.*

Because of this, uncertainty absorption is frequently used, consciously and unconsciously, as a technique for acquiring and exercising power.[20]

Similar observations could be made about people who are placed in positions which allow them to exercise discretion over when and who shall or shall not see another person. A secretary, for example, may have some degree of power over junior executives who have higher rank and earn a larger salary but who are nevertheless dependent upon her for an appointment with the chief executive. A busy executive who insulates himself with assistants to screen his correspondence, arrange his appointment schedule, and carry personal messages to others, creates conditions whereby these assistants may acquire an inordinate amount of power. Although their duties may be seemingly clerical and menial, the fact that they have easy access to the executive, exercise discretion in preparing his schedules, and represent his views, is likely to improve the ability of assistants to render things of value to others in the organization. Certain people might feel, for example, that their chances for a pay raise are better if the executive hears indirectly about an illness in the family, mortgage payments, an impending birth in the family, or about their diligent efforts on the job. Others

[20] James G. March and Herbert A. Simon, *Organizations* (New York: John Wiley & Sons, Inc., 1958), pp. 165–66.

might seek favorable appointment times. Still others might seek "inside" information on the executive's position with respect to certain proposals or plans for the future. The ability to provide these and many other favors gives executive assistants ample opportunity to acquire power.

Physical location within the formal structure also affects the social relations within an organization. Propinquity, for example, facilitates the development of informal organization. It allows people to interact more frequently, to develop closer friendships, and to hold similar attitudes and values.[21] Informal organizations and groups are important in power relations because many values which are unavailable to individuals acting alone may be easily attainable to individuals acting in concert. The reason why a group is able to gain concessions not available to an individual is its ability to exercise greater force. Physical strength, a slowdown or stoppage of operations, and resistance to change are examples of sanctions in which a group is more effective than an individual. Informal organizations, therefore, are an important source of power, and physical location of organization members is a major determinant of the relative importance of the source. Coalitions are discussed again in a later section.

Job Importance. From a functional point of view, everybody in an organization has some degree of power. Every member of an organization supposedly has some job to perform or is responsible for making some contribution to organizational purposes. The amount of power held by any one person may be determined by the essentiality of his job. Some jobs, like that of a treasurer, are very essential to a corporation, and the enterprise cannot function very long without someone filling them. Other jobs, like that of a personnel counselor, may be necessary but not important enough to prevent a corporation from operating for long periods of time without them being filled. From this standpoint, the treasurer has a great deal of power and the personnel counselor has little power.[22] Also, in this context, power is institutional, that is, the amount of

---

[21] John W. Thibaut and Harold H. Kelley, *The Social Psychology of Groups* (New York: John Wiley & Sons, Inc., 1959), pp. 39–40. Thibaut and Kelley cite several studies that show the relationship of proximity to friendship, attitudes, and values.

[22] This functional definition of power is recommended by Robert Dubin, *The World at Work* (Englewood Cliffs, N.J.: Prentice-Hall, Inc., 1959), p. 29.

power held by any person is determined by the importance of his job rather than by personal or other characteristics.

Individual Sources

Expertise. An engineer, a lawyer or an accountant has expert knowledge about a particular speciality because of intensive study and training. Employed where their specialized skills are needed, these people may become extremely valuable and powerful in an organization. They are valuable, first of all, because of their ability to provide services that are needed and wanted by an organization. Of course, professional education is not the only means of acquiring expert knowledge about a job or problem area. Intimate contact, repeated experiences, self-education, and a long-time relationship to a job can be others. It is likely, also, that the professional man would have to supplement his formal education through experience on the job or intensive study of a problem area. However, these means are also available to the nonprofessional man, and it is often the case that a worker with little or no formal education will gain expert knowledge through long and intimate involvement with a job or process. Similarly, a staff specialist may develop expert knowledge and skills about the analytical techniques and information gathering procedures involved in compiling information for decision makers. For example, a statistician may be valuable because of his ability to provide reliable data to those who must make sales forecasts, and a cost specialist may be valuable because of his ability to provide reliable data to those who must make decisions on capital expenditures and budgets. Since the skills possessed by these people are so valuable to the organization, the withdrawal or threat of withdrawal of these services would be detrimental to the organization. Hence, they have power.

The amount of power that attaches to a person with expert knowledge is dependent upon certain conditions. It is dependent, for example, on the availability of other persons having similar expert knowledge. "Power stemming from expertise, . . . is likely to be limited unless it is difficult to replace the expert. Other factors remaining constant, a person difficult to replace will have greater power than a person easily replaceable."[23]

[23] David Mechanic, "Sources of Power of Lower Participants in Complex Organization," *Administrative Science Quarterly,* Vol. 7, No. 3 (December, 1962), p. 358.

Another condition of an expert's power has already been mentioned in the previous section, that is, job importance. While a person may have expert knowledge about a job, he may hold little power because of the relative unimportance of his job. Thus, other factors remaining constant, an expert performing tasks that are important to organizational processes is likely to have more power than an expert performing unimportant tasks.

Interest and Tenure. Oftentimes, there are tasks in an organization that are distasteful to an official with administrative authority, and he will rely on members of his staff to carry out these duties. In other cases, an executive may become so overburdened with administrative duties that he must rely on others for help. In still other cases, the new executive or amateur administrator must rely on the more permanent members of his staff for assistance in fulfilling responsibilities with which he has had little or no experience. In these cases, a subordinate is valuable, too, and may have power over his superior because he is willing to do the "dirty work," because he is in a position to provide or withhold valuable information, or because his lack of cooperation can be detrimental to organizational success. A case in point is provided by Scheff, who studied a large state mental hospital.[24] Hospital administrators were unable to institute a reform program because of opposition from hospital attendants. The power of hospital attendants, according to Scheff, was due in large part to the heavy dependence of ward physicians on attendants. Because Scheff's study is so important to the subject of power, we draw heavily from his research.

The ward physician was a representative of the hospital administration, and in most wards, he was the only representative. As an administrator, the ward physician was responsible for "insuring staff obedience to hospital regulations," "making ward policy," and general supervision of ward attendants. As a physician, he was responsible for the individual treatment of patients. There were several characteristics about the ward physicians' background and job that made the accomplishment of their responsibilities very difficult, to say the least, and they had to rely on ward attendants for help.

One of these characteristics was the short tenure of ward physi-

---

[24] Thomas J. Scheff, "Control Over Policy by Attendants in a Mental Hospital," *Journal of Health and Human Behavior*, Vol. 2, No. 2 (Summer. 1961), pp. 93–105.

cians. The short tenure of physicians in any one ward was due to a
high rate of separations (33 percent per year) and the administrative practice of frequent reassignments. According to Scheff, the
high separation rate was not unusual for the physician group
because they could usually earn more money, make fuller use of
their medical skills, and find better working conditions elsewhere.
The administrative practice of reassignment was for training
purposes; "The administration tried to expose a doctor in training
to a variety of wards."[25] The typical ward physician, therefore, was
a newcomer in the ward to which he was assigned. In contrast, the
ward attendants were more permanent and better organized. Some
supervisory personnel held the same assignment for as long as five
years.

As an administrator, the ward physician was an amateur. His
formal education, which was devoted to the treatment of individual
patients, left him ill equipped to handle duties requiring leadership
and administrative skills. Moreover, the ward physician resented
his administrative responsibilities. According to Scheff: "The
physicians were not only unprepared for administrative duties,
they were also apt to look upon them with distaste. Oriented toward
the individual patient, many considered time spent outside of
psychotherapy or medical treatment as an irritating distraction
from their 'real' job."[26]

Besides his regular duties, the ward physician had many other
duties that required his absence from the ward. "Admission and
physical examination, conferences on various administrative levels,
and in-service training and workshops made demands on his
time."[27] These demands plus the fact that some physicians were
assigned as many as four wards meant that physicians could spend
little more than three to four hours a day in the wards.

These conditions, then, his lack of training and interest in administration, short tenure, heavy burden of administrative duties, and
responsibility to patients, made the ward physician a poor administrator, heavily dependent on ward attendants. This dependence
enabled the ward attendants to use sanctions and, of course, gave
them power.

One type of sanction used by ward attendants on physicians was

[25] *Ibid.*, p. 95.
[26] *Ibid.*
[27] *Ibid.*, p. 96.

the withholding of information. As noted earlier, ward physicians were frequently absent from the wards—sometimes 20 hours during a day and all weekend. As might be expected, they relied on ward attendants for information concerning the behavior of patients. "If the doctor was too demanding of the ward staff, he found that the information he needed to evaluate his patients was not forthcoming, or given only in part."[28]

Another type of sanction used against doctors was the manipulation of patients. It was a general practice, for example, to schedule patients for treatment and consultation with ward physicians by appointment only. Traditionally, the ward attendants attended to patients with minor problems and would not allow patients to see the doctor without an appointment. However, in those instances where ward attendants were dissatisfied with physicians, traditional practice was abandoned. "Patients who would have ordinarily been shunted away from the doctor were encouraged by staff members to accost him with their requests. In such a situation, the physician, whose time on the ward was limited, found it difficult to get off the ward gracefully."[29]

Another type of sanction used by the ward staff was outright disobedience. Some doctors found that their orders were disobeyed, treated lightly, or conveniently misinterpreted. Still another but related type of sanction was the withholding of cooperation. For example, the doctor's legal responsibility to his patients requires that he attend to a host of details such as signing forms for medicine, and the special treatment of patients. According to Scheff:

> Given the time-consuming formal chores of the physician, and his many other duties, he usually worked out an arrangement with the ward personnel, particularly the charge [supervisory attendant], to handle these duties. On several wards, the charge called specific problems to the doctor's attention, and the two of them in effect, would have a consultation. The charge actually made most of the decisions concerning dosage change in the back wards. Since the doctor delegated portions of his formal responsibilities to the charge, he was dependent on her good will toward him. If she withheld her cooperation, the physician had absolutely no recourse but to do all the work himself.[30]

It seems odd indeed that disobedience and the withholding of

---

[28] *Ibid.*
[29] *Ibid.*
[30] *Ibid.*, p. 97.

cooperation could be used as sanctions. Obedience and cooperation are important if not the prime goals of supervision. It is usually the supervisor's main responsibility to obtain obedience and cooperation from subordinates. Also, he usually has the authority to take or recommend disciplinary action (apply sanctions) against those who disobey or are uncooperative. How, then, may a subordinate succeed in gaining power over his superior through means that seemingly are not at his disposal? On the surface, it seems that he would be punished for disobedience or for not cooperating with the boss.

In actual practice, however, there are certain mitigating conditions to the supervisor's ability to apply sanctions. One condition is that the application of sanctions by the supervisor may be subject to review and reversal by his superior, a personnel department, or an arbitrator specified by a union-management agreement. Another mitigating circumstance is that disciplinary action may reflect poorly on the supervisor's ability to command obedience. Still another moderating influence is that disciplinary action may be a highly unpleasant emotional experience. For any one or all of the reasons, the supervisor may seek means other than diciplinary action to obtain cooperation and obedience. He may, for example, allow forbidden or punishable activities, such as smoking, horseplay, sleeping, absence, or lateness, to go unnoticed in return for cooperation on job-oriented activities. In effect, the supervisor, faced with the dysfunctional aspects of his job, supplies subordinates with sanctions (the ability to grant or withhold cooperation) and power to obtain their demands.

A good example of how people in subordinate positions may obtain power is provided by Sykes in his description of conditions in a prison.

To a large extent the guard is dependent on inmates for the satisfactory performance of his duties and like many figures of authority, the guard is evaluated in terms of the conduct of the men he controls—a troublesome, noisy, dirty cellblock reflects on the guard's ability to "handle prisoners," and this forms an important component of the merit rating which is used as the basis for pay raises and promotions. A guard cannot rely on the direct application of forces to achieve compliance, for he is one man against hundreds; and if he continually calls for additional help he becomes a major problem for the shorthanded prison administration. A guard cannot easily rely on threats of punishment, for he is dealing with men who are already being punished near the limits permitted by society, and if the guard insists on constantly using the few negative sanctions available to the institution—the withdrawal of recreation facilities and other privileges, solitary confinement, or loss of good time—he again becomes burdensome to the prison administration which realizes that its apparent dominance rests on some degree of uncoerced cooperation. The guard, then, is under pressure to achieve a smoothly running cellblock not with the stick but with carrot, but here again his stock of rewards is limited. One of the best "offers" he can make is ignoring minor offenses or making sure that he never places himself in a position to discover infractions of the rules.[31]

Thus, this example shows that even when men are placed in the rigid environment of a prison, their behavior does not adhere strictly to the formal hierarchy of authority.

Personal Characteristics. The obvious personal characteristics which may serve as a source of power are physical ones. One person may have power because he is willing and able to defeat or render harm to others. Thus, a subordinate may have power over his peers and even his superior because of his physical strength. The ability to satisfy sexual needs is another physical source of power. The king's mistress, for example, may have power over her paramour for obvious reasons. Another personal attribute which may serve as a source of power is "attractiveness or what some call 'personality.'"[32] A person who is physically attractive and/or has an impressive or engaging personality is likely to be successful in gaining access to other persons. The personable individual may be characterized, for example, by: the executive who is able to get work done in record time by personal appeals to employees; the industrial salesman who is able to gain access and make sales to busy and seemingly inaccessible businessmen; the director of industrial relations who is able to moderate the demands of union officials; the social worker who is able to quell the riotous behavior of a street gang; and the subordinate who is able to get superiors to meet the demands of his fellow employees.

Attractiveness as a source of power may be extended to include "charismatic" qualities. Weber referred to "charisma" as extraordinary personal qualities. According to Weber, "charisma" is:

. . . an extraordinary quality of a person, regardless of whether this quality is actual, alleged, or presumed. "Charismatic authority," hence, shall refer to a rule over men, whether predominantly external or predominantly internal, to which the governed submit because of their belief in

---

[31] Gresham M. Sykes, "The Corruption of Authority and Rehabilitation," *Social Forces*, Vol. 34 (1956), p. 260.

[32] Mechanic, *op. cit.*, p. 360.

the extraordinary quality of the specific person. The magical sorcerer; the prophet, the leader of hunting and booty expeditions, the warrior chieftain, the so-called "Ceasarist" ruler, and, under certain conditions, the personal head of a party are such types of rulers for their disciples, followings, enlisted troops, parties, et cetera. The legitimacy of their rule rests on the belief in and the devotion to the extraordinary, which is valued because it goes beyond the normal human qualities, and which was originally valued as supernatural. The legitimacy of charismatic rule thus rests upon the belief in magical powers, revelations and hero worship.[33]

In this discussion about personal attractiveness, we are talking about something more than a man's verbal persuasive abilities and something more than friendship. We are talking about the total characteristics of a man which may attract others to him. Others seek his approbation, his approval, his guidance, his counsel, and his affection. To the extent that he is able and willing to grant or withhold these gestures (apply sanctions), he has power over those who value or desire them.

Group Sources

Coalitions. As we illustrated with the Jurgensen-Hill versus Philadelphia Eagles episode, the power that is not available to an individual standing alone may be available to a coalition of individuals. A group may have power simply because of its physical abilities to defeat an adversary in battle. A group may have power because of its ability to prevent an organization from functioning. A single employee, for example, who refuses to work unless his working conditions are improved is likely to render little harm and gain no satisfaction from a large corporate employer who rejects his demands. However, a coalition of all employees, or even a major segment of the work force, who agree to strike unless demands are met, can have considerable power over an employer.

It is often the case that groups of people will have power in an organization because they have formed coalitions within their respective occupational speciality. David Mechanic states:

Thus hospitals have administrators, medical personnel, nursing personnel, attendants, maintenance personnel, laboratory personnel, and so on. Universities, similarly have teaching personnel, research personnel, administrative personnel, maintenance personnel, and so on. Each of these

[33] H. H. Gerth and C. Wright Mills, *From Max Weber: Essays in Sociology* (New York: Oxford University Press, Inc., 1958), pp. 295–96.

functional tasks within organizations often becomes the sphere of a particular group that controls activities relating to the task.[34]

Similar observations could be made from Scheff's study of the mental hospital:

> There was a strong feeling of solidarity among the staff in the hospital in the face of attack from the administration. "Whitecoats stick together" was a motto of the attendants. The feeling of solidarity was so strong that it was difficult, even in a staff meeting in which no outsiders were present, for any criticism of a staff member to be voiced.[35]

In the discussion of the expert employee, we indicated that his power was dependent on replaceability and job importance. An expert employee whose job is unimportant or who is easily replaceable is in a relatively weak power position. However, a coalition with other jobholders or other experts who might serve as replacements could display considerable power. While Sonny Jurgensen and King Hill were apparently impotent as individuals making demands on the Eagles' management, their combined efforts could not be ignored or rejected.

MEASURE OF POWER

It is the purpose of this section to introduce further refinements to our previous statements about power and to be more precise about the power relation. We examine two measures of power. One measure pertains to the power of an individual or group in relation to another individual or group. For simplicity, we refer to this measure as "individual power." The other measure pertains to individuals as members of a coalition. We refer to this measure as "power in coalitions." First, we examine individual power.

Individual Power

The power relationship is based on the fact that each party to the relationship possesses something valued by the other party. Thus, each is dependent upon the other for gratification. Dependence provides the basis whereby one party may control the behavior of the other or induce him to produce an intended result. In a previous

---

[34] Mechanic, *op. cit.*, pp. 361–62.
[35] Scheff, *op. cit.*, p. 98.

section of this chapter we discussed Emerson's propositions concerning dependence and power. For example, it was said that the dependence of B in a two-party relationship provides A with the means to influence B's behavior. When A seeks to induce B to produce an intended result, a mutually dependent relation is created. A is now dependent on B for appropriate responses. Thus, each party to the relation is in a position, to some degree, to grant or withhold the things valued by the other. Emerson has shown the power-dependence relation as a pair of equations:[36]

$$Pab = Dba$$
$$Pba = Dab$$

The first equation may be read as "the power of A over B is equal to, and based upon, the dependence of B upon A."[37] The second equation may be read similarly: the power of B over A is equal to, and based upon, the dependence of A upon B. One party to a power relation is more powerful because he is less dependent than the other party. Emerson calls this an unbalanced power relation, and presents it as follows:[38]

$$Pab = Dba$$
$$\vee \qquad \vee$$
$$Pba = Dab.$$

To our previous statements, we would add: the power of A over B is greater than the power of B over A, and (or because) the dependence of B upon A is greater than the dependence of A upon B.

While the simple statement that A has power over B is palpable, it lacks precision. A more precise statement requires references to *scope*. We indicated earlier that power relations have certain dimensions. Power exists over a limited number of people under limited conditions. In other words, a person's or group's power does not extend to all people, and when it does exist, it does not cover all circumstances or all time periods.

Even when the scope is indicated, the statement of power should contain a reference to chance elements; that is, there is a probability that the use or show of force may fail as well as succeed. As we indicated earlier, when an attempt to influence through the use or show of force fails, there is no power relationship. This stipulation

---

[36] Emerson, *op. cit.*, p. 33.
[37] *Ibid.*
[38] *Ibid.*, p. 34.

is made clearer later, but first let us state the other conditions for precision. Precision requires that the statement contain conditional terms. By definition, power is conditioned on the use or show of some particular force. Thus, the sanctions must be identified in the statement. In summary, the statement of power should contain a reference to the following elements:

(a) The *actor* and the *respondent*. In the example used below, the sales manager is the actor and the president is the respondent.
(b) The *act* and the *response*. For example, the act of the sales manager is: threat to resign. The response of the president is: grant a salary increase to the sales manager.
(c) The *scope*. In the example used below, we refer to time ("busy" and "slack" sales periods), persons (president and sales manager), and behavior area (salary).
(d) The *conditional* terms, that is, under what conditions does the response occur?
(e) The *amount of power*, that is, a measure of the chance of success or failure.

A relatively complete and concise statement of A's attempt to influence B through a show of force may be illustrated with the following example: The chances are 8 out of 10 that if A, the sales manager of the Hypothetical Corporation, threatens to resign during the busy season, B, the president, will grant A's request for an increase in salary.[39] It may be said, then, that, on the average, in 8 out of 10 attempts of A to influence B on a salary increase by threatening to resign during the busy season, A has power over B. As a measure of power, we may say that A's power is 0.8.[40]

The statement could be made even more specific with references to the state of the economy, the liquidity and profitability position of the firm, and the mood of the president. For the sake of simplicity, we assume that these other conditions are constant and that they make no difference in our analysis.

The statement: "the sales manager threatens to resign during the busy season *and* the president grants him a raise in salary," contains two *elementary events,* the act and the response, and it is called a *joint event.*[41] Actually, we could make many more state-

<hr />

[39] This discussion follows concepts developed by Dahl, *op. cit.*, pp. 201–15.

[40] Here we deviate from Dahl, *ibid.*, who states that the measure of power, M, is the probability of influence through force, p_1, minus the probability of influence without force, p_2, that is, $M = p_1 - p_2$.

[41] The statistical discussion is adapted from Robert Schlaifer, *Statistics for Business Decisions* (New York: McGraw-Hill Book Co., 1961), chap. viii.

TABLE 7-3

Eight Possible Events in the
President–Sales Manager Relationship
with Respect to the Sales Manager's Salary

Joint Event	Abbreviated Form
Sales manager threatens to resign during busy season *and* president grants salary increase.	Threat, busy, and salary increase
Sales manager threatens to resign during busy season *and* president does not grant salary increase.	Threat, busy, and no salary increase
Sales manager threatens to resign during slack season *and* president grants salary increase.	Threat, slack, and salary increase
Sales manager threatens to resign during slack season *and* president does not grant salary increase.	Threat, slack, and no salary increase
Sales manager does not threaten to resign during busy season *and* president grants salary increase.	No threat, busy, and salary increase
Sales manager does not threaten to resign during busy season *and* president does not grant salary increase.	No threat, busy, and no salary increase
Sales manager does not threaten to resign during slack season *and* president grants salary increase.	No threat, slack, and salary increase
Sales manager does not threaten to resign during slack season *and* president does not grant salary increase.	No threat, slack, and no salary increase

ments indicating several possible joint events. The events are given in Table 7–3. The abbreviated form of the events in the second column of Table 7–3 are used in the subsequent discussion.

Suppose that after some observation and analysis of the power relationship between the president and sales manager on the subject of the sales manager's salary, we are able to assign probability estimates to each of the eight events. In effect, the probability estimates would tell us the relative frequency or proportion of the time that each event takes place in the relationship between the president and the sales manager on the subject of the latter's salary. These probability estimates are known as ordinary or unconditional probabilities and are shown in Table 7–4 at the intersection of the acts and responses (assumed values are used in Table

TABLE 7–4

Hypothetical Ordinary or Unconditional
Probabilities of Joint and Compound Events

Act / Response	Threat, Busy	Threat, Slack	No threat, Busy	No threat, Slack	Total (Compound Event)
Salary Increase	0.28	0.15	0.10	0.05	0.58
No Salary Increase	.07	.05	.15	.15	.42
Total (Compound Event)	.35	.20	.25	.20	1.00

7–4). As noted earlier, the act and response make up a joint event.

Each joint event is mutually exclusive, that is, no two of the events can occur at the same time. However, the joint events have some common elements which allow us to group them into *compound events*. The rule on grouping mutually exclusive events is:

If two or more mutually exclusive events are grouped into a single event, the weight attached to this single event shall be equal to the sum of the weights attached to the original events.[42]

Following this rule, the probabilities for the compound events are shown in the margins of Table 7–4. Following another fundamental rule governing the assignment of probabilities, the sum of the probabilities of joint events must be equal to 1.00. This same rule holds for the sum of the probabilities for compound events and is shown in the lower right hand corner of Table 7–4.

Our analysis does not end with the determination of ordinary or unconditional probabilities, because we have stated that power involves a conditional relationship, that is, the desired response is conditional on some act. We must, therefore, extend our analysis to include conditional probabilities. "The probability which is assigned to an event *A* when it is known that another event *B* has occurred, or which *would* be assigned to *A* if it were known that *B* had occurred, will be called the *conditional* probability of *A* given *B*."[43] Thus, we may be interested in conditional probability of the

[42] Schlaifer, *op. cit.*, p. 12.
[43] *Ibid.*, p. 122.

TABLE 7–5

Four Compound Events in the President–Sales Manager Relationship

Joint Event	Probability	Compound Event	Probability
Threat, busy, and salary increase	0.28		
Threat, busy, and no salary increase	.07		
		Threat, busy	0.35
Threat, slack, and salary increase	.15		
Threat, slack, and no salary increase	.05		
		Threat, slack	0.20
No threat, busy, and salary increase	.10		
No threat, busy, and no salary increase	.15		
		No threat, busy	0.25
No threat, slack, and salary increase	.05		
No threat, slack, and no salary increase	.15		
		No threat, slack	0.20
Total	1.00		1.00

event "the president grants the sales manager a salary increase" *given* the event "the sales manager threatens to resign during the busy season," or in the conditional probability of event "the president grants the sales manager a salary increase" *given* the event "the sales manager does not threaten to resign during the slack season."

According to Table 7–4, the president–sales manager relationship can result in any one of the eight joint events and any one of the six compound events. These possibilities may be shown also in a rearrangement of the events as shown in Tables 7–5 and 7–6. Given the probability of a compound event, we can now determine the conditional probability of an elementary event. Suppose, for example, that

TABLE 7–6

Two Compound Events in the President–Sales Manager Relationship

Joint Event	Probability	Compound Event	Probability
Salary increase and threat, busy	0.28		
Salary increase and threat, slack	.15		
Salary increase and no threat, busy	.10		
Salary increase and no threat, slack	.05		
		Salary increase	0.58
No salary increase and threat, busy	.07		
No salary increase and threat, slack	.05		
No salary increase and no threat, busy	.15		
No salary increase and no threat, slack	.15		
		No salary increase	0.42
Total	1.00		1.00

we knew that the sales manager had threatened to resign during the busy season but we did not know whether or not his salary was increased. We could, however, determine the probability of either response. Since we know that compound event "threat, busy" has occurred, any joint event other than the first two listed in Table 7–5 would be impossible. Thus, we would assign a probability of 0 to the six impossible joint events and make a proportionate assignment of the total probability of 1.00 to the only two joint events that are possible. A proportionate assignment requires that the joint events maintain their same relationship to the compound event. Since the original assignments were 0.28 for the first joint event, 0.07 for the second joint event, and 0.35 for the compound event, the new assignments would be computed as shown in Table 7–7. According to these

TABLE 7–7

Probability of Elementary Event, Given a Compound
Event in President–Sales Manager Relationship

Elementary event given compound event "Threat, busy"	Probability computation of elementary event given that a compound event has occurred
Salary increase	$\dfrac{0.28}{0.35} \times 1.00 = 0.80$
No salary increase	$\dfrac{0.07}{0.35} \times 1.00 = 0.20$
Compound event "Threat, busy"	1.00

computations, we are now able to say that *if* the sales manager threatens to resign during the busy season, there is a probability of 0.80 that the president will grant him a salary increase and a 0.20 probability that the president will not grant him a salary increase. In this example, we have computed the conditional probability of an elementary event given that a certain compound event has occurred. We may generalize:

If e *is an elementary event which is contained in a compound event* A, *the only conditional probability which is reasonable to assign to* e *given* A *is the unconditional probability of* e *divided by the unconditional probability of* A.[44]

---

[44] *Ibid.*, p. 124.

In our example e was either of the elementary events, "salary increase" or "no salary increase," and A was the compound event, "threat, busy."

We may generalize the example further by introducing the notation and formula used by Schlaifer:[45]

$A:$ An elementary event. An act by the actor in the president–sales manager relationship. In our example, the sales manager is the actor and one of his possible acts is "threaten to resign during the busy season."

$P(A):$ The ordinary, simple, or unconditional probability of the elementary event A.

$R:$ An elementary event. A response by the respondent in the power relationship. In our example, the president is the respondent and one of his possible responses is, "grant salary increase to sales manager."

$P(R):$ The ordinary, simple, or unconditional probability of the elementary event R.

$P(R|A):$ The *conditional* probability of the event R *given* the event A; the probability assigned to R when it is known that A has occurred, or which would be assigned to R *if* it were known that A had occurred.

$P(R,A):$ The joint probability of the events R and A; the probability that both R and A will occur. In our example, one of the joint events is, "the sales manager threatens to resign during the busy season *and* the president grants him a salary increase."

The mathematical definition of conditional probability is given by the formula (7–1):

$$P(R|A) = \frac{P(R,A)}{P(A)} \tag{7–1}$$

We have used this equation already in the computations of Table 7–7. Restatement of the president–sales manager relationship according to equation (7–1) would appear as follows:

$$P(\text{salary increase}|\text{threat, busy}) = \frac{P(\text{salary increase and threat, busy})}{P(\text{threat, busy})}$$
$$= \frac{0.28}{0.35} = 0.80$$

$$P(\text{no salary increase}|\text{threat, busy}) = \frac{P(\text{no salary increase and threat, busy})}{P(\text{threat, busy})}$$
$$= \frac{0.07}{0.35} = 0.20$$

[45] *Ibid.*, p. 127–28.

The equation could be applied to the other events of Table 7–5. For example:

$$P(\text{salary increase}|\text{no threat, busy}) = \frac{P(\text{salary increase and no threat, busy})}{P(\text{no threat, busy})}$$

$$= \frac{0.10}{0.25} = 0.40$$

$$P(\text{no salary increase}|\text{no threat, busy}) = \frac{P(\text{salary increase and no threat, busy})}{P(\text{no threat, busy})}$$

$$= \frac{0.15}{0.25} = 0.60$$

In revised form the equation could be applied also in those cases where the response is known to have occurred and we want to know the probability that a certain act has occurred. In the revised form, equation (7–2) is written:

$$P(A|R) = \frac{P(A,R)}{P(R)} \qquad (7\text{–}2)$$

In this application, we would refer to Table 7–6. The computations according to equation (7–2) are as follows:

$$P(\text{threat, busy}|\text{salary increase}) = \frac{P(\text{threat, busy and salary increase})}{P(\text{salary increase})}$$

$$= \frac{0.28}{0.58} = 0.4828$$

$$P(\text{threat, slack}|\text{salary increase}) = \frac{P(\text{threat, slack and salary increase})}{P(\text{salary increase})}$$

$$= \frac{0.15}{0.58} = 0.2686$$

$$P(\text{no threat, busy}|\text{salary increase}) = \frac{P(\text{no threat, slack and salary increase})}{P(\text{salary increase})}$$

$$= \frac{0.10}{0.58} = 0.1724$$

$$P(\text{no threat, slack}|\text{salary increase}) = \frac{P(\text{no threat, slack and salary increase})}{P(\text{salary increase})}$$

$$= \frac{0.05}{0.58} = 0.0862$$

Notes on the Measure of Individual Power

The definition and measure of individual power indicates that under one set of circumstances (behavioral area, time, and actors and respondents), the amount of power possessed by an actor in the power relationship may be different from the amount possessed under a different set of circumstances. For example, in the president–sales manager example, where the sales manager's salary is in question, the sales manager's power is equal to 0.8. On another question such as the pricing of products, the amount of power possessed by the sales manager could be quite small. The president might be unimpressed by the sales manager's threat to resign on the question of pricing. Similarly, in the Milo case, presented in Chapter 4, Rees, the head of industrial relations, seemed to dominate company policy on personnel matters, while Hardy, the assistant plant manager, seemed to dominate in general policy matters.

This observation presents problems with respect to power structure. If the power of an individual is different for each set of circumstances, then there must exist a different power structure for each set of circumstances. Therefore, a formal organization does not have just one power structure but many. The relative status of an individual in any one structure is dependent upon the set of circumstances involved. While these several structures may be combined to make one overall structure, social scientists have not as yet developed gross measures of power.

The difficulties involved in developing an overall measure are quite formidable. An overall measure would require comparisons of individual power. In order to compare the power of different individuals, Dahl states that at least five factors would need to be included in the comparison: (1) differences in the sources or basis of their power; (2) differences in the means or sanctions used in the power relationship; (3) differences in the scope of their power; (4) differences in the number of comparable respondents; and (5) differences in the amounts of power.[46]

The sources of power discussed earlier in this chapter are job assignment or position, location, job importance, expertise, interest and tenure, personal characteristics, and coalitions. In general terms the source of an actor's power ". . . consists of all the resources—opportunities, acts, objects, etc.—that he can exploit in order to affect the behavior of another."[47] When these sources are exploited, they are called the *means or sanctions* of power. Exploitation may involve threats or promises to employ the source or

---

[46] Dahl, *op. cit.*, pp. 205–6.
[47] *Ibid.*, p. 203.

actual use of the source as a sanction. Dahl describes the sanctions available to the President of the United States as: "the promise of patronage, the threat of veto, the holding of a conference, the threat of appeal to the electorate, the exercise of charm and charisma, etc."[48] The *scope* consists of the time, behavioral area, and the actors and respondents in the power relationship. The scope requirements are illustrated in the statement of power involving the president and sales manager. The *number* of respondents was also indicated in the statement. The *amount* of power is stated as a probability measure.

The first two bases of comparison, sources and sanctions, may be considered as properties of actors in the power relationship. While comparisons on the basis of these properties is interesting, they have little meaning in trying to assign relative status to individuals unless some reference is made to the response evoked and the conditions (the last three bases for comparison) under which the responses were forthcoming. Given a method for classifying the properties for comparative purposes, ". . . it would," according to Dahl, "be desirable to have a single measure combining differences in scope, number of comparable respondents controlled . . ."[49] and the amount of power. "But there seems to exist no intuitively satisfying method for doing so."[50] Since there seems to be no way of measuring the relative power of individuals, how can an individual be assigned relative status in a power structure?

Dahl offers some solutions to this problem. First, he indicates that the basis for comparison must be comparable. It does not, for example, make much sense to compare the power of the British Prime Minister over tax legislation in the House of Commons with that of the President over foreign policy decisions in the Senate. It does make sense to compare the two on the same basis, say, tax legislation. Second, the basis of comparison is by necessity arbitrary but it should be relevant enough to provide a criterion for overall power status. For example, tax legislation and foreign policy have enough importance to serve as a basis for determining the relative status of individual senators in the power structure of the Senate. Finally, Dahl, illustrates, by a method of paired compar-

---

[48] *Ibid.*
[49] *Ibid.*, p. 206.
[50] *Ibid.*

isons of voting records, how the senators may be ranked in the power structure.

While it may be possible conceptually to develop measures of individual power and to rank individuals in some power structure, there are serious problems involved in gathering data to "actually" measure and to rank individuals. Imagine, for instance, the difficulties that would be encountered in gathering data to develop probability estimates of the sales manager's power, illustrated in this chapter. A possible alternative when data are not available or are exceedingly difficult to gather, would be to use subjective probabilities where someone estimates the relative frequency of events from experience. Thereafter, the subjective estimates may be adjusted through sampling or further experience.

For our purposes, it is important to recognize that power is a necessity for an organization to function. While it is not the only mode of influence, the organization cannot survive for long without it. It is important, therefore, to understand the sources, means, and scope of power. The measure of power, while limited in practical application, demonstrates the precision required in a statement of power. Its use in this stage of development is one of conceptual convenience, that is, it helps us to understand the concept. Furthermore, it may serve as a guide for developing practical measures and research methods.

Power in Coalitions

Since decisions in organizations are not always made by individuals, we must also consider the power of individuals in groups and subgroups. In order to measure the power of an individual who is a member of a group we must assume that the set of individuals in a group can be defined. For example, we can define a set of six people as $\{A, B, C, D, E, F\}$ and call it a universal set $\mathcal{U}$. This universal set may be composed of a number of subsets. For instance, a subset of the universal set $\mathcal{U}$ may be $\{A, B, C, D\}$ or $\{A, B, D, E, F\}$ or a number of other possible combinations. If each individual is an element, a set with n elements has 2^n subsets. In the case of a set of six members, $2^6 = 64$ subsets are possible.

We are interested in subsets because in committee or group decision making, subsets or coalitions form. Suppose that we want to study decision making in a six-person group where the approval of a decision requires four votes. The subset of four elements needed to approve a decision is a *winning coalition, C*. The subset of nonwinning members is the *losing coalition, $\overline{C}$*, or the nonwinning coalition. If neither C nor $\overline{C}$ is a winning coalition, then one of the coalitions is a *blocking coalition*. A coalition not containing any smaller coalition, which can succeed or win, is a *minimal winning coalition*. In other words, it is the coalition which cannot win if any one member is lost from the coalition. The idea of a minimal winning coalition is of particular importance if we define the power of an individual as his chance of "being critical to the success of a winning coalition."[51] In a situation where the number of outcomes is known, we can determine the power of an individual by counting the number of times that his actions are crucial to the outcomes. In other words, the chance to turn a defeat into a victory for a coalition is a measure of an individual member's power. His vote is the pivot. By computing the number of times that an individual can be a pivot, we have an index of his power. Shapley and Shubik define this index as a measure of "the number of times that the action of the individual actually changes the state of affairs."[52]

Two indices of power, a theoretical index and an empirical index, have been proposed by Shapley and Shubik for the purpose of measuring the power of individuals in decision-making groups. The *theoretical index* is based on the number of times it is possible for a group member to cast the decisive vote. The *empirical index* is based on the actual voting record of an individual group member. An individual's empirical index can be computed, according to Shapley and Shubik, as follows:

He is given no credit for being on the losing side of a vote. If he is on the winning side, when n others voted with him, then he is awarded the probability of his having been the pivot (or blocker, in the case of a defeated motion), which is $1/n + 1$. His probabilities are then averaged over all votes.[53]

Let us illustrate how the theoretical and empirical indices can be computed.

---

[51] For the measure of coalition power we are indebted to L. S. Shapley and Martin Shubik, "A Method of Evaluating the Distribution of Power in a Committee System," *American Political Science Review*, Vol. 48 (1954), pp. 787–92.

[52] *Ibid.*, p. 788.

[53] *Ibid.*, pp. 791–92.

Theoretical Index. The theoretical power index of an individual is determined by computing the frequency with which a member is pivotal in a winning coalition. For example, consider a decision-making committee made up of three managers, *A, B,* and *C.* Assume that each manager has one vote, which is equal in weight to the vote of the others and must be cast on every decision. In terms of the order of voting, there are six possible permutations: *ABC, ACB, CAB, CBA, BCA,* and *BAC.* The possible number of permutations can be determined by *n* factorial or *n!* where *n* is the number of members in the committee.[54] A majority vote or the minimal winning coalition consists of two members. The member who contributes the last vote in making up a majority is considered the pivotal member. Assuming that the members vote in the order shown in the six possible permutations, each member has an equal chance of occupying the pivotal position. The possibilities of a pivotal member and winning coalitions are shown in Table 7–8.

TABLE 7–8

Possible Permutations of Committee Members A, B, and C, Winning Coalitions and Pivotal Members

Pivotal Member (1)	*Permutations of Winning Alignments* (2)	
A	B A C	C A B
B	A B C	C B A
C	A C B	B C A

In each of the six alignments of the three committee members, the winning coalition is underlined and the pivotal member of each winning coalition is indicated in column 1. The total number of pivotal positions held by each person is equal to $1/n$ of the possible alignments, or $(1/n)(n!)$. In the above case, where $n = 3$, we obtain $(1/3)(3 \cdot 2 \cdot 1) = 2$. The total number of pivotal positions held by each person, divided by the total number of alignments, $n!$, or $(1/n)(n!)/n! = 1/n$, is the theoretical index of power for each committee member. Thus, the theoretical power index for each committee member is two sixths, or 0.333. For a four-man group oper-

---

[54] When $n = 1$, $n! = 1$; $n = 2$, $n! = 2 \cdot 1 = 2$; $n = 3$, $n! = 3 \cdot 2 \cdot 1 = 6$; $n = 4$, $n! = 4 \cdot 3 \cdot 2 \cdot 1 = 24$; $n = 5$, $n! = 5 \cdot 4 \cdot 3 \cdot 2 \cdot 1 = 120$; and so on. By definition, $0! = 1$.

ating under the same conditions, the theoretical index is one fourth, or 0.250; for a six-man group it is one sixth, or 0.167; and for an eight-man group it is one eighth, or 0.125. The voting rules of the committee, of course, affect the theoretical power index. The following examples illustrate the way to compute the theoretical power index under various committee voting arrangements.

EXAMPLE A. In a committee consisting of members M, F, S, and P, where each member has an equal vote, the power index is computed by following the procedure outlined above. In this example, $n = 4$, and the power index of each member is $1/n$, or $1/4$. The minimum winning coalition is any three-member coalition, and a blocking coalition is any two-member coalition. In a six-member committee ($n = 6$), the theoretical index of power for each person is $1/n$, or $1/6$. Any coalition of four or more members can win, while any coalition of two or less is a losing coalition. Any three-person coalition is a blocking coalition.

EXAMPLE B. If in the four-member committee of Example A each member has veto power, the theoretical power index for each person is $1/4$. The only coalition that can win is $\{M, F, S, P\}$.

EXAMPLE C. A joint Army, Navy, and Air Force staff committee is composed of nine members. Three of the nine members are senior officers, one from each service. Each of the senior officers has a veto power. Five affirmative votes and no vetoes are needed to ratify any military plan of action. Since the three senior officers have a veto power, a minimal winning coalition requires that they be included in addition to any two other junior (nonveto) officers. Coalitions containing four or less junior officers are losing coalitions. Coalitions with five or six junior members are blocking coalitions, as are any nonwinning coalitions which include at least one senior officer.

EXAMPLE D. In a committee composed of four members, F, M, P, and S, two individuals, F and S, have one vote each, M has three votes and P has two votes. A total of seven votes can be cast, and the committee has a rule that five votes are required to form a winning coalition. In order to compute the index of power, we must determine the number of times a member is in a pivotal position and divide by the total number of alignments. The number of possible alignments ($4! = 24$) and the times that M is pivotal (underlined) are shown in Table 7–9. Thus, M has a theoretical power index of $14/24$. From the same table, we determine that P has a power index of $6/24$, and F and S have an index of $2/24$ each.

TABLE 7-9

Possible Permutations of Committee Members
F, M, S, and P, and Pivotal Members

FMSP	MFSP	FPSM	PFSM	PMSF	MPSF
FMPS	MFPS	FSPM	SFPM	SMPF	MSPF
PMFS	MPFS	MSFP	SMFP	SPFM	PSFM
FSMP	SFMP	PSMF	SPMF	PFMS	FPMS

Empirical Index. In actual practice it is probably not the case that each man in a decision-making group has an equal opportunity to occupy a pivotal position even if the voting rules do not militate against equality. Aside from the particular voting rules, other factors such as psychological, physiological, sociological, and political may affect the way people vote. "Reality" may not permit us to assume that each member of a decision-making group has an equal opportunity to occupy a pivotal position. However, it is still possible to determine the power index from the voting records of group members. Some examples of decision groups where records may be available for examination are the United States Senate, the United Nations Security Council, the board of directors of a corporation, a particular committee of an organization, or a school board.

Let us illustrate the computation of the empirical index of M, a member of the four-man decision-making committee $MSFP$, based on a hypothetical voting record. Assume the voting record of M in a set of 40 decisions indicates that he was a member of a four-man majority winning coalition 12 times, a three-man majority 10 times, a two-man nonwinning minority 10 times, and a one-man minority 8 times. In this case we assume that all of the 40 decisions can be weighted as equally important. To compute M's power index we must determine his chance of being the pivotal man in each of the winning coalitions and multiplying it by the number of wins. In the four-man winning majority, M's probability of occupying the pivot is one fourth or 0.250 multiplied by the number of wins (12). In a nonwinning coalition, M's chance of being the pivot man is zero. The sum of the pivotal probabilities divided by the number of decisions gives M's empirical index

$$\frac{(12 \times 0.250) + (10 \times 0.333) + (10 \times 0.000) + (8 \times 0.000)}{40} = \frac{6.33}{40} = 0.158$$

M's theoretical power index (0.250) is greater than his empirical power index (0.158).

General Procedure. Now that we have examined several types of problems, we can proceed to a general procedure for handling the power index. In the general procedure we are concerned primarily with determining the minimal winning coalition and the theoretical power index (ratio of pivotal chances to total alignments) of individual group members.[55] We must, therefore, find a way of computing a power ratio which takes into account: (1) the total number of coalition alignments; (2) the number of prepivotal permutations for each member; (3) the number of postpivotal permutations for each member; and (4) the number of combinations of winning coalitions.

FIGURE 7–4

Pivotal, Prepivotal and Postpivotal Places for a Six-Man Committee

1 PREPIVOTAL	2 PREPIVOTAL	3 PREPIVOTAL	4 PIVOTAL	5 POSTPIVOTAL	6 POSTPIVOTAL

Before we present the general procedure, perhaps we should take another glance at what is meant by the position of each vote. We assume that voting occurs in some order and not simultaneously. Each vote has a position or place of order. The place of voting is important because the last vote needed to reach a majority is the decisive or pivotal vote or position. Prior votes are called prepivotal, and votes after the pivot vote are labeled postpivotal. For instance, in a six-man committee, operating under voting rules that require a four-vote majority to win, the first three places, as indicated in Figure 7–4, are prepivotal, the fourth place is the pivot, and the fifth and sixth places are postpivotal.

The number of permutations for prepivotal members is $(p - 1)!$, the number of permutations for postpivotal members is $(n - p)!$, and the total number of alignments possible is $n!$. The theoretical power index, I, of a member of a group is given as follows:

$$I = C \frac{(p - 1)! \, (n - p)!}{n!}, \qquad (7\text{--}3)$$

where

p = the number of members needed for a minimal winning coalition.

C = the number of minimal winning coalitions for each p.

---

[55] For this procedure we are indebted to Chris A. Theodore, *Applied Mathematics: An Introduction* (Homewood, Ill.: Richard D. Irwin, Inc., 1965), pp. 102–6.

Another way of defining C in equation (7–3) is that it is the number of r ways that m different members of a committee or group can occupy the prepivotal positions. The number of combinations of a set of m different objects (members), taken r at a time, can be determined by equation (7–4):

$$_mC_r = \frac{m!}{r!\,(m-r)!} \qquad (7\text{–}4)$$

where

m = the number of nonveto group members less one.
r = the number of prepivotal nonveto positions.

In Example A, where $m = 3$ and $r = 2$, the computation of C by equation (7–4) is:

$$_3C_2 = \frac{3!}{2!\,(3-2)!} = \frac{3 \cdot 2 \cdot 1}{2 \cdot 1 \cdot 1} = 3$$

In the four-person committee *MFSP* of Example A, the computation of the theoretical power index of M by equation (7–3) is

$$I = C\frac{(p-1)!\,(n-p)!}{n!} = 3\frac{(3-1)!\,(4-3)!}{4!} = 3\frac{2 \cdot 1 \cdot 1}{4 \cdot 3 \cdot 2 \cdot 1} = \frac{6}{24} = \frac{1}{4}$$

Each of the other three members has a power index of 1/4.

In Example B, for the four-person committee, in which each member has veto power, there is only one winning coalition, $\{M, F, S, P\}$, $C = 1$, $p = 4$, $n = 4$. Thus, the theoretical power index for each person, according to equation (7–3), is:

$$I = C\frac{(p-1)!\,(n-p)!}{n!} = 1\frac{(4-1)!\,(4-4)!}{4!} = 1\frac{3 \cdot 2 \cdot 1 \cdot 1}{4 \cdot 3 \cdot 2 \cdot 1} = \frac{6}{24} = \frac{1}{4}$$

In Example C, where five votes are needed to ratify a plan of action with no vetoes cast by the three senior officers, the minimal winning coalition must include the three senior officers and two nonveto members. If the three veto members occupy the first three positions and the pivot man occupies the fifth position, one position can be permuted among the remaining five nonveto members. Thus, $m = 5$ and $r = 1$. To find the combinations of five members, one at a time, according to (7–4), we have

$$_5C_1 = \frac{m!}{r!\,(m-r)!} = \frac{5!}{1!\,(5-1)!} = \frac{5}{1} = 5$$

and the theoretical power index for each of the nonveto members, indicated by I_t, where $n = 9$, $p = 5$, and $C = 5$, is by (7–3)

$$I_t = C \frac{(p-1)!\,(n-p)!}{n!} = 5\,\frac{(5-1)!\,(9-5)!}{9!} = 5\,\frac{4!\,4!}{9!} = \frac{1}{126}$$

Thus, the theoretical power index of each of the three senior officers, denoted by I_v, is

$$I_v = \frac{1}{3}\left(1 - \frac{6}{126}\right) = \frac{1}{3}\left(\frac{120}{126}\right) = \frac{40}{126} = \frac{20}{63}$$

Notes on the Measure of Power in Coalitions

Certain assumptions of the Shapley-Shubik index need elaboration. Perhaps the most restrictive assumption of the power index is that it is limited to situations in which voting occurs in some prescribed order. Coalitions may exist even in situations where voting occurs simultaneously and secretly. But, the power index model discussed above could not be used if it were impossible to identify the decisive vote and the prepivotal and postpivotal votes.

Another assumption of the power index is that all of the decisions made by a group are of equal importance. This assumption of equality is unlikely to occur. However, this limitation may be handled by assigning a weight to each decision considered in the empirical index. Essentially, this means that each decision must be evaluated as to its relative importance.

The power index, as we have considered it, ignores some pertinent factors which may explain both why some group members seek power and how they organize to obtain power. Sociological, ideological, psychological, and other factors may be important in the formulation of power coalitions. The power index does not attempt to explain these relationships; it merely endeavors to measure the results. It does not attempt to take into account cause and effect relationships. The theoretical index can be used to measure the results that are possible, while the empirical index can be used to measure power in terms of the results that actually occurred. If cause and effect relationships are known in a particular case, the index can be modified accordingly. For instance, if certain sociological or ideological factors account for the formation of a coalition, some of the combinational possibilities are more likely to occur and others are not likely to happen. Some combinational possibilities may have to be eliminated in the computation of C in equation

(7–4). This would affect the pivotal probabilities of some of the group members.

Another limitation centers upon the assumption that nonwinning members of a group are powerless. Glendon Schubert points out that minorities, especially in small groups, are likely to be articulate and to "have a moderating effect upon the acceptance of the majority's decision."[56]

Even with these limitations, the power index can be a useful tool in the analysis of formal organization arrangements made with respect to committee size and voting rules. This suggests that the power index may be an aid in the evaluation and formulation of policies, standards, and rules governing decision-making groups.

A study of the formation of coalitions by William Riker points out that under some experimental conditions group members "create coalitions just as large as they believe will ensure winning and no larger."[57] If further attempts at empirical validation of this conclusion are successful, identifying and measuring coalitional power through such methods as the Shapley-Shubik index can be a valuable tool in the analysis of power.

SUMMARY

The purpose of this chapter is to define power, place it in an organizational perspective, examine its sources, and provide some analytical tools for its measurement. Power is treated as only one of a number of modes of influence. The distinguishing characteristic of power is that it involves coercion.

Power is defined as an ability of an individual or group to induce others to produce an intended result through the use or presentation of force. This type of inducement not only requires the control of sanctions by the power holder but it also involves on the part of the object of power a desire to obtain some values held by the power

---

[56] Glendon Schubert, "The Power of Organized Minorities in a Small Group," *Administrative Science Quarterly*, Vol. 9, No. 2 (1964), p. 151.

[57] William H. Riker, *The Theory of Political Coalitions* (New Haven, Conn.: Yale University Press, 1962), pp. 32–33. Riker indicates that other experimental evidence in support of his conclusion can be found in Theodore Caplow, "A Theory of Coalition in the Triad," *American Sociological Review*, Vol. 21 (1956), pp. 489–93; and W. E. Vinacke and A. Arkoff, "Experimental Study of Coalitions in the Triad," *American Sociological Review*, Vol. 22 (1957), pp. 406–15.

holder. Obtaining intended results through the use or show of force means that a power relationship exists, while failure to obtain intended results means that no power relationship exists. Power is an interpersonal concept. It is based on the fact that each party to the relationship is dependent upon the other for something of value.

In an organizational context, power involves both the acquisition of things valued by others and the ability and willingness to employ possessions as sanctions. Certain organizational, individual, and group attributes provide for the power seeker sources of values.

Power relationships are limited in scope by time, the people involved, and the behavioral area. The limits of power are shown in terms of refining the power concept by the measurement of the amount of individual power and power in coalitions. The amount of individual power is examined as a probability of chances of success or failure. This measure requires the power statement to contain references to (A) the actor and respondent, (B) the act and the response, (C) the scope, and (D) the conditional terms.

The measurement of power in coalitions is expressed as a power index which is based on the chances of a group member to cast the decisive vote in a minimal winning coalition. This index can show possible power results, the theoretical power index, and power results based on actual voting performance, the empirical index.

Power, social, and technical behavior are the basis for the behavior that actually emerges in organization. In the next chapter we examine emergent behavior.

DISCUSSION QUESTIONS AND PROBLEMS

7-1. Is it possible to influence by persuasion in a power relationship? Is the power relationship sustained by the persuasive efforts of the power holder? Explain.

7-2. If both parties to a power relationship are dependent on each other for the gratification of wants, is it not possible to have a standoff where no action takes place? Explain.

7-3. Why is power necessary to the functioning of an organization? Can an organization function without power?

7-4. Speculate about the possibility of a power spillover, that is, the possibility of a power relation in one behavior area, in one time period, or involving a specific number of people, carrying over to other behavior areas, times, or people.

7-5. In what ways can an organization be designed to supply an administrator with more sources of power than formal authority?

7-6. If a manager has sanctions at his disposal, is it possible for one of his subordinates to ignore a command issued without fear of reprisal? Discuss the conditions under which a subordinate may succeed in ignoring a command. Under what conditions would the subordinate fail?

7-7. Both social and power relations entail ties of mutual dependence between the parties involved. What is the difference between social and power relations?

7-8. Can a person in an organization have power without using force? Explain.

7-9. Illustrate several cases in which the scope of a person's power is limited by time and by behavioral area.

7-10. How does a power role differ from a job role? What is the difference between power status and job status?

7-11. A company planning committee consists of five members: the product planner, the production planner, a pricing expert, a cost analyst, and a promotion expert. The company has been experiencing a sales slump.

Top management feels that this slump can be overcome through a change in company promotional policy. With this in mind, top management asks the planning committee to construct a plan which will increase company sales primarily by changing promotion policy. The power structure in the planning committee shows that the promotion expert has power over the product planner, the production planner, the pricing expert, and the cost analyst. The cost analyst has power over the product planner, the production planner, and the pricing expert. The pricing expert has power over the product planner and the production planner, and the production planner has power over the product planner.

Let: *PTP* denote the product planner.
  PNP denote the production planner.
  PGE denote the pricing expert.
  CAT denote the cost analyst.
  PRE denote the promotion expert.

a) Show the given power relations graphically.
b) Show the relationships in (*a*) by means of a power matrix.
   (1) What are the one-step power relationships of each individual?
   (2) What are the two-step power relationships of each individual?

    (3) What is the total number of one- and two-step power advantages for each individual?

    (4) What are the three-step power relationships of each individual?

7–12. In problem 7–11 we have assumed that the power relationships in all instances were unequal. In this problem, assume that the power of the promotion expert equals the power of the cost analyst. Answer parts (*a*) and (*b*) of problem 7–11, using the preceding assumption.

7–13. In problem 7–11 we have assumed that the power relationships in all instances were unequal. In this problem, assume that the power of the promotion expert equals the power of the pricing expert. Answer parts (*a*) and (*b*) of problem 7–11, using this assumption.

7–14. The quality control department (staff) feels that the implementation of a certain sampling procedure will reduce waste from Foreman A's assembly line. The quality control department has no power to force implementation of this procedure on Foreman A. Thus, the implementation of this procedure depends on other factors which the quality control department can and cannot *influence*. The relevant factors are whether or not Foreman A's immediate supervisor can be convinced of the value of the procedure (this is subject to the influence of the quality control department) ; and the length of the present production run. (Quality control feels that the value of the plan will not exceed the cost of the plan unless the present production run will last three months or more after the date of implementation. Quality control cannot influence this factor.) There are eight possible events in the relationship between Foreman A and the quality control department with respect to the implementation of the sampling plan:

Joint Event

A. Supervisor approves plan, enough time to make plan profitable, foreman implements plan.
Abbrev—Approval, time, implemented.

B. Supervisor approves plan, enough time to make plan profitable, foreman does not implement plan.
Abbrev—Approval, time, not implemented.

C. Supervisor does not approve of plan, enough time to make plan profitable, foreman does not implement.
Abbrev—No approval, time, not implemented.

D. Supervisor does not approve plan, enough time to make plan profitable, foreman implements plan.
Abbrev—No approval, time, implemented.

E. Supervisor approves plan, not enough time to make plan profitable, foreman implements plan.
Abbrev—Approval, no time, implemented.

F. Supervisor approves plan, not enough time to make plan profitable, foreman does not implement plan.
Abbrev—Approval, no time, not implemented.

G. Supervisor does not approve plan, not enough time to make plan profitable, foreman implements the plan.
Abbrev—No approval, no time, implemented.

H. Supervisor does not approve plan, not enough time to make plan profitable, foreman does not implement plan.
Abbrev—No approval, no time, not implemented.

The quality control department obtains information on the proportion of the time that each event (approval and no approval time and not enough time) takes place in relation to the implementation of the sampling plan. Available information is given below.

Act / Response	Approval Time	No Approval Time	Approval No Time	No Approval No Time	Total
Implemented	0.30	0.15	0.20		.75
Not implemented	.01			.07	
Total	.31	.25			1.00

a) Fill in the missing probabilities for the joint and compound events in the table.

b) What is the probability that the plan will be implemented given that the supervisor approved the plan and there is time to implement the plan?

c) What is the probability that the plan will be implemented given that the supervisor does not approve the plan and there is no time to implement the plan?

d) What is the probability that the plan will not be implemented given that the supervisor does approve the plan and there is no time to implement the plan?

e) What is the probability that there will be approval of the plan and no time to make the plan profitable given that the plan will be implemented?

f) What is the probability that the plan is not approved and there is no time to make the plan profitable given that the plan will not be implemented.

7-15. The quality control department finds out that the supervisor of Foreman A has just received training on the value and uses of sampling plans. It has also found that the proportion of time that each event occurs changes. New probabilities which take into account the supervisor's training are given below:

Act Response	Approval Time	No Approval Time	Approval No Time	No Approval No Time	Total
Implemented	0.40	0.05	0.25		.80
Not implemented	.01		.04	.10	
Total		.10			1.00

a) Fill in the missing probabilities for the joint and compound events in the table.

b) What is the probability that the sampling plan will be implemented given that the supervisor will not approve and there will be no time to make the plan profitable?

c) What is the probability that the sampling plan will not be implemented given that the supervisor will approve the plan and there will be time to make the plan profitable?

d) What is the probability that the plan will be implemented given that the supervisor will approve the plan and there will be no time to make the plan profitable?

e) What is the probability that there will be no approval and no time given that the plan will be implemented?

f) What is the probability that there will be no approval and there will be time to make the plan profitable given that the plan will not be implemented.

7-16. The examination board for Ph.D. candidates of a large university consists of 11 members. Five of the board members have veto power, and it takes seven votes for a candidate to be accepted.

a) What is the power index of one of the nonveto members?

b) What is the power index of one of the veto members?

7-17. The board of directors of the Slade Company consists of 15 members. Six members, who are major stockholders, have veto power. The other members, who are minor stockholders, have one vote each.

a) If it takes 10 votes to pass a given measure:
   1. What is the power index of a nonveto member?
   2. What is the power index of a veto member?

b) If it takes eight votes to pass a given measure:
   1. What is the power index of a nonveto member?
   2. What is the power index of a veto member?

c) If it takes 12 votes to pass a given measure:
   1. What is the power index of a nonveto member?
   2. What is the power index of a veto member?

d) Comment on your answers to a2, b2, and c2.

7-18. Four men, A,B,C, and D own all of the 3,000 outstanding shares of common stock issued by the Boro Manufacturing Company.

In matters such as the election of the board of directors, a simple majority of votes decides:

a) If A owns 1500 shares, B owns 1 share, C owns 1 share, and D owns 1498 shares, what is the power index of each man?

b) If A always owns 50 percent of the outstanding stock, explain why different distributions in their number of shares held by B, C, or D does not change the power index of B, C, or D.

c) If a person, E, buys one share of D's stock, what is the power index of each stockholder?

d) If in addition to E, 20 more people each buy a share of D's stock, what will be the power index of each stockholder?

7-19. A woman's club is found to have four voting factions w,x,y, and z; w controls 1 vote, x controls two votes; y controls three votes; and z controls four votes.

a) If it takes six votes to win, what is the power index of each faction?

b) If it takes seven votes to win, what is the power index of each faction?

7-20. Consider a five-man decision group. If none of the members has veto power, the power index of each member is $\frac{1}{5}$, the power index of any two members is $\frac{2}{5}$, the power index of any three members is $\frac{3}{5}$, and so on. Show that the power of two members who always vote the same way is equal to 0.5.

8

EMERGENT SYSTEM

The emphasis in traditional theory on the internal workings of an organization and the tendency to think of behavior strictly in terms of a formal structure gave the traditional model the appearance of a closed system, that is, a system closed off from its environment. This tendency to attribute behavior solely to a prescribed structure of relationships also presented a static view of formal organization. We have attempted to show that the formal organization is an open system, that is, a system that exchanges material, energy, and information with its environment. Furthermore, especially in the last three chapters, an attempt is made to show that when people associate on a continuous basis, they elaborate their behavior beyond the original conditions of employment. It was indicated that, in addition to task-oriented behavior, people in formal organizations display social and power behavior. Thus, although a person is employed in an organization to do a job or play a technical role in relation to other jobholders, he elaborates his behavior, creates other relations, and plays other roles in addition to the technical role. This elaboration also creates changes in motives, attitudes, activities, interactions, and, indeed, in the organization itself.[1]

In this chapter and in the following ones, we continue this portrayal of the formal organization as a dynamic system which

---

[1] George C. Homans, *The Human Group* (New York: Harcourt, Brace & World, Inc., 1950), p. 109.

reacts to, and acts upon, its environment. The purpose of this chapter is to show how the technical, social, and power forces interact to create a predominant behavior pattern—the emergent system. Also, in this chapter, set theory is used to illustrate a possible way of classifying behavior patterns in formal organization.

The formal organization, like any other living system, interacts with its environment. In Chapter 1, the example of a business firm was used to show that an organization draws its workers from the community, sells its products or services to consumers, purchases its supplies from other firms, competes with still other firms, and utilizes community resources such as electricity, water, and sewerage. Through wage payments, employee benefit programs, and purchases of goods and services, the business firm affects the welfare of its environment. Similarly, it is affected by, and has an effect on, the culture of its environment. For example, political and religious freedom and democracy are strong cultural influences on American business firms. In turn, capitalism and free enterprise are beliefs which reflect business influence on American society. In the process of interacting, then, the formal organization adapts to and plays a part in molding its environment. In essence, society (the environment) is a suprasystem and has a mutually dependent relation to the formal organization. In addition to these two, there are several more levels in the hierarchy of living systems that exist within the universe. Starting with the cell, James G. Miller has classified living systems into the following seven levels:

1. *Cells* are composed of atoms, molecules, and multi-molecular organelles.
2. *Organs* are composed of cells aggregated into tissues.
3. *Organisms*, of organs.
4. *Groups* (for example, herds, flocks, families, teams, tribes) of organisms.
5. *Organizations*, of groups (and sometimes single individual organisms).
6. *Societies*, or organizations, groups, and individuals.
7. *Supranational systems*, of societies and organizations.[2]

---

[2] James G. Miller, "Living Systems: Basic Concepts," *Behavioral Science*, Vol. 10, No. 3 (July, 1965), p. 213. For similar classification scheme, see Ludwig von Bertalanffy, *Problems of Life* (New York: John Wiley & Sons, Inc., 1952), pp. 23–54. Also see: Kenneth Boulding, "General Systems Theory: The Skelton of Science," *Management Science*, Vol. 2 (1956), pp. 197–208,

SUBSYSTEMS

The levels of systems within the formal organization are called subsystems. Each subsystem is identified by certain objectives, processes, roles, structure, and norms of conduct. The technical, social, and power subsystems have already been identified by these characteristics, but let us summarize the discussion. First, the technical subsystem is examined.

Technical Subsystem

The objectives of formal organization have technical requirements, that is, some work has to be completed to meet the objectives. The formal organization must exchange things of value with its environment. It depends on the environment for survival. In order to obtain life-giving values, it must contribute something in return. The necessity for this mutually advantageous exchange is reflected in the objectives. The behavior patterns of the technical subsystem are directed to these ends. This point may be illustrated by examining the technical processes of a manufacturing firm.

A manufacturing firm performs an *action process* by taking in raw material and transforming it into a finished product. The firm tries to make a mutually advantageous exchange with its environment by producing a product that is desirable to consumers and competitive with the products of other producers in the marketplace. Through the sale of this product, it hopes to recover costs and to make a profit and, therefore, continue to survive.

A firm performs a *communication process* by gathering data about consumer behavior, competitors, and economic conditions, and transforming this information into a sales forecast. The communication process also involves the movement of information from one point to another in the organization. For example, the sales forecast is transmitted to decision centers. A *decision process* is performed when the sales forecast and other information such as data on the cost of resources are searched, alternative courses of action are formulated, and a choice is made on that alternative

---

for a presentation of a hierarchical order that ranges from the individual cell to transcendental systems.

which satisfies organizational objectives. Through the decision process, then, the firm determines what, how much, and for whom to produce. These decisions are communicated further to lower level decision makers who make more detailed decisions on such matters as personnel assignments and machine use. Final implementation is accomplished when decisions are communicated to action centers or to the worker level in the factory organization.

The essentiality of these processes requires that some organizational component be charged with their performance. The basic component of the technical subsystem is a job. A *job* is a group of tasks or activities that can be performed by one man. The person who is assigned to a job, then, must perform certain duties. In essence, he is asked to play a role and this role may involve decision making, communication, and/or action. The requirements of each job are part of the overall requirements of the organizational objectives. The arrangement of jobholders in some relation to other jobholders, such as men working on an assembly line, and/or an authority relationship between superiors and subordinates, is called the *structure* of the system.

In addition to the requirements of each job and the relations with other components, behavior in the technical subsystem is governed by rules, procedures, and policies. The purpose of these regulations is to make sure that jobs are performed as planned and to stabilize behavior so that organization members may develop reasonable expectations of others' work behavior in the organization.

Social Subsystem

What happens when the technical subsystem is activated, that is, when people are placed in jobs and they set out to do work? This question need not be limited to new organizations. Stated in terms that would be applicable to organizations that are already activated or that have a long history of activity, we ask: How do people behave in organizations? Is their behavior limited to work-oriented behavior? The answer to this last question is obvious. From previous discussions, we know that people in formal organizations elaborate their behavior beyond the demands of their jobs. In other words, people in organizations play several different roles besides the role required by the job. One form of this elaboration of roles is social behavior.

In addition to the technical subsystem, every formal organization has within its bounds an informal or social subsystem. This subsystem arises spontaneously from social interaction. Through association in the technical subsystem, people interact; develop sentiments toward each other such as liking, disliking, attraction, or respect; and engage in activities that are other than those required on the job. Social relations become differentiated and hierarchical relationships develop (structure) among members. The hierarchy of the social structure is determined by the amount of friendship and respect that individual members receive from other members. Thus, as we learned in Chapter 6, leaders become differentiated from followers, highly respected members from those who are less highly regarded. The group also develops some unwritten rules of conduct which govern the behavior of its members. These norms specify such matters as how much a worker should produce and how workers should behave toward their boss.

Power Subsystem

People in formal organizations also elaborate their behavior or roles through the power relation. Power has been defined as an ability to induce others to produce an intended result through the presentation of force. While the use of force is not always involved in the power relation, it must be apparent that the power holder will use force if necessary. An executive who has access to or control over sanctions such as demotion, layoff, increase in pay, or promotion, and is unwilling or unable to use such force or sanctions, has authority but not power. The use of force involves the deprivation or rendering of something that is valuable to those who are the object of power. Thus, the power holder must possess, or be in a position to give or withhold, something that is valued by those who are to implement his decisions. The power holder may be an executive who is able and willing to promote, demote, or fire subordinates who value their jobs or a promotion enough to carry out his orders. A subordinate or a person in a position which does not carry formal administrative authority may also have power. The services of an employee may be considered so valuable to an organization that management would readily consent to his demands for higher wages or better working conditions.

There are many sources of power. In Chapter 7, the following are enumerated: formal position, location, job importance, expertise, interest and tenure, personal characteristics, and coalitions. The power subsystem arises as people in the organization use these sources or means to acquire things that are judged valuable by others, make it apparent to others that they are able and willing to use the things of value as sanctions, and finally, successfully implement decisions; that is, they are able to activate the organization or transform a decision into action. Differentiation of power relations evolves into a hierarchy of power centers (structure) as a result of varying degrees of success by those who aspire to power.

Summary of Characteristics

These behavior systems may be subdivided even further to the level of the individual human being, and still further to the nervous

TABLE 8–1
Characteristics of Technical, Social, and Power Subsystems of Formal Organization

Characteristics	Technical Subsystem	Social Subsystem	Power Subsystem
1. Origin	Deliberate employment and arrangement of men and capital to perform tasks required by formal objectives.	Arises spontaneously from social interactions and shared values of men placed in contact with each other.	Arises as people use the various sources of power to acquire things that are judged valuable by others and successfully implement decisions.
2. Processes	Decision, communication, and action.	Interaction, sentiments, and activity.	Politics, decision implementation, and maintenance of order.
3. Structure	Arrangement of jobs in relation to each other. Process and authority relations.	Differentiation based on expressions of sentiments of members for each other. Friendship relations.	Differentiation based on the number of behavior areas controlled.
4. Status	Man holds status because of his ability to meet the job requirements. Status is same as job in importance in the technical structure.	Man holds status because of the sentiments of others in the system. For example, the leader is liked most in the group.	Man holds status because of degree of success attained in implementing his decisions.
5. Roles	Man plays role according to job requirements.	Man plays role according to sentiments, beliefs, attitudes, and social mores.	Man plays opportunistic role.
6. Sources of authority and power	Directly related to the job and is delegated from those who have higher authority.	Informal authority is derived from those who are its subjects. Based on sentiments.	Official position, location, job importance, expertise, interest and tenure, personal characteristics, and coalitions.
7. Norms	Job descriptions, written policies, procedures, and rules.	Values and accepted norms of behavior. Unwritten tacit agreements.	Expediency. That behavior which sustains power. People who are objects of power follow orders of power holder to obtain desired values.

system, the society of cells, and the structure of the cell itself. This discussion is limited to the level of systems as characterized by technical, social, and power behavior. We summarize the distinctions among the systems by the major characteristics shown in Table 8–1.

System Overlays

The distinctions made among technical, social, and power subsystems, while necessary for discussion, are not clearly identifiable in fact. There are behavior patterns that are parts of two subsystems, others that are parts of all three subsystems, and still others that belong to neither of the subsystems. The three subsystems are intertwined by overlapping relations. It is possible, for example, that some power relations are coincident with technical relations. This coincidence is apparent when power is equal to administrative authority, that is, when the holder of administrative authority succesfully employs the sanctions at his disposal to influence the behavior of subordinates. Social relations may also intersect with technical relations when, for example, business is conducted at a social gathering or when social interactions coincide with interactions required by a job.

While it is practically impossible to separate the several types of behavior in a formal organization, the distinction can be made in an abstract way through set theory and the use of Venn diagrams. This abstract approach requires that we make some assumptions about organizational behavior. First, it is assumed that the characteristics of organizational behavior are discernible enough to allow definition and classification. Second, it is assumed that organizational behavior can be observed, counted, and tabulated according to our classifications. Third, it is assumed that there is a finite or fixed amount of behavior in a formal organization.

In order to fulfill our desire to provide an abstract distinction among the subsystems, let us fabricate a situation in which a researcher is placed in an organization in such a manner that he could observe and record all activities according to our three classifications of behavior.[3] Suppose that a tabulation of the findings for

[3] Our hypothetical observer would have a difficult time, to say the very least. Besides the impossible task of being every place and seeing everything, he would have to determine what kind of relationship is involved in each activity. We ignore this methodological difficulty for conceptual convenience.

a particular time period showed that 65 activities had been recorded. Suppose further that the researcher had classified the activities in the following manner:

31 activities involved in technical relations
29 activities involved in power relations
32 activities involved in social relations
20 activities involved in technical and power relations
19 activities involved in technical and social relations
15 activities involved in social and power relations
12 activities involved in technical, social, and power relations

From these gross recordings, a finer distinction among the types of behavior can be made through the use of a Venn diagram, as shown in Figure 8–1. Starting with the last tabulation, which shows 12

FIGURE 8–1

Systems of Behavior in a Formal Organization

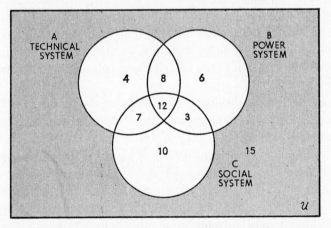

activities classified as belonging to all three systems, we show them at the intersection of the three systems. Proceeding to the next to last tabulation, we are able to complete the intersection of the social and power systems. In like manner, we can complete the diagram. From the diagram, we can be much more specific about the activities observed. For example, the number of activities which involved power relations but not technical relations is $6 + 3 = 9$. It is evident from the diagram that 15 activities fell into none of the classifications. These unclassified activities may have involved, for instance, community projects where some employees were spending some of their time within the organization on a fund-raising campaign.

It is possible to make these same distinctions through set operations. The use of set theory is illustrated at the end of this chapter.

EMERGENT BEHAVIOR

The three subsystems of behavior are *mutually dependent* parts of the larger system, the formal organization. There is also mutual dependence between the parts and the whole of formal organization. The formal organization provides the "reason for being" or, in other words, the justification for existence. For example, a business organization might exist to make and sell steel, a religious organization to save souls, a hospital to save lives, and a baseball team to play baseball. While the subsystems owe their existence to the formal organization, the formal organization is dependent on its subsystems for the successful achievement of its objectives. The technical system, for example, provides the scheme which defines jobs and the relations between jobs, and gives direction to the flow of work. Its purpose is to provide for the efficient accomplishment of organizational objectives. The technical system also provides certain need-satisfying inducements such as wages and job status. The power system provides order and the necessary connection between decision and action. Besides satisfying the organizational need for decision implementation, it also satisfies certain human needs such as the need to hold power.

The social system also satisfies certain human needs such as the need to associate on an intimate basis. The social system fulfills another important purpose in formal organization. In cases where the rules and procedures of the technical system fail to cover a situation requiring action, or where there is a conflict with other rules and procedures, or where they do not specify the best way of performing a task, the social system may fill the vacuum. We may find, for example, that two friends consult to resolve an organizational problem, as when representatives from the production and marketing departments of a business organization meet on an informal basis to resolve discrepancies between sales forecasts and production schedules, or we may find one worker using his friendship with a supply clerk to bypass cumbersome formal procedures for obtaining supplies. Informal behavior arising out of the social system, therefore, may either supplement or supplant the requirements of the technical system and permit more effective and efficient accomplishment of organizational objectives.

Besides the mutual dependence between the formal organization and its subsystems, there is also mutual dependence among the subsystems themselves. The formal organization and each one of its subsystems are a part of the environment of the other subsystems and, as such, influence, and are influenced by, the other subsystems. What in effect happens is that the technical, social, and power forces interact, and through interaction new patterns of behavior emerge which are separate from, but related to, the ways of behaving and thinking that are specified or required by the original systems. We call this new behavior, *emergent behavior.*

To illustrate how the forces interact and how emergent behavior arises, suppose that the management of a business concern attempts to implement changes in the company's work routine and organizational structure. Let us state further that the company finds it expedient to implement these changes because of increased competition from other firms in the industry and because technological advancements have made its existing work routines obsolete. Fearing the loss of their jobs, a possible disruption of social relations, or changes in the power structure, the people who are to be affected decide to resist these changes. Their reactions might emanate from a coalition of forces and might take the form of a restriction of output or an outright refusal to implement the changes. The reaction of managers to this resistance may take several forms, such as punitive action against offenders, or what might be considered a more positive approach, such as giving bonuses in pay to those who are to be affected by the changes. In any event, management actions may cause further responses from those who are to be affected by the change, which will in turn affect future management decision. Action and reaction of this sort is a continual process, and it illustrates the fact that ". . . the forces which affect behavior are in a constant state of mutual dependence."[4]

Compromise

What emerges from this interplay of forces will more than likely represent compromises among the several interest groups participating in the formal organization. There will be compromises

---

[4] Bernard De Voto in the Foreword to George C. Homans, *The Human Group* (New York: Harcourt, Brace & World, Inc., 1950), p. xv.

because the very nature of organization (mutual dependence) dictates that no one group can attain its values without the cooperation of the other groups participating in the accomplishment of organizational objectives. Cooperation with one group will not be forthcoming unless some values or inducements are provided for the other groups. A statement by Herbert Simon underscores this point and dramatically illustrates mutual dependence in organizational behavior. He says that even though one group may be powerful enough to exercise the dominant voice in setting organizational objectives this ". . . does not in any sense imply that the control group exercises an unlimited option to direct the organization in

FIGURE 8–2

Predominance of Emergent System in Formal Organization

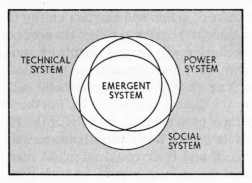

any path it desires, for the power will continue to exist only so long as the controlling group is able to offer sufficient incentives to retain the contributions of the other participants to the organization."[5] Organizational objectives, therefore, must reflect values that appeal in some degree to all participating groups. Since it is virtually impossible to attain goals that provide total satisfaction to all groups, and since no one group can attain its values at the exclusion of others, it is evident that there must be compromise, and emergent behavior is a reflection of this compromise.

Mutual dependence and compromise among the forces of formal organization is best represented by the subsystem where technical, social, and power relations coincide, as shown in the Venn diagram of Figure 8–1. In order to reflect the predominance of the emergent system, the diagram is redrawn in Figure 8–2.

---

[5] Herbert A. Simon, *Administrative Behavior* (New York: Macmillan Co., 1960), p. 119.

Behavior Is Orderly and Purposeful

The compromise among forces allows an explanation of a seeming paradox in formal organizations. People in organizations have, thus far, been characterized as behaving and thinking in ways that are different from, or in addition to, the ways in which they are supposed (that is, according to a predetermined structure) to behave and think. However, virtually all available evidence indicates that actual behavior in formal organizations is orderly and purposeful; that is, actual organizational behavior generally supports and is directed toward the objectives of formal organization.[6] The fact that actual organizational behavior is orderly and purposeful but generally different from formally prescribed behavior is not really a paradox, because organizational objectives change through the process of action and reaction among the parts of the system; and as objectives evolve to reflect the needs of participants, organizational behavior will become oriented towards these goals.

Individual and group participants will contribute to organizational goals as long as they receive personally satisfying inducements in return for their contributions or, in other words, as long as they satisfy their personal goals by helping the formal organization accomplish its goals.[7] When these inducements are not forthcoming, they react, and their reactions might result in activities such as a work stoppage, a slowdown in work pace, resistance to change, or even formal resignation. This is the process of action and reaction described earlier in this section. The result of this action and reaction, as was noted, is a compromise and a change in objectives designed to make them more representative of the values desired by all participants. These views with respect to purposive behavior in organizations parallel those of Simon. He states:

. . . although it is correct to say that organization behavior is oriented toward the organization objectives, this is not the whole story; for the organization objective itself changes in response to the influence of those

---

[6] In *ibid.*, pp. xxiii–xxiv, Simon makes this point in the following manner: "To anyone who has observed administrative organizations, or has concerned himself with their theory, it seems obvious enough that human behavior in organizations is, if not wholly rational, at least in good part intendedly so. Much behavior in organizations is, or seems to be, task oriented—and sometimes efficacious in attaining its goals."

[7] This point is examined more fully in Chapter 15, which is concerned with motivation in organization.

for whom the accomplishment of that objective secures personal values.

The modification of the organization objective usually represents a compromise of the interests of several groups of potential participants, in order to secure their joint cooperation where each group individual is unable to attain its own objectives unaided. Hence, the organization objective will seldom coincide exactly with the personal objectives of even those participants whose interest in the organization lies in its attainment of its goals.[8]

While the modified organizational objective seldom provides total satisfaction to any one participant, its provisions are likely to be more palatable to all participants. The participants in organizations now find that by contributing to organizational goals, they are able to attain their own personal goals. Thus, the more general case in formal organizations may be stated as follows:

> *Organizational objectives are continually changing to reflect the needs of participants and since people in organizations behave in ways that tend to fulfill their needs, their behavior will be directed to the goals of organization.*

We may conclude, therefore, that organizational behavior is generally purposive and orderly.

Structure and Processes

Similar conclusions may be drawn about the structure and processes of the emergent system. The emergent system displays structure and processes which are different from, but related to, the structure and processes of the original subsystems. Interaction among the forces of the subsystems and the environment goes on continually. As a result, the structure and the way that processes are performed are in a continual state of flux. Thus, the *structure* (and the way processes are performed) of the emergent system defines relationships among components only at a given moment in time. This does not mean, however, that behavior in the system is chaotic. After each disturbance or change, the system, like all open systems, tends toward order, that is, it returns to a steady state.

CLASSIFICATION OF BEHAVIOR AND SET THEORY

The purpose of this section is to present a classification of behavior, especially that behavior illustrated in Figures 8–1 and 8–2.

---

[8] Simon, *op. cit.*, p. 114.

Also, set theory is used to illustrate another way of making abstract distinctions among the behavior patterns of a formal organization. Since the formal organization is the totality of all this behavior, it is called a *universal set*.

In general, a *set* is ". . . a well-defined collection of objects."[9] A set must be so well defined that there is no doubt about whether or not a given object belongs to the collection of things under consideration. Sets may be specified in two different ways. One way is to establish the requirements or rules for determining whether or not a given object is contained in a set. The other way involves a complete listing of the objects in the set. "We shall say that the former is a *description* of the set and the latter is a *listing* of the set. For example, a set of four people can be defined as (*a*) the members of the executive committee of the XYZ Corporation, or (*b*) the people whose names are Jones, Smith, Brown, and Green."[10]

Set Operations

Regardless of the classification scheme used, the elements of one set in a formal organization are likely also to be members of another set. When the elements of one set are also members of another set, we say that the latter is a *subset* of the former. The notion of a subset may be understood from our brief review of set operations below. The Venn diagrams of Figures 8–3 and 8–4 are used to

FIGURE 8–3

Subsets and the Universal Set

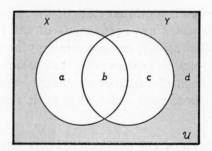

[9] John G. Kemeny, Arthur Schleifer, Jr., J. Laurie Snell, and Gerald L. Thompson, *Finite Mathematics with Business Applications* (Englewood Cliffs, N.J.: Prentice-Hall, Inc., 1962), p. 53.

[10] *Ibid.*, pp. 53–54. © 1962. Reprinted by permission of Prentice-Hall, Inc.

FIGURE 8-4

Disjoint Sets

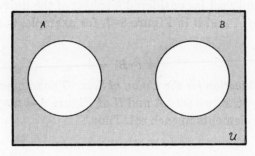

illustrate the discussion. We denote the universal set by $\mathcal{u}$ and let it be the rectangle. The circles within the rectangle are subsets of the universal set. The circles are denoted by upper case letters. The use of lower case letters becomes apparent as we perform set operations.

Intersection. As indicated, the sets X and Y are subsets of the universal set $\mathcal{u}$. The combination of the X and Y sets are also subsets of this same universal set. The intersection of the two sets X and Y form a new set $X \cap Y$. The new set $X \cap Y$, therefore, is a subset of the universal set $\mathcal{u}$ and contains all those elements that belong to both X and Y. We introduce the additional notation $n(X \cap Y)$ to indicate the number of elements in a set. Thus,

$$n(X \cap Y) = b$$

Union. The union of the two sets X and Y also form a new set $X \cup Y$. The new set $X \cup Y$ is a subset of the universal set $\mathcal{u}$ and contains all those elements that belong either to X or to Y or to both. Thus,

$$n(X \cup Y) = a + b + c$$

Complement. A new set is formed by the complement of a given subset. For example, the complement of X, denoted by $\bar{X}$, is the set of all elements of the universal set $\mathcal{u}$ *not* contained in the set X. Thus,

$$n(\bar{X}) = c + d$$

Disjoint. If the two sets X and Y have no elements in common, they are said to be disjoint or mutually exclusive. In Figure 8-4, sets A and B are disjoint because they have no elements in common.

Empty set. A set is empty if it contains no elements of the universal set. The empty or null set, denoted by ϕ, in set theory is similar in importance to the use of zero in the real number system. Hence, the empty set is considered a subset of the universal set. The intersection of A and B in Figure 8–4, for example, is an empty set. Thus,

$$n(A \cap B) = \phi$$

A General Equation for the Union of Sets. The number of elements in the union of the two sets A and B of Figure 8–4 may be obtained by adding the elements in each set. Thus,

$$n(A \cup B) = n(A) + n(B) \tag{8-1}$$

However, this operation is valid only when the two sets A and B are disjoint, that is, they have no elements in common. When the two sets are not disjoint, as illustrated in Figure 8–3, the summation of their elements involves double counting. It is obvious, for example, that the sum of $n(X)$ and $n(Y)$ means that $n(X \cap Y) = b$ is counted twice. Therefore, the general equation (8–2) can be obtained by subtracting $n(X \cap Y)$. Thus,

$$n(X \cup Y) = n(X) + n(Y) - n(X \cap Y) \tag{8-2}$$

The generalized equation (8–2) will hold for any two sets X and Y.

Now, let us perform set operations on the example used previously. Figure 8–1 is used as a point of reference. First, we can consider all activities that were classified under either A or B or C or all three. We are seeking the union of the three sets A and B and C or the new set $A \cup B \cup C$. Thus,

$$n(A \cup B \cup C) = n(A \cap \bar{B} \cap \bar{C}) + n(B \cap \bar{C} \cap \bar{A}) + n(C \cap \bar{A} \cap \bar{B})$$
$$+ n(A \cap B \cap \bar{C}) + n(B \cap C \cap \bar{A}) + n(C \cap A \cap \bar{B}) + n(A \cap B \cap C)$$
$$\tag{8-3}$$

Since we do not have enough information from the original tabulations of the researcher to solve this equation directly, it remains unsolved until we can solve the parts and eventually derive a general equation for the union of three sets. Let us, then, proceed to solving the parts.

Ineffectual Technical Relations. Those formal relations that do not produce a desired effect or that contribute nothing to organization goals are called ineffectual technical relations. An activity that exemplifies this type of relation is when an executive gives an order and it is ignored by his subordinates. In this case, the executive has formal administrative authority but no power or informal influence. This type of behavior is designated by the number of activities or elements in the set $A \cap \bar{B} \cap \bar{C}$. Thus,

$$
\begin{aligned}
n(A \cap \bar{B} \cap \bar{C}) &= n(A) - n(A \cap B) - n(A \cap C) + n(A \cap B \cap C) \\
&= 31 - 20 - 19 + 12 \quad\quad\quad\quad\quad\quad\quad (8\text{--}4) \\
&= 4
\end{aligned}
$$

Illegitimate Power Relations. Those power relations which are not prescribed by either the technical or informal subsystems but, yet, produce a desired result for the power holder are called illegitimate power relations. The behavior that results from this type of relationship is illegitimate in the sense that the role of each participant may not be prescribed by the technical and informal subsystems. Though the results of this relationship may be desired by the power holder, they may be incompatible with the goals of the other subsystems. The previously used illustration about the expert employee demanding a wage increase and getting it represents a desired result as far as the power holder is concerned. In this case, the expert employee has neither formal nor informal authority, but he has power on the question of wages. If the wage increase, however, creates a misalignment in the formal job evaluation plan or a wage incongruency in the informal status structure, it might generally be considered an undesirable result. As far as the technical and informal subsystems are concerned, this is an unintended result. This type of behavior is designated by the number of activities or elements in the set $B \cap \bar{C} \cap \bar{A}$. Thus,

$$
\begin{aligned}
n(B \cap \bar{C} \cap \bar{A}) &= n(B) - n(B \cap C) - n(A \cap B) + n(A \cap B \cap C) \quad (8\text{--}5) \\
&= 29 - 15 - 20 + 12 \\
&= 6
\end{aligned}
$$

Unpurposive Social Relations. The term, "unpurposive social relations" is used to connote those relations that are not prescribed by the technical or power subsystems. For instance, two friends discussing the weather or people doing things together simply because they like to be with each other may be completely unpurposive as far as the technical and power subsystems are concerned. Although these social roles are unintended by the technical and power subsystems, they may satisfy a group norm which expects social conversations and the like among informal group members. The case of unpurposive social behavior is designated by the number of activities or elements in the set $C \cap \bar{A} \cap \bar{B}$. Thus,

$$n(C \cap \bar{A} \cap \bar{B}) = n(C) - n(A \cap C) - n(B \cap C) + n(A \cap B \cap C) \quad (8\text{-}6)$$
$$= 32 - 19 - 15 + 12$$
$$= 10$$

Coincidence of Social Relations and Power Relations. These social relations that coincide with power relations indicate an overlay of the social subsystem with the power subsystem. An example of behavior that results from this type of relationship is when an informal leader is successful in his demands on a fellow employee to slow down his work pace to conform to that of the other members of the group. The informal leader in this case has power through his ability to invoke sanctions such as social ostracism on deviant members of the group. He is fulfilling a social role as well as a power role. This type of behavior is designated by the number of activities or elements in the set $B \cap C \cap \bar{A}$. Thus,

$$n(B \cap C \cap \bar{A}) = n(B \cap C) - n(A \cap B \cap C) \quad (8\text{-}7)$$
$$= 15 - 12$$
$$= 3$$

Coincidence of Social Relations and Technical Relations. Those social relations that coincide with technical relations indicate an overlay of the social subsystem with the technical subsystem. For example, in addition to the technical roles required of people working adjacently on an assembly line, they may also develop friendships. Not only may they be required by the job to interact but they may also want to do it of their own accord. Another example might be where the technical relationship between an executive and his subordinate coincides with their informal relationship in the social subsystem. Since the executive has no power in this case, his appeals for compliance from his subordinate are through their friendship relations. The subordinate in this case may carry out the wishes of the executive because they are friends. This case is designated by the number of activities or elements in the set $A \cap C \cap \bar{B}$. Thus,

$$n(A \cap C \cap \bar{B}) = n(A \cap C) - n(A \cap B \cap C) \quad (8\text{-}8)$$
$$= 19 - 12$$
$$= 7$$

Coincidence of Power Relations and Technical Relations. Those technical relations that coincide with power relations indicate an overlay of the power subsystem with the technical subsystem. An example of this behavior of these relations is when an executive issues an order and it is carried out by his subordinate. The executive in this case has both formal administrative authority and power. In other words, he is successful in his use of the sanctions at his disposal. This type of behavior is designated by the number of activities or elements in the set $A \cap B \cap \bar{C}$. Thus,

$$n(A \cap B \cap \bar{C}) = n(A \cap B) - n(A \cap B \cap C) \qquad (8\text{-}9)$$
$$= 20 - 12$$
$$= 8$$

Coincidence of Technical Relations, Social Relations, and Power Relations. Those technical relations that coincide with power and social relations indicate an overlay of the power subsystem with the social and technical subsystems. An example of this type of overlay is when an executive gives an order and it is carried out by subordinates, but his position in this case is the strongest because he is not only backed by the sanctions of formal administrative authority but also by informal authority. Thus, an uncooperative employee may suffer from the consequence of formal sanctions such as a demotion or reprimand, as well as from social sanctions such as being ostracized by his fellow employees. This case is designated by the number of activities or elements in the set $A \cap B \cap C$. Thus,

$$n(A \cap B \cap C) = n(A \cap B \cap C) \qquad (8\text{-}10)$$
$$= 12$$

All Classified Activities. Now that a solution has been reached for the parts, we may return to our earlier efforts to determine the union of the three sets A and B and C. Again, we are seeking an enumeration of all the activities that were classified. This answer may be obtained by adding equations (8–4) through (8–10) presented above. The number of classified activities obtained in this way would give us the new set $A \cup B \cup C$. Thus,

$$n(A \cup B \cup C) = n(A) + n(B) + n(C) - n(A \cap B) - n(B \cap C)$$
$$-n(A \cap C) + n(A \cap B \cap C) \qquad (8\text{-}11)$$
$$= 31 + 29 + 32 - 20 - 15 - 19 + 12$$
$$= 50$$

Unclassified Activities. Obviously, the difference between the number of recorded activities and the number of classified activities reveals the number of activities that fall into none of the classifications. These activities are designated by the set $\overline{A \cup B \cup C}$. Thus,

$$n(\overline{A \cup B \cup C}) = n(\mathfrak{u}) - n(A \cup B \cup C) \qquad (8\text{-}12)$$
$$= 65 - 50$$
$$= 15$$

The foregoing classification of behavior patterns was presented primarily for conceptual convenience. Thus, the purpose of the analysis is to provide a means for understanding the kinds of patterns that are possible in an organization. There is little practical advantage to this analysis other than the understanding gained about possible behavior patterns and that emergent behavior is the predominant pattern.

SUMMARY

This chapter is devoted to describing the overlay of behavior subsystems within the formal organization. The subsystems are identified as a technical subsystem, a social subsystem, and a power subsystem. Each subsystem is characterized as follows. The *technical subsystem* may be defined as those relations and roles in a formal organization that are prescribed for the coordination of jobs and work activity. The *social subsystem* may be defined as those relations and roles which result from social situations, that is, the interactions and sentiments that people express toward one another; it is characterized by activities such as two friends having lunch together or the members of a group playing some games. The *power subsystem* may be defined as those activities or roles that involve decision and corresponding action, that is, a decision by one party and implementation of that decision by another party. Examples of activities in the power subsystem are a decision by an executive and its implementation by subordinates, and an expert employee demanding a wage increase and getting it. All three of these behavior subsystems exist within the larger system, the formal organization.

Each of these subsystems can be characterized in terms of its objectives, processes, roles, structure, and norms of conduct. In this presentation, behavior is identified in subsystems of overlapping relationships.

The formal organization, taken as a whole, displays characteristics which are different from those of its isolated parts. These characteristics stem from the fact that the subsystems mutually interact with each other and the whole, causing the formulation of new objectives or values that are closer to the needs of all interests rather than of any one force. The new objectives, then, are a blend of interests, a compromise among forces in the formal organization. Since the new goals are more representative of all interests, behavior will be directed to the new goals and will, therefore, be considered purposive and orderly. These new patterns are called the emergent system. The emergent system also displays structure and processes which are different from, but related to, the structure and processes of the original subsystems.

This chapter characterizes formal organization as a system composed of several subsystems. In Chapters 9, 10, 11, 12, 13, and 14, the systems approach is developed further, especially as it may be used in designing and organization.

DISCUSSION QUESTIONS AND PROBLEMS

8-1. If behavior in formal organization invariably deviates from prescribed behavior, how can the existence of orderly and purposive behavior be explained?

8-2. Explain why a business firm, a hospital, a school, and a church can be characterized as systems. Illustrate technical, social, and power subsystems in these types of organizations.

8-3. Is it possible to settle on objectives, processes, and a structure of relations that could lead to the demise or death of a formal organization? Illustrate and explain.

8-4. From your experience in organizations, illustrate some cases in which there is a coincidence of (a) technical and social relations, (b) technical and power relations, (c) social and power relations, and (d) technical, social, and power relations.

8-5. Is it reasonable to conclude that the forces operating within a formal organization generally settle on a workable compromise? Why?

8-6. How does emergent behavior reveal the dynamic nature of a formal organization? Do the dynamics of formal organization mean that the system's behavior is chaotic? Explain.

8-7. In a poll, 570 workers were asked their opinions on the following types of group participation plans: a form of suggestion system, a system of consultative committees, and the Scanlon Plan. In order to save time, the workers were asked to signify either favorable or unfavorable reactions to each plan. The following results were obtained:
   300 favored the suggestion system.
   200 favored the consultative committees.
   400 favored the Scanlon Plan.
   100 favored the suggestion system and the consultative committees.
   140 favored the suggestion system and the Scanlon Plan.
   180 favored the consultative committees and the Scanlon Plan.
   90 favored all three.

Let:
SS denote the suggestion system.
CC denote the consultative committees.
SP denote the Scanlon Plan.

a) How many workers favored the suggestion system but neither the consultative committees nor the Scanlon Plan?

b) How many workers favored the consultative committees but neither the suggestion system nor the Scanlon Plan?

c) How many workers favored the Scanlon Plan but neither the consultative committees nor the suggestion systems?

d) How many workers favored the Scanlon Plan and the consultative committees but not the suggestion system?

e) How many workers favored the Scanlon Plan and the suggestion system but not the consultative committees?

f) How many workers favored the suggestion system and the consultative committees but not the Scanlon Plan?

g) How many workers did not favor any of the three incentive systems?

8-8. Seventy-five workers, who were considering joining a union, were asked to reveal which union they favored. The choices were Union X, Union Y, both, or neither. Thirty-five favored Union X, forty-two favored Union Y, and seven favored both unions. How many workers did not favor either union?

8-9. A supervisor is looking for a man to take a newly created position in systems analysis. The supervisor feels that this position requires knowledge in computer programming, data processing, and information systems. The supervisor obtains the following information from application blanks:

Courses Taken	Abbreviations	Number of Applicants
Computer programming	(CP)	60
Data processing	(DP)	45
Information systems	(IF)	55
Computer programming but neither data processing nor information systems		10
Data processing but neither information systems nor computer programming		15
Information systems but neither data processing nor computer programming		20
Computer programming, data processing, and information systems		5

a) How many applicants had courses in computer programming and data processing but not all three?

    b) How many applicants had courses in data processing and information systems but not all three?

    c) How many applicants had courses in computer programming and information systems but not all three?

    d) If there is a total number of 110 applicants, how many applicants did not have any of the three courses?

8–10. Suppose a business organization called the Worker Corporation consists of people who can be classified as owners, managers, and workers, or some combination of the three. The possible classification combinations for each member of the organization can be shown in the following diagram.

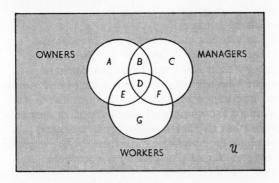

Area *ABDE* indicates the number of those members of the organization who *owned* the organization at a point in time.

Area *BCDF* indicates the number of those members of the organization who were performing a *managerial function* at this point in time.

Area *EDFG* indicates the number of members of the organization who were performing *manual labor* at this point in the time.

Area *A* shows the number of members of the Worker Corporation who own corporation stock but are not managers or workers. An example of this classification would be a secretary who worked for Endurance Company but owned 10 shares of the preferred stock of the Worker Corporation.

Area *B* shows the number of managers of the Worker Corporation who owned stock in the Corporation but are not workers. An example of this classification would be the vice president of marketing who had taken advantage of the stock option plan the company was offering along with his regular salary.

Area *C* shows the number of members of the Worker Corporation who are managers but not owners or workers.

Area *F* shows the number of members of the corporation who are both workers and managers but not owners. Such would be the case of the foreman who also performed some manual labor along with the workers.

Area E indicates the number of members of the organization who were both workers and owners but not managers. An example of this classification is a worker who owns stock in the corporation.

Area G indicates the number of members who are workers but not owners or managers.

Area D shows the number of members of the Worker Corporation who are owners, managers, and workers. A company foreman who owns corporation stock and who performs some manual labor is an example of this classification.

Suppose:

Number of owners	= 40,000
Number of managers	= 5,000
Number of workers	= 16,000
Number who are both owners and managers	= 1,500
Number who are both owners and workers	= 9,000
Number who are both managers and workers	= 1,000
Number who are managers and owners and workers	= 500
Total number of members in the organization	= 50,000

a) Calculate the number of members of the organization who are owners but neither managers nor workers.

b) Calculate the number of members in the organization who are managers but neither owners nor workers.

c) Calculate the number of members in the organization who are workers but neither owners nor managers.

d) Calculate the number of members in the organization who are owners and managers but not workers.

e) Calculate the number of members in the organization who are owners and workers but not managers.

f) Calculate the number of members in the organization who are managers and workers but not owners.

g) Draw a Venn Diagram showing the results of a) through g).

PART III

Organizational Design

MARKOV CHAIN ANALYSIS

In formal organization, there is a constant adjustment and readjustment, alignment and realignment of forces to compensate for imbalances caused by both internal and external disturbances. It is explained in part by the fact that people naturally try to order relationships and to maintain a stable pattern of behavior. It is explained partly by the fact that formal organization is designed to accomplish objectives in an orderly manner and to counteract disturbances that might disrupt stabilized patterns of behavior.

In this part of the book, we are concerned with the problem of the design of organization. Why is it important for the designer of an organization to know about these stabilizing tendencies? There is an obvious answer to this question. The designer tries to develop a system that will accomplish certain objectives. Therefore, he needs to know or have some estimate of the outcome of his design. In other words, he needs to know at which level the system will stabilize or, indeed, whether it will stabilize at all. Also, the designer is concerned with efficient use of resources. Therefore, he needs to know about how long it takes for the system to stabilize; that is, he needs to know the rate at which the system approaches stability. For similar reasons, he may want to know what path this system takes toward the stable condition. The path taken will reveal, for example, whether there is learning in the system. Learning is indicated by a steady improvement in performance. This information is important to the designer because with learning, the system should require less and less resources as it moves through time.

Once the outcome, the rate, and the path have been determined, the designer may proceed with plans if the design promises to achieve objectives efficiently. If the design does not permit efficient goal achievement, he may change either the design, the objectives, or both the design and the objectives. If it is possible, the designer should try to answer these questions about the level of stability and rate and path of behavior before attempting to implement the design or activate the organization. The advantages of this procedure are obvious. The principal benefit is the opportunity afforded to correct defects in the system before they result in misuse of resources.

There are several ways to predict the behavior (outcome, rate, and path) of a system prior to the implementation of a design. One way of predicting behavior, for example, is through a mathematical expression of known or approximately known relationships among variables. This approach has been used very successfully in the aircraft industry, in which it has been discovered that the number of direct man-hours required to produce an airframe can be predicted when the rate at which employees improve performance is known. This approach is illustrated in Chapter 10, where the subject of "learning curves" is discussed.

A system that behaves in ways that are completely predictable is a *deterministic* system. The relationships in the "learning curve" equation are stated in a deterministic way. It is actually only an approximate expression of the relationships, but it provides a "workable" estimate of behavior, that is, an estimate of the man-hours needed and the costs involved in building airplanes.

Generally, the behavior in living systems is not exactly predictable. Behavior in living systems, while not perfectly predictable, usually follows patterns or fits statistical distributions and can be described in probabilistic terms. It is more appropriate, then, to look upon formal organizations as probabilistic systems. In this chapter we present a probabilistic model for predicting behavior—Markov chains.[1] With Markov chains, it is possible to predict

---

[1] In Chapters 11 and 12, we examine the behavior of a system over time through simulation.

behavior in future time periods or experiments, when it is known how a system behaved in a past period or in a previous experiment.

MARKOV CHAINS

Markov chain analysis allows us to determine the level at which a system will stabilize (if it stabilizes at all), the path, and the rate a which it approaches stability. In other words, Markov chains provide a means for predicting the results of implementing an organizational design. The technique reveals the behavior of a system as it passes through successive time periods. The outcome in each period is subject to chance elements. The Markov process, then, is a sequence of probabilistic events. When there is a sequence of experiments in which the outcome of any one experiment is dependent upon the outcome of the immediately preceding experiment, the sequence is called a *Markov process* or a *Markov chain.*[2]

A basic assumption of this presentation is that each experiment has a finite number of outcomes. The outcomes of a Markov chain are called *states.* Thus, the *Markov process* may be described as a ". . . sequence of states through which a system passes at successive points in time."[3] If we start the process in some particular state and we know the probabilities of going from one state to another, that is, the transition probabilities, we can determine the probabilities relating to the whole sequence of states. Suppose, for example, that we label the possible discrete states of a system as a_1, a_2, and a_3; the transition probabilities may then be shown by a *transition diagram*, as in Figure 9–1. The arrows indicate the possible states to which a process can move from a given state. The probabilities indicated have been determined arbitrarily and may be read as the probability of moving from a given state to the state designated by the direction of the arrow. In actual practice, these probabilities would have to be determined from past experience or through a sampling procedure. Alternatively, the probabilities shown in Figure 9–1 may be written as a table of transition probabilities as shown in Table 9–1. Since the elements of each row

---

[2] In this section we draw from John G. Kemeny, Arthur Schleifer, Jr., J. Laurie Snell, and Gerald L. Thompson, *Finite Mathematics with Business Applications* (Englewood Cliffs, N.J.: Prentice-Hall, Inc., 1962), pp. 192–97 and 274–80.

[3] Donald J. Clough, *Concepts in Management Science* (Englewood Cliffs, N.J.: Prentice-Hall, Inc., 1963), p. 220.

TABLE 9–1

Transition Probabilities—Three-State Markov Chain

To State

		a_1	a_2	a_3
From State	a_1	0	0.6	0.4
	a_2	0	0.5	0.5
	a_3	0.4	0	0.6

represent all the possibilities for the process when it is in that particular state, the sum of the elements of each row must equal one. An entry of zero means that the transition from one state to another is impossible.

FIGURE 9–1

Transition Diagram

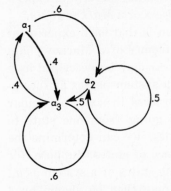

In order to obtain a Markov chain, it is, first of all, necessary to specify the starting position or more properly, the initial state. Given the initial state and the transition probabilities, it is then possible to determine the probabilities of being in all the possible states at successive time periods in the process. Utilizing the transition probabilities of our example and assuming that the process started in state a_1, let us trace the system through five successive time periods. The paths to the various possible states from the initial state a_1 may be shown as a tree diagram in Figure 9–2.

The paths to the eight terminal positions of a_1 from the initial state a_1 is the probability, denoted by $p_{ij}^{(t)}$, where t = time period, i = all the initial states, and j = all the terminal states. The superscript (t) does *not* mean the power of p_{ij}; $p_{11}^{(5)}$ is the probability of being in state a_1 after five successive time periods when the initial state is a_1. It is shown in Figure 9–2 and computed as follows:

$$
\begin{aligned}
p_{11}^{(5)} = &\ (.6 \times .5 \times .5 \times .5 \times .4) + (.6 \times .5 \times .5 \times .6 \times .4) \\
&+ (.6 \times .5 \times .4 \times .4 \times .4) + (.6 \times .5 \times .6 \times .6 \times .4) \\
&+ (.4 \times .4 \times .6 \times .5 \times .4) + (.4 \times .4 \times .4 \times .6 \times .4) \\
&+ (.4 \times .6 \times .4 \times .4 \times .4) + (.4 \times .6 \times .6 \times .6 \times .4) \\
= &\ (.030) + (.036) + (.0192) + (.0432) + (.0192) \\
&+ (.01536) + (.01536) + (.03456) = .21288
\end{aligned}
$$

FIGURE 9-2

Five Successive Time Periods of a Three-State Markov Process That Begins in State a_1

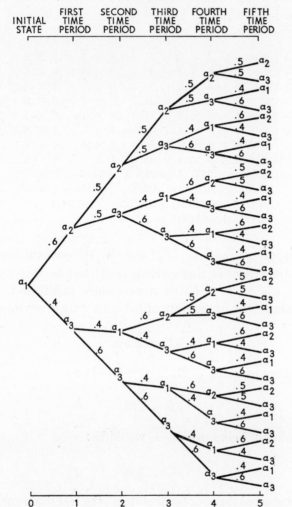

There are also eight terminal positions of the state a_2 from the initial state a_1. The probability of being in state a_2 after five successive time periods is:

$$p_{12}^{(5)} = (.6 \times .5 \times .5 \times .5 \times .5) + (.6 \times .5 \times .5 \times .4 \times .6)$$
$$+ (.6 \times .5 \times .4 \times .6 \times .5) + (.6 \times .5 \times .6 \times .4 \times .6)$$
$$+ (.4 \times .4 \times .6 \times .5 \times .5) + (.4 \times .4 \times .4 \times .4 \times .6)$$
$$+ (.4 \times .6 \times .4 \times .6 \times .5) + (.4 \times .6 \times .6 \times .4 \times .6)$$
$$= (.0375) + (.0360) + (.0360) + (.0432) + (.0240)$$
$$+ (.01536) + (.0288) + (.03456) = .25542$$

There are 16 terminal positions of the state a_3. Considering the paths to these terminal positions of a_3 from the initial state a_1, the probability of being in state a_3 after five successive time periods is computed as follows:

$$
\begin{aligned}
p_{13}^{(5)} =\ & (.6 \times .5 \times .5 \times .5 \times .5) + (.6 \times .5 \times .5 \times .5 \times .6) \\
& + (.6 \times .5 \times .5 \times .4 \times .4) + (.6 \times .5 \times .5 \times .6 \times .6) \\
& + (.6 \times .5 \times .4 \times .6 \times .5) + (.6 \times .5 \times .4 \times .4 \times .6) \\
& + (.6 \times .5 \times .6 \times .4 \times .4) + (.6 \times .5 \times .6 \times .6 \times .6) \\
& + (.4 \times .4 \times .6 \times .5 \times .5) + (.4 \times .4 \times .6 \times .5 \times .6) \\
& + (.4 \times .4 \times .4 \times .4 \times .4) + (.4 \times .4 \times .4 \times .6 \times .6) \\
& + (.4 \times .6 \times .4 \times .6 \times .5) + (.4 \times .6 \times .4 \times .4 \times .5) \\
& + (.4 \times .6 \times .6 \times .4 \times .4) + (.4 \times .6 \times .6 \times .6 \times .6) \\
=\ & (.0375) + (.045) + (.024) + (.054) + (.036) \\
& + (.0288) + (.0288) + (.0648) + (.024) + (.0288) \\
& + (.01024) + (.02304) + (.0288) + (.02304) \\
& + (.02304) + (.05184) = .53170
\end{aligned}
$$

If we had started the process at state a_2, the paths to the various possible states after five time periods could also be shown as a tree diagram in Figure 9–3. Using a procedure identical to the one illustrated above, the probability of being in state a_1 would be:

$$p_{21}^{(5)} = .213$$

The probability of being in state a_2 would be:

$$p_{22}^{(5)} = .255$$

The probability of being in state a_3 would be:

$$p_{23}^{(5)} = .532$$

If we had started the process at state a_3, the tree diagram showing the paths to the various possible states after five time periods could be illustrated as shown in Figure 9–4. The probability of being in state a_1 would be:

$$p_{31}^{(5)} = .213$$

The probability of being in state a_2 would be:

$$p_{32}^{(5)} = .255$$

FIGURE 9–3

Five Successive Time Periods of a Three-State Markov Process That Begins
in State a_2

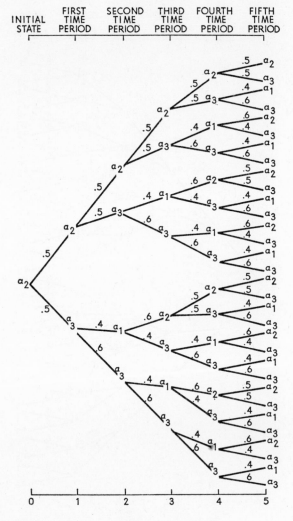

The probability of being in state a_3 would be:

$$p_{33}^{(5)} = .532$$

The results may be shown more conveniently in table form as in
Table 9–2.

Notice that each of the entries in Table 9–2 is a nonzero positive
number, indicating that it is possible to reach every state from each

FIGURE 9–4

Five Successive Time Periods of a Three-State Markov
Process That Begins in State a_3

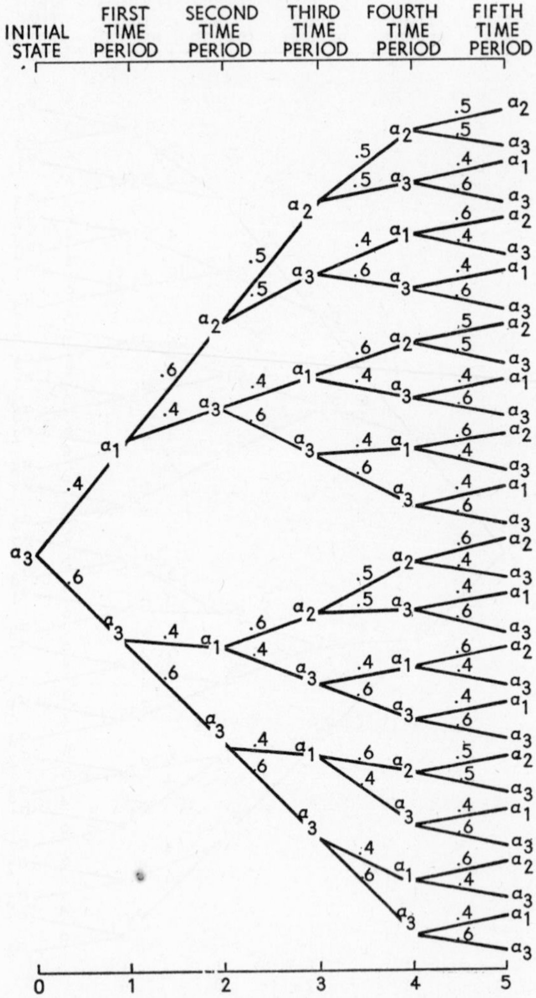

of the other states in five time periods. Also, since all the possible states of the system are represented, the sum of the row entries is still equal to one. We notice also that despite different starting conditions or different initial states, the probabilities of being in each of the respective states are the same. The system displays steady state probabilities and it illustrates an equifinal process. The

TABLE 9-2

Results of Five Time Period, Three-State Markov Chain

To State

		a_1	a_2	a_3
From State	a_1	0.213	0.255	0.532
	a_2	.213	.255	.532
	a_3	.213	.255	.532

steady state and the equifinal process will become clearer as we apply matrix algebra to Markov chains.

Application of Matrix Algebra to Markov Chains

While a tree measure such as the one described above can be constructed to carry the process through as many time periods as desired, a much simpler method is provided through the use of matrix algebra. The transition probabilities of Table 9–1 may be shown as the *transition matrix*, which we call P.

$$P = \begin{matrix} & \begin{matrix} a_1 & a_2 & a_3 \end{matrix} \\ \begin{matrix} a_1 \\ a_2 \\ a_3 \end{matrix} & \begin{pmatrix} 0 & .6 & .4 \\ 0 & .5 & .5 \\ .4 & 0 & .6 \end{pmatrix} \end{matrix}$$

According to the definition of a Markov process, the state of a system in period $t + 1$ is dependent on the state of the system in the immediately preceding period, that is, period t. The general equation of a Markov process, then, may be written

$$p^{(t+1)} = p^{(t)}P \qquad (9\text{--}1)$$

where $p^{(t+1)}$ is a row vector of probabilities which indicate the state of the system in period $t + 1$; $p^{(t)}$ is a row vector of probabilities indicating the state of the system in period t; and P is the matrix of transition probabilities.

Assuming that the initial state of the system and the transition probabilities are known, we can find the state of the system at any time t or in terms of our interests, the time path of the system can be determined by solving equation (9–1) for successive time periods. The procedure is as follows:

$$p^{(1)} = p^{(0)}P$$
$$p^{(2)} = p^{(1)}P$$
$$p^{(3)} = p^{(2)}P$$

$$\cdots$$

$$p^{(t)} = p^{(t-1)}P$$
$$p^{(t+1)} = p^{(t)}P$$

Now let us illustrate this procedure. First, we need to determine the initial state of the system. The starting condition may be stated as a row vector denoted as $p_i^{(0)}$. The subscript i denotes the initial state. Suppose, the process was started in state a_1, then the row vector would appear as $p_1^{(0)}$. The equivalent form for starting the process in state a_1 is

$$p_1^{(0)} = (1\ 0\ 0). \tag{9-2}$$

The reason that equation 9–2 is considered the equivalent form for starting in state a_1 is evident from the first step in the process. Thus:

$$p_1^{(1)} = p_1^{(0)}P = (1\ 0\ 0)\begin{pmatrix} 0 & .6 & .4 \\ 0 & .5 & .5 \\ .4 & 0 & .6 \end{pmatrix} = (0\ .6\ .4).$$

Now, let us continue the process through five time periods:

$$p_1^{(2)} = p_1^{(1)}P = (0\ .6\ .4)\begin{pmatrix} 0 & .6 & .4 \\ 0 & .5 & .5 \\ .4 & 0 & .6 \end{pmatrix} = (.16\ .30\ .54)$$

$$p_1^{(3)} = p_1^{(2)}P = (.16\ .30\ .54)\begin{pmatrix} 0 & .6 & .4 \\ 0 & .5 & .5 \\ .4 & 0 & .6 \end{pmatrix} = (.216\ .246\ .538)$$

$$p_1^{(4)} = p_1^{(3)}P = (.216\ .246\ .538)\begin{pmatrix} 0 & .6 & .4 \\ 0 & .5 & .5 \\ .4 & 0 & .6 \end{pmatrix} = (.2152\ .2526\ .5322)$$

$$p_1^{(5)} = p_1^{(4)}P = (.2152\ .2526\ .5322)\begin{pmatrix} 0 & .6 & .4 \\ 0 & .5 & .5 \\ .4 & 0 & .6 \end{pmatrix} = (.21288\ .25542\ .53170)$$

Notice that the entries of the row vector $p_1^{(5)}$ correspond to the results of the tree measure that started at state a_1 and was carried through five time periods. Recall that this result is shown as the first row of Table 9–2.

If we had started the process at a_2, the Markov process would appear as follows:

$$p_2^{(0)} = (0\ 1\ 0) \tag{9-3}$$

$$p_2^{(1)} = p_2^{(0)}P = (0\ 1\ 0) \begin{pmatrix} 0 & .6 & .4 \\ 0 & .5 & .5 \\ .4 & 0 & .6 \end{pmatrix} = (0\ .5\ .5)$$

$$p_2^{(2)} = p_2^{(1)}P = (0\ .5\ .5) \begin{pmatrix} 0 & .6 & .4 \\ 0 & .5 & .5 \\ .4 & 0 & .6 \end{pmatrix} = (.20\ .25\ .55)$$

$$p_2^{(3)} = p_2^{(2)}P = (.20\ .25\ .55) \begin{pmatrix} 0 & .6 & .4 \\ 0 & .5 & .5 \\ .4 & 0 & .6 \end{pmatrix} = (.220\ .245\ .535)$$

$$p_2^{(4)} = p_2^{(3)}P = (.220\ .245\ .535) \begin{pmatrix} 0 & .6 & .4 \\ 0 & .5 & .5 \\ .4 & 0 & .6 \end{pmatrix} = (.2140\ .2545\ .5315)$$

$$p_2^{(5)} = p_2^{(4)}P = (.2140\ .2545\ .5315) \begin{pmatrix} 0 & .6 & .4 \\ 0 & .5 & .5 \\ .4 & 0 & .6 \end{pmatrix} = (.21260\ .25565\ .53175)$$

Again the entries of row vector $p_2^{(5)}$ correspond to the tree measure that started at a_2 and are shown as the second row of Table 9–2.

If we had started the process at a_3, the Markov process would appear as follows:

$$p_3^{(0)} = (0\ 0\ 1) \tag{9-4}$$

$$p_3^{(1)} = p_3^{(0)}P = (0\ 0\ 1) \begin{pmatrix} 0 & .6 & .4 \\ 0 & .5 & .5 \\ .4 & 0 & .6 \end{pmatrix} = (.4\ 0\ .6)$$

$$p_3^{(2)} = p_3^{(1)}P = (.4\ 0\ .6) \begin{pmatrix} 0 & .6 & .4 \\ 0 & .5 & .5 \\ .4 & 0 & .6 \end{pmatrix} = (.24\ .24\ .52)$$

$$p_3^{(3)} = p_3^{(2)}P = (.24\ .24\ .52) \begin{pmatrix} 0 & .6 & .4 \\ 0 & .5 & .5 \\ .4 & 0 & .6 \end{pmatrix} = (.208\ .264\ .528)$$

$$p_3^{(4)} = p_3^{(3)}P = (.208\ .264\ .528) \begin{pmatrix} 0 & .6 & .4 \\ 0 & .5 & .5 \\ .4 & 0 & .6 \end{pmatrix} = (.2112\ .2568\ .5320)$$

$$p_3^{(5)} = p_3^{(4)}P = (.2112 \ .2568 \ .5320) \begin{pmatrix} 0 & .6 & .4 \\ 0 & .5 & .5 \\ .4 & 0 & .6 \end{pmatrix} = (.21280 \ .25512 \ .53208)$$

The entries of the vector $p_3^{(5)}$ correspond to the results obtained with the tree measure that started at state a_3 and the third row of Table 9-2.

The Steady State

In this presentation, steady state refers to a row in a matrix which is independent of the number of periods. When the values in a row do not change regardless of how many time periods elapse, these values are called steady state probabilities.

When the system ends up in the same state regardless of the initial state, it is called an equifinal process. The tendency toward a steady state and the equifinal process are apparent especially in the application of matrix algebra to Markov chains. As t becomes larger, $p^{(t)}$ approaches some limiting value, and despite the initial state, each process tends toward the same set of limiting values.

The steady state probabilities may be determined through simple algebraic manipulation. Let us denote the steady state probability row vector as w. Since the w vector is constant by definition, the probabilities of being in each state remain the same regardless of how many time periods are examined in the Markov process. If the probabilities describing the Markov process had reached w at time t, then $p^{(t+1)}$, $p^{(t+2)}$, $p^{(t+3)}$ . . . would be equal to w. Thus, from the general equation (9-1) we obtain:

$$p^{(t+1)} = p^tP = wP = w \qquad (9\text{-}5)$$

This result may be demonstrated with our numerical example. Rounding for convenience we assume:

$$w = (.213 \ .255 \ .532)$$

Then,

$$wP = (.213 \ .255 \ .532) \begin{pmatrix} 0 & .6 & .4 \\ 0 & .5 & .5 \\ .4 & 0 & .6 \end{pmatrix}$$

$$= (.213 \ .255 \ .532) = w$$

We see, then, that for a system in a steady state the probabilities of being in each state are constant through time.

It follows, therefore, that if the steady state probabilities are unknown, we may solve for w from equation (9–5)

$$w = wP = (w_1 \ w_2 \ w_3) \begin{pmatrix} 0 & .6 & .4 \\ 0 & .5 & .5 \\ .4 & 0 & .6 \end{pmatrix}$$

$$= (.4w_3, \ .6w_1 + .5w_2, \ .4w_1 + .5w_2 + .6w_3)$$

Since the sum of the elements of the row vector must equal unity, we can solve for all of the probabilities in terms of one of them. The equations are:

$$w_1 = .4w_3$$
$$w_2 = .6w_1 + .5w_2$$
$$w_3 = .4w_1 + .5w_2 + .6w_3$$

Solving in terms of one of them, we obtain:

$$w_2 = 1.2w_1$$
$$w_3 = 2.5w_1$$

Setting the sum of the probabilities equal to one, we solve for w_1 and then substitute to obtain w_2 and w_3.

$$w_1 + w_2 + w_3 = 1$$
$$w_1 + 1.2w_1 + 2.5w_1 = 1$$
$$4.7w_1 = 1$$
$$w_1 = .213$$
$$w_2 = .255$$
$$w_3 = .532$$

It may be seen further that as the transition matrix is raised to higher and higher powers it approaches the matrix W. This tendency is a result of the fact that P is a *regular* transition matrix. A transition matrix is defined to be regular if some power of the matrix has only positive, nonzero elements.[4] It will be found also that each row of the matrix W will be the same probability vector w. These characteristics of the regular transition matrix may be

---

[4] In this book, we do not cover Markov chains that are different from regular chains, such as absorbing Markov chains.

demonstrated by powering the transition matrix of our numerical example

$$P = \begin{pmatrix} 0 & .6 & .4 \\ 0 & .5 & .5 \\ .4 & 0 & .6 \end{pmatrix}$$

$$P^2 = \begin{pmatrix} .16 & .30 & .54 \\ .20 & .25 & .55 \\ .24 & .24 & .52 \end{pmatrix} \qquad P^3 = \begin{pmatrix} .216 & .246 & .538 \\ .220 & .245 & .535 \\ .208 & .264 & .528 \end{pmatrix}$$

$$P^4 = \begin{pmatrix} .2152 & .2526 & .5322 \\ .2140 & .2545 & .5315 \\ .2112 & .2568 & .5320 \end{pmatrix} \qquad P^5 = \begin{pmatrix} .21288 & .25542 & .53170 \\ .21260 & .25565 & .53175 \\ .21280 & .25512 & .53208 \end{pmatrix}$$

Notice that the results of raising the transition matrix to the fifth power are identical to the results obtained in the fifth time period of the Markov process. Thus, each row vector of the matrix $p^{(5)}$ is identical to their respective probability vectors $p_1^{(5)}$, $p_2^{(5)}$, and $p_3^{(5)}$. Notice also that the powered transition matrix approaches the matrix W:

$$W = \begin{pmatrix} .213 & .255 & .532 \\ .213 & .255 & .532 \\ .213 & .255 & .532 \end{pmatrix}$$

We see that each row vector of matrix W is the same as the probability vector w. Thus, by powering the transition matrix we have an alternate way of determining the behavior of a system that displays the characteristics of a Markov process. It should be reemphasized that it is necessary for the transition matrix to be regular for the powers of P to approach W.

We conclude from the exercise that regardless of the initial state or starting condition, if the transition matrix is regular, the probabilities of being in the respective possible states will be very close to a set of limiting values after the system passes through several time periods.

DESIGN OF ORGANIZATION AND MARKOV CHAINS

The designer of organization, as stated earlier in this chapter, is concerned with the steady state probabilities because he wants to know the level at which a system will stabilize, the rate at which it approaches stability, and the path that the system takes toward stability. In this section, we present a hypothetical decision model which evaluates three alternative designs of organization on the basis of the level, rate, and path criteria.

Suppose, a manufacturing firm has been experiencing problems with respect to formulating production schedules and budgets. It seems that the difficulty arises from the firm's inability to process information and make decisions fast enough. In its present form, the firm is organized according to Figure 9–5. Within the present

FIGURE 9–5

Organization Chart of a Manufacturing Firm

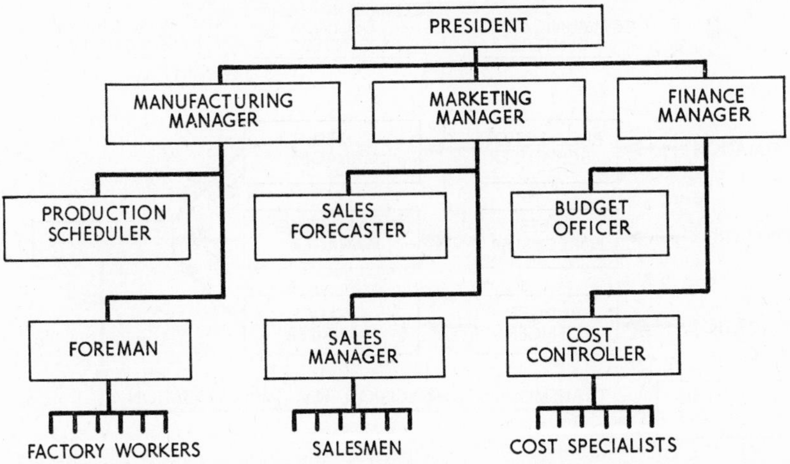

framework of Figure 9–5, the company is considering three alternative designs to solve its problem. The designs to be investigated are represented in Figures 9–6, 9–7, and 9–8 as designs No. 1, No. 2, and No. 3, respectively. A few speculative remarks accompany each design. Each design is tested and compared in the "Analysis" section below.

Design No. 1

Design No. 1 involves an information flow from internal and external sources through the various organizational levels before a final decision on the sales forecast, inventory levels, output, and budget is made by the president. Information is fed to the production scheduler, sales forecaster, and budget officer, who compile and transform the information and send it to their respective superiors, the manufacturing manager, the marketing manager and the finance manager. The latter make decisions related to their particular functions and communicate them to the president as recommendations on the desirable sales forecast, inventory levels, and output. The recommendations may all be similar or they may be divergent. The president is responsible for reconciling them, if necessary, and making a final decision. Conflicting departmental goals may make the president's task of reconciling the recommendations a difficult

FIGURE 9–6

Process Relationships, Design No. 1

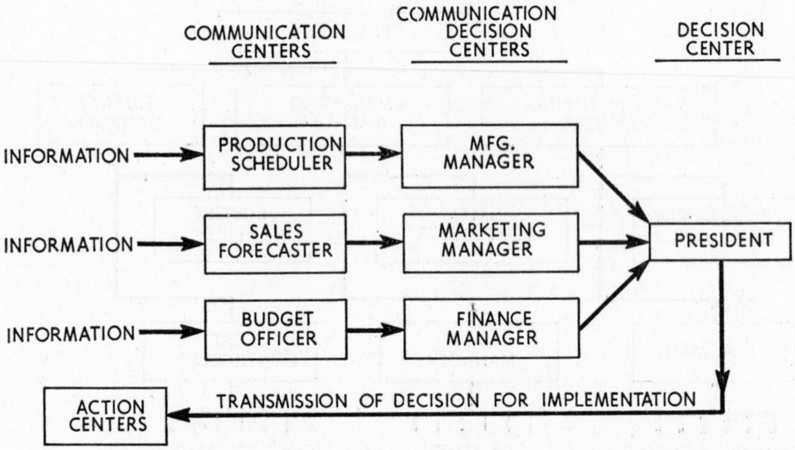

and time-consuming decision. For instance, in making recommendations, the marketing manager, in order to ensure sales revenues, may desire an optimistic sales forecast and high inventory levels. The manufacturing manager's concern for minimizing production costs may reflect itself in a low sales forecast and stable levels of output. The finance manager's recommendations may mirror his concern for "desirable" inventory turnover, accounts receivable turnover, liquidity position, and availability of funds. Subgoal biases in organization may lead to delays. Also, since the information must pass through at least two communication centers before it reaches the final decision-making point, intentional or unintentional distortions and delays are likely to occur.

Design No. 2

Design No. 2 requires that the final decision be made by a committee composed of the manufacturing manager, the marketing

manager, and the finance manager and then transmitted to the
president and the action centers. Information is fed to each of the
department managers by their respective assistants, the production
scheduler, the sales forecaster, and the budget officer. Reconciling
departmental conflicts occur in the committee's direct face-to-face
meetings. Since the departmental managers are responsible for
making a final decision, their perspective on organizational goals is
extended beyond the narrow departmental interests. Actually, each
one of the department managers of the committee is confronted by

FIGURE 9-7
Process Relationships, Design No. 2

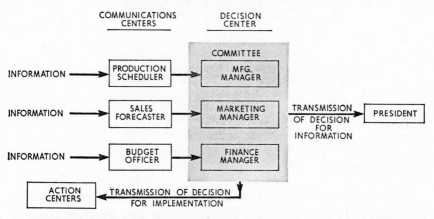

the constraints and problems of all of the departments. We might
expect from this decision-making arrangement a reduction in
delays and distortions over design No. 1 because the information
transmission channel is shorter and the decision center is comprised
of principal members of several interest areas.

Design No. 3

Under design No. 3, the scheduling decision is made by a committee comprised of the three assistants, the production scheduler, the
sales forecaster, and the budget officer. The final decision is transmitted by the committee to the action centers and to the three
department managers, who pass on the decision to the president. In
comparison to the others, design No. 3 has the shortest transmission channel. We might expect the least amount of delays and
distortions in this arrangement.

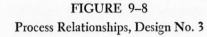

FIGURE 9–8

Process Relationships, Design No. 3

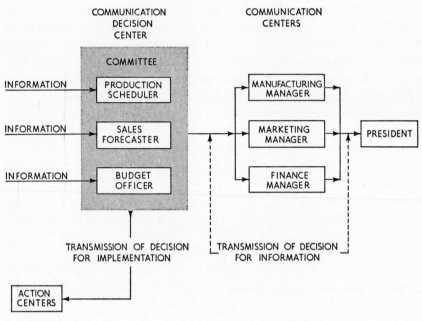

General Procedure

The firm has a standard procedure for the formulation of production schedules and budgets. The schedules and budgets cover a five-week period. The overall plan of production schedules and budgets contain details for each week of the five-week period. The procedure calls for one decision on a production schedule and one decision on a production budget for each week. The overall plan, then, requires 10 decisions—2 for each week. The firm has the additional rule that the overall plan must be completed prior to the first day of the five-week period when they are to be implemented. If a decision has not been reached for one or any of the weekly schedules prior to the first day of the five-week implementation period, then the firm automatically uses the weekly schedule that coincides chronologically in the previous five-week schedule. In order to meet these requirements, decision makers meet once each week in the five weeks prior to the time when the overall schedule is to be implemented. At each meeting, they can make either no decision or any number up to and including 10 decisions required for the next five-week period.

For this illustration, we define performance as the number of decisions made per week. As indicated above, it is possible to make 10 decisions in any one week. Also, there is the time limit on decisions, that is, all decisions for the overall schedules must be completed by the day prior to implementation. Although this rule forces decision makers to make decisions within a specified time period, it is necessary in order to meet the lead-time requirements of production scheduling and budgeting, such as having adequate materials, machinery, manpower, and funds on hand at the proper time and place. If no decision is made within the allotted time, the automatic rule, described above, goes into effect.

Let us examine the history of a single decision through the Markov process. The states of the system are designated as: a_0, a_1, a_2, a_3, and a_4. We say the system is in state a_0 if a decision has been made. It is in state a_1 if one week has passed and no decision has been made, state a_2 if two weeks have passed and no decision has been made, a_3 if three weeks have passed without a decision, a_4 if four weeks have passed with no decision. There is no state a_5 because a decision must be made by the decision makers or by the automatic rule before five weeks have passed.

If a decision has been made within the first week, then there is a transition from state a_0 to state a_0. Here the reasonable assumption is made that schedules and budgets are made on a continuous basis. The system moves from one period where decisions have already been made and the firm is producing an output on the schedule (that is, it is in state a_0) to another period where a decision is made on future schedules and budgets (that is, the system moves from state a_0 to state a_0). If a decision has not been reached within the first week, then there is a transition from state a_0 to a_1. If a decision has been reached within two weeks, then there is a transition from a_1 to a_0; if not, there is a transition from a_1 to a_2. Similar reasoning applies for transitions to and from a_3 and a_4.[5] All of these possibilities can be shown by a transition diagram as indicated in Figure 9–9.

Analysis

Suppose that after studying behavior under the organization designated as design No. 1, we are able to derive the transition

---

[5] This procedure has been adapted from the Group Replacement example presented in Clough, *op. cit.*, pp. 226–31.

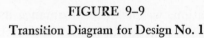

FIGURE 9–9

Transition Diagram for Design No. 1

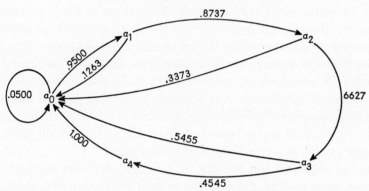

probabilities for one decision as shown in Table 9–3. The entry at the intersection of a_0 and a_0 says there is a probability of 0.05 that a decision will be made in the first week. Again, it is assumed in this condition that the system is already in a_0, that is, it is operating on past schedules or making decisions on future schedules partly on the basis of decisions made on past schedules. There is a probability of 0.95 that a decision will not be made in the first week, shown by

TABLE 9–3

Transition Probabilities for One Decision, Design No. 1.

To State

		a_0	a_1	a_2	a_3	a_4
	a_0	0.0500	0.9500	0	0	0
From State	a_1	0.1263	0	0.8737	0	0
	a_2	0.3373	0	0	0.6627	0
	a_3	0.5455	0	0	0	0.4545
	a_4	1.000	0	0	0	0

the intersection of a_0 and a_1 in Table 9–3. Similarly, assuming that the decision has not been reached in the first week, there is a 0.1263 probability that it will be made in the second week and a 0.873 probability that it will not be made in the second week. If the decision has not been made by the end of the fourth week, it is certain to be made in the fifth week because of the ruling that decisions have to be made before the end of that week either by decision makers or the automatic rule. Thus, the probability of a decision in the fifth week is equal to 1, as shown by the intersection of a_4 and a_0.

The entries of Table 9–3 make up the matrix of transition probabilities P. Before applying the general procedure of equation (9–1), let us first determine the steady-state probability vector w by equation (9–5):

$$w = wP = (w_0, w_1, w_2, w_3, w_4) \begin{pmatrix} .0500 & .9500 & 0 & 0 & 0 \\ .1263 & 0 & .8737 & 0 & 0 \\ .3373 & 0 & 0 & .6627 & 0 \\ .5455 & 0 & 0 & 0 & .4545 \\ 1.000 & 0 & 0 & 0 & 0 \end{pmatrix}$$

$$= (.0500w_0 + .1263w_1 + .3373w_2 + .5455w_3 + 1.000w_4, .9500w_0,$$
$$.8737w_1, .6627w_2, .4545w_3)$$

Solving in terms of one of the elements, we obtain:

$$w_1 = \ldots \ldots = .95w_0$$
$$w_2 = .8737w_1 = .83w_0$$
$$w_3 = .6627w_2 = .55w_0$$
$$w_4 = .4545w_3 = .25w_0$$

Since the sum of the elements of the row vector must equal unity, we first solve for w_0 and then substitute to obtain w_1, w_2, w_3, and w_4.

$$w_0 + w_1 + w_2 + w_3 + w_4 = 1$$
$$w_0 + .95w_0 + .83w_0 + .55w_0 + .25w_0 = 1$$
$$3.58w_0 = 1$$
$$w_0 = .2793$$
$$w_1 = .95w_0 = .2653$$
$$w_2 = .83w_0 = .2318$$
$$w_3 = .55w_0 = .1536$$
$$w_4 = .25w_0 = .0698$$

(Note that the probabilities have been rounded. The sum of the probabilities, therefore, is slightly more than unity.) The steady state probability vector is written as follows:

$$w = (.2793 \quad .2653 \quad .2318 \quad .1536 \quad .0698)$$

The first element of this probability vector is the probability of being in state a_0, that is, the probability of a completed decision.

Recalling that it is possible to make 10 decisions in any one week, we may, therefore, say that once the system reaches equilibrium, the expected number of decisions per week is $(10)(0.2793) = 2.79$. While the decimal part of this result seems unrealistic, it is a result of averaging and may be interpreted as a partially completed decision process.

Let us now trace the Markov process through several time periods to see how the probabilities approach their limiting values. Starting the process in state a_0, we write the equivalent form as follows:

$$p_0^{(0)} = (1\ 0\ 0\ 0\ 0)$$

Recalling the general procedure from equation (9–1) for tracing the process, we have:

$$p^{(1)} = p^{(0)}P$$
$$p^{(2)} = p^{(1)}P$$
$$\cdots$$
$$p^{(t+1)} = p^{(t)}P$$

Solving the equation successively, we obtain:

$$p_0^{(1)} = p_0^{(0)}P = (1\ 0\ 0\ 0\ 0)\begin{pmatrix} .0500 & .9500 & 0 & 0 & 0 \\ .1263 & 0 & .8738 & 0 & 0 \\ .3373 & 0 & 0 & .6627 & 0 \\ .5455 & 0 & 0 & 0 & .4545 \\ 1.000 & 0 & 0 & 0 & 0 \end{pmatrix}$$

$$= (.0500\ .9500\ 0\ 0\ 0)$$

$$p_0^{(2)} = p_0^{(1)}P = (.1225\ .0475\ .8300\ 0\ 0)$$
$$p_0^{(3)} = p_0^{(2)}P = (.2921\ .1164\ .0415\ .5500\ 0)$$
$$p_0^{(4)} = p_0^{(3)}P = (.3433\ .2275\ .1017\ .0275\ .2500)$$
$$p_0^{(5)} = p_0^{(4)}P = (.3515\ .3261\ .2425\ .0674\ .0125)$$
$$p_0^{(6)} = p_0^{(5)}P = (.1898\ .3339\ .2849\ .1607\ .0306)$$
$$p_0^{(7)} = p_0^{(6)}P = (.2660\ .1803\ .2917\ .1888\ .0730)$$
$$p_0^{(8)} = p_0^{(7)}P = (.3105\ .2527\ .1575\ .1933\ .0858)$$
$$p_0^{(9)} = p_0^{(8)}P = (.2918\ .2950\ .2208\ .1044\ .0879)$$
$$p_0^{(10)} = p_0^{(9)}P = (.2712\ .2772\ .2577\ .1463\ .0474)$$
$$p_0^{(11)} = p_0^{(10)}P = (.2627\ .2576\ .2422\ .1708\ .0665)$$
$$p_0^{(12)} = p_0^{(11)}P = (.2870\ .2496\ .2251\ .1605\ .0776)$$
$$p_0^{(13)} = p_0^{(12)}P = (.2870\ .2727\ .2181\ .1492\ .0729)$$
$$p_0^{(14)} = p_0^{(13)}P = (.2766\ .2727\ .2383\ .1445\ .0678)$$

Notice that as we examine more and more time periods, the result gets closer and closer to the steady-state probability vector w. As we noted earlier, the first element of $p_0^{(t)}$ is the probability of being in state a_0 or the probability of a completed decision at time t. When the probability of a completed decision is multiplied times the number of possible decisions in each period, that is, 10 decisions per week, we notice that the result approaches the limiting value of 2.79 decisions per week. The results are shown in Table 9–4.

TABLE 9–4

Expected Number of Decisions per Week, Design No. 1

Time Period t	Probability of Completed Decision at the End of Period t	Expected Number of Completed Decisions at the End of Period t
1	0.0500	0.50
2	.1225	1.23
3	.2921	2.92
4	.3433	3.43
5	.3515	3.52
6	.1898	1.90
7	.2660	2.66
8	.3105	3.11
9	.2918	2.92
10	.2712	2.71
11	.2627	2.63
12	.2870	2.87
13	.2870	2.87
14	.2766	2.77
..	....	...

The expected number of completed decisions at the end of each week and the limiting value of the system are shown graphically in Figure 9–10.

FIGURE 9–10

Behavior and Equilibrium of Design No. 1

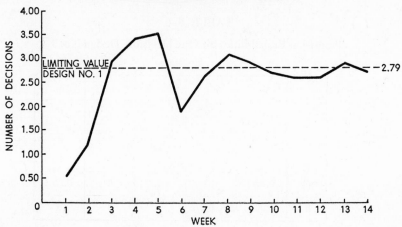

Suppose that after studying behavior under designs No. 2 and No. 3, we are able to derive the transition probabilities of Tables 9–5 and 9–6, respectively. The transition diagram for designs No. 2

TABLE 9–5

Transition Probabilities for One Decision, Design No. 2

To State

		a_0	a_1	a_2	a_3	a_4
	a_0	0.30	0.70	0	0	0
	a_1	0.20	0	0.80	0	0
From State	a_2	0.40	0	0	0.60	0
	a_3	0.60	0	0	0	0.40
	a_4	1.00	0	0	0	0

FIGURE 9–11

Transition Diagram for Design No. 2

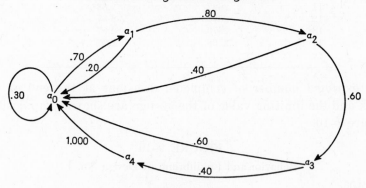

TABLE 9–6

Transition Probabilities for One Decision, Design No. 3

To State

		a_0	a_1	a_2	a_3	a_4
	a_0	0.70	0.30	0	0	0
	a_1	0.40	0	0.60	0	0
From State	a_2	0.60	0	0	0.40	0
	a_3	0.80	0	0	0	0.20
	a_4	1.00	0	0	0	0

FIGURE 9-12
Transition Diagram for Design No. 3

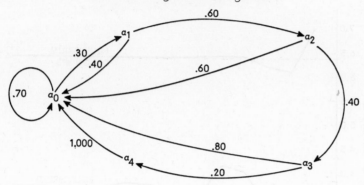

TABLE 9-7
Expected Number of Decisions per Week

Time Period t	Expected Number of Completed Decisions at the End of Period t		
	Design No. 1	Design No. 2	Design No. 3
1	0.50	3.00	7.000
2	1.23	2.30	6.100
3	2.92	3.35	6.190
4	3.43	4.02	6.397
5	3.52	4.14	6.427
6	1.90	3.42	6.387
7	2.66	3.49	6.377
8	3.11	3.71	6.382
9	2.92	3.74	6.384
10	2.71	3.67	6.384
11	2.62	3.62	.
12	2.67	3.66	.
13	2.89	3.68	.
14	2.74	3.67	.
.	.	.	.
.	.	.	.
.	.	.	.
Equilibrium	2.79	3.66	6.384

and No. 3 are in Figures 9–11 and 9–12. From the Markov process, we derive the expected number of decisions per week and the equilibrium condition as shown in Table 9–7. The results of design No. 1 are repeated in this table for purposes of comparison. The behavior of the three systems is shown graphically in Figure 9–13.

FIGURE 9–13

Comparison of Behavior and Equilibria of Designs No. 1, No. 2, and No. 3

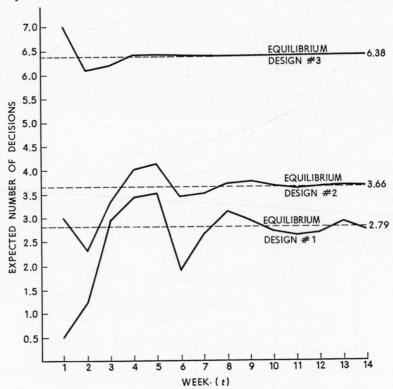

Notes on the Model

It is apparent from Figure 9–13 that behavior under design No. 3 stabilizes at a much higher level of performance, attains stability at a faster rate, and follows a much less erratic time path than either of the two other designs. In terms of the time division, made in Chapter 4, into productive and nonproductive time, it is easy to see that design No. 3 involves less nonproductive time, that is, organization members have to spend less time away from their primary task or less time in meetings in this case.[6] Stated in other terms, design No. 3 is less costly or results in greater productivity. Design No. 3 is less costly in another sense. The executives involved in the decision

---

[6] This conclusion is based on the assumption that all meetings involve an equal amount of time.

process of design No. 3 undoubtedly receive lower salaries than the decision makers of the other designs. Presumably, in design No. 3, there is the added benefit of releasing higher level executives for more important matters.

A word of caution is in order. In order to illustrate a procedure for testing alternative designs of organization, we fabricated tables of transition probabilities which showed design No. 3 to have the best performance. It is not necessarily true that design No. 3 is generally better than designs No. 1 and No. 2 or any other design. We could have devised the transition probabilities to show design No. 1 or No. 2 to have the best performance. Again, we emphasize that we were illustrating a procedure and not trying to convey general impressions about the "best" design. Instead, our emphasis throughout this book is that alternative designs of organization should be evaluated on the basis of objective criteria. The decision to use one design over another should be based on how well it meets these criteria.

DISCUSSION QUESTIONS AND PROBLEMS

9–1. Why is Markov chain analysis important in the evaluation of organization designs?

9–2. Is it necessary to know what characteristics of a particular design cause a system to behave as it does in order to use Markov chain analysis?

9–3. What factors other than level, rate, and path of behavior are important in evaluating a particular design? Can these other factors be incorporated in a predictive model? Explain.

9–4. Is it possible to use a deterministic model to predict behavior in a formal organization? Explain.

9–5. What is the meaning of steady state, and the equifinal process? Distinquish between steady state and equilibrium. In your answer, refer to behavior in formal organization.

9–6. Outline the assumptions of a Markov chain model and discuss their applicability to formal organization.

9–7. Consider a business organization with a continuous flow of information through its various levels. Take, for example, an order to increase production by 10,000 units, which originates at top level n. As the order is relayed through the lower levels of the single-channel organization (n to $n - 1$, $n - 1$ to $n - 2$, $n - 2$ to $n - 3$....

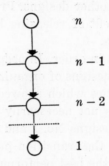

$n - (n - 2)$ to 1), there is a possibility at each level that the order may be altered. We can apply a two-state Markov chain to this problem. The order has *two* possible states in this single-channel organization: state *unaltered*, that is, the order transmitted to a lower level is exactly the same as the original order—for instance, to increase production by 10,000 units; state *altered*, that is, the order transmitted to a lower level is changed—for example, increase production by 1,000 units, or decrease production by 10,000 units. Thus, we can construct a 2 x 2 transition matrix showing the possible states of the order at a given level in the organization. Assume that the probability of going from an unaltered state to an altered state is a, and the probability of going from an altered state to an unaltered state is b, where $0 < a < 1$ and $0 < b < 1$.

a) Construct a transition diagram in terms of the two states.

b) Find the stationary states, w_1 and w_2 from the equation

$$wP = (w_1 w_2) \begin{pmatrix} 1 - a & a \\ b & 1 - b \end{pmatrix}$$

c) Construct two tree diagrams of a Markov chain, tracing the message flow through six levels in the organization. Assume in one diagram that the order begins in an unaltered state at the sixth level. In the other diagram, assume that the order begins in an altered state.

d) Given $a = .1$ $b = .7$, find the stationary state from the equations found in (b).

e) Show that by applying matrix algebra to Markov chains, the same results as that in (d) can be obtained.

9-8. An office supervisor notices that there is an increasing backlog of secretarial work. He traces the cause of this backlog to absenteeism among his secretaries. He wants to know the probability that one of his secretaries will be absent during a given month so he will know how many substitute secretaries to hire. This, he feels, will prevent a backlog of work. He collects data showing the absenteeism of his secretaries for the past year. The supervisor reasons that the probability of a given number of absences this month depends on the number of times a secretary had been absent the previous month. He obtains some past records, and he arrays the data as shown in the following table. The number of absences (states) are shown in the margins of the table, and the transition probabilities are entered at the intersection of absences. An example of how the table may be read is: the probability that a secretary who was absent 2 times last month will be absent 4 times this month is 0.10.

To State

		0	1	2	3	4
	0	.30	.25	.20	.15	.10
From	1	.50	.20	.15	.10	.05
State	2	.55	.15	.10	.10	.10
	3	.60	.15	.15	.05	.05
	4	.65	.20	.10	.04	.01

The matrix shows there have never been more than four absences by any one secretary in a given month.

a) Show that this matrix is regular.

b) Outline the steps required for the supervisor to find the answer to his problems.

9-9. Suppose that the supervisor reasons that the probability of a given number of absences per secretary this week depends on the number of times a secretary had been absent the previous week. From past data, he obtains the following matrix. An example of how the matrix may be read is: the probability that a secretary who was absent 1 time last week will be absent 2 times this week is 0.15.

To State

		0	1	2
	0	.40	.40	.20
From	1	.50	.35	.15
State	2	.60	.30	.10

a) Find the steady state matrix.

b) Give an explanation of the steady state matrix for this problem.

9-10. The methods used to solve for the steady state and the time path of design No. 1 are given in the text.

   a) Use the method shown in the text to solve for the steady states of both design No. 2 and design No. 3.

   b) Use equation (9-1) to show how the time paths of design No. 2 and design No. 3 were obtained.

10

LEARNING

The fact that human beings have the ability to learn is an important consideration for organizational design. It is important, for example, because it affects the size of the organization. In this regard, an airplane manufacturer finds that far fewer man-hours are needed to assemble the 200th unit of a particular aircraft than were needed to produce the 100th unit. He concludes that organization members have "learned" to produce the aircraft with proficiency. Thus, he can produce the airplane with a fewer number of workers. A smaller size should also have an effect on supervision and on the complexity of organizational relationships. Learning is an important consideration, also, because it helps to explain emergent behavior. People learn about their jobs; they learn what to expect from the organization; they learn what to expect from other organization members; and as they learn these kinds of things, they order their relationships and develop orderly patterns of behavior.

Furthermore, the fact that people can acquire knowledge and skills through study, instruction, or experience places a premium on organizational design. First, it is apparent that the design should provide the proper conditions for learning, that is, define tasks and organizational relationships in a manner that enables participants to learn the responses necessary to achieve organizational objectives. Second, the design should change from a condition that once provided a learning situation to one that accommodates on-going production. Under the second condition, that is, after learning, the organization is likely to have a greater capacity to produce. With a greater capacity to produce, the organization can grow and perhaps enter into new and expanded areas of activity. Also, organizational behavior in the learning stage may be limited to reaction and adaptation to environmental changes. As the organization learns to cope with the environment, that is, in the advanced stages of development, it can act and exert a greater influence on its environment. In this stage, it is capable of exercising greater control over its performance by shaping the environment and by timing its actions to be more opportunistic with environmental conditions.[1] We are saying, in effect, that design is not a fixed, one-time arrangement, but it should be changed or made flexible enough to reflect the capacity of its participants, its stage of development (reactive versus active), and the state of its environment.

It is the purpose of this chapter to present models and research evidence of learning behavior. In the first section of this chapter, we report on a model that has been developed through industrial experience—"the learning curve." Although organizational design is considered a factor in the determination of performance, no specific recommendation is given in the literature as to what conditions provide the best opportunity for learning. Nonetheless, it is important to examine this model because it contributes to understanding about organization behavior. In the second and third parts of this chapter, we present the results of experiments that were concerned with learning. In these sections also, we refer to models that predict learning behavior for individuals and groups.

LEARNING CURVES

In the aircraft industry, learning patterns were observed as early as 1925,[2] and a report on their importance for estimating

---

[1] There are many examples to illustrate these stages of development. One example that stands out is the experience of the U.S. Armed Forces in Vietnam.

[2] Miguel A. Requero, "An Economic Study of the Military Airframe Industry" (Wright Patterson Air Force Base, Ohio: Department of the Air Force, October, 1957), p. 213.

costs of airplane assembly was published as early as 1936.[3] These reports indicated that as employees perform the same task over and over again, they become more and more productive, with the result that less and less direct labor is required per unit of output. While this finding hardly seems startling, the additional findings that the improvement in performance followed a regular enough pattern to allow prediction has had tremendous significance to organization planners who must determine future personnel needs, estimate future costs, determine prices for contract bidding, and develop budgets.

In addition, studies have shown that the pattern of improvement was practically the same for different companies in the aircraft industry.[4] This finding has led to the speculation that there is a "general theory" of learning curves. Briefly stated, *learning curve theory is based on the premise that as the total number of units produced doubles, the direct man-hour requirements decline by some constant percentage.* The pattern that is considered most consistent in the aircraft industry is called the "80 percent curve." An "80 percent curve" means that there is a 20 percent reduction in direct man-hour requirements every time production doubles. For example, once production is started on an airplane, it is estimated that the fourth plane requires about 80 percent as much direct labor as the second; the eighth plane requires 80 percent as much direct labor as the fourth; the 200th plane requires 80 percent as much as the 100th, and so on. "Because this rate of improvement seemed to prevail so consistently, it was concluded that the aircraft industry's rate of learning was approximately 80% between doubled quantities. That standard is applied to this day in analyzing a variety of procurement, production, and costing problems within the industry and within particular companies."[5] The 80 percent curve, according to Asher ". . . has been accepted with a universality that can scarcely be imagined by persons outside the airframe industry."[6]

[3] T. P. Wright, "Factors Affecting the Cost of Airplanes," *Journal of the Aeronautical Sciences*, Vol. 3 (February, 1936), pp. 34–40.

[4] In a study of the airframe industry, the Stanford Research Institute found that although each of the companies had different starting points (different amounts of direct labor were used on the first plane), their improvement rates were basically the same. Frank J. Andress, "The Learning Curve as a Production Tool," *Harvard Business Review*, Vol. 32, No. 1 (January–February, 1954), p. 88.

[5] Andress, *op. cit.*, p. 88.

[6] Harold Asher, *Cost-Quantity Relationships in the Airframe Industry* (Santa Monica, Calif.: The RAND Corporation, 1956), p. 17.

Tabular and Graphical Presentation

The learning curve is usually expressed in terms of a relationship between units produced and unit direct labor man-hours or between units produced and cumulative average direct labor man-hours. As we shall see, the same equation may be used to define either relationship. An 80 percent *unit* curve is illustrated in Table 10–1,

TABLE 10–1

Man-Hour Requirements with an 80% Learning Curve with Unit Number Requiring 100,000 Man-Hours

Unit Number (1)	Unit Direct Labor Man-Hours (2)	Cumulative Direct Labor Man-Hours (3)	Cumulative Average Direct Labor Man-Hours (4)
1	100,000	100,000	100,000
2	80,000	180,000	90,000
3	70,210	250,210	83,403
4	64,000	314,210	78,553
5	59,565	373,775	74,755
6	56,157	429,932	71,655
7	53,437	483,369	69,053
8	51,200	534,569	66,821
16	40,960	892,014	55,751
32	32,768	1,467,862	45,871
64	26,214	2,392,453	37,382
128	20,972	3,874,395	30,269
256	16,777	6,247,318	24,404

using 100,000 unit direct labor man-hours as the requirement to produce the first unit of production. Column (1) of Table 10–1 indicates the unit number and column (2) indicates the number of man-hours required to produce the last unit of the number indicated in column (1). Thus, it takes 100,000 man-hours to produce the first unit, 80,000 man-hours to produce the second unit, 70,210 man-hours to produce the third unit, 64,000 man-hours to produce the fourth unit, and so on. Notice that column (2) meets the requirement of an 80 percent curve, that is, a 20 percent decrease in man-hour requirements on doubled quantities produced. Thus, the number of man-hours required to produce the second unit is 80 percent of the number required to produce the first unit, the number required to produce the fourth unit is 80 percent of the number required to produce the second unit, the number required to produce the eighth unit is 80 percent of the number required to produce the fourth unit and so on. The cumulative average direct labor man-hours, column (4) of Table 10–1, is obtained by dividing the cumulative direct labor man-hours, column (3), by the number

FIGURE 10–1

Eighty Percent Learning Curves with Unit Number One Requiring 100,000 Man-Hours

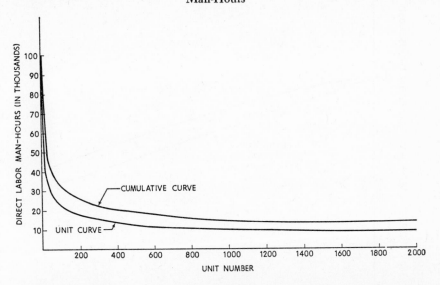

of units in column (1).[7] Notice also that the interim man-hour requirements between doubled quantities are supplied through the eighth unit, that is, units number 3, 5, 6, and 7. These values are supplied to illustrate that consecutive values are needed to derive column (3) of the table. After unit number 8, values are shown only for doubled quantities.

The values for *unit* direct labor man-hours and *cumulative* average direct labor man-hours are plotted in Figure 10–1. The curves illustrate the reduction in man-hours required to produce greater

---

[7] Besides indicating the unit number, column (1) also gives the cumulative units. Thus, column (4) indicates the cumulative average direct labor man-hours *per unit*. This second classification is used in Table 10–3. To avoid confusion with the classification of column (2), the second classification is not used at this point.

and greater amounts of a product. Although the percentage reduction remains constant, the application of this percentage to a diminishing base produces smaller and smaller improvement in the absolute amounts and causes the curve to level off. "This reflects the fact

FIGURE 10–2
Eighty Percent Curve on Log-Log Paper with Unit Number One Requiring 100,000 Man-Hours

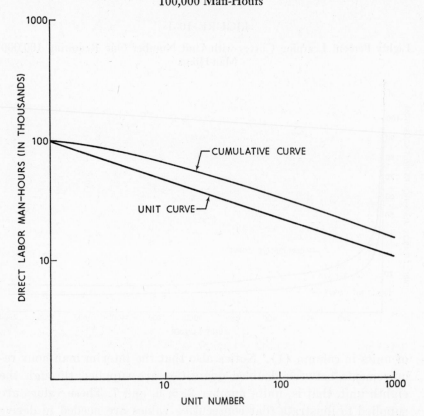

that in actual experience the process of learning a given operation eventually approaches a plateau where relatively little further improvement takes place."[8]

In practice, the unit curve and the cumulative curve are plotted on log-log paper (see Figure 10–2). The reason for this practice is that the curves appear as straight lines on log-log paper and are much easier to project than the curves plotted on ordinary graph paper. The cumulative curve is actually nonlinear, but after the first few units, it takes on the straight-line characteristic and is

---

[8] Andress, *op. cit.*, p. 89.

almost parallel to the unit curve. Thus, after the first few units both curves show approximately the same rate of improvement.

Analytic Model

If the learning curve is defined initially in terms of unit direct labor man-hour requirements, the mathematical expression[9] for this relationship is:

$$Y_x = Kx^b \qquad (10\text{--}1)$$

where

x = the unit number.
Y_x = the number of direct labor man-hours required to produce the xth unit.
K = the number of direct labor man-hours required to produce the first unit.
b = improvement factor, $-1 \le b \le 0$.

If the learning curve is defined initially in terms of cumulative average direct labor man-hour requirements, the mathematical expression is the same as equation (10–1), but the variables and parameters would be defined differently. Thus:

$$Y_x = Kx^b \qquad (10\text{--}2)$$

where

x = any number of completed units.
Y_x = cumulative average direct labor man-hours required to produce any number of units.
K = the number of cumulative average direct labor man-hours to produce the first unit.
b = improvement factor, $-1 \le b \le 0$.

Since the learning curve of our illustration was defined initially in terms of unit direct labor man-hours, we can use equation (10–1) to derive the values for column (2) of Table 10–1 and the unit curve of Figure 10–1. First, let us be more specific about the meaning of the learning percentage, for example, an 80 percent learning curve. The *learning percentage* is defined as the ratio of the unit man-hours required at two different outputs. It is customary to

---

[9] For the derivation of this equation, see W. J. Fabrycky and Paul E. Torgersen, *Operations Economy* (Englewood Cliffs, N.J.: Prentice-Hall, Inc., 1966), p. 104.

derive this ratio for outputs that are different by a factor of 2. The learning percentage is denoted by S. Thus:

$$S = \frac{Y_{2x}}{Y_x} = \frac{K(2x)^b}{Kx^b}$$

or

$$S = 2^b \qquad (10\text{--}3)$$

Since, an 80 percent curve was used in our illustration, we can set S equal to 0.8, solve for b, and use equation (10–1) to illustrate the derivation of a value in column (2) of Table 10–1. Thus:

$$0.8 = 2^b$$

or by using common logarithms, we obtain:

$$\text{Log } 0.8 = b \log 2$$
$$b = \frac{\log 0.8}{\log 2} = \frac{-0.0969}{0.3010}$$

For an 80 percent curve then:

$$b = -0.3219$$

Let us now apply equation (10–1) and find the number of direct labor man-hours needed to build the 16th unit:

$$Y_{16} = 100,000 \ (16)^{-0.3219}$$
$$= \frac{100,000}{16^{0.3219}}$$
$$= \frac{100,000}{0.3219 \log 16}$$
$$= 40,960$$

This value agrees with our tabular unit man-hour requirement for the 16th unit.

Experience with learning curves is not, of course, limited to the aircraft industry. Learning curves are considered applicable in industries such a metalworking, textile, candymaking,[10] construction, petroleum,[11] and maintenance operations.[12]

---

[10] Andress, op. cit., p. 88.

[11] Winifred B. Hirchmann, "Profit from the Learning Curve," Harvard Business Review, Vol. 42, No. 1 (January–February, 1964), pp. 125–39.

[12] C. A. Bennett, "The Application of a Learning Curve to a Maintenance Problem," Proceedings Second Annual Quality Control Symposium of the Dallas–Fort Worth Section, American Society for Quality Control, March 16, 1957.

As might be expected also, there are several learning curves besides the 80 percent curve. Experience seems to indicate that improvement patterns vary with the ratio of human labor to machine operations. In the airframe industry, where the 80 percent curve prevails, three fourths of the direct labor input is in assembly and the remainder is in machine work. Assembly work in the airframe industry involves considerable human effort and, therefore, provides more opportunities for learning than machine-dominated operations. Machines cannot learn to run faster. In those cases, for

TABLE 10–2

Equivalent Improvement Factors for Several Learning Percentages

Learning Percent S	Improvement Factor b
70	−0.5146
71	−0.4942
72	−0.4739
73	−0.4541
74	−0.4345
75	−0.4150
76	−0.3959
77	−0.3771
78	−0.3585
79	−0.3401
80	−0.3219
81	−0.3041
82	−0.2863
83	−0.2688
84	−0.2516
85	−0.2345
86	−0.2176
87	−0.2009
88	−0.1845
89	−0.1681
90	−0.1520

example, where three fourths of operations are machine work and one fourth assembly, ". . . the approximate rate of learning has been found to be 90% rather than 80%. That is, the labor hours drop only 10% between doubled quantities, compared with 20% for the industry generally."[13] The equivalent b values for several different learning curves are provided in Table 10–2. These values are provided for convenience in working problems at the end of this chapter. Let us work one example using a 70 percent learning curve and an initial labor requirement of 90,000 direct labor man-hours on the first unit. We use the same procedure that was

[13] Andress, *op. cit.*, p. 90.

used with the 80 percent curve. This time, we solve for the number
of man-hours required on unit number 20 and obtain the b value
from Table 10–2.

$$Y_{20} = 90,000 \ (20)^{-0.5146}$$
$$= \frac{90,000}{20^{0.5146}}$$
$$= 19,263$$

Logarithmic Function

When the "learning percent" is not known, the parameters b and
K may be derived from raw data. The method for deriving these
values is called regression analysis. Since both equations (10–1)
and (10–2) can be converted to straight-line functions, we use linear
regression analysis.[14] This time we use equation (10–2) for our
illustration (either one could be used). In order to convert the
function $Y_x = Kx^b$ to a straight-line function, we take the loga-
rithm of both sides of the equation so that:

$$\text{Log } Y = \text{Log } K + b \log x \qquad (10\text{–}4)$$

Clearly this is a linear equation of the general form:

$$y = a + bx \qquad (10\text{–}5)$$

where a and b are constant with a indicating the y intercept and b
indicating the slope of the line. The method of least squares in
regression analysis[15] yields the following results for a and b:

$$b = \frac{n(\Sigma \ xy) \ - \ (\Sigma \ x)(\Sigma \ y)}{n(\Sigma \ x^2) \ - \ (\Sigma \ x)^2} \qquad (10\text{–}6)$$

$$a = \frac{\Sigma \ y \ - \ b(\Sigma \ x)}{n} \qquad (10\text{–}7)$$

In equivalent form, b and $\log K$ of equation (10–4) may be stated:

---

[14] On the reliability of the linear learning curve, see Armen Alchian, *Reliability of Progress Curves in Airframe Production*, The RAND Corporation,
Research Memorandum RM 260–1, February 3, 1950. Also see: Asher, *op. cit.*,
p. 129.

[15] Any elementary text in statistics.

$$b = \frac{n \; \Sigma \; (\log x)(\log Y) \; - \; (\Sigma \; \log x)(\Sigma \; \log Y)}{n \; \Sigma(\log x)^2 \; - \; (\Sigma \; \log x)^2} \qquad (10\text{-}8)$$

$$\text{Log } K = \frac{\Sigma \; \log Y \; - \; b \; (\Sigma \; \log x)}{n} \qquad (10\text{-}9)$$

We now illustrate how the values for b and log K are obtained from actual raw data. The data are presented in Table 10–3. The

TABLE 10–3

Raw Data on the Manufacture of Electronic Meters

Column A Month Ending	Column B Labor Hours	Column C Cumulative Labor Hours	Column D Units Completed	Column E Cumulative Units	Column F Cumulative Average Labor Hours per Unit
March–January	3260.2	3260.2	Start-up period—no finished units		
February	2382.5	5642.7	366	366	15.4
March	2483.9	8126.6	168	534	15.2
April	2530.7	10657.3	1392	1926	5.54
May	2717.7	13375.0	920	2846	4.70
June	2696.8	16071.8	865	3711	4.30
July	1081.8	17153.6	520	4231	4.05
August	1177.0	18330.6	625	4856	3.76
September	26.8	18357.4	246	5102	3.59

SOURCE: Francis T. Koen, "Dynamic Evaluation," *Factory*, Vol. 117, No. 9 (September, 1959), p. 100.

data were compiled on a ". . . production run of 5101 electronic meters manufactured over a 9-month period, following several months of start-up time without production."[16]

Using columns E and F of Table 10–3 for x and Y, respectively, we may perform the necessary operations for deriving log K and b. Reproducing columns E and F as x and Y in Table 10–4, and finding logarithms from a table of common logarithms, we obtain $\Sigma \log x = 26.6196$; $\Sigma \log Y = 6.1562$; $\Sigma (\log x)^2 = 89.9581$; and the required summations. From Table 10–4, we have: $n = 8$; $\Sigma (\log x) (\log Y) = 19.6027$. Substituting these values into equation (10–8), we obtain:

$$b = \frac{8(19.6027) \; - \; (26.6196)(6.1562)}{8(89.9581) \; - \; (26.6196)^2}$$
$$= -0.6377$$

---

[16] Francis T. Koen, "Dynamic Evaluation," *Factory*, Vol. 117, No. 9 (September, 1959), p. 100.

TABLE 10–4

Data for Regression Analysis

Cumulative Units from Column E of Table 10-3 x	Cumulative Average Labor Hours per Unit from Column F of Table 10-3 Y	Log x	Log Y	(Log x)²	(Log x) (Log Y)
366	15.4	2.5635	1.1875	6.5715	2.9729
534	15.2	2.7275	1.1818	7.4393	3.2234
1926	5.54	3.2846	.7435	10.7886	2.4421
2846	4.70	3.4542	.6721	11.9315	2.3216
3711	4.30	3.5695	.6335	12.7413	2.2613
4231	4.05	3.6264	.6075	13.1508	2.2030
4856	3.76	3.6862	.5752	13.5881	2.1203
5102	3.59	3.7077	.5551	13.7470	2.0581
Σ		26.6196	6.1562	89.9581	19.6027

Substituting this and tabular values into equation (10–9), we obtain:

$$\text{Log } K = \frac{6.1562 - (-0.6377)(26.6196)}{8}$$
$$= 2.8914$$

We may now rewrite equation (10–4) as follows:

$$\text{Log } Y = 2.8914 - 0.6377 \log x \qquad (10\text{–}10)$$

Equation (10–10) is a straight-line function with the parameters defined as shown. When the line is drawn on log-log graph paper, it gives the "best fit" of the data of columns E and F of Table 10–3. The observed data of columns E and F are shown as points on Figure 10–3. The solid line drawn through the points is the "best fit" line obtained by solving for Y in equation (10–10) when $x = 100$ units and when $x = 1,000$ units. The computations are carried out below:

When x = 100:

$$\text{Log } Y = 2.8914 - 0.6377 \log 100$$
$$= 2.8914 - 1.2754$$
$$= 1.6160$$

FIGURE 10–3

Learning Curve Derived from Raw Data on Production of Electronic Meters

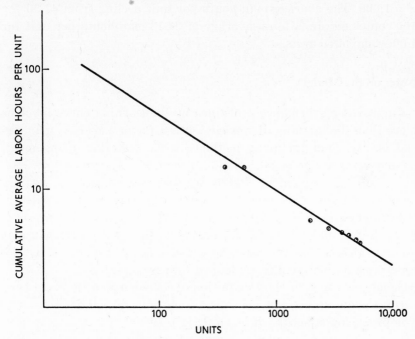

We solve for Y by finding the antilog of 1.6160, thus:

$$Y = 41.30$$

When x = 1,000:

$$\text{Log } Y = 2.8914 - 0.6377 \log 1000$$
$$= 2.8914 - 1.9131$$
$$= 0.9783$$

We solve for Y by finding the antilog of 0.9783, thus:

$$Y = 9.513$$

When these two points, that is $(x = 100, \ Y = 41.30)$ and $(x = 1000, \ Y = 9.513)$, are connected by a straight line, we obtain the "best fit" line or the cumulative curve shown in Figure 10–3. Thus, for any x, we are able to determine Y, the average man-hours per unit, roughly from the graph of Figure 10–3 or precisely by substituting into equation (10–10). Notice the improvement in performance from our computed values of Y when $x = 100$ and $x = 1,000$. The average man-hours per unit decline from 41.30 for 100 completed units to an average of 9.513 man-hours per unit for 1,000 completed units.

Notes on the Model

Improved performance as defined by the learning curve involves more than the learning of workers. Other factors, such as managerial ability, manufacturing methods, tools, materials mangement, quality control, and organizational design, also have an effect upon the rate of improvement. Partly for this reason, several writers have chosen other phrases to describe the improvement pattern. Other names that have been used are "progress curve," "improvement curve," and "experience curve." Another reason for the use of other names is that the learning curve concept does not meet the requirements of learning as defined by psychologists. As expected, psychologists have a rigid definition of learning and they are very careful about specifying the causal factors in a learning situation. The psychologist speaks of learning in terms of stimulus, response, and reinforcement, and he examines these variables in a closely controlled situation (for example, a laboratory experiment). We examine psychological learning in the next two sections of this chapter.

Regardless of the nomenclature used, the significant fact is that there are consistent patterns of behavior, and practitioners have had considerable success in predicting this behavior. Also, it is significant that a considerable part of this behavior, although it has not been precisely isolated, does resemble learning as observed by psychologists in their laboratories. In other words, there are fairly good indications that learning is one of the factors that contributes to the improvement rate.

It appears also that organizational design is an important contributing factor to the improvement rate. According to those who have studied this behavior, improvements in performance do not materialize without improvements in management efficiency and in organization. According to Asher: "Labor costs . . . cannot decline through experience gained by workmen unless management also becomes more efficient. In other words, it is also necessary for management to organize and coordinate the work of all manufacturing departments more efficiently so that parts and assemblies will flow through the plant smoothly and at more rapid rates."[17]

A MODEL FOR INDIVIDUAL LEARNING

Thus far in this chapter, the practical implications of learning have been examined. It was indicated that organization planners have recognized learning as a major organization variable. We illustrated a model which allows for the hypothesis that people in organizations improve their performance over time. Of course, the major assumption of this hypothesis is that conditions in an organization are favorable for learning. Since learning is defined below as a change in behavior, the discussion of the conditions that precipitate learning is reserved for Chapters 15 and 16, which are devoted to organizational change. In this section, we want to examine the major variables that comprise the learning situation and to discuss models that have successfully predicted learning behavior under experimental conditions.

Definitions

Learning may be characterized as a systematic change in behavior that takes place over a period of time and is considered complete when this behavior has stabilized. More specifically, learning may be considered as a stimulus-response relationship, whereby a transition takes place from an initial period when no predictable pattern exists between an environmental condition (stimulus) and the behavior (response) of a subject, to a time when the relationship between the environmental condition and behavior becomes stabilized and predictable.[18] Before discussing the models, let us clarify four terms that are used in learning theory. They are: stimulus element, response, connection, and reinforcement.

Stimulus Elements. A stimulus element is an effector of behavior. The presence of a stimulus means that some change has taken place in the environment of a subject and it has significance to his behav-

---

[17] Asher, *op. cit.*, p. 3. Also see J. R. Crawford and E. Strauss, *Crawford-Strauss Study* (Dayton, Ohio: Air Material Command, 1947) ; J. R. Crawford, *Estimating, Budgeting, and Scheduling,* (Burbank, Calif.: Lockheed Aircraft Corporation, 1944) ; *The Experience Curve, Boeing Airplane Company* (Wichita, Kans., no date) ; and Wright, *op. cit.*

[18] Reed Lawson, *Learning and Behavior* (New York: Macmillan Co., 1960), p. 11.

ior. The presence of a stimulus element was significant in the famous experiments of the Russian physiologist, Pavlov (1849–1936). As a physiologist, Pavlov was interested in the role of salivation in digestion. In some experiments, he placed meat into a dog's mouth and observed, through glass containers attached to the animal's head, the flow of saliva that was stimulated by the meat. As the experiments progressed, he noticed that the dogs began to salivate before the meat was placed in their mouths. Pavlov reasoned that dogs could be conditioned to salivate by artificial means, and he shifted his attention from the study of digestion to experiments on conditioned reflexes. He replaced the sight of meat with the ticking of a metronome in such a way as to associate the two. Meat powder was placed in the dog's mouth after each sounding of the metronome. After several repetitions, a conditioned reflex was produced, and the dog would come to salivate at the sound of the metronome without the meat powder being placed in his mouth. The ticking of the metronome became the stimulus in this experiment.

Response. Response is the change in behavior, an act, or a movement that takes place in the presence of such stimuli. Thus, in the Pavlov experiments, salivation was the response to stimulus of the ticking metronome.

Connection. Connection specifies the response associated with a given stimulus element. In the Pavlov experiments, the dogs were conditioned to salivate (response) to the ticking metronome (stimulus). Therefore, we may say that there was a connection between salivation and the ticking metronome.

Reinforcement. The condition that produces connection of one response instead of another to a particular stimulus is called reinforcement. An experiment by Seward[19] illustrates this concept. Seward used 32 rats in his experiment. He divided the rats into three groups: REWARD Group, REMOVAL Group, and a CONTROL Group. He placed the rats, one at a time, in a small box containing a metal bar. If any of the rats in the REWARD Group pressed the bar, food was dropped into a pan near the bar. The rat was removed from the box after it ate the food. If an animal from

[19] J. P. Seward, "An Experimental Test of Guthrie's Theory of Reinforcement," *Journal of Experimental Psychology*, Vol. 30 (1942), pp. 247–56. We are indebted to Lawson, *op. cit.*, pp. 22–24, for bringing this illustration to our attention.

the REMOVAL Group pressed the bar, it was promptly removed from the box. Nothing happened to the CONTROL rats when they pressed the bar. They were simply removed from the box after five minutes, unless they had pressed the bar 10 seconds prior to removal time.

Seward found that during a training period both the REWARD and REMOVAL Groups showed an increasing tendency to go directly to the bar. In other words, there was a steady decrease in time taken to press the bar after the rats were placed in the box. The CONTROL Group showed highly variable bar-press times over the training period. After the training period, the experimenter put all three groups on the CONTROL Group routine. Both the REWARD and REMOVAL Groups pressed the bar more frequently than the CONTROL Group. Lawson's conclusions about the experiment and how it illustrates stimulus, response, reinforcement, and learning are as follows:

We can conclude that most of the subjects of both the REWARD and REMOVAL Groups had, as we ordinarily say, "learned to press the bar." The CONTROLS had apparently not done so.

For the rats in the REWARD and REMOVAL Groups there had been a definite change in the environment soon after they made a particular response. They showed the kind of response change that we expect to occur when learning is taking place. The control rats had no distinctive event occur after a bar-press; there was no evidence that they ever made this R [response] other than randomly. The difference between the two experimental groups and the control group was, . . . that the experimental rats were reinforced when they pressed the bar, while the control rats were not.[20]

Thus, we may reiterate that the response change that developed in the behavior of the REWARD and REMOVAL rates was a result of reinforcement. In effect, the behavioral changes were a demonstration of learning.

The Estes-Burke Learning Model

Estes[21] developed a model, later refined by Estes and Burke[22] of the learning behavior of human subjects in laboratory experiments.

[20] Lawson, op. cit., pp. 23–24.

[21] William K. Estes, "Toward A Statistical Theory of Learning," Psychological Review, Vol. 57 (1950), pp. 94–107.

[22] W. K. Estes and C. J. Burke, "Application of A Statistical Model to Simple Discrimination Learning in Human Subjects," Journal of Experimental Psychology, Vol. 50 (1955), pp. 81–88.

While there are many possible stimulus elements in a learning situation, Estes used a finite number in his experiment. In the Estes and Burke experiments, there were two stimulus elements. There were two possible responses and two possible reinforcements. The experimental room contained four booths facing a panel of light bulbs. Within a booth, there were two telegraph keys, each beneath a light. Upon illumination of the panel lights in one of two possible patterns (stimulus element), the subjects were asked to depress one of the telegraph keys (response) indicating their prediction of which of the booth lights (reinforcement) would "light up." One of the booth lights would come on following a prearranged schedule of the experimenters, after the subject had made his choice. The task of the subjects was to *learn to predict* which of the "reinforcing" booth lights would illuminate following the stimulus signal on each trial.

The Estes and Burke model successfully predicted the learning behavior of the subjects. Their model is based on the premise that learning is determined by the existence or nonexistence of reinforcement. They concluded: "Correspondences of theory and data, although by no means perfect, tended to support the view that discrimination learning in this situation is a simple resultant of effects of reinforcement and nonreinforcement."[23]

The model predicted that the human subjects would be less than rational in their responses. You would expect a rational subject to maximize "correct responses." "Correct responses," according to the experimenters was a response R_0 matched with a reinforcement A_0 and a response R_1 matched with a reinforcement A_1. Since in one experiment, an R_0 response was followed by an A_0, 50 percent of the time, and a R_1 was never followed by an A_1, you would expect a rational subject to learn to make the R_0 response. This was not the case. As the theory predicted, the subjects displayed less than rational behavior. The subject of rational behavior is taken up again in the next chapter.

GROUP LEARNING

The Estes-Burke model provides a useful device for predicting the learning behavior of individuals. The model presented in this section was used to predict learning by a small group. A group has

[23] *Ibid.*, p. 87.

"learned," according to the assumptions of this model, when the members have organized themselves to perform a given task in an efficient manner. Before describing the model, let us first examine some small-group experiments which appear to display group learning. Our attention is confined to three studies, namely, experiments conducted by Harold J. Leavitt,[24] Harold Guetzkow and Herbert A. Simon,[25] and Rocco Carzo, Jr., and John N. Yanouzas.[26]

Leavitt Experiment

Harold Leavitt conducted experiments with four different communication nets imposed on five-man groups: the wheel net, the circle net, the chain net, and the Y net. In the wheel net, shown in Figure 10-4, one member placed in the most central position had communication access to and from each of the other group members. The circle net, also shown in Figure 10-4, permitted each group member to communicate with the member located on each of his sides. Leavitt used relatively simple problems in which group members had to exchange information in order to identify a symbol held in common by all of the members. This experiment revealed that the groups arranged in a wheel net took less time to complete the task than those groups placed in a circle net.

Guetzkow and Simon Experiment

There have been several refinements of the Leavitt experiment. In one study, Guetzkow and Simon replicated Leavitt's work with the "wheel" and "circle" nets and also tested the effects of an "all-channel" pattern. The three communication nets are illustrated

---

[24] Harold J. Leavitt, "Some Effects of Certain Communication Patterns on Group Performance," *Journal of Abnormal and Social Psychology*, Vol. 46 (January, 1951), pp. 38–50. Leavitt's experiment is based on the theoretical work of Bavelas. See "A Mathematical Model for Group Structures," *Applied Anthropology*, Vol. 7 (1948), pp. 16–30, and "Communication Patterns in Task Oriented Groups," *Journal of the Accoustical Society of America*, Vol. 22 (1950), pp. 725–30.

[25] Harold Guetzkow and Herbert A. Simon, "The Impact of Certain Communication Nets upon Organization and Performance in Task-Oriented Groups," *Management Science*, Vol. 1 (1955), pp. 233–50.

[26] Rocco Carzo, Jr., "Some Effects of Organization Structure on Group Effectiveness," *Administrative Science Quarterly*, Vol. 7 (March, 1963), pp. 393–424; and John N. Yanouzas, "The Relationship of Some Organization Variables to the Performance of Decision Groups" (unpublished dissertation, The Pennsylvania State University, 1963).

in Figure 10–4. In their experiments, Guetzkow and Simon made a basic distinction between the effects of communication restrictions upon task performance and the efforts of groups to organize themselves for such performance. They hypothesized that communication restrictions would not directly effect upon the efficiency with which the task was performed, but only indirectly by ". . . influencing the ability of the members to organize themselves

FIGURE 10–4

Nets Used by Guetzkow and Simon

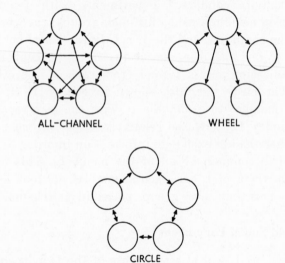

ALL-CHANNEL   WHEEL

CIRCLE

for optimum performance in their line operation."[27] Their empirical findings supported the hypothesis. Although the groups experienced different degrees of difficulty in achieving efficient organizational arrangements, there was no significant difference in times taken to complete the task after they reached an optimum organization.

Although all three groups began the experiment showing different level of performance, eventually each group improved until a plateau was reached where relatively little, if any, improvement occurred. The curves of performance are shown in Figure 10–5.

It is apparent that the aforementioned studies raised some important questions with respect to the question of equifinality.

---

[27] Guetzkow and Simon, *op. cit.*, p. 238.

Would performance levels be the same for groups operating under different communication nets but using the same fixed organizational structure? Recall that Guetzkow and Simon disclosed that

FIGURE 10-5

Performance of Groups in Guetzkow and Simon Experiment

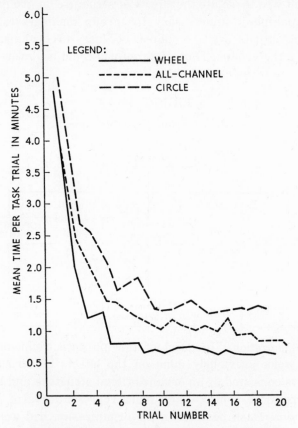

SOURCE: Reproduced from Harold Guetzkow and Herbert A. Simon, "The Impact of Certain Communication Nets upon Organization and Performance in Task-Oriented Groups," *Management Science*, Vol. 1 (1955), p. 242.

differences in performance were really a reflection of differences in the groups' ability to organize and that after they became organized, there was no difference in their performance. Suppose a fixed organization was imposed on the groups and they did not have to spend time in organizing, would their performance still be the same?

Carzo and Yanouzas Experiments

This unanswered question led the authors of this text to engage in further experimental research. Rather than replicate the previous studies, we put the question in general form and sought to test it under different experimental conditions. The purpose of our experiment was to isolate the effects of structure on group performance by making it unnecessary for group members to organize. Organizing efforts were obviated because an organization was imposed on the groups. Thus, their efforts could be devoted entirely to the accomplishment of the task.

FIGURE 10–6

Basic Organizational Structure

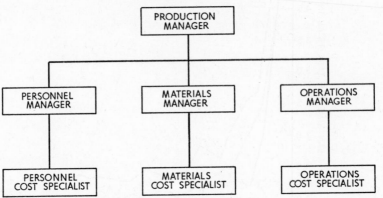

Basic Organization. In quest of this purpose, refinements were made on work previously done on the effects of structure. The refinements consisted of an organizational structure and a problem which were more complex and more representative of industrial organizations. Each position in the organization had a specialized task and a title that was descriptive of, and commensurate with, the task. There was a definite hierarchy consisting of three levels. One central position was located at the top of the hierarchy. The group member who occupied this central position was responsible for coordinating all other tasks in the organization and making final decisions on the assigned problem from an overall analysis. Subordinate managers were responsible for decision making based on their particular area of specialization. The basic organizational structure is shown in Figure 10–6.

Tight and Loose Structures. In addition to the basic structure of Figure 10–6, there were other conditions which specified the communication channels available to subjects. Some groups were organized under a highly restricted communication net called "tight" structures, while others were under a less restricted communication net called "loose" structures. The tight structures were comparable to the "wheel" communication net of the Leavitt, and Guetzkow and Simon, studies. The loose structures were comparable to the "all-channel" communication net of Guetzkow and Simon. The main difference is that we specifically defined the tasks of each subject. Each task was part of a process which was culminated by the decisions of the production manager.

Communication channels open to members under tight and loose structures are shown in Figure 10–7. The tightly structured groups were limited to written communications. Subjects in the tight structure were separated from each other by wooden partitions and allowed to communicate only through the "chain of command" defined by the basic organizational structure and reinforced by the physical seating arrangements of the laboratory.

Two different types of loose structure were employed in the experiment. One was called "Loose Written," and the other, "Loose Oral." As indicated by these labels, the main difference between the two structures was that the groups organized under Loose Written were restricted to written communications while groups organized under Loose Oral were allowed to use oral as well as written communication. The subjects under the loose structures were not separated by partitions. Besides these basic requirements, communication under the loose structures was total, i.e., each subject was allowed to communicate or confer with every other member of the group.

The Problem. A fluctuating sales forecast which extended over 40 periods was given to each group. The production manager was required to make decisions on output and shipments. He made these decisions with the assistance of departmental managers, who submitted recommendations on output and shipments for each period. The groups were measured on three performance variables: total costs, errors, and time per decision.

The Results. The groups initially experienced different levels of performance, but eventually they all improved. When the performance data were averaged for 40 periods, a comparison of

FIGURE 10-7

Communication Patterns under Tight and Loose Structures

LOOSE STRUCTURES—ORAL AND WRITTEN

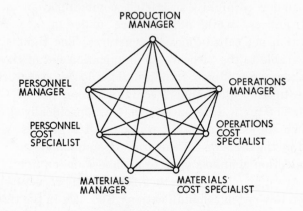

TIGHT STRUCTURE

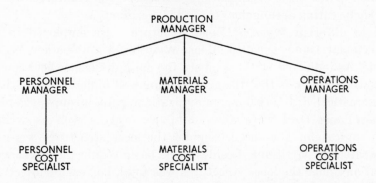

the means of time per decision indicated that both Loose Oral and Loose Written had significantly lower average time per decision than the Tight. A trend analysis revealed, however, that a comparison of means taken alone is insufficient for drawing conclusions about the effects of structure upon group performance.

An examination of the trends of time per decision for all three structures shows that for the first 10 decisions, Tight had the highest, Loose Written had the next highest, and Loose Oral the lowest average time per decision. For the next 15 decisions, Tight still had the highest, and there was no significant difference in the average time taken to make decisions between Loose Written and

Loose Oral. There was no significant difference in the average time per decision between Tight, Loose Written, and Loose Oral for decisions 26 through 40. Prior to the 26th decision, the average time per decision for all three structures steadily declined from a

FIGURE 10–8

Performance of Groups in Carzo-Yanouzas Experiment

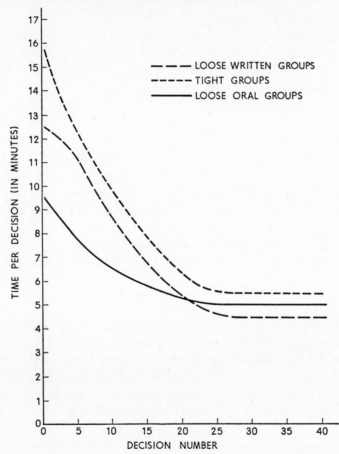

high average time of approximately 16 minutes for Tight, 12 minutes for Loose Written, and 10 minutes for Loose Oral. For decisions 26 through 40, all three structures maintained a level rate of performance at approximately five minutes per decision. See Figure 10–8 for a graphical presentation of these trends.

Initially, then, Loose Oral groups were the fastest in time

required to make decisions. Subsequently, however, Loose Written and Tight learned to make decisions just as fast and in some instances faster than Loose Oral. It took Loose Written groups 10 decisions before they were able to make decisions as fast as Loose Oral. Thereafter, there was no significant difference in their performance. Both of the loose structures were faster than the tight in making decisions until the 26th decision. Thereafter, there was no significant difference between the three groups in average time consumed to make decisions.

Results similar to those on time per decision were obtained on measures of the quality of decisions. Quality of decisions were measured by total costs, average costs, and errors per decision. Both of the loose structures initially produced better decisions than the tight structure. Loose Written and Loose Oral groups made decisions during the early part of the experiment that had lower costs and fewer errors than Tight groups. Loose Oral had the lowest costs and least errors, Loose Written had the next to best performance, and Tight had the poorest performance during the early part of the experiment. Eventually, however, there was no significant difference in performance between the three structures on costs incurred and errors made per decision. In conclusion, then, even when organizing efforts were made unnecessary, groups still displayed the kind of behavior found by Guetzkow and Simon.

A GROUP LEARNING MODEL

A pattern that seems to exist in the studies described above and others not included in the discussion, is that when a task is assigned to a group, its performance improves over time and eventually reaches a plateau where little further improvement is experienced. William H. McWhinney has developed a group learning model which has been used successfully to predict this kind of behavior.[28]

This group learning model includes probability estimates of individual learning. These individual estimates are combined and transformed into a measure of group performance. McWhinney tested the appropriateness of the group learning model with real data

[28] William H. McWhinney, "Isolating Organization Dynamics in a Small Group Experiment," *Sociometry*, Vol. 26 (1963), pp. 354–72. Since the remaining part of this chapter is concerned with McWhinney's group learning model, repeated reference to his work are not made.

taken from the communication network experiments of Guetzkow and Simon,[29] Shure *et al.*,[30] and Cohen, Bennis, and Wolkon.[31]

Individual Learning

Individual learning, according to McWhinney, is concerned with a subject's ability to perform an assigned task. This ability will improve after repeated exposure to the task.

The skills required of subjects by most communication network experiments involve receiving and perceiving incoming messages, computing data, combining data to form a new message, and creating and sending messages. This model assumes that each subject has an equal opportunity to improve his skills during each experimental trial. The learning propositions of this model are as follows.

First, the subjects act only in response to a message stimulus received from other group members or the experimenter.

Second, response time to a stimulus is a function of how well each subject has learned the sequence of acts necessary to produce and send a message.

Third, all subjects have an equal amount of skill at the beginning of the experiment.

Fourth, the difference between the starting skill level and the expected maximum standard occurs at a constant rate. The standard is a parameter that can be established, as in the Guetzkow and Simon experiment, by time study.

Fifth, the receipt of one message on top of another does not slow up the combined response.

These propositions conform to the observation made on real network experiments. By translating the first and second propositions into mathematical expressions, they can be made more rigorous and operational.

---

[29] The Guetzkow and Simon data, *op. cit.*, were combined by McWhinney with the results of a network experiment conducted by Harold Guetzkow and William R. Dill reported in "Factors in the Organizational Development of Task-Oriented Groups," *Sociometry,* Vol. 20 (September, 1957), pp. 175–204.

[30] These data were provided from personal files, but for the research results, see Gerald H. Shure, Miles S. Rogers, Ida M. Larsen, and Jack Tassone, "Group Planning and Task Effectiveness," *Sociometry,* Vol. 25 (September, 1962), pp. 263–82.

[31] These data were provided from personal files, but for the research results, see Arthur M. Cohen, Warren G. Bennis, and George H. Wolkon, "The Effects of Changes in Communication Networks on the Behavioral Problem-solving Groups," *Sociometry,* Vol. 25 (June, 1962), pp. 177–96.

Group Learning

The estimate of the mean time for a subject to respond to a stimulus serves as the basis for a transformation of individual learning rates to a group performance measure. This model takes into consideration the minimal number of interactions or connections necessary to solve a problem under each type of network— wheel, circle, and all-channel. The variety increases as the channels of interaction are opened from the wheel to the all-channel networks. With each type of network there is a minimum number of message sequences which will result in a solution. By combining the mean time for a subject to respond and the number of message sequences, the expected time for each set of sequences leading to a solution can be predicted.

For example, to reach a solution under the wheel network, the minimal number of connections (set of sequences) involves each of the four peripheral subjects in sending a message simultaneously to the center man, who receives, combines, creates, and sends a message sequentially to the four peripheral subjects. This is a five-stage process—four simultaneous messages and four sequential messages.[32]

The group learning model assumes that some pattern of sequences is adopted by the group. This means that the groups organize their interactions in some manner. Thus, the model postulates that the expected time needed to solve a problem should be the same among all groups using a similar pattern of sequences, regardless of the network imposed on a group.

Test of Group Learning Model

The results of the McWhinney tests of the model are shown in Figures 10–9, 10–10, and 10–11 where the theoretical curves derived from the model are compared to plots of actual data.

The group model's appropriateness was tested with real data and parametric values derived from the Guetzkow-Simon-Dill, Shure et al., and Cohen-Bennis-Wolkon network experiments.

The unbroken curves in Figures 10–9, 10–10, and 10–11 represent the theoretical approximations of the time needed to reach a solu-

---

[32] Most of the groups in the network experiments settled on this pattern after the first to fifth trial.

FIGURE 10–9
Theoretical Curves and Mean Observed Times: Wheel Network

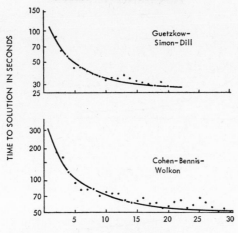

TRIAL NUMBER

SOURCE: Reproduced from William H. McWhinney, "Isolating Organizational Dynamics in Small Group Experiments," *Sociometry*, Vol. 26 (1963), p. 365.

FIGURE 10–10
Theoretical Curves and Mean Observed Times: Circle Network

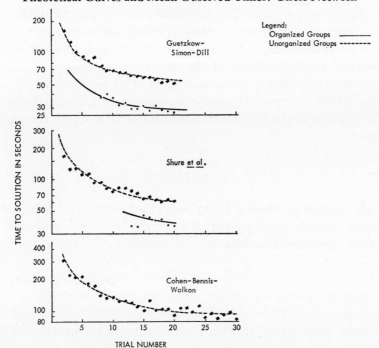

TRIAL NUMBER

SOURCE: Reproduced from William H. McWhinney, "Isolating Organizational Dynamics in Small Group Experiments," *Sociometry*, Vol. 26 (1963), p. 366.

FIGURE 10-11

Theoretical Curves and Observed Mean Times:
All-Channel Networks

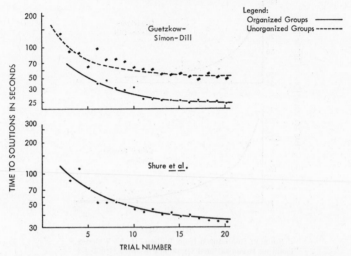

SOURCE: Reproduced from William H. McWhinney, "Isolating Organizational Dynamics in Small Group Experiments," *Sociometry*, Vol. 26 (1963), p. 367.

tion in successive trial periods by each of the organized wheel, circle, and all-channel networks. The scattered points in each of the figures are the actual mean observed times for each network type.

The broken curves in Figures 10-9, 10-10, and 10-11 show the theoretical approximations of the unorganized networks, that is, the groups that did not settle on a pattern of sequences.

The model successfully approximates group learning behavior for both organized and unorganized groups in a fairly reasonable manner.

SUMMARY

This chapter is devoted to an important element of behavior—learning. In this examination of learning, we focus attention on learning curves and models, and on research evidence of learning behavior.

Observations of learning in industry, especially the aircraft industry, reveal the occurrence of learning in repetitive-type jobs. Learning curves derived from experience show that there are consistent patterns of learning in different environmental settings.

This behavior resembles learning as it is observed by psychologists in laboratory experiments.

Individual learning models developed and tested in laboratory experiments reveal that the learning behavior of subjects can be predicted. One such model, the Estes-Burke model, suggests that learning is determined by the existence or nonexistence of reinforcement. Using this model, Estes and Burke successfully predicted behavior of subjects under experimental conditions.

Another learning model, developed by McWhinney, separated individual from group learning, and successfully predicted the latter. Support for the model's validity was found in tests with actual data from laboratory experiments.

DISCUSSION QUESTIONS AND PROBLEMS

10-1. After some study, a business firm found that its factory workers learned according to an improvement factor of $b = -0.75$ when $K = 1,117$.

    a) Formulate the learning curve according to equation (10-2).
    b) Express the equation in logarithmic form.
    c) Plot the curve on log-log paper.
    d) What is the learning percentage?

10-2. The same business firm of problem 10-1 agreed to manufacture for a large customer a product for which it had no previous experience. The company compiled the following data for the first 10 months of production on this product.

Month	Number of Units Produced in Each Month	Cumulative Direct Labor Hours
1	1	1,100
2	2	2,100
3	4	3,430
4	8	5,400
5	16	8,215
6	32	12,411
7	64	18,669
8	128	28,050
9	256	40,880
10	512	59,334

    a) Derive the logarithmic form of equation (10-2) from these data.
    b) Plot the curve on the same log-log paper of problem 10-1. Compare the company's experience on the new product with its experience on other products; that is, compare the two curves, draw conclusions, and make recommedations.

c) What is the learning percentage? Is it better or worse than the learning percentage of problem 10–1?

10–3. On log-log paper, sketch the learning curve, equation (10–2), when $b = -0.60$, and $K = 1,462$. What is the learning percentage for this curve?

10–4. A company experiences the following performance in a 10-month period:

Month	Number of Units Produced in Each Month	Cumulative Direct Labor Hours
1	1	1,000
2	2	1,800
3	4	2,300
4	8	2,700
5	16	3,000
6	32	3,210
7	64	3,360
8	128	3,460
9	256	3,540
10	512	3,610

a) Derive the logarithmic form of equation (10–2) from these data.

b) Plot the curve on the same log-log paper of problem 10–3. Compare the performance as indicated by this curve with that of problem 10–3.

c) What is the learning percentage? Is it better or worse than the learning percentage of problem 10–3?

10–5. The Iron Company produced its 200th casting at a direct labor cost of $22.71 in (*a*), $30.10 in (*b*), and $51.30 in (*c*), below. Assume that direct labor costs $2.50 per hour. Use equation (10–1).

a) With $b = -0.3219$, and $K = 50$, what is the direct labor cost of the 400th casting?

b) When $b = -0.2688$ and $K = 50$, what is the direct labor cost of the 800th casting?

c) When $b = -0.1681$ and $K = 50$, what is the direct labor cost of the 1,600th casting?

10–6. The Toy Company produced 200 bicycles at an average direct labor cost of $6.94 each in (*a*), $4.09 each in (*b*), and $27.92 each in (*c*), below. Direct labor costs $2.50 per hour. Use equation (10–2).

a) When $b = -0.4150$ and $K = 25$, what is the per unit direct labor cost of 400 bicycles?

b) When $b = -0.5146$ and $K = 25$, what is the per unit direct labor cost of 800 bicycles?

c) When $b = -0.1520$ and $K = 25$, what is the per unit direct labor cost of 1,600 bicycles?

10-7. If it takes 30 hours for a small company to complete the first desk of a production run, and the cumulative average direct labor hours decrease by 30 percent between doubled quantities, what will be the average direct labor hours required to complete:
a) 30 desks?
b) 50 desks?

10-8. The Borne Aircraft Company has been awarded a contract that requires it to complete 1,000 tail assemblies per month for each of the next 5 months. Assume that each man works 170 hours per month.
a) When $b = -0.2345$ and $K = 50$, how many men will be required in each month to maintain the production at the desired rate?
b) When $b = -0.3771$ and $K = 50$, how many men will be required in each month to maintain the production at the desired rate?

10-9. Discuss the implications of the learning curve to break-even analysis.

10-10. Why is it important to consider learning in designing an organization? Define what you mean by learning.

10-11. In organization, what are the variables that affect learning? Which of these variables are not included in organizational design? Explain.

10-12. Discuss the variables that most likely affect learning in an aircraft factory, in a hospital, in the army. Explain.

10-13. How can supervisory performance be measured and analyzed through learning curves? What criteria would you use to measure supervisory learning?

10-14. How could learning curves be used to (a) assign workers to jobs, (b) transfer employees, (c) formulate personnel selection policies, (d) negotiate a labor contract, and (e) train employees.

11

BASIC FRAMEWORK FOR ORGANIZATIONAL DESIGN

In the last two chapters, models were presented which allowed us to determine or estimate the value of certain performance variables in a system. The "learning curve" model of Chapter 10, for example, allowed us to estimate the number of direct man-hours required to produce an airplane when the number of man-hours required to produce the first airplane and the learning parameter are known. The Markov analysis of Chapter 9 permitted us to estimate the behavior of a system variable when the probabilities of going from one state to another are known. Both of these models involve a gross approach to the study of formal organization. The discussion of possible applications of Markov analysis, for instance, included detailed descriptions of three organizational designs, but the assumed responses were attributable to the total system. Although certain relationships were implied, there was no analysis of the system's composition and its effect upon performance. In this and the following chapters, we examine the composition of a designed system and illustrate how the relationships among the parts affect performance over time.

PURPOSE OF DESIGN

Formal organization is distinquished from other social systems by the fact that it is designed to accomplish objectives. It is justified on the basis that it can accomplish goals more efficiently; that is, optimum behavior is more likely in formal organization than it is in social groups that have no design. The purpose of design, then, is to provide conditions which facilitate optimal attainment of objectives. In previous discussions, we have attempted to show that people display goal-seeking tendencies even without a formal design, that is, they are intendedly rational in their behavior. However, there are several limitations to rational behavior. Before discussing these limitations, let us review how a living system formulates goals.

The goals of a living system emerge from the interplay of forces operating on and within its boundaries. A "preferential hierarchy of value" evolves and serves as a basis for choosing one course of action over another. Miller describes the characteristic for all living systems in the following manner:

> By the information input of its charter or genetic input, or by changes in behavior brought about by rewards and punishments from its supra-system, *a system develops a preferential hierarchy of values that gives rise to decision rules which determine its preference for one internal steady state value rather than another. This is its purpose.* It is the comparison value which it matches to information received by negative feedback in order to determine whether the variable is being maintained at the appropriate steady state value. In this sense it is normative. The system then takes one alternative action rather than another because it appears most likely to maintain the steady state. When disturbed, this state is restored by the system by successive approximation, in order to relieve the strain of the disparity recognized internally between the feedback signal and the comparison signal.[1]

Although human beings display goal-seeking tendencies and are capable of goal attainment, they never optimize the degree of attainment (except by chance). There are several factors that explain why man is unable to optimize his behavior. For our immediate purposes, we discuss the decisions that he makes on how to behave. A *decision* involves a choice from alternative means for attaining a goal. If the choice optimizes goal attainment, then the decision and behavior are said to be "objectively" rational.[2] However, as Simon points out, actual behavior falls far short of objective rationality.[3]

---

[1] James G. Miller, "Living Systems: Basic Concepts," *Behavioral Science*, Vol. 10, No. 3 (July, 1965), p. 231. [Emphasis is ours.]

[2] Herbert A. Simon, *Administrative Behavior* (New York: Macmillan Co., 1957), p. 76.

[3] *Ibid.*, p. 81.

Limits of Rationality

The outcome of a decision always takes place in some future period. Put in another way, the behavior pattern chosen by a person takes place *in fact* after the decision has been made. It is rational behavior if *in fact* it optimizes the values of the situation. In order to choose an optimum outcome that takes place in a future period, the decision maker must have complete knowledge of all possible behavior patterns and be able to anticipate the consequences of each alternative. More specifically, the requirement states that if a man is to make a rational choice about how to behave in a particular situation, he needs to know about all the possible ways of behaving in that situation. Consider a man who is seeking a new job. In order to make a rational choice, that is, select the best job, he needs to know of every available job in the universe. Even if this information were attainable, it would be practically impossible to assemble, classify, and analyze according to the values sought in the job.

Now, let us take up the problem of anticipating the consequences of various alternatives. There are innumerable factors that affect the outcome of decisions—some, such as the weather, are beyond the control of the decision maker, while others, such as machinery, are controllable. It is virtually impossible to acquire knowledge about all these factors and to determine their effects upon the outcome of decisions. Even if the factors and their effects were known, it is doubtful that humans could make an adequate evaluation of all this information. The human mind simply cannot grasp a very large number of relationships at one time. In addition, the inability to make exact predictions of future events further limits one's knowledge about the consequences of various choices.

Given the limits to human rationality, then, organizational design must remove, as much as possible, the obstacles to optimum behavior, or, improve the chances of achieving the goals of the organization.

The Method of Design

How is the purpose of design accomplished within formal organization? In order to facilitate optimum behavior, the formal organization limits the range of behavioral possibilities of its members. With a narrow range of possibilities available, participants are in a better position to make rational choices than in the case in which the number of possibilities is very large. In addition to information about his own responsibilities and authority, the formal organization provides each member with information about the behavioral possibilities of others and his relationships to others. In this way, each member is in a better position to anticipate the consequences of his action.

Specifically, the formal organization divides work into specialized tasks. Then, by assigning each individual to one particular task, it restricts the behavioral possibilities to the patterns required by a job. Since specialized tasks are usually narrow in scope, it is not difficult for jobholders to acquire knowledge about possible behavioral patterns. In addition, the organization provides rules and procedures which specify how a particular task shall be done and how members shall and shall not behave in various situations.

The information carried in communication channels also facilitates rational behavior. Through communication channels, an organization member receives information that pertains to his assigned task. He receives information through channels of communication that follow the chain of command (the hierarchy of authority). For example, he receives orders and performance evaluations from his superior. There are also information flows that do not follow the chain of command, as when a decision maker, say a foreman in a manufacturing plant, receives information from staff departments about the quality and cost of his department's output. Channels of communication between colleagues or between departments will also carry information pertaining to assigned tasks. For example, information about customer orders, inventories, and output, will be transmitted between the production and the sales departments of a business firm. Another example is provided by a worker on an assembly line who receives information about such matters as quantity and quality of output from workers who perform operations before and after his own operation.

Within a formal organization, then, a person's behavioral alternatives are severely limited. Given the information that he receives about these alternatives, he can anticipate the consequences of his choice better and display greater rationality than would be the case in a situation in which there is no organization.

While an organizational design may advance rationality, it could never achieve objective rationality. The organization is subject to many of the same limits to rationality as is the individual. The organization may have greater capacity for gathering information about alternatives and perhaps it is in a better position to determine the consequences of its choices than an individual, but its resources and its ability to foresee the future are still limited. It is more likely, that the organization strives for what Simon calls "subjective rationality"; that is, it tries to optimize the attainment of goals relative to the actual or available knowledge about alternatives.[4]

The formal organization is limited not only in its ability to foresee future events, but there are limitations in the amount and kind of responses it can evoke from participants. It is doubtful, for example, that an organization could ever achieve or even come close to complete regimentation of its members. It is doubtful, too, that professional members, such as scientists, engineers, and lawyers, would acquiesce to an organization's demands that they perform manual labor as a regular task.

Design, too, can have a destructive effect on the system. It can be detrimental to the extent that it does not produce the values desired by organization members. People have a multitude of motives for participating in the organization, and many of the values that they seek come from the nature of their membership. The way that they are arranged in relation to others (for example, job status), their involvement in the decision process, the amount of authority delegated to positions in an organization, the amount of "red tape" encountered in solving problems, are examples of design features which pertain to membership values.

Design and Efficiency

The fact that organizational design has value to participants implies that it has a broader purpose than just to meet the requirements of the efficiency criterion. Although a particular design seems to be the least costly or the most profitable arrangement of resources, efficiency or the objectives themselves may never be attained because the design does not produce values that elicit cooper-

---

[4] *Ibid.*, p. 76.

ative responses from participants. Thus, the design may be less than optimal.

Any design poses this problem of achieving one set of values while preventing the attainment of some others and producing still others that may have an undesirable effect. The same reasoning applied to the formulation of objectives (Chapter 8), then, also applies to organizational design. The organizational design, as well as the objectives which it is supposed to attain, must produce balanced values. Balance in the sense that they provide sufficient incentives to sustain cooperation from all participants. This stipulation does not destroy or alter the efficiency criterion, but it provides further explanation about the capacity or availability of resources. Usually, when the terms "capacity" or "available resources" are used, there is an implication of physical and/or mental capability. With this stipulation, the meaning is broadened to include not only what people can do but also what they are willing to do. Thus, the purpose of design is still to provide conditions which permit the organization to optimize the attainment of objectives through the efficient use of available resources. For an interesting case of how efficiency with balanced values was accomplished through the systems approach to design, we now examine the parable of the spindle.

THE PARABLE OF THE SPINDLE

Elias H. Porter, a psychologist, writing in the *Harvard Business Review*, stated that organizations should be viewed as systems which process information, and the design of the organization should be evaluated in terms of the capacity it provides to the system to handle information overload.[5] Porter illustrates this frame of reference with a parable about the restaurant industry. In this parable, the president of a large chain of short-order restaurants attended a lecture on human relations problems in business. The lecturer discussed the many pressures that create problems in the human organization. According to the speaker, there are psychological pressures, sociological pressures, conflicts in values, and

[5] Elias H. Porter, "The Parable of the Spindle," *Harvard Business Review*, Vol. 40, No. 3 (May-June, 1962), pp. 58–66. Porter's analysis is drawn from William F. Whyte's study of restaurants, *Human Relations in the Restaurant Industry* (New York: McGraw-Hill Book Co., 1948).

power struggles. The president was impressed and felt that perhaps the pressures discussed in the lecture were the cause of problems in his restaurants but that they were too complex for his managers to comprehend. Therefore, the president decided to ask for help from some social scientists. In an effort to get a broad-ranging analysis, the president asked a psychologist, a sociologist, and an anthropologist to serve as a team of consultants to the company. They were asked to visit the company's several restaurants and to find out why sometimes the waitresses break down in tears, the cooks walk off the job, and the managers get so upset that they summarily fire employees on the spot. Once the consultants had defined the problem, they were asked to recommend solutions.

Since the consultants had different backgrounds and used different methods to analyze problems, they decided to carry out their tasks separately. Each studied the problems according to the methods of his own discipline, and each man made an independent report to management. Although each study and report was made independently of the others, the scientists agreed on when the problems arose and on what would solve the problems. Their reports were identical on the following:

1. The human problems arose primarily during *rush hours*.

2. The solution to these problems was a mechanical device called a *spindle*.

However, the scientists seemed to differ on the causes of the problems. The sociologist defined the causes as status conflict; the psychologist reported a rivalry among the sexes; and the anthropologist said that there was a conflict of values. Here are their reports.

The Sociologist

You have a stress pattern during the rushhours. There is stress between the customer and the waitress and the cook. . . .

There is stress between the waitress and the cook. . . .

There is stress between the waitress and the manager.

And between the manager and the cook. . . .

And the manager is buffeted by complaints from the customer.

We can see one thing which, sociologically speaking, doesn't seem right. The manager has the highest status in the restaurant. The cook has the next highest status. The waitresses, however, are always "local hire" and have the lowest status. Of course, they have higher status than bus boys and dish washers but certainly lower status than the cook, and yet they give orders to the cook.

It doesn't seem right for a lower status person to give orders to a higher status person. We've got to find a way to break up the face-to-face relationship between the waitresses and the cook. We've got to fix it so that they don't have to talk with one another. Now my idea is to put a "spindle" on the order counter. The "spindle" as I choose to call it, is a wheel on a shaft. The wheel has clips on it so the girls can simply put their orders on the wheel rather than calling out orders to the cook.[6]

The Psychologist

Psychologically speaking we can see that the manager is the father figure, the cook is the son, and the waitress is the daughter. Now we know that in our culture you can't have daughters giving orders to the sons. It louses up their ego structure.

What we've got to do is to find a way to break up the face-to-face relationship between them. Now one idea I've thought up is to put what I call a "spindle" on the order counter. It's kind of a wheel on a shaft with little clips on it so that the waitresses can put their orders on it rather than calling out orders to the cook.[7]

The Anthropologist

We anthropologists know that man behaves according to his value systems. Now, the manager holds as a central value the continued growth and development of the restaurant organization. The cooks tend to share this central value system, for as the organization prospers, so do they. But the waitresses are a different story. The only reason most of them are working is to help supplement the family income. They couldn't care less whether the organization thrives or not as long as it's a decent place to work. Now, you can't have a noncentral value system giving orders to a central value system.

What we've got to do is to find some way of breaking up the face-to-face contact between the waitresses and the cook. One way that has occurred to me is to place on the order counter an adaptation of the old-fashioned spindle. By having a wheel at the top of the shaft and putting clips every few inches apart, the waitresses can put their orders on the wheel and not have to call out orders to the cook.[8]

The management of the chain decided to implement their recommendation. A spindle was installed in each of the restaurants. The spindle was highly successful. "It did more to reduce the human relations problems in the restaurant industry than any other innovation of which the restaurant people knew."[9]

Technical and Behavioral Implications

The "Parable of the Spindle" is important because it illustrates the systems approach and it offers solutions to some design prob-

[6] *Ibid.*, pp. 59–60.
[7] *Ibid.*, p. 60.
[8] *Ibid.*, p. 61.
[9] *Ibid.*

lems. In terms of the systems approach, it illustrates the complexity and interdependency of causal factors in the human problems of organization. Scientists from several disciplines not only isolated these causes but also solved the design problem. Although the scientists seemed to differ with regard to the causes of the problem, they really identified several interrelated causes of the problem.

In terms of the design problem, the spindle offered solutions which not only met the efficiency criterion but also lessened the human conflicts. Let us return to Porter's discussion and see how the spindle contributed to the solution of the design problem.

Memory. The spindle serves as a memory device for the cook. After the waitress takes the order, she attaches it to the spindle. The cook no longer has to memorize all the orders, because the information is stored on the spindle. Thus, the cook's job becomes easier, especially during rush hours when the problems of stress arise.

Buffer. The spindle serves as a buffering device. It allows the cook to go about his work while waitresses post their orders. The waitresses do not have to wait until other waitresses give their orders to the cook—several can post their orders on the spindle at the same time. The cook can work at his own capacity; that is, he does not have to adjust his work rate to the input rate of orders. Furthermore, the spindle buffers the cook from face-to-face contacts with the waitresses. Especially during rush hours, therefore, it tends to diminish the stresses of status conflict, of sex rivalry, and of value conflict observed by the social scientists.

Queuing. As a queuing device, the spindle allows the system to place the orders, instead of the waitresses, in the waiting line. By attaching orders to the spindle, the waitresses no longer have to wait in line to pass the information to the cook. Thus, their job is made easier—especially during rush hours.

Visual Display. The spindle with the orders attached is a visual display device for the cook. He can now see several orders at once. When several orders call for the same item, such as a hamburger, he can prepare them all at the same time. Now that he is more efficient, his job is made easier—especially during rush hours.

Feedback. Under the old system, the waitress passed customers' orders to the cook by spoken words. When an error was made, the waitresses often blamed the cook and the cook frequently blamed the waitresses. What did the cook and waitresses learn from these

experiences? Did they learn how to prevent errors? "Indeed not!
The waitresses learned that the cook was a stupid so-and-so, and the
cook learned that the waitress was a scatterbrained so-and-so. This
kind of emotionalized learning situation and strainer-of-interper-
sonal-relations any organization can do without—especially during
the rush hours."[10]

Under the new system, the waitress passed the customer's orders
to the cook in written form and the cook prepared the order directly
from the order slip. If an error was made, the waitress could tell if
she erred in recording the order, and the cook could tell if he
misread the order, by an examination of the order slip. Thus, the
use of the spindle provided feedback to both the waitress and the
cook regarding errors. "The spindle markedly alters the emotional
relationship and redirects the learning process."[11] Porter points out
also that the feedback mechanism engenders new responses. The
cook and waitress, for example, may find that their errors stem
from the difficulties encountered with the order slip itself. There-
upon, they may ask the restaurant manager to use a different form
or order slip. "Now they are working together to solve the system's
problems rather than working against each other and disregarding
the system's problems."[12]

In terms of the design problem then, the solution recommended
by the scientists not only improved efficiency, but the design must
have produced values that were more palatable to the participants,
because it improved human relations in the industry—at least in
the parable. Besides illustrating the design problem, the parable
also revealed two other considerations of organizational design.
One consideration involves overload, that is, how does the system
react to disturbances or to conditions that are other than normal?
Notice that the problems discussed in the parable arose during rush
hours or at a time when the system was overloaded.[13]

The other consideration revealed in the parable is that problems
arise because of the relationships that exist between and among the
components of an organization. The parable focused on the relations between the waitresses and the cook. Our efforts toward de-

---

[10] *Ibid.*, p. 62.

[11] *Ibid.*

[12] *Ibid.*

[13] We discuss design features for handling disturbance or overload later in
this chapter and in the next chapter under the heading of "Control."

signing an organization will be based on process relationships; that is, one component performs a process and it causes another component to act or perform a process. In the parable, for example, the processes could be described in terms of our classification of decision, communication, and action. The customer transforms the information supplied on the menu into a decision. His order (information) is communicated to the waitress, who transforms it into symbols such as HB (hamburger) or BLT (bacon, lettuce, and tomato sandwich) on an order slip. The order is then communicated to the cook by way of the spindle. After reading the order, the cook takes some raw meat (in the case of a hamburger order) and performs an action process, that is, he cooks the meat to the specifications of the order. The completed order is then passed to the waitress, who delivers it to the customer for consumption.

DESIGN FRAMEWORK

The formal organization depends on its decision makers for direction. It depends on decision makers to make wise choices— choices that produce optimum results—choices that are optimum *in fact*. It is important to recognize that the decision process is crucial to organizational success. Organizational design is of little significance if the decision-making process is faulty. It is possible to be very efficient in implementing a poor decision. The design may be adequate, in other words, but the organization fails. It is also possible to implement a good decision improperly through poor design. Thus, the organization may fail not because of the decision-making process, but because of inadequate design. The point is that design is only one of the factors that affect organizational success.

While organizational design cannot ensure good decisions, it can provide some of the elements that are necessary to make and implement good decisions. For example, organizational design can provide communication channels which carry necessary information to and from decision makers. What is done with this information and the kinds of choices that emanate from the decision center is largely a function of the skills possessed by the decision maker. In our framework, we assume that decision-making skills are adequate and that the purpose of design is to provide the conditions which are necessary to make and implement decisions.

Basis for Design

As a basis for design, we treat the formal organization as a system of interconnected components performing processes on flows of matter, energy, and information. In this context, the formal organization transforms matter, energy, and information into different states or output values. These output values are the inducements that make men willing to contribute to the organization. In terms of the economic values of a business firm, for example, the consumer contributes money for the firm's products, the entrepreneur contributes capital for a profit, and employees contribute skills, time, and physical effort for wages.[14] These values are the end product of the flows; they comprise the objectives or desired performance of the system, and through design, decision makers are placed in a position to regulate these flows. By regulating these flows, they are supposed to produce the values agreed upon by participants, that is, meet the organizational objectives. The general framework for organizational design is shown in Figure 11–1.

Desired Performance

The information inputs to the circle labeled "desired performance or desired values or objectives," in Figure 11–1, are messages from environmental and internal forces, and they determine the organizational objectives. As we have indicated, organizational objectives reflect a resolution of interests by these forces. After a working relationship has been established, the agreed-upon goals become the ends toward which organizational processes are directed. Through design the broad overall goals are divided successively until a high degree of specificity is attained, that is, until each member of the organization has one or more goals which he must fulfill. In effect, the goals of the organization are arranged in a hierarchy with ". . . each level to be considered as an end relative to the levels below it and as a means relative to the levels above it. Through the hierarchical structure of ends, behavior attains

----

[14] We discuss these inducements along with psychological and sociological inducements such as membership, security, and recognition values in Chapters 15 and 16.

FIGURE 11-1

General Framework for Organizational Design

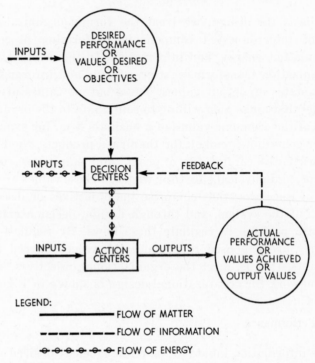

LEGEND:
──────────── FLOW OF MATTER
── ── ── ── FLOW OF INFORMATION
◦-◦-◦-◦-◦-◦ FLOW OF ENERGY

integration and consistency. . . ."[15] The goals represent the "desired performance" of various parts of the system, and since the goals are hierarchical, they are supposed to dovetail and meet the overall goals of the organization.

Actual Performance

The actual performance or output of the system, indicated by a circle at the end of the matter flow of Figure 11-1, is the result of the action process. Decisions are implemented through the action process, and it is through the action centers that decision makers regulate the flows through the system. As a result of noise, bias, and delays in the system (some of which are beyond the control of the organization), actual performance often differs from desired performance. Thus, it is necessary to design the system so that decision

─────────────

[15] Simon, *op. cit.*, p. 63.

makers may monitor actual performance and institute corrective action when it differs significantly from desired performance. A communication channel (or communication channels) connecting decision centers with components that record and measure performance meets this necessity. This communication channel is called a "feedback loop," and the information it carries is called "feedback," as indicated in Figure 11–1.[16]

Processes

The components of formal organization are classified in Figure 11–1 into decision centers and action centers. This classification is according to the critical processes of formal organization. Every living system has critical processes—processes which must be carried out for survival. The human organism, for example, must perform the processes of ingestion, digestion, and excretion. A *process* is defined as the transformation of matter, energy, and/or information over time in a system.[17] We identify two critical processes of formal organization—the decision process and the action process.[18] A *decision process* transforms information through search, formulation of alternatives, and selection of a course of action. The decision process also involves the transformation of energy when the sources of power are used to get others to implement a decision. An *action process* is defined as the transformation of matter from one state to another or movement from one point to another.[19] The meaning and importance of these processes is clarified further below.[20]

---

[16] The problems related to differences between desired and actual performance, feedback, and delays are examined in the next chapter under the subject of control.

[17] Miller, *op. cit.*, p. 209.

[18] It is possible, of course, to break down these critical processes more minutely and identify processes, such as ingestion, in which the organization acquires and transports inputs across its boundaries or the process of distribution, in which the organization distributes matter, energy, and information among components. Since our analysis is not detailed to the extent required by such a breakdown, we have used the grosser classification of decision and action.

[19] Miller, *op. cit.*, p. 193.

[20] Earlier, in Chapter 8, we also identified a communication process. Since both the communication and decision processes involve the transformation and movement of information, we have simplified the presentation by referring only to the decision process.

Structure

As we noted in Chapter 8, the essentiality of these processes requires that some organizational component be charged with their performance. We assume that one component performs only one or a part of one process.[21] The physical arrangement of components is called *spatial relations* of a system. Spatial relations, according to Miller, may be described in the following terms:

> *Containment.* Whether or not a given subsystem or component is within the boundaries of another system or component.
>
> *Number.* The number of subsystems or components in a system. The interrelationships among subsystems or components increase as a direct function of this number.
>
> *Order.* The arrangement of subsystems or components relative to each other along a spatial dimension.
>
> *Position.* The location of components on an absolute, cardinal scale of spatial coordinates.
>
> *Direction.* The relationship of a subsystem or component to a reference point along at least one spatial coordinate.
>
> *Size.* The extent of distance, area of surface, or volume of space occupied by a subsystem or component.
>
> *Pattern.* The form of organization, configuration, or arrangement of subsystems or components within the space occupied by a system.
>
> *Density.* How closely packed subsystems or components are within a system.[22]

In terms of spatial dimensions, the formal organization may be described as existing within a building and as having a definite number of members. Also in spatial terms, each organization member occupies some volume of space and is arranged in some physical relation to others. However, spatial characteristics tell us little about the structure of behavior in formal organization.

Of course, physical conditions affect behavior, but the formal organization with its social-psychological bases of behavior, has no spatial dimension in the same sense as biological and mechanical systems. "The social-psychological basis of social systems comprises

---

[21] This classification of a component by the process it performs has implications about the degree of specialization employed in an organization. It is possible, of course, for a component to perform both processes. For pedagogic reasons, we make the simplifying assumption that one component performs one process or a part of one process.

[22] Miller, *op. cit.*, p. 361. Miller also introduces a temporal dimension and defines most of these relations in terms of time period, *ibid.*, p. 362.

the *role* behavior of members, the *norms* prescribing and sanctioning these behaviors and the *values* in which the norms are imbedded."[23] The physical arrangement, the relationships, and the boundary of parts in biological and mechanical systems can be observed even when the systems are not functioning. The anatomical structures of animals and automobiles, for example, are still present when the systems cease to function.[24] When the formal organization ceases to function, however, there is no identifiable structure; that is, there is no behavior or roles. The formal organization ". . . is a structuring of events or happenings rather than of physical parts and it therefore has no structure apart from its functioning."[25] The "structuring of events" may be characterized in terms of process relations.

A *process relationship* is defined as the transformation of matter, energy, and/or information by one organizational component, and it brings about a decision or action by one or a number of other components, which in turn stimulates further responses from the originator of the process. This cycle or closure in the chain of events is illustrated in Figure 11–1, in which decision centers transmit decisions to action centers for implementation and receive information on actual performance through the feedback channel. In this way, decision centers monitor performance, and when actual performance deviates significantly from desired performance, they make further decisions to correct the problem, and the cycle of events is repeated.

Let us illustrate process relations with reference to the transformation of a raw material into a finished product in a manufacturing firm. The flow of material is shown in Figure 11–2. For simplicity, we have not shown feedback loops in the diagram, but the reader should bear in mind that closure provided by feedback is always present in a system of relations. In the diagram of Figure 11–2, the material enters the system in raw form. Thereafter, it is forged, extruded, milled, lathed, and combined with other parts for final assembly into a finished product. Each component makes some contribution to this transformation, and the completion of work by one component requires that another organizational component

---

[23] Daniel Katz and Robert Kahn, *The Social Psychology of Organizations* (New York: John Wiley & Sons, Inc., 1966), p. 37.

[24] *Ibid.*, p. 31.

[25] *Ibid.*, p. 31.

FIGURE 11-2

Process Relationships Among Components

take up the process. Thus, there is a process relationship among the components.

Critical processes are usually performed at several echelons in the formal organization. For example, in the abbreviated organization chart of a manufacturing firm, Figure 11-3, decisions are made at each level, including the president, vice president, foreman, and workers. Again for simplicity, we have not shown feedback loops. It may not be practicable or possible for the president to make all decisions. Therefore, he assigns part of this responsibility to subordinates, who in turn apportion it further to their subordinates. Allocation of decision-making responsibilites in this manner may also represent an effort to take advantage of specialization. By dividing decisions into numerous constituent decisions and by limiting the scope of each part, the individual decision maker can ac-

FIGURE 11-3

Vertical and Horizontal Process Relationships in Organization

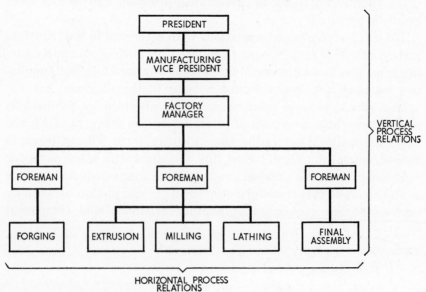

quire expertise in a narrow area of responsibility.[26] The process relation exists because a decision at, say, the top level of the organization creates a need for decisions at the next lower level, which in turn creates a need for decisions at still lower levels. Even at the lowest levels, where behavior possibilities are rather limited, workers make decisions about how they shall fulfill the requirements of their jobs. Thus, specialization of decision-making tasks creates vertical process relationships.

Flows and Processes

When a person is assigned to a job he is asked to play a role, that is, he is asked to perform certain duties. "People are tied together because of the functional interdependence of the roles they play; for example, the worker in the production line depends on the appropriate activity of the man feeding him materials and in turn must add his contribution as the product moves to the next worker."[27] The flows of matter, energy, and information are the connecting links among jobs, components, or roles in a system. Information flows, for example, provide essential connections between the environment and decision centers, between decision centers at different levels, and between decision centers and action centers. Through this kind of flow, the centers can respond to environmental changes, and when necessary, institute appropriate compensating action. The flows of matter refer to material things or anything of substance that flows through the system. Material flows, such as the one illustrated in Figure 11–2, provide connections between specialized components or subsystems which perform a process on the flows.

Energy flows may also refer to material flows because matter can be converted to energy.[28] However, our principal concern with respect to energy is one's ability to produce an effect. For example, an executive who has the authority to promote, demote, and discharge subordinates may be able to produce an intended result by offering or withholding these sanctions. Success in this endeavor implies that there is a power relationship as well as an authority relationship between the executive and his subordinates. Since power is the

[26] Simon, *op. cit.*, p. 137.
[27] Katz and Kahn, *op. cit.*, p. 38.
[28] Miller, *op. cit.*, p. 193.

same as authority in this case, the connections between components are provided by the hierarchy of authority, with the components at one echelon dependent upon the next higher echelon (subordinates reporting to superiors) as a source of authority.

Flows and Decision Process

The decision process may be separated into three phases—the decision itself, transmittal of the decision to action centers for implementation, and the control phase. All three phases involve information flow and/or the transformation of information from one state to another. Although the phases are closely related and might take place almost simultaneously, we separate and examine them below in order to indicate the implications for organizational design.

The Decision. The decision process involves the transformation of information through search, formulation of alternatives, and selection of a course of action that is generally aimed at optimizing the attainment of organizational objectives. To facilitate this process, design provides the decision maker or decision center (as shown in Figure 11–1) with communication channels that carry information about objectives and resources and with information that allows him to formulate alternative uses of the resources. Although the channels of authority are of importance in carrying information, they are not the only channels to be considered for design. The authority channels may, in fact, be unreliable. The tendency to transmit only the "good news" through these channels (recall our discussion in Chapter 5 on the barriers to communication) requires that consideration be given to establishing redundant lines of communication.[29]

Even with the redundant channels, the needs of decision makers are not limited to information that moves upward and downward between levels of an organization. There may be a need for communication channels that provide lateral connections with other decision centers. There may be a need to provide connections to several different sources of information. The following are some examples of sources of information, in addition to the chain of command, that may be important to the decision maker:

---

[29] The question of how many channels is discussed in Chapter 14.

a) Organizational units that gather and analyze statistics such as a market forecast section of a business firm.
b) Organizational units that possess expert knowledge such as an engineering section or a legal division.
c) Organizational members that have expert knowledge gathered through long experience with a particular problem or operation.
d) Informal leaders that have knowledge about employee attitudes.
e) Other organizations, such as suppliers, equipment manufacturers, or consulting firms.

It is possible, of course, to provide an overabundance of information or to provide too many channels of communication. The design problem with respect to the decision process requires a determination of what information is relevant to decision makers and of what communication channels from which sources to provide this information to appropriate decision centers.

Decision Transmittal. After the decision has been made, it is transmitted to action centers for implementation. In this phase of the decision process, information is transmitted not only to "inform" but also to produce the effect intended by the sender. Here, we are not concerned with the clarity of the message, although that is important. We are concerned with the ability of one person or group to induce a desired response from another person or group. We are referring to power relationships. Again, as was emphasized in Chapter 7, there is a difference between coercion and persuasion. There are some information flows that produce an intended effect because of the persuasive ability of the sender with the receiver but it does not have the sustaining effect of a power relationship. There are, of course, other messages that do not produce an intended effect. In these cases, the sender is unable to coerce or persuade the receiver. In the power relationship, the power holder has the ability and willingness to use sanctions. His messages, therefore, have an imperative mood, even though he does not threaten to use sanctions every time he sends a message.

Recall our discussions in Chapter 7, where we said that the use of sanctions involves the deprivation or rendering of something that is considered valuable by those who are the object of power. The power holder has control over something valued by the other party to the relationship. Actually, each party to the relationship controls something that is valued by the other. One party to the relationship tries to achieve an intended result, and, therefore, he *values* the responses of the other party. To obtain the desired responses, he must possess, or be in a position to provide, something of *value* to the other party.

When one party to the relationship fails to respond in the manner desired by the other party, the things of value may be withdrawn or withheld by the controlling party until the desired response is induced. If the application of these sanctions fails to induce the desired response, then the power relationship has changed or never existed. The absence of a power relationship between two parties means that at least one of the parties has nothing valuable enough to induce a desired response from the other party. Unless the organization offers inducements that are sufficient in kind and amount to participants, it will be unable to obtain the cooperation necessary for goal attainment. Thus, we conclude, as before, that power is necessary to initiate and sustain action in a formal organization.

In terms of the design framework of Figure 11–1, we have shown the energy flow as an input to decision centers, indicating connections to sources of power, and as an outflow from decision centers to action centers to indicate the power relationship. It is necessary in the design of organizations to supply decision centers with the ability to use sanctions. In formal organizations, this usually means delegation of authority. However, as we have indicated, authority is not the only element in the power relationship. The characteristics of the man who is assigned to an executive position also has significance to the power relationship; that is, his personality, skills, and general demeanor are also important elements. His power position may be enhanced by a design that provides connections to other sources of power. For example, his skills or expertise may be developed by proper channeling of information. Strategic location of an executive with respect to the lines of communication may give him an advantage in his relations with subordinates. According to Simon: "The superior who possesses such advantages of information will have much less occasion to invoke the formal sanctions of authority than the superior whose subordinates are in a better position than he, from the standpoint of information, to make the decision."[30] Also, through design, the executive is made less dependent on any one subordinate when he is provided with redundant channels of communications and operating components.

---

[30] Simon, *op. cit.*, p. 139.

Control Phase. The control phase of the decision process is necessary because actual performance often differs from desired performance. As we indicated in our discussion of actual performance above, it is necessary to design the system with communication channels that feed back information about actual performance so that decision makers may formulate alternatives to correct significant deviations from desired performance.[31]

Flows and Action Process

Action processes, which involve the transformation of matter-energy from one state to another or its movement from one point to another, are performed on several different flows through the organization. Forrester, for example, lists five different flows of a business firm on which the action process may be performed. According to Forrester, there is: a *materials flow,* such as the flow of physical goods through a factory; an *orders flow,* such as the flow of customers' orders, requisitions for new employees, or contracts for new plant space; a *money flow,* such as the transmittal of payments to a supplier or receipts from customers; a *personnel flow,* such as men leaving a training program to take a job assignment; a *capital equipment flow,* such as the flow of equipment or factory space from equipment manufacturers or builders to production line capability and further to obsolescence or to a depreciated state.[32]

Subsystems on Each Flow

On each flow, there is need for the critical processes of decision and action. The decision process is necessary to determine the best allocation of resources. The action process is necessary to implement the decision or perform the required transformation and movement of whatever is carried in the flow. Each flow has an end

---

[31] Since "control" is the subject of Chapter 12, we leave it at this point.

[32] Jay W. Forrester, *Industrial Dynamics* (Cambridge, Mass.: M.I.T. Press, Massachusetts Institute of Technology, 1961), pp. 70–71. Forrester also lists an information flow which provides connections among the other five flows. Thus, it would not be appropriate to list it in conjunction with the action process. Besides, we have already indicated its importance as a connecting link. There are exceptions to the use of information flows strictly as a connecting link. For example, in the case of a firm that produces public opinion polls, information would be the main throughput of the organization.

product or output values. Furthermore, there are objectives, a desired performance, or values expected from each flow. In short, it is necessary for each flow to pass through at least one subsystem that is designed according to the framework of Figure 11-1.

We can illustrate a subsystem designed according to the framework of Figure 11-1 by depicting the flow of personnel through a formal organization. In the flow of personnel, employees are re-

FIGURE 11-4

Personnel Subsystem

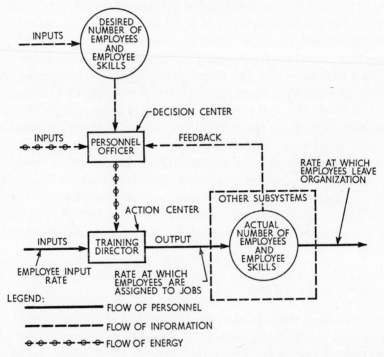

LEGEND:

────────────── FLOW OF PERSONNEL

── ── ── ── ── FLOW OF INFORMATION

⬦–⬦–⬦–⬦–⬦–⬦ FLOW OF ENERGY

cruited, hired, trained, assigned to a job, and leave the organization for reasons such as retirement, sickness, dismissal, or resignation. In this illustration, it is assumed that the personnel officer has the authority to make the recruitment, hiring, training, and assigment decisions. Let us assume further that the authority to fire rests with the decision maker of the subsystem where the employee is assigned. The personnel subsystem is shown in Figure 11-4. For simplicity, the training director is the only action center shown in the diagram. The personnel officer is the decision center of this subsystem. As the decision center, he determines how fast employees will be processed on their way to job assignments, that is, he regulates the flow of personnel up to the point where employees assume the responsibilities of a particular job in another subsystem. Thereafter, the decision center of the subsystem where the employee is assigned will regulate the flow (except in cases such as retirement, sickness, or resignations). When actual performance is fed back from the other subsystems, the personnel officer compares the actual with desired performance, and when there is a significant difference, he makes a control decision or determines what corrective action, if any, is required.

The Total System

The totality of all subsystems with their interconnections make up the system of formal organization. The subsystems are connected by flows of matter, energy, and/or information. Notice in Figure 11-4 how the personnel subsystem is connected to other subsystems. Its output on the personnel flow is the input to other subsystems. The feedback loop provides another connection. Through this connection, the personnel officer receives information about the actual performance of his subsystem. In the simulation model below, we see that performance depends on the difference between the input and output quantities. In the diagram of Figure 11-4, it depends on the difference between "the number of employees that are assigned to jobs" and "the number of employees that leave the organization." Still other connections are provided by the inputs to the personnel subsystem. They are employee inputs that come from the organization's environment in the case of new employees and others that come from other subsystems when existing organization members are processed through the training program. Inputs to the personnel officer provide connections to the sources of power and help to establish the power relationship (or connection) between decision centers and action centers.

The objectives of a subsystem are either imposed by a suprasystem or established through interaction of the two systems. In either event, the goals of a subsystem are a means for attaining higher level objectives. Thus, the goals of each subsystem are a subgoal of the total system's goals and, as the name indicates, each subsystem is a constitutent part of a larger system. The attainment of subsystem goals is a part of the performance required to achieve overall goals. Since the goals and performance of each subsystem are parts of a larger system and since the subsystems are interconnected by the flows of matter, energy, and information, organizational design must focus on the total system rather than on any particular part.

In order to optimize the attainment of the goals of the total system, it might be necessary to utilize an inefficient or suboptimal design for one or more of the subsystems. The systems approach requires the selection of a design that produces the greatest overall result. Let us now turn to a model that illustrates total system behavior.

A SIMULATION MODEL

In order to be more specific about the general framework for organizational design, as shown in Figure 11–1, we draw upon the important work of Jay W. Forrester.[33] Professor Forrester has developed a mathematical model which describes certain system characteristics of business firms. We have already mentioned the several flows of his model earlier in this chapter. By supplying inputs to the model, such as the pattern of consumer purchases, and making certain assumptions about decision rules and desired levels of performance, one is able to observe how the system as a whole behaves. Models such as the one developed by Forrester enable us to determine the effects of various organizational designs through simulation rather than through actual experience. In other words, we may determine the effects of organizational design through experiments with a mathematical model instead of conducting experiments in a real organization, where they would disrupt operations and would likely involve considerable costs.

The formulations are so complex and the computations are so involved that full presentation of the Forrester model in this book would be practically impossible. Instead, we present a simplified version as developed by Donald J. Clough.[34] The Clough version is concerned with only one sector of the business firm's operations, the factory subsystem. A more complete version would include others,

---

[33] Forrester, *op. cit.*

[34] Donald J. Clough, *Concepts in Management Science* (Englewood Cliffs, N.J.: Prentice-Hall, Inc., © 1963), chap. XIV. Adapted by permission of Prentice-Hall, Inc.

such as a wholesale subsystem and a retail subsystem. The simulation model, shown in Figure 11–5, is presented according to the framework of Figure 11–1. Notice that there are subsystems within the factory subsystem. They are represented by the two decision

FIGURE 11–5

Simple Model of a Factory System

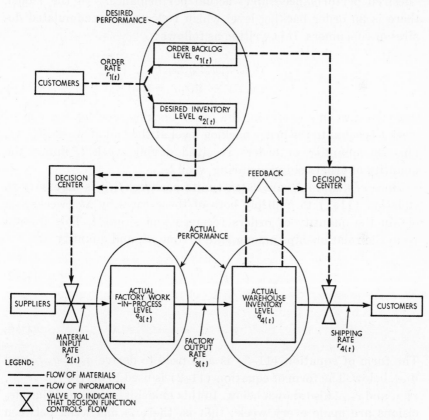

LEGEND:

—— FLOW OF MATERIALS
– – – FLOW OF INFORMATION
⋈ VALVE TO INDICATE THAT DECISION FUNCTION CONTROLS FLOW

centers. Each has a decision function which regulates flow at two different points on the materials throughput. As material moves through the system, it is transformed from a raw state to finished products; it spends some time in storage; and it is finally shipped to customers. For simplicity, we have not identified action centers in the diagram, but their existence is apparent by the fact that there is a factory output rate and a shipping rate. In portraying it this way, we want to make it explicit that decision centers regulate the flow

of material. A valve on the materials flow symbolizes regulation of
the flow. In actuality, this regulatory function is accomplished by
decision centers through their control over action centers.

Level Equations

Notice that the model uses the word "level" where we have used
"desired performance" and "actual performance." In the model,
there is an order backlog level which reflects the accumulated desires of consumers. It is written as follows:

$$Order\ Backlog\ Level$$
$$q_{1(t)} = q_{1(t-1)} + \Delta t(r_{1(t)} - r_{4(t)}) \tag{11-1}$$

According to this equation, the order backlog level at the end of
week t is equal to the order backlog level at the end of week $(t-1)$,
plus the quantity of orders received during week t, minus the
quantity of orders shipped during week t.

Since $r_{1(t)}$ and $r_{4(t)}$ are rates (units per week), it is necessary in
equation (11–1) to multiply both of these rates by Δt (weeks) to
obtain the quantity of orders received and shipped. This follows
from the relationships among rate r, time Δt, and quantity q:

$$r = \frac{q}{\Delta t} \tag{11-2}$$

or

$$q = \Delta t \cdot r \tag{11-3}$$

The form of equation (11–3) is also used to derive $q_{2(t)}$, $q_{3(t)}$, and
$q_{4(t)}$, below. The form of equation (11–2) is used to derive $r_{1(t)}$, $r_{2(t)}$,
$r_{3(t)}$, and $r_{4(t)}$, also shown below. In this model it is assumed that decisions are made every week; that is, there is one week between
decisions, or Δt equals one week.

Inventories serve several purposes. The general function of an
inventory or level is to allow ". . . the inflow rates to differ, over
limited intervals, from the outflow rates."[35] Thus, by maintaining
an inventory of goods, a manufacturer does not have to synchronize
production with consumption. It may be uneconomical for him to
adapt his production schedule to the random behavior of consumers.

---

[35] Forrester, *op. cit.*, p. 86.

Even when demand follows a regular pattern, inventories may be desirable to cushion against demand change and to gain the advantages of a stable production schedule. A manufacturer may also obtain "economies of scale" by building inventories. For example, savings may result from purchases of large lots and from long production runs. He may wish to buy in large lots to obtain quantity price discounts. Through long production runs, he avoids the costs that result from changing setups on production equipment. The desired inventory level, therefore, expresses the desires of management to service sales readily and to cushion the company against fluctuations in sales. It is a *subgoal* of the organization. The desired inventory level is written as follows:

Desired Inventory Level

$$q_{2(t)} = 5 \frac{\Delta t}{10} (r_{1(t-9)} + \cdots + r_{1(t)}) \tag{11-4}$$

This equation is stated as a "moving average" quantity, and it tends to "smooth" the effects of a fluctuating order rate. As Clough states: "Smoothing the information in this way allows the inventory goal to follow the general trend in orders. But it prevents the drastic fluctuations in $q_{2(t)}$ that might occur if the goal is based solely on the most recent order rate $r_{1(t-1)}$."[36] The desired inventory level at the end of week t, equation (11-4), is five times the "moving average" quantity ordered in the 10 weeks of $(t - 9)$ through t.

The other level equations reflect actual performance. The first equation represents the actual factory work-in-process level. For simplicity, a feedback loop and a decision function are not shown for this level. The emphasis in this illustration is on the actual warehouse inventory level, which is covered after the work-in-process level equation:

Actual Factory Work-in-Process Level

$$q_{3(t)} = q_{3(t-1)} + \Delta t(r_{2(t)} - r_{3(t)}) \tag{11-5}$$

The work-in-process level refers to the amount of material or goods in the manufacturing process at a particular period of time. It is as if we stopped all operations and counted the amount of goods in the factory. Another way of obtaining the same result is to use equation

---

[36] Clough, *op. cit.*, p. 376.

(11–5), which states that the factory work-in-process level at the end of week t is equal to the work-in-process level at end of week $(t - 1)$ plus the input quantity of material during week t, minus the output quantity from the factory during week t.

The actual warehouse inventory level is the main performance variable in this illustration and is given by the equation:

Actual Warehouse Inventory Level

$$q_{4(t)} = q_{4(t-1)} + \Delta t(r_{3(t)} - r_{4(t)}) \tag{11–6}$$

According to equation (11–6), the actual warehouse inventory level at the end of week t is equal to the warehouse inventory level at the end of week $(t - 1)$, plus the input quantity from the factory during week t, minus the quantity of goods shipped to customers during week t.

Decision Functions or Flow Rate Equations

As we indicated above, decisions regulate the flow of material through the system. Also, decisions are made on the basis of comparisons of actual performance and desired performance. When actual performance differs significantly from desired performance, decision makers choose a course of action that tends to adjust the flow of materials and performance. This process reflects interdependence and the cycle or closure in the chain of events in the system. It may be described as follows: the desired inventory level $q_{2(t)}$ and the actual warehouse inventory level $q_{4(t)}$ are inputs to the decision center; the output of the decision center regulates the material inflow rate $r_{2(t)}$; the material inflow rate $r_{2(t)}$ and factory output rate $r_{3(t)}$ affect the factory work-in-process level $q_{3(t)}$; the factory output rate $r_{3(t)}$ and the shipping rate $r_{4(t)}$ affect the actual warehouse inventory level $q_{4(t)}$, which in turn affects decisions. In this case, decisions regulate flow rates, flow rates determine levels, and levels affect decisions.

In the model under consideration, decisions are expressed as rate equations, that is, in units per week. Furthermore, the rate equation does not change. It is a "decision rule" or set policy. In the decision rule for the material input rate, it is assumed that the supplier's capacity is fixed at 50 units per week. Using the form of equation (11–2), we write the rule for the material input rate:

Material Input Rate

$$r_{2(t)} = 20 \cdot \frac{q_{2(t-1)}}{q_{4(t-1)}} \quad \text{if} \quad 20 \cdot \frac{q_{2(t-1)}}{q_{4(t-1)}} \leq 50$$

or

$$r_{2(t)} = 50 \quad \text{if} \quad 20 \, \frac{q_{2(t-1)}}{q_{4(t-1)}} \geq 50 \tag{11-7}$$

According to this equation, the decision rule says that the material input rate during week t will be governed by the ratio of the desired inventory level to the actual inventory level at the end of week $(t-1)$ times 20. Since the supplier's capacity is fixed at 50 units per week, the rule also says that $r_{2(t)}$ will not exceed this rate.

The factory output rate, in the form of equation (11-2) is given by the equation:

Factory Output Rate

$$r_{3(t)} = \frac{q_{3(t-1)}}{4\Delta t} \tag{11-8}$$

According to equation (11-8), the decision rule says that the factory output rate during week t will be one fourth of the work-in-process level at the end of week $(t-1)$.

The decision rule for the shipping rate depends on the order backlog level, the actual inventory level, and shipping capacity, which is fixed at 35 units per week. Again we follow the form of equation (11-2) and state the shipping rate equation as follows:

Shipping Rate

$$r_{4(t)} = \frac{q_{1(t-1)}}{\Delta t} \quad \text{if} \quad \frac{q_{1(t-1)}}{\Delta t} \leq \frac{q_{4(t-1)}}{\Delta t} \leq 35$$

or

$$r_{4(t)} = \frac{q_{4(t-1)}}{\Delta t} \quad \text{if} \quad \frac{q_{4(t-1)}}{\Delta t} \leq \frac{q_{1(t-1)}}{\Delta t} \leq 35$$

or

$$r_{4(t)} = 35 \quad \text{if} \quad \frac{q_{1(t-1)}}{\Delta t}, \quad \frac{q_{4(t-1)}}{\Delta t} \geq 35 \tag{11-9}$$

According to equation (11-9), the decision rule states that the number of units shipped during week t will be equal to either the backlog level at the end of week $(t-1)$, or the warehouse inventory level at the end of week $(t-1)$, or the shipping capacity of 35 units per week, whichever is smallest.

Simulation of Behavior

Now that we have defined the elements that affect the flow of values through this rather simple system, its dynamic nature may be illustrated through simulation, that is, we may trace its behavior through time. Clough begins the simulation procedure by assuming that the system starts out in an equilibrium condition. In equilibrium, the flow rates and levels are held constant at the following values:

$r_{1(t)}$ = 20 units per week.
$r_{2(t)}$ = 20 units per week.
$r_{3(t)}$ = 20 units per week.
$r_{4(t)}$ = 20 units per week.
$q_{1(t)}$ = 20 units.
$q_{2(t)}$ = 100 units.
$q_{3(t)}$ = 80 units.
$q_{4(t)}$ = 100 units.

The customer order rate $r_{1(t)}$ is designated as an *exogenous* variable. As an exogenous variable, it represents an influence from the environment, and it is assumed to be beyond the control of the company. The order rate remains constant at 20 units per week until the 13th week. During the 13th week, it is assumed that customers increase their orders by 50 percent to 30 units per week. Thereafter, it is held at this rate. Given the design and decision rules, the purpose of this experiment is to determine how long it takes for the system to stabilize or indeed to find out whether it will stabilize at all. Also, we want to know at what level the system will stabilize, that is, we want to know whether or not it will achieve its objectives. Recall, that we sought this same information from the Markov chain model of Chapter 9.

The values for each of the system's variables are shown in Table 11–1. Since it was assumed that the system was in equilibrium during the first 12 weeks, it was not necessary to repeat the values for each of these weeks. Thus, the values for the first 10 weeks are not shown, but they are the same as those values shown for weeks 11 and 12 in Table 11–1. As a sample calculation, we derive the value for actual factory work-in-process level, using equation (11–5), for week 20:

$$q_{3(20)} = q_{3(19)} + \Delta t(r_{2(20)} - r_{3(20)})$$
$$= 131 + 1\,(46 - 33)$$
$$= 144$$

Thus, the work-in-process level at end of week 20 is 144 units. This value is shown in the table for the 20th week. The values in Table 11–1 are calculated to the nearest integer.

The results of Table 11–1 are plotted in Figure 11–6. A reading of Table 11–1 and Figure 11–6 indicates that the purposes of the experiment have been met. First, we are able to determine that the system does stabilize after the 50 percent increase in the customer order rate. Second, we are able to determine approximately when the system stabilizes. The two performance variables, actual factory work-in-process level and actual warehouse inventory level, approach an equilibrium condition at about the 50th week. Third, we are able to determine whether or not the system achieves objectives or desired performance. We conclude that the system is unable to

FIGURE 11–6

System Responses to Change in Order Rate

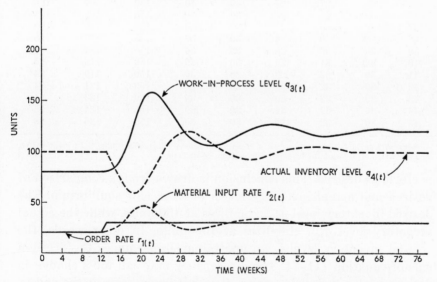

SOURCE: Reproduced from Donald J. Clough, *Concepts in Management Science* (Englewood Cliffs, N.J.: Prentice-Hall, Inc., © 1963), p. 380. Reprinted by permission of Prentice-Hall, Inc.

TABLE 11-1
Simulation of System Behavior

Week t	Rate $r_{1(t)}$ Exoge-nous	Rate $r_{2(t)}$	Rate $r_{3(t)}$	Rate $r_{4(t)}$	Level $q_{1(t)}$	Level $q_{2(t)}$	Level $q_{3(t)}$	Level $q_{4(t)}$
11	20	20	20	20	20	100	80	100
12	20	20	20	20	20	100	80	100
13	30	20	20	20	30	105	80	100
14	30	21	20	30	30	110	81	90
15	30	24	20	30	30	115	85	80
16	30	29	21	30	30	120	93	71
17	30	34	23	30	30	125	104	64
18	30	39	26	30	30	130	117	60
19	30	43	29	30	30	135	131	59
20	30	46	33	30	30	140	144	62
21	30	45	36	30	30	145	153	68
22	30	43	38	30	30	150	158	76
23	30	39	40	30	30	150	157	86
24	30	35	39	30	30	150	153	95
25	30	32	38	30	30	150	147	103
26	30	29	37	30	30	150	139	110
27	30	27	35	30	30	150	131	115
28	30	26	33	30	30	150	124	118
29	30	25	31	30	30	150	118	119
30	30	25	30	30	30	150	113	119
31	30	25	28	30	30	150	110	117
32	30	26	28	30	30	150	108	115
33	30	26	27	30	30	150	107	112
34	30	27	27	30	30	150	107	109
35	30	27	27	30	30	150	107	106
36	30	28	27	30	30	150	108	103
37	30	29	27	30	30	150	110	100
38	30	30	28	30	30	150	112	98
39	30	30	28	30	30	150	114	96
40	30	31	29	30	30	150	116	95
41	30	32	29	30	30	150	119	94
42	30	32	30	30	30	150	121	94
43	30	32	30	30	30	150	123	94
44	30	32	31	30	30	150	124	95
45	30	32	31	30	30	150	125	96

SOURCE: Donald J. Clough, *Concepts in Management Science* (Englewood Cliffs, N.J.: Prentice-Hall, Inc., © 1963), p. 379. Reprinted by permission of Prentice-Hall, Inc.

perform as desired. This conclusion is drawn from a comparison of desired and actual inventory levels in their new equilibrium. The desired inventory level $q_{2(t)}$ stabilizes at 150 units, while the actual inventory level $q_{4(t)}$ stabilizes at 100 units. In other words, the desired inventory level is an unattainable goal under the decision rule of equation (11–7). The discrepancy may call for a change in design, goals, or decision rules. It is left as exercise at the end of this chapter for the student to solve this problem.

Notes on the Model

In the simulation model of this chapter and the Markov chain model of Chapter 9, the same criteria were used for judging the adequacy of a system's design. We measured the performance of the system and determined whether or not it would stabilize, the length of time it took to stabilize, and the level at which it stabilized. While the analysis of both models is concerned with a system's performance, the simulation model allows us to examine the internal parts of the system and some determinants of behavior. We noticed, for example, that the subgoals of the system (the desired inventory level) changed with a change in inputs (the customer order rate). We noticed also that the decision rule (the material input rate) "built in" or designed into the system prevented the attainment of the desired goal. With the kind of information provided by the simulation model, we not only have a basis for judging performance, but we also have a basis for making design changes. Thus, we may continue experiments with different design features.

For simplicity, the relationships in the simulation model are defined to be deterministic; that is, it assumes that we can predict exactly how the parts of a system will interact. A more realistic model would require that the relationships be defined in probabilistic terms. However, a probabilistic model would add undue complexity at this point where we are stressing fundamentals of design.

SUMMARY

This chapter presents a basic framework for organizational design. We define organizational goals in terms of some desired performance or a "preferential hierarchy of values." Formal organizational design is justified on the basis that it can optimize the attainment of the desired goals through efficient use of available resources. Formal design attempts to remove, as much as possible, the impediments to rational behavior. Generally, formal design facilitates rationality by limiting the range of behavior possibilities of its participants.

In this basic framework for design, organization is viewed as a system of interdependent components performing processes on flows of matter, energy, and information. The system exchanges values with its environment and it transforms matter, energy, and information into different states or output values. The critical processes performed at several echelons of formal organization are the decision process and the action process. The flows of matter, energy, and information are the connecting links among the decision and action centers which bring about the production of the desired values or outputs. Through feedback loops it is possible to compare actual performance of the system to desired performance.

Forrester's dynamic model is used to illustrate the flows of a system. Given certain decision rules, the behavior of a system is simulated. Through the simulation, we can measure the performance of the system and determine whether or not it will stabilize, the length of time it takes to stabilize, and the level at which it may stabilize. This approach also permits us to examine the internal components of the system as determinants of behavior, and to make judgments concerning the adequacy of actual performance.

DISCUSSION QUESTIONS AND PROBLEMS

11-1. What is meant by optimal behavior? How does organization remove impediments to optimal behavior? Give several illustrations.

11-2. In systems terms, discuss how the spindle solved the efficiency and human relations problems. Is the spindle idea applicable to other organizations? Illustrate.

11-3. How do the basics of organizational design suggested in this chapter differ from traditional organization theory?

11-4. How can the Forrester model be useful to the organization designer? What is meant by simulation?

11-5. If organizational design is concerned primarily with efficiency, why should it be of any importance to the participants in organization?

11-6. How does the design of an organization affect the decision-making process and the action process?

11-7. Are the values of the participants of formal organization inconsistent with the efficiency criterion? Explain.

Start the simulations called for in the following problems in the 13th week. Levels and rates at the end of the 12th week $(t = 12)$ are:

$$r_{1(t)} = 20 \qquad q_{1(t)} = 20$$
$$r_{2(t)} = 20 \qquad q_{2(t)} = 100$$
$$r_{3(t)} = 20 \qquad q_{3(t)} = 80$$
$$r_{4(t)} = 20 \qquad q_{4(t)} = 100$$

Equations which describe the original factory system are as follows:

$$r_{1(t)} = \text{order rate (exogenous variable)}$$

$$r_{2(t)} = 20 \cdot \frac{q_{2(t-1)}}{q_{4(t-1)}} \text{ if } 20 \cdot \frac{q_{2(t-1)}}{q_{4(t-1)}} \leq 50$$
or

$$r_{2(t)} = 50 \text{ if } 20 \cdot \frac{q_{2(t-1)}}{q_{4(t-1)}} \geq 50$$

$$r_{3(t)} = \frac{q_{3(t-1)}}{4\Delta t}$$

$$r_{4(t)} = \frac{q_{1(t-1)}}{\Delta t} \text{ if } \frac{q_{1(t-1)}}{\Delta t} \leq \frac{q_{4(t-1)}}{\Delta t} \leq 35$$
or

$$r_{4(t)} = \frac{q_{4(t-1)}}{\Delta t} \text{ if } \frac{q_{4(t-1)}}{\Delta t} \leq \frac{q_{1(t-1)}}{\Delta t} \leq 35$$
or

$$r_{4(t)} = 35 \text{ if } \frac{q_{4(t-1)}}{\Delta t}, \frac{q_{1(t-1)}}{\Delta t} \geq 35$$

$$q_{1(t)} = q_{1(t-1)} + \Delta t \, (r_{1t} - r_{4t})$$

$$q_{2(t)} = \frac{5\Delta t}{10} \, (r_{1(t-9)} + r_{1(t-8)} + \ldots + r_{1(t)})$$

$$q_{3(t)} = q_{3(t-1)} + \Delta t \, (r_{2(t)} - r_{3(t)})$$

$$q_{4(t)} = q_{4(t-1)} + \Delta t \, (r_{3(t)} - r_{4(t)})$$

The order rate, r_1, rises to 30 units per week during the 13th week.

Notice from the simulation shown in the chapter that the equilibrium of the actual warehouse inventory level ($q_{4(t)}$) does not reach the desired warehouse inventory level ($q_{2(t)}$). Also, the actual warehouse inventory level does not reach its equilibrium until the 63rd week.

11-8. *a*) Simulate the performance of the factory system when:

$$r_{3(t)} = \frac{q_{3(t-1)}}{2\Delta t}$$

Allow the rest of the system's relationships to remain the same

b) Simulate the performance of the factory system when:

$$r_{3(t)} = \frac{q_{3(t-1)}}{\Delta t}$$

    c) Compare the results of the original simulation and the simulations of 11–1 (*a*) and 11–1 (*b*) in terms of actual warehouse inventory reaching desired warehouse inventory; compare the results in terms of the number of weeks it takes the actual warehouse inventory level to reach its equilibrium.

11–9.

    a) Simulate the performance of the factory system when:

$$r_{3(t)} = \frac{q_{3(t-1)}}{4\Delta t}$$

$$q_{2(t)} = \frac{5\Delta t(r_{1(t-1)} + r_{1(t)})}{2}$$

and the rest of the relationships remain the same.

    b) Simulate the performance of the factory system when:

$$r_{3(t)} = \frac{q_{3(t-1)}}{\Delta t}$$

$$q_{2(t)} = \frac{5\Delta t(r_{1(t-1)} + r_{1(t)})}{2}$$

    c) Make general conclusions regarding the number of weeks it takes for $q_{4(t)}$ to reach its equilibrium; make general conclusions regarding the actual attainment of the desired inventory level.

11–10. The managers of the factory systems discussed in the chapter have found that actual warehouse inventory level will rise if the desired warehouse level rises, and vice versa.

    a) Simulate the performance of the system if the desired warehouse inventory is:

$$q_{2(t)} = \frac{3.33\Delta t(r_{1(t-1)} + r_{1(t)})}{2}$$

and

$$r_{3(t)} = \frac{q_{3(t-1)}}{2\Delta t}$$

and the original relationships describing the factory system remain the same.

    b) Simulate the performance of the system if the desired warehouse inventory is:

$$q_{2(t)} = \frac{7\Delta t(r_{1(t-1)} + r_{2(t)})}{2}$$

and

$$r_{3(t)} = \frac{q_{3(t-1)}}{2\Delta t}$$

c) Simulate the performance of the system if the desired warehouse inventory is:

$$q_{2(t)} = \frac{8\Delta t(r_{1(t-1)} + r_{1(t)})}{2}$$

and

$$r_{3(t)} = \frac{q_{3(t-1)}}{2\Delta t}$$

d) What conclusions can the managers make regarding the relationships of the actual warehouse inventory level at equilibrium to the desired inventory level?

11-11.

a) How can the relationships describing the performance of the factory system be changed so that the equilibrium of the actual warehouse inventory level is equal to the desired warehouse inventory level? Hint: the results of 11–10 may be helpful. Also, remember that $r_{1(t)}$, the order rate, has increased from 20 to 30. Assume:

$$r_{3(t)} = \frac{q_{3(t-1)}}{2\Delta t}$$

b) Simulate the performance of the factory system, using the decision rules you formulated in 11–11 (a). Assume:

$$r_{3(t)} = \frac{q_{3(t-1)}}{2\Delta t}$$

12

CONTROL

The formal organization is subject to many influences which may cause its performance to deviate markedly from expectations. These influences may come from its environment as in the case of a business firm suffering a decrease in sales due to increased advertising expenditures or price reductions by a competitor. Internal disturbances may arise from machine breakdowns, unwise decisions, or employee resistance to company policy. In any case, disturbances or deviations from planned behavior are a fact of life to the formal organization. Therefore, it is necessary for the design of formal organization to have features which allow it to monitor its own performance and to make corrections whenever that performance deviates significantly from expectations. When a system performs as planned, it is said to be under control. It is the purpose of this chapter to examine characteristics which affect the control of performance in formal organization.

Living systems are capable of self-regulation by a *natural* control device. Through this control device, the system maintains steady-state performance despite disturbances or changes in its environment. It detects changes in the environment, makes compensating adjustments, and holds behavior within desired limits. This control device is known as a *homeostat*. One example of this homeostatic quality is the ability of animals to maintain a relatively constant body temperature when exposed to changing climatic conditions. When body blood is cooled, certain centers in the brain are stimulated to ". . . 'turn on' heat producing mechanisms of the body, and the body temperature is monitored back to the center so that temperature is maintained at a constant level."[1] The body also displays homeostasis by maintaining a constant level of oxygen, carbon dioxide, solids, and fluids. The self-regulating characteristic was also evident in our discussions of higher level systems. The informal organization, for example, controls the behavior of its members through the establishment of norms and the application of sanctions against those who deviate from these unwritten rules of behavior.

DESIGN FOR CONTROL

There are many examples of systems that are *designed* to be self-regulating such as ship steering systems, guided missile systems, and antiaircraft fire control systems. Thermostatic control of room temperature is a classic example of a system that is designed to be self-regulating. Although the thermostat is a physical system, it displays some basic characteristics of formal organization. Therefore, we describe its operation and make references to the organizational processes of decision, communication, and action. First, the purpose of control is to make sure that a system performs according to expectations or to some standard. To accomplish this purpose, the control process involves at least the following four steps:

1. Establishment of a standard.
2. Measurement of performance.
3. Comparison of performance against standard.
4. Corrective action when performance deviates significantly from standard.

Now, let us see how the thermostat system illustrates the control process. Suppose we have the problem of designing a classroom. The objective of the design is to determine and create physical conditions that would provide a maximum opportunity for learning. Thus, we would need to make decisions on such matters as room size, number and arrangement of chairs, lighting, color scheme of walls, and room temperature. Obviously, room temperature is not

---

[1] Ludwig von Bertalanffy, "General System Theory," *General Systems*, Vol. 1 (1956), p. 5.

the only variable in the learning situation, and the design of a system to maintain temperature at desired levels would require coordination with other systems of the educational institution. In essence, the apparatus for temperature control is a subsystem.

Suppose it has been decided that the "ideal" room temperature is 72° F. This decision is the *standard of performance*, and it is communicated to the thermostat by a decision maker setting a dial on the instrument. As a mechanism for control, the thermostat *measures* the temperature of the room, and *compares* the measurement against the standard. When the actual temperature is less than standard, the thermostat initiates action or decides that action must be taken to restore the temperature to the desired level. This decision is then communicated to an action center (a furnace) which, in effect, is "turned on" by the message and proceeds to take *corrective action*. When the temperature of the classroom is returned to the desired level, the thermostat, which is constantly monitoring the temperature of the room, sends a "turn off" message to the action unit. This process goes on continually to maintain room temperature at a constant level.

Another classic example of a designed self-regulating system is the Watt governor, which was invented in 1788 by James Watt as a means of controlling the output of a steam engine. It is shown in Figure 12–1. The gears at the bottom of the vertical shaft link the governor to the output shaft of the engine. The arm at the top of the vertical shaft links the governor to the valve that controls the input of steam to the engine. When the engine starts, the governor begins to spin and the flyballs are forced outward and upward by centrifugal force. As the engine increases in speed, the flyballs rise higher, and their arms tend to close the valve which supplies the input to the engine. Thus, as the engine tends to exceed a given speed, the movement of the flyballs tends to close off the supply of energy, and this slows the engine down to the desired speed. Conversely, if the engine fails to attain the given speed, the inward and downward movement of the flyballs tends to open the input valve, supplying more energy, which increases the speed of the engine to the desired rate. In this manner, a constant rate of output is attained.

Each of the examples of automatic control provided above displays the property of feedback. In each case, the actual performance of the system is measured and compared against some standard. This information is then "fed back" to the system, and when

FIGURE 12-1
The Watt Governor

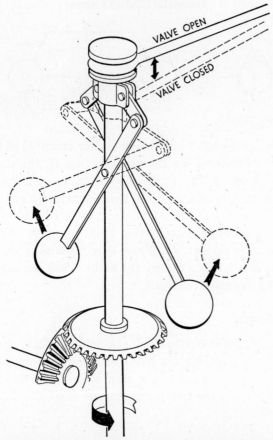

there is a deviation from standard, called "error," the system is actuated to take corrective action. This feature is essential to any automatic control system and it is called negative feedback. Negative feedback means that when the performance of a system departs from standard, the error reported back causes the system to reduce the error. The existing error, then, brings about its own reduction. According to Tustin, the basic scheme of automatic control may be shown as diagrammed in Figure 12-2.[2]

---

[2] Arnold Tustin, *The Mechanism of Economic Systems* (Cambridge, Mass.: Harvard University Press, 1953), pp. 6–7. Used by permission of Heinemann Educational Books, Ltd., London.

FIGURE 12-2

Basic Relationships in
Automatic Control Systems

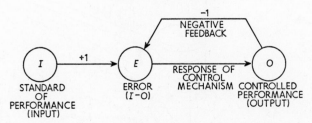

According to Figure 12-2 and to our earlier example of the thermostat, the dial setting on the thermostat, that is, the desired classroom temperature of 72° F., is the input, I, to the system. The actual classroom temperature is the output, O, of the system. The difference between input and output $(I-O)$ is the error, E. The error, E, has a positive contribution from input, I, and a negative contribution from output, O. When there is an error, the control mechanism is activated to reduce the error. Thus, automatic control is exercised by negative feedback.

Effect of Feedback

Another way of stating the feedback principle is to say that there is interdependence among the parts of organization. To illustrate, suppose we have two parts to a system A and B. The interdependent relation between the two parts may be shown as follows:

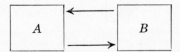

The diagram tells us that A affects B and B affects A. "When this circularity of action exists between the parts of a dynamic system, feedback may be said to be present."[3] According to our definition of a system as a set of interdependent elements, then, feedback is a basic characteristic of any system.

Let us now show a general expression for the feedback effect as developed by Tustin.[4] Suppose we have a simple system with a single feedback loop as shown in Figure 12-3.

---

[3] W. Ross Ashby, *An Introduction to Cybernetics* (New York: John Wiley & Sons, Inc., 1965), p. 53.

[4] Tustin, *op. cit.*, pp. 7-9.

FIGURE 12–3

Simple System with Single
Feedback

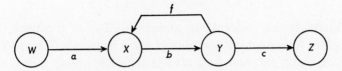

According to the diagram of Figure 12–3, there is a sequence of dependence between the successive quantities W, X, Y, and Z. The factors of dependence are shown as a, b, c, and f. Without feedback, the quantity X is determined by aW, but with the addition of feedback loop f, the quantity X is determined as follows:

$$X = aW + f Y \qquad (12\text{–}1)$$

The quantity Y is determined by:

$$Y = b X \qquad (12\text{–}2)$$

Substituting equation (12–2) for Y in equation (12–1), we obtain:

$$X = a W + f b X$$

Rearranging, we obtain:

$$\frac{X}{W} = a + f b \frac{X}{W}$$

$$\frac{X}{W} - f b \frac{X}{W} = a$$

$$\frac{X}{W} (1 - f b) = a$$

$$\frac{X}{W} = \frac{a}{1 - fb}$$

Letting $f b = k$, we have:

$$\frac{X}{W} = a \left(\frac{1}{1 - k} \right) \qquad (12\text{–}3)$$

As we said above: Without feedback, the quantity X is determined by aW, or $X/W = a$. However, with feedback, the ratio X/W is written as shown in equation (12–3). "The general rule for the effect of feedback k is therefore that the quantity to which it is applied, and therefore also all quantities in the sequence subsequent to this quantity are multiplied by $\left(\dfrac{1}{1-k}\right)$."[5]

To illustrate this general rule about the effect of feedback, Tustin applies it to introductory portions of Lord Keynes's *General Theory of Employment, Interest, and Money*. The Keynesian model as presented by Tustin is shown in Figure 12-4. According to this model, income Y is made up of money spent on the production of consumer

FIGURE 12-4

Dependence in the Keynesian Model

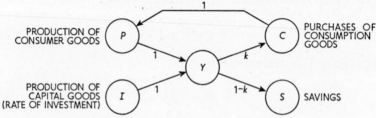

goods P, and on the production of capital goods I (that is, machinery, buildings, and so on). These incomes are used to purchase consumer goods C, or are saved S. P and I may be considered as inputs to Y, and C and S as outputs from national income Y. To exercise control in this system, that is, to maintain a balance between input and output, there must be feedback between C and P. The amount spent on consumption is a fraction k of Y and the remaining fraction $(1-k)$ of Y is savings. Thus:

$$C = k\,Y \qquad (12\text{-}4)$$

and

$$S = (1 - k)\,Y \qquad (12\text{-}5)$$

Since the production of consumption goods will be consumed over time, the model requires that $P = C$ and the feedback loop from C to P have a factor of unity. Thus, k is the feedback coefficient, which means that any variation in the sequence Y, C, P, Y, is "fed back" k

[5] *Ibid.*, p. 8.

times the initial variation. It follows then, that the sequence show-ing the relationship between investment I, and income Y, has the form of equation (12–3) or

$$\frac{Y}{I} = 1 \left(\frac{1}{1 - k}\right)$$

and

$$Y = I \left(\frac{1}{1 - k}\right) \tag{12-6}$$

The factor $\left(\dfrac{1}{1-k}\right)$ is known as the "investment multiplier" and is multiplied times an increment in investment to show the effect of increased investment on national income.

Rearranging equation (12–6), we obtain:

$$I = (1 - k)\, Y \tag{12-7}$$

This equation for investment is identical to that for savings, equa-tion (12–5). Thus, we derive Keynes's proposition that savings equal investment or $S = I$.

POSITIVE AND NEGATIVE FEEDBACK

When a variation caused by disturbance is carried through the feedback loop and is perpetuated or amplified, *positive feedback* is said to exist. When the disturbance carried through the feedback loop is counteracted so that the variation from steady state is diminished or damped, *negative feedback* exists.

Positive feedback loops are not undesirable. It is a legitimate purpose of a formal organization to amplify disturbance or varia-tions in the system. A physical example of desirable positive feedback is a power-assisted brake on an automobile. ". . . power-assisted brakes use machinery which detects the small manual move-ments made, and enlarges them until the force applied is capable of stopping a vehicle in motion."[6] An organization which tries to increase the productivity of its members and a business organization which tries to stimulate sales growth are other examples of legiti-mate uses of positive feedback.

---

[6] Stafford Beer, *Cybernetics and Management* (New York: John Wiley & Sons, Inc., 1964), p. 30.

Delays

Even with negative feedback, it is possible for a system to display unstable behavior. Recall that negative feedback exists when forces in the system tend to counteract variations and return the system to a steady state. However, when *delays* exist in the system, a variation by one of the quantities in the feedback loop may be perpetuated; that is, the behavior of the system will display continuous oscillation instead of settling down. Tustin states the rule as follows: "Thus any system with negative feedback will maintain a continuous oscillation when disturbed if (*a*) the time delays in response at some frequency add up to half a period of oscillation, and (*b*) the feedback effect is sufficiently large at this frequency.[7] In general, for linear systems, the effect of feedback with delays may be stated as follows:

In a linear system, that is, roughly speaking, a system in which effects are directly proportional to causes, there are three possible results. If the feedback, at the frequency for which the lag is half a period, is equal in strength to the original oscillation, there will be a continuous steady oscillation which sustains itself. If the feedback is greater than the oscillation at that frequency, the oscillation builds up; if it is smaller, the oscillation will die away.[8]

Tustin illustrates these rules by diagrams and explanation as shown in Figure 12–5.

Now let us see how negative and positive feedback loops are coupled in a business situation.

Coupled Feedback Loops

The following model was also developed by Professor Jay W. Forrester.[9] In this case, he talks about behavior of customers and the feedback of their attitudes and needs to decision-making centers in a business firm. A company has many linkages with the marketplace.

---

[7] Arnold Tustin, "Feedback" in a *Scientific American* book, *Automatic Control* (New York: Simon & Schuster, Inc., 1955), p. 16. Copyright © 1952 by Scientific American, Inc. All rights reserved.

[8] *Ibid.*, pp. 16–17.

[9] Jay W. Forrester, *Industrial Dynamics* (Cambridge, Mass.: M.I.T. Press, Massachusetts Institute of Technology, 1961). In this section, we draw from: Jay W. Forrester, "Modeling of Market and Company Interactions," *Proceedings: Marketing and Economic Development* (Chicago: American Marketing Association, September, 1965), pp. 353–64.

FIGURE 12–5

Oscillations in Feedback Systems

Oscillation is inherent in all feedback systems. The drawing at top shows that when a regular oscillation is introduced into the input of a system (*lighter line*), it is followed somewhat later by a corresponding variation in the output of the system. The dotted rectangle indicates the lag that will prevail between equivalent phases of the input and the output curves. In the three drawings below, the input is assumed to be a feedback from the output. The first of the three shows a state of stable oscillation, which results when the feedback signal (*thinner line*) is opposite in phase to the disturbance of a system and calls for corrective action equal in amplitude. The oscillation is damped and may be made to disappear when, as in the next drawing, the feedback is less than the output. Unstable oscillation is caused by a feedback signal that induces corrective action greater than the error and thus amplifies the original disturbance.

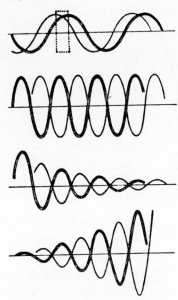

In keeping with our earlier discussions, the idea of feedback loops is used to describe these linkages. Outputs of the company include a product which has a *price*, a level of *quality*, and a *suitability* to market needs. Output also includes *delivery delays* which reflect the company's ability to meet incoming orders, and *sales effort* which, of course, reflects efforts to stimulate sales. Feedback to the company includes the flow of *orders* and *payments* from customers. Information about *customer attitudes* toward price, quality, delivery delay, and product suitability, is also fed back to the company. Thus, as the company produces a product at a particular price and quality level, customers develop attitudes about these attributes of the product, and when this information is fed back to management, it will affect future decisions about price and quality. Linkages between the company and the market are shown in Figure 12–6.

There are also interconnections among the feedback loops. Suppose, for example, that price is reduced; this may reduce revenues or payments to the firm, which may cause it to spend less on quality. Lower quality in turn, may cause a decrease in customer orders. It is possible, of course, for a price reduction to stimulate greater

FIGURE 12-6

Company-Market Linkages

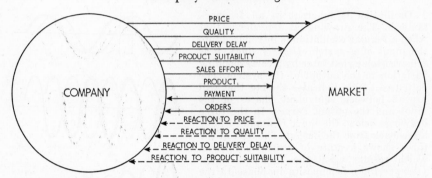

SOURCE: Jay W. Forrester, "Modeling of Market and Company Interactions," *Proceedings: Marketing and Economic Development* (Chicago: American Marketing Association, September, 1965), p. 355.

sales, and, therefore, amplify the effect through the system. Given these linkages between a business firm and the market, it is fruitful to think in terms of positive or negative feedback effects.

Forrester illustrates these effects by examining the possible growth and decline of a new product. In his illustration of positive feedback, he uses the elements of sales effectiveness, sales rate, revenue, sales budget, and sales effort. Positive feedback is illustrated in Figure 12-7. Sales effectiveness reflects market acceptance of the product and is measured by the ease by which the product can be sold. Sales effort at some level of sales effectiveness produces a sales rate which, in turn, produces sales revenue. Part of the sales revenue is used in the sales budget to pay for future sales effort. Now suppose sales effectiveness is at a relatively high level, ". . . then a given sales effort will produce a sales rate and budget higher than necessary to sustain the initial sales effort. Under these favorable circumstances, sales effort leads to a growing sales budget which then supports an increasing sales effort."[10] Amplification or the positive feedback effect continues until one of the quantities in the closed sequence changes, as, for example, when sales effectiveness changes to reflect diminishing consumer acceptance of the product. Positive feedback may also amplify, decline, or decay. For example, when sales effectiveness is low, sales effort will produce a sales rate and revenue that does not justify the amount allocated in the budget to support that effort. Thereafter, a reduc-

---

[10] Forrester, *op. cit.*, p. 356.

FIGURE 12-7

Positive Feedback in Sales Growth

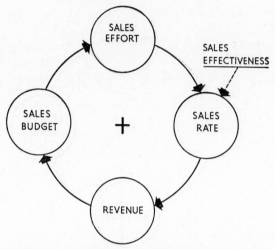

SOURCE: Jay W. Forrester, "Modeling of Market and Company Interactions," *Proceedings: Marketing and Economic Development* (Chicago: American Marketing Association, September, 1965), p. 357.

tion in the budget and sales effort will reduce sales, causing further reductions in budget, sales effort, and sales.

Let us see how negative feedback causes the system to stabilize. In his illustration of a negative feedback loop, Forrester relates the sales rate, order backlog, delivery delay, and sales effectiveness as shown in Figure 12–8. In this part of the model, it is assumed that sales effort remains constant and is more than adequate to support the sales rate. It is assumed also that production capacity is fixed. "Under these circumstances, sales rate will exceed production capacity and the order backlog will increase. The increase in the order backlog will continue until the resulting increase in delivery delay becomes sufficient that some customers become unwilling to wait for delivery."[11] Customer dissatisfaction with delivery delays will make the product less salable and cause sales effectiveness to decline. Sales effectiveness will decline until the sales rate falls to the production capacity. The system will stabilize as long as delays are relatively short.

Delays exist at each point in the loop, however, and as they become excessive, they cause instability. As the delivery delay, for example, becomes longer, customer dissatisfaction does not show

---

[11] *Ibid.*, p. 357.

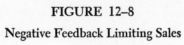

FIGURE 12–8

Negative Feedback Limiting Sales

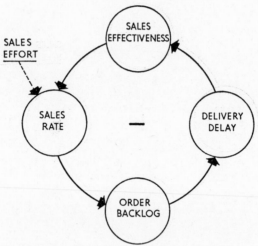

SOURCE: "Modeling of Market and Company Interactions,"
Proceedings: Marketing and Economic Development (Chicago:
American Marketing Association, September, 1965), p. 358.

immediately in the sales rate because many orders are already
committed to the company. It takes some time before discrepancies
between the sales rate and capacity are recognized as backlog. Also,
delivery delay is extended because of increases in the order backlog.
An increase in the sales rate, then, may go unnoticed until delivery
delay and order backlog become excessive. By this time, customers
express their dissatisfaction by buying less, causing the sales rate
to decline below production capacity. Delays cause the system to
overcorrect. Instead of returning the sales rate to the production
capabilities of the company, as would be expected from negative
feedback, the sales rate goes below production capacity. As the sales
rate goes below production capacity, order backlog and delivery
delay also decrease unduly. When sales rise again, the system swings
in the opposite direction and thereafter may oscillate perpetually.

Formal organizations have both negative and positive feedback
loops. Furthermore, these loops are usually interdependent. In the
Forrester model, this interdependence means that the loops are
coupled as shown in Figure 12–9. The behavior of a system with
coupled feedback loops may be simulated as shown in Figure 12–10.
With limited production capacity, the positive feedback loop will
amplify an increased sales rate until the production capacity limit

FIGURE 12–9

Coupled Negative and Positive Feedback Loops

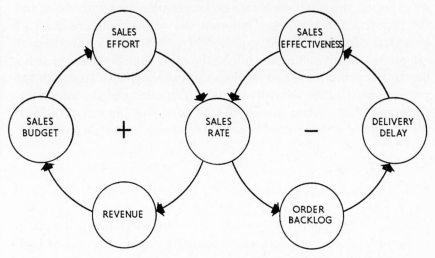

SOURCE: Jay W, Forrester. "Modeling of Market and Company Interactions," *Proceedings: Marketing and Economic Development* (Chicago: American Marketing Association, September, 1965), p. 361.

FIGURE 12–10

Growth and Stagnation in Sales

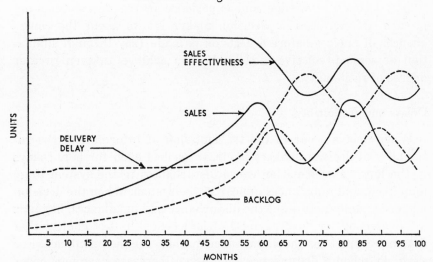

SOURCE: Jay W. Forrester, "Modeling of Market and Company Interactions," *Proceedings: Marketing and Economic Development* (Chicago: American Marketing Association, September, 1965), p. 361.

is reached. In the simulation of Figure 12–10, the sales rate grows until the 60th month, when the production capacity limit is reached. At capacity, the production rate no longer increases with sales, and the negative feedback loop becomes the primary determinant of behavior. "During the early period of growth, sales effectiveness remains constant and high while at the same time the delivery delay remains constant and low. As the sales rate begins to approach the production capacity, the delivery delay increases and the sales effectiveness falls."[12] After month 60, the delays in the negative feedback loop cause the system to oscillate rather than settle down.

Rationality

In an organizational context, feedback is essential because it provides information which helps the decision maker to approach rationality. We defined *rationality* as the ability to formulate alternatives and to make choices which optimize results. Recall also that, in Chapter 11, we listed "the inability to know about the consequences of choices" as a limitation on rationality. A feedback connection (by organizational design) between performance and decision centers helps to reduce this limitation by providing a means whereby decision makers may gain knowledge about the consequences of past decisions. While knowledge of the consequences of past decisions may not be the best basis for future decisions, it provides some knowledge and experience in the decision-making process. Of course, if a decision maker knows about the consequences of choices before a decision is made (say through simulation or some predictive model), he can achieve an even greater degree of rationality.

Delays and Rationality

When delays occur in the transmission of information, the rationality of decision makers is circumscribed even further. Delays in the flow of information cause disturbances in the system to go unnoticed, and imbalances appear in the system. When the decision maker is finally notified of the disturbance and imbalances, he tends to "overshoot" or "overcorrect." His decisions reflect choices that not only correct for the disturbance but also for the imbalance. For example, when a disturbance such as an increased customer order rate goes unnoticed, an imbalance occurs because inventories de-

---

[12] *Ibid.*, p. 360.

crease. The decision maker tries to make adjustments not only to compensate for greater sales but also to restore inventories to desired levels. Thus, his decisions tend to amplify rather than dampen the effect of the disturbance. This condition can be illustrated by using the simulation model of the last chapter. Equation (11–7), the material input rate, was stated as follows:

Material Input Rate

$$r_{2(t)} = 20 \cdot \frac{q_{2(t-1)}}{q_{4(t-1)}} \quad \text{if} \quad 20 \cdot \frac{q_{2(t-1)}}{q_{4(t-1)}} \leq 50$$

or

$$r_{2(t)} = 50 \quad \text{if} \quad 20 \cdot \frac{q_{2(t-1)}}{q_{4(t-1)}} \geq 50$$

The material input rate during week t is governed by the ratio of desired to actual inventory level at the end of week $(t-1)$, according to this equation. Clough calls this decision rule a "fast" replenishment because it is based on the previous week's inventory levels. In other words, there is practically no delay (one week) between the time that decision makers find out about the state of the system (in this case, compare the actual inventory level with the desired inventory level), and when necessary, make decisions that involve corrective action (that is, adjust the flow rate), and the time that the decision is implemented. Through simulation of behavior under this "fast" decision rule, we found that the system was able to adjust and stabilize after a disturbance caused by an increase in the customer order rate. The system's behavior is shown in Figure 11–6, page 355.

Now what would happen if there were a delay in the communication channels. Suppose that a three-week delay existed between the time that the state of the system changed and the time that adjustments were made in the material input rate. Equation (11–7) would now be written as equation (12–9):

Material Input Rate

$$r_{2(t)} = 20 \cdot \frac{q_{2(t-4)}}{q_{4(t-4)}} \quad \text{if} \quad 20 \cdot \frac{q_{2(t-4)}}{q_{4(t-4)}} \leq 50$$

or

$$r_{2(t)} = 50 \quad \text{if} \quad 20 \cdot \frac{q_{2(t-4)}}{q_{4(t-4)}} \geq 50 \qquad (12\text{–}9)$$

According to the decision rule of equation (12-9), the material input rate during week t is the ratio of the desired inventory level to the actual inventory level at the end of week $(t-4)$ times 20 units per week. Thus, three weeks pass before the material input rate is adjusted to reflect a change in the state of the system. As before, the system is constrained by the supplier's capacity of 50 units per week.

This "delayed" decision rule has a dramatic effect on the behavior of the system. The results of the calculations for the simulation

TABLE 12-1
Simulation of System's Behavior

Week t	Rate $r_{1(t)}$	Rate $r_{2(t)}$	Rate $r_{3(t)}$	Rate $r_{4(t)}$	Level $q_{1(t)}$	Level $q_{2(t)}$	Level $q_{3(t)}$	Level $q_{4(t)}$
11	20	20	20	20	20	100	80	100
12	20	20	20	20	20	100	80	100
13	30	20	20	20	30	105	80	100
14	30	20	20	30	30	110	80	90
15	30	20	20	30	30	115	80	80
16	30	20	20	30	30	120	80	70
17	30	21	20	30	30	125	81	60
18	30	24	20	30	30	130	85	50
19	30	29	21	30	30	135	93	41
20	30	34	23	30	30	140	102	34
21	30	42	26	30	30	145	118	26
22	30	50	30	26	34	150	138	30
23	30	50	35	30	34	150	153	35
24	30	50	38	34	30	150	165	39
25	30	50	41	30	30	150	174	50
26	30	50	44	30	30	150	180	64
27	30	50	45	30	30	150	185	79
28	30	50	46	30	30	150	189	85
29	30	50	47	30	30	150	192	102
30	30	47	48	30	30	150	192	120
31	30	38	48	30	30	150	181	138
32	30	35	45	30	30	150	171	153
33	30	29	43	30	30	150	157	166
34	30	25	39	30	30	150	143	175
35	30	22	36	30	30	150	129	181
36	30	20	32	30	30	150	117	183
37	30	18	29	30	30	150	106	182
38	30	17	27	30	30	150	96	179
39	30	17	24	30	30	150	89	173
40	30	16	22	30	30	150	83	165
41	30	16	21	30	30	150	78	156
42	30	17	20	30	30	150	75	146
43	30	17	19	30	30	150	73	135
44	30	18	18	30	30	150	73	123
45	30	19	18	30	30	150	74	111

SOURCE: Donald J. Clough, *Concepts in Management Science* (Englewood Cliffs, N.J.: Prentice-Hall, Inc., 1963), p. 381. © 1963. Reprinted by permission of Prentice-Hall, Inc.

are shown in Table 12–1. The revised model assumes the same initial equilibrium conditions and the same equations, except equation (11–7), used in calculating the values for Table 11–1. Under the "fast" rule, the system was able to dampen oscillations caused by the change in the customer order rate. Under the "delayed" rule, however, the system amplifies and perpetuates the oscillations caused by the disturbance, shown in Figure 12–11. This condition, as we have noted above, illustrates how the system tends to overcorrect.

FIGURE 12–11

System Responses to a Change in Order Rate

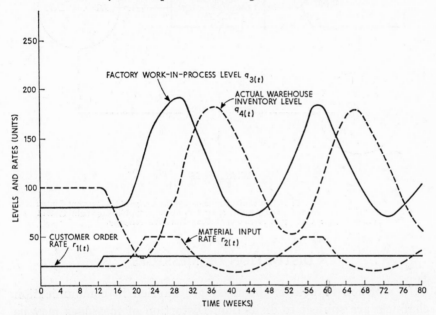

SOURCE: Donald J. Clough, *Concepts in Management Science* (Englewood Cliffs, N.J.: Prentice-Hall, Inc., 1963), p. 382. © 1963. Reprinted by permission of Prentice-Hall, Inc.

Notice that the disturbance in $r_{1(t)}$ occurs in period 13 but, the material input rate, $r_{2(t)}$, does not change until period 17, three weeks after the disturbance. Meanwhile, the desired inventory level, $q_{2(t)}$, is increasing and the actual warehouse inventory level, $q_{4(t)}$, is decreasing. Thus, the decision rule is affected not only by the disturbance or change in $r_{1(t)}$ but also by the imbalance between $q_{2(t)}$ and $q_{4(t)}$. As a result, the system behaves as shown in Figure 12–11.

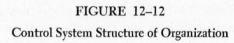

FIGURE 12–12

Control System Structure of Organization

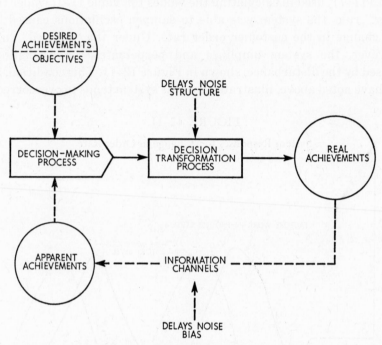

SOURCE: Edward B.Roberts, "Industrial Dynamics and the Design of Management Control Systems," in Bonini, Jaedicke, and Wagner, *Management Controls*, p. 103. Copyright © 1964 by McGraw-Hill, Inc. Used by permission of McGraw-Hill Book Company.

DISTORTION OF MESSAGES

In addition to delays, the messages carried in communication channels are subject to distortion. Distortion of messages may be intentional, such as the case when statistical data are averaged or smoothed to make the system less sensitive to short-term fluctuations. An example of unintentional distortion is when a subordinate reports only the "good" news to his superior. He is reluctant to report "bad" news, because it might have an unfavorable effect on the boss's opinion of his ability. While the distortion by the subordinate may be intentional, it is unintentional on the part of the system. In any event, distorted information tends to limit the rationality of decision makers. If decision makers base their decisions on delayed and distorted information supplied to them through communication channels, then the assumptions upon which they base their decisions will have little relation to fact. Roberts portrays the problem as shown in Figure 12–12.[13] According to this diagram, decisions are transformed into action through processes that are affected by distortions and delays. As a result, actual performance is often different from desired performance—the problem of control. Furthermore, the apparent performance reported back to decision makers through feedback loops is different from the actual performance of the system for the same reasons of

FIGURE 12–13

Theoretical Quality Control System

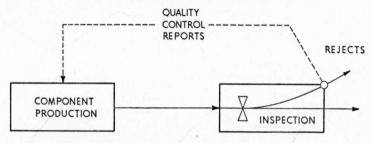

SOURCE: Edward B. Roberts, "Industrial Dynamics and the Design of Management Control Systems," in Bonini, Jaedicke, and Wagner. *Management Controls*, p. 121. Copyright © 1964 by McGraw-Hill, Inc. Used by permission of McGraw-Hill Book Company.

distortion and delay. Roberts points out that the "real" system of relationships is often disguised ". . . because of its numerous sources of noise or random behavior and due to its often lengthy time delays between cause and effect."[14] Roberts uses a quality control system, shown in Figure 12–13, to illustrate this point. Of course, the purpose of this system is to control the quality of manufacturing output. The diagram of Figure 12–13, according to Roberts, is the feedback system that is *apparent* to the designers of quality control systems. The parts produced by the production process of this system are inspected for defects, and rejects are either discarded or reworked. The performance of the system is measured, recorded, and reported back to production. When it has been determined through statistical quality control methods that the system is "out of control," corrective action is taken.

---

[13] Edward B. Roberts, "Industrial Dynamics and the Design of Management Control Systems," in Charles P. Bonini, Robert K. Jaedicke, and Harvey M. Wagner, *Management Controls*, pp. 102–26. Copyright © 1964 by McGraw-Hill, Inc. Used by permission of McGraw-Hill Book Company.

[14] *Ibid.*, p. 102.

Roberts questions the effectiveness of such quality control systems. There is good reason to question the effectiveness of such systems, considering the performance curves of what Roberts calls "a typical system." The curves are shown in Figure 12–14. Assuming that the swings in the reject rate are wide enough to indicate that the system is "out of control," corrective action may take the form of machine adjustments which cause the production rate to

FIGURE 12–14

Quality Control System Performance

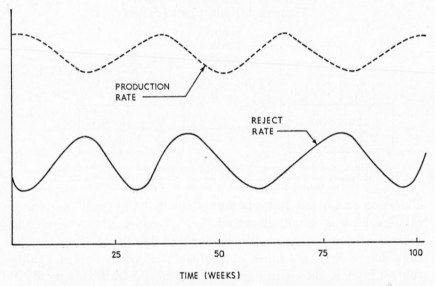

TIME (WEEKS)

SOURCE: Edward B. Roberts, "Industrial Dynamics and the Design of Management Control Systems," in Bonini, Jaedicke, and Wagner, *Management Controls*, p. 121. Copyright © 1964 by McGraw-Hill, Inc. Used by permission of McGraw-Hill Book Company.

fall temporarily. The periodicity of the reject rate suggests to the manager that quality is subject to seasonal fluctuations, but he is unable to validate this assumption.

Roberts explains that a better understanding of the system's behavior can be obtained through simulation. Through computer simulation of such a system, a two-year run of results was produced. Throughout the run, production quality was held constant. He concludes that if the same results could be produced while holding production quality constant, the performance of the system (the oscillations of the reject rate and production) must be attributable to something other than a seasonal fluctuation in quality—perhaps a behavioral influence.

A more complete analysis which would include the *total* factory system reveals behavorial influences. The more complete system is shown in Figure 12–15. According to the flows shown in this diagram, parts are produced and inspected. Rejects are discarded, and acceptable parts are forwarded for further processing to the assembly operation. After final assembly, the finished product (say, electronic tubes) is given a final test. If the final test produces too many failures, the assembly manager complains to the quality con-

FIGURE 12–15

More Complete Representation of Quality Control System

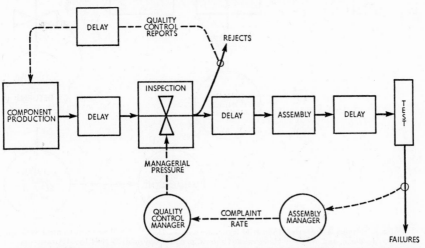

SOURCE: Edward B. Roberts, "Industrial Dynamics and the Design of Management Control Systems," in Bonini, Jaedicke, and Wagner, *Management Controls*, p. 122. Copyright © 1964 by McGraw-Hill, Inc. Used by permission of McGraw-Hill Book Company.

trol manager. As these complaints mount, the quality control manager puts pressure on inspectors and tells them to be more careful. As a result of this pressure, the inspectors reject far more parts. They now reject any part of questionable quality, and these include parts that are actually acceptable. As the reject rate increases, there are fewer failures of the final assembled product, but now the production rate decreases because there are fewer parts available for final assembly. The assembly manager, who is now satisfied with quality, starts to complain about the poor production rate. As a result, inspectors become less careful and tend to loosen inspection standards. The reject rate declines, the production rate increases, and the assembly manager renews his complaints about quality. The cycle repeats over and over again, and with normal

FIGURE 12–16

Total Quality Control System

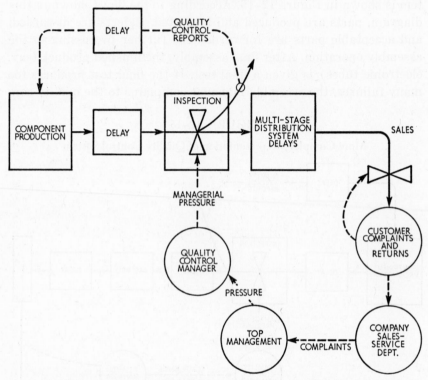

SOURCE: Edward B. Roberts, "Industrial Dynamics and the Design of Management Control Systems," in Bonini, Jaedicke, and Wagner, *Management Controls*, p. 124. Copyright © 1964 by McGraw-Hill, Inc. Used by permission of McGraw-Hill Book Company.

delays, the performance of the system suggests seasonal fluctuations in quality. "Thus, a system intended to assure control of product quality actually creates serious fluctuations of rejects, component production, and tube failures, all attributed to unknown factors "out of our control.'"[15]

When the definition of the system is expanded to include customers and the channels of distribution, such as the sales department, wholesalers and retailers, the situation becomes more serious because of the delays and influences introduced into the problem by these elements. The expanded diagram is shown in Figure 12–16. It may take a long time before customer complaints and returns are reflected in lower sales (customers may use the product for some

---

[15] *Ibid.*, p. 123.

time before noticing its defects) and still longer before top management recognizes customer dissatisfactions and applies pressure to the quality control manager.

One of the points of this discussion is that quality control involves more than the production facility and inspectors. Also, there are more feedback loops than the statistical reporting system. Furthermore, there are behavioral variables that enter into the quality control system. *For effective control, then, it is important to design the system to include all important elements and the vital communication channels so that reliable information is "fed back" to decision centers and decisions specifying corrective action are reliably "fed to" appropriate action centers.* This conclusion is not just applicable to quality control systems but to any activity of the organization. It means that the design must incorporate many elements and feedback loops, even though they cross departmental lines and the boundary of the organization. In the quality control illustration, for example, a definition of the total system included not only the production facility and inspection department but final assembly, the sales department, distribution channels, top management, and customers.

DISCONTINUITIES IN THE SYSTEM

There are many reasons for delays of matter, energy, and information through the system. One reason for delays is discontinuities in the system. In the flow of information, for example, components connected by channels of communication may have different capacities for processing messages. The receiver may not have the capacity to process messages at the rate that is commensurate with the arrival rate. At the other end of the channel, the sender may not have the capacity to send messages as quickly as the receiver is able to process them. Also, the receiver's processing time and the times that messages arrive may occur on a random basis, causing either the receiver or the messages to wait. In any event, discontinuities cause delays in the flow of information through the system.

One way of solving the problem of discontinuities is to add more components to the system. By adding components, processing becomes more continuous and delays are reduced. In terms of the costs involved, the addition of components increases the costs of components while it decreases the costs of delays. In the next chapter, we present an analytical model, the waiting line model, which allows us to determine the optimum number of components for a system faced with the ever present delay problem. In Chapter 14, a model is presented which allows us to determine the optimum number of components in an information system.

SUMMARY

Formal organization must have features which allow it to control its own performance. The formal organization is subject to many influences which cause actual performance to deviate markedly from desired performance. Therefore, it is necessary to monitor and correct performance when it differs significantly from standards.

The control process involves (1) establishment of performance standards, (2) measurement of performance, (3) comparison of actual performance against standards, and (4) corrective action when performance deviates significantly from standards.

Feedback loops are essential to the control process. They are the communication channels which carry information about disturbances in the system. When a disturbance reported through feedback loops is amplified, positive feedback is said to exist. When a disturbance is counteracted so that deviations from standard are damped or diminished, negative feedback is said to exist. Both positive and negative feedback loops exist in an organization and are coupled or interdependent.

Distortion, bias, and noise in a system cause erroneous information to be carried in feedback loops. In designing a system, it is necessary to provide information channels to decision makers from proper sources of information and from decision centers to proper action centers so that control can be exercised.

DISCUSSION QUESTIONS AND PROBLEMS

12–1. How do delays and distortions of feedback messages affect rationality in decision making?

12–2. Why does formal organization, which is composed of human beings capable of self-regulation, require a design for control?

12–3. Under what conditions should positive feedback loops be designed in the formal organization?

12–4. Is it possible for feedback to have an adverse effect on performance and achievement. Explain.

12–5. Enumerate and discuss the possible design features to overcome the feedback problems of delays and distortion.

12–6. Develop an organizational design for cost control. Discuss the possible behavioral problems of such a system. Also consider the conflicts with efforts to maintain quantity and quality control.

12–7. Develop a control system that would involve several performance variables such as quantity, cost, quality, and time.

Assume for the following simulations that

$$
\begin{array}{ll}
r_{1(t)} = 20 & q_{1(t)} = 20 \\
r_{2(t)} = 20 & q_{2(t)} = 100 \\
r_{3(t)} = 20 & q_{3(t)} = 80 \\
r_{4(t)} = 20 & q_{4(t)} = 100
\end{array}
$$

for weeks 9, 10, 11, and 12. Begin the simulation at the end of the 13th week when the order rate rises to 30 units per week.

Base your equation changes on the following relationships:

$$r_{1(t)} = 30 \text{ when } t > 12$$

$$r_{2(t)} = 20 \cdot \frac{q_{2(t-4)}}{q_{4(t-4)}} \text{ if } 20 \cdot \frac{q_{2(t-4)}}{q_{4(t-4)}} \leq 50, \text{ or}$$

$$r_{2(t)} = 50 \text{ if } 20 \cdot \frac{q_{2(t-4)}}{q_{4(t-4)}} \geq 50$$

$$r_{3(t)} = \frac{q_{3(t-1)}}{2\Delta t}$$

$$r_{4(t)} = \frac{q_{1(t-1)}}{\Delta t} \text{ if } \frac{q_{1(t-1)}}{\Delta t} \leq \frac{q_{4(t-1)}}{\Delta t} \leq 35, \text{ or}$$

$$r_{4(t)} = \frac{q_{4(t-1)}}{\Delta t} \text{ if } \frac{q_{4(t-1)}}{\Delta t} \leq \frac{q_{1(t-1)}}{\Delta t} \leq 35, \text{ or}$$

$$r_{4(t)} = 35 \text{ if } \frac{q_{1(t-1)}}{\Delta t}, \frac{q_{4(t-1)}}{\Delta t} \geq 35$$

$$q_{1(t)} = q_{1(t-1)} + \Delta t(r_{1(t)} - r_{4(t)})$$

$$q_{2(t)} = \frac{5\Delta t}{10}(r_{1(t-9)} + r_{1(t-8)} + \ldots + r_{1(t)})$$

$$q_{3(t)} = q_{3(t-1)} + \Delta t(r_{2(t)} - r_{3(t)})$$

$$q_{4(t)} = q_{4(t-1)} + \Delta t(r_{3(t)} - r_{4(t)})$$

12–8. The managers of the factory system of Chapter 12 reasoned that if all rates were based on the same amount of delay $(t - 4)$, the factory system would stabilize. More specifically, the managers hoped that the actual inventory level would cease to fluctuate and would stabilize at one level.

Thus, management introduced uniform delays into the system through the rate changes. The resultant system relationships are:

$$r_{1(t)} = 30 \text{ when } t > 12$$

$$r_{2(t)} = 20 \cdot \frac{q_{2(t-4)}}{q_{4(t-4)}} \text{ if } 20 \cdot \frac{q_{2(t-4)}}{q_{4(t-4)}} \leq 50, \text{ or}$$

$$r_{2(t)} = 50 \text{ if } 20 \cdot \frac{q_{2(t-4)}}{q_{4(t-4)}} \geq 50$$

$$r_{3(t)} = \frac{q_{3(t-4)}}{2\Delta t}$$

$$r_{4(t)} = \frac{q_{1(t-4)}}{\Delta t} \text{ if } \frac{q_{1(t-4)}}{\Delta t} \leq \frac{q_{4(t-4)}}{\Delta t} \leq 35, \text{ or}$$

$$r_{4(t)} = \frac{q_{4(t-4)}}{\Delta t} \text{ if } \frac{q_{4(t-4)}}{\Delta t} \leq \frac{q_{1(t-4)}}{\Delta t} \leq 35, \text{ or}$$

$$r_{4(t)} = 35 \text{ if } \frac{q_{1(t-4)}}{\Delta t}, \frac{q_{4(t-4)}}{\Delta t} \geq 35$$

Management reasoned that the level relationships would not have to be changed.

a) Simulate the performance of the factory system.

b) Where has management erred?

12-9. What can management do in terms of changing the system's relationships in order to stabilize the performance of the factory system? It is impossible to reduce the delays.

a) Simulate the performance of the system, using relationships which you have developed.

b) If the actual warehouse inventory level, $q_{4(t)}$, stabilizes, does it stabilize at the desired level?

12-10. How can management change the relationships of the factory system so that the equilibrium of the actual warehouse inventory, $q_{4(t)}$, is equal to the desired warehouse inventory level, $q_{2(t)}$? Assume that the delays are impossible to reduce. Simulate performance of the system, using the relationships you have developed. Hint: Refer to problem 11-11.

13

WAITING LINE THEORY AND ORGANIZATIONAL DESIGN

There are many reasons for delays in an organization. A *delay* occurs anytime that the flow of matter, energy, or information is interrupted. The main reason for delays is the fact that throughputs of the system are processed and processing takes time. Consider, for example, the flow of material through a factory system. The very fact that material has to be transformed from one state to another interrupts its flow through an organization. This kind of delay hardly seems worth mentioning, because without the delays associated with processing times, there would be no need to direct the flow of matter, energy, and information through an organization. However, suppose that delays could be decreased by adding components to the system, that is, by increasing the number of jobs or adding more men to the task. Then, the problem is to determine how many components should be added. It is a problem because output does not necessarily increase (or delays do not decrease) indefinitely with increases in the number of components. In this regard, recall the familiar "law of diminishing returns," which states:

An increase in some inputs relative to other fixed inputs will cause total output to increase; but after a point the extra output resulting from the same additions of extra inputs is likely to become less and less. This falling off of extra returns is a consequence of the fact that the new

389

"doses" of the varying resources have less and less of the fixed resources to work with.[1]

Similarly, we show in Chapter 14 that an increase in the number of communication channels does not continually improve the chances of messages passing correctly through the system. After a point, the addition of channels adds less and less to the chances of successful communication. It seems then, that there is some optimum point—a point at which the benefits attained by adding components are exceeded by the added costs. In this chapter, a model is examined that allows us to determine the optimum number of components in a system. First, however, we need to be more specific about the problem.

DISCONTINUITIES IN THE SYSTEM

Another aspect of the problem is revealed when delays are examined in terms of discontinuities in a system. In the flow of information, for example, components connected by channels of communication may have different capacities for processing messages. The receiver may not have the capacity to process messages at a rate that is commensurate with the arrival rate. A discontinuity exists in this case because the sender has a greater capacity or simply sends messages quicker than the receiver is able to process them. In any event, messages have to wait or the flow of information is interrupted not only because of processing times but also because of the time spent in line waiting for service. Our concern in this chapter is with this aspect of the problem, that is, the waiting line problem.

By adding components at the receiving end, the time that messages have to wait in line for processing tends to be reduced. In terms of the costs involved, the addition of components increases the cost of components while it decreases the costs incurred as a result of interruptions in the flow of information or the costs involved in requiring messages to wait. Thus, there are opposing costs to the waiting line problem. In general, the objective of the waiting line model is to determine the number of components that minimizes the sum of these costs.

---

[1] Paul A. Samuelson, *Economics* (6th ed.; New York: McGraw-Hill Book Co., 1964), p. 27.

Another type of discontinuity occurs in a system when: (1) items in a flow arrive at a subsystem for processing at irregular time intervals, and/or; (2) the subsystem providing service has variable service time. To illustrate this variability, let us describe a flow that involves workers going to a stock room to withdraw supplies. In this case, irregular intervals between arrivals occur when, for example, there are long periods of time in which no workers arrive to withdraw supplies and other times when several workers arrive almost simultaneously. This same variability is likely to occur in the service provided by men working in the stock room. Some requests for supplies can be filled very quickly while others may take longer periods of time. If a worker arrives at the stock room for supplies and the clerk is busy, the worker must wait. At other times, when no workers are calling for service, the clerk is idle. Again, we have the problem of determining how many components or clerks should be employed in the system. As before, the addition of components increases the total cost of the components while it reduces the costs associated with workers spending their time idly waiting in line.

It is likely, too, that these events occur on a random basis, that is, we would be unable to predict exactly the times of arrival and service. Arnold Kaufmann defines random behavior as follows: "An event appears to occur in a random manner (or by chance) if the causes for its occurrence are independent and so numerous that it is impossible for us to know them all and to single out the laws that govern the occurrence of the event."[2] Throughout our discussion the assumption is made that events occur in a random manner but follow a statistical distribution from which we can determine the probability of their occurrence.

The problem of delays is the subject of waiting line or queuing theory. Our purpose in this chapter is to present some aspects of the theory and to show its application to problems of organizational design. In this endeavor, we develop and solve a model of the waiting line problem. Before presenting the model let us provide a brief illustration of its application to a problem of organizational design. Since several illustrations are employed in this chapter, we label this first illustration, "Example 1."

---

[2] Arnold Kaufmann, *Methods and Models of Operations Research* (Englewood Cliffs, N.J.: Prentice-Hall, Inc., 1963), p. 79.

EXAMPLE 1

Suppose a manufacturing organization has four departments with 10 machines in each department. Assume that these machines break down on a random basis and require maintenance to be restored to running order. When a machine breaks down, we say it arrives for service. Assume that the times required by repairmen to restore machines to running order are also random. Since machine breakdowns (arrivals for service) and service times are random events, there will be times when machines break down while repairmen are busy and other times when there are no breakdowns while repairmen stand idle. There is an obvious economic problem associated with this situation. If a machine arrives for service and there is no repairman available to provide service, the machine must wait and, therefore, is unable to produce revenue for the firm. In other words, when a machine is disabled and waiting for maintenance, the firm incurs an idle-machine cost in the form of lost revenue. During the times when no service is required and there are repairmen available to provide service, the men must wait and the firm incurs the costs of having idle repairmen. Once the probability distributions of arrival rates and service times have been ascertained, we can, through the waiting line model, determine the average number of machines waiting in line and the average number of idle repairmen in the system. Given this information, the cost per machine-hour and the cost per man-hour, we can then develop a total cost function which includes both the cost of machines waiting in line and the cost of idle repairmen. The firm may reduce the number of machines waiting for service by adding more repairmen to the system. However, the addition of more repairmen will increase the cost of idle repairmen. If the firm seeks an optimum economic position, it will seek to minimize the combined costs of machines waiting and idle repairmen.

Now how does this waiting line problem affect the design of organizations? To answer this question, suppose that we know the cost per machine-hour for various combinations of repairmen assigned to service a particular number of machines. The values are shown in Table 13–1.[3] The derivation of the values in the table will

[3] The table and the analysis presented in this chapter on the relation of waiting lines and organizational design are adapted from D. G. Malcolm, "Queuing Theory in Organization Design," *Journal of Industrial Engineering* (Official Publication of the American Institute of Industrial Engineers, Inc., 345 E. 47th St. N.Y.), Vol. 6 (November–December, 1955), pp. 19–26.

TABLE 13–1
Hourly Cost for Combinations of Machines and Repairmen

Number of Machines (1)	Number of Repairmen (2)	Cost per Machine-Hour (3)
10	2	$1.34
20	4	1.24
30	5	1.18
40	6	1.16
50	8	1.15
60	9	1.13
70	10	1.12
80	11	1.11
90	12	1.11
100	14	1.10

be explained later. At this point, let us explain that the number of repairmen shown in column (2) of Table 13–1 is the least cost (expressed as cost per hour) assignment for the number of machines in column (1). For example, after examining the possible combinations of repairmen to service 20 machines, it was found that four men was the least-cost assignment. The least-cost assignment for 30 machines was five repairmen and so on. The costs per machine-hour are shown in column (3). Table 13–1 indicates that as the size of the repairmen's group gets larger and is responsible for a greater number of machines, costs per machine-hour decrease.

Let us now examine three possible organizational designs of the maintenance activity. Recall that there were four departments and 40 machines in the organization. Using the data from Table 13–1, maintenance activity, when organized according to Figure 13–1,

FIGURE 13–1
Maintenance Serving All Departments

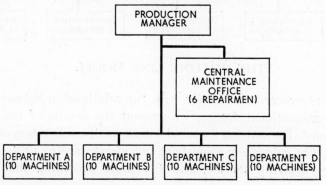

FIGURE 13-2

Maintenance Serving Two Departments

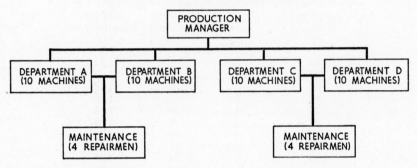

where six repairmen are assigned to maintain the entire 40 machines, would result in a total cost of 40 machines × $1.16 = $46.40 per hour. Organized according to Figure 13-2, where the assignment is four repairmen to each of two groups of 10 machines, the total cost would be 40 machines × $1.24 = $49.60 per hour. Organized according to Figure 13-3, where two men are assigned to each of four groups of 10 machines, the total cost would be 40 machines × $1.34 = $53.60 per hour. It is apparent that the centralized maintenance activity of Figure 13-1 is the least-cost design.

FIGURE 13-3

Maintenance Serving One Department

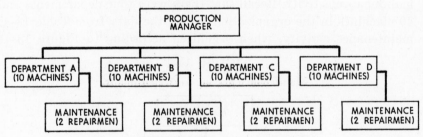

THE WAITING LINE MODEL

Before proceeding further with the relationship between delays and organizational design, we present the details of the waiting line model. The waiting line model deals with a subsystem of organization. The subsystem consists of two elements: (a) units demanding or requiring service, and (b) units providing that service.

TABLE 13-2

Examples of Waiting Line Problems

Units Demanding Service	Nature of Service	Units Providing Service
Machines	Machine repair	Maintenance men
Customer	Haircut	Barber
Patient	Medical treatment	Doctor
Trucks	Unload and load	Dock crew
Planes	Landing	Runways
Airline passenger	Ticket sale	Ticket seller

There are many situations where waiting line problems occur. A few examples are listed in Table 13-2. The process underlying the structure of a waiting line problem has already been discussed. Units demanding service arrive at a service station on a random basis. If the service station is busy, a waiting line is formed. The structure is illustrated in Figure 13-4.

FIGURE 13-4

Structure of Waiting Line Problem

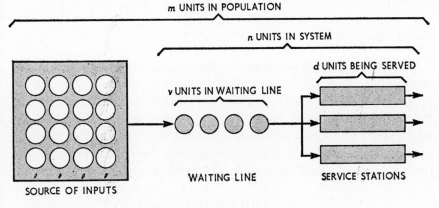

m UNITS IN POPULATION

n UNITS IN SYSTEM

d UNITS BEING SERVED

v UNITS IN WAITING LINE

SOURCE OF INPUTS

WAITING LINE

SERVICE STATIONS

Distribution of Arrival and Service Times

As noted, random arrivals at a service station mean that a demand for service occurs by chance and that its occurrence is an independent event. Thus, an arrival for service in one period is independent of arrivals in any other period. Through statistical analysis, the probability of events can be determined. It is assumed that these probabilities do not change with time. Thus, the probabilities in one period are the same as in any other period. Further, it is assumed that arrival rates or the number of arrivals per time period follow a Poisson distribution with the mean arrival rate designated by the Greek letter lambda (λ). If this is true, then, the time between arrivals will follow a negative exponential distribution with an average time between arrivals of $1/\lambda$. If the reader is not familiar with Poisson and negative exponential distributions, he can proceed with the analysis by accepting on faith that λ and $1/\lambda$ are theoretically valid (this same faith is needed below with μ and $1/\mu$). This measure of the average time between arrivals for service may also be interpreted as a measure of average time that units are running without a need for service. In our example, in which machine breakdowns are defined as arrivals for service, $1/\lambda$ is the average running time of machines between the completion of any one repair and the following breakdown.

It is assumed that the service rate or number of services completed per time period also follows a Poisson distribution with the average service rate designated by the Greek letter mu (μ). As before, a Poisson distribution with a mean service rate μ, means that the service times will follow a negative exponential distribution with average service time of $1/\mu$.

Queue Discipline

The *queue discipline* refers to the method by which the units demanding service are selected for service. The most common procedure is to serve units in the order of their arrival, that is, on a first-come, first-served basis. The system shown in Figure 13–5 illustrates a first-come, first-served basis of service. Another method would be to select units on some priority basis. An example of this basis of selection is a doctor who accepts appointments as well

FIGURE 13–5

Single-Station System

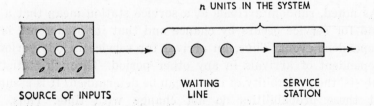

SOURCE OF INPUTS   WAITING LINE   SERVICE STATION

as "walk-in" patients, where the latter are served in between appointments or have to wait until the appointment patients have been served. In some systems several queue disciplines may be used. In a supermarket, for example, customers may select the server among the check-out counters available for service. Some markets have "quickie lines," however, in which customers with 10 items or less are processed through a separate check-out counter. Throughout the chapter, we assume the simple first-come, first-served queue discipline.

Inputs to the System

Inputs to the system may come from a finite population or an infinite population. A finite population refers to a limited source of potential inputs, while an infinite population refers to an unlimited or extremely large source. The example presented earlier in this chapter described a finite population of 40 machines. Other examples of finite populations might include the number of machine operators in a factory building who draw tools from a tool crib, patients in a hospital, or trucks in a motor pool. Examples of an essentially infinite population might include potential customers of a bank drive-in window, automobiles served by a toll station of a turnpike, and airline passengers at a ticket counter.

INFINITE POPULATION

The simplest of waiting line models is the single-station system serving an infinite population, illustrated in Figure 13–5. Examples of waiting lines in this type of system are customers waiting to be checked out at a grocery store where there is only one check-out counter, patients waiting to see a doctor, and customers waiting to be served in a barber shop where there is only one barber.

In the single-station model, we make the usual assumptions about Poisson and exponential distributions for arrival rates and service times. Also, we assume the first-come, first-served queue discipline. For the model, an index which indicates the utilization of the service station is called the service factor and is denoted by the Greek letter psi (ψ). It is the ratio of the average service time $1/\mu$ and the average time between arrivals for service $1/\lambda$. Thus:

$$\psi = \frac{1/\mu}{1/\lambda} = \frac{\lambda}{\mu}, \text{ where } 0 < \lambda/\mu < 1. \qquad (13\text{–}1)$$

Average Number of Units in the System

Recall that the system of the waiting line model was defined to include the waiting line and the service channels. The probability that there are n units in the system is given by the formula:[4]

$$p_n = \left(\frac{\lambda}{\mu}\right)^n \left(1 - \frac{\lambda}{\mu}\right), \text{ where } n = 0, 1, 2, 3, 4, \ldots$$

In terms of equation (13-1), p_n may be written:

$$p_n = \psi^n(1 - \psi) \text{ where } 0 < \psi < 1, \text{ and } n = 0, 1, 2, \ldots$$

When $n = 0$.

$$p_0 = 1 - \psi. \tag{13-2}$$

The probability of zero units in the system, equation 13-2, may also be interpreted as the probability that the service facility is idle.

When

$$n = 1, \quad p_1 = \psi(1 - \psi) = \psi p_0.$$
$$n = 2, \quad p_2 = \psi\psi(1 - \psi) = \psi^2 p_0.$$
$$n = 3, \quad p_3 = \psi^3 p_0.$$

$$n \geq 1, \quad p_n = \psi^n p_0 = \psi^n(1 - \psi). \tag{13-3}$$

Given the probability of n units in the system, we can now determine the average number of units in the system by the method of finding a weighted average. In a simplified example, shown in Table 13-3, we use a finite case where there are a limited number of units in the system. The second column of Table 13-3 (a) shows the number of times the corresponding number in column one occurred in the system. The sum of their products divided by the sum of the frequencies gives the weighted average. Table 13-3 (b) shows that this same weighted average may be obtained by using relative frequencies, each of which is $\frac{1}{36}$ as large as the corresponding frequency of Table 13-3 (a). If we use relative frequency as analogous to probabilities, the example may be used to determine $\bar{n}$, the

---

[4] Here we use standard formulae, but we follow the waiting-line models presented by Arnold Kaufmann, *Methods and Models of Operations Research* (Englewood Cliffs, N.J.: Prentice-Hall, Inc., 1963). For derivation of the formulas, see his chaps. iii and viii.

TABLE 13-3
A Weighted Average

(a)			(b)		
Number in System	Frequency	Product	Number in System	Relative* Frequency	Expectation*
0	14	0	0	0.3889	0
1	10	10	1	.2778	0.2778
2	6	12	2	.1667	.3334
3	4	12	3	.1111	.3333
4	2	8	4	.0555	.2220
	36	42		1.00	1.1665

Weighted Average $= \dfrac{42}{36} = 1.167$ | Weighted Average $= \dfrac{1.167}{1.00} = 1.167$

* Slight differences because of rounding.

average number of units in the system or what is known as mathematical expectation:

$$\bar{n} = 0 \cdot p_0 + 1 \cdot p_1 + 2 \cdot p_2 + 3 \cdot p_3 + 4 \cdot p_4$$
$$= 0(0.3889) + 1(0.2778) + 2(0.1667) + 3(0.1111) + 4(0.0555)$$
$$= 1.167.$$

In more general terms we write:

$$\bar{n} = \sum_{n=0}^{4} np_n, \text{ where } \sum_{n=0}^{4} p_n = 1$$

$$= 1.167.$$

Recall, however, that we are dealing with an infinite population. Therefore, the average number units in the system is given by:

$$\bar{n} = 0 \cdot p_0 + 1 \cdot p_1 + 2 \cdot p_2 + 3 \cdot p_3 + \ldots + np_n + \ldots$$

or, in general:

$$\bar{n} = \sum_{n=0}^{\infty} np_n, \text{ where } \sum_{n=0}^{\infty} p_n = 1$$

From equation (13-3), we may rewrite the equations for $\bar{n}$:

$$\bar{n} = 0(1 - \psi) + 1(\psi)(1 - \psi) + 2(\psi)^2(1 - \psi) + 3(\psi)^3(1 - \psi) + \ldots$$
$$+ n(\psi)^n (1 - \psi) + \ldots$$

$$= \sum_{n=0}^{\infty} n\psi^n (1 - \psi)$$

$$= (1 - \psi) \sum_{n=0}^{\infty} n\psi^n$$

Through the use of calculus, the result for the average number of units in the system is obtained. It is:

$$\bar{n} = \frac{\psi}{1 - \psi} \tag{13-4}$$

Average Number of Units in Waiting Line

If we let v be the number of units in the waiting line and d the number of units being served, then v plus d is equal to n, the number of units in the system. Since it was assumed that only one unit can be served in each service facility at a time, and if s is designated as the number of service stations, then:

$$n = d, \text{ if } n \leq s,$$
$$n = v + d, \text{ if } n > s.$$

As soon as n becomes larger than s, there are units in the waiting line. Since we are dealing with one service facility, $d = 1$, thus:

$$v = n - 1, \text{ where } n > 0.$$

The average number of units in the waiting line is also obtained according to the procedure of mathematical expectation. Thus:

$$\bar{v} = 1 \cdot p_2 + 2 \cdot p_3 + 3 \cdot p_4 + 4 \cdot p_5 + \ldots + (n - 1)p_n + \ldots$$

$$= \sum_{n=2}^{\infty} (n - 1)p_n$$

or

$$v = \sum_{n=2}^{\infty} np_n - \sum_{n=2}^{\infty} p_n$$

or

$$v = \sum_{n=0}^{\infty} np_n - \sum_{n=0}^{1} np_n - \sum_{n=0}^{\infty} p_n + \sum_{n=0}^{1} p_n$$

Since

$$\sum_{n=0}^{\infty} np_n = \bar{n}, \ \sum_{n=0}^{1} np_n = p_1, \ \sum_{n=0}^{\infty} p_n = 1, \text{ and } \sum_{n=0}^{1} p_n = p_0 + p_1,$$

we rewrite :

$$\bar{v} = \bar{n} - p_1 - 1 + p_0 + p_1$$
$$= \bar{n} - 1 + p_0$$

Since:

$$n = \frac{\psi}{1 - \psi} \text{ equation (13-4), and since equation (13-2),}$$

$p_0 = 1 - \psi$ can be rearranged to:

$-\psi = -1 + p_0,$

then, $\bar{v}$ may be rewritten as follows:

$$v = \frac{\psi}{1 - \psi} - \psi$$

$$= \frac{\psi^2}{1 - \psi} \tag{13-5}$$

Average Waiting Time in the Line

Let $\bar{w}$ be the average waiting time in the line, then:

$$\bar{w} = \frac{\bar{v}}{\lambda}$$

Since:

$$\bar{v} = \frac{\psi^2}{1 - \psi} \text{ equation (13-5)}$$

We rewrite:

$$\bar{w} = \frac{\psi^2}{1 - \psi} \cdot \frac{1}{\lambda}$$

Since $1/\lambda$ may be written:

$$\frac{1}{\lambda} = \frac{1}{\mu} \cdot \frac{1}{\lambda/\mu}$$

$$= \frac{1}{\mu} \cdot \frac{1}{\psi}$$

Then:

$$\bar{w} = \frac{\psi^2}{1 - \psi} \cdot \frac{1}{\mu \psi}$$

$$= \frac{\psi}{1 - \psi} \cdot \frac{1}{\mu}$$

Since:

$$\bar{n} = \frac{\psi}{1 - \psi} \text{ equation (13-4)}$$

Then:

$$\bar{w} = \frac{\bar{n}}{\mu} \tag{13-6}$$

Average Time in the System

Let $\bar{s}$ represent the average time in the system which, of course, includes the service time of the one unit being served. Then:

$$\bar{s} = \frac{\bar{n}}{\lambda} \qquad (13\text{-}7)$$

Summary of Pertinent Equations

We will now restate the pertinent equations for analyzing a waiting line problem with a single service station.

Service Factor

$$\psi = \frac{\lambda}{\mu} \text{ where } 0 < \lambda/\mu < 1. \qquad (13\text{-}1)$$

Probability that the Service Station is Idle

$$p_0 = 1 - \psi \qquad (13\text{-}2)$$

Average Number of Units in the System

$$\bar{n} = \frac{\psi}{1 - \psi} \qquad (13\text{-}4)$$

Average Number of Units in the Waiting Line

$$\bar{v} = \frac{\psi^2}{1 - \psi} \qquad (13\text{-}5)$$

Average Waiting Time in the Line

$$\bar{w} = \frac{\bar{n}}{\mu} \qquad (13\text{-}6)$$

Average Time in the System

$$\bar{s} = \frac{\bar{n}}{\lambda} \qquad (13\text{-}7)$$

Before applying these equations to a problem, let us explain the restraint $(0 < \lambda/\mu < 1)$ placed on equation (13-1). The requirement that the measure exceed zero is, of course, obvious for any operating system. The requirement $\lambda/\mu < 1$ means that service rate μ must always exceed the arrival rate λ. This restraint is necessary in the waiting line model because if units arrive for service faster on the average than they can be processed, the waiting line will become very long. This result is shown in Figure 13-6, where we show the relationship between the service factor ψ and the average number of units waiting in line, $\bar{v}$. As ψ approaches one, $\bar{v}$ approaches

FIGURE 13-6

Average Number of Units in Waiting Line and Service Factor

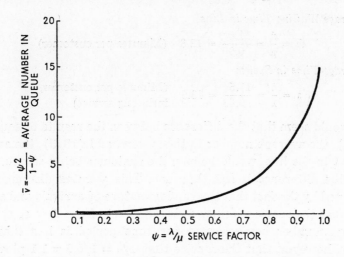

$\psi = \lambda/\mu$ SERVICE FACTOR

infinity. This conclusion also holds for the equations (13–4) and (13–6). Thus, as ψ approaches unity, the average number of units in the system and average waiting time in the line approach infinity.

EXAMPLE 2

Suppose a grocery store has one check-out counter. Arrival rates and service rates both follow a Poisson distribution. Customers arrive at the counter on the average of 50 per hour, and the cashier can process an average of 54 per hour. Thus:

$\lambda = 0.83$ arrivals per minute.
$\mu = 0.90$ service completions per minute.

Service Factor

$$\psi = \frac{\lambda}{\mu} = \frac{0.83}{0.90} = 0.92 \qquad (13\text{–}1)$$

Idle Time of Cashier

$$p_0 = 1 - \psi = 1 - 0.92 = 0.08 \text{ (Cashier is idle 8 percent} \qquad (13\text{–}2)$$
$$\text{of the time)}$$

Average Number of Units in System

$$\bar{n} = \frac{\psi}{1 - \psi} = \frac{0.92}{0.08} = 11.5 \qquad \begin{array}{l}\text{(Customers in system including} \\ \text{the one being served)}\end{array} \qquad (13\text{–}4)$$

Average Number of Units in Waiting Line

$$\bar{v} = \frac{\psi^2}{1 - \psi} = \frac{0.8464}{0.08} = 10.6 \quad \text{(Customers in line)} \qquad (13\text{--}5)$$

Average Waiting Time in Line

$$\bar{w} = \frac{\bar{n}}{\mu} = \frac{11.5}{0.90} = 12.8 \quad \text{(Minutes per customer)} \qquad (13\text{--}6)$$

Average Time in System

$$\bar{s} = \frac{\bar{n}}{\lambda} = \frac{11.5}{0.83} = 13.9 \quad \begin{array}{l}\text{(Minutes per customer,} \\ \text{including service)}\end{array} \qquad (13\text{--}7)$$

It would seem that the difference between the results of equations (13–4), the average number in the system, and (13–5), the average number in the line, would be one, the customer being served. However, the difference is less than one. This seeming discrepancy is explained by the fact that the random nature of arrivals and service will cause the service facility to be idle part of the time so that the average number being served per time period is less than one. Notice, however, that the service time $1/\mu = 1/0.9 = 1.1$ plus average waiting time in line $\bar{w} = 12.8$ is equal to the average waiting time in the system $\bar{s} = 13.9$ minutes.

It is likely that some customers will be displeased about the 13.9-minute check-out time. As a result, the store will probably lose customers. Obviously, the waiting time of customers and the possibility of lost sales can be reduced by redesigning the system to include more service stations. Adding more stations would create a multiple-station system as shown in Figure 13–4. However, the addition of more check-out counters, while reducing the amount of time that customers have to spend at the check-out counters, would increase the amount of time that cashiers stand idle. The store has the economic problem, therefore, of determining the optimum number of check-out counters. In other words, it will try to minimize the combined costs of lost sales and idle time of cashiers. The economic implications of adding more stations will be examined more thoroughly after we present the analysis for systems with finite populations.

FINITE POPULATION

A waiting line system that has a limited population poses a different problem from the case of an infinite population. In the finite system, the probability of arrivals is affected by the number in the waiting line. When a unit arrives (for example, a machine breakdown) for service or is waiting in line, it cannot arrive again (that is, the machine cannot break down again) until it has been serviced. The number in the line, then, may be a significant proportion of the population, and the probability of arrivals is dependent on the number of units in the line. The structure of a finite system is shown in Figure 13–7. In the case of infinite population, arrivals are independent of the number waiting in line because theoretically anyone can arrive for service (for example, consider the possible arrivals at a check-out counter of a supermarket). Therefore, the mathematical formulations for the finite case are different and much more complicated than those for the infinite case. Fortunately, tables exist which make it easier to arrive at solutions for finite queuing problems. Peck and Hazelwood[5] have developed queuing tables for populations from 4 through 250. We have reproduced these tables for populations from 4 through 15 and for 20, 30, and 40 in Appendix A. Before explaining the use of these tables, let us provide definitions for the model.

N = number of units in the population.
M = number of service stations.
T = average service time.
U = average productive time or running time.
W = average waiting time.
X = service factor.
F = efficiency factor.

The Service Factor

The service factor is a function of average service time and average productive time, and is written:

$$X = \frac{T}{T + U} \tag{13–8}$$

The meaning of the service factor can be illustrated in the following way. Suppose a machine operates for an average of 60 hours and then it requires an average of 20 hours in repair. This means that $X = 0.25$, or machines spend 25 percent of running time U, and service time T, in repair.

---

[5] L. G. Peck and R. N. Hazelwood, *Finite Queuing Tables* (New York: John Wiley & Sons, Inc., 1958).

Efficiency Factor

The efficiency factor is a function of average service time, average productive time, and average waiting time. The efficiency factor F is the percentage of total time that machines are running and/or being serviced (that is, the percentage of time that machines are not waiting), and is written:

$$F = \frac{T + U}{T + U + W}.$$ (13-9)

Equation (13-9) is a measure of the overall efficiency of the system and is unique to the finite model. Recall that we indicated that the difference between the infinite and finite models was the fact that the finite model considered the effect of the number in the waiting line on demands for service. When there is a finite population, a unit waiting in line for service cannot arrive again or generate demand. Equation (13-9), then, is a measure of the reduction in the number of units running and demanding service. This effect is illustrated below.

Average Number of Units Being Serviced

If there were no waiting line, the average number of units being serviced would be $(NT)/(T + U)$. However, the waiting line effect requires that this ratio be reduced by F. Hence:

$$\begin{aligned} H &= \frac{FNT}{T + U} \\ &= \left(\frac{T + U}{T + U + W}\right)\left(\frac{NT}{T + U}\right) \\ &= \frac{NT}{T + U + W} \end{aligned}$$ (13-10)

Since equation (13-10) is equivalent to FNX, we may write:

$$H = FNX$$ (13-11)

Average Number of Units Running or Productive

If there were no waiting line, the average number of units running would be $(NU)/(T + U)$. Reducing this ratio by the factor F, as required in the finite model, means that the average number of units running is written:

$$J = \frac{FNU}{T + U}$$

$$= \left(\frac{\prime T + U}{T + U + W}\right)\left(\frac{NU}{T + U}\right)$$

$$= \frac{NU}{T + U + W} \qquad (13\text{-}12)$$

Since equation (13–12) is equivalent to $NF\ (1 - X)$, we may write:

$$J = NF(1 - X) \qquad (13\text{-}13)$$

Average Number of Units Waiting for Service

The average number of units waiting for service may be expressed as N times the percentage of total time that is waiting time. Thus:

$$L = \frac{NW}{T + W + U} \qquad (13\text{-}14)$$

The same result may be obtained in terms of equation (13–9). Since equation (13–9) may be read as the percentage of total time that units are not waiting, $1 - F$ is the percentage of time that units wait for service. Hence, the average number of units waiting for service is written:

$$L = N(1 - F). \qquad (13\text{-}15)$$

The tables of Appendix A are classified by N, the size of the population. Within each size of N, data are further classified by X, the service factor; M, the number of service stations; and F, the factor of efficiency. Given N, X, and M, we may obtain F for use in the equations of the model. The use of the tables becomes evident from the following illustrations.

EXAMPLE 3

In order to determine the effectiveness of a system, we first examine a hypothetical situation involving one repairman attempting to service a number of identical machines. Effectiveness is defined as the ability of the system to keep machines running. As a measure of effectiveness, we introduce E, percent machine running time. It is the average number of machines running, equation (13–13), expressed as a percent of the total number of machines, N. Thus:

$$E = \frac{J}{N}$$
$$= \frac{NF(1 - X)}{N}$$
$$= F(1 - X) \tag{13-16}$$

Assume that $N = 10$, $M = 1$, and $X = 0.1$. From Appendix A, we obtain $F = 0.832$. Thus:

$$E = 0.832(0.90)$$
$$= 0.7488.$$

On the average, then, machines are running 74.88 percent of the time. Now let us determine how much time machines have to spend in the system. Equation (13–14) can be rearranged to obtain W, the average waiting time:

$$L = \frac{NW}{T + W + U}$$
$$L(T + W + U) = NW$$
$$L(T + U) = NW - LW$$
$$L(T + U) = W(N - L)$$
$$W = \frac{L(T + U)}{N - L} \tag{13-17}$$

The average number of units waiting, L, is obtained from equation (13–15). Thus:

$$L = 10(0.168)$$
$$= 1.68$$

Assume that the machines operate for an average of 27 hours and then require an average of 3 hours repair, that is, $T = 3$ and $U = 27$. Substituting these values into equation (13–17), we obtain:

$$W = \frac{1.68(30)}{8.32}$$
$$= 6.06$$

Each machine, then, must wait an average of 6.06 hours before it receives service. It spends another $T = 3$ hours being serviced, which makes a total of 9.06 hours in the system. The long downtime of machines and the percent running time measure seem to indicate that the system could be improved. There are really two questions involved: Would it be beneficial for the organization to add more repairmen (service stations) to the system? If so, how should they be organized? These questions are answered in the next two sections, where we examine a multiple-station system with a finite population and present economic criteria for making a decision.

MULTIPLE-STATION SYSTEM, FINITE POPULATION

The multiple-station system is illustrated in Figure 13–7. The diagram shows the closed characteristic of the system where the serviced units return to the source with a probability of arrival affected by the number in line.

In our discussion of the single-station system, we presented a situation with one repairman maintaining 10 machines. We found that machines were running 74.88 percent of the time and that each

FIGURE 13–7

Multiple-Station System, Finite Population

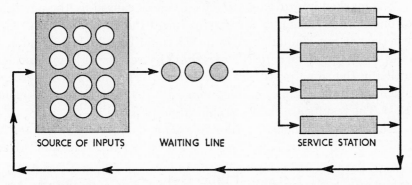

SOURCE OF INPUTS   WAITING LINE   SERVICE STATION

machine had to spend 9.06 hours in the system after breakdown. Let us determine if one additional repairman will improve the situation. Again, we assume that there are $N = 10$ machines and the same service factor $X = 0.1$, but we increase the number of repairmen to $M = 2$. Again, we examine E, percent running time, equation (13–16). The F value is derived from the tables of Appendix A. Thus:

$$E = 0.981(0.90)$$
$$= 0.8829$$

The addition of one repairman has increased effectiveness from a point where machines were running 74.88 percent of the time to the point where they are running 88.29 percent of the time. Now let us determine how the addition of one repairman has affected the time spent in the system. First, we obtain L, the average number of units waiting, from equation (13–15). Using the F value already derived for E above, we find:

$$
\begin{aligned}
L &= 10(1 - 0.981) \\
&= 10(0.019) \\
&= 0.19
\end{aligned}
$$

Substituting this value and the assumed values of $T = 3$ and $U = 27$, into equation (13–17), we obtain:

$$
\begin{aligned}
W &= \frac{0.19(3 + 27)}{10 - 0.19} \\
&= 0.581
\end{aligned}
$$

The addition of one repairman, then, reduces the average time spent in the system from 9.06 hours to 3.581 hours. The time spent waiting in line is reduced from 6.06 hours to 0.581 hours. Thus, we may conclude that it is very beneficial to add one repairman to the system.

The marked improvement in effectiveness caused by the addition of one service station or repairman raises the question again as to whether or not similar improvements could be achieved by adding even more repairmen to the system. The results of computations utilizing the same procedure detailed above for finding E, percent machine running time, by equation (13–16), are shown in Table 13–4. The results are shown graphically in Figure 13–8.[6]

The results of calculations for $N = 20$ and of several values for X and M are shown in Table 13–5 and Figure 13–9. Notice that after

TABLE 13–4

Percent Machine Running Time

$$N = 10$$
$$X = 0.1$$

Number of Repairmen M	Percent Machine Running Time E
1	74.88
2	88.29
3	89.82
.	.
.	.
.	.
Limit	90.00

---

[6] As noted earlier in this chapter, this method has been adapted from Malcolm, *op. cit.* Malcolm uses the detailed formulations of the finite waiting line model, while we use the tables of Peck and Hazelwood, *op. cit.*

FIGURE 13–8

Limiting Performance of the System

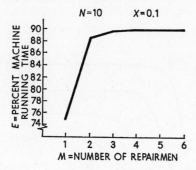

an initial improvement, the system stabilizes or levels off as it approaches the limit of $E = 0.90$. The rate of improvement levels off after M becomes greater than $(X)(N)$. After a certain point, therefore, adding more repairmen results in no practical improvement to the system. This characteristic of the system suggests, as Malcolm concludes, ". . . that at some point the man added will cost more in wages than the increase in machine running time is

TABLE 13–5

Percent Machine Running Time

$N = 20$

Number of Repairmen M	Service Factor X			
	0.1	0.2	0.3	0.4
1	45.00			
2	79.02	40.00		
3	87.75	58.88	35.00	
4	89.55	71.60	46.48	
5	89.91	77.04	56.56	37.44
6	.	79.04	63.49	44.64
7	.	79.76	67.27	50.70
8	.	79.92	68.95	55.08
9	.	.	69.65	57.72
10	.	.	69.86	59.04
11	.	.	.	59.64
12	.	.	.	59.88
13	.	.	.	59.94
.	.	.	.	.
.	.	.	.	.
.	.	.	.	.
Limit	90.00	80.00	70.00	60.00

FIGURE 13–9

Limiting Performance of the Systems

$N = 20$

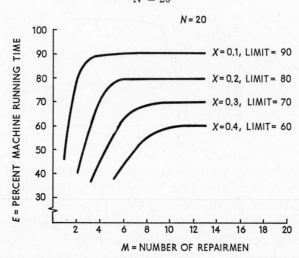

worth."[7] In order to find this point, the costs involved and the decision criteria must be defined. This is our next task.

DECISION CRITERIA

When a machine breaks down and has to wait for service, the company incurs a loss or cost equivalent to the revenue that the machine would have earned had it been running. We have seen that machine waiting time can be reduced and its percent running time increased by adding more repairmen to the system. In order to decrease the cost of idle machines, then, the cost of repairmen must increase. Thus, the objective of the decision model is to determine the number of repairmen that will minimize the combined costs of repairmen and idle machines.

Implications for Organizational Design

For purposes of organizational design, the objective function must not only solve for the optimum number of service stations but also for the optimum size of service stations (number of repairmen in each crew). Thus, the objective function may be stated:

---

[7] *Ibid.*, p. 22.

Objective: Determine the number of repairmen and crew size that will minimize the combined costs of repairmen and idle machines.

We designate the cost (or revenue lost) per machine hour as c_1 and the cost per hour for repairmen as c_2. Both c_1 and c_2 are constant. Since E is the percentage of machines running $(1 - E)$ is the percentage of machines not running, and $c_1(1 - E)$ is the hourly nonproductive cost per machine. Since M is the number of service stations or repairmen, $c_2(M/N)$ is the hourly cost of repairmen per machine. The total hourly cost per machine is written, therefore, as:

$$TC_a = c_1(1 - E) + c_2(M/N) \qquad (13\text{--}18)$$

The subscript of total cost, TC, is used to distinguish equation (13–18) from (13–20) and (13–21).

Table 13–6 presents values for E, percent running time, for combinations of M and N with $X = 0.1$. Notice that E, percent running time, approaches the limit of 90.00 percent for combi-

TABLE 13–6

Percent Running Times

$X = 0.1$

Number of Service Stations M	N = Number of Units to be Serviced									
	10	20	30	40	50	60	70	80	90	100
1	74.88	45.00								
2	88.29	79.02	59.76							
3	89.82	87.75	80.91	67.05						
4		89.55	87.57	82.08	71.37					
5		89.91	89.37	87.57	82.89	74.16				
6			89.82	89.19	87.48	83.52	76.14			
7				89.73	89.10	87.48	83.97	77.67		
8				89.91	89.64	89.01	87.48	84.33	78.84	
9					89.91	89.64	89.01	87.57	84.69	79.74
10						89.82	89.55	88.92	87.57	84.96
11						89.91	89.82	89.55	88.92	87.57
12							89.91	89.82	89.46	88.83
13								89.91	89.73	89.46
14									89.91	89.73
15										
16										89.91
17										
18										
19										
20										

nations of M and N. This characteristic is in accord with our discussion of limiting performance and the illustrations of Figures 13–8 and 13–9. We look to Table 13–6 for E and solve equation (13–18) for various sizes of M and N. Throughout, it is assumed $c_1 = \$8$, $c_2 = \$2$, and $X = 0.1$. Here are some sample computations:

Computation 1

$$N = 20$$
$$M = 2$$
$$TC_a = \$8(1 - 0.7902) + \$2(2/20)$$
$$= \$1.88$$

Computation 2

$$N = 30$$
$$M = 5$$
$$TC_a = \$8(1 - 0.8937) + \$2(5/30)$$
$$= \$1.18$$

Computation 3

$$N = 40$$
$$M = 6$$
$$TC_a = \$8(1 - 0.8919) + \$2(6/40)$$
$$= \$1.16$$

These values and others are presented in Table 13–7 for $N = 20$, $N = 30$ and $N = 40$. Notice that the minimum values are boxed in Table 13–7 for each size of N. These and the minimum values for other sizes of N and M are produced in Table 13–8. Notice that Table 13–8 is a reproduction of Table 13–1 with the addition of the column for percent running time.

TABLE 13–7

Hourly Costs for the System

$c_1 = \$8$ $c_2 = \$2$ $X = 0.1$

Repairmen M	Total Hourly Cost per Machine $TC_a = c_1(1 - E) + c_2(M/N)$		
	$N = 20$	$N = 30$	$N = 40$
1	\$4.50		
2	1.88	\$3.35	
3	1.28	1.73	\$2.79
4	$\boxed{1.24}$	1.26	1.63
5	1.31	$\boxed{1.18}$	1.24
6		1.21	$\boxed{1.16}$
7			1.17
8			1.21

TABLE 13–8

Minimum Cost Solutions

$$X = 0.1 \qquad c_1 = \$8 \qquad c_2 = \$2$$

Machines N	Solutions		Percent Machine Running Time E
	TC_a	M	
10	1.34	2	88.29
20	1.24	4	89.55
30	1.18	5	89.37
40	1.16	6	89.19
50	1.15	8	89.64
60	1.13	9	89.64
70	1.12	10	89.55
80	1.11	11	89.55
90	1.11	12	89.46
100	1.10	14	89.73

Again, we conclude as we did earlier in the chapter that the minimum cost solutions shown in Table 13–8 indicate that it is better to organize into larger groups of repairmen assigned to a greater number of machines. In accord with our earlier analysis, where Figures 13–1, 13–2, and 13–3 were used to illustrate possible organizational designs, a centralized maintenance office was found to be the most economical with a total cost per hour of $46.40. It was better to organize a central office with six repairmen responsible for 40 machines than either of the other two arrangements—one where four repairmen were assigned to two groups of 10 machines, and the other where two repairmen were assigned to maintain each of four groups of 10 machines. Also, with a group size of six rather than two, the percent running time increased from 88.29 percent to 89.19 percent.

Effects of Crew Size

A basic assumption of the waiting line model applied to maintenance men servicing machines was that the size of the crew had no effect on performance. Thus, we concluded that it was better to organize into the largest group of repairmen assigned to the greatest number of machines. However, if we consider that relations increase exponentially as components are added to a system, this premise about group size is tenuous. Also, there are technical problems caused by centralizing the maintenance men. For example, the maintenance men located centrally would probably have to walk longer distances to service machines than men who are decentralized and located closer to machines. Furthermore, there might be greater delays in communications to men in centralized locations than to men located closer to the scene of possible machine breakdowns.

Let us assume that the effect of crew size may be designated by a factor B and is written:

$$B = 1 + gN, \text{ where } g > 0 \qquad (13\text{--}19)$$

When multiplied times $(1 - E)$, the factor B has the effect of increasing the percentage of machines not running. Thus, in order to incorporate the effect of crew size into the total cost equation, we revise equation (13–18):

$$TC_b = c_3 B (1 - E) + c_4(M/N) \qquad (13\text{--}20)$$

To illustrate the effect of crew size, let us return to the repairmen example and assume, as before, that $c_3 = \$8$, $c_4 = \$2$, and $X = 0.1$. Furthermore, let us assume that $g = 0.01$ in equation (13–19). Obtaining values for E from Table 13–6, Tables 13–7 and 13–8 would be revised as shown in Tables 13–9 and 13–10. We now conclude that it is better to organize according to Figure 13–2 with four repairmen assigned to two groups of 10 machines. The total cost of this arrangement would be 40 machines $\times$ \$1.40 = \$56.00. The arrangement of Figure 13–1 would now require seven repairmen to maintain the entire 40 machines and would have a total cost

TABLE 13–9

Hourly Costs for the System Including the Effect of
Crew Size

$c_3 = \$8 \qquad c_4 = \$2 \qquad X = 0.1 \qquad g = 0.01$

Repairmen M	Total Hourly Cost per Machine $TC_b = c_3B(1 - E) + c_4(M/N)$			
	$N = 10$	$N = 20$	$N = 30$	$N = 40$
1	\$2.41	\$5.38		
2	|1.43|	2.22	\$4.32	
3	1.50	1.48	2.19	\$3.84
4		|1.40|	1.55	2.21
5		1.47	|1.44|	1.64
6			1.46	1.51
7				|1.50|
8				1.53

TABLE 13–10

Minimum Cost Solutions Including the Effect of
Crew Size

$c_3 = \$8$ $\qquad$ $c_4 = \$2$ $\qquad$ $X = 0.1$ $\qquad$ $g = 0.01$

Machines N	Solutions		Percent Machine Running Time E
	TC_b	M	
10	1.43	2	88.29
20	[1.40]	4	89.55
30	1.44	5	89.37
40	1.50	7	89.73

of 40 machines × \$1.50 = \$60. Organized according to Figure 13–3, where two men are assigned to each of four groups of 10 machines, the total cost would be 40 machines × \$1.43 = 57.20. Hence, we see that the effect of crew size with $g = 0.01$ requires a different organizational design from the case where crew size was not considered.

Notes on the Model

Certain assumptions of the waiting line model require elaboration. Perhaps the most serious assumption is that the service factor X is constant. The learning behavior of people in organizations would suggest that the service rate might improve over time. Thus, in the case of machines and repairmen, you would expect that after repeated exposures to the same machines, repairmen would require less time to provide service. However, we have hypothesized that performance, as it is affected by learning, stabilizes at some limiting rate. Therefore, we may assume that the waiting line model uses a service rate that reflects this stability of rate.

Another assumption of the model discussed is that effectiveness could be improved only by adding more service stations. There are, of course, other ways to increase effectiveness, that is, improvement of units demanding service so as to reduce their demands for service. For example, the percent running times of machines could possibly be increased by redesign of the machines or by implementing technological improvements, so that they would require less maintenance. If these factors were to be included in the model, then the costs of increased investment would have to be considered.

Perhaps the greatest reservation that should be made about the waiting line model is that it deals with a subsystem of the organization. While decision criteria allow us to find an optimum assignment for the subsystem, this assignment may be less than optimum for the total system. The decision criteria for the waiting line model, for example, may give an optimum where there is a relatively large amount of waiting time and relatively little idle time. In the case of a business organization, the long waiting time indicated by the model may be inconsistent with the firm's desire to maintain an image of prompt service to customers. Another illustration of inconsistency between the subsystem and the total system may be the case where the waiting line model indicates a centralized design for an organization which follows a policy of decentralization. Obviously, the needs of the total system are paramount and should prevail in any differences that exist between it and its parts. However, the waiting line model and its accompanying decision criteria provide an objective means for solving the delay problem in a subsystem of the organization. It, therefore, provides a base for making decisions of broader scope. This point is especially important in cases where no objective means exist for solving total system problems.

We need to emphasize also that the organizational schemes used in Figure 13–1, 13–2, and 13–3 were determined on an arbitrary basis. The solution of the waiting line model does not determine an optimum organizational design. It does determine the optimum number of components and crew size or process flows of items such as materials, machine breakdowns, information, and customers. Several organizational arrangements were possible in the crew-size example. A centralized design could have been used with any crew size. For example, repairmen in the two-man and four-man crews could also operate from a central maintenance office. While each crew would be responsible for the maintenance of machines in particular departments, their orders could come from one supervisor in the maintenance office. As we indicated above, the needs of the total system are paramount in determining the design of a subsystem.

However, this rule does not mean that the needs or conditions of the subsystem are ignored. What is an optimum for a subsystem is important information for designing the whole system. For example, the solution of the model for crew size indicated that it was best to organize with a crew of six repairmen responsible for 40 machines. Now suppose it had been determined that decentralization is the best design for the total system. With the knowledge that (1) the optimum for the subsystem is a crew size of six repairmen, and (2) that it is not feasible to decentralize the crew since they should be responsible for the entire 40 machines, then, it might be wise to make an exception at this level of the organization by centralizing the crew in one office.

There are waiting line models that approach a total system concept. These models deal with multiphase systems or systems in a series. A single-channel multiple-phase system, as shown in Figure 13–10, involves units waiting in line for the first service, and after

FIGURE 13–10

Single-Channel, Multiple-Phase System

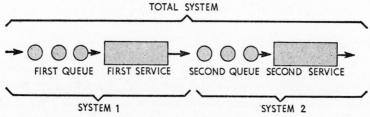

TOTAL SYSTEM

FIRST QUEUE   FIRST SERVICE   SECOND QUEUE   SECOND SERVICE

SYSTEM 1   SYSTEM 2

being serviced in System 1, they wait in line for the second service in System 2. To illustrate total system equations, we again refer to Kaufmann.[8] First, we assume:

$$\psi_1 = \lambda/\mu_1 < 1, \qquad \psi_2 = \lambda/\mu_2 < 1$$

Then, for an infinite population, the following equations hold:

	System 1	*System 2*	*Total System*
Average number of units in the line	$v_1 = \dfrac{\psi_1^2}{1 - \psi_1}$	$v_2 = \dfrac{\psi_2^2}{1 - \psi_2}$	$v = v_1 + v_2$ $= \dfrac{\psi_1^2}{1 - \psi_1} + \dfrac{\psi_2^2}{1 - \psi_2}$
Average number of units in the system	$\bar{n}_1 = \dfrac{\psi_1}{1 - \psi_1}$	$\bar{n}_2 = \dfrac{\psi_2}{1 - \psi_2}$	$\bar{n} = \bar{n}_1 + \bar{n}_2$ $= \dfrac{\psi_1}{1 - \psi_1} + \dfrac{\psi_2}{1 - \psi}$
Average number of units being serviced	$\bar{d}_1 = \psi_1$	$\bar{d}_2 = \psi_2$	$\bar{d} = \bar{d}_1 + \bar{d}_2$ $= \psi_1 + \psi_2$

[8] Kaufmann, *op. cit.*, p. 376.

WAITING LINE THEORY AND SPAN OF SUPERVISION

One of the basic problems of organizational design is the determination of how many employees should report directly to one supervisor. We discussed this problem in Chapters 3 and 4. In Chapter 4, we concluded that the optimum number of subordinates for a supervisor depends on local conditions, that is, upon the skills of the supervisor, the skills of subordinates, the nature of the work, and the existing social and power relationships at the local level. The relationships of supervisor and subordinates may, therefore, be considered as a subsystem of behavior. Insofar as local conditions are reflected in the frequency of contacts between supervisor and subordinates and the time it takes for the supervisor to service the needs of subordinates, the span-of-supervision problem may be solved through the application of waiting line theory.

The Waiting Line Model[9]

In terms of the finite model of waiting line theory, supervisors would be considered service stations or M. Subordinates would be classified as units demanding service or N in the model. We may use reasoning that is similar to that employed in our analysis of machines and repairmen. When subordinates leave their jobs to call on a supervisor, the company incurs a loss or cost equivalent to the revenue that the worker would have earned had he been working. In this model, we want to determine the number of subordinates that will minimize the combined costs of supervision and idle subordinates. In this model we are constrained by the "unity of command" doctrine, that is, everybody in the organization has one boss, or $M = 1$.

We designate the cost (or revenue lost) per subordinate hour as c_5 and the cost per hour of supervision as c_6. We assume that both c_5 and c_6 are constant. In this case, we designate E as the percentage of subordinates working and $(1 - E)$ as the percentage of subordinates not working, that is, calling on supervisors. Then, $c_5 (1 - E)$ is the hourly idle cost per subordinate. Since M is the number of service stations or supervisors, $c_6 (M/N)$ is the hourly supervisory cost per subordinate. The total cost function, then, is

[9] Adapted from Lawrence S. Hill, "The Application of Queuing Theory to the Span of Control," *Academy of Management Journal*, Vol. 6, No. 1 (March, 1963), pp. 58–69.

identical to equation (13–18) with the exception that in the present
case we use different labels. Thus, we write:

Total Hourly Cost per Subordinate

$$TC_c = c_5(1 - E) + c_6(M/N) \qquad (13\text{–}21)$$

EXAMPLE 4

Assume a situation where a supervisor's contacts with subordinates last on the average of 1.3 minutes or $T = 0.02174$. Assume also that the time between arrivals for service or the average working time of workers is $U = 0.25$ hours, that is, subordinates work on the average of 15 minutes and then have to call on their supervisor for help or service. From equation (13–8), we obtain:

$$X = \frac{0.02174}{0.25 + 0.02174}$$
$$= 0.08$$

Starting with a design where there are four workers reporting to one supervisor, $M = 1$, the system efficiency factor from Appendix A is:

$$F = 0.978$$

Thus, it is apparent that the system is extremely efficient with a 4:1 supervisor-subordinate ratio. In other words, there is a very high

TABLE 13–11

Total Costs per Hour in Supervisor-Subordinate Relationship

$X = 0.08 \qquad M = 1 \qquad c_5 = \$3 \qquad c_6 = \$6$

Number of Subordinates N	System Efficiency Factor F	Working Time $E = F(1 - X)$	Hourly Idle Costs per Subordinate $c_5(1 - E)$	Supervisory Costs per Subordinate $c_6(M/N)$	Total Hourly Costs per Subordinate $TC_c = c_5(1 - E) + c_6(M/N)$
4	0.978	0.899	$0.303	$1.50	$1.803
5	.969	.891	.327	1.20	1.527
6	.958	.881	.357	1.00	1.357
7	.946	.870	.390	0.857	1.247
8	.932	.857	.429	0.750	1.179
9	.917	.844	.468	0.667	1.135
10	.899	.827	.519	0.600	1.119
11	.878	.808	.576	0.545	1.121
12	.855	.787	.639	0.500	1.139
13	.830	.764	.708	0.462	1.170
14	.803	.739	.783	0.429	1.213
15	.774	.712	.864	0.400	1.264

percentage of subordinates working. As we increase the number of workers reporting directly to this supervisor, system efficiency steadily decreases. The results are shown in Table 13–11. It follows, of course, that the percentage of workers not working $(1 - E)$, would increase as the number of subordinates increases. As expected, supervisory costs decrease and subordinate idle costs increase as the number of subordinates increases. There is a point where assigning more subordinates to a supervisor would cease to be beneficial. From Table 13–11, column six, the optimum assignment for one supervisor, when $X = 0.08$, is 10 subordinates. The cost functions are illustrated in Figure 13–11, where it is shown graphically that the minimum total cost is at 10 subordinates.

FIGURE 13–11

Total Costs and Number of Subordinates

$$X = 0.08 \qquad M = 1 \qquad c_5 = \$3 \qquad c_6 = \$6$$

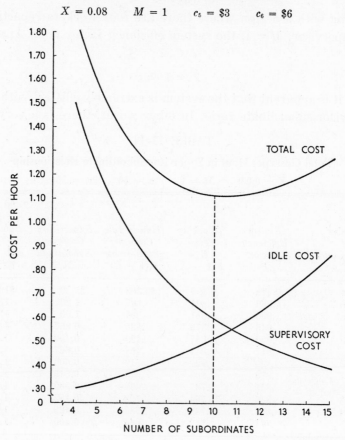

NUMBER OF SUBORDINATES

EXAMPLES 5 AND 6

In Table 13–12, we present an example where contacts between supervisor and subordinate last on the average of 0.957 minutes or $T = 0.01595$. The average productive time of workers is $U = 0.25$ hours. The service factor is $X = 0.06$. Notice that with a lower service factor than the system of the previous example the number of subordinates can be increased profitably. According to Table 13–12 and Figure 13–12, the optimum assignment for one supervisor, when $X = 0.06$, is 13 subordinates.

For further comparison, we present another example in Table 13–13, where $T = 0.02777$, $U = 0.25$, and $X = 0.1$. According to column six, the optimum assignment for one supervisor, when $X = 0.1$, is nine subordinates.

A comparison of the total cost curves for each of three examples is presented in Figure 13–13. This figure graphically illustrates

TABLE 13–12

Total Costs per Hour in Supervisor-Subordinate Relationship

$X = 0.06 \quad M = 1 \quad c_5 = \$3 \quad c_6 = \$6$

Number of Subordinates N	System Efficiency Factor F	Working Time $E = F(1-X)$	Hourly Idle Costs per Subordinate $c_5(1-E)$	Supervisory Costs per Subordinate $c_6(M/N)$	Total Hourly Costs per Subordinate $TC_c = c_5(1-E) + c_6(M/N)$
4	0.988	0.929	$0.213	$1.50	$1.713
5	.983	.924	.228	1.20	1.428
6	.978	.919	.243	1.00	1.243
7	.972	.914	.258	0.857	1.115
8	.965	.907	.279	0.750	1.029
9	.957	.899	.303	0.667	0.970
10	.949	.892	.324	0.600	0.924
11	.939	.883	.351	0.545	0.896
12	.928	.872	.384	0.500	0.884
13	.916	.861	.417	0.462	0.879
14	.902	.848	.456	0.429	0.885
15	.887	.834	.498	0.400	0.898
16	.870	.818	.546	0.375	0.921
17	.851	.800	.600	0.353	0.953
18	.830	.780	.660	0.333	0.993
19	.808	.759	.723	0.316	1.039
20	.785	.738	.786	0.300	1.086
21	.761	.715	.855	0.286	1.141
22	.736	.692	.924	0.273	1.197
23	.711	.668	.996	0.261	1.257

FIGURE 13-12

Total Costs and Number of Subordinates

$X = 0.06 \quad M = 1 \quad c_s = \$3 \quad c_b = \$6$

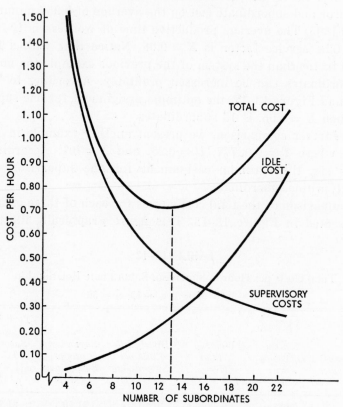

how differences in the service factor for contacts between supervisor and subordinate can affect the optimum span of control.

Note on the Model Applied to Span of Supervision

The waiting line model applied to the problem of span of supervision was constrained by the "principle" of organization—unity of command, which states that no one in the organization should report to more than one boss. Constrained by the one-boss rule, our approach was to hold $M = 1$, that is, hold to one supervisor, and to examine the system with various sizes of N, that is, vary the number of subordinates. This approach was different from our previous approach where we applied the model to machines and

TABLE 13-13

Total Costs per Hour in Supervisor-Subordinate Relationship

$X = 0.1 \quad M = 1 \quad c_5 = \$3 \quad c_6 = \$6$

Number of Subordinates N	System Efficiency Factor F	Working Time $E = F(1 - X)$	Hourly Idle Costs per Subordinate $c_5(1 - E)$	Supervisory Costs per Subordinate $c_6(M/N)$	Total Hourly Costs per Subordinate $TC_c = c_5(1 - E) + c_6(M/N)$
4	0.965	0.8685	\$0.3945	\$1.50	\$1.8945
5	.950	.855	0.435	1.20	1.635
6	.932	.8388	0.4836	1.00	1.4836
7	.912	.8208	0.5376	0.857	1.3946
8	.889	.8001	0.5997	0.750	1.3497
9	.862	.7758	0.6726	0.667	1.3396
10	.832	.7488	0.7536	0.600	1.3536
11	.799	.7191	0.8427	0.545	1.3877
12	.764	.6876	0.9372	0.500	1.4372
13	.727	.6543	1.0371	0.462	1.4991
14	.690	.621	1.137	0.428	1.5650
15	.653	.5877	1.2369	0.400	1.6369

repairmen. It can be shown through waiting line theory that the unity of command doctrine requires more supervisors than a design that allows subordinates to report to any of a group of supervisors, that is, hold N constant and vary M. In order to solve for the optimum in a multiple-reporting arrangement, we would follow the machine-repairman approach used earlier. Problems with multiple-reporting arrangements are included in the problem section at the end of the chapter.

While a multiple-reporting arrangement in which subordinates report to any supervisor requires less supervisors than an arrangement that adheres to the unity of command rule, its practicality is questionable. The necessity for establishing accountability and providing unity of direction is probably an overwhelming requirement in organizational design.

The necessity for directing all parts of the organization toward the accomplishment of overall objectives means that accountability, unity of direction, and unity of command are important requirements of the total system. It is likely, then, that the needs of the total system would lead to a rejection of a multiple-reporting arrangement even though it requires fewer supervisors. Thus, the one-boss rule is another illustration of how total system requirements constrain the design of subsystems. However, as we demon-

FIGURE 13-13

Total Costs and Number of Subordinates

$$X = 0.1 \qquad T = 0.02777$$
$$U = 0.25$$

$$X = 0.08 \qquad T = 0.02174$$
$$U = 0.25$$

$$X = 0.06 \qquad T = 0.01595$$
$$U = 0.25$$

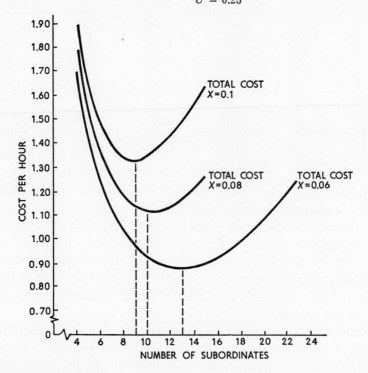

strated, the waiting line model may still be used within the unity of command constraint.

SUMMARY

The object of this chapter is to focus upon one type of discontinuity—the case of a difference between services demanded and services offered. The problem is a common one in the real world in which people, equipment, materials, information, and vehicles form waiting lines or queues in order to obtain some kind of service. The focal point of the waiting line problem is to determine the optimum number of components for a system. Essentially, this involves opposing costs—the cost of adding service components versus the cost of waiting in line for service.

In this chapter, we presented several waiting line models and showed how they can be applied to organizational design. In order to do this, we made several assumptions: (1) that although behavior may occur on a random basis, it can be expressed in terms of a statistical distribution; and (2) arrivals for service and service times follow a negative exponential distribution. In finite situations, the waiting line problem is simplified by the use of Finite Queuing Tables.

In the following chapter we are concerned with the problem of adding components in order to attain system reliability.

DISCUSSION QUESTIONS AND PROBLEMS

13–1. Arrivals at a warehouse loading platform average six trucks per hour. The dock crew can load a truck in an average of 7.5 minutes. Arrival rates and service rates resemble the Poisson distribution. Assume an infinite population.

a) Determine the average number of trucks in the system.
b) Determine the average number of trucks in the waiting line.
c) Determine the average waiting time in the line.
d) Determine the average waiting time in the system.

13–2. People arrive at a cafeteria check-out counter every 30 seconds. The cashier can compute and collect an average of 140 order slips an hour. Arrival rates and check-out rates resemble a Poisson distribution. Assume an infinite population.

a) Determine the average number of people in the system.
b) Determine the average number of people in the waiting line.
c) Determine the average waiting time in the line.
d) Determine the average waiting time in the system.

13–3. Every Friday, employees of a large university arrive at the Bursar's office to receive their paychecks. There is one pay clerk, and he can distribute 500 checks per hour. If 20 employees arrive every minute to receive their checks, determine the average waiting time in the line. Assume an infinite population.

13–4. Forty secretaries work in an office where there is one water cooler. Arrivals at the cooler average six secretaries per hour. The arrival rate resembles the Poisson distribution. The average length of time to get a drink is exponentially distributed and is 15 seconds.

a) What is the average number of secretaries waiting in line?
b) Assuming the secretaries work an eight-hour day and work at 80 percent of capacity, what is the average time spent doing productive work?

13–5. A dispensary in a steel plant employing 40 workers handles minor injuries and illnesses occurring during the workday. The fixed costs of the dispensary are $100 per week, and the wages paid to the nurses are $2 per hour. (Assume a 40-hour week.) Arrival rates and service rates are Poisson distributed. The service factor is 0.3, and the average arrival rate is 4 workers per hour. The opportunity cost of employees who use the dispensary is $3 per hour.

    a) Determine the average service time of the dispensary.

    b) Determine the optimum number of nurses needed to service the employees if the mean service times were:

        (1) 10 minutes.

        (2) 11.8 minutes.

13–6. Using the information given in problem 13–5, determine the optimum number of nurses if:

    a) The service factor was 0.1.

    b) The service factor was 0.2.

13–7. A fleet of 30 trucks is serviced by 1 repairman. Breakdowns follow the Poisson distribution and occur on the average of one every five hours. The service factor of the repairman is 0.05. The opporturnity cost per truck during a breakdown is $10 per hour. The repairman is paid $3.50 per hour. Using the finite queuing tables:

    a) Determine the effectiveness of the system.

    b) Determine the optimum number of repairmen needed in order to maximize effectiveness.

    c) Determine the optimum number of repairmen needed, considering the decision criteria.

13–8. In a manufacturing plant, there are 40 machines whose breakdowns approximate the Poisson distribution. It is estimated that when a machine breaks down the company is losing $8 per hour per machine. Repairman wages are $4 per hour. The average service time per machine is found to be one hour. The machines average two breakdowns per eight-hour day. Due to the nature of the output, a maximum running time is desired; however, the management also wishes to minimize its costs. Provide sufficient information for management to make a rational decision concerning the optimum number of repairmen to use. (Use the finite queuing tables.)

13–9. The production division of the LBS corporation is having efficiency problems with its span of supervision. The production manager has 12 subordinates under his supervision. A subordinate spends about 30 minutes with the manager during a conference. Conferences take place on the average of one every two hours. Thus, the production manager has little time to do anything else but give advice. In your solution to the problem, assume that subordinates can have more than one supervisor.

a) Determine the optimum number of supervisors to hire if the objective is to minimize total cost per man-hour of nonproductive operations. Subordinates are worth $2 per hour and supervisor's time is worth $7 per hour.

b) Determine the average number of subordinates waiting for service for all values of M you have found.

13-10. In the military, a company commander has four platoon leaders reporting directly to him. Assume that the platoon leaders' time is worth $2.50 per hour and the company commander's time is worth $3.50 per hour. Average contact time is 15 minutes, and time between contacts is two hours.

a) What is the service factor?

b) What are total nonproductive costs per hour for the company commander and his platoon leaders?

c) What is the optimum number of platoon leaders that should report to the company commander? Use:
1) The service factor from this problem.
2) The service factor from problem 13-9.

13-11. A hospital supervisor has seven nurses reporting to her. The supervisor's time is worth $6 per hour, and nurses are worth $3 per hour. Assume the average time per contact is 15 minutes and the service factor is 0.1.

a) What is the average time between calls for service?

b) Determine the percent waiting time per subordinate.

c) Determine the average productive time of subordinates.

d) Determine whether or not the 7 to 1 ratio of nurses to supervisors is optimum.

13-12.° A newly organized manufacturing plant has 60 machines. The management cannot decide whether to centralize or decentralize its repairmen. A service factor of 0.15 is estimated. The repairmen are paid $3.50 per hour, and the lost revenue during machine breakdowns is $10 per hour. (Make use of Table 13-6.)

a) Prepare a table similar to Table 13-7 for N's of 15, 30, and 60.

b) Prepare a table similar to Table 13-8 for N's of 15, 30, and 60.

c) Should the repairmen be centralized or decentralized? If decentralized, how?

13-13.° A milk plant has 80 trucks used for delivery. A crew of mechanics is centrally organized to repair the trucks when they break down. The service factor is 0.1. Mechanics are paid $3 an hour, and lost revenue for each truck during breakdowns is $5 per hour. The supervisor is thinking of decentralizing the mechanics. What should the supervisor do? (Use N-values of 10, 20, 40, and 80. Assume $g = 0.1$.)

13-14. A hospital has a staff of 60 nurses. The nurses report to one of

several supervisors when a problem arises which the nurses cannot
handle. The supervisor's time is worth $5 an hour, and the nurses
are worth $100 for a 40-hour week. A centralized organization is
presently used. The hospital is considering switching to a decentralized organization with each nurse reporting to one supervisor. To aid you in your decision, prepare tables similar to
Table 13–7 and Table 13–8 in the text. (Assume a service factor
of 0.2 and that $g = 0.3$). Use: $N = 4, 5, 6, 10, 12, 15$.

13–15.° An income tax center is composed of 60 agents. The duty of the
agent is to investigate cases of tax default. An agent has the
authority to settle any account without the approval of the supervisor. In some instances, an agent must contact a supervisor—for
example, for legal advice. Since very few contacts are necessary,
the service factor is low $(X = 0.03)$. The supervisor receives $5
per hour, and the agents are worth $3 per hour. Assume that the
cases are homogeneous in nature and that a centralized pool of
supervisors could serve the needs of the 60 agents. There are two
ways to organize the tax center: alternative No. 1, centralize; alternative No. 2, various ways of decentralization. Which alternative
gives the lowest hourly cost per agent?

a) Use equation (13–18).

b) Use equation (13–20) ; assume $g = 0.1$.

* For these problems, consult L. G. Peck and R. N. Hazelwood,
Finite Queuing Tables (New York: John Wiley & Sons, Inc., 1958).

14

SYSTEM RELIABILITY IN ORGANIZATIONAL DESIGN

On April 18, 1958, Andrei Gromyko, the foreign minister for the Soviet Union, charged that the United States was endangering world peace by sending its Strategic Air Command jet bombers loaded with nuclear bombs across the Arctic areas in the direction of the borders of the Soviet Union. He said atomic war could descend on the world as a result of "the slightest mistake on the part of an American technician from carelessness, miscalculation or a faulty conclusion on the part of some American officer. The Soviet Government protests the United States actions," Mr. Gromyko declared, "and demands that the practice of sending bombers carrying atomic and hydrogen bombs in the direction of the Soviet Union's borders be stopped immediately."[1] Representatives of the U.S. government replied quickly with strong denials. James Hagerty, the Presidential press secretary said: "Mr. Gromyko's statements are not true." The State Department in a formal statement said: "It is categorically denied that the U.S. Air Force is conducting provocative flights."[2]

The charges made by the Soviet Union were in reference to the practice "bombing runs" of the Strategic Air Command. The purpose of these practice missions was to develop combat-ready crews and a deterrent force against a possible enemy attack. Besides the

---

[1] Reported in *The New York Times*, Vol. 107, No. 36,610 (April 19, 1958), pp. 1–2. © 1958 by The New York Times Company. Reprinted by permission.

[2] Reported in *Time*, Vol. 71, No. 17 (April 28, 1958), p. 15.

enormous problems of organizing a deterrent force, the Armed Forces had to design a system that "could not fail," that is, a system that eliminated the chance that a mechanical, electronic, or human failure could cause a war. In the words of the Air Force, the system had to be "Fail Safe." According to *Time:*

> Fail Safe is a cold-war projection of an engineering principle used for decades in aircraft design and around dangerous machinery. The principle: if a device can fail, it must be assumed that it will fail, and it must be designed so that its failure will do minimal or no harm. Fail safe on U.S. railroads, for example, means "the dead man's throttle." If an engineer dies at the controls, his pressure on a foot pedal or hand lever is released, and the train automatically goes into an emergency stop.[3]

The name of the system has been changed. Instead of "Fail Safe," it is now called the "Positive Control" system.

Were the Armed Forces successful? Is there a possibility of war because of mechanical, electronic, or human error? After several weeks of personal investigation, Donald Robinson answered this question and gave a detailed explanation in a magazine article.[4] Since the article is so concise and to the point, major portions of it are reproduced below.

> The truth is this. U.S. Air Force . . . safeguards are now so effective that there is not one chance in a million of a mechanical, electronic, or human failure causing war.
>
> In the event of an attack on the United States or its allies, a conference phone call would instantly be set up between the President, Secretary of Defense . . . , the Joint Chiefs of Staff, the commander of NORAD [North American Air Defense Command], General Power [the Commander in Chief of the Strategic Air Command], and others. Should the President decide on a counterattack, orders would be given to General Power with the others listening in.
>
> The Pentagon makes sure that nothing will go wrong with this procedure. Several methods of communication are employed to link the President with his military chiefs wherever they may be. At frequent intervals, dry runs are held in which the President and the others practice their emergency roles.
>
> The safeguards that SAC takes against unauthorized actions by its own personnel are as thorough. No person is allowed to be in a SAC plane

---

[3] *Ibid.*, p. 16.

[4] Donald Robinson, "How Safe is Fail-Safe?" *This Week* (January 27, 1963), pp. 4–7. Reprinted from THIS WEEK Magazine. Copyrighted 1963 by the United Newspapers Magazine Corporation. Although the author discussed both Air Force and Navy defense systems, we limit the excerpts to those parts of the article that cover the Air Force system.

alone. He can't even approach a nuclear armed SAC plane by himself. Every nuclear armed SAC plane is patrolled by armed sentries who won't allow anyone to come near unless he is in the company of at least one other authorized individual. Each has to show his SAC credentials.

The "Positive Control" system moves into top gear as soon as an alert is ordered. It is a miracle of checks and double checks to forestall any conceivable error.

The System Has Five Steps

1. The alert order is flashed directly from SAC headquarters to each SAC unit in code by radio and other electronic means. It tells what war plan is to be implemented, which targets are to be hit. Several officers in the unit Command Post—majors or lieutenant colonels with at least ten years' service—must decode the message individually, check it with one another, and then authenticate it, before bombers fly.

2. Meanwhile, klaxons are screaming and the bomber crews are racing to their planes. The officer in charge of the unit's codes is the pivotal man now. He supplies three crew members on each plane with the day's codes.

These codes are changed every day, and in some cases every hour. This is to prevent an enemy nation from penetrating them. SAC is always on guard against the possibility that a third power—Communist China, for example—might transmit false radio messages to our bombers in an effort to provoke war between us and the U.S.S.R.

The codes are protected more closely than the U.S. Mint. A few months ago, a SAC bomber crashed on foreign soil. Within ten minutes, orders had gone out to every SAC base and plane in the world to abandon the code of the wrecked bomber.

3. The minute the crews board their aircraft, they start the engines and wait for radio instructions from the unit Command Post. These tell them if the alert is another practice or the real thing.

4. Should it be the real thing, the jet bombers start roaring down the runways and up into the sky—giant B-52's each with six men aboard, B-47's and B-58's each with three men in its crew, all bearing fantastic stores of thermonuclear destruction.

Each bomber is heading toward specific enemy targets. None can fly anywhere near enemy territory, though, without further directive. Each has a "Positive Control" point, outside the Russian radar early-warning line, beyond which it cannot pass until it receives a coded message from SAC telling it to "Go."

This is the most significant portion of the "Positive Control" system. Unless a bomber receives this "Go" order, it automatically returns to its base.

Silence from SAC means just one thing. The plane must turn home.[5]

5. The final provision of the "Positive Control" system concerns the "Go" message itself. No fabled little black box, or any other mechanical

---

[5] Italics were added by the authors.

gadget, can distort the message. The order is always transmitted verbally by radio.

It requires three men to decode it. Therefore no one man can, by error or design, mislead the other members of the crew into thinking that they have been directed to "Go." Nor can any plane broadcast a false "Go" order to other SAC bombers in the air.

What would happen if a deranged pilot decided to drop a bomb on Russia without orders?

He can't do it. It takes at least three men to fly a SAC bomber and each one of them must take individual action for its nuclear weapons to be armed.

What if the Commander-in-Chief of SAC were to become unbalanced and attempt to start a war?

SAC has thought of that too. General Power has instructed the SAC Control Center not to accept any executive order—including his own—without being positive of its authenticity. The command post must check the validity of any orders received.

SAC's "Positive Control" system . . . has been 100 per cent successful for the past 16 years. Despite all the rumors to the contrary, not one U.S. bomber has been launched by mistake.

The world need not fear the United States will ever start an accidental war.

According to the account by Robinson, then, we may conclude that the "Fail Safe" system is very reliable. Let us now examine a system that proved to be very unreliable.

Pearl Harbor

The surprise attack on Pearl Harbor by the Japanese on December 7, 1941 has been called "the greatest military disaster in American history."[6] The attack lasted 110 minutes and when it was over ". . . 2,403 Americans—mostly sailors on the battleships were dead or dying; 1,178 more had been wounded; the battle force of the Pacific Fleet had been destroyed, with four battleships sunk or capsized and the remaining four damaged. . . ."[7] Several other vessels were destroyed or badly damaged and almost half of the American military planes were destroyed or disabled. Japanese losses were nominal. Our military forces were almost totally unprepared for the attack. This fact seems almost incredible in view of the events that preceded the disaster.

---

[6] Samuel Eliot Morison, "The Lessons of Pearl Harbor," *Saturday Evening Post*, Vol. 234, No. 43 (October 28, 1961), p. 20.

[7] T. N. Dupuy, "Pearl Harbor—Who Blundered?" *American Heritage*, Vol. 13, No. 2 (February, 1962), p. 80.

Colonel T. N. Dupuy has written a detailed account of, and commentary on, the events immediately preceding the disaster, during the critical days when the existing system was put to the test. To the student of organizational systems, the pattern of events described furnishes a classic example of a system that failed to carry important messages and implement command decisions. The system was unreliable. Colonel Dupuy states the problem well:

A well-planned and brilliantly executed surprise attack by Japanese carrier-based aircraft was launched against the major American bastion in the Pacific. The United States government, its senior military leaders, and its commanders in Hawaii had had sufficient information to be adequately warned that an attack was possible, and had had time to be prepared to thwart or to blunt the blow. The information was largely ignored; the preparations were utterly inadequate.

At the time the attack occurred, four professional military men held key posts: in Washington, General George C. Marshall, Army Chief of Staff and his Navy counterpart, Admiral Harold R. Stark, Chief of Naval Operations; in Oahu, Hawaii, Lieutenant General Walter C. Short, commander of the Hawaiian Army Department and Rear Admiral Husband E. Kimmel, commander of the U.S. Pacific Fleet.

The following discussion is based on Colonel Dupuy's account of the sequence of events, of the reactions of those in responsible positions, and of the actions taken by them.[8]

That the professional military men individually had the knowledge needed to put them on the alert and to make them suspicious of Japan is clear from the following:

a) They shared the established opinion among military men that a clash with Japan for control of the Pacific was inevitable and that in that clash the Pearl Harbor base and the Pacific Fleet were vital factors.

b) In 1940, the Japanese secret codes were cracked, a procedure the War Department named "Magic." Through Magic code radio intercepts each of the military men in positions of importance was provided with information about Japanese intentions and plans for the attack as they developed, right up to December 7, the day the attack occurred.

Why then, did the system fail? Colonel Dupuy's account suggests some answers. One is that each commander (Kimmel and Short)

---

[8] *Ibid.*, pp. 65–81.

assumed that the other knew his business and that "to probe into the other's shop would be an unpardonable and resented intrusion. As a result, the liason essential to any sort of joint or concerted operation . . . was almost nonexistent. Each commander, then, was working in a partial vacuum."[9]

It becomes evident, too, in reading Colonel Dupuy's account that important messages were received, mainly by way of Magic code radio intercepts, but were misunderstood or not taken seriously enough to be acted upon. For example, it was known in this way that the Japanese were concentrating a large proportion of their military strength in the Indochina and South China areas, but that the aircraft carriers that later carried out the attack on Pearl Harbor were nowhere to be found. The significance of this was disregarded.

On November 25, Admiral Stark sent a warning to Admiral Kimmel in Hawaii that "neither the President nor the Secretary of State would be surprised over a Japanese surprise attack," but he thought it was likely to come in the Philippines.

It was known, too, as early as November 24, that the chances of a favorable outcome of the negotiations with Japanese envoys were small. On November 25, General Marshall and Admiral Stark learned that Secretary of State Hull had given the Japanese envoys a statement of the American position that would almost surely be interpreted by the Japanese government as "practically putting an end to negotiations."

The civilian authorities relied upon the military men to carry out existing war plans and to be ready for any attack. Secretary of State Hull said, "I have washed my hands of it, and it is now in the hands of you [General MacArthur] and Knox and the Army and the Navy." Finally, at this time, steps for security were taken by Kimmel and Short, but they were inadequate and uncoordinated.

Even on the morning of December 7, when intercepted Japanese messages clearly indicated that something was about to happen, there was still time to make some preparations. However, the personality of General Marshall (for example, he did not want to be disturbed during off-duty hours), poor organization, and mismanagement prevented that possibility. As described by Colonel Dupuy:

By 8 A.M. [2:30 A.M. Hawaii time] the last part of the Japanese memorandum—Part Fourteen—had been intercepted, transcribed, and was

9 *Ibid.*, p. 68.

ready for distribution. Both Army and Navy intelligence officers were slightly surprised at its mild tone: "The Japanese Government regrets . . . that it is impossible to reach an agreement through further negotiations."

Stark got it in his office. Marshall was taking his Sunday morning recreational ride at Fort Myer: the message would await his arrival— usually at about 11 A.M. All others concerned got it. Meanwhile two other messages had been intercepted by Magic, and Colonel Rufus Bratton, executive officer in G–2, was so upset by them he tried vainly to get them to the Chief of Staff.

One of the messages ordered the embassy to destroy immediately its one remaining cipher machine plus all codes and secret documents. The other read:

"Will the Ambassador please submit to the United States Government (if possible to the Secretary of State) our reply to the United States at 1 P.M. on the 7th, your time."

It will be remembered that General Marshall did not take kindly to interruptions in his off-duty hours. So, despite the limited area of his ride—an automobile or motorcycle from Fort Myer headquarters could have intercepted him in fifteen minutes at most—not until his return to his quarters at ten-thirty did Marshall learn that an important message was awaiting him. He reached his office in the Munitions Building at about 11:15, to find General Gerow, General Miles, and Colonel Bratton there. Bratton handed him the three intercepted messages—the memorandum, the instructions to destroy codes and papers, and the instruction to deliver the Japanese answer at 1 P.M. precisely.[10]

Colonel Dupuy describes the action taken by General Marshall when he received the memorandum, and the ensuing events on December 7, as follows:

He [Marshall] immediately called Stark, who had read all three messages. A warning should be sent at once to all Pacific commanders, Marshall felt; Stark hesitated; he felt all had already been alerted. Marshall stated that in view of the "one o'clock" item he would apprise Army commanders anyway.

Hanging up, he reached for a pencil and drafted his instruction to DeWitt, Western Defense Command; Andrews, Panama Command; Short, Hawaiian Command; and MacArthur, Philippine Command. It took him about three minutes. He read it to the group:

"The Japanese are presenting at 1 P.M. E.S.T. today, what amounts to an ultimatum. Also they are under orders to destroy their code machine immediately. Just what significance the hour set may have, we do not know, but be on alert accordingly."

As he was ordering Bratton to send it out at once, Stark telephoned back. Would Marshall please include in his dispatch the "usual expression

---

[10] *Ibid.*, p. 78.

to inform the naval officers?" Marshall quickly added the words "Inform naval authorities of this communication." He sent Bratton on his way, instructing him to return as soon as the message had been delivered to the message center.

Bratton was back in five minutes; he had delivered the message personally to the officer in charge of the message center, Colonel French.

Marshall, obviously more perturbed than any of those present had ever before seen him, asked Bratton how much time would be consumed in enciphering and dispatching the message. Bratton didn't know. So back he was rushed to find out.

Marshall, it developed, was pondering whether or not he should telephone a warning—especially to MacArthur. Time was running out; not much more than one hour remained. Marshall had a "scrambler" phone on his desk, which permitted secure long-distance conversations with similar phones in the headquarters of overseas commanders; eavesdroppers would hear only unintelligible gibberish. Marshall, however, must have had some private reservations as to the efficacy of the scrambler mechanism, and apparently feared that the Japanese might have some way of deciphering the conversation. A telephone call which could not be kept secret might precipitate Japanese action; it would almost certainly indicate we had broken their secret code. Would it be worth it?

Bratton reported back that the process would take about thirty minutes.

"Thirty minutes until it is dispatched, or thirty minutes until it is received and decoded at the other end?"

Business of rushing back to the message center again, while the big office clock ticked away. Bratton charging back, announced that the message, decoded, would be in the hands of the addressees in thirty minutes. It was not precisely noon. In Hawaii it was only 6:30 A.M. Marshall, satisfied, made no further follow-up.

Had he done so he would have found out that Colonel French at the message center was having some troubles. To San Francisco, Panama, and Manila the warning sped without delay. But the War Department radio, so Colonel French was informed, had been out of contact with Hawaii since 10:20 that morning. French decided to use commercial facilities: Western Union to San Francisco, thence commercial radio to Honolulu. This was a normal procedure; usually it would mean but little further delay. French never dreamed of disturbing the Chief of Staff by reporting such trivia. So Marshall's warning was filed at the Army Signal Center at 12:01 P.M (6:31 A.M in Hawaii) : teletype transmission to San Francisco was completed by 12:17 P.M (6:47 A.M in Hawaii), and was in the Honolulu office of RCA at 1:03 P.M Washington time (7:33 A.M in Hawaii). Since that was too early for teletype traffic to Fort Shafter, RCA sent it by motorcycle messenger. He would, as it turned out, be delayed through extraordinary circumstances.[11]

---

[11] *Ibid.*, p. 78–79.

The circumstances that delayed the messenger were these:

> The Nisei RCA messenger boy carrying General Marshall's message speedily found himself involved in trouble. Not until 11:45 could he thread his way through traffic jams, road blocks, and general confusion to reach the Fort Shafter signal office, which was itself swamped in traffic by this time.
>
> Not until 2:58 P.M Hawaiian time—9:58 that evening in bewildered Washington—was the message decoded and placed on Short's desk. He rushed a copy to Admiral Kimmel, who read it, remarked—perhaps unnecessarily—that it was not of the slightest interest any more, and dropped it into the wastebasket.[12]

Colonel Dupuy summarizes and assesses responsibility for Pearl Harbor as follows:

> No disaster of the magnitude of Pearl Harbor could have occurred without the failure—somewhere and somehow—of leadership. A total of eight separate official investigations searched for scapegoats, and found them. The disaster remained a political football long after the last three of these investigations. And much confusion and argument still exist.
>
> Yet through this welter of discord, some facts and conclusions stand out. Today, twenty years later, in another time of crisis, they hold important lessons.
>
> It makes no difference, in assessing responsibility, that exceptional Japanese military skill, shrouded by deceit and assisted by almost incredible luck, accomplished its mission. Nor, indeed, does it matter that—as adjudicated in the always brilliant light of afterthought—Japan might well have inflicted defeat upon our Pacific Fleet and our Army forces in Hawaii regardless of how well alerted they may have been on December 7, 1941.
>
> It makes no difference, so far as responsibility for the disaster itself was concerned, whether the war could have been prevented by wiser statesmanship or more astute diplomacy—though this would have required a wholehearted and unified national determination which did not exist in America in 1941 and the years before. It makes no difference that on December 7 the President and the Secretary of State—like the civilian Secretaries of War and Navy—had their eyes fixed on the Japanese threat in Southeast Asia. They had repeatedly warned the military men that war had probably become unavoidable.
>
> What *does* matter is that the civilian statesmen—however deft or clumsy, shrewd, or shortsighted—performed their difficult tasks of diplomacy and of administration confident that the military men would carry out their professional responsibilities by doing everything humanly possible to prepare for a war so clearly impending. They had every right to

---

[12] *Ibid.*, p. 80.

expect that—within the limits of scanty means available—the Armed Forces would be ready for any contingency.

The confidence and expectations of civilian leadership and of the nation were tragically dashed that Sunday morning. . . .

Military failures were responsible for Pearl Harbor.

In Washington the most important of these were the following:

1. The War Department staff, over which General Marshall presided, was at the time a complicated but "one-man" shop, where delegation of responsibility was the exception rather than the rule. When Marshall was absent, the operational wheels tended to freeze. This situation was to some extent due to cumbersome organization, to some extent due to the personality of the Chief of Staff.

2. General Marshall, in a letter to General Short on February 7, 1941, stressed that "the risk of sabotage and the *risk involved in a surprise raid by air and submarine* (underscore supplied) constitute the real perils of the (Hawaiian) situation." Yet, although definitely warning General Short on November 27 of the threat of war, and ordering him to report the measures he would take in response, Marshall did not check up on those measures; moreover, he was unaware that Short had done no more than to take routine precautions against sabotage. And General Gerow, heading the War Plans Division of General Marshall's General Staff—as he testified later in taking full responsibility for this slip—had not made any provision for following up operational orders. The net result was that both Marshall and Short remained the whole time in blissful ignorance of a vital misinterpretation of orders.

3. Marshall and Admiral Stark—and indeed all members of their staffs who knew the situation—permitted themselves to be hyponotized by the concrete evidence of the aggressive Japanese build-up in Southeast Asia which threatened our Philippines outpost. This theme, it will be remembered, ran as background to nearly all the warnings sent Hawaii. Thus succumbing to the illusory diagnosis of "enemy probable intentions," both top commanders ignored the danger implicit in our inability to locate at least four Japanese carriers.

4. Finally, on December 7, having indicated his full realization of the significance of the "one o'clock" intercept—that less than two hours now separated peace and war—and having decided not to use his "scrambler" telephone, Marshall failed to require surveillance and positive report on the delivery of his final warning.[13]

A COMPARISON OF SYSTEMS

As Colonel Dupuy points out, the American people have every right to expect the Armed Forces of the United States to be ready for any contingency. At Pearl Harbor, the military system failed

---

[13] *Ibid.,* p. 81.

miserably. On the other hand, the military "Positive Control" system has been extremely successful. While there are many reasons for the failure at Pearl Harbor, the most important reason for organizational design was the fact that decisions were made on a unilateral basis and communications followed a single channel. The result of this practice was that important decisions and communications were delayed or easily blocked. At the top levels of the military organization, this practice was evidenced by the tendency of Marshall's staff to become inoperative in the general's absence; the reluctance of staff people to disturb General Marshall on his off-duty hours—even though important Japanese messages had been intercepted; the failure of General Marshall and his staff to "check up on" whether or not adequate preparations had been made for the anticipated attack; the failure of General Marshall to use more than one channel of communication in issuing the "final warnings"; and the failure of General Marshall to check "on the delivery of his final warning." At the operating level, this practice was evidenced by the tendency of Admiral Kimmel, commander of the Pacific Fleet, and General Short, commander of the Army forces, to act independently (". . . each commander assumed the other knew his business . . . the liaison essential to any sort of joint or concerted action . . . was almost nonexistent"); the reluctance of the commanders to exchange information, for example, reports of Japanese ship movements received by Kimmel and the independent intelligence reports received by both men, and the warnings of November 27, were not discussed by the two commanders. Another striking example at the operating level was that the attack planes were detected by radar on December 7, and the system failed to carry this information to a command position. The radar crew sighted the attack planes while they were still 110 miles away. On reporting their findings to the duty officer, they were told to "forget it." The biggest blunder at the operating level was, of course, the failure of Short and Kimmel to take adequate precautionary measures against attack, even though they were forewarned.

Obviously, Robinson's purpose in writing about the more successful "Positive Control" system was to impress readers with the safeguards taken to prevent "accidental war." While the prevention of "accidental war" is not the purpose of the U.S. defense system, it is a very important constraint and undoubtedly affects the design of the system. Contrary to the Pearl Harbor situation, it is evident that in the "Positive Control" system decisions are made on a multilateral basis and that more than one channel is used for communications. In more technical language, the requirements that the President consult with top civilian and military officials before ordering a counterattack, that more than one man decode messages, that more than one man fly the aircraft, and that more than one man arm the nuclear weapons, appear similar to efforts in systems design to have enough *components in parallel* so as to maximize the probability that the system will function properly. In general, the concern is with the reliability of systems.

MEASURES OF SYSTEM RELIABILITY

In order for a system to function properly, it is necessary that certain of its individual components function properly. One way of improving the probability that a system will function properly is to duplicate or add parallel components to the system. However, by adding components, we also increase the probability that the system will function inadvertently. Thus, with more channels of communication there may be a greater probability that missiles will be launched when they should not or that SAC bombers will proceed past the "Positive Control" point when they should return to their home base. It remains, therefore, to develop a procedure for determining the optimum number of parallel components in a system.[14]

Let us begin by examining communication systems that operate under the simple assumption that accidental behavior is impossible. More specifically, we assume that the system has two possible responses :

1. The system operates correctly, or
2. The system fails completely.

Under this simple assumption, the system does not produce an incorrect signal. Later, we examine systems that do have the possibility of operating inadvertently. Throughout our discussion, it is

---

[14] The procedure that follows was developed by: Robert Gordon,"Optimum Component Redundancy for Maximum System Reliability," *Operations Research*, Vol. 5 (1957), pp. 229–43. Also see John G. Kemeny, Arthur Schleifer, Jr., J. Laurie Snell, and Gerald L. Thompson, *Finite Mathematics with Business Applications* (Englewood Cliffs, N.J.: Prentice-Hall, Inc., 1962), pp. 215–21.

assumed that the ability of one component in a system to function is independent of the other components' ability to function.

Single-Channel System

A very simple communication system of four components, A, B, C, D, is shown in Figure 14–1. While each component of System S_1 is connected with the other components, the ability of any one to

FIGURE 14–1

Communication System S_1

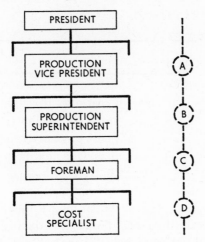

function correctly is independent of the abilities of the others. However, it is obvious from the diagram of Figure 14–1 that the System S_1 cannot function correctly (or process messages through the system) unless all components function correctly. System S_1 may be illustrated in a practical situation by a simple line arrangement in which cost data are reported through a business organization, as shown in Figure 14–2. System S_1 is superimposed in the diagram to show its component counterpart in the production activity of the business. This same detail could be shown for other activities of the business, such as marketing and finance.

FIGURE 14–2

Business Organization and System S_1

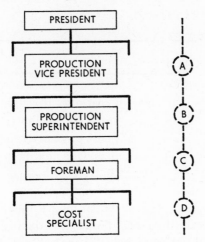

Suppose that a component of type A has a probability of functioning correctly of 0.9, type B functions correctly with a probability of 0.7, type C with a probability of 0.8, and type D with a probability of 0.6. Since each component is independent, we may determine the probability that the total system will function correctly from the following general equation:

$$P(S_1) = P(A) \cdot P(B) \cdot P(C) \cdot P(D) \qquad (14-1)$$

Thus:

$$P(S_1) = (0.9)(0.7)(0.8)(0.6)$$
$$= 0.3024$$

Two-Channel System

We could increase the overall system reliability or improve the probability that the entire system will function properly by creating another system identical to, but independent of, S_1 and placing the two systems in parallel as shown in Figure 14–3. Thus, the overall System S_2 will function properly if either of the two Subsystems S_1 function properly.

FIGURE 14–3

Communication System S_2

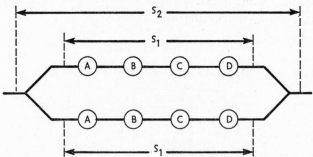

Again, using the reporting of cost data through a business organization, we may illustrate System S_2 as shown in Figure 14–4. According to this arrangement, cost data are reported through two separate and independent channels. One channel represents the line organization of the production activity whose cost reports eventually reach the president. The other channel is the staff organization of the financial vice president which makes independent studies of production costs and reports its findings to the president.

We can determine the probability that S_2 will function correctly

FIGURE 14-4

Business Organization and System S_2

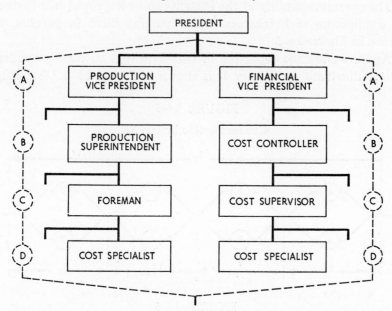

by first indicating the probability that it will *not* function correctly. If $P(S_2)$ is the probability that S_2 will function correctly, then $[1 - P(S_2)]$ is the probability that it will not function correctly. Both subsystems of type S_1 must fail to function correctly in order for System S_2 to function improperly. This condition may be written as follows:

$$1 - P(S_2) = [1 - P(S_1)] [1 - P(S_1)]$$
$$= [1 - P(S_1)]^2$$

From this condition, we may write the probability that S_2 will function properly as follows:

$$P(S_2) = 1 - [1 - P(S_1)]^2 \qquad (14-2)$$

Substituting the known value of $P(S_1)$ in equation (14-2), we have:

$$P(S_2) = 1 - [1 - 0.3024]^2$$
$$= 1 - [0.4866]$$
$$= 0.5134$$

Comparing $P(S_1)$ and $P(S_2)$, we see that the reliability of the system has been improved. Obviously, the addition of an independent system in parallel increases the probability of functioning properly.

The overall reliability of the system can be improved still further by duplicating each component and putting them in parallel, as shown in Figure 14–5.

Again we use the reporting of cost data in a business organization to illustrate the system. It is shown in Figure 14–6. Obviously,

FIGURE 14–5

Communication System S_3

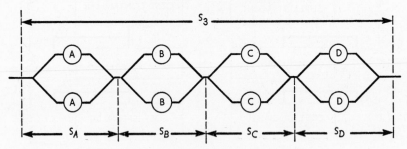

FIGURE 14–6

Business Organization and System S_3

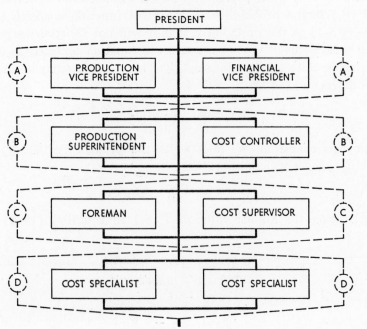

System S_3 has all the advantages of S_2 plus the additional advantage that reports from components can be passed through one or two other components.

Communication System S_3 will function correctly as long as one component in every pair functions correctly. It will not function properly only if *both* components of any pair fails. If $P(S_A)$ is the probability that S_A will function properly then $[1 - P(S_A)]$ is the probability that it will fail. Both components of type A must fail in order for S_A to fail. Thus:

$$1 - P(S_A) = [1 - P(A)] [1 - P(A)]$$
$$= [1 - P(A)]^2$$

It follows, therefore, that the probability that S_A will function properly is:

$$P(S_A) = 1 - [1 - P(A)]^2 \qquad (14\text{-}3)$$

Similar reasoning holds for $P(S_B)$, $P(S_C)$ and $P(S_D)$. Hence the probability that S_3 is reliable is:

$$P(S_3) = [P(S_A)] [P(S_B)] [P(S_C)] [P(S_D)]$$
$$= [1 - (1 - P(A))^2] [1 - (1 - P(B))^2]$$
$$[1 - (1 - P(C))^2] [1 - (1 - P(D))^2] \qquad (14\text{-}4)$$

Substituting the known values of $P(A)$, $P(B)$, $P(C)$, and $P(D)$, we have:

$$P(S_3) = [1 - (1 - 0.9)^2] [1 - (1 - 0.7)^2] [1 - (1 - 0.8)^2]$$
$$[1 - (1 - 0.6)^2]$$
$$= (0.99)(0.91)(0.96)(0.84)$$
$$= 0.7265$$

Comparing $P(S_3)$ to $P(S_2)$, we see that the reliability of the system was improved by putting two of each type of component in parallel.

Three-Channel System

The system can be improved still further by putting three of each type of component in parallel as shown in Figure 14–7.

The probability that System S_4 will function properly is:

$$P(S_4) = [P(S_A)] [P(S_B)] [P(S_C)] [P(S_D)]$$
$$= [1 - (1 - P(A))^3] [1 - (1 - P(B))^3] [1 - (1 - P(C))^3]$$
$$[1 - (1 - P(D))^3] \qquad (14\text{-}5)$$

FIGURE 14-7

Communication System S_4

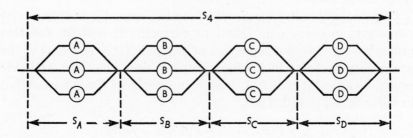

Substituting the known values of $P(A)$, $P(B)$, $P(C)$, and $P(D)$, we have:

$$P(S_4) = [1 - (1 - 0.9)^3] [1 - (1 - 0.7)^3] [1 - (1 - 0.8)^3] [1 - (1 - 0.6)^3]$$
$$= (0.999) (0.973) (0.992) (0.936)$$
$$= 0.903$$

Again, we have increased the reliability of the system by adding components in parallel. We could illustrate System S_4 by adding to the illustration of Figure 14-6 an agency which is charged with the responsibility of reporting cost data such as an engineering activity, or a personnel activity.

Systems S_3 and S_4, illustrated in Figure 14-6, require unorthodox organization, unorthodox in the sense that it deviates from the traditional design of line and staff and unity of command. Designs patterned after S_3 and S_4 are more reliable than systems that follow traditional organizational structure. In terms of a probability measure of reliability, it can be shown that systems of the type S_3 and S_4 are always more reliable than their counterpart in the traditional design. For example, let us compare two systems with four components—one designed according to S_3 and the other according to traditional design following the rule of unity of command. The designs are shown in Figure 14-8. For the sake of simplicity, let us assume that components A and B are reliable with a probability measure where $0 < p < 1$.

The probability that S_3 is reliable can be written as follows:

$$P(S_3) = [1 - (1 - p)^2] [1 - (1 - p)^2]$$
$$= [1 - (1 - p)^2]^2$$
$$= 4p^2 - 4p^3 + p^4$$
$$= p^2(4 - 4p + p^2) \qquad (14-6)$$

FIGURE 14–8

Comparison of Designs

SYSTEM S_3	TRADITIONAL

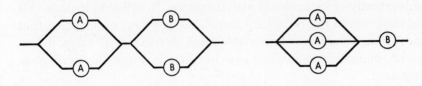

The probability that the traditional design is reliable can be written as follows:

$$P(\text{traditional}) = [1 - (1 - p)^3]p$$
$$= (3p - 3p^2 + p^3)p$$
$$= 3p^2 - 3p^3 + p^4$$
$$= p^2(3 - 3p + p^2) \qquad (14\text{–}7)$$

If S_3 is better than the traditional design, then the difference between equations (14–6) and (14–7) should be greater than zero, that is, if:

$$P(S_3) - P(\text{traditional}) > 0; \text{then } P(S_3) > P(\text{traditional})$$

Substituting, we have:

$$p^2(4 - 4p + p^2) - p^2(3 - 3p + p^2) = p^2(1 - p) > 0$$

Thus, we have shown in terms of a probability measure of reliability that System S_3 is always better than the traditional design.[15]

A More Comprehensive Model

It is evident that the probability of functioning correctly can be made as large as we please by adding enough of each type of component in parallel. However, the addition of components is likely to increase the costs and space requirements of the system. The systems designer, therefore, must decide whether the increased reliability is worth the costs associated with adding components to the systems.[16] There is still another consideration that should be

---

[15] This discussion is adapted from *ibid.*, p. 220, Exercise 4.

[16] Recall that this type of decision was examined in Chapter 13.

included in the cost model which most likely occupies primary importance in the design of systems such as the "Positive Control" system. This consideration stems from the fact that while an addition in the number of components increases the probability of successful operation, the probability that the system will function inadvertently or by accident also increases. In order to include this consideration in the reliability model, the previous assumption that inadvertent behavior is impossible must be relaxed. The new definition of component reliability now includes four possible responses. They are:

1. The component operates when it is *not* required to operate.
2. The component operates when it is required to operate.
3. The component does not operate when it is *not* required to operate.
4. The component does not operate when it is required to operate.

Gordon defines the probabilities for each of these responses in the following manner:

$p_1 =$ probability of inadvertent operation, such as would result from: a relay closing caused by vibration rather than by an input signal; a solenoid valve closing caused by a crossed electrical wire that improperly furnishes an input signal; or a spring-operated, normally closed valve opening under the influence of line pressure if an internal spring breaks.

$p_2 =$ probability of operating properly when an input signal is imposed.

$p_3 =$ probability that a component does not operate when no input signal is imposed.

$p_4 =$ probability that a component does not operate in response to a proper input signal.

By these definitions it is evident that

$$p_1 + p_3 = 1$$
$$p_2 + p_4 = 1$$

The normal definition of reliability is actually a combination of p_2 and p_3 which represents the desired responses. The p_1 and p_4 probabilities represent the undesired responses.[17]

General Form of Reliability Model

Through combinatorial analysis and algebraic manipulation, Gordon develops the following general equation for determining the

---

[17] Gordon, *op. cit.*, p. 235.

overall reliability of a system. In terms used above, the probability
that the system will function properly is:

$$P_m = p_3^{2m} [1 - (1 - p_2)^m] \qquad (14\text{--}8)$$

where m is the number of components in parallel. For example, if
we examine a simple case of four components in parallel as shown
in Figure 14–9, equation (14–8) would be written as follows:

$$P_4 = p_3^8 [1 - (1 - p_2)^4]$$

Equation (14–8) reduces to the conventional definition of reliability, p_2, the probability of functioning properly when the input
signal is put into the system, and p_3, the probability of not functioning properly when there is no signal. It is obvious from Figure
(14–9), that for the system to function correctly, only one compo-

FIGURE 14–9

Communication System S_5

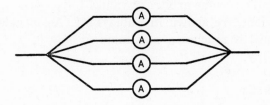

nent need function when a message is put into the system. However,
when there is no message, all components must not function, for the
system to function correctly.

When there are n sets of components in parallel, the general
equation for overall probability of success expands to:

$$\begin{aligned} P_{m,n} &= (P_m)^n \\ &= p_3^{2mn} [1 - (1 - p_2)^m]^n \end{aligned} \qquad (14\text{--}9)$$

A system of three sets of four components in parallel is illustrated
in Figure 14–10. According to equation (14–9), the probability that
System S_6 will function properly is:

$$P_{4.3} = p_3^{2 \cdot 4 \cdot 3} [1 - (1 - p_2)^4]^3$$

It is apparent from equations (14–8) and (14–9) where
$0 < p_3 < 1$, $0 < p_2 < 1$, and $m \geqslant 1$, that an increase in the number
of components m will not improve the reliability of the system, P_m,
indefinitely. In fact, for some combinations of p_2 and p_3, P_m will

FIGURE 14-10

Communication System S_6

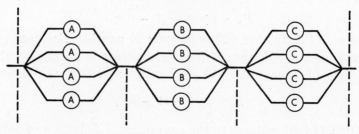

decrease steadily. We see from equation (14–8), for example, that as m increases without bound, the term $(1 - p_2)^m$ decreases and approaches zero and the term $[1 - (1 - p_2)^m]$ increases and approaches the limit, 1. Furthermore, as m increases, p_3^{2m} approaches zero. Depending on the values of p_2 and p_3, P_m may at first increase, reach a maximum, and decrease steadily, or decrease steadily for all values of $m > 1$. Let us demonstrate the behavior of P_m for several values of m. We assume arbitrary values for p_2 and p_3. The results of computations are shown in Table 14–1. As m gets larger, P_m increases until it reaches a maximum at $m = 3$, and then it decreases steadily.

Decision Criteria

With respect to system reliability, then, it is the task of the systems designer to choose the number of components m that will

TABLE 14-1

Solutions for P_m for Several Values of m

$$p_2 = 0.65$$
$$p_3 = 0.97$$

Number of Components in Parallel m	$(1 - p_2)^m$	$[1 - (1 - p_2)^m]$	p_3^{2m}	Probability that System Will Function Correctly $P_m = p_3^{2m} [1 - (1 - p_2)^m]$
1	0.35	0.65	0.9409	0.6116
2	.123	.877	.8853	.7764
3	.043	.957	.8329	.7971
4	.015	.985	.7837	.7719
5	.0053	.9947	.7374	.7335
6	.0019	.9981	.6938	.6925
7	.00067	.99933	.6528	.6524
8	.00023	.99977	.6142	.6141

maximize P_m, the probability of correct functioning. The decision rule for this task may be stated as follows:

Decision Rule:
    Given values for p_2 and p_3, increase m as long as $P_{m+1} > P_m$.

Since m may assume only positive integral values, we can illustrate a rough[18] application of the decision rule by a graphical presentation, as shown in Figure 14–11. In addition to plotting the data of Table 14–1, we also show curves for other combinations of p_2 and

FIGURE 14–11

Behavior of P_m for Arbitrary Values of p_2 and p_3 and Various Sizes of m

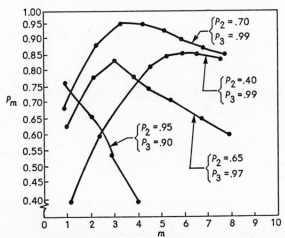

p_3. When $p_2 = 0.70$ and $p_3 = 0.99$, P_m is maximum when $m = 3$. When $p_2 = 0.65$ and $p_3 = 0.97$, P_m is maximum when $m = 3$. When $p_2 = 0.40$ and $p_3 = 0.99$, P_m is maximum when $m = 6$. When $p_2 = 0.95$ and $p_3 = 0.90$, P_m decreases steadily for $m > 1$, and, therefore, we conclude that P_m is maximized when $m = 1$.

Instead of stating the decision rule in terms of given or arbitrary

---

[18] A precise statement for determining the maximum P_m would require the use of differential calculus. Thus P_m would be maximized where $dP_m/dm = 0$. However, this exercise requires undue manipulation for the determination of m, where P_m is maximized. This point may be appreciated from the general equation for an optimum m:

$$m = \frac{ln\ [2ln\ p_3\ /ln\ p_3^2(1-p_2)]}{ln\ (1-p_2)}$$

values of p_2 and p_3, the decision rule may be stated in terms of all combinations of p_2 and p_3. First, we form the ratio:[19]

$$t_m = \frac{P_{m+1}}{P_m} \tag{14-10}$$

The decision rule may then be stated as follows:

Decision Rule:
Increase m as long as $t_m > 1$.

In order to simplify manipulation, let $q = 1 - p_2$, then

$$t_m = \frac{p_3^{2(m+1)} (1 - q^{m+1})}{p_3^{2m} (1 - q^m)}$$

Since

$$(1 - q^{m+1}) \text{ factors to } (1 - q)(1 + q + q^2 + q^3 + \cdots + q^m)$$

and

$$(1 - q^m) \text{ factors to } (1 - q)(1 + q + q^2 + q^3 + \cdots + q^{m-1})$$

Then

$$t_m = \frac{p_3^{2(m+1)} (1 - q) (1 + q + q^2 + q^3 + \cdots + q^m)}{p_3^{2m} (1 - q) (1 + q + q^2 + q^3 + \cdots + q^{m-1})}$$

or

$$= \frac{p_3^2 (1 + q + q^2 + q^3 + \cdots + q^m)}{(1 + q + q^2 + q^3 + \cdots + q^{m-1})}$$

This equation may be written:

$$t_m = p_3^2 \left[\frac{(1 + q + q^2 + q^3 + \cdots + q^{m-1})}{(1 + q + q^2 + q^3 + \cdots + q^{m-1})} + \frac{q^m}{(1 + q + q^2 + q^3 + \cdots + q^{m-1})} \right]$$

or

$$= p_3^2 \left[1 + \frac{q^m}{(1 + q + q^2 + q^3 + \cdots + q^{m-1})} \right] \tag{14-11}$$

---

[19] From: Kemeny, Schleifer, Snell, and Thompson, op. cit., pp. 218–19.

For:

$m = 1, 2, 3, 4, 5$

$$t_1 = p_3^2 [1 + q]$$

$$t_2 = p_3^2 \left[1 + \frac{q^2}{1 + q}\right]$$

$$t_3 = p_3^2 \left[1 + \frac{q^3}{1 + q + q^2}\right]$$

$$t_4 = p_3^2 \left[1 + \frac{q^4}{1 + q + q^2 + q^3}\right]$$

$$t_5 = p_3^2 \left[1 + \frac{q^5}{1 + q + q^2 + q^3 + q^4}\right]$$

We show a sample calculation to illustrate the derivation of the values for p_3 when $m = 5$ and $p_2 = 0.60$. Where

$q = 1 - p_2$

$= 1 - 0.60 = 0.40$

Since we are interested in whether or not $t_m > 1$ over values of p_2 and p_3, set $t_1 = 1$, $t_2 = 1$, $t_3 = 1$, $t_4 = 1$, and $t_5 = 1$, and solve for p_3 or p_2. Therefore, when $m = 5$ and $t_5 = 1$:

$$1 = p_3^2 \left[1 + \frac{(0.4)^5}{1 + 0.4 + (0.4)^2 + (0.4)^3 + (0.4)^4}\right]$$

$$= p_3^2 \left[1 + \frac{0.01024}{1.6496}\right]$$

$$= p_3^2 [1 + 0.006207]$$

$$p_3^2 = 0.99386$$

$$p_3 = 0.99691$$

Other values for p_3 are shown in Table 14–2.

TABLE 14–2
Solutions for p_3 for Several Values of p_2, $m = 5$

$$t_5 = 1 = p_3^2 \left(1 + \frac{q^5}{1 + q + q^2 + q^3 + q^4}\right)$$

p_2	$1 + \dfrac{q^5}{1 + q + q^2 + q^3 + q^4}$	p_3^2	p_3
0.0	1.200000	0.83333	0.91288
0.1	1.144194	0.87397	0.93485
0.2	1.097477	0.91118	0.95450
0.3	1.060607	0.94285	0.97102
0.4	1.033726	0.96737	0.98355
0.5	1.016129	0.98412	0.99203
0.6	1.006207	0.99386	0.99691
0.7	1.001705	0.99829	0.99914
0.8	1.000256	0.99974	0.99987
0.9	1.000009	0.99998	0.99999
1.0	1.000000	1.00000	1.00000

The values for p_2 and p_3 from Table 14–2, where $m = 5$, are plotted in Figure 14–12. Using this same procedure, we derive values for p_2 and p_3, when $m = 1$, $m = 2$, $m = 3$, $m = 4$, and $m = 5$. These values are also plotted in Figure 14–12.

FIGURE 14–12

Graphical Analysis for Decisions on Optimum m

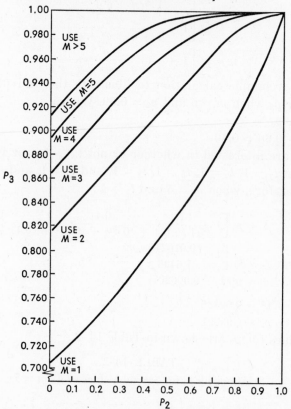

For all pairs of p_2 and p_3 that lie below $t_1 = 1$, we use one component or $m = 1$. For all p_2 and p_3 that lie between $t_1 = 1$ and $t_2 = 1$, we use two components or $m = 2$. When p_2 and p_3 fall between $t_2 = 1$ and $t_3 = 1$, we choose three components and so on. For example, when $p_2 = 0.60$ and $p_3 = 0.80$, choose $m = 1$; when $p_2 = 0.80$ and $p_3 = 0.96$, choose $m = 2$; when $p_2 = 0.20$ and $p_3 = 0.98$, choose $m > 5$.

DESIGN IMPLICATIONS

Numerous examples could be cited to illustrate the attempts of

organizations to increase the reliability of systems by adding redundant channels of communication. The "Positive Control" system
has already been cited as one example where channels of communication are duplicated. The Inspector General's office in military
organization is another example. The efforts of business organizations to gather information about the market for their products is
still another illustration of channel duplication. In addition to the efforts of internal marketing research departments, some companies
employ independent consulting firms to gather market information.
It is not unusual for these same manufacturers to ask wholesalers
and retailers of their products to submit periodic reports to the
company on inventories and sales. Another example of channel
duplication is a business organization which employs a public
accounting firm to audit its financial records, even though this
work has already been done by its own accounting department.
It makes this "double check" to ensure the accuracy of reporting. In
terms of system reliability, the business organization is trying to
increase the probability that the condition of its financial records is
reported through the system.

Obviously, the necessity to duplicate channels stems from the
belief that the human system tends to malfunction. For example,
consider the organizational problem of distortions in upward and
downward communication. This problem is discussed in Chapter 5.
In that chapter we noted that the two necessary design features of
specialization and coordination create status relationships which
tend to inhibit the free flow of communication. Let us review the
discussion. The separation of work into specialized jobs requires a
coordinating function so that the efforts of individual jobholders
may be directed to the overall task. The coordinating function
creates status relationships, with the coordinator as the superior
and the specialized jobholders as subordinates. The superior in the
status relationship has two responsibilities which work at cross-
purposes. As a decision maker, he requires full and complete information from subordinates. His other responsibility requires him to
evaluate the performance of subordinates. Realizing that the superior appraises their performance, subordinates are reluctant to give
him information that reflects unfavorably on their performance.
Thus, the superior will likely get less than full and complete information. "In fact," McMurry states, "much information provided the
chief executive by his subordinates is either unintentionally or

willfully and maliciously inaccurate."[20] Besides the subordinates' fears of performance appraisal, McMurry offers some additional reasons for distortions in upward communications:

No subordinate wishes to have his superiors learn of anything which *he* interprets to be actually or potentially discreditable to him. Hence, he consciously and intentionally endeavors to screen everything that is transmitted upward, filtering out those items of information which are potentially threatening.

He learns what his superiors desire to hear. Hence, he becomes adept not only at avoiding the unpleasant, but also at "stressing the positive." Though the individual subordinate may consciously be entirely sincere and accountable, his personal anxieties, hostilities, aspirations, and system of beliefs and values almost inevitably shape and color his interpretation and acceptance of what he has learned and is expected to transmit.

Each subordinate is often desirous of impressing the top manager with the superiority of *his* contributions to the enterprise—and, by the same token, of the pitiful inadequacy of the contributions of his rivals in other divisions and departments of the company. *Special pleading* of this nature is often most seriously misleading. How can the chief executive know which protagonist is telling the truth? In most instances, he cannot be sure. If he depends solely upon his own judgment, he will probably be wrong at least as often as he is right.

Another source of error arises from the fact that the position of chief executive is one for which there is often substantial competition and rivalry. Hence, the incumbent is not always surrounded and supported by allies and friends, despite his staff's frequent servility, obsequiousness, and dramatic protestations of loyalty. While most subordinates would hesitate to give their chief executive a final push into the abyss, many are not at all reluctant to sit by and let him stumble into it blindly.

Finally, and from the viewpoint of upward communication of the greatest consequence, there is the inability of many chief executives to comprehend and accept valid information even when it is brought to their attention. No wonder top managers are seldom told "the whole truth and nothing but . . ." by their subordinates.[21]

In Chapter 5, we also recognized that the status relationship creates a distortion in downward communication. In his efforts to maintain the status difference, the superior is less than candid in his relationship with subordinates. He does not wish to admit mistakes or reveal conditions which could reflect adversely on his ability and judgment.

---

[20] Robert N. McMurry, "Clear Communication for Chief Executives," *Harvard Business Review*, Vol. 43 (March–April, 1965), pp. 131–32.

[21] *Ibid.*, p. 132.

The Problem

There are, of course, other reasons for a system to function *improperly*. We have discussed many of these problems in the chapter on nonformal behavior. Rather than review these discussions, our purpose here is to discuss the possibility that optimum design for system reliability requires an unorthodox organizational structure. We reviewed the problem of distortions in upward and downward communication because it illustrates the point so well.

There are important advantages to orthodox design features, such as specialization, coordination, and the status differences of superior and subordinate. However, as noted, orthodox design features may have an adverse effect on system reliability, such as the tendency to distort communication. Depending on the values of p_2 and p_3, optimum system reliability may indicate an unorthodox design. The design problem, then, is to decide whether the reliability gained by adding communication channels is worth the advantages given up by deviating from orthodox design.

Some Guidelines

There are few objective means to resolve this dilemma between system reliability and orthodox design. In extreme cases such as the "Positive Control" system, the demand for system reliability is so overwhelming that the design dictated by the model of this chapter prevails. In other words, the advantages of orthodox design are considered of low value compared to the need for system reliability. At the other extreme there are organizations, such as a combat unit in battle, where the demand for an orthodox design is absolute. However, there are few organizations that fall under these extremes.

There are designs that meet the requirements of both models. The use of independent channels such as the employment of a public accounting firm has already been mentioned. Another widely used procedure is committee-type management. To illustrate how committees meet the needs of systems reliability and orthodox design, let us expand our model of the business organization as shown in Figure 14–13. The positions shown on the chart are those occupied by people in the organization who would be concerned with the closely related problems of production rates, sales rates, and inventory levels. Production personnel must have information about sales forecasts, desired levels of finished goods inventories, and existing inventory levels, in order to prepare production and inventory schedules. Marketing personnel must know about production rates and inventory levels in order to prepare sales promotion campaigns and delivery schedules. Financial personnel are concerned about the costs involved in both production and marketing and the cash

FIGURE 14-13

Orthodox Design of a Manufacturing Firm

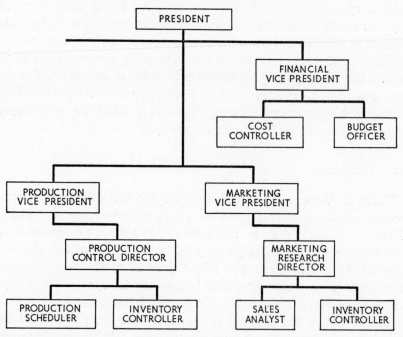

that must flow to support these activities. According to the orthodox design shown in Figure 14–13, the president is the coordinator of these activities. Information from any particular activity must pass through its responsible executive and then to the president, who presumably must reconcile differences and then communicate his decision down through these same channels. From the previous discussion, we know that this type of system is subject to the serious problem of distortion. The reliability of this system could be improved with an arrangement that approximates Systems S_5 and

S_6. This arrangement may be accomplished in a system of committees. In order to maintain the benefits of orthodox design, we can arrange these committees outside of, or in addition to, the established organization. The committee arrangement is shown in Figure 14–14. According to this arrangement, the Production, Inventory, Sales Committee prepares a report which may consist of current and projected sales rates, inventory level, and production schedules. When completed, this report is submitted to the Coordinating Committee, which in turn prepares a report outlining sev-

FIGURE 14–14

Committee Arrangement in Addition to Orthodox Design

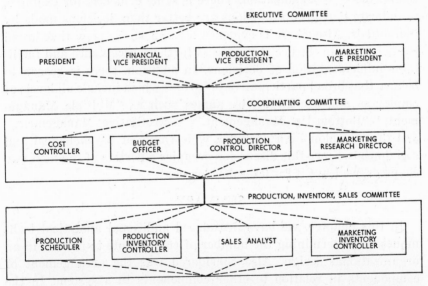

eral alternative courses of action depending on costs, availability of cash, sales promotion efforts, and production economies made possible through equipment purchases. The report is submitted to the Executive Committee which makes a final decision. The final decision is then implemented through normal procedures of the orthodox organization.

As indicated by the broken lines in Figure 14–14, each member is informed about the report submitted to his committee. When a committee report is prepared by the Coordinating Committee, for example, and submitted to the Executive Committee, this is the same as if each component member of the lower committee has sent the same message to every component member of the higher committee. However, the system shown in Figure 14–14 is more than a communication system; it is also a decision system. Thus, information put into the system goes through some transformation. Each committee performs some degree of synthesis, analysis, and decision making. Since this is more than a communication system, we cannot apply the reliability model to this system, but we are generally confident from our comparison of System S_3 with the orthodox design that the committee system is more reliable. Furthermore, when the committee system is added to the design of Figure 14–13, the benefits of orthodoxy and reliability are obtained.

Research studies indicate that there are additional benefits to committee-type organization. There is some evidence, for example, to indicate that group decisions are better than decisions made by individuals. Also, there is evidence to support the view that broad participation in the decision process furthers acceptance and facilitates implementation of decisions. In addition, there is reason to believe that broad participative programs which include all levels of employees and are known by names such as "Multiple Management," "Bottom-Up Management," "Consultative Management," and the "Scanlon Plan" fulfill a wide range of psychological and social needs. Since this discussion occupies a portion of the next two chapters, we leave it for later development.

SUMMARY

In this chapter, we have introduced additional analytical techniques for determining the number of components to include in an organizational design. Also considered was the arrangement of components in relation to other components in a system. In the waiting line model of Chapter 13, total costs were used as the criteria for determining the number and arrangement of components in a system. In this chapter, the criterion used for judgment was the system's reliability, that is, the probability that a system will function as it is supposed to function.

It was shown that the probability of functioning correctly could be increased by adding components in parallel to a system. However, it was shown that the addition of components also increases the probability that a system will function inadvertently or by accident. A model was presented which allows us to choose a design that maximizes the probability of functioning correctly.

Since noise, bias, and distortion are always present in a human situation, system reliability is a major problem in the design of formal organization. The problem was illustrated in descriptions of the system that existed prior to the attack on Pearl Harbor and the system that exists currently in the U.S. Air Force "Positive Control" system.

DISCUSSION QUESTIONS AND PROBLEMS

14–1. Diagram the "Positive Control" system, showing decision and action centers and information flows.

14–2. Would it be valid to conclude that every organization should have redundant channels of communication, that is, channels in addition to the ones provided by the hierarchy of authority? Explain.

14–3. What other criteria, besides the probability analysis of this chapter, would be appropriate for an evaluation of organization design? Could these other criteria be combined with the probability measures to provide overall criteria for selecting one organizational design over another? Explain.

14–4. Is the model of this chapter appropriate for a system in which messages must undergo substantial alteration before reaching their final destination? Explain.

14–5. What are some of the disadvantages of a system designed according to Figure 14–14?

14–6. If component A has a probability of functioning correctly of 0.6, component B has a probability of functioning correctly of 0.4, component C has a probability of functioning correctly of 0.8, and component D has a probability of functioning correctly of 0.9, what is the probability that.
  a) System S_1 will operate correctly?
  b) System S_2 will operate correctly?
  c) System S_3 will operate correctly?
  d) System S_4 will operate correctly?

14–7. If one component of type D is known to be defective, what is the probability that the following systems will function correctly (use the information given in problem 14–6)?
  a) S_1?
  b) S_2?
  c) S_3?
  d) S_4?

14–8. The manager of a baseball team has three equally effective "components" (the third base coach, the manager, and the first base coach) through which signals are transmitted to the batter. The probability that the batter will bunt the ball when the bunt signal is given by the third base coach is 0.8. The same probability applies between the manager and the first base coach and the manager and the batter. The manager knows that the reliability of a communication system between the batter and two of the components is 0.9. The manager does not want to use more than two components to transmit the signals in order to minimize the probability that the opposing team will "steal" the signals. How large must p_3 (the probability that the batter will not bunt when the bunt signal is not given) be for the above conditions to exist?

14–9. The Slade Company has a market forecasting department which predicts sales trends. The probability that this department will recognize and transmit market information which indicates a down trend in sales is 0.90. The Slade Company could also hire any of a number of consulting firms to gather market information and make sales forecasts. Assume that the forecasting department and the individual consulting firms each have a probability of 0.98 of not forecasting a downtrend in sales when there are no indicators of a downtrend.

 a) What is the optimum number of components that should comprise the market forecasting system so that the probability of the sales forecast being correct is maximized? Use Figure 14–12 to verify your results.

 b) What is the maximum probability?

14–10. A helicopter rescue system was established in Vietnam in 1966. This rescue system ensures that a helicopter is flying back and forth over a given area at all times. If a soldier is wounded and needs immediate attention, his commanding officer is instructed to light a red smoke flare to signal the helicopter. From casualty statistics, the Army found that 95 percent of the soldiers with wounds requiring immediate attention lived if they received medical attention within one hour. The probability that one helicopter patrolling a given area will see the smoke flare and transport the soldier to a medical station within one hour is 0.3. The probability that the helicopter pilot will respond to a flare sent by the enemy and thus become involved in combat is 0.1.

 a) What is the optimum number of helicopters the Army should employ in a given area in order to maximize the probability that wounded soldiers will receive attention within one hour?

 b) What is the maximum probability?

14–11. The Bell Company is designing a camera for the Surveyor experiments to take pictures of the moon. When the Surveyor lands on the moon, a signal is to be transmitted from earth to the Surveyor. The probability that the camera system will receive the signal and began taking pictures is 0.99. The probability that the camera system will not take pictures without a signal is 0.80.

a) How many camera systems should be installed in order to maximize the probability that the pictures are taken when the signal is given?

b) What is the reliability of the system in problem 14–11a?

14–12. A switch on a railroad track is operated electrically from a central office. The probability that the switch will open when it receives a signal from the central office is 0.2. The probability that the switch will open without an electric signal from the office is 0.04.

a) How many switches should be used to maximize the probability that the switch will open?

b) What is the maximum probability?

PART IV

Elements of Change

15

MOTIVATION IN ORGANIZATION

Why does a person join a formal organization and make contributions toward its goals? He joins and contributes because the organization offers him something that is personally satisfying. Through membership in an organization, he hopes to satisfy certain needs or desires—he hopes to fulfill some of his personal goals. His goals may be fulfilled by material benefits such as money wages, or they may be fulfilled by intangible benefits such as the feelings he has when he contributes to a charitable or religious organization. He may derive much satisfaction from the goals of the organization. The goals of the Peace Corps, for example, may be very attractive to its members. In any event, he values what the organization has to offer and, therefore, submits willingly to its demands.

There is little disagreement with the premise that man participates in an organization to fulfill some of his personal goals. However, there is disagreement about *what* motivates man and the *strength* of different factors of motivation. On the strength of factors, for example, there is the argument about whether material factors such as money are stronger motivators than other factors such as social status. In the first part of this chapter, we summarize some of these arguments. The explanations of man's behavior range from broad historical and philosophical arguments to reasoning confined to stimulus-response models.

Later in the chapter, we explain that membership in an organization involves a contractual relationship. Individuals offer their services to an organization in exchange for things that are personally valuable. The organization, in turn, offers them the things of value in return for their contributions or cooperation. In essence, there must be a mutually advantageous exchange between the parties to the relationship.

Even though he is required to perform certain tasks, to abide by rules, and to carry out the orders of superiors, an individual in a formal organization is subject to other pressures that influence his behavior. For example, there are the pressures of the informal organization. Several behavior patterns in formal organization have already been discussed. The point that we wish to make at this juncture is that the members of an organization have some choice on how to behave. How they choose to behave is a major question discussed in this chapter. For conceptual convenience, we present three analytical models which help to explain how a person chooses to behave.

The general purpose in this chapter is to help the reader to understand the complex subject of human motivation in formal organization. We review some pertinent literature on the subject and examine some analytical models. We hope to shed some light on the questions of what motivates man and how he chooses to behave. Let us begin with a review of literature.

EXPLANATION BY HISTORIANS

Several historians have tried to understand motivation by studying the rise and fall of civilizations. H. J. Muller[1] offered a so-called "tragic view" of history. He felt that there was no general reason for the rise and fall of civilizations. There are others, less skeptical than Muller, who argue that while generalizations about all civilizations are impossible, the factors affecting any one civilization can be isolated. There are still others who believe that generalizations are possible. Arnold Toynbee, Max Weber, and Ellsworth Huntington, for example, have stated that sufficient similarities among the events accompanying the rise and fall of civilizations allow general explanation. Characteristics of the environment, religion, climate, geography, race, and the human anatomy have been offered as common elements in the cultural growth and decline of civilizations.

Arnold Toynbee, while rejecting a general environmental theory,

---

[1] H. J. Muller, *The Uses of the Past* (London: Oxford University Press, 1957), pp. 20–26.

proposed a modified theory as an explanation of the genesis of civilization.[2] Toynbee attributed growth to a moderate amount of "challenge in the environment."[3] He hypothesized that the desiccation of northern Africa, presented a challenge. Men, who had been living a nomadic life, were stimulated to settle in one place where they dammed rivers, irrigated the land, and cultivated natural resources. Toynbee's hypothesis may be classified as a challenge-response model of motivation.

Max Weber[4] hypothesized that Protestantism was the cause for the economic vigor and growth of Western nations, ultimately resulting in industrial capitalism. Amintore Fanfani, the Italian economics professor and politician, argues that Catholicism is the motivating force behind the growth of capitalism.[5]

Ellsworth Huntington hypothesized that climatic factors have played an instrumental role in motivating people of the great civilizations.[6] He argues that great civilizations develop in moderate climates with a temperature range of 40° to 60° F., and this explains why no great civilizations have flourished in the extreme temperatures of the tropical zone and polar areas of the world. However important climate may be in motivating people toward greatness, this theory does not explain why there exist significant differences in growth among the nations which are located in the moderate climate zone. For instance, why are there vast differences between the average per capita income of Poland and Germany?

Questions of a similar nature can be raised about each of the general theories which attempt to explain why certain civilizations grew and then declined. The difficulty with these theories, as might be expected, is that they are too general. However, individual and group motivation cannot be understood without an understanding of the broad physical and cultural influences within which men live. For instance, it would be difficult to understand why the Egyptians were motivated to build the colossal pyramids in the midst of an

---

[2] Arnold J. Toynbee, *A Study of History* (London: Oxford University Press, 1934), Vol. I, pp. 205–338.

[3] The use of the term "environment" by Toynbee includes both physical and social environment.

[4] Max Weber, *The Protestant Ethic and the Spirit of Capitalism*, trans. T. Parsons (New York: Charles Scribner's Sons, 1930).

[5] Amintore Fanfani, *Catholicism, Protestantism, and Capitalism* (New York: Sheed & Ward, 1935).

[6] Ellsworth Huntington, *Civilization and Climate* (New Haven, Conn.: Yale University Press, 1915), chap. xiii.

arid land unless we were aware of the fact that they manifested their respect for their leaders by making sacrifices. How can we explain the motivation of the Athenians to build the Acropolis unless we realize that the desire for aesthetic beauty was a powerful motivating force. Similarly, how will future generations be able to understand the accomplishments of man during the 19th and 20th centuries unless they understand the motivating forces of our time. Accomplishments such as the construction of the Panama Canal, the Golden Gate Bridge, interstate turnpikes, the Aswan Dam, the Volga Dam, Telstar, and so on, suggest that the motivating force of the 19th and 20th centuries is based on material achievements.[7]

SOCIOECONOMIC EXPLANATIONS

More than 50 years have elapsed since Sigmund Freud, William McDougall, and other social scientists lamented about man's ignorance of the variables which motivate the human being. Not until recent years has any significant progress been made in the discovery of the major elements of man's nature.

Humoral Models

During the Middle Ages and Renaissance, analyses of the elements of man were confined primarily to the humoral distillations—black bile (melancholic), yellow bile (sanguine), blood (choleric), and phlegm (phlegmatic). These human characteristics were derived from the four cosmic elements of earth, air, fire, and water.[8] With the aid of this method of analysis, each man was classified as melancholic, sanguine, choleric, phlegmatic, or some combination of these types. The "humor model" of man endured until the 17th century, when Harvey's discovery of the circulation

---

[7] For an explanation of the psychological relationship between the Protestant ethic and the material achievements of modern capitalism, see Marian R. Winterbottom, "The Relation of Need for Achievement to Learning Experiences in Independence and Mastery," in J. W. Atkinson (ed.), *Motives in Fantasy, Action, and Society* (Princeton, N.J.: D. Van Nostrand Co., Inc., 1958), pp. 453–78.

[8] Charles Sherrington, *Man on His Nature* (New York: Macmillan Co., 1941), chap. i.

of the blood made it a highly questionable basis for explaining human behavior.[9]

Instinct and Drive Models

The era of Darwinism introduced ideas such as instincts and drives to explain motivation. William McDougall, perhaps, more than anyone else, proposed the idea of instincts—"those inborn appetites and hungers without which every 'human organism' would become incapable of activity of any kind."[10] Psychologists were prolific with newly discovered instincts during this era. For instance, in his explanation of the "mainspring of men," Whiting Williams proposed that the "key to human behavior is to be found less in the effort to save our physiological skin than in the effort to save our social 'face.' "[11] For Thorstein Veblen, the chief "instinctive proclivity" of life, that is, the instinctive disposition required for the continuation of life, is the "sense or instinct of workmanship." Veblen believed that the instinct of workmanship is a "consistent, ubiquitous, and resilient" disposition which affects all the other instinctual proclivities of man.[12] Others attempted to elaborate this theory by classifying various types of instincts. A study conducted by L. L. Bernard reveals that approximately 14,000 instincts have been proposed,[13] and E. C. Wilm explored the history of theories of instinct back to the Roman philosophers (circa 64–546 B.C.).[14]

Economic Man Model

The classical economics model of human behavior assumes, first, that man is conscious of his material needs such as food, clothing,

---

[9] Gordon W. Allport, *Personality: a Psychological Interpretation* (New York: Henry Holt & Co., 1937), pp. 64–65.

[10] William McDougall, *An Introduction to Social Psychology* (New York: Methuen & Co., Ltd., 1908).

[11] Whiting Williams, *Mainsprings of Men* (New York: Charles Scribner's Sons, 1925), p. 146.

[12] Thorstein Veblen, *The Instinct of Workmanship* (New York: Macmillan Co., 1914), especially chap. i.

[13] L. L. Bernard, *Instincts: A Study of Social Psychology* (New York: Henry Holt & Co., 1924), p. 220.

[14] E. C. Wilm, *The Theories of Instinct* (New Haven, Conn.: Yale University Press, 1925).

and shelter, and he behaves in a manner to maximize these material rewards.[15] For instance, the pursuit of material self-interest for the entrepreneur means the maximization of profit, and for the laborer it means the maximization of wages.

The economic-man model is a simple reward-response mechanism. Economic rewards produce a given response or performance, and more rewards stimulate more response.

Modern economists have stated that this materialistic model is an oversimplification of reality. For instance, Joseph Schumpeter suggested that the profit motive is not the only motivating force behind economic achievement, but that the entrepreneur is not void of "hedonistic motives," which range from "spiritual ambition down to mere snobbery."[16] The following quotation provides an elaboration of Schumpeter's meaning of "hedonistic adaptation" as it is related to motivation of the entrepreneur:

> First of all there is the dream and the will to found a private kingdom, usually, though not necessarily a dynasty. . . . Then there is the will to conquer: the impulse to fight, to prove oneself superior to others, to succeed for the sake, not of the fruits of success, but of success itself. The financial result is a secondary consideration, mainly valued as an index of success and as symptom of victory. . . . Finally, there is the joy of creating, of getting things done, or simply exercising one's energy and ingenuity.[17]

According to Schumpeter the pursuit of nonmonetary rewards such as fame, pride, prestige, satisfaction from creating, are relevant elements of motivation which cannot be ignored in the explanation of the "psychology of entrepreneurial activity."[18] Although the economic man model has lost favor, a similar type of stimulus-response mechanism, but more complex than the former, has been used to explain motivation. This model might be labeled a multiple stimuli-response model of motivation because more than just economic rewards were considered as incentives that make man willing to work. According to this model, man is motivated as much by psy-

---

[15] Adam Smith, *The Wealth of Nations* (Cannan edition; New York: Random House Inc., 1937).

[16] Joseph A. Schumpeter, *The Theory of Economic Development* (Cambridge, Mass.: Harvard University Press, 1961), p. 93. Translated by Redvers Opie.

[17] *Ibid.*, p. 93.

[18] *Ibid.*, pp. 93–94. This view is not limited to Schumpeter. See Edward S. Mason, "Apologetics of Managerialism," *Journal of Business*, Vol. 31 (January, 1958), pp. 1–11.

chological and sociological factors as he is by the economic rewards. Rewards include not only money but also job security, type of supervision, intrinsic job satisfaction, opportunity to socialize, recognition, opportunities for advancement, and others.

The multiple stimuli-response model included some organizational variables which were ignored previously. But even the multiple stimuli-response model is relatively simple, because it does not explain the relative importance of variables in determining man's behavior patterns.

Need-Satiation Model

A more complex theory of motivation, proposed by A. H. Maslow,[19] takes into consideration the order of human needs and satiation of needs. This approach to motivation theory may be labeled the "need-satiation" theory, and it is based on two propositions. The first proposition states that man has a hierarchy of needs, some of which are basic needs and others of which are growth needs, but both are motivators. Maslow's hierarchy includes basic needs such as physiological, safety, belongingness and love, and esteem needs, and a growth need which he calls self-actualization.[20] Self-actualization refers to a need for self-fulfillment according to each man's potential. For example, if a man has the potential to be a novelist, he must write novels to satisfy the self-actualization need.

The second proposition states that as each need in the hierarchy is fulfilled or satiated, it no longer is the prime factor in motivating human behavior. The next higher need in the hierarchy emerges as the prime motivator.

Maslow argues that "healthy people have sufficiently gratified basic needs for safety, belongingness, love, respect, and self-esteem so that they are motivated primarily by trends to self actualization. . . ."[21]

This theory of a hierarchy of needs was conditioned by Maslow in the following ways: First, various degrees of fixity of the hier-

---

[19] *Motivation and Personality* (New York: Harper & Bros., 1954), especially pp. 80–92.

[20] This dichotomy was presented by Abraham Maslow in a paper titled "Deficiency Motivation and Growth Motivation," in Marshall R. Jones (ed.), *Nebraska Symposium on Motivation, 1955* (Lincoln, Nebr.: University of Nebraska Press, 1955), pp. 1–30.

[21] *Ibid.*, p. 2.

archy can exist, and for some people, there may be some reversal in the order of the hierarchy. Second, satisfaction of needs is of a relative nature. Third, the needs may exist in man on a conscious or subconscious level. Fourth, behavior has multiple determinants which extend outside of the area of motives. Finally, basic needs are much more universal than we would expect from observing culturally specified behavior. Although Maslow does not classify his theory as an instinct theory, he suggests that basic needs to some degree are hereditary in their determination.[22]

In summary, the instinctoid-type models have attempted to define motivation in terms of physiological and sociopsychological needs and drives. According to this trend of thought, behavior is a result of these needs, and behavioral variations are due to differences in needs. The economist's variation of instinct theory implies that man has an instinct to maximize his economic position. Given this instinct, man behaves in an economically rational manner, and the economist has reduced this behavior to an explainable and calculable process. This trend of thought has been particularly meaningful in attempting to explain motivation in economically oriented organizations. The historian's explanation is placed on a much grosser plane of analysis, for he uses physical and cultural characteristics to explain the rise and decline of various civilizations and nations. The significant aspect of this approach is that it directs attention to the broad environmental climate which must be considered in attempting to understand motivation within organizations of a particular time and place. Although in this discussion we are concerned primarily with the explanation of motivation within an organization, we cannot lose sight of the fact that motivational forces largely governed by a cultural enviornment affect the behavior of man at work.

MOTIVATION AND EXCHANGE

Since we are concerned with human motivation in organization, in this section the focus of attention is on how the individual decides on the exchange of his efforts for some kind of reward. Our concern with motivation in organization implicitly assumes that the individual is energized to participate in an organization. The key issue for the individual, then, is to find a particular organization to

---

[22] Maslow, *Motivation and Personality*, *op cit.*, pp. 98–104.

match his preferences. The organization seeks individuals who possess certain job skills. In the first part of this section we are concerned with the matching of individual and organizational preferences, and the latter part involves a set of concepts which explain the complex exchange decision.

Preferences and Selection

In varying degrees of clarity and certainty, the individual as well as the organization has a set of preferences. The organization selects those individuals who appear to possess the values desired by the organization, and the individual, more or less, seeks the organization most suitable to his preferences.

In addition to some minimum level of motivation required of the individual, at least enough to motivate him to participate in organization,[23] the organization offers the individual a set of values that are designed to pattern his behavior toward its goals. The assumption that an individual is already motivated or energized when he joins an organization is consistent with psychological theory. In D. O. Hebb's notion, the motive concept explains the "patterning and direction" of activities rather than the overall intensity.[24] In the same vein, Abraham Maslow suggests that the individual is not a passive agent; he is an active agent who does something to causes or stimuli.[25] *In essence, the individual as a live organism is "energized" to act, and the organization provides him with "patterning and direction" of behavior.*

The organizational preferences represent a set of norms which define expected behavior as differentiated from unacceptable behavior, that is, legitimate behavior is distinguished from illegitimate behavior, right from wrong, fair from unfair, adequate from inadequate, and so on. The set of preferences provided in each organization is founded on the basis of the acceptable limits established by society, the past experiences of the organization, and the individual-organization bargaining process.[26]

---

[23] Called the "motivation to participate," by Herbert A. Simon and James G. March, *Organization* (New York: John Wiley & Sons, Inc., 1958), chap. iv.

[24] D. O. Hebb, *The Organization of Behavior* (New York: John Wiley & Sons, Inc., 1949), especially chap. viii.

[25] Maslow, *op. cit.*, p. 30.

[26] Richard M. Cyert and James G. March, *Behavioral Theory of the Firm* (Englewood Cliffs, N.J.: Prentice-Hall, Inc., 1963), chap. iii.

The organization does not employ individuals on a random basis, but rather, individuals are selected on the basis of (1) evidence of a capacity for sustained activity, (2) personal attitudes toward organization, (3) willingness to submit to some degree of direction, and (4) work skills and aptitudes, as well as other variables. Robert Dubin points out that society also performs the same function when it rejects "those individuals who are so dissociated from reality that their activity bears no relationship to the immediate environment."[27]

Exchange of Values

The receipt of expected individual contributions assists the organization in obtaining its given goals, and it also reinforces and sustains the organizational expectations. The individual possesses certain values or inputs which the organization needs, for instance, mental, manual, and social skills, age, seniority, sex, and others, and the organization holds some values which the individual seeks to acquire, for example, money, seniority benefits, job status, intrinsic job rewards, and others. Each part is willing to surrender some of these values, but in return each expects to receive a mix of rewards for providing these values.[28] When the inducements supplied by the organization are sufficient in quantity and kind to gain the continued contributions of members and when the contributions of members are sufficient in quantity and kind to sustain the organization (that is, to permit it to survive and grow), the system is said to be in steady state or state of equilibrium.

ANALYTICAL TECHNIQUES FOR CHOOSING BEHAVIOR PATTERNS

In this section we present three analytical techniques which help us to understand how people choose among possible behavior patterns. It is a basic premise of these techniques that man is rational. He chooses to behave in a certain way because that behavior pattern promises to produce some values that optimize the attainment

---

[27] Robert Dubin, *The World of Work* (Englewood Cliffs, N.J.: Prentice-Hall, Inc., 1958), p. 214.

[28] The idea of an exchange system was suggested by Herbert A. Simon, *Administrative Behavior* (New York: Macmillan Co., 1957), especially chap. vi; and Dubin, *op. cit.*, chap. xii.

of his personal goals. His evaluation of the rewards associated with each kind of behavior depends in part upon how much of the reward is already in his possession. For example, a man's evaluation of a money reward will depend on the size of his bank account. Supposedly, a man with a relatively large account will have a lower evaluation of a money reward than a man who has a small account or no money at all in his possession. Similarly, a man with a full stomach will be motivated less by a promise of food than a man who is hungry. This consideration in the process of choosing a behavior pattern is called the utility concept. It will become clearer as we examine the analytical techniques.

The first technique is a model of consumer behavior—a consumer who must choose how he will divide his resources among several products. While a consumer deciding upon expenditures for several products may have little relevance to the way people behave in organization, it does reveal the decision promises of an individual decision maker faced with several alternatives. It gives us a general idea about how people can make rational choices among possible behavior patterns in organization. The remaining techniques—indifference analysis, and activity-satisfaction analysis—are more applicable to an organizational setting.

Marginal Utility Analysis

For an illustration of how the individual reaches a solution with respect to his contributions, we can use an analytical technique developed in economic theory. An individual who contributes his skills and energy to an organization in return for some rewards is similar in some ways to a consumer who demands goods and service (rewards) from a business firm for some amount of money (contributions) he is willing to spend.

Economic theory explains consumer demand in terms of prices charged for goods and services. As unit price is decreased, the quantity of a good demanded by a consumer increases. Figure 15–1 illustrates the relationship between product price and the quantity of dress shirts that would be demanded by a hypothetical consumer, Mr. Jones.

Each of the points on the demand curve (DD') represents a unit price and the corresponding quantity of dress shirts that Mr. Jones would purchase. The downward sloping demand curve simply

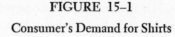

FIGURE 15–1

Consumer's Demand for Shirts

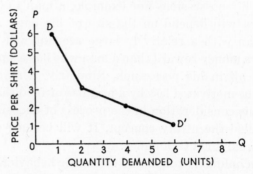

means that Mr. Jones would buy more units of a product if the unit price were reduced. The underlying explanation of the downsloping characteristic of the demand curve is based on three economic concepts—the income and substitution effects, and the law of diminishing marginal utility.

The *income effect* means that with a constant money income a consumer will purchase more dress shirts or other goods if the price is reduced. For instance, with a constant money income of $6, Mr. Jones will purchase one dress shirt priced at $6 per unit. But if the unit price is reduced to $3, he will either purchase two dress shirts or he will purchase one dress shirt and free some income for the purchase of other commodities. The real income of Mr. Jones is increased by a decrease in the price of some commodity that he demands. Also, an increase in the unit price of a dress shirt would reduce his real income.

The *substitution effect* means that a consumer with a fixed income may substitute some goods that have become more attractive due to a decrease in unit price for others. A decline in the unit price of a dress shirt means that the consumer may substitute dress shirts for other commodities. Mr. Jones may buy dress shirts instead of sport shirts, polo shirts, and other types of shirts. The opposite substitution would occur if the price of dress shirts were increased.

The *law of diminishing marginal utility* provides another explanation of the downsloping characteristic of the demand curve. This law states that even though additional units of a good may increase the total utility, the marginal utility of each unit of successive new units of a good tends to decrease. The relationship of utility to the quantity consumed of the hypothetical shirt consumer is illustrated in Table 15–1 and Figure 15–2. As the quantity of dress shirts consumed increases from one to six, the total utility increases from zero to sixteen, but the marginal utility per unit decreases from six to zero. This decline, giving rise to the law of diminishing marginal utility, stated in terms of satisfaction, means that as a consumer acquires more and more of a good he derives less and less additional satisfaction from its use.[29]

Assuming that Mr. Jones has a limited money income, he must make a decision as to what goods he wants and how much of each good he will purchase. The consumer, in other words, will attempt

TABLE 15–1	FIGURE 15–2
Quantity of Consumption and Utility	Quantity of Consumption and Utility

Quantity of Dress Shirts Consumed	Total Utility	Marginal Utility
0.............	0	
		6
1.............	6	
		4
2.............	10	
		3
3.............	13	
		2
4.............	15	
		1
5.............	16	
		0
6.............	16	

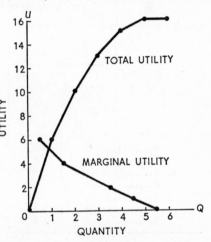

to determine the market collection which provides maximum utility or what has been labeled by economists as "equilibrium of utility." The basic premise of this "equilibrium" process is that the consumer arranges his expenditures so that an equality exists among the ratios of product marginal utility to product price of each good in the consumer's market collection. Once the consumer reaches an equilibrium position among all the marginal utilities of the goods in his collection, he will not alter his pattern of consumption as long as his income, his preferences, the quality, and the price of the goods remain the same.

---

[29] Paul A. Samuelson, *Economics: An Introductory Analysis* (6th ed.; New York: McGraw-Hill Book Co., 1964), p. 429.

The condition of consumer equilibrium for different goods may be written as follows:

$$\frac{MU_1}{P_1} = \frac{MU_2}{P_2} = \frac{MU_3}{P_3} = \cdots \frac{MU_n}{P_n} = \text{Common } MU \text{ per income dollar}$$

This equality can be illustrated if we suppose that Mr. Jones is confronted by a total market collection of three goods—X, Y, and Z. The price per unit for these goods is $1, $2, and $3 respectively. Table 15–2 contains Mr. Jones's marginal utility of each product in

TABLE 15–2

Combinations of Utility-Maximization

Quantity of Units	Product X Price = $1		Product Y Price = $2		Product Z Price = $3	
	Marginal Utils (MU)	Marginal Utility per Dollar (MU/P)	Marginal Utils (MU)	Marginal Utility per Dollar (MU/P)	Marginal Utils (MU)	Marginal Utility per Dollar (MU/P)
0.......	0	0	0	0	0	0
1.......	6	6	16	8	27	9
2.......	[5]	5	14	7	21	7
3.......	4	4	12	6	18	6
4.......	3	3	10	[5]	15	[5]
5.......	3	3	9	4½	14	4⅔
6.......	2	2	8	4	12	4

terms of marginal utils (MU) and his marginal utility per dollar (MU/P). From the above we know that the algebraic solution to this problem is:

$$\frac{MU_X}{P_X} = \frac{MU_Y}{P_Y} = \frac{MU_Z}{P_Z} = \text{Common } MU \text{ per income dollar.}$$

Suppose that Mr. Jones has a fixed income of $22; then, by substituting various combinations of X, Y, and Z from Table 15–2 we find that the solution is:

$$\frac{5}{1} = \frac{10}{2} = \frac{15}{3} = 5$$

This means that Mr. Jones maximizes his utility if he purchases 2 units of X, 4 units of Y, and 4 units of Z, because the ratio of marginal utility to price for each of these quantities is equal (5). These values are shown in boxes in Table 15–2. The total utility of this collection of goods is 144 utils, and the cost of this selection is equal to $[(2 \times \$1) + (4 \times \$2) + (4 \times \$3)]$ or \$22. If Mr. Jones has more or less than \$22 of income to spend on X, Y, and Z, then he must find another solution. For an income of \$16, Mr. Jones would maximize his utility by purchasing 1 unit of X, 3 units of Y, and 3 units of Z. The marginal utility per dollar for each product is 6 and the total utility is 114 utils. An income of \$33 would allow Mr. Jones to buy 3 units of X, 6 units of Y, and 6 units of Z, yielding a total utility of 191 utils.

The combination of 2 units of X, 4 units of Y, and 4 units of Z permits Mr. Jones to spend all of his \$22 income in a manner that maximizes his utility by equating the marginal utility of X, Y, and Z. This selection of products represents an equilibrium position. In order to make this analysis possible, it is necessary to assume that marginal utility is measurable—a most difficult, if not impossible problem.

Indifference Analysis

An alternative type of consumer preference analysis, which circumvents the problem of measuring marginal utility accurately, involves graphical analysis using indifference curves. Instead of using products as we did in the previous example, we use work and leisure to indicate possible uses of an individual's energy. In order to show the benefits of different approaches, first we show how the problem may be solved by marginal utility analysis and then arrive at the same solution by indifference curves.

Suppose that Mr. Jones has a limited amount of energy, which can be allocated between work and leisure in any way he chooses. His job as a commission salesman allows him this freedom to control the use of his efforts. He can earn more income by working harder, but by working harder he has less energy to spend on leisure-time activities. In order to maximize his satisfaction, Mr. Jones will first have to determine the marginal utility of the energy spent on work and leisure. Assume that an hour spent in work requires more energy than an hour spent in leisure. Instead of a unit of money, let us designate P as a unit of energy, and say that an hour of work requires four energy units and an hour of leisure requires two energy units. Table 15–3 summarizes Mr. Jones marginal utility (assumed) for energy spent in work and leisure. As more energy is spent in work and leisure, the marginal utility decreases to reflect the law of diminishing marginal utility. The decrease in marginal utility is assumed to set in after 20 hours of work and after 10 hours of leisure. Suppose that Mr. Jones's energy is fixed at 200 units. By

TABLE 15–3

Marginal Utility of Time Spent in Work and Leisure

Time	Work		Leisure	
Total	Marginal Utility per Energy Unit (MU)	Marginal Utility per Energy Unit (MU/P)	Marginal Utility per Energy Unit (MU)	Marginal Utility per Energy Unit (MU/P)
10	352	88	230	115
20	352	88	210	105
30	320	80	180	90
40	312	78	160	80
50	304	76	150	75
60	300	75	146	73
70	296	74	140	70
80	292	73	136	68
90	288	72	134	67
100	284	71	132	66

substituting various values of work and leisure from Table 15–3, we find that the utility-maximizing solution is:

$$\frac{MU_W}{P_W} = \frac{MU_L}{P_L} = \text{Common } MU \text{ per energy unit}$$

$$\frac{320}{4} = \frac{160}{2} = 80$$

Mr. Jones is willing to work in order to obtain the benefits derived from an income. He may be willing to participate in an organization if a contribution is made, directly or indirectly, to his personal goals. However, our analysis shows that he is not willing to allocate all his energy to work, because leisure-time activities also yield some desirable benefits. According to the marginal utility analysis, Mr. Jones will maximize benefits if he works 30 hours per week and engages in leisure 40 hours per week. This allocation fully utilizes his available energy of $[(30 \times 4) + (40 \times 2)]$ or 200 units per week.

We can obtain the same solution through indifference curves. Suppose that Mr. Jones can tell us his preferences for various combinations of work and leisure-time activities. Let us say that he can give his preference for combinations for which he is indifferent. The indifference curve U_2, in Figure 15–3, represents various

FIGURE 15–3

Indifference Curves and Feasibility Line

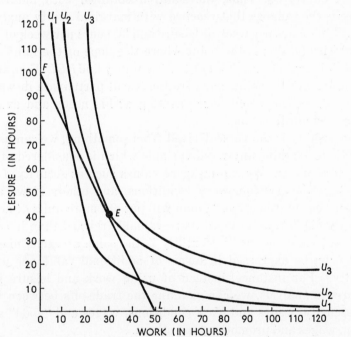

combinations of work and leisure acceptable to Mr. Jones. The curve tells us, for example, that Mr. Jones is indifferent to: 120 units of leisure and 10 units of work; 95 units of leisure and 15 units of work; 40 units of leisure and 30 units of work; or 20 units of leisure and 60 units of work. Each combination is neither better nor worse than each of the others to Mr. Jones. Curves U_1 and U_3 in Figure 15–3 are other sets of work-leisure combinations that represent lower and higher levels of satisfaction for Mr. Jones. Although an indifference curve does not yield the optimum choice, it allows us to move one step closer to a solution by describing how Mr. Jones relates work to leisure.

Suppose we impose on the indifference curves a feasibility line, *FEL*, which shows the amount of energy available to devote to work and leisure-time activities. Mr. Jones can work up to 50 hours per week and engage in leisure zero hours per week, or he may be idle 100 hours per week and work zero hours per week, or any combination in between.

If Mr. Jones seeks to maximize satisfaction, he will select the point at which his feasibility line is tangent to the highest indifference curve, U_2. Thus, the solution obtained with indifference curves is the same as that reached with marginal utility analysis— point E, 40 hours per week of leisure and 30 hours per week of work. Geometrically, this is the point where the slope of the indifference curve U_2 is equal to the slope of the feasibility line *FEL*. Equilibrium is attained at this point, and Mr. Jones will participate in work 30 hours and in leisure 40 hours as long as his needs and available energy remain the same.

Since utility is the value derived from something, we can use this analysis to examine any work variable which is considered of some value to a person. We can measure values such as security, friendship, good supervision, work conditions, and others if we accept Homans' assumption that "a man will put out more units of activity within a given time to get a more valuable reward than he will to get a less valuable one."[30] If utility is the same as value, marginal utility can be expressed in terms of additional value per unit of activity.[31] For instance, instead of using work and leisure in the preference analysis, we can examine the trade-offs between wages and security, wages and work conditions, wages and "good" supervision, wages and promotion, and others.

Activity-Satisfaction Analysis

Another way of expressing the relationship is to determine what amount of activity a person is willing to offer in order to obtain rewards. A person seeks rewards to satisfy some needs or desires. He

---

[30] George C. Homans, *Social Behavior: Its Elementary Form* (New York: Harcourt, Brace & World, Inc., 1961), p. 41.
[31] *Ibid.*

will exert physical and mental activity in some relation to need satiation. In this section, we examine motivation in terms of the relationship between satisfaction (gained from rewards) and performance (productivity).

An oversimplified and perhaps widely glamorized version of the relationship is that a satisfied worker will work harder and produce more than an unsatisfied worker. While this seems to be a reasonable solution, research evidence reveals the opposite effect, that is, the unsatisfied man will work harder. The "happy" man is not necessarily the best worker. There are complicating factors in the satisfaction-productivity relationship. Part of the complexity may be attributed to difficulties of determining causes for satisfaction.[32] As we learned, there are many interrelated determinants of man's behavior in organization. When an organization member says he is satisfied it is difficult to determine the sources of his satisfaction. For instance, is a worker's statement of satisfaction based on his liking for the type and amount of work he performs, the pay he receives, the opportunity to make friendships, or the justification it provides for being away from home? Furthermore, the effect of *satisfaction* upon *satisfaction* raises an important question. In other words, does the satisfaction already received have an effect upon additional increments of satisfaction? A general solution is suggested by Nancy Morse on the basis of her study of white-collar workers: "The greater the amount the individual gets, the greater his satisfaction and, at the same time, the more the individual still desires, the less his satisfaction."[33] According to Morse, satisfaction is determined by both what a worker wants or aspires to obtain from a situation, and what he already has obtained from it, and though satisfaction may determine an individual's willingness to participate in an organization, it does not determine directly his level of productvity.[34]

Another matter which complicates the satisfaction-productivity relationship is the worker's perception of fairness in the distribu-

---

[32] See Nancy Morse, *Satisfaction in the White-Collar Job* (Ann Arbor, Mich.: Survey Research Center for Social Research, University of Michigan, 1953), pp. 4–5 and 110–12. A. Zaleznik, C. R. Christensen, and F. J. Roethlisberger, *The Motivation, Productivity, and Satisfaction of Workers* (Boston: Division of Research, Graduate School of Business Administration, Harvard University, 1958), chaps. viii and ix.

[33] Morse, *Satisfaction in the White-Collar Job, op. cit.*, p. 28.

[34] *Ibid.*, p. 112.

tion of rewards as they relate to his contribution.[35] This perception of fairness appears under such titles as "distributive justice," "relative deprivation," "cognitive dissonance," "fair exchange," and "status congruency." The worker's concept of a fair exchange of contributions and reward is not always compatible with the logic of the technical subsystem, or for that matter, it may differ from the norms of the social subsystem. For example, two workers performing the same job and receiving an equal amount of reward may have different feelings about the compensation. One may feel deprived, the other may be satisfied. The feeling of deprivation may be based on a comparison of the time and effort that others contribute for the rewards they receive, or it may be based on external factors or social "investments"[36] such as expected differentials due to age, sex, education, race, social status, and other factors.

George Homans has developed a model which shows in an abstract way the relationship between satisfaction, activity, personal goals, and the amount of rewards already received. He argues that given certain personal goals, a person will be less motivated to emit activity as his reward approaches these goals.[37] Satisfaction, according to Homans, depends upon the predetermined goal level and the level and amount of reward already obtained. Satisfaction can be defined as:

---

[35] For theoretical considerations and research evidence concerning this concept, see Leon A. Festinger, *A Theory of Cognitive Dissonance* (Evanston, Ill.: Row, Peterson & Co., 1957) ; Homans, *op. cit.;* Elliott Jaques, *Equitable Payment* (New York: John Wiley & Sons, Inc., 1961) ; M. Patchen, *The Choice of Wage Comparisons* (Englewood Cliffs, N.J.: Prentice-Hall, Inc., 1961); Zaleznik, Christensen, and Roethlisberger, *op. cit.;* L. R. Sayles, *Behavior of Industrial Work Groups* (New York: John Wiley & Sons, Inc., 1958) ; S. N. Adams, "Status Congruency as a Variable in Small Group Performance," Vol. 32 (1953–54), pp. 16–22; J. A. Davis, "A Formal Interpretation of the Theory of Relative Deprivation," *Sociometry*, Vol. 22 (1959), pp. 280–96; G. Lenski, "Status Crystallization," *American Sociological Review*, Vol. 19 (1954), pp. 405–13; M. N. Richter, "The Concept of Cognitive Dissonance," *Journal of Psychology*, Vol. 60 (1965), pp. 291–94; J. S. Adams, "Toward An Understanding of Equity," *Journal of Abnormal and Social Psychology*, Vol. 67 (1963), pp. 422–36; J. S. Adams and W. B. Rosenbaum, "The Relationship of Worker Productivity to Cognitive Dissonance About Wage Inequities," *Journal of Applied Psychology*, Vol. 46 (1962), pp. 161–64.

[36] The term "investment" was used by George Homans to represent "features of past histories and backgrounds" that a man considers in evaluating his worth to an organization. See Homans, *op. cit.*, pp. 74–75.

[37] The Homans model, *op. cit.*, pp. 265–82, resembles the hierarchy-of-needs approach proposed by Maslow, *op. cit.*, pp. 80–106, in that a satiated need ceases to operate as a motivator. The mathematical conceptualization of satisfaction and reward that follows was adopted from Homans, *op. cit.*, pp. 278–81.

$$S = a\left(\frac{R}{G - R}\right) \qquad (15\text{-}1)$$

where

G = the predetermined goal level.
R = r (amount of activity) = total amount of reward received.
r = the unit of reward.
a = perceived justice per unit of reward.

As rewards keep adding up and approaching the predetermined goal level, the total satisfaction increases. Satisfaction increases and approaches infinity, as the rewards a person receives get close to his personal goals. In this expression of satisfaction, we assume that a person has a fixed reward goal for a given period of time and that rewards can be defined in terms of some standard unit. For instance, we can express Mr. Jones's satisfaction, if we assume that his goal is to earn an income of $G = \$200$ per week and that he is rewarded in standardized units of $r = \$20$ for each unit that he sells. The perceived justice per unit of reward, a, represents a ratio of the reward unit received over what he feels it should be, based on the activity Mr. Jones must contribute in order to obtain a unit of reward.[38]

Let us illustrate perceived justice in the case of Mr. Jones's reward of r = \$20. He feels that he should be paid \$25. Thus, his perceived justice per unit of reward is $a = \$20/\$25 = 0.80$. The selling effort necessary to obtain revenues is Mr. Jones's investment cost for the rewards he receives. It is this cost that enters into his assessment of rewards. The assessment may be based on a comparison of his reward-contribution ratio with the ratio of other XYZ Company salesmen or with salesmen working for other firms. By some standard of distributive justice, Mr. Jones feels that the rewards he receives should be proportional to his contribution and in line with the reward-contribution ratio of others engaged in similar activities. Although in most of the illustrations we use money or wages as the reward, other inducements can be considered in a similar way.[39]

---

[38] The constant a is defined here as perceived justice, but it could include a number of other psychological and sociological variables. The same is true also for the constants of proportionality b and c which are introduced subsequently.

[39] One approach to assessing the individual's needs is by measuring the strength of his needs for achievement, which has been defined as a general disposition to derive success from "success in competition with some standards of excellence." See David C. McClelland, John W. Atkinson, Russell A. Clark, and Edgar L. Lowell, *The Achievement Motive* (New York: Appleton-Century-

Both externally mediated rewards, such as wages, promotions, and co-worker acceptance, and internal rewards such as ego-involvement, pride in work, and others may contribute to satisfaction.[40]

Using equation (15-1) with $G = \$200$, $r = \$20$, and $a = 0.80$, satisfaction is shown to increase in Table 15-4. The curve S_1, in Figure 15-4 indicates the relationship between satisfaction and reward. G is the desired level of reward, and as R approaches G, Mr. Jones's satisfaction increases rapidly. The curve S_2 in Figure 15-4 shows the relationship between satisfaction and reward in a case where Mr. Jones feels that he is overpaid. The perceived justice per unit of reward is 1.20. Instead of deprivation, in this case Mr. Jones may have guilt feelings.

The other variable of interest to us is the amount of effort or frequency of activity, F_A. The frequency with which a man is willing to contribute activity is directly proportional to the difference between his personal goal and the amount of reward received, that is, it depends on $G - R$. It also depends on the frequency of reward, F_R, or the frequency with which the activity is rewarded.[41] The frequency of activity can be expressed by:

$$F_A = bF_R \, (G - R) \qquad (15-2)$$

where F_A is the frequency of activity, F_R is the frequency of reward, and b is the constant of proportionality.

The assumptions underlying this expression are as follows. First, need satiation is related to motivation.[42] Presumably, if a satiated need ceases to operate as a motivator, the frequency of contributing

Crofts, Inc., 1953) ; Henry A. Murray, *Explorations in Personality* (New York: Oxford University Press, Inc., 1938) ; J. W. Atkinson, "Towards Experimental Analysis of Human Motivation in Terms of Motives, Expectancies, and Incentives," in J. W. Atkinson (ed.), *Motives in Fantasy, Action, and Society* (Princeton, N.J.: D. Van Nostrand Co., Inc., 1958), pp. 288–305; Herbert H. Meyer, William B. Walker, and George H. Litwin, "Motive Patterns and Risk Preferences Associated with Entrepreneuriship," *Journal of Abnormal and Social Psychology*, Vol. 63 (1961), pp. 570–74; Herbert H. Meyer and William B. Walker, "Need for Achievement and Risk Preferences as they Relate to Attitudes Toward Reward Systems and Performance Appraisal in an Industrial Setting," *Journal of Applied Psychology*, Vol. 45 (1961), pp. 251–56.

[40] See Victor H. Vroom, *Work and Motivation* (New York: John Wiley & Sons, Inc., 1964), pp. 264–67.

[41] Homans, *op. cit.*, pp. 278–80.

[42] This assumption is in accord with Maslow's proposition that satisfied need ceases to be operative as a motivator. See Maslow, *op. cit.*

activity decreases as the need becomes more satisfied or as R approaches G. Second, it is possible to reward activity at a constant ratio; that is, as an individual contributes a unit of activity he receives a unit of reward.[43] For instance, the commission salesman, Mr. Jones, receives $20 for every sales unit he sells. Since the frequency of a man's rewards depends on the frequency of his activity, which varies with $G - R$, then F_R is also directly proportional to $G - R$. Thus, $F_R = c(G - R)$, where c is the constant of proportionality. Substituting $c(G - R)$ for F_R in equation (15–2), we obtain equation (15–3)

$$F_A = bc\ (G - R)\ (G - R)$$
$$= bc\ (G - R)^2 \qquad\qquad (15\text{–}3)$$

Thus, the frequency of contributing an activity F_A decreases and becomes zero as the difference between G and R approaches zero, that is, when $G = R$. As the rewards earned by Mr. Jones approach the $200 reward level during a given week, he will decrease the frequency of contributing selling activities, or in simple terms, he will not work as hard as before.

Using equation (15–3) with $G = \$200$, $r = \$20$, $b = 0.8$, and $c = 1.0$, the frequency of contributing activity by Mr. Jones, as shown in Table 15–4, decreases as R approaches G and as satisfaction increases. As shown in Figure 15–4, a man works hardest when he is least satisfied. When he is most satisfied, he is least willing to do extra work for added rewards. "For reasons of this sort we cannot say that, in general, the more satisfied a man is with a reward the harder he will work to get it. Under many circumstances, indeed, the reverse is likely to be the case: the less satisfied he is the harder he works."[44] This conclusion should be approached with some caution because the satisfaction-activity relationship is complex.

The complexity of this relationship can be illustrated by changing the second assumption concerning the constancy of rewarding activity to a condition of infrequent reward or lump-sum reward received upon completion of a task. Under these conditions, the inverse relationship does not hold. For instance, if Mr. Jones were

---

[43] For some support of this assumption, see B. F. Skinner, *Science and Human Behavior* (New York: Macmillan Co., 1953), pp. 102–4.

[44] Homans, *op. cit.*, p. 280.

TABLE 15-4

Relationship of Rewards, Satisfactions, and Activity

G = $200   r = $20

Cumulative Reward Units (In Dollars) R	Satisfaction		Frequency of Activity F_A
	a = 0.80 S_1	a = 1.20 S_2	
$ 20	0.09	0.13	25.92
40	0.20	0.30	20.48
60	0.34	0.51	15.68
80	0.53	0.80	11 52
100	0.80	1.20	8.00
120	1.20	1.80	5.12
140	1.87	2.80	2.88
160	3.20	4.80	1.28
180	7.20	10.80	0.32
200			

FIGURE 15-4

The Effect of Perceived Justice on Satisfaction

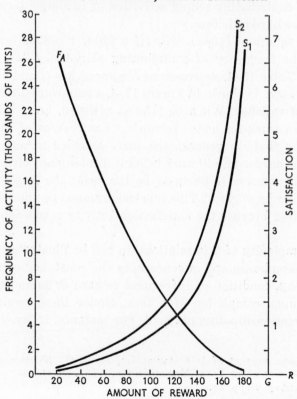

rewarded once every week in a lump sum of $200 provided he met some imposed sales quota, as he approached the sales quota he might work harder and longer to ensure himself of the $200 reward. An author approaching the completion of a book, or a student nearing graduation, might act in a similar manner.[45] This simple model shows how a person may adapt his behavior with respect to satisfaction and activity contributed under two conditions—frequent reward and infrequent reward. Each condition brings about a different adaptation of behavior.

The complexity of motivation is compounded even more if we take into consideration a situation involving a shift in the desired reward goal.

Shift of Desired Goal

Though the assumption of a fixed goal may be reasonable, at least for short periods of time, in the long run an individual's aspirations may change. As a person acquires more knowledge, skills, experiences, seniority, and other similar investments, the amount needed to satisfy, that is, his level of aspiration, may increase. Or as a person ages, loses physical skills, forgets knowledge, becomes less sociable, his goals may shift downward.

In the process of attaining a suitable exchange, the individual and the organization may go through an adjustment of reward goals. For several reasons, the individual may not be able to satisfy his needs. If for instance, the individual lacks physical, mental, or social ability, or if his bargaining position is weakened because of some other reason, then the individual may be forced into lowering his reward goals. If a person's activities aimed at the attainment of monetary reward, friendship, security, power, position, and so on, lead, time after time, to failure, the individual may lower his reward goals in order to avoid repeated frustrations. In other words, motivation to achieve need satisfaction may be altered on the basis of past personal success or failure.

By successive compromises between the individual and the organization, a new solution may be reached as a result of lowering of goals by one or both. The opposite may also be true. Over an extended period of time, the individual and the organization may elevate their expectations. An improvement in individual skills, for

---

[45] For a more complete discussion of the lump-sum reward conditions, see Homans, *op. cit.*, pp. 280–81.

example, development of new and better manual abilities, improvement of social skills by learning how to work with other people, and learning more about the technical aspects of work, may result in an upward shift of the individual's goals. Because of environmental changes, improved technology, job training, better raw materials, new services, products, and processes, and other changes, the organization may expect more from the individual. The shifting of goals is a very real and likely phenomenon. Homans,[46] March and Simon,[47] and others have hypothesized that an upward change in the level of expectations means that the amount of rewards needed to satisfy a person also increases. Field and experimental research suggests that this hypothesis is valid. Nancy Morse observed in her study of white-collar workers that "the amount of satisfaction which a person derives from a particular situation depends upon what he wants from the situation (i.e., what he aspires for) and what the situation provides."[48] Morse suggests that the differences in need satisfaction between two groups, treated in opposite ways with respect to the supervision they received, are attributable to differences in aspiration levels. The group with a relatively higher aspiration level was less satisfied than the group with a lower aspiration level. The least satisfied group was given a less restrictive type of supervision, that is, "general supervision" as opposed to the other group which received "close supervision." It appears that the general supervisory pattern shifted the aspiration levels of the group members for pay and promotion upward.

The Morse findings suggest that the aspiration level of a worker may shift because of organizational arrangements. A more general hypothesis proposes that the individual's level of aspiration is determined by environmental factors, such as economic and social background, informal group norms, culture, and organizational policies and standards, and personal factors, for example, previous performance, habits, personality, and physiology.[49]

[46] Homans, *op. cit.*, pp. 274–75.

[47] James G. March and Herbert A. Simon. *Organizations* (New York: John Wiley & Sons, Inc., 1958), pp. 48–52.

[48] Morse, *op. cit.*, p. 139.

[49] For a discussion of the concept of aspiration level and bibliographic references on studies of aspiration, see Kurt Lewin, Tamara Dembo, Leon Festinger, and Pauline S. Sears, "Level of Aspiration," in J. McV. Hunt (ed.), *Personality and Behavior Disorders*, (New York: Ronald Press, 1944), Vol I, pp. 333–78; Gardner Lindzey (ed.), *Handbook of Social Psychology*, (Cam-

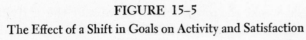

FIGURE 15-5

The Effect of a Shift in Goals on Activity and Satisfaction

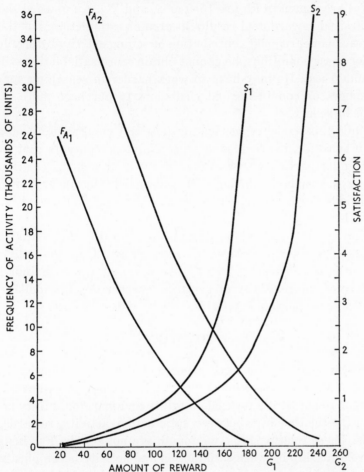

A shift of the reward goal for our hypothetical salesman, Mr. Jones, will have an affect upon satisfaction and frequency of activity. Let us suppose that for some reason Mr. Jones shifts his income goal from $200 to $260 per week with all other conditions remaining the same, that is, $r = \$20$, $a = 0.8$, $b = 0.8$, and $c = 1.0$. The original curves depicting satisfaction and frequency of activity are shown in Figure 15-5 as S_1, and F_{A1}. By shifting the reward goal

bridge, Mass.: Addison-Wesley Publishing Co., 1954), Vol. I, pp. 208–9; and H. J. Eysenck (ed.), *Handbook of Abnormal Psychology* (New York: Basic Books, Inc., 1961), pp. 284–97.

to $260 per week, the satisfaction curve and the activity curves shift upward and to the right. The new satisfaction and activity curves are shown in Figure 15-5 as S_2 and F_{A2}. An upward shift of the desired reward goal results in greater satisfaction, but this requires a more frequent contribution of selling activity by Mr. Jones. Under these conditions, he cannot obtain more satisfaction without an added cost. He may have to work harder in searching for new customers or convincing old customers to purchase more of the goods he sells.

While this model of motivation does not generalize all of motivated behavior, it provides us with analytical concepts that can be used under particular conditions. There is no general relationship among the variables included in the model, but under particular conditions, for instance, when activity is rewarded frequently, this model is useful.

This entire discussion of activity, reward, and satisfaction hinges upon the value placed on certain rewards by the individual. The satisfaction-activity solution is different for each individual because of the relativity of rewards whether they are dollars, leisure time, promotion, supportive supervision, or others.

SUMMARY

In this chapter, we have attempted to examine motivation in terms of a person's decision to work and exchange his skills and abilities for rewards. We focused on utility and marginal utility as well as on the relationships between satisfaction, activity, rewards, and goals. These relationships, we found, are not simple. For instance, the relationship between satisfaction and activity is complicated by other variables—the frequency of rewards, and the shifting of goals.

DISCUSSION QUESTIONS AND PROBLEMS

15-1. Do people generally behave in a rational manner to achieve personal goals? Explain.

15-2. In terms of Maslow's "hierarchy of needs," is it necessary for a person to fulfill lower order needs before the higher order needs take over as motivators? For example, does a hungry person worry about self-actualization?

15-3. Can organizational goals and individual needs be satisfied simultaneously? What can be done to promote the attainment of organizational goals while endeavoring to provide need satisfaction for organizational participants?

15–4. How is an organization able to pattern the behavior of an individual toward its goals?

15–5. To what extent can financial rewards provide need satisfaction for employees?

15–6. Why does an individual submit to efforts to pattern his behavior? Does there have to be some agreement or compromise with the organization about rewards and behavior?

15–7. Compare the idea of satisfaction in indifference curve analysis and in activity-satisfaction analysis.

15–8. Evaluate the following statements:
   a) "The more workers are satisfied, the more they will produce."
   b) "The only way to run a ship efficiently is to establish rules and make sure the men stick to them."
   c) "You can't motivate a lazy man."
   d) "In a large organization, it is easy for a man to lose his motivation."
   e) "Subordinates are highly motivated around the time that salary increases and promotions are decided."
   f) "After a long season, the players lost their motivation in the championship game."

15–9. The Green Company produces and sells office equipment. The management of the Green Company wants to determine how to assign each of three newly hired salesmen to each of three territories. Yearly sales potential in territory 1 is $50,000; in territory 2, $70,000; and in territory 3, $250,000.

Each prospective salesman is given a battery of personnel tests upon applying for a job with the Green Company. The results of these tests show:

Salesman	Yearly Goal
A	$35,000
B	10,000
C	20,000

Each salesman is paid on a commission basis, 10% of sales for the first $100,000 sales and 15% of sales on all sales above $100,000. How would you make assignments to a territory to maximize each salesman's satisfaction? Assume that each salesman feels that he is neither underpaid nor overpaid for the selling activities he will perform.

The following information pertains to problems 15–10, 15–11, and 15–12.

The Lenox Company manufactures and sells three models of vacuum cleaners. Relevant data available on each model are as follows:

Model	Unit Selling Price $	Unit Variable Costs $	Unit Contribution to Profit and Fixed Costs ($)	Average Selling Time Required (Hours/ Unit)
A................100	80	20	1.5
B................150	112	38	3.0
C................200	140	60	4.0

Mr. Cooper, Lenox's salesman in territory 1, wishes to attain a yearly salary of $10,000. He feels he is underpaid for the work he performs. Lenox salesmen are paid, on a commission basis, 6% of sales. Mr. Cooper feels he should earn 8% on the sales he makes. Mr. Cooper's philosophy of selling is "to maximize his commission."

Mr. Cooper averages 36 hours per week performing selling activities for Lenox. He works 50 weeks per year. Assume F_A and F_R are constant.

15-10. *a*) If Mr. Cooper adheres to his philosophy of selling, which model will he concentrate on?

b) What will be Mr. Cooper's level of satisfaction if he adheres to his philosophy?

c) How would the results of Mr. Cooper's selling philosophy affect the achievement of company objectives (maximizing contribution to profit and fixed costs)?

d) What would be Mr. Cooper's level of satisfaction if he tries to achieve company objectives?

15-11. The Lenox Company has been experiencing unusually low sales of models B and C and unusually high sales of model A. After an investigation, management found that the low sales of model B and model C were caused by the high average selling time per unit of models B and C relative to the average time required to sell a unit of model A. Thus, management has decided to increase advertising for model B and model C in an effort to reduce the average time required to sell a unit of model B and model C.

a) How much must the average time required to sell a unit of model B and model C be reduced so that Mr. Cooper has equal preference as to the model he sells?

b) What will be Mr. Cooper's level of satisfaction?

c) Since Mr. Cooper has nothing to gain by "pushing" one model over another, he decides to allocate equal selling time to each model. How much contribution to fixed costs and profit will he generate?

15–12. Management could have gotten Mr. Cooper to show equal preference toward each of the three models by changing the commission rates for model B and model C (instead of changing the average time required to sell a unit of model B and model C).

  a) What would the commission rates be changed to if Mr. Cooper is to show equal preference toward models A, B, and C? Assume that the commission on model A will remain at 6% of sales of model A.

  b) What would be Mr. Cooper's level of satisfaction?

  c) How much would Mr. Cooper contribute to fixed costs and profit?

  d) Why would management choose to change the average time required to sell a unit of model B and model C rather than change the commission on model B and model C?

15–13. There exist those unusual people (the opposite of Mr. Jones) in our society whose satisfaction increases very little with increased cumulative rewards and whose frequency of activity increases the more cumulative rewards they receive. Such a person may be described by "the more he gets the more he wants."

  a) Revise the equation for satisfaction so that it applies to this type of person.

  b) Revise the equation for frequency of activity and frequency of reward.

15–14. Mr. Smith owns and operates a drive-in restaurant. Mr. Smith earns $30 per day after all expenses are paid. Normally, Mr. Smith keeps the drive-in open 10 hours per day, five days per week. Also, he has found that he earns $3 per hour each hour over 10 hours he keeps his restaurant open each day. Assume that $F_R = 1$, $a = 1$, $b = 1$; and that Mr. Smith's weekly income goal is $150.

  a) Calculate Mr. Smith's frequency of activity and level of satisfaction at the end of each day for one week.

  b) Before Mr. Smith opened the restaurant on Wednesday morning, he decided he wanted to buy a new golf bag the following weekend. Thus, Mr. Smith had to earn an extra $60 by the time he closed Friday evening. Calculate Mr. Smith's frequency of activity and level of satisfaction at the end of each day for one week.

16

ORGANIZATIONAL CHANGE

In the last chapter, we were concerned with the factors that affect an individual's behavior. However, the factors that change an individual's behavior may not create change in an organization. The formal organization is like an individual in that there are forces operating within it that try to maintain a steady-state pattern of behavior. As might be expected, the forces of formal organization are much more powerful and diverse than those of the individual. In consequence, organizational forces have greater abilities to resist change and maintain the steady state. The interdependence of parts means that change (when it is organizational change) not only affects an individual's behavior but it reverberates throughout the organization and affects the behavior of others and possibly the relationships among individuals.

DEFINITION OF CHANGE

Partially through design features such as feedback and control and partially through sociopsychological factors such as norms of informal organization, the forces operating within the system try to counteract disturbances and maintain stabilized patterns of behavior. In order to induce change, the magnitude of a disturbance must be great enough or appealing enough so that the internal forces are unable to compensate or are unwilling to return the system to the former state of affairs.

Operationally, the steady state of a system may be defined in terms of a statistical distribution. When the mean and variance of a statistical distribution which describes the pattern of behavior in a system are constant over time, the system is said to have a steady-state pattern of variation, that is, the probabilities of events are constant over time.[1] When the mean and/or the variance of the distribution describing the pattern have changed significantly, it may be said that a change in the system has occurred. While not all of the studies discussed in this chapter apply this criterion to test for change, it is implied, at least, that change involves a significant difference from a previous stabilized pattern of behavior.

Change to a New Steady State

The shift from a steady-state pattern of behavior may result in a number of other states. For example, there is the possibility of movement from a stabilized pattern to complete random behavior. The more general case, and the one which we emphasize, is the movement from one steady-state pattern of behavior to another steady-state pattern of behavior. Once change has been induced in a system, the movement away from one steady state will be characterized by the efforts of group members to establish a new stabilized pattern of behavior or steady state. To illustrate this movement, we refer again to the Harwood experiments of Coch and French.[2]

As mentioned earlier, the research at the Harwood Manufacturing Company involved experimental efforts to overcome worker resistance to change. The company which had tried to introduce changes in the jobs and methods of its production workers, found worker attitudes to be markedly negative and their behavior revealed a general resistance to the changes. In other words, they tried to hold to the steady state or the established pattern of behavior. Coch and French used the field-forces theory of Kurt Lewin to explain this behavior.

According to Kurt Lewin, a state of equilibrium can exist in social life even though it undergoes a change. Lewin called this steady state "quasi-stationary equilibrium," and he used the con-

---

[1] W. J. Fabrycky and Paul E. Torgersen, *Operations Economy* (Englewood Cliffs, N.J.: Prentice-Hall, Inc., 1966), p. 194.

[2] Lester Coch and John R. P. French, Jr., "Overcoming Resistance to Change," *Human Relations*, Vol. 1 (August, 1948), pp. 512–32.

cept to describe change processes which are kept at some given level by "opposing field forces."[3] The field forces operate in such a way that opposition to an increase is strengthened as the increase approaches the equilibrium level, and at the same time other forces are strengthened against a decrease as the decrease comes closer to the level of equilibrium. This idea is illustrated in Figure 16–1.

For example, a change such as an increase in the expected unit output prescribed by the technical subsystem may be opposed by

FIGURE 16–1

Quasi-Stationary Equilibrium

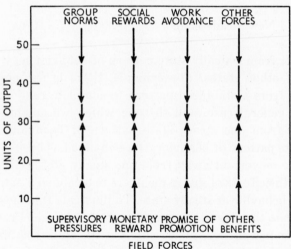

SOURCE; Lester Coch and John R. P. French, Jr., "Overcoming Resistance to Change," *Human Relations*, Vol. 1 (August, 1948).

the output norm of the social subsystem. Inducements such as an increase in supervisory pressure, an increase in monetary rewards, promises of promotion, and other benefits may be used by the technical subsystem to change unit output. However, opposing field forces such as individual and group pressures may increase as the output level approaches an equilibrium level. Figure 16–1 illustrates an equilibrium level established at 30 units by two sets of opposing forces. In this illustration the field forces are composed of behavioral elements of the technical and social subsystems, but other forces and other combinations may prevail in establishing a steady-state position.

---

[3] Kurt Lewin, "Frontiers in Group Dynamics," *Human Relations*, Vol. 1 (1947), pp. 5–42.

In the Coch and French experiment, workers were divided into four groups. One group, called the "control group," was simply told about the job changes. The three other groups, called "experimental groups," were allowed to participate in formulating as well as implementing the changes.

The productivity results, in terms of units of output per hour, for the control group (nonparticipation group) over a 30-day period

FIGURE 16–2

Quasi-Stationary Equilibrium for Nonparticipating Group

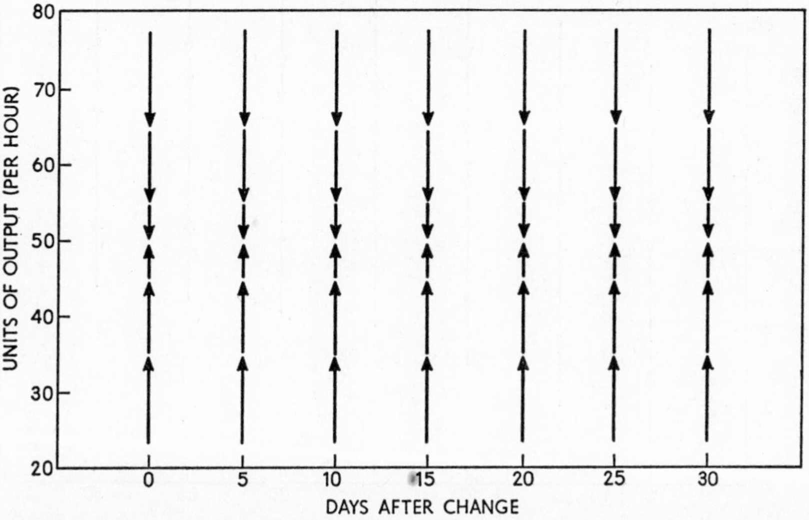

SOURCE; Lester Coch and John R. P. French, Jr., "Overcoming Resistance to Change," *Human Relations*, Vol. 1 (August, 1948).

after the job changes were introduced, remained at about 50 units per hour. The resultant field forces, depicted in Figure 16–2 by arrows, appear to be equal at the level of 50 units per hour. The productivity level remained constant because the resultant upward forces were equal to the resultant downward forces.

The results of the experimental groups (participation groups), depicted in Figure 16–3, show that although the output level increased from 50 units per hour to approximately 73 units per hour, the increase appears to be approaching a quasi-stationary equilibrium at about 70 units per hour.

The control group resisted change and maintained the prechange level of output, whereas the participative groups accommodated change and increased output to a higher level. The increase in output, however, stabilized at about 70 units per hour.

The Harwood experiments reveal that workers may or may not resist change. Whether or not change is resisted depends partly on the method of organizing for change. These experiments suggest

FIGURE 16–3

Quasi-Stationary Equilibrium for Participation Groups

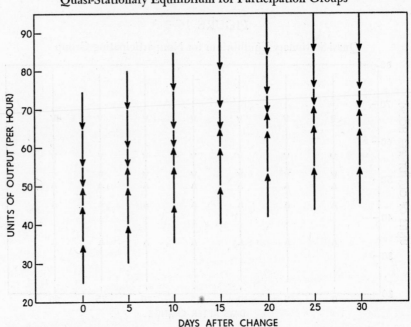

Source: Lester Coch and John R. P. French, Jr., "Overcoming Resistance to Change," *Human Relations*, Vol. 1 (August, 1948).

that worker resistance to change can be reduced if the organizational structure and processes are designed in a manner which allows worker participation in planning change. In other words, through participation the workers act as the change agent. In terms of organizational stability, these research results illustrate change as the movement from one steady state to a higher steady state.

Some Conditions of Change

It is evident that in the experimental groups Coch and French used a major variable of change, that is, through group discussion and decision making they were able to overcome the forces operating to maintain established behavior patterns of the system. However, as researchers found in a later experiment, there are important conditions that must be met before group discussion and decision operate as a major variable of change. In the later experiment conducted in a footwear department of a Norwegian factory by J. R. P. French and others, the researchers were unsuccessful in their efforts to raise the level of production.[4] As was the case with the Coch and French experiments, the concern of the research at the Norwegian factory was with the effects of increased worker participation on production, labor-management relations, and job satisfaction. There were, according to the researchers, eight possible areas of worker participation: (1) designing and selecting new articles (footwear); (2) allocating to the work groups the articles to be produced; (3) deciding the need for training and the length of training; (4) setting up the division of labor within a work group; (5) assigning jobs within the work group; (6) constituting and reconstituting work groups; (7) setting the piece rate; and (8) deciding about the level of production. After discussions with management and the union, the researchers had to exclude areas of decision making. "Decisions about the level of production were excluded because the workers already had a maximal influence in setting their production level. The piece-rate setting was considered to be a bargaining procedure between management and the union."[5] The researchers were allowed to use only four areas of decision making in the experiment: allocation of the articles to the work groups; length of training; division of labor; and assignment of jobs within the work groups.

According to the investigators, worker participation in the discussions and decisions on change did not affect production because the four areas of decision making were not very relevant to production and the pattern of participation was not "legitimate" to workers. The importance of the decision areas and the fact that workers already exerted "maximal influence" in setting production levels meant that participation was a "weak" variable for inducing change in the Norwegian factory. The Norwegian workers had a strong tradition for participation through union representatives.

[4] John R. P. French, Jr., Joachim Israel, and Dagfinn As, "An Experiment on Participation in a Norwegian Factory," *Human Relations*, Vol. 13 (1960), pp. 3–19.

[5] *Ibid.*, p. 9.

Thus, the "legitimate pattern of participation" to the workers was through union representatives rather than through the direct participation of the experiment. These findings supported the hypotheses of the investigators which state that in order for increased participation to affect production, labor-management relations, and job satisfaction, four conditioning variables must be present: (1) the decisions are important; (2) the content of the decisions are relevant to the dependent variable; (3) the participation is considered legitimate; and (4) there is no resistance to the *methods* of managing the change.[6]

SYSTEMS APPROACH AND CHANGE

The systems approach, which stresses the interrelatedness of the parts of organization, requires that we study the effects of change not just on one part in isolation from the other parts but also the effects of change on all of the parts and the relationships among the parts. This means, according to Mary Parker Follett, ". . . that when a factor is added to or subtracted from a situation, you have not that situation minus or plus that factor, for all the rest will be changed.[7] She gave an example to illustrate this point:

You see it in a board of directors. One man leaves and all the rest become a little different. The influence of that board of director as a total is not the same as it was minus that man's influence, because his withdrawal, by changing slightly every other man, has made the total different. Every business man knows that the president of a company in relation to one board of director may be very different from that same president in relation to another board.[8]

In another example, Follett reports a discussion with a businessman who describes the effects of coordination as follows:

If my heads of departments tell me that Department D and Department E are co-ordinated, and then I find that Department D and Department E are exactly the same as they were before, then I know that what I have been told is not true; they are not co-ordinated. If they have been co-ordinated, then the parts will be changed, that is, the practice of Department D will differ in some respects from what it was before co-ordination.[9]

[6] *Ibid.*, p. 17.

[7] Henry C. Metcalf and L. Urwick, *Dynamic Administration* (New York: Harper & Bros., 1941), p. 192.

[8] *Ibid.*, pp. 192–93.

[9] *Ibid.*, p. 193.

Effects of Change

There are several studies, in addition to the ones already cited, which have attempted to determine the effects of changing an organizational variable. In this section, we report on some of these studies and discuss the changes brought about by the research.

Structure and Change. The interrelatedness of the parts of a system can be illustrated by referring to several field studies. James Worthy found that cooperation among employees improved after a change of structure at Sears, Roebuck and Company.[10] By "flattening" the organizational structure (that is, eliminating hierarchical levels), by decreasing individual and subunit specialization, and by increasing primary face-to-face relationships of the employees, was it possible to obtain more spontaneous cooperation. Worthy claims that by reducing the technically prescribed, impersonalized relationships, thus relying more on primary relationships, conflict is reduced at both the worker and managerial levels.

In a longitudinal field study of organizational growth, Mason Haire found that there exists a relationship between changes in the size of a firm and its shape.[11] In organizational terms, he claims that as "inside" employees (for example, production, inventory control, inspection, maintenance workers) increase by a cube function, the "outside" employees (for instance, salesmen, receptionists, purchasing agents, shipping workers) increase by a square function. The cube of the number of "inside" employees and the square of the "outside" employees, in each of the industries studied, provide a reasonably good fit to a straight line.[12]

---

[10] James C. Worthy, "Organizational Structure and Employee Morale," *American Sociological Review*, Vol. 15 (1950), pp. 169–79.

[11] See Mason Haire, "Size, Shape, and Function in Industrial Organizations," *Human Organization*, Vol. 14 (1956), pp. 17–22, and, also in *Modern Organization Theory* (New York: John Wiley & Sons, Inc., 1959), chap. x. Haire's findings are supported by another similar study: Seymore Levy and Gordon Donhowe, "Exploration of a Biological Model of Industrial Organization," *Journal of Business*, Vol. 35 (October, 1962), pp. 335–42.

[12] Criticisms expressed about the use of a biological model to explain organizational growth and change claim that (1) the model lacks parsimony; (2) the terms "inside" and "outside" are not defined clearly, nor are the terms appropriate for social organization; (3) the model does not yield testable prediction; and (4) generally, predictive validity is lacking. See, Jean Draper and George B. Stroher, "Testing a Model for Organization Growth," *Human Organization*, Vol. 22 (1956), pp. 180–94.

508 FORMAL ORGANIZATION: A SYSTEMS APPROACH

This study suggests that one element of an organizational system, the staff function, tends to increase especially where the "destructive forces" are the greatest. These forces operate at "the areas of coordination and control," and at the peripheral areas where the system is exposed to the environment.

Processes and Change. Significant changes in the organization need not arise only from an alteration of the formal structure; they can occur also through the alteration of processes of any of the subsystems. A change in the action processes of the technical subsystem can affect any of the dimensions of the social organization and vice versa.

Empirical evidence concerning this point has been reported in several cases. Charles R. Walker found that an action process change due to the introduction of new technology in the production of seamless tubing not only affected some elements of the technical subsystem, but it also caused an alteration in the social structure of the work groups.[13]

Floyd C. Mann and L. R. Hoffman found in their study of automation in the electric power industry that an action process change due to new technology affected not only the size of the work groups but also the social processes of both employee groups and the superior-subordinate relationships.[14] In a case which involved an action process change due to the introduction of electronic data processing, Floyd C. Mann and L. K. Williams observed an interplay that resulted in changes in the technical and social subsystems and in the communication process between the personnel of the accounting and sales departments. The decision processes were also affected.[15]

Personnel and Change. Significant changes also can occur because of changes in the personnel employed by the organization. In a study of a large automobile plant, extending over a three-year period, Robert H. Guest reported that the actual behavioral patterns, as measured by interactions, sentiments, and activities of the workers and supervisors, changed significantly with a change in plant manager.[16]

---

[13] Charles R. Walker, *Toward the Automatic Factory* (New Haven, Conn.: Yale University Press, 1957).

[14] Floyd C. Mann and L. R. Hoffman, *Automation and the Worker: A Case Study of Social Change in Power Plants* (New York: Henry Holt & Co., 1960).

[15] Floyd C. Mann and L. K. Williams, "Observations on the Dynamics of a Change in Electronic Data Processing Equipment," *Administrative Science Quarterly*, Vol. 5 (Fall, 1960), pp. 217–56.

[16] Robert H. Guest, *Organizational Change: The Effect of Successful Leadership* (Homewood, Ill.: Richard D. Irwin, Inc., and Dorsey Press, 1962).

Guest found that while no basic changes were made in the formal organizational structure, substantial changes occurred in the pattern of interactions and sentiments of the organization participants due to a change in plant manager. Under the new plant manager, a greater proportion of communications were originated by subordinates and directed to superiors than under the deposed leader. "Fewer emergencies and more time to plan" was another result of the new leadership. The shift in the pattern of interactions was accompanied by a marked change in sentiments from negative to positive as expressed by the workers about top management. The reason for the shift was attributed by Guest to the workers' perceptions of the behavior of their supervisors. The workers felt that they were given a greater opportunity to express their opinions to top management. Meetings between groups of workers and management, under the new plant manager, were no longer perceived as a stage for punishing individuals by open criticism, but rather they were viewed by the workers as rewarding experiences. The meetings reinforced what the workers had learned through experience with their own superiors in individual interactions.

In general, the mode of social behavior closely approximated the type of behavior expected among friends and neighbors in the culture which prevailed outside of the work situation. During the annual automobile model changeover, the performance of this plant improved as measured by production costs, quality, safety, labor grievances, turnover, and absenteeism. Performance was not only better in terms of previous time periods but it was better than the performance of other similar plants.

Major Organizational Variables and Change

A change in one of the parts of formal organization does not necessarily mean that the total organization will change. While the parts are interrelated, the change in one part may have an imperceptible effect on the other parts. For example, a minor executive who attends a management development program may have his attitudes changed or he may acquire new management skills, but his organizational role may be so insignificant that the changes have no effect on the organization. Also, while a change in one part of the organization may induce responses from the other parts, the responses may be a counteraction which effectively suppresses or nullifies the effects of the change. In order to induce organizational change, then, it may be necessary to make drastic revisions in the total system or to introduce changes in many parts of the organization at once.

Change at General Electric. This approach was illustrated by the General Electric Company, which changed to decentralization after operating since its inception under a highly centralized type of management. The company implemented the change by making a complete "overhaul" of its organization and ways of managing. Imagine the problems encountered by this company that counted its sales in billions of dollars and numbered its employees in hundreds of thousands, that had plants and offices located virtually in every state of the United States and several foreign countries, and that had a long tradition of centralized management.

The reorganization which took place between 1951 and 1952 converted the highly centralized organization into 20 decentralized divisions made up of 70 relatively autonomous operating departments. This resulted in the shifting or transferring of approximately 2,000 management personnel. Many organizational changes were made. Executives with line authority working in functionally centralized departments were reassigned to service departments and were given staff authority. Some reassignments were viewed by the managers as shifts to lower level positions in the organization. In some cases, executives in charge of large departments with many assistants and coordinators were relieved of their responsibilities as department heads and shifted to other duties. The organizational change provided Ralph Cordiner, the president of the firm, with an opportunity to eliminate some positions. For example, assistants and coordinators were eliminated. According to Cordiner, "An assistant is really a prop for a manager who can't get his own work done," and a "coordinator is an official with a vested interest in keeping two more or less important people apart."[17]

Some of the new organizational assignments required department managers, for the first time in General Electric's long history, to be responsible for making their own decisions. Furthermore, managers were no longer required to make their decisions according to a long list of organizational prescriptions.

The shifts were not limited only to organizational changes. Many executives were reassigned to new geographical areas. For in-

---

[17] William B. Harris, "The Overhaul of General Electric," *Fortune*, Vol. 52, No. 6 (December, 1955), p. 115.

stance, executives were forced to move with their families from Schenectady to New York City, from Bridgeport, Connecticut, to Louisville, Kentucky, and from Pittsfield, Massachusetts, to Rome, Georgia.

Morse-Reimer Experiment. Although there has been widespread acceptance of decentralization as an effective method of organizing, there has been little testing or experimentation to determine its effectiveness.[18] One study which did test the effects of decentralization was conducted through the research programs of the Survey Research Center of the University of Michigan by Morse and Reimer in a business organization.[19] While the results of their study are important and are discussed below, our interest at this juncture is not so much in the effectiveness of decentralization as in what was required to induce the changes required by the experiment.

The researchers sought to test two hypotheses. The hypotheses, which formulated the relationship between decision-making roles and satisfaction and productivity, are as follows:

Hypothesis I:
An increased role in the decision-making processes for rank and file groups increases their satisfaction (while a decreased role in decision making reduces satisfaction).

Hypothesis II:
An increased role in decision making for rank and file groups increases their productivity (while a decreased role in decision making decreases productivity).[20]

The experiments were conducted in one department of the company. The rank-and-file members were nonunionized and were engaged in relatively routine work. The department had four parallel divisions. Prior to the experiment, each division was similar with respect to decision-making authority, productivity and satisfaction

---

[18] The central idea of decentralization is to allocate decision-making authority to the lowest possible level in the organization. There is a serious definitional problem involved in any discussion of this concept. As mentioned previously, there is the obvious problem that stems from the fact that all organizations are decentralized to some extent. There is, for example, decision-making authority involved in a worker's choice to make body movements or to "turn on" the power that starts a machine. Thus, it is necessary in any discussion of this concept to specify what is being decided upon, the people involved, and the time period covered by the decision.

[19] Nancy C. Morse and Everett Reimer, "The Experimental Change of a Major Organizational Variable," *Journal of Abnormal and Social Psychology,* Vol. 52 (1956), pp. 120-29.

[20] *Ibid.,* p. 121.

(as measured by the investigators), type of work, type of personnel, and type of supervisory structure. According to the research plan, the decision-making role of rank-and-file members in two of the divisions was increased and in the other two divisions, their decision-making role was decreased. In other words, in two divisions, the degree of decentralization was increased, and in the other two divisions, it was decreased. For simplicity, we call the divisions with an increased decision-making role "decentralized" and the divisions with a decreased decision-making role, "centralized."

The researchers recognized that the change in decision-making roles required by the experiment could not be realized without involving the entire organization. The roles at one level could not be changed, for example, without changing the roles at all other levels in the organization. Hence, in the decentralized divisions, the changes would require rank-and-file employees to assume the additional decision-making duties of first-line supervisors, first-line supervisors to give up their previous duties and to operate as division managers, division managers to assume the duties of department heads, and department heads to operate as top-management officials coordinating the department's work with other departments. Thus, the researchers followed a total systems approach to implement the changes.[21] First, they felt that the roles had to be *legitimized* by top management officials. In this endeavor, the executive vice president introduced the proposed changes to employees as new company policy.[22] Second, there were formalized structural changes. In the decentralized divisions, ". . . authority was delegated by upper management to lower levels in the hierarchy with the understanding that they would redelegate it to the clerical work group."[23] In the centralized divisions, ". . . authority was given to the higher line officials to increase their role in the running of the divisions and to the staff officials to increase their power to institute changes. . . ."[24] Third, ". . . there were training programs for the supervisors of the divisions to ensure that the formal changes would result in actual changes in relations between people."[25]

The researchers successfully implemented the changes required

[21] Daniel Katz and Robert L. Kahn, *The Social Psychology of Organization* (New York: John Wiley & Sons, Inc., 1966), p. 427.

[22] *Ibid.*, p. 428.

[23] Morse and Reimer, *op. cit.*, p. 121.

[24] *Ibid.*, pp. 121–22.

[25] *Ibid.*, p. 122.

by the experimental design. Katz and Kahn, who were the directors of the experimental program, describe the changes as follows:

The experimental manipulations were successful in creating two different social subsystems for the two sets of divisions. In the [decentralized divisions] the clerical work groups did in fact make a variety of group decisions on matters of importance to them, such as recess periods, the handling of tardiness, work methods, and work processes. Some work groups were more active than others in getting together to discuss and decide on how their section should operate, but all groups in this program assumed group responsibility for the operations of the section. In the [centralized divisions], on the other hand, the employees were less involved than before in the regulation and control of their own activities. Previously they had little direct influence on decisions, but they did have some degree of influence on their supervisors and division managers with whom they had direct contact. Now decisions were made at the departmental level, and employees were completely removed from affecting the control process. The measurement of the changes perceived by the employees in the two program corroborates the effectiveness of the experimental manipulations. In the [decentralized divisions] the clerks saw decision-making activities as less a function of higher organizational levels than before the experiment, whereas in the [centralized divisions] the clerks now perceived all policies and procedures as determined to a very high degree at levels above their own.[26]

The results of the experiment revealed that individual satisfaction of group members increased significantly in the decentralized divisions and decreased significantly in the centralized divisions. Both decision-making systems increased productivity, but the centralized divisions showed a greater increase. Thus, the results supported the first hypothesis but not the second.

The fact that the centralized divisions were able to increase productivity more than the decentralized divisions is explained partially by the work situation and the method of measuring this performance variable. The divisions had no control over the amount of work scheduled. "The amount of work done by the divisions was completely dependent upon the flow of work to them. . . ."[27] The volume of work done was fixed. The only way that productivity could be increased, therefore, was to reduce the number of clerks.

Both the decentralized and the centralized divisions increased productivity by reducing the number of clerks. However, the reduction of clerks in the decentralized divisions was accomplished when

[26] Katz and Kahn, *op. cit.*, p. 429.
[27] Morse and Reimer, *op. cit.*, p. 75.

the girls decided not to replace members who left for normal reasons such as marriage, while in the centralized divisions the number of clerks assigned to tasks was reduced by executive order. Since the volume of work was fixed for all of the divisions, the greater productivity increases for the centralized divisions could be expected. Katz and Kahn conclude that with the cooperative spirit engendered among the girls in the decentralized divisions, ". . . they could hardly be expected to dismember their group if no one was willing to leave, and they showed no inclination to do so. If the girls themselves could have determined their quotas of work, there would have been more opportunity for increases in productivity. . . ."[28] The researchers and the directors of the Survey Research Center speculate that if the experiment had been allowed to continue for a longer period, the gains of the centralized divisions would have been reversed and the gains in productivity of the decentralized divisions would have continued.

Again, we emphasize that while the differences in productivity gains are interesting and important for the study of formal organization, our primary interest in this chapter is the systems approach to induce change. The Morse-Reimer experiment successfully induced change through the systems approach. Let us now turn our attention to the sociotechnical aspects of the systems approach.

Linking the Technical and Social Subsystems

Oftentimes, an organization finds it necessary to implement changes in order to take advantage of a technological innovation or to correct inefficient practices. Several studies have shown that when technical changes are introduced without due regard for the social subsystem, the inevitable result is a failure to realize the sought-after improvements. "Where, as has frequently happened, the resulting work organization has failed to satisfy the social and psychological needs of its members, their attitudes on task performance have inhibited the full realization of technological potential and lowered productivity."[29]

Trist-Bamforth Study. A study by Trist and Bamforth of the longwall method of mining in the British coal industry attempted to

---

[28] Katz and Kahn, *op. cit.*, p. 432.

[29] A. K. Rice, *Productivity and Social Organization: The Ahmedabad Experiment* (London: Tavistock Publications, Ltd., 1958), p. 4.

examine the interrelatedness between the technical and social sub-systems of formal organization.[30] As a result of technological inno-vations, companies in the industry decided to institute the long-wall method of coal mining. The effect of this change was a breakdown in established social patterns in the mines.

The old method of mining involved a cycle of three phases—digging the coal, loading it into tubs, and advancing the coal face. Under the old method, miners formed in groups of six, two for each shift. Each miner had the skills to perform all three phases of the cycle. The members of the group on one shift would take up the cycle wherever the previous shift had left off, regardless of the phase or part of the phase that had been completed. Each man was paid the same wages, the amount being dependent upon the output of the six-man group. The composition of each group was deter-mined by the members themselves. The men were allowed to select their partners and set their own standards of output.

The long-wall method required that each of the three phases of mining be assigned to a separate shift, that is, the first shift did all of the digging, the second shift performed all of the loading, and the third shift was engaged in advancing the coal face. Perform-ance measures and payment were based on the shift task as opposed to total output. In terms of skills, the old method required each miner to use several skills, while the long-wall method involved more specialization.

The introduction of the long-wall method resulted in a number of problems. By specializing, miners were less able to handle some of the underground hazards of mining. Shifting miners from one job to another became more difficult. Disruptions in production re-quired more management attention because miners were generally less willing to stop their own work to help others correct problems. When digging, loading, or advancing the coal face was disrupted, miners working on the last shift were called upon to bring the cycle back into balance. This debilitated the morale of the other shifts, because it provided the miners of the last shift with a superior bargaining position.

Some of the mines did not convert completely to the conventional long-wall method. They adopted what was called the "composite

---

[30] E. L. Trist and K. W. Bamforth, "Some Social and Psychological Conse-quences of the Long-Wall Method of Coal-Getting," *Human Relations*, Vol. 4 (1951), pp. 3–38.

long-wall method." Under the composite method, the mines maintained the six-man group responsibility for the three phases of the production cycle. As was the case in the other pits, the miners had to learn new skills to run the new machinery. The composite method was different from the conventional long-wall method in that workers were not restricted to a specialized job. Workers in the composite pits were allowed to rotate among several jobs and, therefore, developed several skills. In effect, the benefits of the old system were retained. Possessing several skills, members of a team could complete one phase of the production cycle during a shift and move to the next phase during the same shift. Workers on the next shift took up the cycle, regardless of the phase. Each group could select its own members and the earnings of each worker were based on the productivity of the group.

The composite method of long-wall mining allowed the adoption of technological advancements while preserving the existing social subsystem. The composite method also preserved the links between the technical and social subsystems of the mines. Evidence of the link between subsystems was the way that miners coordinated their own work under the composite method. Since each group was responsible for all phases of the cycle and had the skills to complete it, workers moved easily from task to task and moved the work as far along as possible on a shift. There was an easy transition from one shift to another, again, because of the multiple skills of the workers, but mostly because workers on different shifts were "chosen" members of a group and they were compensated as a group. Under the conventional long-wall method, management had to coordinate all work, because the workers were relegated to specialized jobs and could not move to different tasks. Furthermore, payment methods under the long-wall method fostered a spirit of competition rather than cooperation. Instead of working together to maintain the productivity of the group and to focus on the overall task, workers concentrated on specialized tasks (the basis of reward) with little or no regard for other jobs. The petty arguments and grievances over which specialized group was responsible for slowdowns was further evidence that the induced technical change tended to pull the forces apart rather than pull them together for the welfare of the system.

When the researchers compared pits that used the conventional long-wall method to pits that used the composite long-wall method, they found marked differences in performance. Performance comparisons revealed that the composite method was superior in terms of productivity and reduced absenteeism. Productivity as measured by output per man-shift was 5.3 tons for the composite system and 3.5 tons for the conventional system. Absenteeism was two and one half times higher under the conventional method than the composite method. Trist and Bamforth hypothesized that under the conventional method "self-compensatory" absenteeism occurred, that is, absenteeism to compensate for the undesirable conditions of conventional long-wall mining.

It appears that the social subsystem played an important role in the coal-mining task. It facilitated coordination and the maintenance of underground safety, and in general it helped organize the task, though not in a formally prescribed manner, to advance the attainment of organizational goals. The conventional method did not work as expected because it tended to break the links between the technical and social subsystems.[31]

Rice's textile studies. Another research effort that illustrates the necessity for linking the technical and social subsystems was the study of A. K. Rice.[32] The study was conducted in India at the textile mills of the Ahmedabad Manufacturing and Calico Printing Company, Ltd. The problem faced by the research team dealt with the introduction of modern machinery. Not only did the new machinery fail to raise productivity but it caused social and pyschological problems for both management and the workers.

The results of introducing automatic looms were disappointing to management. The automatics were set up in a new experimental shed with the latest type of lighting and humidity control to overcome tropical conditions. The company followed the American and British practice of assigning workers to specialized operations. American and Japanese standards, modified for Indian conditions, were used to determine the number of workers assigned to the different operations. The hours of work were the same as for the rest of the mill. As might be expected, management was very interested and paid considerable attention to the shed. The morale of the shed appeared to be good, the supervisors enjoyed good relations

---

[31] A study reported by R. T. Golembiewski concerning a change in work flow in the U.S. Patent Office supports this conclusion. See Robert T. Golembiewski, *Behavior and Organization: O & M and the Small Group* (Skokie, Ill.: Rand McNally & Co., 1962).

[32] A. K. Rice, *op. cit.*

with the workers, the group had a reputation for competence and hard work, and virtually all of the technological problems had been solved, but the efficiency and the quality of output was no better than that experienced on ordinary looms. "Technological change had not led to the expected productive change."[33]

The method of specialization required that each worker perform one task on a number of looms. For example, in the shed, there were eight weavers to care for the 224 automatic looms. Each weaver was responsible for 24 or 32 looms, depending upon his skills. "Once looms were loaded and set up, the eight weavers were responsible for keeping them running, discovering reasons for stoppages, mending broken warp threads, and dealing with minor entanglements."[34] The other jobs in the shed (there were 21 other workers) were set up on a basis similar to those of the weavers.

In contrast to the production process of the ordinary looms, the automatic looms involved a continuous process in which all activities had to be performed simultaneously. The ordinary looms involved a cyclic process in which workers could experience the psychological rewards that come from the completion of a whole task. Since jobs were so specialized on the automatic looms, completion of a whole task was not possible. With the exception of a few jobholders, the result of specializing to this degree created an aggregate of individuals who were virtually independent of each other. No stable pattern of relationships could develop, there was no group structure, and no self-government among the workers. Thus, there were few social rewards to be gained from the organizational design of the shed. In addition, the degree of specialization and the fact that different workers were assigned to different numbers of machines created much confusion with regard to the responsibilities of each man. Also, there was no way to group workers conveniently for supervision. The lack of any overt difficulties under these trying conditions was, according to Rice, a tribute to the quality of relations between supervisors and workers and their tolerance for confusion in responsibility and authority.

There appeared to be two possible ways to gain the advantages of the automatic looms. The first was to strengthen the existing management system by increasing the number of supervisors and by tightening inspection. The second was to reorganize by creating a

---

[33] *Ibid.*, p. 51.
[34] *Ibid.*, p. 54.

link between the technical and social subsystems whereby an internal structure would develop among groups responsible for a whole task. The dangers of the first possibility were that it would increase the cost of supervision and it would risk a "vote of no confidence" from the workers. "The workers would not only continue to experience the discomfort of their unstructured confusion but would feel further coerced and policed. In consequence, they might be expected to increase their resistance to greater effort and productivity."[35]

In view of the potential consequences of the first possibility and the belief that there was a need for an internally structured work group responsible for a "whole task," the researchers recommended that management adopt the second possibility. The design required that workers be formed into groups. Each group would contain workers with skills to perform a "total task" and would be responsible for a group of looms. The groups would be set up by mutual choice of the workers. In this way it was hoped that the groups would experience a "closure in terms of the total task performed" and develop the sought-after internal structure. The proposed reorganization was so appealing that it was rapidly accepted and implemented by both management and the workers.

Except for some minor difficulties, the results showed that the experiment was highly successful. The workers' enthusiasm for the plan presented a "remarkable picture." Weavers ran to repair broken yarn on stopped looms. Other members of the group also ran to help the weavers. Workers carrying 200-pound beams on their shoulders were seen trotting. The motivation was so high that supervisors had to stay in the shed to prevent members of groups from remaining on the job during meal breaks or returning early from the breaks. This supervisory effort was necessary because Indian law specifies that no worker shall be at his workplace during the meal break. Efficiency, which was the actual output expressed as a percentage of the potential output (that is, output that would result if the looms ran continuously), rose from an average of 80 percent before the reorganization to about 95 percent in the final phase of the experiment. Damage, expressed as the percentage of cloth rejected by inspectors, fell from an average of 32 percent before the reorganization to about 20 percent in the final phase of the experiment.

The new design, which created a social system and merged it

---

[35] *Ibid.*, p. 61.

with the technical system, allowed the workers to perform their tasks effectively and to derive benefits which satisfied their social and psychological needs adequately. Rice concluded that: "A work organization that does not satisfy the social and psychological needs of its members will inhibit the full realization of technological potential."[36]

Likert's Linking-Pin Model. The idea of linking subsystems is incorporated in an organizational model proposed by Rensis Likert. The fundamental characteristic of the Likert model, concerning a "motivational approach to organization," involves several system concepts.[37] Based on a considerable amount of research, Likert has developed an integrative organizational model that encourages the internalization of organizational objectives by involving all of the participants in group decision making concerning task-related problems. The essential concepts of Likert's model are: (1) group processes are efficacious in maximizing motivation of participants in organizations; (2) group overlapping creates linkages in the hierarchy that channels motivation toward group goals; (3) group linkages provide a network of feedback loops; and (4) representation in decision making facilitates change.[38]

This theory emphasizes the value of linking together various components of an organization by overlapping group memberships. Figure 16–4 reveals how an organization can be linked, according to Likert, "by means of people who hold overlapping group memberships."[39] The values derived from this linking-pin arrangement are threefold. First, decision making is based on group processes. Second, each group at a given level has a representative in a higher level decision-making group. Third, individuals representing lower level groups can perform an information feedback function. The underlying assumption of this model is that individuals seek, and are satisfied by, involvement in the decisions that govern their work conditions.

While this model provides conditions for channeling motivation through social satisfactions derived from primary group relation-

---

[36] *Ibid.*, p. 251.

[37] Rensis Likert, *New Patterns of Management* (New York: McGraw-Hill Book Co., 1961), chap. viii.

[38] For a brief description and evaluation of the Likert model, see Daniel Katz, "The Motivational Basis of Organizational Behavior," *Behavioral Science*, Vol. 9 (April, 1964), pp. 131–46.

[39] Rensis Likert, "A Motivational Approach to a Modified Theory of Organization and Management," in Mason Haire (ed.), *Modern Organization Theory* (New York: John Wiley & Sons, Inc., 1959), pp. 184–217.

ships, it does not violate the logic of the hierarchical authority structure of the technical subsystem. The members of the organization serve as linking-pins between organization levels, and, at the same time, the decisions are personally mediated and feedback channels are provided.[40]

The Likert model, the French, Trist and Bamforth, Morse and Reimer, and Rice experiments are integrative or systems approaches that attempt to increase the performance of organization

FIGURE 16–4

Likert's Linking-Pin Organization Model

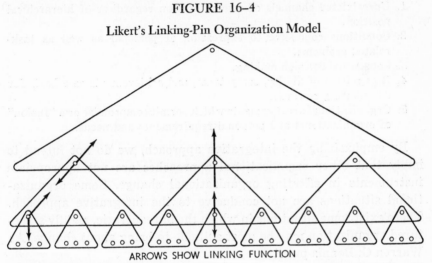

ARROWS SHOW LINKING FUNCTION

SOURCE: Rensis Likert, *New Patterns of Management* (New York: McGraw-Hill Book Co., 1961), p. 113.

through member participation. The rationale to increasing participation is that involvement in decision making presumably commits the participants to their decision, increases the likelihood of successful execution and implementation, and satisfies some higher order needs. Increasing participation means involving more individuals in decision making at lower levels in the organization than with the traditional approach. Under the integrative type of organization, therefore, it is necessary to increase the number of

---

[40] Other integrative models have been proposed. See E. Wight Bakke, *The Fusion Process* (New Haven, Conn.: Yale University, Labor and Management Center, 1955); Charles P. McCormick, *Multiple Management* (New York: Harper & Bros., 1938); Douglas McGregor, *The Human Side of Enterprise* (New York: McGraw-Hill Book Co., 1960); William B. Given, Jr., *Bottom-Up Management* (New York: Harper & Bros., 1949); William F. Whyte, *Man and Organization* (Homewood, Ill.: Richard D. Irwin, Inc., 1959); Elliott Jaques, *The Changing Culture of a Factory* (London: Tavistock Publications, Ltd., 1951).

communication channels and feedback loops and to widen the distribution of information.

Empirical data in support of the integrative approach is insufficient for validation purposes. Tests that have been undertaken are at best equivocal,[41] and some tests disclose negative results.[42] Yet, the integrative principle has drawn considerable attention and loyalty as a method of effecting organizational change. This principle is based upon a system of values which pervades the American concept of democracy. These beliefs include the following:

1. Unrestricted channels of communication regardless of hierarchical position.
2. Conditions conducive to expression of personal as well as task-related problems.
3. Consensual decision making.
4. Recognition of ability, competence, and achievements as a basis for distributing rewards.
5. Organizational arrangements which permit compromise or a "fusion" of organizational and personal requirements and needs.

By emphasizing the integrative approach, we do not intend to imply that other organizational approaches are not appropriate instruments in effecting organizational change. Some organizational situations are not conducive to the integrative approach. There exist some situations in which the bureaucratic, rigidly structured organization may be most suitable to bring about change. As Warren G. Bennis put it:

. . . Specifically, for simple tasks under static conditions, an autocratic centralized structure, such as has characterized most industrial organizations in the past, is quicker, neater, and more efficient. But for adaptability to changing conditions, for "rapid acceptance of a new idea," for "flexibility in dealing with novel problems, generally high morale and loyalty . . . the more egalitarian or decentralized type seems to work better."[43]

---

[41] R. Harrison, "Impact of the Laboratory on Perceptions of Others by the Experimental Group," in Chris Argyris, *Interpersonal Competence and Organizational Effectiveness* (Homewood, Ill.: Richard D. Irwin, Inc. and Dorsey Press, 1962), pp. 261–71; Robert R. Blake, "Typical Laboratory Procedures and Experiments," *An Action Research Program for Organization Improvement* (in Standard Oil Company) (Ann Arbor, Mich.: Foundation for Research on Human Behavior, 1960), pp. 7–29.

[42] Reinhard Bendix, *Work and Authority in Industry* (New York: John Wiley & Sons, Inc., 1956); pp. 319–40; Warren G. Bennis, "Bureaucracy and Social Change: An Anatomy of a Failure" (Boston: Massachusetts Institute of Technology, School of Industrial Management, multilithed., 1962).

[43] Bennis, *Changing Organization, op. cit.,* pp. 19–20. Part of this quote appears in Bennis', "Towards a 'Truly' Scientific Management: The Concept of Organization Health," *General Systems,* Vol. 7 (1962).

SUMMARY

This chapter is devoted to an examination of variables that induce change in an organization. Change is defined as a shift from one established stable pattern of behavior (steady state) to another stable pattern. In order to induce change, the change variable has to be major or strong enough to overcome the forces that try to maintain the established steady state.

Research studies suggest that for variables to be instruments of change, they must: (1) have the support of power elements such as management and unions, that is, they must be legitimized; (2) not disturb the emergent system or create a new framework which promises to satisfy social and psychological needs of participants adequately as well as the material needs of the organization; (3) provide organizational arrangements which permit those that are affected, to control, as much as possible, their own work activities; and (4) allow organizational members to participate in the decisions required to implement change.

DISCUSSION QUESTIONS

16–1. What are some of the reasons for the tendency of organization members to resist change?

16–2. What are some possible ways to gain the acceptance of organization members and prepare them for the implementation of change?

16–3. Compare the conditions at Harwood with those at the Norwegian factory and explain why French and his associates were able to raise productivity in the one experiment and not in the other.

16–4. Why is the legitimization of the instruments of change so important to participants of the organization?

16–5. Why is it important to provide for or create a social structure when implementing a change? How is it possible to provide for the social and psychological needs of participants when a change requires a disruption of existing social relationships?

16–6. What implications does a systems approach have for the preparations required to achieve a change as it was intended?

16–7. Why is it possible for the social subsystem to perform managerial functions such as coordination better than management?

16–8. Compare the money costs involved in trying to achieve a change through the participation of those who are to be affected to a change that is implemented by executive order.

16–9. Compare the Trist-Bamforth study with the Rice study with respect to the importance of the sociotechnical system.

16–10. Is it possible to create a social system within the formal organization? Explain.

Epilogue

Epilogue

Epilogue

Over the years one of the most recurring issues of mankind has been the problem of how to organize. One of the aspects of this problem revolves around the question of the proper balance between the promises of materialistic organizational efficiency and individual freedom. The uneasy balance between organizational efficiency and other human values has been the subject of considerable discussion and speculation among philosophers, anthropologists, political scientists, and others.

Ancient Greek philosophers, more than 2,000 years ago, speculated at great lengths on the origin and essence of organization. Although they were not concerned primarily with economic and institutional organizations, Greek philosophers discussed and hypothesized about the organization of the city-state.

Aristotle perceived the state as a means toward a "good life," while Plato completely subordinated the individual to the state. Plato's subordination of the individual was complete, for it ranged from state regulation of property to the application of principles of eugenics for the improvement of the racial quality of the Athenians.

This controversy has not been confined to the organization of the ancient Greek city-state, for the same issue was reexamined during the 17th and 18th centuries. The two positions taken are the "social contract" theory and the "social mold" theory, each of which in some ways reflect the arguments expounded by the Greek philosophers.

Thomas Hobbes in the *Leviathan* argued that men are by nature self-seeking, brutish, and aggressive; to avoid anarchy it was
necessary for groups of men to unite in a society that would pre-
serve peace and order.[1] Émile Durkheim advocated the superiority
of society over the individual in both time and space because society
brings the individual into being through a particular "mold."[2] Jean
Jacques Rousseau stated the same problem in 1762:

> The problem is to find a form of association which will defend and
> protect with the whole common force the person and good of each associ-
> ate, and in which each, while uniting himself with all, may still obey
> himself alone, and remain as free as before. This is the fundamental
> problem.[3]

During the two centuries that have elapsed since this statement
was made, what has been done to resolve the problem?

With the emergence of industrialization and large-scale enterprises, the initial solution to this problem, according to Max
Weber,[4] was based on nepotism, emotionalism, cruelty, and other
irrational practices. The reaction against these irrational practices
was what Weber called "bureaucracy" and what has been labeled in
this book as traditional organization theory. This social invention
was aimed at introducing rationality into organization.

According to traditional theory, organization is based on the
work that has to be done in order to attain the predetermined goals
of the formal organization. The formal goals are used to derive a
method of organizing and controlling scarce resources in an
efficient manner. The method is based on a rational appeal to define,
measure, calculate, and predict organizational behavior. This rational method of organizing places an emphasis on work, division
of labor, a well-defined hierarchy of authority, and a system of
administrative policies, procedures, and rules.

While the traditional organization theory, according to some of
its proponents "is logically consistent," "has stood the test of time,"

---

[1] Thomas Hobbes, *Leviathan* (London: J. M. Dent & Sons, Ltd., 1914), esp.
Part 2, chap. xvii.

[2] Émile Durkheim, *The Rules of Sociological Method*, tr. by Sarah S.
Solovay and John H. Mueller (8th ed.; Glencoe, Ill.: Free Press, 1938), chap.
vi.

[3] Jean Jacques Rousseau, *The Social Contract*, tr. by Charles Frankel (New
York: Hafner Publishing Co., Inc., 1949), p. 1.i.

[4] H. H. Gerth and C. Wright Mills, *From Max Weber: Essays in Sociology*
(New York: Oxford University Press, Inc., 1958), pp. 196–98.

and "works in practice" it has been subjected to a searching examination. The criticisms reveal that it is too narrow in scope, ignores many important human values, and lacks precision, adaptability, and a comprehensive framework.

TODAY

Rousseau's statement is a perplexing legacy that has been handed down from generation to generation. The same question is being asked today about the organization of industrial enterprises as well as others such as hospitals, schools, and ecclesiastic organizations. A contemporary organizational theorist, Chris Argyris, reflects the same age-old dilemma as follows:

. . . How is it possible to create an organization in which the individual may obtain optimum expression and, simultaneously, in which the organization itself may obtain optimum satisfaction of its demands?[5]

Other contemporary organizational theorists reflect the same dilemma. For instance, Chester I. Barnard poses the problem as a conflict facing the executive in terms of "efficiency" (satisfying personal needs) versus "effectiveness" (satisfying the productivity needs of organization).[6] The same cross-currents are referred to as the "personalizing process" and the "socializing process" by E. Wight Bakke;[7] "Theory X" and "Theory Y" by Douglas McGregor;[8] and "pyramids and people" by Harold J. Leavitt.[9]

In recent years a number of theoretical and practical propositions have been made to resolve some of the criticisms of traditional theory. While the recommendations offered are far too numerous to mention, they can be classified under several theories—leadership, structure, exchange, and adaptation.

---

[5] Chris Argyris, "The Individual and Organization: Some Problems of Mutual Adjustment," *Administrative Science Quarterly*, Vol. 2, No. 2 (1957), p. 24.

[6] Chester I. Barnard, *The Functions of the Executive* (Cambridge, Mass.: Harvard University Press, 1938), pp. 19–20.

[7] E. Wight Bakke, *The Fusion Process* (New Haven, Conn.: Labor and Management Center, Yale University, 1935), pp. 4–5.

[8] Douglas McGregor, *The Human Side of Enterprise* (New York: McGraw-Hill Book Co., 1960), chaps. iii and iv.

[9] Harold J. Leavitt, *Managerial Psychology* (Chicago: University of Chicago Press, 1958), pp. 257–62.

Leadership

Leadership theory suggests that the autocrat should be replaced by someone who is sensitive to the needs of his subordinates. To be "employee oriented" means to listen to subordinates and attempt to understand them and their problems, to keep them well informed about what is going on and particularly about what is expected of them, and to be fair and consistent in applying rules, especially in distributing rewards. These are the supervisory conditions which, according to Herzberg, Mausner, and Snyderman are "hygienic": that is, they are analogous to medical hygiene as it operates to remove health hazards.[10]

Other leadership theories do not attempt to prescribe the "right" conditions, but rather emphasis is placed upon the combination of leader, followers, and situation. Leadership is viewed as an interaction of two parties—a leader and followers. The "right" style of leadership used in a particular case must be suited to the leader, the followers, and the situation.[11]

Exchange

Another explanation of organizational behavior is based on the premise that an organization exchanges values with its participants.[12] It offers various "inducements" or "payments" to participants in return for the values that are demanded by the organization. The employee-participant offers his time, effort, and talent to the organization in return for payments. If the inducements are adequate, the participant is motivated to deal with the organization. The inducements offered to employee-participants are not limited to monetary rewards. The Hawthorne experiments revealed that man seeks satisfaction of social needs at work. This suggests that needs

[10] Frederick Herzberg, Bernard Mausner, and Barbara Block Snyderman, The Motivation to Work (New York: John Wiley & Sons, Inc., 1966), chap. xii.

[11] R. Tannebaum and W. H. Schmidt, "How to Choose a Leadership Pattern," Harvard Business Review, Vol. 36 (March–April, 1958), pp. 95–101.

[12] For example, see: Herbert A. Simon, Administrative Behavior (New York: Macmillan Co., 1960), chap. vi; Alfred Kuhn, The Study of Society: A Unified Approach (Homewood, Ill.: Richard D. Irwin, Inc., and Dorsey Press, 1963); Peter M. Blau, Exchange and Power (New York: John Wiley & Sons, Inc., 1964); and George C. Homans, Social Behavior: Its Elementary Forms (New York: Harcourt, Brace & World, Inc., 1961).

such as recognition, affiliation, achievement, and involvement can be used as payments to induce cooperation.

Structure

Some theorists believe that in order to change behavior and attitudes the structure of the organization must be modified. The formal hierarchy, specialization, and role specification, designed to meet the technical needs of the organization, must be modified to accommodate latent identities, social needs, and personal development of the employees. For example, both Rensis Likert and James C. Worthy suggest that this can be accomplished by altering the bureaucratic structure. Likert's linking-pin theory induces group cooperation, sharing of responsibility and lower level participation in decision making.[13] Worthy sees in his "flat" organization a method of inducing more integration as opposed to specialization, decentralization vis-à-vis centralization of authority, and personal development.[14] Some of the practical models developed to accomplish similar results are "multiple management," "Scanlon plan," "bottom-up management," "consultative hierarchy," "job enlargement," and "participative management."

Adaptation

Some of the recommendations discussed above require adaptation of individual behavior on the part of organization participants. Distributing power, decision making, information, opportunities for advancement, and growth more evenly throughout the organization may require some preparation for the change. Especially those occupying the "have-not" positions may have to adapt their behavior in order to accept and benefit from decentralization, independent decision making, freer communications, and group collaboration. For example, Likert's linking-pin theory implies a shift from an autocratic superior with submissive and passive subordinates to a more equal balance of power among all group participants.

The principal methods that have emerged for adapting individual

[13] Rensis Likert, *New Patterns of Management* (New York: McGraw-Hill Book Co., 1961), chap. viii.

[14] James C. Worthy, "Organizational Structure and Employee Morals," *American Sociological Review*, Vol. 15 (1950), pp. 169–79.

behavior in organization include client-centered counseling and sensitivity training.

Traditional organizational theory may be inadequate and not in tune with contemporary organizational realities. But, judging it by the number of reactions it has sparked, traditional theory has served a useful purpose. At the very least it has been an easy target to hit, a good straw man to knock down. The first thrust has provided a number of resolutions for the individual-organization conflict. These methods mediate between organizational goals and personal needs.

THE FUTURE

The boundaries of rationality have been expanded to include a better understanding of organizational behavior and problems, but the world of tomorrow promises many changes. While some solutions exist for the individual-organization problem, in the future, organization will face a new set of problems arising from environmental changes. Changes in science, technology, education, demography, government, and composition of the population will require the organization, above all, to be more adaptable.

Forecasts about the future of organization, mostly based on what Warren Bennis calls "thin ice,"[15] have been plentiful. The prognostications range from Orwellian utopias in the distant future to man-machine systems which are already foreseeable.

Revolutionary Predictions

Many different theorists have made forecasts about organization in the future. Revolutionary predictions cover the spectrum from Clark Kerr's "New Bohemianism" to C. P. Snow's apprehensions concerning the emergence in organization of a new breed of 20th-century machine destructionists—"intellectual Luddites."

Kerr, Dunlop, Harbison, and Myers envision that, increasingly, work will be "programmed." This means that there will exist fewer opportunities for creativity and discretion on the job, but the individual will spend fewer hours per week at work. The creation of this "New Bohemianism" means that leisure and not work will

---

[15] Warren Bennis, "Beyond Bureaucracy," *Trans-action*, Vol. 2, No. 5 (1965), p. 34.

provide man with more opportunities for freedom, creativity, and satisfaction.[16] According to this prophecy, the apprehensions about "unhuman organizations,"[17] "creatures garbed in distinctive gray flannel uniforms," "executive suites in crystal palaces," "robot executives," and the like will cease to be important or relevant.

New technological developments in information processing and control systems, according to Harold J. Leavitt and Thomas L. Whisler will have an effect upon organizational structure.[18] What will emerge is an organizational structure that resembles a football balanced on a church bell. The middle-levels of management will be reduced and reorganized. The football part, consisting mostly of an elite oligarchy of innovators, operations researchers, mathematical programmers, computer experts, and "committors" will have more individual autonomy to carry out applied research than lower management levels. The demarcation between these elite and the lower levels will be marked and impenetrable.

C. P. Snow foresees the danger, especially in government, of the decision-making "circle" shrinking with the development of the computer.[19] Only a "tiny circle of computer boys" will be familiar with decision rules and the new computer art. The scientists and administrators who are in the decision-making seat today will not be able to gain the literacy needed for the computer in addition to their own specialties. They will cease to occupy decision-making positions, and they may turn out to be the "intellectual Luddites."

While these predictions are aimed at the distant future, several moderate forecasts have been made about the more immediate future.

Moderate Predictions

In his assessment of the "new science of management decision," Herbert A. Simon forecasted that the hierarchical form of organi-

---

[16] Clark Kerr, John T. Dunlop, Frederick H. Harbison, and Charles A. Myers, *Industrialism and Industrial Man* (Cambridge, Mass.: Harvard University Press, 1960), pp. 294–96.

[17] Harold J. Leavitt, "Unhuman Organizations," *Harvard Business Review*, Vol. 40, No. 4 (1962), pp. 90–98.

[18] Harold J. Leavitt and Thomas L. Whisler, "Management in the 1980's," *Harvard Business Review*, Vol. 36 (1958), pp. 41–48.

[19] Sir Charles Percy Snow, "Scientists and Decision Making," in Martin Greenberger (ed.), *Management and the Computer* (Cambridge and New York: Published jointly by M.I.T. Press and John Wiley & Sons, Inc., 1962), pp. 3–34.

zation is not likely to be replaced.[20] Departmentation will continue
to be the basis of organizing activities. The principal change is
likely to alter the relative importance of the patterns of specialization. Purpose departmentation may become more important than it
is today. For instance, in a business organization of the future, differences between manufacturing, marketing, finance, and engineering are not likely to be as marked as they are today. Product-type departments will be more important as organizations become more and
more service oriented.

The forecast made by Warren Bennis is based on the premise
that the real *coup de grâce* against bureaucracy is its "ethical-moral
posture" which is incongruent with today's environment and hope-
lessly out of step with the changing environment expected in the
future. To survive, organization will have to be more flexible and
adaptive. In the future, organization must incorporate an "or-
ganic-adaptive" structure. People will be organized, not hierarchically according to rank and role, but "flexibly and functionally
according to skill and professional training."[21]

It appears that the amount of organization is not likely to decrease in the near future. Based on the premise that organizing is a
simple and natural human response to a complex task, organization
is likely to remain as a general problem solver for a long time. This
premise is supported by psychological research which points out
that it is a natural tendency for man to program himself by seeking
to find general problem-solving routines. This is also a historical
fact. Arnold Toynbee has pointed out that the genesis of the first
civilization came about through organization. When the nomads of
northern Africa were faced with the enormous problems of dessica-
tion, their response was to organize. By damming the Nile River,
irrigating the land, and tilling the arid soil, nature was coaxed to
produce a bountiful harvest.

Breaking down the task, departmentalizing activities, programming decisions, sequencing operations, and channeling authority
and communications are contemporary attempts to employ general
problem-solving routines. These attempts to organize involve two
important features—to divide a task into parts and subdivide if
necessary, and to arrange the parts in a hierarchical form. It is

---

[20] Herbert A. Simon, *The New Science of Management Decision* (New York:
Harper & Bros., 1960), pp. 49–50.

[21] Bennis, *op. cit.*, p. 35.

unlikely that these basic features will be discarded in the future. This is the best that finite intelligence has been able to produce.

Regardless of what organizational system is developed, in the final analysis, its viability will depend on how it is applied. Achievement and success are a product of more than just an organizational structure. Bertalanffy stated this well:

. . . The real values of humanity are not those which it shares with biological entities, the function of an organism or a community of animals, but those which stem from the individual mind. Human society is not a community of ants or termites, governed by inherited instinct and controlled by the laws of the superordinate whole; it is based upon the achievements of the individual and is doomed if the individual is made a mere cog in the social machine. This, I believe, is the ultimate precept a theory of organization can give: not a manual for dictators of any denomination more efficiently to subjugate human beings by the scientific application of Iron Laws, but a warning that the Leviathan of organization must not swallow the individual without sealing its own inevitable doom."[22]

---

[22] Ludwig von Bertalanffy, "General Systems Theory," *General Systems*, Vol. 1 (1950), p. 10.

APPENDIX

Finite Queuing Tables*

*From L. G. Peck and R. N. Hazelwood, *Finite Queuing Tables* (New York: John Wiley & Sons, Inc., 1958), pp. 3-18, 25-27, 42-45, and 54-57.

POPULATION 4

X	M	F	X	M	F	X	M	F	X	M	F
.015	1	.999	.155	2	.994		2	.954		1	.384
.022	1	.998		1	.916		1	.696	.700	3	.926
.030	1	.997	.160	2	.994	.330	3	.996		2	.695
.034	1	.996		1	.910		2	.950		1	.357
.038	1	.995	.165	2	.993		1	.683	.750	3	.905
.042	1	.994		1	.904	.340	3	.996		2	.657
.046	1	.993	.170	2	.993		2	.945		1	.333
.048	1	.992		1	.899		1	.670	.800	3	.880
.052	1	.991	.180	2	.991	.360	3	.994		2	.621
.054	1	.990		1	.887		2	.936		1	.312
.058	1	.989	.190	2	.990		1	.644	.850	3	.852
.060	1	.988		1	.874	.380	3	.993		2	.587
.062	1	.987	.200	3	.999		2	.926		1	.294
.064	1	.986		2	.988		1	.619	.900	3	.821
.066	1	.985		1	.862	.400	3	.992		2	.555
.070	2	.999	.210	3	.999		2	.915	.950	3	.786
	1	.984		2	.986		1	.595		2	.526
.075	2	.999		1	.849	.420	3	.990			
	1	.981	.220	3	.999		2	.903			
.080	2	.999		2	.984		1	.572			
	1	.978		1	.835	.440	3	.988			
.085	2	.999	.230	3	.999		2	.891			
	1	.975		2	.982		1	.551			
.090	2	.999		1	.822	.460	3	.985			
	1	.972	.240	3	.999		2	.878			
.095	2	.999		2	.980		1	.530			
	1	.969		1	.808	.480	3	.983			
.100	2	.999	.250	3	.999		2	.864			
	1	.965		2	.977		1	.511			
.105	2	.998		1	.794	.500	3	.980			
	1	.962	.260	3	.998		2	.850			
.110	2	.998		2	.975		1	.492			
	1	.958		1	.780	.520	3	.976			
.115	2	.998	.270	3	.998		2	.835			
	1	.954		2	.972		1	.475			
.120	2	.997		1	.766	.540	3	.972			
	1	.950	.280	3	.998		2	.820			
.125	2	.997		2	.968		1	.459			
	1	.945		1	.752	.560	3	.968			
.130	2	.997	.290	3	.998		2	.805			
	1	.941		2	.965		1	.443			
.135	2	.996		1	.738	.580	3	.964			
	1	.936	.300	3	.997		2	.789			
.140	2	.996		2	.962		1	.429			
	1	.931		1	.724	.600	3	.959			
.145	2	.995	.310	3	.997		2	.774			
	1	.926		2	.958		1	.415			
.150	2	.995		1	.710	.650	3	.944			
	1	.921	.320	3	.997		2	.734			

539

POPULATION 5

X	M	F	X	M	F	X	M	F	X	M	F
			.120	2	.995	.250	3	.995	.420	3	.966
				1	.927		2	.955		2	.826
.012	1	.999	.125	2	.994		1	.712		1	.471
.019	1	.998		1	.920	.260	3	.994	.440	4	.996
.025	1	.997	.130	2	.993		2	.950		3	.960
.030	1	.996		1	.914		1	.695		2	.807
.034	1	.995	.135	2	.993	.270	3	.994		1	.451
.036	1	.994		1	.907		2	.944	.460	4	.995
.040	1	.993	.140	2	.992		1	.677		3	.953
.042	1	.992		1	.900	.280	3	.993		2	.787
.044	1	.991	.145	3	.999		2	.938		1	.432
.046	1	.990		2	.991		1	.661	.480	4	.994
.050	1	.989		1	.892	.290	4	.999		3	.945
.052	1	.988	.150	3	.999		3	.992		2	.767
.054	1	.987		2	.990		2	.932		1	.415
.056	2	.999		1	.885		1	.644	.500	4	.992
	1	.985	.155	3	.999	.300	4	.999		3	.936
.058	2	.999		2	.989		3	.990		2	.748
	1	.984		1	.877		2	.926		1	.399
.060	2	.999	.160	3	.999		1	.628	.520	4	.991
	1	.983		2	.988	.310	4	.999		3	.927
.062	2	.999		1	.869		3	.989		2	.728
	1	.982	.165	3	.999		2	.919		1	.384
.064	2	.999		2	.987		1	.613	.540	4	.989
	1	.981		1	.861	.320	4	.999		3	.917
.066	2	.999	.170	3	.999		3	.988		2	.708
	1	.979		2	.985		2	.912		1	.370
.068	2	.999		1	.853		1	.597	.560	4	.986
	1	.978	.180	3	.999	.330	4	.999		3	.906
.070	2	.999		2	.983		3	.986		2	.689
	1	.977		1	.836		2	.904		1	.357
.075	2	.999	.190	3	.998		1	.583	.580	4	.984
	1	.973		2	.980	.340	4	.999		3	.895
.080	2	.998		1	.819		3	.985		2	.670
	1	.969	.200	3	.998		2	.896		1	.345
.085	2	.998	.200	2	.976		1	.569	.600	4	.981
	1	.965		1	.801	.360	4	.998		3	.883
.090	2	.998	.210	3	.998		3	.981		2	.652
	1	.960		2	.973		2	.880		1	.333
.095	2	.997		1	.783		1	.542	.650	4	.972
	1	.955	.220	3	.997	.380	4	.998		3	.850
.100	2	.997		2	.969		3	.976		2	.608
	1	.950		1	.765		2	.863		1	.308
.105	2	.997	.230	3	.997		1	.516	.700	4	.960
	1	.945		2	.965	.400	4	.997		3	.815
.110	2	.996		1	.747		3	.972		2	.568
	1	.939	.240	3	.996		2	.845		1	.286
.115	2	.995		2	.960		1	.493	.750	4	.944
	1	.933		1	.730	.420	4	.997		3	.777

X	M	F
	2	.532
.800	4	.924
	3	.739
	2	.500
.850	4	.900
	3	.702
	2	.470
.900	4	.871
	3	.666
	2	.444
.950	4	.838
	3	.631

POPULATION 6

X	M	F	X	M	F	X	M	F	X	M	F
				1	.932		1	.736		3	.969
			.105	2	.994	.210	3	.994		2	.848
				1	.925		2	.955		1	.499
.010	1	.999	.110	2	.993	.220	1	.714	.340	4	.995
.017	1	.998		1	.917		4	.999		3	.966
.022	1	.997	.115	3	.999		3	.993		2	.837
.026	1	.996		2	.992		2	.948		1	.485
.030	1	.995									
.032	1	.994		1	.909	.230	1	.693	.360	4	.994
.034	1	.993	.120	3	.999		4	.999		3	.958
.038	1	.992		1	.991		3	.992		2	.814
.040	1	.991		1	.900		2	.941		1	.460
.042	1	.990	.125	3	.999	.240	1	.672	.380	5	.999
.044	1	.989		2	.990		4	.999		4	.992
.046	1	.987		1	.892		3	.991		3	.949
.048	2	.999	.130	3	.999		2	.934		2	.790
	1	.986		2	.989		1	.652		1	.436
.050	2	.999		1	.882	.250	4	.999	.400	5	.999
	1	.985	.135	3	.999		3	.989		4	.990
.052	2	.999		2	.988		2	.926		3	.939
	1	.984		1	.873		1	.632		2	.766
.054	2	.999	.140	3	.999	.260	4	.999		1	.415
	1	.982		2	.986		3	.987	.420	5	.999
.056	2	.999		1	.863		2	.918		4	.987
	1	.981	.145	3	.999		1	.613		3	.928
.058	2	.999		2	.985	.270	4	.998		2	.742
	1	.979		1	.853		3	.985		1	.396
.060	2	.999	.150	3	.998		2	.909	.440	5	.999
	1	.978		2	.983		1	.594		4	.984
.062	2	.999		1	.843	.280	4	.998		3	.916
	1	.976	.155	3	.998		3	.983		2	.719
.064	2	.999		2	.981		2	.900		1	.378
	1	.974		1	.833		1	.577	.460	5	.998
.066	2	.999	.160	3	.998	.290	4	.998		4	.981
	1	.973		2	.980		3	.981		3	.903
.068	2	.998		1	.822		2	.890		2	.695
	1	.971	.165	3	.998		1	.560		1	.362
.070	2	.998		2	.978	.300	4	.997	.480	5	.998
	1	.969		1	.812		3	.978		4	.977
.075	2	.998	.170	3	.998		2	.880		3	.889
	1	.964		2	.976		1	.543		2	.673
.080	2	.997		1	.801	.310	4	.997		1	.347
	1	.958	.180	3	.997		3	.976	.500	5	.997
.085	2	.997		2	.971		2	.870		4	.972
	1	.953		1	.779		1	.528		3	.875
.090	2	.996	.190	3	.996	.320	4	.996		2	.650
	1	.946		2	.966		3	.973		1	.333
.095	2	.996		1	.757		2	.859	.520	5	.996
	1	.940	.200	3	.995		1	.513		4	.966
.100	2	.995		2	.961	.330	4	.996		3	.859

X	M	F
	2	.629
	1	.320
.540	5	.995
	4	.960
	3	.843
	2	.609
	1	.309
.560	5	.994
	4	.953
	3	.826
	2	.589
	1	.298
.580	5	.992
	4	.946
	3	.809
	2	.570
	1	.287
.600	5	.991
	4	.937
	3	.792
	2	.552
	1	.278
.650	5	.985
	4	.913
	3	.747
	2	.512
.700	5	.977
	4	.884
	3	.704
	2	.476
.750	5	.966
	4	.851
	3	.662
	2	.444
.800	5	.950
	4	.815
	3	.623
	2	.417
.850	5	.930
	4	.777
	3	.588
.900	5	.904
	4	.739
	3	.555
.950	5	.872
	4	.702
	3	.526

POPULATION 7

X	M	F	X	M	F	X	M	F	X	M	F
			.090	2	.994	.180	4	.999	.300	5	.999
				1	.930		3	.994		4	.993
.009	1	.999	.095	2	.993		2	.956		3	.961
.016	1	.998		1	.921		1	.720		2	.827
.020	1	.997	.100	3	.999	.190	4	.999		1	.473
.023	1	.996		2	.992		3	.993	.310	5	.999
.026	1	.995		1	.912		2	.949		4	.992
.030	1	.994	.105	3	.999		1	.694		3	.956
.032	1	.993		2	.991	.200	4	.999		2	.813
.034	1	.992		1	.902		3	.991		1	.458
.036	1	.991	.110	3	.999		2	.941	.320	5	.999
.038	1	.990		2	.990		1	.669		4	.991
.040	1	.988		1	.892	.210	4	.999		3	.950
.042	2	.999	.115	3	.999		3	.989		2	.799
	1	.987		2	.988		2	.932		1	.444
.044	2	.999		1	.881		1	.645	.330	5	.999
	1	.986	.120	3	.999	.220	4	.998		4	.990
.046	2	.999		2	.987		3	.987		3	.945
	1	.984		1	.870		2	.922		2	.785
.048	2	.999	.125	3	.999		1	.622		1	.431
	1	.983		2	.985	.230	4	.998	.340	5	.999
.050	2	.999	.125	1	.858		3	.985		4	.988
	1	.981	.130	3	.998		2	.912		3	.939
.052	2	.999		2	.983		1	.600		2	.771
	1	.979		1	.847	.240	4	.998		1	.419
.054	2	.999	.135	3	.998		3	.983	.360	5	.998
	1	.978		2	.981		2	.902		4	.985
.056	2	.999		1	.834		1	.579		3	.926
	1	.976	.140	3	.998	.250	4	.997		2	.743
.058	2	.999		2	.979		3	.980		1	.396
	1	.974		1	.822		2	.890	.380	5	.997
.060	2	.998	.145	3	.997		1	.559		4	.981
	1	.972		2	.977	.260	4	.997		3	.912
.062	2	.998		1	.810		3	.977		2	.715
	1	.970	.150	3	.997		2	.879		1	.375
.064	2	.998		2	.974	.260	1	.540	.400	5	.996
	1	.967		1	.797	.270	4	.996		4	.976
.066	2	.998	.155	3	.997		3	.973		3	.896
	1	.965		2	.972		2	.866		2	.688
.068	2	.998		1	.784		1	.522		1	.357
	1	.963	.160	3	.996	.280	4	.995	.420	5	.995
.070	2	.997		2	.969		3	.969		4	.970
	1	.960		1	.771		2	.854		3	.879
.075	2	.997	.165	3	.996		1	.504		2	.662
	1	.953		2	.966	.290	5	.999		1	.340
.080	2	.996		1	.758		4	.994	.440	6	.999
	1	.946	.170	3	.995		3	.965		5	.994
.085	2	.995		2	.963		2	.840		4	.963
	1	.939		1	.745		1	.488		3	.861

X	M	F	X	M	F
.440	2	.636		2	.439
	1	.325	.700	6	.986
.460	6	.999		5	.926
	5	.992		4	.794
	4	.955		3	.610
	3	.842		2	.408
	2	.612	.750	6	.978
	1	.311		5	.898
.480	6	.999		4	.752
	5	.990		3	.571
	4	.947		2	.381
	3	.823	.800	6	.966
	2	.589		5	.865
	1	.298		4	.711
.500	6	.999		3	.536
	5	.987	.850	6	.949
	4	.937		5	.829
	3	.803		4	.671
	2	.567		3	.504
	1	.286	.900	6	.926
.520	6	.998		5	.790
	5	.984		4	.635
	4	.926	.950	6	.896
	3	.782		5	.751
	2	.546		4	.601
.540	6	.998			
	5	.980			
	4	.915			
	3	.762			
	2	.527			
.560	6	.997			
	5	.976			
	4	.902			
	3	.741			
	2	.509			
.580	6	.996			
	5	.971			
	4	.889			
	3	.721			
	2	.492			
.600	6	.995			
	5	.966			
	4	.875			
	3	.701			
	2	.476			
.650	6	.992			
	5	.948			
	4	.836			
	3	.654			

POPULATION 8

X	M	F	X	M	F	X	M	F	X	M	F
			.080	1	.932		3	.994		1	.478
			.085	3	.999		2	.956	.270	5	.999
.009	1	.999		2	.993		1	.717		4	.992
.015	1	.998		1	.922	.165	4	.999		3	.956
.018	1	.997	.090	3	.999		3	.993		2	.818
.022	1	.996		2	.992		2	.952		1	.461
.024	1	.995		1	.912		1	.702	.280	5	.999
.026	1	.994	.095	3	.999	.170	4	.999		4	.990
.030	1	.992		2	.991		3	.992		3	.950
.032	1	.991		1	.901		2	.947		2	.802
.034	1	.990	.100	3	.999		1	.688		1	.445
.036	1	.989		2	.989	.180	4	.999	.290	5	.998
.038	2	.999		1	.889		3	.990		4	.989
	1	.987	.105	3	.999		2	.938		3	.944
.040	2	.999		2	.988		1	.659		2	.785
	1	.986		1	.876	.190	4	.998		1	.430
.042	2	.999	.110	3	.999		3	.988	.300	5	.998
	1	.984		2	.986		2	.927		4	.987
.044	2	.999		1	.863		1	.632		3	.937
	1	.983	.115	3	.998	.200	4	.998		2	.769
.046	2	.999		2	.984		3	.985		1	.416
	1	.981		1	.849		2	.916	.310	5	.998
.048	2	.999	.120	3	.998		1	.606		4	.985
	1	.979		2	.981	.210	4	.997		3	.929
.050	2	.999		1	.835		3	.982		2	.753
	1	.977	.125	3	.998		2	.904		1	.403
.052	2	.999		2	.979		1	.581	.320	5	.997
	1	.975		1	.821	.220	4	.997		4	.982
.054	2	.998	.130	3	.997		3	.979		3	.921
	1	.972		2	.976		2	.891		2	.737
.056	2	.998		1	.807		1	.558		1	.390
	1	.970	.135	3	.997	.230	4	.996	.330	5	.996
.058	2	.998		2	.973		3	.975		4	.980
	1	.968		1	.792		2	.878		3	.913
.060	2	.998	.140	3	.996		1	.536		2	.721
	1	.965		2	.970	.240	5	.999		1	.378
.062	2	.997		1	.777		4	.995	.340	5	.996
	1	.962	.145	3	.996		3	.971		4	.977
.064	2	.997		2	.967		2	.863		3	.904
	1	.959		1	.762		1	.515		2	.705
.066	2	.997	.150	4	.999	.250	5	.999		1	.367
	1	.956		3	.995		4	.994	.360	6	.999
.068	2	.997		2	.964		3	.967		5	.994
	1	.953		1	.747		2	.849		4	.970
.070	2	.996	.155	4	.999		1	.496		3	.885
	1	.950		3	.994	.260	5	.999		2	.674
.075	2	.995		2	.960		4	.993		1	.347
	1	.942		1	.732		3	.962	.380	6	.999
.080	2	.995	.160	4	.999		2	.833		5	.992

X	M	F	X	M	F
	4	.963		6	.988
	3	.865		5	.945
	2	.644		4	.839
	1	.329		3	.662
.400	6	.999		2	.446
	5	.990	.580	7	.998
	4	.954		6	.985
	3	.844		5	.935
	2	.616		4	.821
	1	.312		3	.641
.420	6	.998		2	.431
	5	.987	.600	7	.998
	4	.943		6	.981
	3	.821		5	.924
	2	.589		4	.802
.440	6	.997		3	.621
	5	.983		2	.417
	4	.932	.650	7	.995
	3	.798		6	.969
	2	.564		5	.893
.460	6	.996		4	.755
	5	.979		3	.576
	4	.919		2	.385
	3	.775	.700	7	.992
	2	.541		6	.952
.480	6	.995		5	.856
	5	.974		4	.708
	4	.905		3	.535
	3	.752	.750	7	.986
	2	.519		6	.929
.500	7	.999		5	.816
	6	.994		4	.665
	5	.968		3	.500
	4	.890	.800	7	.977
	3	.728		6	.901
	2	.499		5	.774
.520	7	.999		4	.624
	6	.992		3	.469
	5	.961	.850	7	.963
	4	.874		6	.867
	3	.706		5	.733
	2	.480		4	.588
.540	7	.999	.900	7	.942
	6	.990		6	.829
	5	.953		5	.694
	4	.857		4	.556
	3	.683	.950	7	.913
	2	.463		6	.789
.560	7	.999		5	.658

POPULATION 9

X	M	F	X	M	F	X	M	F	X	M	F
			.075	3	.999	.150	4	.999		3	.956
				2	.994		3	.992		2	.820
.008	1	.999		1	.928		2	.950		1	.461
.014	1	.998	.080	3	.999		1	.695	.250	5	.998
.017	1	.997		2	.993	.155	4	.999		4	.990
.020	1	.996		1	.917		3	.991		3	.950
.022	1	.995	.085	3	.999		2	.945		2	.802
.025	1	.994		2	.991		1	.679		1	.443
.028	1	.992		1	.904	.160	4	.999	.260	5	.998
.030	1	.991	.090	3	.999		3	.990		4	.988
.032	1	.990		2	.989		2	.940		3	.942
.034	2	.999		1	.891		1	.663		2	.784
	1	.988	.095	3	.999	.165	4	.998		1	.427
.036	2	.999		2	.988		3	.989	.270	5	.997
	1	.987		1	.877		2	.934		4	.985
.038	2	.999	.100	3	.998		1	.647		3	.934
	1	.985		2	.985	.170	4	.998		2	.765
.040	2	.999		1	.862		3	.988		1	.411
	1	.983	.105	3	.998		2	.929	.280	5	.997
.042	2	.999		2	.983		1	.631		4	.983
	1	.981		1	.846	.180	4	.998		3	.926
.044	2	.999	.110	3	.998		3	.985		2	.747
	1	.979		2	.981		2	.916		1	.396
.046	2	.999		1	.830		1	.602	.290	6	.999
	1	.977	.115	3	.997	.190	4	.997		5	.996
.048	2	.998		2	.978		3	.981		4	.980
	1	.974		1	.814		2	.902		3	.917
.050	2	.998	.120	3	.997		1	.574		2	.728
	1	.972		2	.975	.200	4	.996		1	.383
.052	2	.998		1	.797		3	.978	.300	6	.999
	1	.969	.125	3	.996		2	.887		5	.995
.054	2	.998		2	.971		1	.548		4	.977
	1	.967		1	.780	.210	5	.999		3	.907
.056	2	.997	.130	4	.999		4	.995		2	.710
	1	.964		3	.996		3	.973		1	.370
.058	2	.997		2	.968		2	.872	.310	6	.999
	1	.961		1	.763		1	.524		5	.994
.060	2	.997	.135	4	.999	.220	5	.999		4	.973
	1	.957		3	.995		4	.994		3	.897
.062	2	.997		2	.964		3	.968		2	.692
	1	.954		1	.746		2	.855		1	.358
.064	2	.996	.140	4	.999		1	.501	.320	6	.999
	1	.950		3	.994	.230	5	.999		5	.993
.066	2	.996		2	.960		4	.993		4	.969
	1	.947		1	.729		3	.963		3	.886
.068	2	.995	.145	4	.999		2	.838		2	.675
	1	.943		3	.993		1	.481		1	.347
.070	2	.995		2	.955	.240	5	.999	.330	6	.999
	1	.939		1	.712		4	.991		5	.992

POPULATION 9 (Continued)

X	M	F	X	M	F	X	M	F
.330	4	.965		2	.463		4	.633
	3	.875	.500	7	.997		3	.476
	2	.658		6	.984	.750	8	.991
	1	.337		5	.939		7	.950
.340	6	.999		4	.834		6	.863
	5	.991		3	.659		5	.736
	4	.960		2	.444		4	.592
	3	.863	.520	7	.996		3	.444
	2	.641		6	.979	.800	8	.983
	1	.327		5	.927		7	.926
.360	6	.998		4	.814		6	.823
	5	.988		3	.636		5	.693
	4	.950		2	.427		4	.555
	3	.838	.540	7	.995	.850	8	.972
	2	.609		6	.974		7	.895
.380	6	.997		5	.915		6	.781
	5	.984		4	.793		5	.653
	4	.937		3	.614		4	.523
	3	.813		2	.411	.900	8	.954
	2	.580	.560	8	.999		7	.858
.400	7	.999		7	.993		6	.740
	6	.996		6	.968		5	.617
	5	.979		5	.901	.950	8	.927
	4	.924		4	.772		7	.818
	3	.787		3	.593		6	.702
	2	.553		2	.397			
.420	7	.999	.580	8	.999			
	6	.994		7	.992			
	5	.973		6	.962			
	4	.908		5	.886			
	3	.760		4	.750			
	2	.527		3	.573			
.440	7	.999		2	.383			
	6	.992	.600	8	.999			
	5	.967		7	.989			
	4	.892		6	.954			
	3	.734		5	.870			
	2	.504		4	.730			
.460	7	.998		3	.555			
	6	.990	.650	8	.997			
	5	.959		7	.981			
	4	.874		6	.930			
	3	.708		5	.827			
	2	.482		4	.679			
.480	7	.998		3	.513			
	6	.987	.700	8	.995			
	5	.949		7	.968			
	4	.854		6	.899			
	3	.683		5	.781			

X	M	F	X	M	F	X	M	F	X	M	F
.008	1	.999	.070	3	.999		1	.680		1	.453
.013	1	.998		2	.994	.145	4	.999	.230	5	.998
.016	1	.997		1	.926		3	.990		4	.988
.019	1	.996	.075	3	.999		2	.941		3	.947
.021	1	.995		2	.992		1	.662		2	.794
.023	1	.994		1	.913	.150	4	.998		1	.434
.025	1	.993	.080	3	.999		3	.989	.240	5	.997
.026	1	.992		2	.990		2	.935		4	.986
.028	1	.991		1	.899		1	.644		3	.938
.030	1	.990	.085	3	.999	.155	4	.998		2	.774
.032	2	.999		2	.988		3	.987		1	.416
	1	.988		1	.883		2	.928	.250	6	.999
.034	2	.999	.090	3	.998		1	.627		5	.997
	1	.986		2	.986	.160	4	.998		4	.983
.036	2	.999		1	.867		3	.986		3	.929
	1	.984	.095	3	.998		2	.921		2	.753
.038	2	.999		2	.984		1	.610		1	.400
	1	.982		1	.850	.165	4	.997	.260	6	.999
.040	2	.999	.100	3	.998		3	.984		5	.996
	1	.980		2	.981		2	.914		4	.980
.042	2	.999		1	.832		1	.594		3	.919
	1	.978	.105	3	.997	.170	4	.997		2	.732
.044	2	.998		2	.978		3	.982		1	.584
	1	.975		1	.814		2	.906	.270	6	.999
.046	2	.998	.110	3	.997		1	.579		5	.995
	1	.973		2	.974	.180	5	.999		4	.976
.048	2	.998		1	.795		4	.996		3	.908
	1	.970	.115	3	.996		3	.978		2	.712
.050	2	.998		2	.971		2	.890		1	.370
	1	.967		1	.776		1	.549	.280	6	.999
.052	2	.997	.120	4	.999	.190	5	.999		5	.994
	1	.963		3	.995		4	.995		4	.972
.054	2	.997		2	.967		3	.973		3	.896
	1	.960		1	.756		2	.873		2	.692
.056	2	.997	.125	4	.999		1	.522		1	.357
	1	.956		3	.994	.200	5	.999		6	.999
.058	2	.996		2	.962		4	.994	.290	5	.993
	1	.953		1	.737		3	.968		4	.968
.060	2	.996	.130	4	.999		2	.854		3	.884
	1	.949		3	.994		1	.497		2	.672
.062	2	.996		2	.958	.210	5	.999		1	.345
	1	.945		1	.718		4	.992	.300	6	.998
.064	2	.995	.135	4	.999		3	.961		5	.991
	1	.940		3	.993		2	.835		4	.963
.066	2	.995		2	.952		1	.474		3	.872
	1	.936		1	.699	.220	5	.998		2	.653
.068	3	.999	.140	4	.999		4	.990		1	.333
	2	.994		3	.991		3	.954	.310	6	.998
	1	.931		2	.947		2	.815		5	.990

POPULATION 10 (Continued)

X	M	F	X	M	F	X	M	F
	4	.957	.460	8	.999		6	.915
	3	.858		7	.995		5	.809
	2	.635		6	.979		4	.663
.320	6	.998		5	.930		3	.500
	5	.988		4	.822	.650	9	.999
	4	.952		3	.646		8	.988
	3	.845		2	.435		7	.954
	2	.617	.480	8	.999		6	.878
.330	6	.997		7	.994		5	.759
	5	.986		6	.973		4	.614
	4	.945		5	.916		3	.461
	3	.831		4	.799	.700	9	.997
	2	.600		3	.621		8	.979
.340	7	.999		2	.417		7	.929
	6	.997	.500	8	.999		6	.836
	5	.983		7	.992		5	.711
	4	.938		6	.966		4	.571
	3	.816		5	.901	.750	9	.994
	2	.584		4	.775		8	.965
.360	7	.999		3	.598		7	.897
	6	.995		2	.400		6	.792
	5	.978	.520	8	.998		5	.666
	4	.923		7	.989		4	.533
	3	.787		6	.958	.800	9	.988
	2	.553		5	.884		8	.944
.380	7	.999		4	.752		7	.859
	6	.993		3	.575		6	.747
	5	.971		2	.385		5	.625
	4	.906	.540	8	.997		4	.500
	3	.758		7	.986	.850	9	.979
	2	.525		6	.949		8	.916
.400	7	.998		5	.867		7	.818
	6	.991		4	.729		6	.705
	5	.963		3	.555		5	.588
	4	.887	.560	8	.996	.900	9	.963
	3	.728		7	.982		8	.881
	2	.499		6	.939		7	.777
.420	7	.998		5	.848		6	.667
	6	.987		4	.706	.950	9	.938
	5	.954		3	.535		8	.841
	4	.866	.580	8	.995		7	.737
	3	.700		7	.977			
	2	.476		6	.927			
.440	7	.997		5	.829			
	6	.984		4	.684			
	5	.943		3	.517			
	4	.845	.600	9	.999			
	3	.672		8	.994			
	2	.454		7	.972			

POPULATION 11

X	M	F	X	M	F	X	M	F	X	M	F
				1	.929		2	.946		3	.955
			.066	3	.999		1	.672		2	.818
.007	1	.999		2	.993	.135	4	.998		1	.454
.012	1	.998		1	.923		3	.990	.210	5	.998
.015	1	.997	.068	3	.999		2	.939		4	.988
.018	1	.996		2	.993		1	.652		3	.947
.020	1	.995		1	.917	.140	4	.998		2	.795
.022	1	.994	.070	3	.999		3	.988		1	.432
.023	1	.993		2	.992		2	.932	.220	5	.997
.025	1	.992		1	.911		1	.633		4	.985
.026	1	.991	.075	3	.999	.145	4	.998		3	.937
.028	1	.990		2	.990		3	.986		2	.772
.030	2	.999		1	.895		2	.925		1	.413
	1	.988	.080	3	.999		1	.614	.230	6	.999
.032	2	.999		2	.988	.150	4	.997		5	.996
	1	.986		1	.878		3	.985		4	.982
.034	2	.999	.085	3	.998		2	.917		3	.927
	1	.984		2	.985		1	.596		2	.749
.036	2	.999		1	.860	.155	4	.997		1	.395
	1	.982	.090	3	.998		3	.982	.240	6	.999
.038	2	.999		2	.982		2	.908		5	.995
	1	.980		1	.840		1	.578		4	.978
.040	2	.999	.095	3	.997	.160	5	.999		3	.916
	1	.977		2	.979		4	.996		2	.726
.042	2	.998		1	.820		3	.980		1	.379
	1	.974	.100	3	.997		2	.900	.250	6	.999
.044	2	.998		2	.976		1	.562		5	.994
	1	.971		1	.799	.165	5	.999		4	.974
.046	2	.998	.105	3	.996		4	.996		3	.904
	1	.968		2	.972		3	.978		2	.703
.048	2	.997		1	.778		2	.890		1	.364
	1	.964	.110	4	.999		1	.546	.260	6	.999
.050	2	.997		3	.995	.170	5	.999		5	.993
	1	.961		2	.967		4	.995		4	.970
.052	2	.997		1	.756		3	.975		3	.891
	1	.957	.115	4	.999		2	.881		2	.681
.054	2	.996		3	.994		1	.531		1	.350
	1	.953		2	.963	.180	5	.999	.270	6	.998
.056	2	.996		1	.735		4	.994		5	.991
	1	.948	.120	4	.999		3	.969		4	.964
.058	2	.995		3	.993		2	.861		3	.877
	1	.944		2	.957		1	.503		2	.660
.060	2	.995		1	.714	.190	5	.999	.280	6	.998
	1	.939	.125	4	.999		4	.992		5	.990
.062	3	.999		3	.992		3	.963		4	.959
	2	.994		2	.952		2	.840		3	.862
	1	.934		1	.693		1	.477		2	.639
.064	3	.999	.130	4	.999	.200	5	.998	.290	6	.997
	2	.994		3	.991		4	.990		5	.987

X	M	F	X	M	F	X	M	F	X	M	F
	4	.952		4	.844	.540	4	.669	.850	10	.984
	3	.847		3	.673		3	.505		9	.932
	2	.620		2	.454	.560	9	.998		8	.848
.300	7	.999	.420	8	.999		8	.990		7	.748
	6	.997		7	.994		7	.963		6	.642
	5	.985		6	.977		6	.900	.900	10	.970
	4	.945		5	.927		5	.792		9	.899
	3	.832		4	.819		4	.647		8	.807
	2	.601		3	.644		3	.487		7	.707
.310	7	.999		2	.433	.580	9	.997		6	.606
	6	.996	.440	8	.998		8	.986	.950	10	.946
	5	.982		7	.992		7	.954		9	.860
	4	.937		6	.970		6	.884		8	.765
	3	.816		5	.912		5	.770		7	.670
	2	.582		4	.794		4	.625			
.320	7	.999		3	.616		3	.470			
	6	.995		2	.413	.600	9	.996			
	5	.979	.460	8	.998		8	.983			
	4	.929		7	.989		7	.944			
	3	.800		6	.962		6	.866			
	2	.565		5	.894		5	.748			
.330	7	.999		4	.768		4	.605			
	6	.994		3	.591		3	.455			
	5	.976		2	.395	.650	10	.999			
	4	.920	.480	8	.997		9	.993			
	3	.784		7	.986		8	.969			
	2	.549		6	.952		7	.914			
.340	7	.999		5	.876		6	.820			
	6	.993		4	.742		5	.696			
	5	.972		3	.567		4	.559			
	4	.911	.500	9	.999	.700	10	.998			
	3	.767		8	.996		9	.986			
	2	.533		7	.981		8	.949			
.360	7	.998		6	.941		7	.877			
	6	.990		5	.856		6	.772			
	5	.964		4	.717		5	.648			
	4	.891		3	.545		4	.519			
	3	.735	.520	9	.999	.750	10	.996			
	2	.504		8	.994		9	.975			
.380	7	.997		7	.976		8	.922			
	6	.987		6	.929		7	.835			
	5	.953		5	.835		6	.725			
	4	.868		4	.693		5	.606			
	3	.703		3	.524	.800	10	.991			
	2	.478	.540	9	.999		9	.957			
.400	8	.999		8	.992		8	.888			
	7	.996		7	.970		7	.791			
	6	.982		6	.915		6	.681			
	5	.941		5	.813		5	.568			

POPULATION 12

X	M	F	X	M	F	X	M	F	X	M	F
				2	.993	.125	4	.998		2	.828
				1	.922		3	.990		1	.462
.007	1	.999	.064	3	.999		2	.939	.190	5	.998
.012	1	.998		2	.992		1	.649		4	.989
.015	1	.997		1	.916	.130	4	.998		3	.950
.017	1	.996	.066	3	.999		3	.988		2	.804
.019	1	.995		2	.992		2	.932		1	.438
.021	1	.994		1	.909		1	.627	.200	5	.997
.022	1	.993	.068	3	.999	.135	4	.998		4	.986
.024	1	.992		2	.991		3	.986		3	.940
.025	1	.991		1	.902		2	.923		2	.778
.026	1	.990	.070	3	.999		1	.607		1	.416
.028	2	.999		2	.990	.140	4	.997	.210	6	.999
	1	.988		1	.895		3	.984		5	.996
.030	2	.999	.075	3	.999		2	.915		4	.982
	1	.986		2	.988		1	.587		3	.929
.032	2	.999		1	.876	.145	5	.999		2	.753
	1	.984	.080	3	.998		4	.997		1	.397
.034	2	.999		2	.985		3	.982	.220	6	.999
	1	.982		1	.855		2	.905		5	.995
.036	2	.999	.085	3	.998		1	.569		4	.979
	1	.979		2	.982	.150	5	.999		3	.917
.038	2	.998		1	.834		4	.996		2	.728
	1	.976	.090	3	.997		3	.979		1	.379
.040	2	.998		2	.978		2	.896	.230	6	.999
	1	.973		1	.811		1	.551		5	.994
.042	2	.998	.095	3	.996	.155	5	.999		4	.974
	1	.970		2	.974		4	.995		3	.904
.044	2	.998		1	.788		3	.976		2	.703
	1	.966	.100	4	.999		2	.885		1	.362
.046	2	.997		3	.996		1	.534	.240	6	.998
	1	.963		2	.970	.160	5	.999		5	.992
.048	2	.997		1	.764		4	.995		4	.969
	1	.959	.105	4	.999		3	.973		3	.890
.050	2	.996		3	.995		2	.875		2	.679
	1	.954		2	.965		1	.518	.250	6	.998
.052	2	.996		1	.740	.165	5	.999		5	.991
	1	.950	.110	4	.999		4	.994		4	.963
.054	2	.995		3	.994		3	.970		3	.874
	1	.945		2	.959		2	.864		2	.655
.056	2	.995		1	.717		1	.503	.260	6	.997
	1	.939	.115	4	.999	.170	5	.999		5	.989
.058	3	.999		3	.992		4	.993		4	.957
	2	.994		2	.953		3	.967		3	.858
	1	.934		1	.693		2	.852		2	.633
.060	3	.999	.120	4	.999		1	.489	.270	7	.999
	2	.994		3	.991	.180	5	.998		6	.997
	1	.928		2	.946		4	.991		5	.986
.062	3	.999		1	.671		3	.959		4	.949

X	M	F	X	M	F	X	M	F	X	M	F
	3	.842		4	.853		5	.806		10	.991
	2	.611		3	.684		4	.663		9	.964
.280	7	.999		2	.463		3	.500		8	.908
	6	.996	.380	8	.999	.520	9	.997		7	.821
	5	.983		7	.994		8	.986		6	.712
	4	.941		6	.977		7	.957		5	.595
	3	.825		5	.930		6	.892	.750	11	.997
	2	.591		4	.826		5	.783		10	.982
	7	.999		3	.652		4	.639		9	.941
.290	6	.995		2	.438		3	.481		8	.869
	5	.980	.400	8	.998	.540	10	.999		7	.773
	4	.933		7	.991		9	.996		6	.666
	3	.807		6	.970		8	.982		5	.556
	2	.572		5	.914		7	.946	.800	11	.994
.300	7	.999		4	.798		6	.874		10	.967
	6	.994		3	.621		5	.759		9	.910
	5	.977		2	.417		4	.616		8	.826
	4	.923	.420	8	.997		3	.463		7	.728
	3	.789		7	.988	.560	10	.999		6	.625
	2	.553		6	.961		9	.994	.850	11	.987
.310	7	.998		5	.895		8	.977		10	.945
	6	.993		4	.770		7	.935		9	.873
	5	.973		3	.593		6	.854		8	.783
	4	.913		2	.397		5	.736		7	.686
	3	.771	.440	9	.999		4	.594		6	.588
	2	.536		8	.996		3	.446	.900	11	.975
.320	7	.998		7	.984	.580	10	.999		10	.914
	6	.991		6	.950		9	.992		9	.831
	5	.968		5	.875		8	.971		8	.741
	4	.902		4	.742		7	.922		7	.648
	3	.753		3	.567		6	.834	.950	11	.953
	2	.520	.460	9	.999		5	.713		10	.876
.330	7	.998		8	.994		4	.574		9	.789
	6	.990		7	.979	.600	10	.998		8	.702
	5	.963		6	.938		9	.989			
	4	.891		5	.853		8	.964			
	3	.736		4	.715		7	.907			
	2	.504		3	.543		6	.814			
.340	8	.999	.480	9	.998		5	.691			
	7	.997		8	.992		4	.555			
	6	.988		7	.973	.650	11	.999			
	5	.958		6	.924		10	.995			
	4	.879		5	.830		9	.980			
	3	.718		4	.688		8	.940			
	2	.490		3	.520		7	.866			
.360	8	.999	.500	9	.998		6	.762			
	7	.996		8	.990		5	.640			
	6	.983		7	.965		4	.513			
	5	.945		6	.909	.700	11	.999			

POPULATION 13

X	M	F	X	M	F	X	M	F	X	M	F
				1	.923		3	.990		1	.466
.007	1	.999	.060	3	.999		2	.942	.170	5	.998
.011	1	.998		2	.992		1	.652		4	.990
.014	1	.997	.062	1	.916	.120	4	.998		3	.957
.016	1	.996		3	.999		3	.988		2	.821
.018	1	.995		2	.992		2	.934		1	.452
				1	.909		1	.629	.180	5	.997
.020	1	.994	.064	3	.999	.125	4	.998		4	.988
.021	1	.993		2	.991		3	.986		3	.947
.023	1	.992		1	.901		2	.925		2	.793
.024	1	.991	.066	3	.999		1	.607		1	.427
.025	2	.999		2	.990	.130	4	.997	.190	6	.999
	1	.990		1	.893		3	.984		5	.997
.026	2	.999	.068	3	.999		2	.916		4	.984
	1	.989		2	.989		1	.585		3	.935
.028	2	.999		1	.885	.135	5	.999		2	.766
	1	.987	.070	3	.999		4	.997		1	.405
.030	2	.999		2	.988		3	.982	.200	6	.999
	1	.985		1	.877		2	.906		5	.995
.032	2	.999	.075	3	.998		1	.565		4	.980
	1	.982		2	.985	.140	5	.999		3	.923
.034	2	.999		1	.854		4	.996		2	.738
	1	.979	.080	3	.998		3	.979		1	.385
.036	2	.998		2	.981		2	.895	.210	6	.999
	1	.976		1	.830		1	.546		5	.994
.038	2	.998	.085	3	.997	.145	5	.999		4	.976
	1	.973		2	.977		4	.995		3	.909
.040	2	.996		1	.805		3	.976		2	.710
	1	.969	.090	4	.999		2	.884	.220	6	.998
.042	2	.997		3	.996		1	.528		5	.993
	1	.966		2	.973	.150	5	.999		4	.970
.044	2	.997		1	.780		4	.994		3	.894
	1	.961	.095	4	.999		3	.973		2	.684
.046	2	.997		3	.995		2	.872	.230	6	.998
	1	.957		2	.968		1	.511		5	.991
.048	2	.996		1	.753	.155	5	.999		4	.964
	1	.952	.100	4	.999		4	.994		3	.877
.050	2	.996		3	.994		3	.969		2	.658
	1	.947		2	.962		2	.860	.240	7	.999
.052	2	.995		1	.727		1	.495		6	.997
	1	.941	.105	4	.999	.160	5	.999		5	.988
.054	3	.999		3	.993		4	.993		4	.957
	2	.995		2	.956		3	.965		3	.860
	1	.936		1	.702		2	.847		2	.634
.056	3	.999	.110	4	.999		1	.480	.250	7	.999
	2	.994		3	.992	.165	5	.998		6	.997
	1	.929		2	.949		4	.992		5	.986
.058	3	.999		1	.677		3	.961		4	.949
	2	.993	.115	4	.998		2	.834		3	.842

X	M	F	X	M	F	X	M	F	X	M	F
.260	2	.610		4	.857		6	.909		5	.661
	7	.999		3	.689		5	.808		4	.530
	6	.996		2	.466		4	.665	.600	11	.999
	5	.983	.340	8	.999		3	.501		10	.993
	4	.940		7	.995	.480	10	.999		9	.976
	3	.823		6	.980		9	.996		8	.936
	2	.588		5	.939		8	.985		7	.864
.270	7	.999		4	.843		7	.955		6	.761
	6	.995		3	.671		6	.891		5	.640
	5	.979		2	.452		5	.782		4	.513
	4	.931	.360	8	.998		4	.639	.650	11	.997
	3	.804		7	.992		3	.481		10	.986
	2	.567		6	.973	.500	10	.999		9	.958
.280	7	.999		5	.922		9	.994		8	.901
	6	.993		4	.813		8	.980		7	.815
	5	.975		3	.637		7	.943		6	.708
	4	.920		2	.427		6	.871		5	.591
	3	.784	.380	9	.999		5	.757	.700	12	.999
	2	.548		8	.997		4	.614		11	.994
.290	7	.998		7	.989		3	.461		10	.974
	6	.992		6	.964	.520	10	.998		9	.931
	5	.971		5	.903		9	.992		8	.859
	4	.909		4	.782		8	.974		7	.765
	3	.765		3	.605		7	.930		6	.659
	2	.529	.400	9	.999		6	.850		5	.549
.300	7	.998		8	.996		5	.732	.750	12	.998
	6	.990		7	.985		4	.591		11	.987
	5	.966		6	.953		3	.444		10	.955
	4	.897		5	.681	.540	10	.998		9	.896
	3	.745		4	.752		9	.989		8	.813
	2	.512		3	.576		8	.966		7	.717
.310	8	.999	.420	9	.999		7	.916		6	.615
	7	.997		8	.994		6	.828	.800	12	.995
	6	.988		7	.979		5	.707		11	.975
	5	.960		6	.940		4	.569	.900	11	.927
	4	.884		5	.858	.560	11	.999		10	.852
	3	.726		4	.722		10	.997		9	.769
	2	.496		3	.549		9	.986		8	.684
.320	8	.999	.440	9	.998		8	.958	.950	12	.959
	7	.996		8	.992		7	.900		11	.889
	6	.986		7	.972		6	.806		10	.810
	5	.954		6	.926		5	.684		9	.729
	4	.871		5	.833		4	.549			
	3	.707		4	.693	.580	11	.999			
	2	.480		3	.524		10	.995			
.330	8	.999	.460	10	.999		9	.982			
	7	.996		9	.997		8	.948			
	6	.983		8	.989		7	.882			
	5	.947		7	.964		6	.783			

	m	P
.006	1	.999
.011	1	.998
.013	1	.997
.015	1	.996
.017	1	.995
.019	1	.994
.020	1	.993
.022	1	.992
.023	1	.991
.024	2	.999
	1	.990
.025	2	.999
	1	.989
.026	2	.999
	1	.988
.028	2	.999
	1	.985
.030	2	.999
	1	.983
.032	2	.999
	1	.980
.034	2	.998
	1	.977
.036	2	.998
	1	.973
.038	2	.998
	1	.969
.040	2	.997
	1	.965
.042	2	.997
	1	.961
.044	2	.997
	1	.956
.046	2	.996
	1	.950
.048	2	.995
	1	.945
.050	3	.999
	2	.995
	1	.939
.052	3	.999
	2	.994
	1	.932
.054	3	.999
	2	.993
	1	.925
.056	3	.999

	m	P
	2	.993
	1	.918
.058	3	.999
	2	.992
	1	.910
.060	3	.999
	2	.991
	1	.902
.062	3	.999
	2	.990
	1	.894
.064	3	.999
	2	.989
	1	.885
.066	3	.998
	2	.988
	1	.876
.068	3	.998
	2	.987
	1	.866
.070	3	.998
	2	.985
	1	.856
.075	3	.998
	2	.982
	1	.830
.080	3	.997
	2	.977
	1	.803
.085	4	.999
	3	.996
	2	.973
	1	.775
.090	4	.999
	3	.995
	2	.967
	1	.746
.095	4	.999
	3	.994
	2	.961
	1	.718
.100	4	.999
	3	.992
	2	.954
	1	.690
.105	4	.999
	3	.991
	2	.947
	1	.663

	m	P
.110	4	.998
	3	.989
	2	.938
	1	.637
.115	4	.998
	3	.987
	2	.929
	1	.613
.120	4	.997
	3	.985
	2	.919
	1	.589
.125	5	.999
	4	.997
	3	.982
	2	.909
	1	.567
.130	5	.999
	4	.996
	3	.980
	2	.897
	1	.547
.135	5	.999
	4	.995
	3	.976
	2	.885
	1	.527
.140	5	.999
	4	.994
	3	.973
	2	.873
	1	.509
.145	5	.999
	4	.994
	3	.969
	2	.859
	1	.492
.150	5	.999
	4	.992
	3	.965
	2	.846
	1	.476
.155	5	.998
	4	.991
	3	.961
	2	.831
	1	.460
.160	5	.998
	4	.990

	m	P
	3	.956
	2	.817
	1	.446
.165	5	.998
	4	.988
	3	.950
	2	.802
	1	.433
.170	6	.999
	5	.997
	4	.987
	3	.945
	2	.787
	1	.420
.180	6	.999
	5	.996
	4	.983
	3	.932
	2	.757
	1	.397
.190	6	.999
	5	.995
	4	.978
	3	.918
	2	.727
.200	6	.999
	5	.993
	4	.973
	3	.902
	2	.697
.210	6	.998
	5	.991
	4	.967
	3	.885
	2	.669
.220	7	.999
	6	.997
	5	.989
	4	.960
	3	.867
	2	.642
.230	7	.999
	6	.997
	5	.986
	4	.952
	3	.848
	2	.616
.240	7	.999
	6	.996

	5	.983	.310	2	.461		4	.675	.560	11	.998
	4	.943	.320	8	.998		3	.510		10	.991
	3	.828		7	.994	.440	10	.999		9	.973
	2	.592		6	.978		9	.996		8	.932
.250	7	.939		5	.935		8	.985		7	.859
	6	.995		4	.837		7	.956		6	.757
	5	.980		3	.663		6	.896		5	.637
	4	.932		2	.446		5	.790		4	.510
	3	.807	.330	8	.999		4	.647	.580	11	.997
	2	.569		7	.992		3	.487		10	.988
.260	7	.998		6	.974	.460	10	.999		9	.965
	6	.993		5	.926		9	.994		8	.917
	5	.975		4	.820		8	.980		7	.839
	4	.921		3	.645		7	.945		6	.734
	3	.786		2	.433	.460	6	.875		5	.615
	2	.548	.340	8	.998		5	.763		4	.493
.270	7	.998		7	.991		4	.620	.600	12	.999
	6	.992		6	.970		3	.466		11	.996
	5	.970		5	.916	.480	10	998		10	.985
	4	.909		4	.804			.991		9	.956
	3	.764		3	.627		8	.973		8	.902
	2	.528		2	.420		7	.931		7	.817
.280	8	.999	.360	9	.999		6	.852		6	.711
	7	.997		8	.996		5	.735		5	.595
	6	.990		7	.987		4	.594	.650	12	.998
	5	.965		6	.959	.500	11	.999		11	.991
	4	.896		5	.895		10	.997		10	.970
	3	.743		4	.771		9	.988		9	.927
	2	.510		3	.593		8	.965		8	.857
.290	8	.999	.380	9	.999		7	.915		7	.764
	7	.997		8	.995		6	.829		6	.659
	6	.987		7	.981		5	.709		5	.549
	5	.958		6	.947		4	.571	.700	13	.999
	4	.882		5	.871	.520	11	.999		12	.996
	3	.723		4	.738		10	.996		11	.982
	2	.492		3	.563		9	.984		10	.949
.300	8	.999	.400	9	.998		8	.956		9	.890
	7	.996		8	.992		7	.898		8	.808
	6	.985		7	.975		6	.805		7	.713
	5	.951		6	.932		5	.684		6	.612
	4	.868		5	.845		4	.549	.750	13	.999
	3	.702		4	.706	.540	11	.999		12	.990
	2	.476		3	.535		10	.994		11	.966
.310	8	.999	.420	10	.999		9	.979		10	.918
	7	.995		9	.997		8	.944		9	.846
	6	.982		8	.989		7	.879		8	.760
	5	.944		7	.967		6	.781		7	.666
	4	.852		6	.915		5	.659		6	.571
	3	.682		5	.818		4	.529	.800	13	.997

	12	.981
	11	.942
	10	.880
	9	.801
	8	.714
	7	.625
.850	13	.992

	12	.964
	11	.909
	10	.837
	9	.756
	8	.672
.900	13	.983
	12	.937

	11	.870
	10	.793
	9	.714
.950	13	.964
	12	.900
	11	.827
	10	.752

				2	.992	.105	4	.998	.155	4	.988
				1	.914		3	.989		3	.950
.006	1	.999	.056	3	.999		2	.936		2	.801
.010	1	.998		2	.991		1	.626		1	.430
.013	1	.997	.058	3	.999	.110	4	.998	.160	6	.999
.015	1	.996		2	.990		3	.986		5	.997
.017	1	.995					2	.926		4	.987
.018	1	.994		1	.896		1	.600		3	.944
.019	1	.993	.060	3	.999	.115	5	.999		2	.785
.021	1	.992		2	.989		4	.997		1	.417
.022	1	.991		1	.887		3	.984	.165	6	.999
.023	2	.999	.062	3	.999		2	.915		5	.996
	1	.990		2	.988		1	.576		4	.985
.024	2	.999		1	.877	.120	5	.999		3	.938
	1	.989	.064	3	.998		4	.996		2	.768
.025	2	.999		2	.987		3	.981		1	.404
	1	.986		1	.867		2	.903	.170	6	.999
.026	2	.999	.066	3	.998		1	.553		5	.996
	1	.986		2	.985	.125	5	.999		4	.982
.028	2	.999		1	.856		4	.996		3	.931
	1	.984	.068	3	.998		3	.978		2	.752
.030	2	.999		2	.984		2	.890	.180	6	.999
	1	.981		1	.845		1	.532		5	.994
.032	2	.998	.070	3	.998	.130	5	.999		4	.977
	1	.977		2	.982		4	.995		3	.915
.034	2	.998		1	.833		3	.974		2	.720
	1	.974	.075	3	.997		2	.877	.190	6	.998
.036	2	.998		2	.978		1	.512		5	.993
	1	.970		1	.804	.135	5	.999		4	.972
.038	2	.997	.080	4	.999		4	.994		3	.898
	1	.965		3	.996		3	.970		2	.688
.040	2	.997		2	.973		2	.863	.200	6	.998
	1	.961		1	.774		1	.493		5	.991
.042	2	.996	.085	4	.999	.140	5	.999		4	.965
	1	.955		3	.995		4	.993		3	.879
.044	2	.996		2	.967		3	.966		2	.658
	1	.950		1	.743		2	.848	.210	7	.999
.046	2	.995	.090	4	.999		1	.476		6	.997
	1	.943		3	.994	.145	5	.998		5	.988
.048	3	.999		2	.961		4	.991		4	.957
	2	.995		1	.712		3	.961		3	.859
	1	.937	.095	4	.999		2	.833		2	.629
.050	3	.999		3	.992		1	.459	.220	7	.999
	2	.994		2	.953	.150	5	.998		6	.996
	1	.930		1	.682		4	.990		5	.985
.052	3	.999	.100	4	.998		3	.956		4	.947
	2	.993		3	.991		2	.817		3	.838
	1	.922		2	.945		1	.444		2	.603
.054	3	.999		1	.653	.155	5	.997	.230	7	.999

6	.995	4	.835	7	.962	8	.932
5	.981	3	.661	6	.906	7	.861
4	.937	2	.444	5	.806	6	.760
3	.816	.310 8	.998	4	.663	5	.640
2	.578	7	.992	3	.500	4	.513
.240 7	.998	6	.973	.420 10	.999	.540 12	.999
6	.993	5	.924	9	.994	11	.996
5	.977	4	.818	8	.981	10	.987
4	.925	3	.641	7	.950	9	.964
3	.793	2	.430	6	.885	8	.917
2	.554	.320 9	.999	5	.776	7	.839
.250 7	.998	8	.997	4	.633	6	.735
6	.992	7	.990	3	.476	5	.617
5	.972	6	.968	.440 10	.998	4	.494
?50 4	.913	5	.914	9	.992	.560 12	.999
3	.770	4	.800	8	.975	11	.995
2	.533	3	.622	7	.936	10	.983
.260 8	.999	.330 9	.999	6	.862	9	.954
7	.997	8	.997	5	.747	8	.900
6	.990	7	.988	4	.605	7	.817
5	.966	6	.963	3	.455	6	.711
4	.899	5	.902	.460 11	.999	5	.595
3	.747	4	.782	10	.997	.580 12	.998
2	.512	3	.604	9	.988	11	.993
.270 8	.999	.340 9	.999	8	.967	10	.977
7	.997	8	.996	7	.920	9	.942
6	.987	7	.985	6	.837	8	.881
5	.959	6	.957	5	.718	7	.794
4	.884	5	.890	4	.579	6	.688
3	.725	4	.764	.480 11	.999	5	.575
2	.494	3	.587	10	.995	.600 12	.997
.280 8	.999	.360 9	.998	9	.984	11	.990
7	.996	8	.994	8	.957	10	.970
6	.984	7	.979	7	.902	9	.929
5	.952	6	.942	6	.812	8	.862
4	.869	5	.864	5	.691	7	.771
3	.703	4	.729	4	.555	6	.666
2	.476	3	.555	.500 11	.998	5	.555
.290 8	.999	.380 10	.999	10	.993	.650 13	.999
7	.995	9	.997	9	.979	12	.994
6	.981	8	.991	8	.945	11	.979
5	.943	7	.971	7	.882	10	.947
4	.852	6	.926	6	.786	9	.890
3	.681	5	.835	5	.665	8	.811
2	.460	4	.695	4	.533	7	.716
.300 8	.998	3	.526	.520 12	.999	6	.615
7	.993	.400 10	.999	11	.997	.700 13	.997
6	.977	9	.996	10	.990	12	.987
5	.934	8	.987	9	.972	11	.962

	10	.914
	9	.844
	8	.759
	7	.666
	6	.571
.750	14	.999
	13	.993
	12	.974
	11	.935
	10	.874
	9	.796
	8	.710
	7	.622
.800	14	.997
	13	.985
	12	.953
	11	.900
	10	.829
	9	.749
	8	.667
.850	14	.994
	13	.970
	12	.923
	11	.858
	10	.783
	9	.706
	8	.627
.900	14	.986
	13	.945
	12	.885
	11	.814
	10	.741
	9	.667
.950	14	.968
	13	.910
	12	.842
	11	.772

.005	1	.999
.009	1	.998
.011	1	.997
.013	1	.996
.014	1	.995
.015	1	.994
.016	1	.993
.017	1	.992
.018	2	.999
	1	.991
.019	2	.999
	1	.990
.020	2	.999
	1	.989
.021	2	.999
	1	.987
.022	2	.999
	1	.986
.023	2	.999
	1	.984
.024	2	.999
	1	.982
.025	2	.999
	1	.980
.026	2	.998
	1	.978
.028	2	.998
	1	.973
.030	2	.998
	1	.968
.032	2	.997
	1	.962
.034	2	.996
	1	.955
.036	2	.996
	1	.947
.038	3	.999
	2	.995
	1	.938
.040	3	.999
	2	.994
	1	.929
.042	3	.999
	2	.993
	1	.918
.044	3	.999
	2	.992

.046	1	.906
	3	.999
	2	.991
	1	.894
.048	3	.999
	2	.989
	1	.881
.050	3	.998
	2	.988
	1	.866
.052	3	.998
	2	.986
	1	.851
.054	3	.998
	2	.984
	1	.835
.056	3	.997
	2	.982
	1	.819
.058	3	.997
	2	.980
	1	.802
.060	4	.999
	3	.997
	2	.978
	1	.785
.062	4	.999
	3	.996
	2	.975
	1	.768
.064	4	.999
	3	.996
	2	.972
	1	.751
.066	4	.999
	3	.995
	2	.969
	1	.733
.068	4	.999
	3	.995
	2	.966
	1	.716
.070	4	.999
	3	.994
	2	.962
	1	.699
.075	4	.999
	3	.992
	2	.953

.080	1	.659
	4	.998
	3	.990
	2	.941
	1	.621
.085	4	.997
	3	.987
	2	.928
	1	.586
.090	5	.999
	4	.997
	3	.984
	2	.913
	1	.554
.095	5	.999
	4	.996
	3	.980
	2	.896
	1	.526
.100	5	.999
	4	.995
	3	.975
	2	.878
	1	.500
105	5	.999
	4	.993
	3	.970
	2	.858
	1	.476
.110	5	.998
	4	.992
	3	.964
	2	.837
.115	5	.998
	4	.990
	3	.958
	2	.816
.120	6	.999
	5	.997
	4	.988
	3	.950
	2	.793
.125	6	.999
	5	.997
	4	.986
	3	.942
	2	.770
.130	6	.999
	5	.996

	4	.983
	3	.933
	2	.748
.135	6	.999
	5	.995
	4	.980
	3	.923
	2	.725
.140	6	.998
	5	.994
	4	.976
	3	.912
	2	.703
.145	6	.998
	5	.993
	4	.972
	3	.900
	2	.682
.150	7	.999
	6	.998
	5	.991
	4	.968
	3	.887
	2	.661
.155	7	.999
	6	.997
	5	.990
	4	.963
	3	.874
	2	.641
.160	7	.999
	6	.997
	5	.988
	4	.957
	3	.860
	2	.622
.165	7	.999
	6	.996
	5	.986
	4	.951
	3	.845
	2	.604
.170	7	.999
	6	.995
	5	.983
	4	.945
	3	.830
	2	.587
.180	7	.998

POPULATION 20 (Continued)

X	M	F	X	M	F	X	M	F	X	M	F
	6	.994		6	.961		5	.788		8	.918
	5	.978		5	.901		4	.643		7	.845
	4	.930		4	.780	.320	11	.999		6	.744
	3	.799		3	.599		10	.997		5	.624
.190	2	.555	.260	9	.998		9	.992	.420	13	.999
	8	.999		8	.994		8	.977		12	.997
	7	.998		7	.983		7	.944		11	.991
	6	.991		6	.953		6	.878		10	.977
	5	.971		5	.884		5	.768		9	.949
	4	.914		4	.755		4	.624		8	.896
	3	.768		3	.576	.330	11	.999		7	.815
	2	.526	.270	10	.999		10	.997		6	.711
.200	8	.999		9	.998		9	.990		5	.595
	7	.997		8	.992		8	.973	.440	13	.999
	6	.988		7	.978		7	.935		12	.995
	5	.963		6	.943		6	.862		11	.987
	4	.895		5	.867		5	.748		10	.969
	3	.736		4	.731		4	.605		9	.933
	2	.500		3	.555	.340	11	.999		8	.872
.210	8	.999	.280	10	.999		10	.996		7	.785
	7	.995		9	.997		9	.987		6	.680
	6	.985		8	.990		8	.967		5	.568
	5	.954		7	.973		7	.924	.460	14	.999
	4	.874		6	.932		6	.846		13	.998
	3	.706		5	.848		5	.729		12	.993
	2	.476		4	.708		4	.588		11	.982
.220	8	.998		3	.536	.360	12	.999		10	.958
	7	.994	.290	10	.999		11	.998		9	.914
	6	.980		9	.996		10	.993		8	.846
	5	.943		8	.988		9	.981		7	.755
	4	.852		7	.967		8	.954		6	.651
	3	.677		6	.920		7	.901		5	.543
.230	9	.999		5	.828		6	.812	.480	14	.999
	8	.998		4	.685		5	.691		13	.996
	7	.992		3	.517		4	.555		12	.990
	6	.975	.300	10	.998	.380	12	.999		11	.974
	5	.931		9	.995		11	.996		10	.944
	4	.828		8	.985		10	.989		9	.893
	3	.649		7	.961		9	.973		8	.819
.240	9	.999		6	.907		8	.938		7	.726
	8	.997		5	.808		7	.874		6	.625
	7	.989		4	.664		6	.777	.500	14	.998
•	6	.969		3	.500		5	.656		13	.995
	5	.917	.310	11	.999		4	.526		12	.985
	4	.804		10	.998	.400	13	.999		11	.965
	3	.623		9	.993		12	.998		10	.929
.250	9	.999		8	.981		11	.994		9	.870
	8	.996		7	.953		10	.984		8	.791
	7	.986		6	.893		9	.962		7	.698

X	M	F	X	M	F	X	M	F
	6	.600		7	.583		16	.886
.520	15	.999	.650	17	.999		15	.833
	14	.997		16	.997		14	.778
	13	.992		15	.989		13	.722
	12	.979		14	.973	.950	19	.981
	11	.954		13	.943		18	.943
	10	.911		12	.898		17	.894
	9	.846		11	.837		16	.842
	8	.764		10	.767		15	.789
	7	.672		9	.692			
	6	.577		8	.615			
.540	15	.999	.700	17	.998			
	14	.996		16	.991			
	13	.988		15	.976			
	12	.972		14	.948			
	11	.941		13	.905			
	10	.891		12	.849			
	9	.821		11	.783			
	8	.738		10	.714			
	7	.648		9	.643			
	6	.556	.750	18	.999			
.560	15	.998		17	.993			
	14	.994		16	.980			
	13	.984		15	.954			
	12	.963		14	.913			
	11	.926		13	.859			
	10	.869		12	.796			
	9	.796		11	.733			
	8	.713		10	.667			
	7	.625	.800	19	.999			
.580	16	.999		18	.996			
	15	.997		17	.984			
	14	.991		16	.959			
	13	.978		15	.920			
	12	.952		14	.869			
	11	.908		13	.811			
	10	.847		12	.750			
	9	.772		11	.687			
	8	.689	.850	19	.998			
	7	.603		18	.988			
.600	16	.999		17	.965			
	15	.996		16	.927			
	14	.988		15	.878			
	13	.970		14	.823			
	12	.938		13	.765			
	11	.889		12	.706			
	10	.824	.900	19	.994			
	9	.748		18	.972			
	8	.666		17	.935			

POPULATION 30

X	M	F	X	M	F	X	M	F	X	M	F
				1	.853		3	.986		5	.991
			.038	3	.998		2	.918		4	.967
.004	1	.999		2	.986	.064	5	.999		3	.879
.007	1	.998		1	.827		4	.997		2	.634
.009	1	.997	.040	3	.997		3	.984	.110	7	.999
.010	1	.996		2	.983		2	.906		6	.997
.011	1	.995		1	.800	.066	5	.999		5	.988
.012	1	.994	.042	3	.997		4	.996		4	.959
.013	1	.993		2	.980		3	.982		3	.857
.014	2	.999		1	.772		2	.897		2	.605
	1	.991	.044	4	.999	.068	5	.999	.115	7	.999
.015	2	.999		3	.996		4	.995		6	.996
	1	.989		2	.977		3	.979		5	.985
.016	2	.999		1	.744		2	.885		4	.950
	1	.987	.046	4	.999	.070	5	.999		3	.833
.017	2	.999		3	.996		4	.995		2	.579
	1	.985		2	.972		3	.976	.120	7	.998
.018	2	.999		1	.716		2	.873		6	.994
	1	.983	.048	4	.999	.075	5	.996		5	.981
.019	2	.999		3	.995		4	.993		4	.939
	1	.980		2	.968		3	.969		3	.808
.020	2	.998		1	.689		2	.840		2	.555
	1	.976	.050	4	.999	.080	6	.999	.125	8	.999
.021	2	.998		3	.994		5	.998		7	.998
	1	.973		2	.963		4	.990		6	.993
.022	2	.998		1	.663		3	.959		5	.977
	1	.969	.052	4	.999		2	.805		4	.927
.023	2	.997		3	.993	.085	6	.999		3	.783
	1	.965		2	.957		5	.997	.130	8	.999
.024	2	.997		1	.639		4	.987		7	.997
	1	.960	.054	4	.998		3	.948		6	.991
.025	2	.996		3	.992		2	.766		5	.972
	1	.954		2	.951	.090	6	.999		4	.914
.026	2	.996		1	.616		5	.996		3	.758
	1	.948	.056	4	.998		4	.984	.135	8	.999
.028	3	.999		3	.991		3	.934		7	.997
	2	.995		2	.944		2	.732		6	.989
	1	.935		1	.595	.095	6	.999		5	.966
.030	3	.999	.058	4	.998		5	.994		4	.899
	2	.994		3	.989		4	.979		3	.734
	1	.918		2	.936		3	.918	.140	8	.999
.032	3	.999		1	.574		2	.697		7	.996
	2	.992	.060	5	.999	.100	6	.998		6	.987
	1	.899		4	.997		5	.993		5	.960
.034	3	.999		3	.987		4	.973		4	.884
	2	.990		2	.927		3	.899		3	.710
	1	.877		1	.555		2	.664	.145	8	.998
.036	3	.998	.062	5	.999	.105	7	.999		7	.995
	2	.988		4	.997		6	.997		6	.984

POPULATION 30 (Continued)

X	M	F	X	M	F	X	M	F	X	M	F
	5	.952		8	.990		11	.996		10	.962
	4	.867		7	.973		10	.989		9	.924
	3	.687		6	.932		9	.975		8	.861
.150	9	.999		5	.845		8	.944		7	.771
	8	.998		4	.699		7	.885		6	.666
	7	.993	.200	11	.999		6	.789	.310	15	.999
	6	.980		10	.998		5	.666		14	.996
	5	.944		9	.995	.260	13	.999		13	.996
	4	.849		8	.985		12	.998		12	.990
	3	.665		7	.963		11	.994		11	.977
.155	9	.999		6	.913		10	.986		10	.953
	8	.997		5	.814		9	.967		9	.909
	7	.992		4	.665		8	.930		8	.840
	6	.976	.210	11	.999		7	.864		7	.749
	5	.935		10	.997		6	.763		6	.645
	4	.830		9	.992		5	.641	.320	15	.999
	3	.644		8	.980	.270	13	.999		14	.998
.160	9	.999		7	.952		12	.997		13	.994
	8	.997		6	.892		11	.992		12	.987
	7	.990		5	.782		10	.981		11	.971
	6	.972		4	.634		9	.959		10	.943
	5	.924	.220	11	.999		8	.915		9	.893
	4	.811		10	.996		7	.841		8	.820
	3	.624		9	.989		6	.737		7	.727
.165	9	.999		8	.974		5	.617		6	.625
	8	.996		7	.938	.280	14	.999	.330	15	.999
	7	.988		6	.868		13	.998		14	.997
	6	.967		5	.751		12	.996		13	.993
	5	.913		4	.606		11	.989		12	.983
	4	.792	.230	12	.999		10	.976		11	.965
	3	.606		11	.998		9	.949		10	.931
.170	10	.999		10	.994		8	.898		9	.876
	9	.998		9	.985		7	.818		8	.799
	8	.995		8	.965		6	.712		7	.706
	7	.986		7	.923		5	.595		6	.606
	6	.961		6	.842	.290	14	.999	.340	16	.999
	5	.901		5	.721		13	.998		15	.998
	4	.773		4	.580		12	.994		14	.996
	3	.589	.240	12	.999		11	.986		13	.990
.180	10	.999		11	.997		10	.969		12	.979
	9	.997		10	.992		9	.937		11	.957
	8	.993		9	.981		8	.880		10	.918
	7	.980		8	.955		7	.795		9	.858
	6	.948		7	.905		6	.688		8	.778
	5	.874		6	.816		5	.575		7	.685
	4	.735		5	.693	.300	14	.999		6	.588
	3	.555		4	.556		13	.997	.360	16	.999
.190	10	.999	.250	13	.999		12	.992		15	.997
	9	.996		12	.998		11	.982		14	.993

X	M	F	X	M	F	X	M	F	X	M	F
	13	.984		9	.681		20	.996		23	.996
	12	.967		8	.606		19	.991		22	.991
	11	.937	.460	19	.999		18	.981		21	.982
	10	.889		18	.997		17	.965		20	.965
	9	.821		17	.993		16	.938		19	.940
	8	.738		16	.985		15	.901		18	.906
	7	.648		15	.970		14	.850		17	.865
.380	17	.999		14	.944		13	.799		16	.818
	16	.998		13	.906		12	.740		15	.769
	15	.995		12	.855		11	.679		14	.718
	14	.986		11	.793		10	.617		13	.667
	13	.975		10	.724	.560	22	.999	.700	25	.998
	12	.952		9	.652		21	.997		24	.995
	11	.914	.480	20	.999		20	.994		23	.989
.400	10	.857		19	.998		19	.986		22	.977
	9	.784		18	.995		18	.973		21	.958
	8	.701		17	.989		17	.952		20	.930
	7	.614		16	.977		16	.920		19	.894
	17	.999		15	.957		15	.878		18	.853
	16	.996		14	.926		14	.828		17	.808
	15	.992		13	.881		13	.772		16	.762
	14	.982		12	.826		12	.714		15	.714
	13	.964		11	.762		11	.655	.750	26	.998
	12	.933		10	.694	.580	23	.999		25	.994
	11	.886		9	.625		22	.998		24	.986
	10	.823	.500	20	.999		21	.996		23	.972
	9	.748		19	.997		20	.990		22	.950
	8	.666		18	.992		19	.980		21	.920
.420	18	.999		17	.983		18	.963		20	.883
	17	.997		16	.967		17	.936		19	.842
	16	.994		15	.941		16	.899		18	.799
	15	.986		14	.904		15	.854		17	.755
	14	.972		13	.854		14	.802		16	.711
	13	.948		12	.796		13	.746	.800	27	.998
	12	.910		11	.732		12	.690		26	.993
	11	.856		10	.667		11	.632		25	.984
	10	.789	.520	21	.999	.600	23	.999		24	.966
	9	.713		20	.998		22	.997		23	.941
	8	.635		19	.994		21	.993		22	.909
.440	19	.999		18	.988		20	.986		21	.872
	18	.998		17	.975		19	.972		20	.832
	17	.996		16	.954		18	.949		19	.791
	16	.990		15	.923		17	.918		18	.750
	15	.979		14	.880		16	.877	.850	28	.998
	14	.960		13	.827		15	.829		27	.993
	13	.929		12	.767		14	.776		26	.981
	12	.883		11	.705		13	.722		25	.960
	11	.824		10	.641		12	.667		24	.932
	10	.755	.540	21	.999	.650	24	.999		23	.899

X	M	F
	22	.862
	21	.823
	20	.784
	19	.745
.900	29	.999
	28	.992
	27	.977
	26	.953
	25	.923
	24	.888
	23	.852
	22	.815
	21	.778
.950	29	.993
	28	.973
	27	.945
	26	.912
	25	.877
	24	.842

X	M	F	X	M	F	X	M	F	X	M	F
				2	.987		3	.970		3	.814
				1	.809		2	.832	.095	8	.999
.004	1	.999	.032	3	.997	.060	5	.998		7	.998
.006	1	.998		2	.983		4	.992		6	.993
.007	1	.997		1	.769		3	.965		5	.979
.008	1	.996	.034	4	.999		2	.812		4	.931
.009	1	.995		3	.997	.062	6	.999		3	.780
.010	1	.994		2	.979		5	.996	.100	8	.999
.011	2	.999		1	.730		4	.991		7	.997
	1	.992	.036	4	.999		3	.960		6	.991
.012	2	.999		3	.996		2	.792		5	.973
	1	.990		2	.974	.064	6	.999		4	.912
.013	2	.999	.038	4	.999		5	.997		3	.745
	1	.988		3	.995		4	.989	.105	8	.999
.014	2	.999		2	.968		3	.954		7	.996
	1	.985	.040	4	.999		2	.771		6	.988
.015	2	.999		3	.994	.066	6	.999		5	.965
	1	.981		2	.960		5	.997		4	.891
.016	2	.998	.042	4	.998		4	.988		3	.712
	1	.977		3	.992		3	.947	.110	9	.999
.017	2	.998		2	.952		2	.751		8	.998
	1	.973	.044	4	.998	.068	6	.999		7	.995
.018	2	.998		3	.991		5	.996		6	.985
	1	.967		2	.942		4	.986		5	.955
.019	2	.997	.046	4	.998		3	.940		4	.868
	1	.961		3	.989		2	.731	.115	9	.999
.020	2	.997		2	.931	.070	6	.999		8	.998
	1	.953	.048	5	.999		5	.996		7	.993
.021	2	.996		4	.997		4	.984		6	.981
	1	.945		3	.987		3	.932		5	.944
.022	3	.999		2	.918		2	.711		4	.843
	2	.995	.050	5	.999	.075	6	.998	.120	9	.999
	1	.935		4	.997		5	.994		8	.997
.023	3	.999		3	.984		4	.977		7	.991
	2	.995		2	.904		3	.908		6	.975
	1	.924	.052	5	.999	.080	7	.999		5	.931
.024	3	.999		4	.996		6	.998		4	.816
	2	.994		3	.981		5	.991	.125	9	.999
	1	.911		2	.888		4	.969		8	.996
.025	3	.999	.054	5	.999		3	.880		7	.989
	2	.993		4	.995	.085	7	.999		6	.969
	1	.897		3	.978		6	.997		5	.916
.026	3	.999		2	.870		5	.986		4	.790
	2	.992	.056	5	.999		4	.959	.130	10	.999
	1	.882		4	.994		3	.849		9	.998
.028	3	.998		3	.974	.090	7	.999		8	.995
	2	.989		2	.852		6	.995		7	.986
	1	.847	.058	5	.998		5	.984		6	.962
.030	3	.998		4	.993		4	.946		5	.899

X	M	F	X	M	F	X	M	F	X	M	F
	4	.763	.170	12	.999		14	.998		12	.956
.135	10	.999		11	.998		13	.996		11	.924
	9	.998		10	.995		12	.991		10	.870
	8	.993		9	.988		11	.980		9	.798
	7	.982		8	.971		10	.958	.290	13	.999
	6	.953		7	.933		9	.917		16	.997
	5	.880		6	.856		8	.850		15	.993
	4	.737		5	.733		7	.758		14	.986
.140	10	.999	.180	12	.999	.240	15	.999		13	.972
	9	.997		11	.997		14	.997		12	.947
	8	.992		10	.992		13	.994		11	.906
	7	.978		9	.982		12	.987		10	.847
	6	.943		8	.959		11	.972		9	.773
	5	.860		7	.910		10	.945	.300	18	.999
	4	.712		6	.820		9	.896		17	.998
.145	10	.999	.190	13	.999		8	.822		16	.996
	9	.996		12	.998		7	.728		15	.991
	8	.989		11	.995	.250	16	.999		14	.981
	7	.973		10	.989		15	.998		13	.963
	6	.932		9	.974		14	.996		12	.934
	5	.840		8	.943		13	.992		11	.888
.150	11	.999		7	.882		12	.982		10	.824
	10	.998		6	.783		11	.963		9	.748
	9	.995	.200	13	.999		10	.929	.310	19	.999
	8	.987		12	.997		9	.873		17	.997
	7	.967		11	.993		8	.794		16	.994
	6	.919		10	.984	.260	16	.999		15	.987
	5	.818		9	.964		15	.998		14	.975
.155	11	.999		8	.924		14	.995		13	.953
	10	.998		7	.853		13	.988		12	.919
	9	.994		6	.747		12	.976		11	.867
	8	.984	.210	14	.999		11	.952		10	.801
	7	.960		13	.998		10	.911		9	.725
	6	.905		12	.996		9	.849	.320	19	.999
	5	.796		11	.990		8	.766		13	.998
.160	11	.999		10	.977	.270	17	.999		17	.996
	10	.997		9	.951		15	.997		16	.992
	9	.992		8	.902		14	.992		15	.983
	8	.980		7	.821		13	.984		14	.968
	7	.952		6	.713		12	.968		13	.942
	6	.889	.220	14	.999		11	.939		12	.902
	5	.775		13	.997		10	.891		11	.847
.165	12	.999		12	.994		9	.823		10	.778
	10	.996		11	.985		8	.739	.330	19	.999
	9	.990		10	.969	.280	17	.999		18	.998
	8	.976		9	.936		16	.998		17	.995
	7	.943		8	.877		15	.995		16	.989
	6	.873		7	.789		14	.989		15	.978
	5	.753	.230	15	.999		13	.978		14	.959

X	M	F	X	M	F	X	M	F	X	M	F
	13	.929		20	.991		18	.886	.600	30	.999
	12	.884		19	.983		17	.844		29	.998
	11	.825		18	.970		16	.798		28	.996
	10	.756		17	.948	.520	27	.999		27	.992
.340	20	.999		16	.918		26	.998		26	.985
	19	.998		15	.877		25	.996		25	.973
	18	.996		14	.828		24	.992		24	.956
	17	.993		13	.772		23	.984		23	.933
	16	.985	.440	24	.999		22	.973		22	.903
	15	.972		23	.998		21	.955		21	.869
	14	.949		22	.996		20	.930		20	.831
	13	.914		21	.992		19	.897		19	.791
	12	.865		20	.985		18	.859	.650	32	.999
	11	.804		19	.973		17	.815		30	.997
	10	.734		18	.954		16	.768		29	.993
.360	21	.999		17	.927	.540	28	.999		28	.986
	19	.997		16	.890		26	.997		27	.975
	18	.993		15	.845		25	.993		26	.959
	17	.987		14	.793		24	.987		25	.938
	16	.975	.460	25	.999		23	.976		24	.911
	15	.955		23	.997		22	.960		23	.879
	14	.925		22	.993		21	.937		22	.844
	13	.881		21	.987		20	.907		21	.807
	12	.826		20	.977		19	.871	.700	33	.999
	11	.762		19	.960		18	.830		32	.997
.380	21	.999		18	.935		17	.786		31	.994
	20	.997		17	.902	.560	28	.999		30	.988
	19	.994		16	.860		27	.997		29	.978
	18	.988		15	.812		26	.994		28	.963
	17	.978		14	.760		25	.989		27	.943
	16	.961	.480	25	.999		24	.979		26	.917
	15	.934		24	.997		23	.965		25	.888
	14	.895		23	.994		22	.944		24	.855
	13	.845		22	.989		21	.917		23	.821
	12	.787		21	.979		20	.883	.750	35	.999
.400	22	.999		20	.965		19	.844		34	.998
	21	.998		19	.942		18	.802		33	.995
	20	.995		18	.912	.580	29	.999		32	.990
	19	.990		17	.874		28	.998		31	.981
	18	.981		16	.829		27	.995		30	.967
	17	.965		15	.780		26	.990		29	.948
	16	.942	.500	26	.999		25	.982		28	.923
	15	.907		25	.998		24	.969		27	.895
	14	.862		24	.995		23	.950		26	.865
	13	.808		23	.990		22	.925		25	.833
	12	.749		22	.982		21	.894	.800	36	.999
.420	23	.999		21	.969		20	.857		35	.997
	22	.998		20	.949		19	.817		34	.992
	21	.996		19	.921		18	.775		33	.984

X	M	F
	32	.971
	31	.952
	30	.929
	29	.903
	28	.874
	27	.843
.850	37	.998
	36	.995
	35	.988
	34	.975
	33	.957
	32	.935
	31	.909
	30	.881
	29	.853
.900	38	.998
	37	.992
	36	.980
	35	.963
	34	.940
	33	.915
	32	.886
.950	39	.997
	38	.986
	37	.969
	36	.946
	35	.921

Indexes

AUTHOR INDEX

A

Abegglen, James C., 17
Adams, J. S., 488
Adams, S. N., 488
Affinito, M., 183
Alchian, Armen, 300
Anderson, A. R., 86
Andress, Frank, 293, 296, 298, 299
Argyris, Chris, 74, 75, 528
Arkoff, A., 228
Ås, D., 98, 505, 506
Ashby, Ross W., 366
Asher, Harold, 293, 300, 305
Atkinson, J. W., 472, 489

B

Bakke, E. Wight, 143, 521, 529
Bales, R. F., 159
Bamforth, K. W., 515
Barnard, C. I., 96, 140, 529
Beegle, J. A., 174
Beer, Stafford, 13, 369
Bendix, Reinhard, 522
Bennett, C. A., 298
Bennis, Warren G., 98, 183, 317, 319, 522, 532, 534
Berkowitz, L., 157
Bernard, L. L., 473
Bertalanffy, Ludwig von, 14, 15, 18, 20, 363, 535
Bierstedt, Robert, 191
Blake, Robert R., 13, 522
Blau, Peter M., 5, 120, 121, 530
Bonini, Charles P., 381, 384
Bonney, M. E., 174
Borgatta, Edgar F., 158, 159, 162, 176
Boulding, Kenneth E., 11, 236
Bradley, D. F., 15
Brown, Donaldson, 57
Brown, Wilfred, 99
Browne, C. G., 175
Burgess, E. W., 143
Burke, C. J., 307, 308

C

Calvin, M., 15
Caplow, Theodore, 144, 228
Cartwright, D., 191
Carzo, R., Jr., 309, 312–16
Chase, Stuart, 109, 110, 111, 114
Christensen, C. R., 487, 488
Clark, R. A., 489
Clough, Donald J., 263, 348, 351, 355, 356, 378, 379
Coch, Lester, 7, 97, 501
Cohen, Arthur M., 317, 319
Cordiner, Ralph J., 61
Crawford, J. R., 305
Cyert, Richard M., 427

D

Dahl, R. A., 192, 211, 218, 219, 221
Dale, Ernest, 53, 57, 85
Dalton, Melville, 129–36
Davis, J. A., 488
Davis, Keith, 144
Davis, Ralph, 54
Dearden, John, 56
Dembo, Tamara, 494
DeVoto, Bernard, 244
Dickson, W. J., 18, 115, 116
Dill, William R., 317, 319, 320
Donhowe, Gordon, 507
Draper, Jean, 507
Drucker, Peter F., 58
Dubin, Robert, 123, 191, 200, 478
Dunlop, John T., 533
Dupuy, T. N., 434–40
Durkheim, Émile, 528

E

Emerson, H., 53
Emerson, R. M., 189, 192, 210
Estes, William K., 307, 308
Eysenck, H., 495

F

Fabrycky, W. J., 297, 501
Fanfani, Amintore, 471

Faunce, D., 174
Fayol, Henri, 25, 27, 44, 45, 47, 48, 49, 54, 56, 78
Festinger, L., 119, 157, 488, 494
Follett, Mary P., 20, 506
Fordham, S., 89
Form, W. H., 198
Forrester, Jay W., 345, 348, 350, 370, 372, 373, 375, 376
French, John R. P., Jr., 7, 97, 98, 191, 501, 505, 506

G

Gerth, H. H., 25, 27, 208, 528
Given, William B., 100, 521
Golembiewski, R. T., 517
Gomberg, W. R., 98
Goodacre, D. M., III, 176
Gordon, Robert, 442
Gordon, W. Allport, 473
Graicunas, V. A., 45, 47
Greenberger, Martin, 533
Greenwalt, C. H., 108
Gronlund, N. E., 174
Guest, Robert H., 73, 74, 508
Guetzkow, Harold, 309, 310, 317, 319, 320
Gulick, Luther, 25, 29, 79, 87

H

Haire, Mason, 507
Hall, Earnest J., 13
Hamilton, I., 45, 47
Harbison, Frederick, 17, 533
Harris, William B., 59, 62, 510
Harrison, R., 522
Hazelwood, R. N., 405, 410, 412
Healy, James H., 84
Hebb, D. O., 477
Henderson, A. M., 50
Herzberg, Frederick, 530
Hickson, D. J., 148
Hill, Lawrence S., 420
Hirchmann, Winifred B., 298
Hittle, J. D., 50, 51
Hobbes, Thomas, 528
Hoffman, L. R., 98, 508
Holden, Paul E., 54
Homans, George C., 14, 18, 19, 143, 144, 158, 235, 244, 486, 488, 490, 491, 493, 494, 530
Hoslett, S. D., 119
Hughes, J. W., 142
Hunt, J. McV., 494
Huntington, Ellsworth, 471

I

Indik, B. P., 86
Israel, J., 98, 505, 506

J

Jacobs, J. H., 159, 175
Jaedicke, Robert K., 381, 384
Jaques, Elliott, 99, 488, 521
Jenkins, J. G., 176
Jennings, H. H., 159, 174
Johnson, A. D., 174
Jones, Marshall R., 475
Jules, H., 86

K

Kahn, Robert L., 157, 339, 341, 512, 513
Kaplan, A., 186, 190
Katz, Daniel, 157, 339, 341, 512, 513, 520
Kaufmann, Arnold, 391, 398, 419
Kelley, H. H., 119, 200
Kemeny, J. G., 194, 249, 263, 442, 449, 454
Kerr, Clark, 533
Kerr, W., 175
Kerstetter, L., 174
Klein, Josephine, 157
Koen, Francis T., 301
Koontz, H., 49, 54
Kuhn, Alfred, 530

L

Larsen, Ida M., 317
Lasswell, H. D., 186, 190
Lawler, E. E., 85, 86
Lawrence, Paul R., 149
Lawson, Reed, 305, 307
Leavitt, Harold J., 309, 529, 533
Lenski, G., 488
Levy, Seymore, 507
Lewin, Kurt, 494, 502
Likert, Rensis, 520, 531
Lindzey, Gardner, 158, 159, 162, 176
Linton, Ralph J., 142, 143
Litwin, George H., 490
Lombard, George F., 157
Lowell, Edgar L., 489
Luce, D. R., 168

M

Maier, N. R. F., 98
Malcolm, D. G., 392, 410, 412
Malone, M., 186
Mann, Floyd C., 508
March, James G., 200, 477, 494

Maslow, A., 475, 476, 477, 488, 490
Mason, Edward S., 474
Mausner, Bernard, 530
Mayo, Elton, 108, 109, 157
McClelland, David C., 489
McCormick, Charles P., 100, 521
McDougall, William, 473
McGregor, Douglas, 97, 521, 529
McMurry, Robert N., 458
McWhinney, William H., 316, 317, 319
Mead, George H., 143
Mechanic, David, 202, 207, 209
Meltzer, L., 85
Merton, Robert K., 118
Metcalf, Henry C., 20, 506
Meyer, Herbert H., 490
Miller, Delbert C., 198
Miller, James G., 236, 325, 337, 338, 341
Mills, C. Wright, 25, 27, 209, 528
Misumi, J., 98
Mooney, James D., 25, 27, 28, 48, 49, 52, 53, 55
Moreno, J. L., 159, 174
Morison, Samuel E., 434
Morse, Nancy, 487, 511, 512, 513, 514
Mouton, Jane S., 13
Muller, H. J., 470
Murray, H. A., 490
Myers, C. A., 17, 533

N

Nieman, L. J., 142
Northway, M. C., 174

O

O'Donnell, C., 49, 54

P

Park, R. E 143
Parsons, T., 50
Patchen, M., 159, 488
Peck, L. G., 405, 410, 412
Perry, Albert B., 168
Pfiffner, John M., 24
Porter, Elias H., 329, 331, 333
Porter, L. W., 85, 86

R

Raven, Bertram, 191
Read, W. H., 120
Reiley, Alan C., 25
Reimer, Everett, 511, 512, 513, 514
Requero, Miguel A., 292
Rice, A. K., 514, 517, 518, 519, 520
Richter, M. N., 488
Ridgeway, V. F., 120

Riker, W. H., 228
Roberts, Edward B., 381, 384
Robinson, Donald, 432
Roethlisberger, F. J., 18, 76, 115, 116, 139, 487, 488
Rogers, Miles S., 317
Rosenbaum, W. B., 488
Rousseau, Jean Jacques, 528
Rowland, H., 148
Roy, D., 148

S

Salter, J., 85
Samuelson, Paul A., 4, 390, 481
Sargent, J., 174
Sayles, L. R., 147, 488
Schachter, Stanley, 157
Scheff, T. J., 203, 204, 205, 209
Schellendorf, B., 51
Schlaifer, Robert, 211, 213, 215, 216
Schleifer, Arthur, Jr., 248, 263, 442, 449, 454
Schmidt, W. H., 530
Schubert, Glendon, 228
Schumpeter, Joseph A., 474
Schwartz, M. S., 38
Scott, William G., 101
Scott, W. Richard, 5
Sears, P. S., 494
Seashore, Stanley E., 157
Seiler, J. A., 149
Seward, J. P., 306
Shapley, L. S., 221
Sherrington, Charles, 473
Sherwood, Frank P., 24
Shubik, M., 221
Shure, Gerald H., 317, 319, 320
Simon, Herbert A., 8, 71, 77, 79, 200, 245, 246, 247, 309, 310, 317, 319, 320, 325, 328, 336, 341, 344, 477, 478, 494, 530, 534
Skinner, B. F., 491
Smith, Adam, 474
Smith, Richard A., 16
Snell, J. Laurie, 194, 248, 263, 442, 449, 454
Snow, C. P., 533
Snyderman, Barbara B., 530
Speroff, B., 175, 176
Stanton, A. H., 38
Stieglitz, Harold, 93–96
Stogdill, R. M., 159
Strauss, E., 305
Stroher, George B., 507
Suojanen, Waino, 88
Swanson, Guy E., 157
Sykes, G. M., 148, 207

T

Tannebaum, R., 130
Tassone, Jack, 317
Taylor, Frederick W., 25, 26
Teichroew, Daniel, 89
Theodore, Chris A., 225
Thibaut, J., 119, 201
Thompson, G. L., 194, 263, 442, 449, 454
Tolstoy, Leo, 23
Torgersen, Paul E., 297, 501
Toynbee, Arnold J., 471
Trist, E. L., 515
Turner, A. N., 73
Turner, R. H., 123, 124, 125
Tustin, Arnold, 365, 366, 368, 370

U

Urwick, Lyndall F., 20, 25, 45, 46, 47, 48, 79, 81, 87, 506

V

Van Zelst, R. H., 175
Veblen, Thorstein, 473
Vinacke, W. E., 228
Vroom, Victor H., 490

W

Wagner, Harvey M., 381, 384
Walker, Charles R., 72, 73, 508
Walker, W. B., 490
Warkov, S., 86
Weber, Max, 471
Whisler, Thomas L., 533
Whyte, William F., 148, 329, 331, 333, 521
Williams, L. K., 508
Williams, Whiting, 473
Wilm, E. C., 473
Winterbottom, Marion R., 472
Wolkon, George H., 317, 319
Worthy, James C., 68, 72, 76, 85, 507 531
Wright, T. P., 292

Y

Yanouzas, J. N., 309, 312–16

Z

Zaleznik, Abraham, 121, 487, 488
Zander, Alvin, 191
Zeleny, L. D., 174

GENERAL INDEX

A

Action centers, 336
Action process
  change, 508
  definition, 337
  design, 337
  flows, 345
  technical subsystems, 237
Activity
  definition, 143
  element of behavior, 143
  frequency, 490
  reward, 490
  satisfaction, 491–92
Administration
  communication, 77
  coordination, 77
  decision making, 77
  horizontal specialization, 77
  specialization, 77
  unity of command, 77
  vertical specialization, 77
Administration in traditional theory,
  43
Administrative level, 122
Administrative unit, 64
  departmentation, 65
Ahmedabad Manufacturing and Calico
  Printing Company, Ltd., 517
American Brake Shoe Company, 100
Analytical techniques for choosing behavior
  income effect, 480
  indifference curve analysis, 483
  law of diminishing marginal util-
    ity, 480–81
  marginal utility analysis, 479
  patterns, 478
  substitution effect, 480
Appeal channels, 98, 101
Aspiration
  activity, 489
  levels, 487, 494

Aspiration—*Cont.*
  organizational arrangements,
    494–95
  shift in level, 493
Attitudes, 7, 75
Authority, 48
  administrative, 49, 96–97
  administrative unit, 65
  amount, 55
  army staff concept, 50
  business organization, 53
  channels, 342
  compulsory staff, 53
  definition, 48
  delegation, 55
  departmentation, 65, 67
  dispersion, 55, 67
  division, 96
  functional, 54
  functional management, 54
  legal, 49
  line and staff, 50
  line and staff conflict, 125–26
  military staff, 50
  official, 49
  operating, 57
  policymaking, 57
  power relationship, 344
  religious organization, 52
  residual, 56
  service activities, 67
  source, 49
  span of supervision, 68
  staff independence, 53
  supreme coordinative power, 49
Authority channels, 342

B

Balance, 329
Basic framework for organizational
  design, 324
Behavior
  analytical techniques, 478
  elaboration, 18–19
  formal, 117

581

Behavior—*Cont.*
  illegitimate relations, 251
  limits of rationality, 251
  measurement, 157–76
  nonformal, 107
  nonformal social, 117–18
  ordered, 246
  power and social, 253
  power and technical, 252
  purposive, 246
  random, 391
  rational, 327
  role, 338
  simulation, 354–57
  social and technical, 252
  spontaneous, 17–18
  steady-state, 14–15
  task-oriented, 117
  technical, power, and social, 253
  unpurposive, 251
Beliefs
  functions, 147–49
  shared, 5, 147–49
Bureaucracy, 26

C

Centralization, 56
Centralized control with decentralized
  responsibility, 57
Centralized divisions, 511–14
Charisma, 207, 219
Chestnut Lodge Sanitarium, 38
Classification of behavior, 116
  formal, 117
  nonformal social, 117
  nonformal task-oriented, 117
Cliques
  definition, 167
  identification, 167–69
Closed systems, 14, 15, 235
Coalitions
  blocking, 221
  empirical power index, 224–25
  losing, 221
  measure of power, 220–28
  source of power, 208–9
  theoretical power index, 222–24, 227
  winning, 221
Coercion, 186, 191, 343
Cognitive dissonance; *see* Distributive
  justice
Communication, 119
  barriers, 119–20, 457
  channels, 327, 334–42
  learning, 308–16
  processes, 237
  redundant lines, 342

Communication—*Cont.*
  structure, 311–16
  vertical, 119
Communication process, 237
  technical subsystem, 237–38
Communication systems, 442
Components in parallel, 442
Compound event, 213, 215
Compromise of goals, 244, 493
Conditional probability, 213, 216
Conflict
  line and staff, 125–29
  organization and personal goals,
    246
  power struggles, 129–30
Contact time, 92
  frequency, 87
Control, 362
  communication channels, 431, 433
  comparison, 363–64
  corrective action, 363–65
  delays, 370
  delays and rationality, 376
  design, 363
  discontinuities, 385, 390
  distortions, 380
  effect of feedback, 366
  homeostat, 362
  measurement, 363–64
  process, 363
  purpose, 363
  rationality, 376
  standards, 363–64
  thermostat, 363
  Watt governor, 365
Coordination, 29, 93, 121
Coordinator, 119
Critical processes, 337
  decision making, 340
Cube-square law, 507

D

Decentralization, 56
  centralized control, 57
  General Electric, 58
  General Motors, 57
  Port of New York Authority, 63
  practice, 57
  span of control, 88
Decentralized divisions, 511–14
Decision, 325, 342
Decision criteria, 412, 452
  decision rules for reliability, 453–54
  effects of crew size, 414–17
  implications for organizational de-
    sign, 412

Decision making, 77, 335
  productivity, 511–14
  satisfaction, 511–14
Decision process, 145, 237, 334, 337
  control phase, 345
  decision, 342
  decision transmittal, 343
  design, 337, 345
  flow rate, 352
  flows, 342
Delays, 370, 373, 374, 377, 389
  communication, 436, 438, 439, 441
  control, 370
  feedback, 370
  quality control, 381
  rationality, 376–77
  waiting line theory, 389
Departmentation, 29
  clientele, 34
  dispersion of authority, 67
  function, 36
  functional, 30
  place, 33, 39
  purpose, 30, 34
  size of administrative unit, 65
Design, 107
  buffer, 332
  communication systems, 443–49, 460–62
  control, 363
  efficiency, 328
  explicit purpose, 11
  feedback, 332
  Markov Chain analysis, 274
  memory, 332
  method, 327
  purpose, 324
  queuing, 332
  visual display, 332
  waiting line theory, 392–94, 403–4, 406–9, 421–22, 423–24
Design and efficiency, 328
Design framework, 334
  actual performance, 336
  basis, 335
  desired performance, 335
  flows and action process, 345
  flows and design process, 342
  flows and processes, 341
  norms, 339
  processes, 337
  role, 339
  structure, 338
  subsystems on each flow, 345
  total system, 347
  values, 339
Deterministic system, 262, 357

Diamond Crystal Salt Co., 37
Diminishing marginal utility, 480–81, 484
Discontinuities, 385
  waiting line theory, 390
Distortion, 380
  messages, 380–81
  quality control system, 381
Distributive justice
  definition, 487
  motivation, 488
  satisfaction, 488–89, 492
Division of authority
  appeal channels, 100
  bottom-up management, 100
  consultative hierarchy, 99
  Harwood experiments, 97
  multiple management, 100
  participative management, 98
  resistance to change, 97
Dysfunctions of formal organization, 118
  communication, 457–58
  communications distortions, 119
  informal pressures, 124
  line and staff conflicts, 125
  problems of structure, 118
  rules and procedures, 122
  rules and work processes, 119
  specialization, 72
  status relationship, 119

E

E. I. duPont de Nemours and Co., 35
Economic man, 107, 474
Effectiveness, 90, 96
  organizational structure, 308–16
Efficiency, 28, 333
  allocation of resources, 9–10
  criterion, 11–12
  definition, 8, 12
  individual, 90–91
  organization, 89, 92
  span of control, 91
  supervisory, 91
  a three-level organization, 91
  total efficiency, 91
Efficiency criterion, 11, 329
Elementary event, 211, 215
Emergent behavior, 243, 244
  compromise, 244
  orderly and purposeful, 246
  structure and processes, 247
Emergent system, 235
  compromise, 244–46
  power subsystem, 237–38
  social subsystem, 238–39

Emergent system—*Cont.*
  structure and processes, 247
  technical subsystem, 239–40
Energy flows, 341
Entropy, 14–15
Environment, 16
Equifinality, 263, 272
Equilibrium, 4, 7, 14, 283, 286, 379
  change, 501–4
  marginal utility, 482
Error, 365
Exchange
  fairness, 488
  indifference analysis, 483
  marginal utility, 479
  motivation, 476
  preference and selection, 477
  system, 124
  values, 478

F

Fail Safe, 432
Farm Bureau Insurance Co., 37
Fayol's bridge, 78
Feedback, 337, 366–67
  change, 522
  coefficient, 368
  control, 366–67
  coupled loops, 370–71
  delays, 370
  design, 332–33
  effects, 366–67
  loop, 337, 347, 368
  negative, 369
  oscillations, 371
  performance monitoring, 339
  positive, 369
  single loop, 367
Finite population—Waiting line theory, 404
  average number of units being served, 406
  average number of units running or productive, 406
  average number of units waiting for service, 407
  efficiency factor, 406
  illustrations, 406, 421, 423
  multiple-station system, 409
  service factor, 405
Flat organization, 85
Flows, 341–47
  action process, 342
  capital, 345
  decision process, 342, 352
  equations, 352
  material, 345

Flows—*Cont.*
  men, 345
  money, 345
  orders, 345
  subsystems, 345–46
Force, 187
  ability to use, 188
  presentation, 187
  threat, 188
  use, 187
Ford Motor Company, 15
Formal authority, 130
Formal organization
  characteristics, 6, 12
  compared to social organization, 141
  definitions, 6
  description, 6
  efficiency, 9–12
  purpose, 6
  relation with environment, 16
  as a system, 13–14
  traditional organization theory, 23–69
  why study it, 11
Formal structure, 145
  line and staff, 128
Frequency of activity, 490–91, 495–96
Friendliness, 145
Friendship choice, 164
Friendship patterns, 164
  cubed matrix of friendships, 166
  matrix of symmetrical relationships, 166
  simple, 164
  squared matrix of friendships, 165

G

General Dynamics Corporation, 15
General Electric Company, 58–63
General Motors Corporation, 57
General systems theory
  concepts, 19–20
  gestalt psychology, 19–20
  movement, 19
  whole man approach, 19
German Army—Western Front, 83
German Army Corps (World War II), 52
Glacier Metal Company of Great Britain, 99
Goals, (see Objectives)
Grapevine, 144
Group learning, 308
  basic organization, 312
  Carzo and Yanouzas experiment, 312

Group learning—*Cont.*
  Guetzkow and Simon experiment, 309
  Leavitt experiment, 309
Group learning model, 316
  test model, 318–20

H

Harwood Manufacturing Company, 97–98, 501–4
Hawthorne experiments, 109
  bank wiring room, 115
  interview program, 114
  lighting experiment, 110
  mysterious something, 109
  relay assembly test room, 111
  unknown factor, 113
Hierarchy of needs, 475
Homeostat, 362
Horizontal process relationship, 340
Human values, 96

I

Indifference analysis
  curves, 485
  explanation, 483
  preference, 483
Individual power
  measure, 209
  rules of probability, 213, 215–16
Inducements; *see* Rewards
Infinite population—Waiting line theory, 397
  arrival rate, 396
  average number of units in system, 398
  average number of units in waiting line, 400
  average time in system, 402
  average waiting time in line, 401–2
  service factor, 397–98
  service rate, 396
  waiting line model, 397
  weighted average, 398–99
Influence, 186, 189, 191
Informal leader, 141
Informal organization, 140
  characteristics, 140
  controlling behavior, 148
  defining goals, 147
  functions, 147–49
  illustration of processes and structure, 145
  norms, 141
  prescribing conduct, 147
  shared values, 147

Informal organization—*Cont.*
  social processes, 143
  status and role, 142
Information
  flows, 343
  sources of, 342–43
Interaction, 5
  content, 144
  definition, 144
  direction, 144
  frequency, 144
  length, 144
  type, 144
Interdependence
  problem, 13–14
Institutionalization, 88

J

Job definition, 238
Job enlargement, 73–74
  British coal mines, 515–17
  Indian textile mills, 517–20
Joint event, 211, 215

L

Law of diminishing returns
  waiting line theory, 389–90
Leadership, 530
Learning, 291
  definition, 305
Learning curves, 292
  analytical model, 297
  cumulative curve, 295–96
  definition, 293
  learning percentage, 297–98
  logarithmic function, 300
  log-log presentation, 206
  regression analysis, 300
  unit curve, 295–96
  use of in industry, 292, 303
Learning model, 305
  connection, 306
  Estes learning model, 307
  individual, 305, 317
  reinforcement, 306
  response, 306
  stimulus elements, 305
Level of stability, 261–62
Line authority, 50
Linking
  linking-pin model, 520–22
  linking-pin organization
  subsystems, 347–48
Lockheed Missiles and Space Company, 93–96

M

Marginal utility
  definition, 479
  motivation, 479
Markov chain analysis, 261
Markov process, 263
  application of matrix algebra, 269
  application to organizational design, 274
  design of organization, 274
  general procedure, 278
  limiting value, 272
  matrix algebra, 266
  notes on model, 286
  steady state, 272
  steady state vector, 272
  transition diagram, 263–64
  transition tree, 264–68
  W matrix, 274
Matrix analysis
  cliques, 167–69
  cubed matrix, 167–69
  friendships, 161–62, 165–66
  Markov chain process, 261
  multiplication rules, 162
  mutual choice, 166–69
  power matrices, 273–74
  power relations, 193–97
  regular matrix, 273
  squared matrix, 165–66
  symmetrical, 166–69
  transition matrix, 264
  transition probabilities, 264
Matrix analysis applications
  education, 174
  industry, 174–76
  military, 176
  power, 195–96
  Slade illustration, 169
McCormick and Company, 100
Measure of power, 209
  coalitions, 220
  empirical index, 224
  general procedure, 225
  individual power, 209
  notes on measure of individual power, 217
  notes on the measure of power in coalitions, 227
  theoretical index, 222
Messages, 380
Method of design, 327
Milo Fractionating Center, 130–36
Motivation
  economic man, 473
  exchange, 476

Motivation—*Cont.*
  exchange and values, 478
  explanation by historians, 470
  humoral models, 472
  income effect, 480
  instincts and drives, 473
  need-satiation, 475
  productivity, 487
  substitution effect, 480
Motivation in organization, 469
Multiple-station system, 409
  effects of crew size, 415
  illustration, 421
Multiple stimuli-response model, 475
Mutual dependence
  cliques, 167–69
  emergent behavior, 243–44
  emergent system, 244–45
  feedback, 366
  matrix, 166–69
  Parable of the Spindle, 329
  power, 189

N

Need satiation, 490
Negative feedback, 365–74
Noise, 381
Nonformal behavior, 107
  economic man, 107
  norms, 115
  self-interest doctrine, 108
  social, 117–18
  social organization, 115
  social value, 115
  task oriented, 123
Nonproductive time
  definition, 89
  Markov chain analysis, 286
Norms, 5, 115, 141–42, 147–49, 339

O

Objectives, 76, 329, 335, 347
  multiple, 76
  rewards, 489
  satisfaction, 488
  shift of goals, 493
  social, 147
Open door policy, 101
Open systems, 14–15
Operating level, 121
Order, 4
Orderliness, 4
Organizational change, 500
  conditions, 504–6
  definition, 500–501
  effects, 507–9
  feedback, 522

Organizational change—*Cont.*
  General Electric, 510–11
  Likert's linking-pin model, 520–22
  links between technical and social
      subsystems, 514–20
  major variables, 509–14
  Morse-Reimer experiments, 511–14
  participation, 501–6
  personnel, 508–9
  processes, 508
  Rice textile studies, 517–20
  steady state, 501–4
  structure, 507
  Trist-Banforth study, 514–17
Oscillation, 371
Overload, 333
Overshoot or overcorrect, 376, 379

P

Parable of the Spindle, 329–34
  systems approach, 329
  technical and behavioral implica-
      tions, 331
Participation
  Harwood experiments, 98
Path, system approaches stability,
      261–62
Pearl Harbor, 434–42
Perceived justice, 489
Personnel subsystem, 346
Persuasion, 186, 191, 343
Philadelphia Eagles professional foot-
      ball team, 183–85
Poisson distribution
  waiting line theory, 396
Politics, 198
Port of New York Authority, 31, 32,
      36
Positive control system, 432–34, 441–
      42
Positive feedback, 369–70, 372, 374
Positive and negative feedback, 369
  coupled feedback loops, 370
  delays, 370
Power, 182
  ability to influence through force,
      188
  act, 211
  actor, 211
  amount, 211, 219
  behavior area, 190
  conditional terms, 211
  definition, 186
  formal authority, 130
  illustration, 183
  mutual dependence, 189
  people, 190, 219

Power—*Cont.*
  perspective, 190
  presentation of force, 187
  respondent, 211
  response, 211
  scope of, 190, 211, 219
  structure, 193–97
  time period, 190
  use of force, 187
Power process, 198
Power relationship, 343
  sanctions, 344
Power structure, 193–97
Power struggles, 129
  Milo study, 130
Power subsystem, 242–45
Preferential hierarchy of values, 325
Principles, 27, 28
Probabilistic system, 262
Problems of traditional theory, 71
Process
  change, 508
  critical, 337, 340
  design, 337
  flows, 341
  formal, 145–46
  horizontal, 340
  power, 129
  relationships, 339
  social, 116, 143–45
  vertical, 340
Process relationship, 339
Productive time, 89, 90, 423
Productivity
  centralized organization, 511–14
  decentralized organization, 511–14
Purpose of design, 324

Q

Quality control system, 381
Quasi-stationary equilibrium, 501–4
Queuing theory, 391; *see also* Waiting
      line theory

R

Random behavior, 391
Rate buster, 5, 149
Rate, system approaches stability,
      261–62
Rationality
  control, 376
  delays, 376–77
  limits, 326
  objective vs. subjective, 325–28
Redundancy
  communication channels, 444
  flows and decision process, 342, 344

Redundancy—*Cont.*
  four-channel system, 451
  measure of reliability, 442
  three-channel system, 447
  two-channel system, 444
Regulations; *see* Rules
Relations
  illegitimate, 251
  power and social, 253
  processes, 339
  spatial, 338
  technical and power, 252
  technical, power, and social, 253
  technical and social, 252
  unpurposive, 251
Relations and behavior, 251
  coincidence of power relations and
    technical relations, 252
  coincidence of social relations and
    technical relations, 252
  coincidence of technical relations,
    social relations, and power re-
    lations, 253
  illegitimate power relations, 251
  ineffectual technical relations, 250
  unpurposive social relations, 251
Resistance to change, 7, 97
Reward-contribution ratio, 489
Rewards
  activity and satisfaction, 490, 494
  contributions, 477–78, 481, 484–85,
    487–88
  goals, 489
  marginal utility, 479
Role
  behavior, 339
  definition, 142
  differentiation, 5
  emergence, 5, 6
  expectations, 5
  status, 142–43
Rules
  dysfunctional, 122
  procedures, 122
  work processes, 121–24

S

Sanctions
  power, 186, 188
  power relationship, 344
  social, 5, 140–41
Satisfaction, 488–90, 494–95
  curves, 492, 495
  frequency of activity, 492
  maximization, 483–86
  motivation, 487
  productivity, 487

Scalar principle, 28
Sears Roebuck Company, 85
Self-actualization, 475
Self-interest, 107
Self-interest doctrine, 107–8, 474
Sentiments; *see also* Friendliness;
    Friendship choice
  definition, 144
  social order, 5
Service factor
  arrival rate, 395–96
  average service time, 396
  average time between arrivals, 396
  finite population, 405–6
  infinite population, 397–98
  negative exponential distribution,
    398
  Poisson distribution, 396
  restraints, 402
  service rate, 395–96
Set operations, 248
  complement, 249
  disjoint, 249
  empty set, 249
  general equation for the union of
    sets, 250
  intersection, 249
  union, 249
Set theory, 247
Shared beliefs, 141
Shift of goals, 493–96
  effects on activity and satisfaction,
    495
Simulation, 348–56
  decision functions or flow rate equa-
    tions, 352
  level equations, 350
  notes, 357
Slade Company, 149–57, 169–74
  group norms, 154
  group performance, 155–56
  informal groups in the plating de-
    partment, 152
  informal processes, 151–54
  plating room layout, 153
  structure, 150–51
Social communication, 144
Social order, 5–6
Social organization, 115
  characteristics, 140
  definition, 140
  description, 140
  origin, 6
  processes, 143–45
  purpose, 140

Social organization and behavior, 139
  informal pressures, 124–25
  processes, 143
  role, 142
  status, 142
  structure, 5, 145–47, 239
Social processes
  activity, 143
  interaction, 144
  sentiments, 144
Social role, 143
Social subsystem, 242–45
Social value, 115
Sociometric analysis, 157
  based on friendships, 161–62, 165–66
  choice and data, 158
  definition, 158
  multiplication rules, 162
  sociogram, 159–60
  sociometric matrix, 161
Soldiering, 25
Sources of power, 197
  coalitions, 208
  expertise, 202
  interest and tenure, 203
  job importance, 201
  location, 199
  personal characteristics, 207
Span of management, 44; see also
    Span of supervision
Span of supervision, 44, 79
  cross relations, 47
  dilemma, 86
  direct group relations, 46
  direct single relations, 46
  duration of time, 87
  flat versus tall organization, 81
  Fordham model, 88
  frequency of contacts, 87
  illustrations, 421, 423
  important considerations, 87
  limitations of supervisor, 45
  limited resources, 80
  Lockheed model, 93
  multiple reporting arrangement,
    425
  narrow span, 45
  notes on waiting line model, 424
  possible relationships, 46, 87
  principle of, 48
  problem, 80
  Sears Roebuck Company, 85
  size of supervisory unit, 44
  span of control, 48
  waiting line theory, 420
Spatial relations, 338

Specialization, 72
  administration, 77
  attitudes, 76
  decision making, 77, 340
  dysfunction, 72
  efficiency, 73
  horizontal, 77
  multiple channel of communications,
    79
  multiple objectives, 76
  vertical, 77
Staff authority, 50
Staff concept
  business organization, 53–54
  compulsory staff service, 53
  military organization, 50–52
  religious organization, 52–53
Staff independence, 53
Standard of Performance, 364
Standards, 5
State of system, 263
  initial state, 264
  possible states, 264–67
Status
  congruency, 488
  defined, 142
  differences, 121
  relationship, 119
  role, 142–43
Status structure, 141
Steady state
  behavior, 14–16
  definition, 272
  description, 273, 281
  Markov process, 272
  state of imbalance, 15
  tendency toward, 7, 15–16
  vector, 281–82
Structure, 5, 116
  characteristics, 338
  communications, 308–16
  design framework, 338
  dysfunctions, 118–21
  emergent system, 247
  learning, 311–16
  power, 193–97
  problems, 118–21
  social, 145–47
Structure and change, 507
Structuring of events, 339
Subordinates, 119
Subset, 248
Subsystems, 237
  characteristics, 240
  flows, 345–46
  links, 347–48

Subsystems—*Cont.*
  objectives, 347
  overlapping, 241
  power, 239–40
  social, 238–39
  technical, 237–38
Superior, 119
Suprasystem, 236
Survey Research Center of the University of Michigan, 511
System
  characteristics, 12–14, 332
  definition, 13
  delays, 370
  discontinuities, 385, 390
  distortions, 381
  emergent, 235
  formal organization, 12–13
  living, 15
  natural, 6–7
  open; *see* Open systems
  overlays, 241–42
  reliability, 431
  state of imbalance, 15
  waiting line theory, 388, 418
System reliability, 431
  comprehensive model, 449
  decision criteria, 452
  design implications, 456
  four-channel system, 451
  guidelines, 459
  measures, 442
  problems, 459
  single-channel system, 443
  three-channel system, 447
  two-channel system, 444
System reliability model
  design implications, 456
  general form, 450
  graphical analysis, 456
System reliability in organizational design, 431, 452, 459
Systems approach and change, 506

T

Technical role, 142
Technical subsystem, 242–45
Thermostat, 364, 366
Total system, 347
Traditional organization theory, 23
  in brief, 28
  bureaucracy, 26–27
  bureaucratic organization, 27
  coordination, 29
  coordinative principle, 27
  departmentation, 29–38

Traditional organization theory—
    Cont.
  efficiency, 28
  functional management, 26
  functional principle, 28
  principles, 27–28
  problems, 71
  scalar principle, 28
  soldiering, 25
  span of supervision, 71
  staff principle, 28
  work, 28
Transition diagram, 263–64, 284–85
Transition matrix, 272–73, 281
  regular, 273
Transition probabilities, 264, 280, 284–85

U

Uncertainty absorption, 200
Unintended relationships, 127
United States Army
  infantry division, 38
  Northern France, 82
Unity of command, 43–44
  specialization, 79

V

Values, 116, 147
  chain of command, 331
  power, 189
  social system, 339
Vertical process relationship, 341

W

Waiting line theory, 389
  application to design problem, 392–94
  decision criteria, 412
  delay, 389
  discontinuities, 390
  distribution of arrival and service times, 395–96
  effects of crew size, 415
  equations—finite population, 405–8
  equations—infinite population, 402
  finite population, 404
  infinite population, 397–404
  inputs to system, 397
  model, 394
  multiple reporting arrangement, 425
  multiple station—finite population, 409–12
  queue discipline, 396

Waiting line theory—*Cont.*
  random behavior, 391
  span of supervision, 420–26
Watt governor, 364–65
Western Electric Company
  Hawthorne plant, 18, 108–16

Whole task
  change, 516, 518–19
Work, 28
Works Committee, 99–100
Works Council, 99–100

This book has been set in 10 point Century Expanded, leaded 3 points and 9 point Century Expanded, leaded 2 points. The Chapter numbers are in 48 point Delphian Open Title; Part numbers are in 24 point Venus Bold Extended. Chapter and Part titles are in 18 point Venus Bold Extended. The size of the type page is 27 by 45½ picas.